# TWENTY-FIRST CENTURY PERSPECTIVES ON THE SCHOLARSHIP OF AV DICEY

This book reassesses AV Dicey's legacy in political and legal thought through the reflections of leading scholars who consider his importance not only in today's British constitutional and legal culture but also in other foreign constitutional cultures.

Every student in law and in politics, every law faculty and most legal practitioners in the world are aware of who Albert Venn Dicey (1835–1922) was and what he wrote. Yet, this fame does not mean that Dicey's legacy is not controversial and debated in the present world. This book considers why Dicey's late Victorian constitutional and political thinking is still alive. In spite of all the transformations that have taken place in public law in the UK in the last hundred years, the book argues that Dicey managed to grasp and to crystallise something of the British political identity and culture. Hence the long-lasting fire-power of his constitutional and political thinking.

The book also considers that there is something even more prescient in Dicey's writings, for the UK but also for countries that have adopted his understanding of the rule of law and/or of parliamentary government. Dicey identified one of the most fundamental political issues at stake: the nature of the relationship between public law and democracy. The book looks closely at the alliance between public law and democratic spirit. This alliance needs to be reassessed from a legal, historical and comparative perspective. This edited collection, gathering authors from different countries, from various legal systems and from diverse backgrounds, tackles this task.

# Twenty-First Century Perspectives on the Scholarship of AV Dicey

*The Enduring Legacy of a Victorian Constitutionalist*

Edited by
Catherine Marshall
and
Céline Roynier

•HART•
OXFORD • LONDON • NEW YORK • NEW DELHI • SYDNEY

HART PUBLISHING

Bloomsbury Publishing Plc

Kemp House, Chawley Park, Cumnor Hill, Oxford, OX2 9PH, UK

1385 Broadway, New York, NY 10018, USA

29 Earlsfort Terrace, Dublin 2, Ireland

HART PUBLISHING, the Hart/Stag logo, BLOOMSBURY and the Diana logo are trademarks of Bloomsbury Publishing Plc

First published in Great Britain 2024

First published in hardback, 2024

Paperback edition, 2026



A catalogue record for this book is available from the British Library.

A catalogue record for this book is available from the Library of Congress.

Library of Congress Control Number: 2024944067

ISBN: PB: 978-1-50997-506-8
ePDF: 978-1-50997-509-9
ePub: 978-1-50997-508-2

Typeset by Compuscript Ltd, Shannon

# ACKNOWLEDGEMENTS

A long time ago, while discussing – as one does at University – who would be in our top three of the great English constitutionalists, we decided that AV Dicey would definitely make it close to the top. The other two were Bolingbroke and Bagehot. As the centenary of the death of Dicey was approaching, we decided to celebrate it with an international conference in France. On our list of guests from across the Channel (sadly our finances would not allow us to extend the invitations across the Atlantic), we had included a list of British scholars who to our amazement and delight all agreed to join us in June 2022 in Paris. We were also pleased to see that our French colleagues would join us with enthusiasm. What we learned during these two glorious days was that AV Dicey could be either loved or hated and that his legacy was much more enduring than we had even anticipated.

This book is the result of those days and the inspiration the conversations gave us. With it, we were able to reach many more colleagues and friends across the world, this time, to try and fill in the missing links of Dicey's continuing legacy.

On our quest, we were helped by a number of friends and colleagues. Even if we are solely responsible for what is written in the introduction and have approved all the articles written, we can safely say that this book is the product of many minds as we had countless conversations about many parts of the work which transformed our ways of thinking about Dicey. We are indebted to all our contributors for trusting us with such a project and for their constant work on several drafts. They all gave invaluable suggestions, kind criticism and generous support to get the manuscript published.

Our special thanks go to Timothy Endicott who made many introductory meetings possible in Britain, and gave much needed encouragement always at the right time. The same goes for Mark Walters who immediately agreed to take part in the book even though we could not invite him to Paris in June 2022. Both gave help with much kindness.

Our warm thanks also go to our University, CY Cergy Paris University (formerly the Université de Cergy-Pontoise), and our two research centres, Agora for Catherine and the Centre de Philosophie Juridique et Politique (CPJP) for Céline, that generously supported us throughout the years. A second University, the Université Paris Panthéon Assas and the Institut Michel Villey played a big part in making the initial conference possible and we would like to thank most sincerely Professors Olivier Beaud and Denis Baranger, who supported our project from the very beginning, along with Thibault Desmoulins for his invaluable help.

We are likewise very grateful to Kate Whetter and Verity Stuart at Hart, for their interest in the subject and for their patient help in bringing it to fruition. Our thanks are extended to the anonymous referee who gave support to the book whilst giving ideas which pushed us into rewriting parts he/she felt could be strengthened. With Julian Marshall who read the first drafts and Sarah Bentley, who thoughtfully and relentlessly copy-edited the final version, they all made the book a reality.

Catherine would like to thank Balliol College at the University of Oxford where she was accepted as *Oliver Smithies Visiting Fellow* and allowed to spend two terms in 2023, doing her research there, whilst being funded and welcomed in a way she will never forget. During that time, she was able to meet some of the contributors of the book and meet new ones. The Fellowship has had a long-lasting impact on this work.

Céline would also like to thank the Institut Universitaire de France (IUF) that helped make this publication possible.

Lastly, we both have an enormous debt of gratitude to our families – husbands and our four daughters, Emma and Daphne for Catherine and Lili and Camille for Céline – who all had to put up with the long hours spent on the project and our infatuation with a long dead, rather odd, Victorian constitutionalist. In all fairness and with love, we dedicate this book to them.

Catherine Marshall and Céline Roynier
*May 2024*

# CONTENTS

## PART III
## DICEY BEYOND BORDERS



## PART IV
## DICEY vs DICEY

# LIST OF CONTRIBUTORS

**Aurélien Antoine** is professor of law at the Jean-Monnet University, Saint-Étienne.

**NW Barber** is Professor of Constitutional Law and Theory, Trinity College, University of Oxford.

**Gregory Bligh** is Senior lecturer in Public Law, Sciences Po Lyon.

**Sir Vernon Bogdanor CBE** is Professor of Government, King's College, London.

**Richard Cullen** is Adjunct Professor in Law, University of Hong Kong, and previously Professor of Business Law, Monash University, Melbourne.

**Dr Nicholas Dickinson** is Bingham Early Career Fellow in Constitutional Studies, Balliol College, University of Oxford.

**Timothy Endicott** is Vinerian Professor of English Law, All Souls College, University of Oxford.

**Nicolas Gabayet** is Professor of Public Law, Jean Monnet University, Saint-Etienne.

**Michael Greve** is Professor of Law, Antonin Scalia Law School, George Mason University.

**Thibault Guilluy** is Professor of Public Law, University of Lorraine.

**Alan S Kahan** is Professor of British Civilisation, University of Paris-Saclay.

**Michael Lobban** is Professor of Legal History and Senior Research Fellow, All Souls College, University of Oxford.

**Catherine Marshall** is Professor in British Studies, CY Cergy Paris University.

**Iain McLean** is Senior Research Fellow in Politics, Nuffield College, University of Oxford.

**Alex Middleton** is Fellow in History, St Hugh's College, University of Oxford.

**Françoise Orazi** is Professor in British Studies, Lumière University Lyon 2.

**Marie Padilla** is Senior Lecturer, University of Bordeaux.

**Scot Peterson** is Departmental Lecturer in British Politics, Department of Politics and International Relations, University of Oxford.

**Céline Roynier** is Professor of Public Law, CY Cergy Paris University, and a junior member of the Institut Universitaire de France.

**Adam Tomkins** is John Millar Professor of Public Law, University of Glasgow.

**Mark D Walters** is Professor of Law, Faculty of Law, Queen's University, Ontario.

# Introduction

CATHERINE MARSHALL AND CÉLINE ROYNIER

> What is striking about [Dicey] is the hiatus between the major distortions with reality … which are contained in his detailed description of existing Law and the great accuracy of the descriptive equations (the famous 'principles') that he coined about the legal system. He discovered everything in advance, questions and answers included. Or at least, it is difficult to do better than to struggle within the nets he has set.[1]

## Why Dicey and Why Now?

In 1680 – a few years prior to the 'Glorious Revolution' – a book was published, gathering treatises from Thomas Williams, Thomas Risden and Matthew Hale under the title *Excellency and Praeheminence of the Law of England, above all other Humane Lawes in the World*. This title tells two things about the relationship between the English jurists and their national law. First, English law is good, the best in the world. Such a statement is not very original for the times; since the writings of Fortescue[2] and others before him, English lawyers had praised their law and shown that it was much better than, for instance, French law. Second, the title implies that the only law above English law is divine law, as English law is 'above all other *human* lawes in the world' (emphasis added).[3] The preface explains that 'English law … was ordained with Public consent of many, pro conservatione Regis et regni et in utilitatem Reipublicae. And therefore it is also called *lex Politica* …'.[4]

Most English lawyers show that English law and common law are political in essence and AV Dicey (1835–1922) is undoubtedly part of this tradition. Nevertheless, this is without considering democracy and Dicey lived 'his period

[1] D Baranger, *Ecrire la constitution non-écrite. Une introduction au droit politique britannique* (Paris, Presses Universitaires de France, 2008) 188 (translation by C Marshall and C Roynier).

[2] J Fortescue, *De Laudibus Legum Angliae*, SB Chrimes (ed) (Cambridge, Cambridge University Press, 1942).

[3] T Williams, *Excellency and Praeheminence of the Law of England, above all other Humane Lawes in the World* (London, Assign of R and E Atkins, 1680).

[4] ibid 10.

as a revolutionary one'.[5] *His* law of the Constitution was threatened,[6] in many ways, by democracy. The democratisation process – further secured by the Prime Minister William Gladstone's 1885 Third Reform Act – implied, in the long run, votes for women, Home Rule for Ireland and, during his lifetime, what Dicey disparagingly called 'collectivism' (as opposed to Benthamism, which was supposed to be 'individualist').[7] Even if Dicey denied doing so, he defended his interpretation of the English Constitution against this democratisation: teaching the law of the Constitution as a Vinerian professor amounted to defending the Constitution. Almost in spite of himself, Dicey changed his original intellectual project: from 'expounder', he became 'defender',[8] and his vision of the Constitution became the law of the Constitution.[9] He joined Bracton, Fortescue, Coke, Blackstone, and Bagehot in the tradition of praising the law. But which tradition was he defending? Was it the all-encompassing tradition of common law, based on an intertwined relationship between law and politics? Or the burgeoning constitutional positivism of his period, which understood law as command? How could these two opposing ways of combining law with politics flourish in the Victorian democratisation of political life? This is the fundamental relationship at stake in the following essays.

This intense constitutional upheaval while Dicey was writing about the Constitution is not devoid of similarities during the last 50 years, in which the English Constitution has been battered. As Vernon Bogdanor has written, 'the Old Constitution [is] under strain'[10] because of the United Kingdom's accession to the European Union and its membership, because of devolution, because of democratisation (reform of the House of Lords), because of the Human Rights Act and the incorporation of the provisions of the European Convention on Human Rights into British law, because of Brexit, and because of the development of judicial review in the 1960s. The majority of United Kingdom citizens have seen many evolutions, and at least some have perceived threats from the interfering role of the European Union/European Economic Community. In the process,

[5] R Weill, 'Dicey Was Not Diceyan' (2003) 62 *The Cambridge Law Journal* 474–93, 485.

[6] M Loughlin, *Public Law and Political Theory* (Oxford, Oxford University Press, 1992) 156: 'In later life Dicey therefore felt that developments in society and politics were threatening the idea of the British constitution which he had thought to formulate in 1885'.

[7] AV Dicey, *Lectures on the Relation between Law and Public Opinion in England in the Nineteenth Century* (London, MacMillan, 1905).

[8] AV Dicey, *Introduction to the Study of the Law of the Constitution*, R Michener (ed) (Indianapolis, Liberty Fund, 1982, reprint of the 1915 Macmillan edition), cxxvii: 'At the present day students of the constitution wish neither to criticise, nor to venerate, but to understand; and a professor whose duty it is to lecture on constitutional law, must feel that he is called upon to perform the part neither of a critic nor of an apologist, nor of an eulogist, but simply of an expounder; his duty is neither to attack nor to defend the constitution, but simply to explain its laws'.

[9] ibid.

[10] V Bogdanor, *The New British Constitution* (Oxford, Hart Publishing, 2009) ch 2. See also P Craig, 'Six Dimensions of Public Law. Pressure-testing the UK and EU Systems' in E Fischer et al (eds), *The Foundations and Future of Public Law* (Oxford, Oxford University Press, 2020) 399.

the Victorian 'English' Constitution has become the 'British' Constitution, even if 'Anglo-British' would be a better description.[11]

For Bogdanor and many along with him, such threats have led to an opposition between an 'Old Constitution' and a 'New Constitution'.[12] Some put it differently and assert that the British Constitution is undergoing 'a profound moment of constitutional fluidity'[13] but the idea – ie that the Constitution is changing – remains the same. From a constitutional perspective, the main problem the British Constitution has been facing through democratisation, be it via devolution or Brexit, has been the absence of a clear conveyor of the will of the people as constituent power.[14] By contrast, the identification of the will of the people as constituent power is quite clear – even if it is often fictitious – in written constitutions: the political sovereign is the legal sovereign, in whom legal and political powers are conceptually fused. In contrast, however, Dicey made a seminal distinction between the legal sovereign (the King-in-Parliament) and the political sovereign (the people, or, more accurately, 'the electoral body').[15] In a decisive period for democracy, this distinction is something Dicey needed to protect. He even defended the Constitution at the expense of his own theory: the evolution of his writings about referendums are probably the most striking example of his intellectual evolution. Dicey died in 1922, after a long life dedicated to constitutional law and politics. This longevity, of course, required him to change his mind and to tone down some of his theories. As is well identified in the following essays, the evolutions and opportunities for contradictions were and remain numerous in Dicey's work.

In truth, throughout his life AV Dicey had to tackle the issue of change and transition, and this made him an enduring landmark of the twentieth and twenty-first centuries. In the words of Martin Loughlin and Matthew Arnold:

> In codifying the British constitution he attempted … to blend … the modern institutional forms and the culture of the ancient constitution. In that sense he expressed the anxiety of Victorians who were 'wandering between two worlds, one dead, the other powerless to be born'.[16]

Post-Brexit days are similar to this Victorian period and are sometimes described as 'threshold times'. Arendt described it beautifully: these were times between a 'no longer' and a 'not yet'.[17] The post-Brexit political dramas, followed by attacks

[11] I Ward, *The English Constitution. Myths and Realities* (Oxford, Hart Publishing, 2004). Concerning Dicey more specifically, see MD Walters, *A.V. Dicey and the Common Law Tradition: A Legal Turn of Mind* (Cambridge, Cambridge University Press, 2020) 8–10.

[12] V Bogdanor, *The New British Constitution*.

[13] A Tomkins quoted by S Douglas-Scott, 'Brexit and the Challenges of a Post-sovereign Legal Landscape' in *The Foundations and Future of Public Law* (Oxford, Oxford University Press, 2020) 390.

[14] See D Baranger, 'Brexit as a Constitutional Decision' (2018) 21 *Jus Politicum* 287.

[15] Dicey, *The Law of the Constitution* 286–87.

[16] Loughlin, *Public Law and Political Theory* 153.

[17] H Arendt, *On Revolution* (London, Penguin Books, 1963) 205: 'If these legends could teach anything at all, their lesson indicated that freedom is no more the automatic result of liberation than

on the British Constitution by at least two Prime Ministers, have exposed the fragility of the system.[18]

Transition thinking such as Dicey's can be useful in examining post-Brexit Britain and also, more generally, to think about constitutionalism in a context of change.[19] The continuity of identity through change is at the core of British constitutionalism, as JWF Allison has asserted.[20] Dicey's French counterpart, Emile Boutmy, pleasingly defined the English Constitution as 'a walking path'.[21] The continuity of this forever-changing identity[22] concerned Dicey and it is obvious that his anxieties are echoed in the present-day political 'uneasiness' – to borrow Locke's term.[23] As will be seen in the following essays, Dicey managed to remedy his anxiety: what if this success was due to the fact that he was the first one who understood how to combine constitutional form with substance in a satisfactory language? What if British constitutional identity and the general idea carried by constitutionalism is this plain but fundamental belief that a body of law that is common – ie that it applies to the whole political community – is the best weapon against arbitrary power? Fundamentally, Dicey forces us to question the definitions of legal and political constitutionalism by endlessly blurring the lines between law and politics. At the end of the 1970s, John Griffith criticised Dicey for such a lack of focus. For Griffith, laws were 'merely statements of a power relationship and nothing more' and constitutions were statements of 'authority'.[24] The two were not compatible, making Dicey's attempt at removing constitutional sovereignty from the political whilst grounding it in common law either plainly wrong or impossible to square with his different inspirations (from Bracton, Fortescue, Coke, Blackstone, and Bagehot to Austin). But what if Dicey's genius was his capacity to reconcile what is irreconcilable: that is, rooting constitutional positivism in the political Constitution of his people?

the new beginning is the automatic consequence of the end. The revolution – so at least it must have appeared to these men – was precisely the legendary hiatus between end and beginning, between a no-longer and a not-yet.'

[18] A Blick and P Hennessy, *The Bonfires of the Decencies. Repairing and Restoring the British Constitution* (London, Haus Publishing, 2022). See also J Bowers, 'Conventions, the Rule of Law and Declining Standards: What Happens when Good Chaps do not Behave' in J Bowers, *Downward Spiral. Collapsing Public Standards and How to Restore Them* (Manchester, Manchester University Press, 2024) ch 15.

[19] See M Russell et al, 'Rebuilding and Renewing the Constitution: Options for Reform' (Report 204, July 2023) https://www.ucl.ac.uk/constitution-unit/publications/reports.

[20] JWF Allison, *The English Historical Constitution. Continuity, Changes and European Effects* (Cambridge, Cambridge University Press, 2007) 205.

[21] E Boutmy, *Études de droit constitutionnel: France, Angleterre, États-Unis* (Paris, E Plon, Nourrit et Cie, 1885) 2.

[22] Some would say that the United Kingdom constitutional order is 'unsettled', N Walker quoted by S Douglas-Scott, *The Foundations and Future of Public Law* 394: 'Both EU and UK legal and constitutional orders are unstable, and to use Neil Walker's characterisation, "unsettled"' (N Walker, 'Our Constitutional Unsettlement' (2014) *Public Law* 529).

[23] J Locke, *An Essay Concerning Human Understanding* (London, Penguin Classics, 1998).

[24] J Griffith, 'The Political Constitution' (1979) 42 *Modern Law Review* 1, 19.

Thus, it is important to take a fresh look[25] at Dicey's constitutional discourse: just as the turning point of the nineteenth to the twentieth century put pressure on the 'Constitution d'Angleterre' based on the 'wrong' idea that powers were separated in this Constitution – Walter Bagehot was the one who formulated this in the first place – so was the turn of the twentieth century for Diceyan political law. Because the century between 1922 and 2022 saw very important changes in constitutional law, not only in the United Kingdom but also in many countries throughout the world thanks to decolonisation and the development of constitutional justice, this book is based on a broad and comprehensive approach. First, perspectives on Dicey's scholarship are interdisciplinary, a cross-fertilisation of law and history of political ideas. Second, given that constitutionalism and democratisation are, if not universal, at least global concerns, Dicey's scholarship has to be considered through foreign – by this we mean non-British – lenses. Commenting on British constitutionalism is, and has always been, a universal intellectual exercise. The essays collectively attempt to answer four questions: (1) How did Dicey's *Law of the Constitution* rescue the English Constitution? (2) Do we *need* Dicey's *Law of the Constitution* today to understand the United Kingdom Constitution? (3) Or to understand other constitutional systems? (4) And what do we *want* to keep from Dicey's scholarship for ourselves today?

## Part I: Was Dicey a Follower or a Legal 'Disrupter'? Rescuing the English Constitution

The concept of *lex politica* involved religious assumptions. Within the common law tradition, religious grounds for public law can be identified in the writings of Coke, Selden, Hale, and Blackstone,[26] for whom sovereignty ultimately relied on faith, government, and the premise that promises had to be kept under the aegis of a Christian God.[27] Of course, the 'anti-common law' stream – that also forms

[25] There are already many studies about the scope of Dicey's doctrines, eg RA Cosgrove, *The Rule of Law: AV Dicey. A Victorian Jurist* (London, MacMillan, 1980); P McAuslan and JF McEldowney (eds), *Law, Legitimacy and the Constitution. Essays Marking the Centenary of Dicey's Law of the Constitution* (London, Sweet and Maxwell, 1985); AV Dicey and JWF Allison (ed), *The Oxford Edition of Dicey*, vols 1 & 2 (Oxford, Oxford University Press, 2013); Allison, *The English Historical Constitution*; Walters, *A.V. Dicey and the Common Law Tradition*.

[26] Blackstone quoted by Loughlin, *Public Law and Political Theory* 147, writing about Parliament: 'It can, in short, do everything that is not *naturally* impossible .... True it is, that what Parliament doth, no authority *upon earth* can undo' (emphasis added). About the relations between common law, constitutionalism and Christianism, see DC Smith, 'Sir Edward Coke' in RH Helmholz and M Hill (eds), *Great Christian Jurists in English History* (Cambridge, Cambridge University Press, 2017) 93–114; N Aroney and I Leigh, *Christianity and Constitutionalism* (Oxford, Oxford University Press, 2022); HJ Berman, *Law and Revolution II. The Impact of Protestant Reformation on the Western Legal Tradition* (Cambridge, Belknap Press of Harvard University, 2003).

[27] For instance: GJ Postema (ed), *Matthew Hale. On the Law of Nature, Reason, & Common Law. Selected Jurisprudential Writings* (Oxford, Oxford University Press, 2017) 209: 'The governed have an interest in the protection of a governor by his stipulation to them, and the governor hath an interest

a tradition with authors like Hobbes, Bentham, and Austin – started to secularise political law (or right) but not, precisely, with common law language. Bagehot may have paved the way for this worldliness of the common law but his 'dignified parts' of the Constitution are still anchored in a religious way of thinking in which the concept of deference has a great role to play.[28] Dicey was therefore at the right place at the right moment: at the crossroads between the 'high road' to public law and the asserted superiority of the English common law, although he had no pretention of being a constitutionalist.[29] In his seminal work *An Introduction to the Study of the Law of the Constitution*, which was reedited eight times during his lifetime, Dicey manifestly managed to find the right language, grammar and web of relationships to teach constitutional law and, even more importantly, to anchor constitutional law in the English legal tradition. The three most important principles that he coined – the sovereignty of Parliament, the rule of law, and the conventions of the Constitution – did not come out of the blue.

The first part of this volume, 'Dicey: Follower or Legal 'Disrupter'?' is not so much about identifying Dicey's inspirations – it is common knowledge that his absolutist conception of the sovereignty of the Westminster Parliament was directly inspired by J Austin's jurisprudence for instance – as it is about understanding what shade Dicey used for his constitutional big picture. In this sense, Chapter 1, written by **Michael Lobban**, gives many subtle answers thanks to his archaeology of Dicey's thought and makes us understand that one of the forces of his jurisprudence was that he managed to combine legal and constitutional positivism with historiographical interpretations.[30] It is consequently clear that the way Dicey defined the rule of law came straight from the classical common law tradition[31] and that his conventions of the Constitution cannot be understood without reference to the conventional Constitution developed in *The Growth of the English Constitution* written by the Whig historian EA Freeman in 1872.[32] What Lobban also makes clear is that Dicey was not unaware that constitutional conventions could be abused if the political sovereign did not follow the law or decided to impose his view too heavily. In the words of Gladstone, the British system relied far too much on 'the good sense and the good faith of those who work it',[33] leaving ample space for the Constitution to be moulded by the

in the subjection of the governed by their stipulation, and the governed have an interest in the mutual subjection one of another by a mutual stipulation between themselves and the common concernment one of another. And this fides publica [public faith or fidelity] hath twisted both governors and governed into one body. And therefore God hath set to his seal, so natural justice hath set to her seal to this universal and eternal truth, fides est servanda [promises or agreements must be kept.]'.

[28] C Marshall, *Political Deference in a Democratic Age. British Politics and the Constitution from the Eighteenth Century to Brexit* (Cham, Palgrave Macmillan, 2021).

[29] Baranger, *Ecrire la constitution non-écrite* 141.

[30] M Lobban, 'Bentham and Dicey', see ch 1 below.

[31] Dicey, *Law of the Constitution* 107. See also C Roynier, *Le problème de la liberté dans le constitutionnalisme britannique* (Paris, Classiques Garnier, 2019) 47–57.

[32] M Lobban, 'Bentham and Dicey', see ch 1 below; eg Walters, *A.V. Dicey and the Common Law Constitutional Tradition* 106–107.

[33] WE Gladstone, *Gleanings of Past Years*, vol 1 (London, John Murray, 1879) 245.

legislators and politicians of the day – as the present post-Brexit set of politicians have demonstrated.

Beyond constitutional conventions, the definition of sovereignty is also crucial for constitutional law as discussed by **Gregory Bligh**,[34] who shows how difficult it is to build a consistent concept of sovereignty in a political culture where no state, in the Continental sense of the term, exists. Bligh reinvests the Diceyan opposition of legal and political sovereignty in order to show that Dicey was simultaneously Austinian and Benthamite. He explains how *Law of the Constitution* 'distinguishes the legal sovereignty of the King in Parliament and the political sovereignty of the "electoral body"' whilst not rejecting the historical validity of the constitutional morality of the Constitution. This is of supreme value in understanding what happened at the time of the psycho-parliamentary drama of the Brexit years and around the *Miller* cases. Bligh also retrieves the Benthamite narrative of the 'Public Opinion Tribunal' by showing how the whole constitutional edifice, through the extension of the suffrage, moved from a Victorian individualistic liberalism to the first layers of a type of socialism which would have an impact on the ways in which legislation was made in the twentieth century. In this sense, Dicey warned how the forever-changing Constitution could be threatened – which is essentially what has happened in the last few years in Britain.

Probably also because his first love was international private law[35] and given that he was experienced in the resolution of systemic conflicts, Dicey managed to renew the reflection about political authority by replacing the appeal to foundational religion with an unprecedented blend of legal positivism, historical interpretation, and common law immanentism. This capacity to think anything and everything at the same time is typical of the classical common law tradition.[36] This new combination rescued something of the English constitutional tradition, but according to **Adam Tomkins**, this had a price: the definitive burial of the *Constitution d'Angleterre* of the eighteenth century. Tomkins[37] refutes the belief, quite frequently displayed, that Dicey created or revived an 'Ancient constitution'[38] that was subsumed by upheavals in public law in the beginning of the twentieth century. For him, rather, Dicey and Bagehot put in place important and long-lasting foundations of the British Constitution for the twenty-first century. Yet by doing so – and it is particularly true for Dicey – they buried the eighteenth century *Constitution d'Angleterre* because they also saw what Montesquieu could not see, that the separation of powers did not operate across the Channel in the

[34] G Bligh, 'Austinian Qualms. Dicey on Sovereignty', see ch 2 below.

[35] AV Dicey, *On Conflict of Laws*. It is still edited today under: Dicey, Morris, and Collins, *The Conflict of Laws*, 16th edn (London, Sweet and Maxwell, 2022).

[36] About what is particular to the common law as a legal culture, see D Baranger, 'Angleterre (Culture juridique)' in S Rials and D Alland (eds), *Dictionnaire de la culture juridique* (Paris, Presses Universitaires de France, 2003) 52–59.

[37] A Tomkins, 'Dicey and Bagehot: What is Left of the Nineteenth-Century Constitution in Twenty-First Century Britain?', see ch 3 below.

[38] On this discussion see Loughlin, *Public Law and Political Theory* 150 ff.

way Montesquieu had thought – rather that, in the words of Bagehot, the fusion of legislative and political powers was at work. In a way, Dicey chose his own intellectual heritage. That is why his writings have such foundational force, but this is also the most vulnerable and questionable dimension of his legal art because these choices may look arbitrary. Dicey explicitly made *epistemological* decisions but in the field of constitutional law; these necessarily amount to *political* choices. The consequences of these decisions are quite clear in the last two chapters of the first part of this volume. The first, by **Françoise Orazi**, asserts that there are matters about which Dicey's thinking seems to change, but that, in reality, he implemented a deep and well-anchored philosophy. In Orazi's research, the letter against women's vote illustrates strong Diceyan philosophical assumptions[39] which reverse JS Mill in *The Subjection of Women* (1869).[40] Orazi states that the utilitarian argument can be used (or abused) both ways: either, in Mill's sense, by saying that the principle of utility proves that men will lose from women's removal from the public political sphere or, in Dicey's odd pamphlet, that the utility of women's participation in political life is not a proven benefit for the country. Dicey's rejection of Home Rule is made on the same grounds, which may lead the reader to question the use Dicey made of a utilitarian ethos. The second answer is along similar lines where **Alex Middleton** shows that Dicey's *Law and Public Opinion*[41] discusses political change. Focusing on the growth of public imperialism, Middleton sheds light on the way Dicey tried to explain political changes in the nineteenth century through analysing the development of English imperialism.[42] Twisting Benthamite principles to their limit, Dicey ended up exalting imperialism as 'a political religion, for it is public spirit touched with emotion', to fit his own political agenda. Dicey changed his mind – he meandered politically – but he was also eager to explain political changes at a national level, still holding on to a legal narrative. In the end, both Orazi and Middleton show he ended up losing touch with the needs and evolutions of his day. Thus, Dicey is both a follower and a disrupter.

Dicey invented a new combination of the political resources that were available to him and his *Law of the Constitution* rescued the English Constitution. Dicey managed to connect the principle of democracy as a principle of legitimacy with the constitutional system. He created a new circuit between the Constitution and society through his reflections about the relationship between law and public opinion, through his conventions of the Constitution, and his writings about referendums. However, he had concerns about political legitimacy: he saw how it could be abused.[43] In a way, he politicised common law by anchoring it

[39] F Orazi, 'Dicey's *Letters to a Friend on Votes for Women*', see ch 4 below.

[40] JS Mill, *The Subjection of Women* (London, Longmans, Green, Reader, and Dyer, 1869).

[41] Dicey, *Lectures on the Relation between Law and Public Opinion.*

[42] A Middleton, 'AV Dicey on English Imperialism', see ch 5 below.

[43] It is no coincidence that the centenary book of Dicey's first edition of *Law of the Constitution* focuses on legitimacy, and starts with the note that Britain is slowly undergoing an 'incipient crisis in constitutional arrangements': P McAuslan and JF McEldowney (eds), *Law, Legitimacy and the Constitution. Essays Marking the Centenary of Dicey's Law of the Constitution* (London, Sweet and Maxwell, 1985) 2.

in three common legal and political discourses: the discourse of power and might (indivisible and absolute sovereignty) that implied legal positivism; the discourse of limits (rule of law) that was necessary if law was defined, even subtly, by voluntarism; and a discourse that related the two through practical philosophy and produced political legitimation.[44] Conventions are made to 'secure that Parliament, or the Cabinet which is indirectly appointed by Parliament, shall in the long run give effect to *the will of that power which in modern England is the true political sovereign of the state* ...'.[45] By doing so, Dicey also made choices. Are these choices still relevant today in understanding the United Kingdom Constitution?

## Part II: Dicey Put to the Test: Do We Need to Save Dicey's Law of the Constitution?

It is ironic that the phrase 'AV Dicey high priest of constitutional orthodoxy' is everywhere to be found, while this mid-Victorian constitutionalist wanted to be an 'expounder', not a 'defender' and even less an 'oracle' of the British Constitution. Dicey did not refer to any religious belief or faith in his legal writings but he assuredly created a kind of new religion: *The Law of the Constitution*. This new creed was based on legal positivism on one hand and on epistemological positivism on the other. As for the former dimension, Dicey may 'have presented a highly skewed account of British Constitutional law' by 'ignoring' the immunities and privileges of the Crown[46] in his *Introduction* and prevented a certain kind of public law from appearing in Britain. But much more than his predecessors, he had a concept of law that was close to voluntarism, since for him Parliament 'has ... the right to *make or unmake* any law whatever'.[47] Law was defined as produced by will, even if this will has to be authorised. Dicey unveiled and therefore invented the law *in* the Constitution: not only did he assert that constitutional law was not a question of morality (or at least, not only)[48] but also, to some extent, that the British Constitution and its institutions obeyed general principles – general laws – as well as rules that had to be identified by legal science. He has been considered by most specialists as using, in one way or another, an analytical method. As JWF Allison explains in *The English Historical Constitution*, 'his method was that of observation and objective description through the composition of sets of categories and the division or subdivision of their components'.[49] If Dicey actually separated the historical from the legal and the constitutional, he also separated, at

[44] See Baranger, *Ecrire la constitution non-écrite* 151.

[45] Dicey, *Law of the Constitution* 424.

[46] M Loughlin, 'The Concept of the State' in M Sunkin and S Payne (eds), *The Nature of the Crown. A Legal and Political Analysis* (Oxford, Oxford University Press, 1999) 64.

[47] Dicey, *Law of the Constitution* 3.

[48] J Austin, *The Province of Jurisprudence Determined* (New York, Prometheus Books, 2000) 257–68.

[49] Allison, *The English Historical Constitution* 8; Loughlin, *Public Law and Political Theory* 13–17.

face value, what is legal and what is political; the best example, of course, was his distinction between legal and political sovereignty.[50] In other words, he separated rules from facts, and rules from principles and it may be no coincidence that this analytical method appeared in constitutional law at the same time as precedents were being theorised.[51]

However, as Loughlin and Allison have shown, Dicey was not always consistent with his analytical method. One does not have to go into detail to notice Diceyan inconsistency: let us only think of one of the components of the rule of law. According to Dicey, the second component of the rule of law was 'that here every man, whatever his rank of condition, is subject to the ordinary law of the realm and amenable to the jurisdiction of the ordinary tribunals'.[52] This mention of the 'ordinary law of the realm' connects Dicey's rule of law and Constitution to the common law tradition. In fact, this connection gives a quite dizzying historical depth to Dicey's Constitution and a strong anchor in English political culture that cannot be pulled up. Dicey's analytical method was a way for him to cut the 'Constitution d'Angleterre' from its historical Whig roots, to 'dispose of it'[53] in order to find even more solid ground formed by common law *and* the 'Ancient Constitution'.[54] Indeed, Dicey managed to build a system of constitutional appropriation without resorting to the Whig account of the Constitution which was based on the 'spirit' of the English people.[55] Unlike Bagehot, he did not resort to the national character of the English and their love of freedom, embodied in their 'Constitution'. In other words, Dicey managed to create a dynamic constitutional system generated by, and benefiting, a community of political and practical experiences. The community was then in a position to claim the Constitution as its 'property' and as a trust. It was not an entity (the people or the nation), it was common experience, and if it was not democracy, it was one of its *sine qua non* conditions. It is as if Dicey was giving formal sense to his Constitution: its past (the ground), its common political experience, and its future (the horizon). By giving this formal and evolutionary sense to the Constitution, Dicey may have created a constitutional dogma.

The second part of this book, 'Dicey Put to the Test', aims to verify whether this dogma passes the test of time and is still of constitutional value. In Chapter 6, **Vernon Bogdanor** lists what is still useful in Dicey's legacy. He contrasts Dicey's central doctrines with the most important changes from the second half of the

[50] Dicey, *Law of the Constitution* 27–28.

[51] JH Baker, *An Introduction to English Legal History*, 4th edn (Oxford, Oxford University Press, 2007) 96–201; CK Allen, *Law in the Making* (Oxford, Clarendon Press, 1927).

[52] Dicey, *Law of the Constitution* 114.

[53] Sentence borrowed from C Harlow, 'Disposing of Dicey: From Legal Autonomy to Political Discourse' (2002) 48 *Political Studies* 356.

[54] Loughlin, *Public Law and Political Theory* 150–53.

[55] Contra: Allison, *The English Historical Constitution* 165–85, 185: 'However scant in analysis, it amply illustrates a whig version of the history in that constitution'.

twentieth century to the first twenty years of the twenty-first. More precisely, Bogdanor puts to the test four doctrines that were held by Dicey:[56]

1. the legal doctrine that Parliament is sovereign;
2. the political doctrine that the unity of the United Kingdom is best preserved by maintaining the unitary state, federation being unsuited to British conditions;
3. the political doctrine that there is no stable *via media* such as 'Home Rule' or 'devolution' lying between the unitary state and federalism;
4. the moral doctrine that there are certain things which a sovereign Parliament ought not to do and which would therefore be unconstitutional.

The need to go back to the meaning of sovereignty is analysed by Bogdanor in the post-Brexit vote of 2016 in which the sovereignty of the people came into conflict with the sovereignty of Parliament. Another important evolution is how, since 1997, the British state has transferred part of its power to allow the creation of devolved bodies. The last strong challenge to the Diceyan myth raised by Bogdanor is the rise of the power of the courts through judicial review which, in the end, has codified certain aspects of the Constitution. The paradox he exposes is that Brexit uncovered the cracks in the old veneer of the system, which can no longer be ignored.

Chapter 7, by **Aurélien Antoine**, assesses Dicey's influence in the *Miller 1* and *Miller 2* Supreme Court judgments. On the subjects of 'parliamentary sovereignty, rule of law, royal prerogative, government responsibility (accountability), constitutional conventions, and the referendum', Dicey's writings are considered by the Court as being fundamental. Nonetheless, Antoine reveals the use – which was different in the two judgments – of Dicey's basic constitutional jurisprudence on all these points.[57] Antoine demonstrates the malleability of Dicey's ideas and how they can be easily used by judges to suit their own vision. He strips away the different layers of decisions in the two cases to reveal a simplification of the complexity of Dicey's thought. In the end one wonders if this is to say that Dicey's contradictions and flexible definitions end up meaning everything and nothing, or whether his spirit infuses the way in which judgments are made, denying the possibility of thinking outside Dicey's box? For Ian Ward, the sombre reality would be that 'like the Cheshire cat in *Alice in Wonderland*, the Diceyan smile remains, but the juristic Cat has all but disappeared; only with the increasingly sour and melancholic Dicey, it would be rather more appropriate to envisage a grimace than a smile'.[58]

In the next chapter, **Timothy Endicott** – the present Vinerian professor of English law – does not fully remove the Cheshire cat scowl by focusing on

[56] V Bogdanor, 'What is Left of Dicey's Constitution?', see ch 6 below.
[57] A Antoine 'Dicey in the *Miller 1* and *Miller 2* Judgments', see ch 7 below.
[58] I Ward, *The English Constitution. Myths and Realities* (Oxford, Hart Publishing, 2004) 37.

'parliamentary executive'. He puts the idea to the test and deals with the question of the survival of the constitutional structure in the present British Constitution. Relying on the nomination of the Prime Minister by the monarch, Endicott leads a global reflection about the evolution (or non-evolution) of political legitimacy in the British Constitution.[59] Challenging Dicey by showing the value of 'the parliamentary executive', Endicott makes clear that the House of Common is the arena, 'the forum', in which the executive is held accountable by the legislative to a much greater extent than Dicey ever valued.

The section continues to examine the legitimacy in Dicey's constitutional and political jurisprudence. **Nick Barber**, through a retrospective glance, focuses on the question of what Dicey forgot when he defined the rule of law. He shows that there is more about Dicey than just Austin[60] when exploring the connections between the British Empire and the rule of law. Of course, this question is crucial today for the reassessment of the posterity of his jurisprudence. Barber discusses the rule of law in the context of imperialism but in another way than simply as a means of political domination. What comes out is how Dicey's rule of law is embedded first and foremost in the English historical past. Thus, once superimposed on the peoples of the countries of the British Empire, the spirit of liberty at the heart of the rule of law cannot have the same force but does end up eroding the concept of Empire.

Dicey's constitutional concepts thus remain necessary in the twenty-first century for anyone seeking to understand the British Constitution. Dicey may no longer be a high priest but in 1885, in the first edition of his *Introduction to the Study of the Law of the Constitution*, whether we like it or not, he codified a part of the British Constitution, and gave us a language with which to discuss it, then and now. As with any codification, Dicey's law of the Constitution indicates what belongs to the past, to the present, and to some extent, even to the future.

## Part III: Dicey Abroad: Do We Need Dicey's Law of the Constitution Outside England?

'Dicey beyond Borders' deals with the effect of Dicey's doctrines on territories other than England and with the way these doctrines were transposed into other common law systems. Here Dicey appears as more political and less theoretical than in the two previous parts of this book.

If Dicey's contradictions have been underlined for Britain, they are no less problematic for the countries of the former Empire. As these four chapters make clear,

[59] T Endicott, 'The Parliamentary Executive', see ch 8 below.
[60] NW Barber, 'What Dicey Forgot', see ch 9 below.

Dicey's belief in the London Parliament as 'the absolute sovereign of the British Empire'[61] carried with it a number of unsolved questions, the most contentious of which was the concept of a unified Empire on which parliamentary sovereignty had a real impact. The diversity of the countries of the former Empire and their lack of constitutional unity made the Diceyan approach irreconcilable with any type of constitutional logic, except perhaps for monarchical sovereignty.[62] This spatial test of Dicey's works leads to liberty through the rule of law, whether Dicey wanted it or not.

To start this section, **Thibault Guilluy**[63] focuses on the question of Irish Home Rule for which Dicey is famous, in that he rejected it violently. He sheds light on Dicey's distinctive constitutional theory by analysing the assumptions of Dicey's doctrine about Irish Home Rule and illustrates that Dicey's theory is more subtle than is generally believed. He helps understand how Dicey's concepts can be adapted to other constitutional systems, as Dicey himself altered his theory in order to support his anti-devolution doctrine. For him, any dilution of power – either through devolution or federalism – would be fatal to the unity of the state, and a form of parliamentary sovereignty Dicey would never contemplate. Guilluy demonstrates that Diceyan English constitutionalism is inherently conservative, weary of constitutional experimentations for moral reasons. Once again, what emerges is a Dicey not shying away from using political morality to justify his legal theory. That this is problematic is an understatement for one who was purporting to do the opposite in his magnum opus *The Law of the Constitution*. What also appears, between disapproving lines, is what could be Dicey's theory of federalism, given how federal systems can work, keeping in mind the United States example.

The three other chapters of this section are less about constitutional theory than about the way Dicey's constitutional thoughts, doctrines, and concepts were adapted in other constitutional systems. It is interesting to note that, paradoxically, Dicey's abstract approach to British constitutional law opened the door to comparative jurisprudence. **Michael Greve**[64] follows Guilluy's discussion of federalism in the United States, not so much about the concept of sovereignty or Dicey's and Bryce's journeys in the United States,[65] but rather with Dicey's concept of the rule of law. The discussion is dedicated to the importance of Dicey's ideas when administrative law appeared in the United States of America. Greve shows to what extent the debate about administrative law, until the adoption of the Administrative Procedure Act in 1946, was structured according to

[61] Dicey, *Law of the Constitution*, 1st edn, 355.

[62] S Douglas-Scott, *Brexit, Union, and Disunion. The Evolution of British Constitutional Unsettlement* (Cambridge, Cambridge University Press, 2023) 240.

[63] T Guilluy, 'Dicey's Theory of the British Constitution in the Light of the Home Rule Question', see ch 10 below.

[64] M Greve, 'Dicey in America: The Rule of (Administrative) Law, a Century Later', see ch 11 below.

[65] Walters, *A. V. Dicey and the Common Law Constitutional Tradition* 67–69.

Dicey's ideas about the rule of law. He also makes clear that Dicey's idea about the arbitrariness of administrative law was in existence throughout the rise of this body of law. Likewise, Greve shows how Dicey has resurfaced in constitutional and legal United States debates as a force to be reckoned with. Interestingly, Greve underlines how the administrative state cannot understand difficulties related to the rule of law without understanding the common law background on which such ideas rest. The United States Constitution may be codified and rigid in substance, yet it stems, in part, from a common law tradition which rooted rights in the constitution/body of the free Englishmen of England. Ignoring this nugget of the past means ignoring what is certainly the most valuable element, beyond Dicey's mistakes and idiosyncrasies.

As far as Canada is concerned, things are obviously different because Canada has a written Charter of Rights and Freedoms. **Nicholas Dickinson**[66] contrasts Dicey's rule of law, which was based on an unwritten constitution, with a written constitutional culture of rights. He assesses Dicey's concepts when it is necessary to combine local traditions with abstract principles, and to understand the 'judicialisation of politics'.[67] If there is a bit of Dicey left at the core of the Canadian system, it is more the spirit of liberty than anything left in a system which has become everything Dicey would have disapproved of: federal, dualistic, favouring the rights of First Nations, parliamentary, 'constrained', and in favour of legal collectivism. Yet Dickinson demonstrates how Dicey's 'constitutional conservatism' can be like an old ghost to vanquish in the renewed Canada of the twenty-first century.

The last chapter in this section concerns Hong Kong, which was a British protectorate where Dicey's doctrines were transposed in a totally different political and constitutional context. **Richard Cullen**[68] explains how Dicey's concepts were combined with what he calls 'authoritarian legality'. He confirms that Diycean doctrines and concepts 'took a life of [their] own':[69] not only did they do so by the different ways they were interpreted by constitutionalists but also because they were transposed to other constitutional and political cultures which made them their own. This is a testament to the enduring legacy of Diceyan liberty much more than to his Victorian constitutional heritage.

Consequently, the last issue to be faced today is what we want to save out of Dicey's constitutional law? At the heart of it lies one fundamental idea: British liberty. What this liberty really is, and what rights defend it, are other questions that Dicey did not bother with, believing, along with Austin, that existing laws were enough. Yet, in the twenty-first century, this is no longer sustainable.

[66] N Dickinson, 'Resolving Dicey's Contradictions? Rights, Freedoms and Parliamentary Sovereignty in Canada', see ch 12 below.

[67] ibid.

[68] R Cullen, 'Dicey in Hong Kong', see ch 13 below.

[69] Loughlin, *Public Law and Political Theory* 159.

## Part IV: Dicey vs Dicey: What do We want to Save in Dicey's Constitution?

Dicey's contradictions are the negative reflections of the richness of his constitutional jurisprudence. This fourth part, 'Dicey vs Dicey', gives some examples of the many reflections of Dicey that currently exist. As Dicey's *Law of the Constitution* codified, at least in part, the British Constitution, his constitutional thinking today forms the basis of the British Constitution: like any constitutional source, it is interpreted in ways that more or less comply with what he asserted. In the words of Peter Oliver, as 'any teacher of first year constitutional law will know, once Dicey's doctrine is in place in the minds of law students it is very difficult to dislodge it'.[70] Nevertheless, let us try to do so, because if there is a tradition of interpretation of Dicey's doctrines, there is also a tradition of interpretation autonomous from Dicey's original intent. How far is this tradition of interpretation from Dicey's original purpose?[71]

**Marie Padilla** uses the distinction between 'trace' and 'aura' to identify what the substantive 'Dicey' (no longer used as a surname) and references to him mean today. Padilla reveals that this distinction, initially made by the French historian Boucheron about Benjamin, could be used to understand what 'Dicey' means today, or more exactly, what function his doctrines have in public law discussions and what kind of space his writings occupy. Here, the opposition lies between Dicey – the man – and Dicey – the author. According to Padilla, what Boucheron called the 'aura' is useful to decipher some projects. Applying this theory of 'aura' to MD Walters's *A.V. Dicey and Common Law Constitutionalism*, Padilla shows that the use of the Dicey's aura enabled Walters to reconstruct a legal narrative that demonstrated the roots of common law constitutionalism at the time by Dicey and before him, by Coke. Dicey then became one of the fathers of common law constitutionalism. This notion was famously coined by TRS Allan and summarised by JWF Allison in the following terms: 'Allan's theory is not one of constitutionalism without a constitution'. For Allan, a constitution is a 'common law constitution' – in the sense that 'the rule of law serves in Britain as a form of constitution' in the absence of a higher constitutional law of a written constitution: 'it is in this fundamental sense that Britain has a *common law constitution*: the ideas and values of which the rule of law consists are reflected and embedded in the ordinary common law'.[72] From the perspective of a history of political thought, common law constitutionalism is deeply connected to political liberalism as it is based on the principle of liberal constitutionalism.

[70] PC Oliver, *The Constitution of Independence. The Development of Constitutional Theory in Australia, Canada, and New Zealand* (Oxford, Oxford University Press, 2005) 350.

[71] M Padilla, 'Between *Traces* and *Aura*, Dicey's Many Lives in Contemporary Public Law Scholarship', see ch 14 below.

[72] Allison, *The English Historical Constitution* 31.

But what sort of political liberalism does Dicey stand for? This is precisely what **Alan Kahan** looks at in his intentionally provocative contribution,[73] in which he shows that Dicey was more important for the history of liberalism than Locke. Kahan suggests that there was a 'before Dicey' and an 'after Dicey'. In this sense, Dicey, through his doctrine about poverty and the rejection of state interventionism, produced a decisive contribution to the line of demarcation between 'ancient liberalism' and 'modern liberalism'.[74] Dicey really was a man of his times and a product of his social class but his understanding of Victorian liberty ended up being a source of inspiration for a number of twentieth-century liberal thinkers, from Hayek to Shklar. Kahan opposes Dicey as a classic liberal and Dicey as an ancient liberal and helps us think outside of both a constitutional and a liberal way of thinking.

Following the same line of thought – that there are many positive and negative versions of Dicey, but from a public law perspective – **Nicolas Gabayet**[75] sheds light on one of the most famous 'contradictions' of Dicey's, MD Walters' 'blind spot'.[76] Here, it is Dicey's refusal to acknowledge that there actually was something like a *droit administratif* developing in Britain at the turn of the nineteenth century. This blind spot brings us back to an internal conflict between Dicey's political convictions and his scientific approach. Gabayet asserts that one of the explanations for such a Diceyan blind spot was his rejection of collectivism and state interventionism – such a rejection, as shown by Gabayet, also having a posterity of its own.

To conclude this final section, **Iain McLean** and **Scot Peterson**[77] tackle Dicey's dark sides head on. They point out Dicey's many inconsistencies and changes of mind during his lifetime: about women's vote and about the referendum. While Marie Padilla insists that Dicey's legacy could be manipulated, this last contribution stands as its mirror and shows that all these contradictions were intrinsic to Dicey.[78] The discussion about the contradictions between Dicey's own political positions and the implications of his constitutional doctrines and scientific choices, as well as the identification of a far-fetched tradition of interpreting Dicey's writings, was clearly crystallised in Weill's famous article 'Dicey Was Not Diceyan' published in 2003.[79] Weill insisted that Dicey was more consistent than many may think. According to her, despite the fact that Dicey's distinction between a legal and a political meaning of sovereignty might have sounded quite clear-cut, Dicey had a more subtle and complex concept of popular sovereignty which he supported. **McLean** had already tackled some of the problems in 2010 in a chapter

[73] AS Kahan, 'AV Dicey and the History of Liberalism', see ch 15 below.
[74] ibid, Kahan's opposition couple.
[75] N Gabayet, 'Dicey's Influence on English Administrative Law', see ch 16 below.
[76] Walters, *AV Dicey and the Common Law Constitutional Tradition* (Cambridge, Cambridge University Press, 2020) 299.
[77] I McLean and S Peterson, 'No, Really, Dicey Was Not Diceyan', see ch 17 below.
[78] ibid.
[79] Weill, 'Dicey Was Not Diceyan' 485.

entitled 'The Contradictions of Professor Dicey' in his book *What's Wrong with The British Constitution*.[80] This time, with **Peterson**, the charge against Dicey is not only that he contradicted himself but that he did so willingly for political elitist reasons, to the extent of destroying his own liberal legacy. Read with the other chapters of this section, McLean and Peterson force the reader to look at Dicey in a different and rather unpleasant light.

In order to comply with the adversarial principle, **MD Walters** who has produced one of the most enduring works on Dicey with his elegant book *A.V. Dicey and the Common Law Constitutional Tradition*, makes his case in the conclusion[81] of this collection of essays about Dicey and his legacy.

At the end of the day, what is there in Dicey that we want to keep for ourselves? The most striking fact is that there is no consensus about him, nor about his legacy and in truth, there never was, whether in Britain or abroad. However, any constitutionalist would agree that AV Dicey is a central character in the history of constitutional law. Disagreements and lack of consensus begin when it comes to constitutionalism, that is to say, not constitutional law but the ideology that underpins this body of law and the rules of political power. Some will say that Dicey's doctrine favoured freedom through sovereignty and rule of law, whereas others assert that no principle of liberty can stem from a man who held that 'constitutionalism could be maintained by the British practice of "democracy tempered by snobbishness"'.[82] This edited collection nevertheless shows that two things are unquestionable. First, that Dicey's tradition of interpretation lives on and has a life of its own on an international scale: like Hans Kelsen (1881–1973), Dicey belongs to a global legal heritage. Second, that in a world in which democracy no longer equates to the values of human rights, the main Diceyan postulate of his rule of law, according to which freedom is safe as long as law is common, may be his most enduring legacy. More than anything, more than the man himself, whatever one thinks about him today, that is what *we* want to keep.

[80] I McLean, *What's Wrong with The British Constitution* (Oxford, Oxford University Press, 2010) 128–40.

[81] MD Walters, 'The High Priest of Orthodox Constitutional Theory: AV Dicey Revisited', see ch 18 below.

[82] Loughlin, *Public Law and Political Theory* 144.

# PART I

# Dicey: Follower or Legal 'Disrupter'?

# 1

# Bentham and Dicey

MICHAEL LOBBAN

In his *Lectures on the Relation between Law and Public Opinion during the Nineteenth Century*, AV Dicey identified the mid-nineteenth century as the 'period of Benthamism': 'from 1825 onwards the teaching of Bentham exercised so potent an influence that to him is fairly ascribed that thorough-going though gradual amendment of the law of England which was one of the main results of the Reform Act'.[1] Dicey's interpretation of 'Benthamism', which associated it strongly with individualism and *laissez-faire*, proved highly influential, though its accuracy as a depiction of Bentham's own position has been much contested.[2] Nor is it exactly clear how deep Dicey's reading of Bentham was, and how far his vision of 'Benthamism' was shaped by reading Leslie Stephen's work on *The English Utilitarians* or Élie Halévy's *La Formation du Radicalisme Philosophique*.[3]

Bentham's work ranged very broadly. It encompassed a theory of law and an analysis of legal concepts to be found in his early jurisprudential writings, some of which were published by Etienne Dumont in 1802 in *Traités de Législation Civile et Pénale*.[4] It was here that he developed his theory of law as a command, a version of which would be popularised in the work of his follower John Austin. It included a utilitarian theory of legislation, expounded in his *Introduction to the Principles of Morals and Legislation*[5] where he set out the groundwork of a code of civil and penal law which would identify the interests which needed protection and defined the offences which caused injuries to such interests. It also

[1] AV Dicey, *Lectures on the Relation between Law and Opinion in England during the Nineteenth Century*, 2nd edn (London, MacMillan and Co, 1914) 126.

[2] See JB Brebner, 'Laissez Faire and State Intervention in Nineteenth-Century Britain' (1948) 8 *Journal of Economic History* 59; D Roberts, 'Jeremy Bentham and the Victorian Administrative State' (1958–9) 2 *Victorian Studies* 193; O MacDonagh, 'The Nineteenth-Century Revolution in Government: a Reappraisal' (1958) 1 *Historical Journal* 52; H ParrisPollo, 'The Nineteenth-Century Revolution in Government: a Reappraisal Reappraised' (1960) 3 *Historical Journal* 117; LJ Hume, 'Bentham and the Nineteenth-Century Revolution in Government' (1967) 10 *Historical Journal* 361.

[3] L Stephen, *The English Utilitarians*, vol 1 (London, Duckworth, 1900); E Halévy, *La Formation du Radicalisme Philosophique* (Paris, F Alcan, 1901–1904).

[4] J Bentham, *Traités de Législation Civile et Pénale* (Paris, Bossange, Masson et Besson, 1802).

[5] J Bentham, *Introduction to the Principles of Morals and Legislation*, HLA Hart and JH Burns (eds) (Oxford, Clarendon Press, 1996).

included a *Constitutional Code*,[6] in which he designed a constitution which would include securities against misrule by those holding political power, and set out both the 'powers and duties of the several servants of the Community' and how officials should obtain and lose power.[7] Along the way, he left a mass of papers, published and unpublished, with projects for the reform of legal institutions, civil procedure, and criminal justice.

Bentham left behind him a group of 'philosophic radicals' – including James Mill, Edwin Chadwick, and John Stuart Mill, who edited his *Rationale of Judicial Evidence* – but his main projects were not taken up by his successors. The common law was not abolished and replaced by a code, and the Constitution was not recast on Benthamic lines. Bentham's jurisprudence did, however, cast a strong influence on the way later generations of jurists thought about law and law reform.[8] Those whose way of thinking was influenced by Bentham included Dicey. He admired the analytical method pioneered by Bentham and wrote a number of treatises on legal topics which sought to arrange the material of the common law around sets of logically defined rules.[9] There has been much debate over how far Dicey's constitutional thought, and his aim to write a treatise on the *law* of the Constitution, was indebted to the Benthamic tradition. In writing his book, *Introduction to the Study of the Law of the Constitution*, Dicey used some of the language of sovereignty to be found in the works of Bentham and his follower John Austin, and set out to resolve some of the flaws he found in Austin's definitions so that it might better reflect actual practice. However, as shall be seen, Dicey's vision of the Constitution was also highly influenced by a common lawyers' vision, which saw the Constitution in very different terms. Dicey's modified version of Austin – which posited a legal sovereign constrained by a politically sovereign electorate – did not sit comfortably with his common lawyer's vision of the rule of law; and nor did his understanding of conventions provide the bridge he had promised between legal and political sovereignty. A deeper reading of Bentham might have helped Dicey better to identify and resolve the theoretical tensions inherent in his own vision of the Constitution.

## I. Dicey and 'Benthamism'

Like many mid-Victorian liberals, Dicey admired the clarification of legal concepts which had been effected by Bentham and his followers. By the time Dicey began

[6] J Bentham, *Constitutional Code* in *The Works of Jeremy Bentham*, vol 10, J Bowring (ed) (Edinburgh, William Tait, 1843).

[7] J Bentham, *First Principles Preparatory to Constitutional Code*, P Schofield (ed) (Oxford, Oxford University Press, 1989) 3. On Bentham's political thought, see especially P Schofield, *Utility and Democracy: The Political Thought of Jeremy Bentham* (Oxford, Oxford University Press, 2006).

[8] M Lobban, *The Common Law and English Jurisprudence, 1760–1820* (Oxford, Clarendon, 1991).

[9] AV Dicey, *A Treatise on the Rules for the Selection of the Parties to an Action* (London, W Maxwell, 1870); *The Law of Domicil as a Branch of the Law of England, Stated in the Form of Rules* (London, Stevens and Sons, 1879); *A Digest of the Law of England with Reference to the Conflict of Laws* (London, Stevens and Sons, 1897).

his career, analytical jurisprudence was associated more with Austin than Bentham, thanks to the publication of Austin's *Lectures on Jurisprudence*.[10] Austin's project was narrower than Bentham's, for whom the analysis of legal concepts was merely the starting point of a much larger project of utilitarian reform, which included all aspects of law. Austin's concern was primarily with the building blocks of private law: the concepts of property and contract, which explained how rights were established, and the concepts of delict or crime, which dealt with violations of those rights. He sought to provide a legal terminology by elucidating the 'notions which the human mind is compelled to form, and the distinctions which it is necessitated to make, by the mere existence of a body of law of any kind', at least in a civilised society.[11] It was a language which jurists would be able to use to clarify their ideas, a set of tools any lawyer or legislator needed to give effect to his purposes.

Dicey admired this analytical project, stating that Austin had explained 'the elementary terms of legal logic' with a lucidity 'which makes misapprehension or forgetfulness impossible'. Austin had 'freed from all mistiness and confusion … the terms which constitute the elements of the logic of law'.[12] Indeed, Dicey defended Austin's conceptual analyses from Sir Henry Maine's criticisms, saying that the latter's critique of Austin in his *Early History of Institutions*[13] was 'the least satisfactory part of his work' since it confounded history with logic. For Dicey, it was self-evident that a lawyer who wished to understand the law needed to know the meaning of the legal concepts which defined property and contract: it was all the more necessary for the English lawyer, since so much of the law of England was left to judicial development. It was here that Austin provided the tools: 'When you have once imbibed Austin's doctrine as to the meaning of the law, you can no more use the term vaguely than after you have studied Ricardo you can doubt what is meant by rent'.[14] For mid-century liberals, just as Ricardo provided the economic language for *laissez-faire*, so Austinian analysis provided its jurisprudential concepts.

Dicey certainly associated Bentham and his school with *laissez-faire*. In *Law and Opinion*, he argued that 'though *laissez faire* is not an essential part of utilitarianism, it was practically the most vital part of Bentham's legislative doctrine, and in England gave to the movement for the reform of the law, both its power and its character'.[15] Bentham's utilitarian theory was in fact more complex than

[10] J Austin, *Lectures on Jurisprudence, or, The Philosophy of Positive Law*, 4th edn (London, John Murray, 1873).

[11] JS Mill, 'Austin on Jurisprudence', *The Collected Works of John Stuart Mill*, vol 21, JM Robson and S Collini (eds) (Toronto, University of Toronto Press, 1984) 168.

[12] AV Dicey, 'Maine's Early History of Institutions' (1875) 20: 509 *The Nation* 225. Here, he defended Austin's concept of sovereignty from Maine's attacks. Contrast his later comment that Austin's theory of sovereignty was not a 'deduction from abstract theories of jurisprudence' but was rather 'suggested by the position of the English Parliament, just as Austin's analysis of the term "law" is at bottom an analysis of a typical law, namely, an English criminal statute': AV Dicey, *Introduction to the Law of the Constitution*, 6th edn (London, MacMillan and Co, 1902) 69–70.

[13] H Maine, *Lectures on the Early History of Institutions* (London, John Murray, 1875).

[14] AV Dicey, 'The Study of Jurisprudence' (1880) 5 (5th ser) *Law Magazine and Review* 382–83, 386.

[15] Dicey, *Law and Opinion* 147.

this suggested. For Bentham, the central utilitarian object of legislation was to secure the 'happiness of the body politic'. He identified four subordinate ends of legislation through which the greatest happiness was to be achieved: they were 'to provide for subsistence; to secure abundance; to befriend equality; to maintain security'. Of these, it was the final one which was the most important, and the most closely connected to law,[16] for it was law which secured for the individual a sphere of personal liberty by protecting him from injuries at the hands of others.[17] Bentham suggested that law could not promote subsistence or abundance directly: this was done by nature. But law could provide for them indirectly by securing for individuals the fruits of their work. The potential tensions between these ends – and in particular the tension between security and equality – left open the degree of state intervention which would be needed in any Benthamic state.[18] However, contemporaries of Dicey certainly read his work as encouraging a regime of *laissez-faire* which would be facilitated by his reformist vision of law.

When it came to civil law, Bentham's successors agreed that the presence of a robust system of law enforced by coercive authority was an essential prerequisite for a settled political society, to provide security for person and property. Rather than looking to legislation as a means to promote the greatest happiness of the greatest number, they saw the law as a neutral structure which allowed people to pursue their own vision of happiness. Bentham's importance in this process (as Dicey himself explained) was twofold: he set 'before reformers an ideal to be attained by the amendment of the law'; and he determined 'the method, i.e., the legislative means, by which the amendment of the law might be best affected' [*sic*].[19] For Dicey, what Bentham supplied was not the idea of an interventionist legislature with a programme to advance happiness, but rather a programme to sweep away the technical and procedural abuses of the old common law.[20] In his view, *laissez-faire* was embedded in the very principles of Bentham's utilitarian legislation: since legislation was a science whose aim was to promote utility, and since every individual was the best judge of his own happiness, 'therefore legislation should aim at the removal of all those restrictions on the free action of an individual which are not necessary for securing the like freedom on part of neighbours'.[21] The corollaries he drew from these principles were 'that the law ought to extend the sphere and enforce the obligation of contract, and that, as

[16] 'If no direct laws are made respecting subsistence, this object will be neglected by no one. But if there are no laws respecting security, it will be useless to have made laws respecting subsistence': J Bentham, 'Principles of the Civil Code' in *The Works of Jeremy Bentham* 303.

[17] Bentham, 'Principles of the Civil Code' 302.

[18] See PJ Kelly, *Utilitarianism and Distributive Justice: Jeremy Bentham and the Civil Law* (Oxford, Clarendon, 1990); GJ Postema, 'Bentham's Equality-Sensitive Utilitarianism' (1998) 10 *Utilitas* 144; M Quinn, 'A Failure to Reconcile the Irreconcilable? Security, Subsistence and Equality in Bentham's Writings on the Civil Code and on the Poor Law' (2008) 29 *History of Political Thought* 320.

[19] Dicey, *Law and Opinion* 165.

[20] ibid 205–206.

[21] ibid 146.

regards the possession of political power, every man ought to count for one and no man ought to count for more than one'.[22]

This vision of the role of law in mid-Victorian society was shared by Dicey's friends and contemporaries. For them, Austin's jurisprudence explained the legal concepts associated with property and contract, the protection of which devotees of *laissez-faire* saw as the minimum essential functions of government. For instance, in his *Principles of Political Economy*, John Stuart Mill described the prime function of government to be the protection of person and property, as well as securing the performance of contracts.[23] Mill argued against state intervention, describing a 'circle of liberty' surrounding every person which helped to define the sphere of 'authoritative' state intervention:[24] it was the state's role to protect certain rights, the most important of which was not to be hurt or have one's freedom impaired by another.[25] Mill proceeded to offer a philosophical justification for the existence of the kinds of rights of person, property, and contract analysed by Austin and the lawyers. This vision of the legitimate sphere of authoritative state intervention appeared to put at its centre the core areas of the common law of property and obligations. For Mill, the main problem with English law was not with its substantive rules but with its complicated and costly procedures, which often made it impossible to know what one's rights were. 'The law everywhere ostensibly favours at least pecuniary honesty and the faith of contracts,' he argued, 'but if it affords facilities for evading those obligations, by trick and chicanery … to that extent the law is demoralizing, even in regard to pecuniary integrity'.[26] Like Dicey, Mill was an enthusiast for Benthamite reforms of technical procedure.[27]

We can trace a similar vision in the 'individualistic minimum' described by Dicey's friend Henry Sidgwick in his *Elements of Politics* at the end of the century.[28] Sidgwick pointed out that 'the legislation of modern civilised communities' was primarily framed on the basis 'that what one sane adult is legally compelled to render to others should be merely the negative service of non-interference, except

[22] ibid 149–50.

[23] JS Mill, *Principles of Political Economy* in *The Collected Works of John Stuart Mill*, vol 3, JM Robson (ed), intro by VW Bladen (Toronto, University of Toronto Press, 1965) 880.

[24] '[T]here is a part of the life of every person who has come to years of discretion', Mill wrote, 'within which the individuality of that person ought to reign uncontrolled either by any other individual or by the public collectively': Mill, *Principles of Political Economy* 938.

[25] JS Mill, *Utilitarianism* in *The Collected Works of John Stuart Mill*, vol 10, JM Robson (ed), introductions by FEL Priestley and DP Dryer (Toronto, University of Toronto Press, 1969) 255.

[26] Mill, *Principles of Political Economy* 886.

[27] Mill also argued for property law reform in areas – such as primogeniture, entails and inheritance – which interfered with the freedom to use one's own property as one wished.

[28] H Sidgwick, *The Elements of Politics*, 1st edn (London, MacMillan and Co, 1891). The phrase 'individualistic minimum' connoted the 'necessary' as opposed to the 'optimal' functions of government. By the time *The Elements of Politics* was first issued in 1891, the heyday of Victorian *laissez-faire* ideology had passed and Sidgwick himself argued that there was an important role for legislation beyond the individualistic minimum.

so far as he has voluntarily undertaken to render positive services'.[29] Sidgwick's discussion of the individualistic minimum as applied to property, contract, and tort largely reflected the approach of the common law courts of his day, and indeed drew heavily on the work of analytical jurists such as TE Holland. Significantly, the individualistic minimum which Sidgwick described was one which did not require legislation. In Austinian vein, he argued that the notions of 'government' and 'law' were closely connected, insofar as it was the government which issued general commands backed by penalties which it enforced.[30] However, the core function of government in securing the individualistic minimum consisted of (first) assessing whether any infringements of the rights had occurred in the case in question, and (second) taking steps to compel adequate redress. This required the existence of both a judiciary and an executive. However, 'the obvious inference from law to a legislature is not quite so indispensable as it seems', he wrote, 'if we suppose the action of government to be strictly confined to the "individualistic minimum"'. Many of the rules enforced by government did not arise from express legislation: they had been brought to the degree of precision which they had now attained 'by a series of judicial decisions which ostensibly declared or applied rules or principles of right handed down from time immemorial'. Moreover, he added that this kind of 'judicial quasi-legislation is, even in a highly civilised society, the best machinery for introducing such improvements as may be required in the definition of the fundamental rights and duties that constitute the "individualistic minimum"'.[31]

The conception of *laissez-faire* individualism found in such works reflected a widely-held mid-Victorian view that the essential functions of state did not require an activist legislator. It suggested that the entities of property, person, and contract to be protected by the state were unproblematic. Rather than being the subject of political contention, they could be left to judicial development. The idea that the law should be developed by judges was of course anathema to Jeremy Bentham: but it was one which his follower John Austin endorsed. It was also endorsed by Dicey. In *Law and Opinion*, he pointed out that nine-tenths of the law of contract and almost all of the law of torts were judge-made.[32] While he conceded that judges were influenced by the public opinion of their era, Dicey stressed that '[j]udicial legislation aims to a far greater extent than do enactments passed by Parliament, at the maintenance of the logic or the symmetry of the law'.[33] The decisions made by judges were influenced 'by the ideas and theories of writers on law' which meant that '[i]f an author of ingenuity has reduced some branch of the law to a consistent scheme of logically coherent rules, he supplies exactly

[29] Sidgwick, *Elements of Politics*, 1st edn, 38.
[30] H Sidgwick, *The Elements of Politics*, 2nd edn (London, MacMillan and Co, 1897) 19.
[31] Sidgwick, *Elements of Politics*, 1st edn, 324.
[32] Dicey, *Law and Opinion* 362. For Austin's views on judicial legislation, see WE Rumble, *The Thought of John Austin* (London, Athlone Press, 1985) ch 4.
[33] ibid 364.

the principles of which a Court is in need'.[34] Judicial legislation aimed at certainty and the maintenance of a fixed legal system. While Dicey recognised that the opinions of judges often reflected the ideas of an earlier age, he also thought that their opinions 'may sometimes rise above the ideas prevalent at a particular era'.[35] By reasoning logically on particular cases, judges developed 'general and reasonable rule[s] of decision'. This contrasted with Parliament, which mostly paid little regard to general principles and 'attempts to meet in the easiest and most off-hand manner some particular grievance or want'. Rather than being guided by logic, it acted in response to such pressure as 'powerful bodies can bring to bear'.[36] Dicey's comparison of judicial and parliamentary legislation revealed an old-fashioned common lawyer's preference for the former.[37]

## II. Sovereign Power

By the time of his death in 1832, Jeremy Bentham had devoted ten years to developing a distinct code of constitutional law which would set out both the powers and duties of those in government. Bentham's theory had changed significantly over the course of his long life. In his early work, *A Fragment on Government*, Bentham argued that a sovereign's legislative power was without legal limit. Instead of being limited by law, the sovereign's power was determined by the people's habit of obedience: if enough people disobeyed a law of which they disapproved, a 'juncture of resistance' would be reached which would dissolve the government and the state.[38] Already in his early work, there were signs of some qualifications. In the *Fragment*, he suggested that a supreme body might be 'limited by express convention', where the convention provided a 'common signal' for disobedience 'which, in other cases, we despaired of finding'.[39] In his unpublished writings from this era, he also wrote of rulers limiting themselves by constitutional laws *in principem*, through which rulers bound themselves by a declaration of their will which was enforced not by the political sanction under their own control (which was the hallmark of a law *in populum*) but by the moral sanction of the people. Such laws set new markers for the people's habit of obedience.[40] In his later works, particularly the *Constitutional Code*, Bentham elaborated on his theory of constitutional law, looking more deeply at the relationship between the

[34] ibid 365.
[35] ibid 368.
[36] ibid 370–71n.
[37] See eg D Lieberman, *The Province of Legislation Determined: Legal Theory in Eighteenth-Century Britain* (Cambridge, Cambridge University Press, 1989) ch 2.
[38] J Bentham, *A Fragment on Government* in *A Comment on the Commentaries and a Fragment on Government* JH Burns and HLA Hart (eds) (Oxford, Oxford University Press, 1977) 484.
[39] Bentham, *Fragment on Government* 485, 489.
[40] J Bentham, *Of the Limits of the Penal Branch of Jurisprudence*, P Schofield (ed) (Oxford, Clarendon, 2010) 86–89.

sovereign ruler and the people. He now distinguished between two aspects of sovereignty, located in the supreme operative power and the supreme constitutive power. The supreme operative power was made up of the public functionaries 'to whose power it is intended, on each occasion, the conduct of all the other members of the community in question shall be subjected'.[41] This body was made up of the governors and stood in effect in the shoes of the party Bentham had in his earlier work designated as the sovereign. It was omnicompetent, and had plenary lawmaking powers, including the power to make the Constitution.[42] The supreme constitutive power in Bentham's code lay in the people, who had the power of 'locating and eventually dislocating' those who held the operative power, and who were consequently sovereign.[43] This was in effect a way of rethinking and developing the earlier notion of the sovereign being constituted by the people's habit of obedience.

The *Constitutional Code* aimed to be a system which built in accountability and good rule. In order to obviate the risk of corruption, the possessors of the supreme operative power had to depend on the holders of the supreme constitutive power – the people – for their positions. As Bentham explained, '[i]n every political state the whole body of public functionaries constituting the supreme operative, require to be considered in the character of corruptors and corruptees': to obviate this danger (at least in republics), 'the constitutive authority is placed over the supreme operative, with dislocating power with relation to it'.[44] Bentham's constitutional structure was designed to obviate the risk of corruption by ensuring that the officials' interest would always coincide with their duty. At the heart of this system was the notion of transparency, which ensured that governors would always be subject to the 'Public Opinion Tribunal':[45] it would be the public which constantly superintended those in power, ensuring that they acted in accordance with the interests of the community as a whole. 'Dislocability and puniability of members excepted', Bentham wrote, 'the Public Opinion Tribunal is to the Supreme Constitutive what the Judiciary is to the Supreme Legislative'.[46]

Bentham's wider constitutional ideas were set forth in the *Constitutional Code*, which was edited by John Bowring in 1843 in his *Works of Jeremy Bentham* and was readily available to Dicey's generation. However, mid-century jurists thinking about the nature of sovereignty did not look to this radical work. Instead, they looked to John Austin's version, which put forward a simpler theory, based on ideas found in *A Fragment on Government*. Like the early Bentham, Austin spoke of the sovereign as being constituted by a people's habit of obedience. Unlike Bentham, he did not explore in any detail how the people whose obedience gave

[41] Bentham, *Constitutional Code* 9.

[42] See F Rosen, *Bentham, Byron, and Greece: Constitutionalism, Nationalism, and Early Liberal Political Thought* (Oxford, Clarendon, 1992) 65–66.

[43] Bentham, *Constitutional Code* 98.

[44] ibid 69.

[45] Schofield, *Utility and Democracy* 259–63.

[46] Bentham, *Constitutional Code* 157.

power to the sovereign might exercise its control. In Austin's view, this was not a matter of law, but of positive morality. For Austin, '[s]upreme power limited by positive law, is a flat contradiction in terms'.[47] The limits which the people might in practice impose on a sovereign – and which he would in turn follow – were not material for a book on legal concepts. Austin did not pick up the nuances in Bentham's work. For instance, whereas Bentham had drawn attention to confederations such as the German Empire, the Dutch Republic, and Switzerland as examples of sovereigns limited by convention, when Austin discussed such entities, it was simply to identify exactly where the true illimitable legal sovereignty lay in them.[48]

Like his contemporaries, Dicey engaged with Austin rather than Bentham when discussing sovereignty. He began his critique by attacking one of the weakest points of Austin's discussion, his attempt to locate which determinate persons held sovereign power in England: in Austin's version, they were the King, Lords, and the electorate which elected members of the Commons. This was low-hanging jurisprudential fruit, for many critics pointed out the flaws in Austin's quest to find a factual sovereign whose commands were habitually obeyed.[49] In common with many critics, Dicey thought that Austin's notion that the MPs who exercised actual sovereign power by passing legislation were trustees for the electors created far more problems than it solved. In Dicey's view, Austin had used this device to enable him to explain why Parliament was not in fact omnipotent, but 'its powers are practically limited in more ways than one'.[50] This was an unlikely explanation of Austin's reasons for making this argument, since his notion of the habit of obedience already exercised a control mechanism. In fact, Austin was attempting to resolve the dilemma of locating which particular people held sovereign power once a parliament had been dissolved in anticipation of an election.

Dicey's critique of Austin led him to explore further the nature of the relationship between sovereign and people. Although Dicey himself followed Austin in acknowledging that the sovereign could be practically limited by the people's habit of obedience (which Dicey described as an 'external limit' on sovereign power), he seized on the mention of the electorate to introduce his own modification of the Austinian theory, by introducing a new distinction between legal sovereignty and political sovereignty. In Dicey's version, Parliament had legal sovereignty,

[47] Austin, *Lectures* 270.

[48] In composite states, 'the sovereignty of each of the united societies, and also of the larger society arising from the union of all, resides in the united governments as forming one aggregate body', while in confederated states 'the several compacted societies are not one society, and are not subject to a common sovereign … a system of confederated states is not essentially different from a number of independent governments connected by an ordinary alliance': Austin, *Lectures* 267, 269.

[49] See J Bryce, 'The Nature of Sovereignty' in his *Studies in History and Jurisprudence*, vol 2 (Oxford, Oxford University Press, 1901) 49; Sidgwick, *Elements of Politics*, 1st edn, 23–25; DG Ritchie, 'On the Conception of Sovereignty' (1891) 1 *Annals of the American Academy of Political and Social Science* 385.

[50] Dicey, *Law of the Constitution* 73.

since it was not subject to any legal limitations, and since its will was enforced in the courts. Political sovereignty rested with the electors, whose will was 'ultimately obeyed by the citizens of a state'. This was 'a political, not a legal fact', for the courts took no notice of that will, though Parliament would, at least 'in the long run'. As Dicey put it, 'as things now stand, the will of the electorate, and certainly of the electorate in combination with the Lords and the Crown, is sure ultimately to prevail on all subjects to be determined by the British government'.[51]

In making these arguments, Dicey was not only influenced by his desire to unpack Austin's clumsy identification of where sovereignty lay in England. He wanted to describe the actual working of the present Constitution, while maintaining the view of both Austin and the common lawyers that Parliament had supreme unlimited lawmaking powers. Dicey saw Parliament as the most important political actor. He shared neither Bagehot's political view that the real centre of power in the English Constitution lay with the Prime Minister and Cabinet, nor Anson's legal view that sovereignty was divided between the executive and legislative branches.[52] In his view, the Constitution provided for representative government, the essence of which was that 'the legislature should give effect to the will of the political sovereign, i.e. of the electoral body, or of the nation'.[53] If this was a vague definition of what constituted the political nation, Dicey elaborated in *Law and Opinion* that (at least for the Philosophic Radicals) these relevant electors were the middle class voters, a class 'so wide' that their interests would 'coincide with the interest of the whole people'; a class whose parliamentary representatives 'would study to promote the greatest happiness of the greatest number, *i.e.* of the whole community'.[54]

Dicey thereby modified the Austinian theory of sovereignty by introducing the 'political sovereign'. He was not content with a theory in which the authority of the sovereign was constituted by a simple habit of obedience; but neither was he interested in recasting constitutional law in a new form, in the manner of Bentham. Instead, he wished to analyse an existing Constitution which he thought was already working properly. However, there were a number of problems with Dicey's approach. As Henry Sidgwick pointed out, his use of the same word – sovereignty – to connote 'two such very different kinds of power' was 'highly dubious'.[55] Dicey did not fully work out the nature of the relationship between these two 'sovereigns', to show how the legal sovereign was constituted or constrained. Rather than setting out a constitutional theory of the relationship between sovereign and people, as Bentham had, or leaving the question of the political limits on a sovereign to the realm of 'positive morality' or political

[51] ibid 70.

[52] WR Anson, *The Law and Custom of the Constitution*, vol 1 (Oxford, Clarendon, 1907) 4: 'there is a real dualism in our constitution, the Crown in Parliament and the Crown in Council'.

[53] Dicey, *Law of the Constitution* 373.

[54] Dicey, *Law and Opinion* 161.

[55] Sidgwick, *Elements of Politics*, 2nd edn, 658.

science, as Austin had, Dicey introduced common law elements. These elements may have described how common lawyers understood the working of the Constitution, but they did not meet the challenge of explaining how and why the sovereign Parliament was constrained. In the end, as shall be seen, Dicey's constraints would prove to be no more robust than Austin's.

## III. The Common Law Constitution

Although they were central to his constitutional story, Dicey explored neither the foundations of the authority of Parliament and the judiciary nor the relationship between them. Seeking to provide students with a description of the central features of the existing Constitution and how distinct institutions operated, he restated the assumptions of lawyers in the common law tradition, rather than working out how exactly the elements of the Constitution interacted. Although he spoke of a sovereign legislature which was subject in some way to a distinct political sovereign, Dicey argued that 'the constitution is the result of the ordinary law of the land'. General constitutional principles, such as those which related to personal liberty, had been developed through common law judgments. The position of the Crown and its servants had been determined by the courts and Parliament extending 'the principles of private law'. If there was no *droit administratif*, it was because '[t]his idea is utterly unknown to the law of England, and indeed is fundamentally inconsistent with our traditions and customs'.[56] In articulating these views, he drew on the work of a variety of historians, jurists, and political scientists who had traced the growth of the English Constitution from its ancient foundations. Indeed, in the preface to the first edition of *Law of the Constitution*, Dicey wrote that '[n]ot a page of my lectures could have been written without constant reference to writers such as Blackstone, Hallam, Hearn, Gardiner, or Freeman'. However, as shall be seen, although Dicey's view of history was informed by these writers, he did not use them to develop a theory to explain the foundations of law.

Such works might have provided materials for a theory of a customary Constitution. For instance, EA Freeman's *The Growth of the English Constitution from the Earliest Times* explained how the legal institutions of the Constitution which were in place by the end of the reign of Edward I had developed out of a customary ancient common law. 'The prerogative of the Crown, the privilege of Parliament [and] the liberty of the subject' rested largely 'on that somewhat shadowy yet very practical creation, that mixture of genuine ancient traditions and of recent devices of lawyers' known as the common law.[57] For this writer,

[56] Dicey, *Law of the Constitution* 199.

[57] EA Freeman, *The Growth of the English Constitution from the Earliest Times* (London, MacMillan, 1872) 107–108. For a discussion of the 'Whig' historians who influenced Dicey, see JW Burrow, *A Liberal Descent* (Cambridge, Cambridge University Press, 1981) ch 6.

it was clear 'that our judicial and our parliamentary institutions are closely connected, that both sprang out of the primitive Assemblies' found in 'the immemorial Teutonic constitution' of 'our forefathers' and that 'things which now seem so unlike our popular juries and the judicial powers of the House of Lords are in truth both of them fragments of the judicial powers which Tacitus speaks of as being vested in those primitive Assemblies'.[58] In making this point, Freeman drew on Francis Palgrave's 1823 *Rise and Progress of the English Commonwealth*, which argued that 'the ancient modes of administering the laws have produced the political constitution'. 'Parliament in its present form', Palgrave continued, 'is entirely founded upon the legal Constitution by which it was preceded; and the authorities exercised by the aristocratical and popular branches of the legislature, have arisen from the ancient distribution of the powers of remedial and corrective justice'.[59] Palgrave's history suggested the slow development of a constitution, as the practices of a vigilant people ossified into law. By far the most powerful factor behind the development of the Constitution was 'the silent legislation of precedent', as occasional acts became usages or customs, which in turn became laws. Attracting little attention at first, they grew into full vigour.[60] The great institutions of the kingdom, including trial by jury or Parliament itself, did not arise from any preconceived system, but grew out of particular circumstances and practices.[61] For Palgrave, the history of English law was one:

> in which the exercise of power has been transferred from the Sovereign to his Counsellors and to the Courts which bear his name, a process by which the ancient royal prerogatives, arbitrary and indefinite in their nature, have either been coerced by the law, or shared with those who have become the organs of the national influence and authority.

In this process, 'the steady empire of the law has been substituted for an uncertain, and therefore arbitrary, rule'.[62]

Besides these works on the growth of the Constitution, there was a long tradition in common law thought dating back to Sir Edward Coke which accorded a prime position to the judiciary in developing a common law Constitution on the foundations of community custom.[63] A modern version of this could be seen in Frederick Pollock's *Expansion of the Common Law*, which argued that the royal judges appointed in the thirteenth century saw themselves as 'servants of the law

[58] Freeman, *Growth of the English Constitution*, 18, 80–81.

[59] F Palgrave, *The Rise and Progress of the English Commonwealth* (London, John Murray, 1832) 2–3.

[60] Palgrave, *Rise and Progress* 315.

[61] Thus, the jury was neither the product of a deliberate policy, nor an ancient Saxon institution, but was (Palgrave argued) a product of a Norman innovation which 'expand[ed] from its primitive germ. Had it not been for the constant exercise of the functions which the people of England possessed when they assisted in the administration of the law, they would never have been qualified to claim their political rights': Palgrave, *Rise and Progress* 276.

[62] Palgrave, *Rise and Progress* 280–81.

[63] See further M Lobban, *A History of the Philosophy of Law in the Common Law World* (Dordrecht, Springer, 2007) ch 2.

first and the king afterwards' and continued 'the work of the ancient tradition, inasmuch as the uniformity which they established was not according to the king's pleasure, but according to law'.[64] Pollock traced their approach to law to that found in the ancient county court, which had 'no external authority to look to' but had to 'find its own law', in the custom of the community.[65] In these courts, where decisions were made by suitors (rather than royal judges) 'there was always some man, or a small group of men, whose opinion about a disputed point of custom did in fact carry great weight'.[66] In a similar way, the judges of the superior courts would cultivate their own expertise.

Despite his familiarity with these works, Dicey was not interested in developing a historical theory of the Constitution. It was not only that he was aware that other historical writers, focusing on later political history, presented a different vision of constitutional development.[67] More importantly, he insisted that his work was one of law, not history, and drew a firm line between historical and legal exposition. In an otherwise complimentary review of Kenelm Digby's *Introduction to the History of the Law of Real Property*, Dicey criticised Digby's attempt to combine what he saw as two different methods: 'You may deal with law either historically or analytically; you may, that is to say, either trace the growth of legal conceptions and institutions, or else analyse logically the nature of such conceptions and show their place in a logically arranged plan'.[68] For a lawyer, Dicey noted, 'the primary object of study is the law as it now stands; he is only secondarily occupied with ascertaining how it came into existence'.[69] It was clear that he did not think that a theory of the Constitution could be derived from history. In the *Law of the Constitution*, Dicey praised Freeman's *Growth of the English Constitution*, but argued that his tracing of English constitutional forms to the Teutonic assemblies of the high Middle Ages was 'mere antiquarianism': it 'has no direct bearing on the rules of constitutional law in the sense in which these rules can become the subject of legal comment'. Dicey added that historians like Freeman were 'infected with a love which, in the eyes of a lawyer, appears inordinate, for the germs of our institutions, and seem to care little about their later developments'.[70]

Dicey did not have a romantic vision of an ancient unchanging Constitution, or of a customary Constitution in which the common law stood above the Crown.

[64] F Pollock, *The Expansion of the Common Law* (London, Stevens and Sons, 1904) 46. Pollock's reference to 'suitors' connoted 'suitors of the court', who were obliged to attend, rather than litigants.

[65] Pollock, *Expansion of the Common Law* 44: 'the law of the land may be said to live in the witness of the county and the hundred'.

[66] ibid 45.

[67] Referring to SR Gardiner's multi-volume *History of England from the Accession of James I to the Outbreak of the Civil War, 1603–1642*, Dicey said that 'the historian who most nearly meets the wants of lawyers is Mr Gardiner': *Law of the Constitution* 16.

[68] AV Dicey, 'Digby on the History of English Law' (1875) 21: 545 *The Nation* 374.

[69] Dicey, *Law of the Constitution* 15.

[70] ibid 14, 16.

The work of historians like William Stubbs taught him that in every stage of society 'a number of different principles, which are often at bottom scarcely inconsistent with each other, exert co-ordinate influence, no one being fully carried out'.[71] From Stubbs, he also took the point that there was a difference between the form of the Constitution and its substance. One of the lessons of Stubbs's *Constitutional History* was that 'the English constitution, like all medieval institutions, has been from the first a mass of fictions', with the result that it 'retains in its form the character of an age of which the spirit has passed away from the modern world'. Consequently, Dicey did not draw on history to explain the source of parliamentary or judicial authority. Neither did he put forward any other theory. Like many of his predecessors from Coke to Blackstone, he simply asserted parliamentary sovereignty as a legal fact, and left the origins of judicial power unaddressed.

## IV. The Rule of Law and the Role of the Judges

Next to parliamentary sovereignty, the rule of law was the second pillar of Dicey's Constitution. He associated the concept both with Parliament and with the judiciary. The idea of its importance to the English Constitution may have suggested itself to Dicey from his reading of William Stubbs in the early 1870s.[72] Reviewing Stubbs's *Constitutional History*, Dicey drew attention to one 'essential peculiarity of English political development': the fact that, 'through a fortunate combination of circumstances, the rule of law was established in England at a time when it was unknown in every other great country of Europe'.[73] Stubbs's history traced the establishment of a single, unified rule of law to the reign of Henry II, when a centralised system of royal justice emerged.[74] Rudolph Gneist's *History of the English Constitution* also showed that the establishment of a system of uniform and equal laws was to be attributed to the power of the Crown in the later middle ages. Such works suggested that the rule of law, a national and common law, was to be associated with a national, supreme government ruling through law. The rule of law equated to the absence of arbitrary or discretionary power: in Dicey's age, '[t]he supremacy of the law necessitates the exercise of Parliamentary sovereignty'.[75]

The rule of law was also closely associated with the judiciary. Defining what he meant by the rule of law, when introducing the topic in his book, Dicey identified three features, each of which related to the work of the courts: that no one could be

[71] AV Dicey, 'Stubbs's Constitutional History of England' (1875) 20: 505 *The Nation* 153.

[72] W Stubbs, *Select Charters and Other Illustrations of English Constitutional History from the Earliest Times to the Reign of Edward I* (Oxford, Clarendon, 1870) 21: 'The reign of Henry II initiates the rule of law'; *cf* J Kirby, 'Dicey and English Constitutionalism' (2019) 45 *History of European Ideas* 33, 39.

[73] Dicey, 'Stubbs's Constitutional History of England' 154.

[74] See W Stubbs, *The Constitutional History of England*, vol 1 (Oxford, Clarendon, 1874) 552–53.

[75] Dicey, *Law of the Constitution* 354.

punished save by law; that public officials were as accountable to ordinary law as private citizens; and that the general principles of the Constitution were 'the result of judicial decisions determining the rights of private persons in particular cases brought before the Courts'. This suggested that many of the rights associated with the English Constitution had been developed in case law, subject to amendments and additions made by Parliament. Furthermore, it was the courts which offered an additional security for the rule of law, in case Parliament passed arbitrary legislation: for '[p]owers, however extraordinary, which are conferred or sanctioned by statute, are never really unlimited, for they are confined by the words of the Act itself, and, what is more, by the interpretation put upon the statute by the judges'.[76] The centrality of the judges in Dicey's vision was also to be seen in the fact that what defined a valid statute was its enforcement by the courts.

The role of the judges was clearly central in Dicey's constitutional thought. He recognised that they had played a major part in developing the rights and liberties enjoyed by modern Englishmen. In his review of Freeman's book, Dicey rejected the author's 'amiable delusion that at some unknown period Englishmen possessed the freedom which in fact has only been the prize of centuries of long contest with arbitrary power'.[77] Instead, English liberties were the result of particular decisions in particular contexts. Indeed, it was the very fact that England had a 'judge-made constitution' which arose from conflicts in the courts and was not 'created at one stroke' which had generated the otherwise misleading idea that the English government was 'a sort of spontaneous growth so closely bound up with the life of a people that we can hardly treat it as a product of human will'.[78]

However, Dicey devoted relatively little attention to exploring the precise nature of common law reasoning and its relationship to the development of the Constitution. The closest he got in *Law of the Constitution* (in a section discussing the absence of any competing legislative power to Parliament) was to describe judges in Austinian terms as subordinate legislators, acting 'with the assent and subject to the supervision of Parliament'.[79] To understand how they operated, Dicey here pointed the reader to Pollock's essay on 'The Science of Case Law' for further elaboration.[80] In an earlier work on 'The Development of the Common Law', he had set out a Mainite view of legal development which downplayed the role of the judiciary in the modern age, suggesting that the age of judicial innovation through

[76] ibid 357.

[77] AV Dicey, 'Freeman's Growth of the English Constitution' (1872) 15: 376 *The Nation* 170.

[78] Dicey, *Law of the Constitution* 192.

[79] ibid 58.

[80] In that essay, Pollock had described the work of the judges as a kind of inductive science using the data of precedents, guided by an 'ideal standard of scientific and harmony', which reflected 'the collective opinion of legal experts' who were 'long trained in legal habits of mind'. Pollock also described a developing law, in which 'the mutual reaction of professional opinion and decided cases is to prevent the ideal conceptions and the actual results from ever becoming inconveniently remote from one another': F Pollock, 'The Science of Case Law' in his *Essays in Jurisprudence and Ethics* (London, MacMillan, 1882) 251–52.

fiction had been overtaken first by equity, and then by legislation.[81] A further hint of Dicey's view of judicial innovation can be found in his comment on Coke's famous spat with James I in the *Case of Proclamations* over who had the right to pronounce law. This was a conflict, he noted, which established a rule 'essential to the very existence of the constitution', but it had been effected by an argument of Coke's which had been 'pedantic', 'artificial' and 'unhistorical'. For Dicey, this case showed that 'there are social conditions under which legal fictions or subtleties afford the sole means of establishing that rule of equal and settled law which is the true basis of English civilisation'.[82] It was only when he came to writing the lectures for *Law and Opinion* that Dicey devoted much attention to the nature of judicial legislation; but even then, the focus of his attention was largely on matters of private law, and sought to show how judges managed to keep the law in line with public opinion, without delving more deeply into the nature of the judicial mind.

Dicey did not think it necessary to elaborate on judicial technique when discussing the rule of law. This was because, for Dicey, the rule of law was not a matter of technique but a state of mind. In his reviews of the works of historians such as Stubbs and Gneist, he pointed out that the notion of the rule of law found in their works was associated primarily with aspects of the national character and its form of government. Noting that 'one essential merit' of English institutions 'has been to secure the rule of law', Dicey's review of Stubbs's book identified this with the 'spirit' rather than the 'form' of these institutions'.[83] In his review of Gneist, Dicey also identified 'the determination of Englishmen to be ruled by law' with the 'English character'. Strong central government and the rule of law were complementary: 'What the nation has detested is a government wanting in strength, wanting sympathy with the nation, and lacking respect for law … which expressed the will of the nation'.[84] In identifying the importance of 'character', Dicey was invoking a concept often mentioned by late nineteenth-century jurists discussing the Constitution. For instance, Sheldon Amos, professor of jurisprudence at University College London from 1869, wrote that '[t]he sentiments which mould the framework of the Constitution must possess a stability and duration which tend to impress upon those who share them a permanent type which is called "character"'.[85] For James Bryce, 'Constitutions are the expression

[81] AV Dicey, 'The Development of the Common Law' (1871) 21 *Macmillan's Magazine* 287, which argued that the common law judges in the later Middle Ages had used fictions 'to expand the existing system, so as to afford protection for new rights not recognised' hitherto. But once the common law began to ossify (by the reign of Edward I), its forms 'were not sufficiently plastic to afford protection for all the rights which, as society advanced, had gradually obtained recognition', and later modifications in law needed the intervention of Chancery and legislation, which (as emanations of royal authority) were aspects of sovereign power able to 'supply justice when the regular tribunals failed to do so'.

[82] Dicey, *Law of the Constitution* 18.

[83] AV Dicey, 'Stubbs's Constitutional History of England' (1875) 20: 505 *The Nation* 153.

[84] AV Dicey, 'Gneist's History of the English Constitution' (1886) 42: 1095 *The Nation* 532.

[85] S Amos, *Fifty Years of the English Constitution, 1830–1880* (London, Longmans Green and Co, 1880) 6.

of national character, as they in their turn mould the character of those who use them'.[86] Similarly, Pollock argued that the judges who developed the common law 'were thoroughly imbued with the national character'.[87] Dicey himself noted that the commitment to the supremacy of law which was a hallmark of the English Constitution was itself a 'trait of national character which is as noticeable as it is hard to portray'.[88]

It was this character which infused the judiciary. In Dicey's argument, the judges who controlled potentially arbitrary legislation by interpretation

> are influenced by the feelings of magistrates no less than by the general spirit of the common law, [and] are disposed to construe statutory exceptions to common law principles in a mode which would not commend itself either to a body of officials or to the Houses of Parliament, if the Houses were called upon to interpret their own enactments.[89]

This was a rather vague invocation of an *esprit de corps* found among judges. It did little to explain it as a normative principle of the common law and did not explicitly offer a theory of adjudication which could show how and why they would ensure that each new decision would remain coherent with the wider body of principles to be teased from the common law. In short, Dicey's Constitution contained no guarantee that the rule of law would be upheld by the judges – it was simply a trait of the English character, which they shared.

## V. Constitutional Conventions

The notion that the rule of law was to be contrasted with the rule of arbitrary discretion had a long pedigree in English political thought. For many earlier theorists, the challenge had been to articulate a theory to ensure that rulers would abide by the rule of law. Addressing this problem, John Locke's anti-absolutist *Two Treatises of Government* presented a theory of government created by a social contract, which established and defined the powers of a supreme legislature. In Locke's theory, governments had to rule by laws passed by a legislature authorised by the sovereign people; and if the social contract were broken, the people had a right to rebel, for 'having no appeal upon earth they have a liberty to appeal to Heaven'.[90] For Bentham, the fictitious social contract was far too flimsy and uncertain a device to secure a rule of laws which reflected the will of the people; and

[86] J Bryce, 'Flexible and Rigid Constitutions' in his *Studies in History and Jurisprudence*, vol 1 (New York, Oxford University Press, 1901) 123, 125.
[87] Pollock, *Expansion of the Common Law* 59. See further N Duxbury, *Frederick Pollock and the English Juristic Tradition* (Oxford, Oxford University Press, 2004) 147–56.
[88] Dicey, *Law of the Constitution* 183.
[89] ibid 357.
[90] J Locke, *Two Treatises of Government*, P Laslett (ed) (Cambridge, Cambridge University Press, 1988) 379 (§ 168).

so he constructed a more systematic constitutional theory with built-in checks of accountability. These theories in effect sought to show how a supreme governing power could be made accountable to the people.

For Dicey, the constitutional guarantee that those holding legislative power would not use it arbitrarily or tyrannically came through conventions. He borrowed this idea from EA Freeman's history. Freeman noted that all the legal building blocks of the Constitution had been put in place by the end of the reign of Edward I.[91] Although the political conditions of this era were entirely different, the 'King, Lords and Commons' already had 'nearly the same strictly legal powers, which they still keep'. What changed in the interim was not the 'outward form' of the Constitution but its 'practical working'. Britain's later constitutional history was a record of 'those silent changes whose gradual working has wrought out for us a conventional Constitution alongside of our written law'.[92] This conventional Constitution was not a matter of law: 'We now have a whole system of political morality, a whole code of precepts for the guidance of public men, which will not be found in any page of either the Statute or the Common Law'. This meant that there could be 'offences against the Constitution which are not offences against the Law'.[93] The notion that the legal structure of the Constitution gave a very misleading view of its practical operation was hardly new to Freeman; but the concept of conventions promised to provide a sharper tool for analysing the Constitution.

It was not a tool which impressed Dicey at first. When he reviewed Freeman's book in 1872, he was critical, noting that the author was 'unfortunately … nothing of a lawyer'.[94] In particular, he rejected Freeman's contention that conventions were nearly as strictly obeyed as rules of positive law. In this review, Dicey took the view that conventions were understandings which varied across time and context: 'They are not understood in exactly the same sense by all persons and all parties, and are, it must be added, extremely likely to be misunderstood'.[95] A conventional Constitution had the 'merit … of leaving a large number of questions, and especially the question of the exact distribution of the sovereign power, unsettled'.[96] Its demerits included 'the spirit of fiction which it fosters amongst the people who are ruled by it' which led people to forget 'the immense

[91] As Freeman put it, constitutional history before that reign was an inquiry into something which had passed away, and was the 'domain of antiquaries'; from that point on, 'it is an inquiry into laws which, whenever they have not been formally repealed, are in full force at this day' and so was 'the domain of lawyers': EA Freeman, 'The Continuity of English History' in *Historical Essays*, first ser, 3rd edn (London, MacMillan and Co, 1875) 40, 41.

[92] Freeman, *Growth of the English Constitution* 86–87; *cf* ES Creasy, *The Rise and Progress of the English Constitution*, 3rd edn (London, Richard Bentley, 1856) 14.

[93] ibid 108–109.

[94] Dicey, 'Freeman's Growth of the English Constitution' 169.

[95] ibid 170.

[96] ibid 188. He went on 'The English public … are … profoundly well satisfied with their constitutional arrangements, yet there exists an immense difference of opinion on what would seem the question, both what is and what ought to be the power of the crown'.

advantage … of calling things by their right names'. At this stage, Dicey appeared to regard conventions as indeterminate and largely unreliable. A decade later, his opinion of Freeman's work had clearly improved, for he introduced his discussion of the topic in *Law of the Constitution* with a lengthy quotation from it. Following Freeman, he pointed out that the conventions of the Constitution were not laws, since they were not recognised or enforced by the courts of law. They were instead the 'understandings which make up the constitutional morality of modern England'. These conventional 'rules or customs' which were 'constantly acted upon' were largely about how the Crown and the two Houses of Parliament should exercise their powers.[97]

Dicey's list of conventions echoed those found in Freeman. They included the conventions that the majority party in the Commons had a right to have their leaders placed in office; that the Cabinet was collectively responsible to Parliament; and that the Lords should give way to the Commons. Dicey also identified a convention that in an emergency, Parliament should be summoned to give ministers the powers needed to protect the state, and that in the meantime ministers should take any steps – including breaking the law – to restore order, trusting to a future indemnity. In Dicey's view, conventions had a particular constitutional function:

> [t]heir end is to secure that Parliament, or the Cabinet which is indirectly appointed by Parliament, shall in the long run give effect to the will of that power which in modern England is the true political sovereign of the state – the majority of the electors or (to use popular though not quite accurate language) the nation.[98]

They provided the bridge between the legal and political sovereigns.

In contrast to his treatment of judges – whose fidelity to constitutionalism was assumed – Dicey felt it necessary to devote a chapter to explaining the sanctions which ensured that conventions would be observed. He thought it necessary to do this to demonstrate that they were not simply a realm of background morality which might or might not be observed; and thereby to make an advance on Austin's thin description of the relationship between the sovereign and the people's habit of obedience. Dicey dismissed the idea that the moral power of public opinion would ensure compliance. As he saw it, to make this argument was 'like maintaining the kindred doctrine that the conventions of international law are kept alive solely by moral force', a proposition which he thought only 'a few daydreamers' would believe.[99] Instead, the true sanction which ensured compliance with 'the fundamental principles of the Constitution and the conventions in which these principles are expressed' was the 'fact that the breach of these principles and of these conventions will almost immediately bring the offender

[97] Dicey, *Law of the Constitution* 362, 366.
[98] ibid 372.
[99] He also dismissed the argument that the fear of impeachment was the threat that impelled ministers and parliamentarians to follow conventions: Dicey, *Law of the Constitution* 386–87.

into conflict with the Courts and the law of the land', since any ministry which acted without the support of Parliament or which attempted not to call it would be unable to collect tax, or maintain an army.

This was a weak argument. It sat uncomfortably with Dicey's identification of a convention that in times of emergency ministers might need to break the law to preserve order. It also failed to explain why the legal sovereign could not prolong its own life indefinitely. Dicey was particularly interested in the Septennial Act of 1716, in which a Parliament elected for three years had extended its life to seven. He used this example in the first part of his book precisely to demonstrate the legal sovereignty of a Parliament and to show that Austin's theory that MPs were trustees for an electorate which shared part of legal sovereignty was false.[100] Later, when discussing conventions, he noted that the Septennial Act would never have been passed had it been preceded by an 'appeal to the electorate'. In 1716, the electorate's opinion had not been canvassed, but times had changed: 'under the conditions of modern political life, the understandings which exist with us as to the right of dissolution' of Parliament would ensure that any such major constitutional legislation would now always be preceded by an election. However, this argument was simply a matter of assumption on Dicey's part, for he failed to demonstrate why and how the convention regarding dissolution – which 'underlies all those constitutional conventions which, in one way or another, are intended to produce harmony between the legal and the political sovereign power' – would invariably be followed. Indeed, in the same breath he conceded that 'Crown, Cabinet, and Parliament may conceivably favour constitutional innovations which do not approve themselves to the electors', which did not promise any effective guarantee of control by the latter.[101]

Dicey's discussion of conventions in effect described the practices of his day, without showing that they were constitutional devices which could ensure that the legislator was controlled. In the end, his conventions were simply matters of political morality, rather than law. As he put it,

> The conventions of the constitution now consist of customs which (whatever their historical origin) are at the present day maintained for the sake of ensuring the supremacy of the House of Commons, and ultimately, through the elective House of Commons, of the nation. Our modern code of constitutional morality secures, though in a roundabout way, what is called abroad the 'sovereignty of the people'.[102]

If the role of conventions was to provide the jurisprudential bridge between the legal and the political sovereign, it was a weak one, and one which offered little advance on Austin's theory that the sovereign power could be constrained by positive morality – the expectations of the community over which the sovereign ruled which constituted the sovereign by its habit of obedience. Dicey's theory relied on

[100] Dicey, *Law of the Constitution* 45, 72.
[101] ibid 381.
[102] Dicey, *Law and Opinion* 374.

'constitutional morality' to ensure that the 'political sovereign' would be obeyed, but he gave no greater understanding of why rulers would follow it, other than that it was part of their character to do so.

It was far from offering the kind of constitutional guarantees so carefully worked out in Bentham's *Constitutional Code*. Nor could Dicey's theory be seen as a version of Bentham's earlier theory of constitutional laws *in principem*, whereby a sovereign issued constitutional commands binding to himself as a result of the moral sanction exerted by the populace. Even if Dicey's conventions were characterised as stable 'rules or customs', they gave no clear signals to the people. According to Dicey, the point at which the House of Lords had to give way to the Commons in any clash was 'determined by anything which conclusively shows that the House of Commons represents on the matter in dispute the deliberate decision of the nation'. Similarly, the Crown had the right to dismiss a ministry with a majority and dissolve Parliament when 'an occasion has arisen on which there is fair reason to suppose that the opinion of the House is not the opinion of the electors'. Both these questions were matters of political judgement, rather than law: they were in no way exercises of political sovereignty, either in terms of giving or enforcing rules. Dicey was discussing constitutional practice in a time of change, but this was hardly law.[103] In the end, the effectiveness of the constitutional conventions which were intended to ensure that the legal sovereign would follow the wishes of the political sovereign came down to a question of character: whether those holding power would follow the conventions, or mould them to the perceived needs of the day.

[103] In Dicey, 'Freeman's Growth of the English Constitution' (Part II) 189, Dicey argued that by admitting that they were bound by the clearly expressed will of the people, the House of Lords had begun a process of introducing the notion of a referendum (in substance if not in form) as a principle of English politics.

# 2

# Austinian Qualms: Dicey on Sovereignty

GREGORY BLIGH

## I. Introduction

This chapter defends the view that AV Dicey's work reveals a robust theory of authority through his articulation of the 'legal sense' and the 'political sense' of the concept of sovereignty. It is through the concept of 'authority' that the problem of 'voluntary servitude'[1] came gradually to be restated to characterise a relation of domination excluding a direct use of, and need for, coercion.[2] Where the authority of a superior is *recognised*, the person in a position of inferiority obeys spontaneously in fact, although he is either free to disobey or would face little likelihood of having to suffer the consequences of disobedience. Of course, political authority is supported by the means to punish through the exercise of violence to overcome occasional acts of disobedience. But where the 'mass of the people'[3] are motivated merely by the anticipation and fear of coercion, a governing minority can no longer count on spontaneous obedience on a large scale,[4]

[1] See É de La Boétie, 'Discours de la servitude volontaire' [1576] in *Œuvres complètes*, P Bonnefon (ed) (Paris, J Rouam & Cie, 1892) 9, 13–14.

[2] A Kojève, *La notion de l'autorité* (Paris, Gallimard, 2004) 57–61; H Arendt, 'What is Authority?' in *Between Past and Future* (New York, Viking Press, 1961) 92–93, 106; C Perelman, 'Autorité, idéologie et violence' in *Éthique et droit* (Brussels, Éditions de l'Université de Bruxelles, 2012) 399–409. This chapter thus focuses on 'de facto', not 'de jure', authority in the sense highlighted by J Raz, *The Authority of Law*, 2nd edn (Oxford, Oxford University Press, 2009) 4.

[3] AV Dicey, *Introduction to the Study of the Law of the Constitution*, 10th edn (London, Macmillan, 1959) 265; *Lectures on the Relation Between Law and Public Opinion in England during the Nineteenth Century*, 2nd edn, (London, Macmillan, 1963) lxix; J Austin, *The Province of Jurisprudence Determined* (Cambridge, Cambridge University Press, 1995 [1885]) (VI) 263.

[4] In Hartian terms, the internal point of view towards valid rules of law would be 'confined to the official world': HLA Hart, *The Concept of Law*, 3rd edn (Oxford, Oxford University Press, 2012 [1961]) 115, 117. At this point of dissolution of the authority of law – or breakdown of voluntary servitude – private citizens are led to act as Holmes's 'bad man', conditioning their obedience to law on the legal consequences of disobedience and the likelihood of punishment. See OW Holmes, 'The Path of the Law' (1897) 10 *Harvard Law Review* 457, 459.

and is thus faced with a 'crisis of authority'.[5] Dicey wrote enlightening passages about the spontaneous obedience of the governed to the political power of those who govern.

The difficulty is confronted squarely in his seminal works *Introduction to the Study of the Law of the Constitution* and *Lectures on the Relations Between Law and Public Opinion*.[6] In each book, Dicey quotes at length a passage from David Hume's restatement of the problem of voluntary servitude in the essay *Of the First Principles of Government*:

> Nothing appears more surprising to those who consider human affairs with a philosophical eye, than the easiness with which the many are governed by the few; and the implicit submission, with which men resign their own sentiments and passions to those of their rulers. When we inquire by what means this wonder is effected, we shall find, that, as force is always on the side of the governed, the governors have nothing to support them but opinion. It is therefore on opinion alone that government is founded; and this maxim extends to the most despotic and most military governments, as well as to the most free and most popular.[7]

The core of my claim is that, despite these references to Hume,[8] it is through a critical engagement with John Austin's concept of 'sovereignty'[9] that Dicey was able to apply the problem of voluntary servitude to the province of constitutional law.[10] As a result, this chapter will approach the study of Dicey's concept of authority through a discussion of the nature and extent of Austin's influence.

[5] In the sense highlighted by A Gramsci, *Selections From the Prison Notebooks*, Q Hoare and G Nowell Smith (eds and transl) (New York, International Publishers, 1971) 305.

[6] AV Dicey, *Introduction to the Study of the Law of the Constitution* 77–78; *Lectures on the Relation between Law and Public Opinion in England during the Nineteenth Century* 2. The pagination of the tenth edition of *Law of the Constitution* is reproduced in the margins of AV Dicey, *Lectures Introductory to the Study of the Law of the Constitution. The Oxford Edition of Dicey*, vol I, JWF Allisson (ed) (Oxford, Oxford University Press, 2013).

[7] Hume, 'First Principles of Government' 16. Cited in Dicey, *Law and Public Opinion* 2; *Law of the Constitution* 77.

[8] It is perhaps noteworthy that Hume is not cited in intellectual biographies of Dicey: MD Walters, *AV Dicey and the Common Law Constitutional Tradition* (Cambridge, Cambridge University Press, 2020); RA Cosgrove, *The Rule of Law: Albert Venn Dicey, Victorian Jurist* (London, Macmillan, 1980); nor is Dicey mentioned in Postema's reconstruction of Hume's constitutional jurisprudence: GJ Postema, *Bentham and the Common Law Constitutional Tradition*, 2nd edn (Oxford, Oxford University Press, 2019 [1986]) chs 3–4. Dicey thus appears to be referring to a general statement of the problem of voluntary servitude to be found in Hume.

[9] References to Austin's work in Dicey's *Law of the Constitution* and *Law and Public Opinion* are mainly to J Austin, *Lectures on Jurisprudence*, vol 1, 4th edn, R Campbell (ed) (London, John Murray, 1879). This volume of the *Lectures* includes *The Province of Jurisprudence Determined* (Austin, *Lectures* 81–348). More specifically, Dicey's references are to passages of the sixth lecture of Austin's *Province* dedicated to the analysis of the concept of sovereignty (Austin, *Lectures* 224–348). See eg Dicey, *Law and Public Opinion* 413.

[10] It is not necessary to this argument to claim that Austin was an admirer of Hume. Indeed, Hume receives little or no attention in the main works devoted to Austin: WL Morison, *John Austin* (Stanford, Stanford University Press, 1982); RN Moles, *Definition and Rule in Legal Theory. A Reassessment of HLA Hart and the Positivist Tradition* (Oxford, Basil Blackwell, 1987); WE Rumble, *The Thought of John Austin* (London, Athlone Press, 1985); WE Rumble, *Doing Austin Justice. The Reception of John*

Austin's style of analytical jurisprudence did indeed exert attraction over Dicey,[11] and would no doubt have provided a natural backdrop for constitutional theory-building at the time.[12] Dicey's long critical discussion of the Austinian concept of sovereignty through his distinction between the 'legal' and the 'political' senses of sovereignty remained the heart of his analysis of the illimitable character of the law-making powers of the King-in-Parliament from the first to the final edition of *Law of the Constitution*.[13] These insights are taken up and elaborated on, I will argue, in *Law and Public Opinion*. With a difference of emphasis, Walter Bagehot (who Dicey also read)[14] insisted that the historical existence of a 'deferential community' was the hidden factor upon which England's unwritten Constitution relied for its stability.[15] The present chapter will nevertheless bring into focus the importance of John Austin, who insisted unambiguously on voluntary servitude as the foundation of *every* stable system of government

*Austin's Philosophy of Law in Nineteenth Century England* (London, Continuum, 2005); M Freeman and P Mindus (eds), *The Legacy of John Austin's Jurisprudence* (Dordrecht, Springer, 2013). On Postema's account, Austin would find himself in the Benthamite camp against the common law tradition represented by Hume: see Postema, *Bentham and the Common Law* 261–62. Hume, however, is also recognised as a precursor of utilitarianist thought in F Rosen, *Classical Utilitarianism from Hume to Mill* (London, Routledge, 2003) 48–57. See also M Lobban, *A History of Philosophy of Law in the Common Law World, 1600–1900* (Dordrecht, Springer, 2007) 156. Both Austin and Bentham cite Hume in reference to his use of the notion of 'utility': Austin, *Province* (IV) 86; J Bentham, *A Fragment on Government* (Cambridge, Cambridge University Press, 1988 [1776]) (I, §36) 51.

[11] Cosgrove, *Albert Venn Dicey* 23–28; Rumble, *Doing Austin Justice* 191–95. See also M Lobban, *The Common Law and English Jurisprudence, 1760–1850* (Oxford, Clarendon Press, 1991) 288. Given the inconsistent use of Austin's concept of sovereignty (see below), Dicey might simply have drawn on his analytical style of jurisprudence as a convenient method to relegate the historical view of the Constitution. See JWF Allison, *The English Historical Constitution. Continuity, Change, and European Effects* (Cambridge, Cambridge University Press, 2007) 11–12.

[12] Whether Austin's positions were accepted *or rejected* as a sound starting point: Rumble, *Doing Austin Justice* 4, 9. Not only was Austinian analytical positivism a source of inspiration of Holland's widely circulated textbook of jurisprudence in Dicey's lifetime – see TE Holland, *Elements of Jurisprudence*, 11th edn (Oxford, Clarendon, 1910 [1880]) – it was also a stable point of reference to push back against. It is through express reaction to Austin that influential authors could develop their own original approaches – such figures as HS Maine, *Ancient Law*, 10th edn (Boston, Beacon Press, 1884 [1861]) 6–8; *Lectures on the Early History of Institutions* (New York, Henry Holt & Co, 1888) 358, 383 ff); JC Gray, *The Nature and Sources of Law* (New York, Columbia University Press, 1909) vii, 6, 63 ff; J Salmond, *Jurisprudence*, 6th edn (London, Sweet & Maxwell, 1920 [1902]) 6, 47, 127, 470; CK Allen, *Law in the Making*, 7th edn (Oxford, Clarendon, 1963 [1927]) 2 ff, 65, or indeed later on Hart, *Concept of Law* chs 1–3.

[13] Dicey, *Law of the Constitution* 70–85. This can be ascertained with ease thanks to Allisson's *Oxford Edition of Dicey*, vol 1.

[14] Dicey, *Law of the Constitution* 19; Dicey, *Law and Public Opinion* xxv.

[15] W Bagehot, *The English Constitution* M Taylor (ed) (Oxford, Oxford University Press, 2001 [1867]) 34–37. See C Marshall, *Political Deference in a Democratic Age. British Politics and the Constitution from the Eighteenth Century to Brexit* (Cham, Palgrave Macmillan, 2021) ch 4. This conditioned, in turn, a reciprocal attitude of self-restraint in those who exercise government as expressed in the 'good chap theory of government': A Blick and P Hennessy, *The Bonfire of the Decencies. Repairing and Restoring the British Constitution* (London, Haus Publishing, 2022) 3–4. Catherine Marshall (*Political Deference* ch 5) focuses on Bagehot's influence on Dicey, but does not discuss Austin's. This chapter will do the opposite. Of course, our arguments need not be mutually exclusive.

('the most despotic ... *as well as* the most free' (emphasis added),[16] as Hume writes). In doing so, this study will propose a candid reading not only of Dicey, but also, mediately, of Austin who is often read in overly simplistic terms.[17]

The nature of Austin's influence in Dicey's work turns out, on closer inspection, to be counterintuitive. First, Dicey's claim to have accepted Austin's conception of sovereignty in a 'strictly legal sense'[18] is simply incorrect (see section II.A below). This observation takes a step in the direction of constitutional lawyers such as Trevor Allan and Mark Walters, who have challenged the perception of Dicey as a 'high priest of orthodox constitutional theory' in the Austinian tradition.[19] Their aim, however, is to propose a contemporary interpretivist reconstruction of Dicey's understanding of law as a form of reasoned institutional discourse.[20] The thrust of my argument is different[21] (see section II.B below). Indeed, a core of lasting Austinian influence will be highlighted here in Dicey's lack of any robust concept of the state (see section II.C below). Second, although the Vinerian Professor claimed to have distanced himself from *The Province of Jurisprudence Determined* in highlighting and discussing a 'political aspect' of sovereignty,[22] this is precisely where his line of reasoning appears to mirror Austin's (see section III.A). This raises specific challenges given the close articulation within Dicey's work of the concepts of political sovereignty and of *public opinion* (see section III.B). A breakthrough in scholarship, following authors such as Philip Schofield or Gerald Postema, has led to a sharp distinction between Austin and Bentham's respective forms of legal positivism, and to a revaluation of the role of public opinion in Bentham's later political philosophy.[23] It is nevertheless unclear how aware Dicey was of (or influenced by) Bentham's work on the relation between sovereignty and public opinion (see section III.C). Here again, this chapter makes the claim that there is at least a core of Austinian influence in Dicey's positions that could have got him – no doubt did get him – on the right path in his analysis of the relation of authority.

[16] Hume, 'First Principles of Government' 16.

[17] See Rumble, *Doing Austin Justice* 7–8.

[18] Dicey, *Law of the Constitution* 73.

[19] Walters, *Dicey and the Common Law* 129, 358–68.

[20] TRS Allan, *The Sovereignty of Law. Freedom, Constitution, and Common Law* (Oxford, Oxford University Press, 2013); Walters, *Dicey and the Common Law.*

[21] I have difficulty joining Walters in the view that Dicey *himself* could have held proto-interpretivist views very peculiar to the jurisprudential debates of the 1970s onwards, although his work manifestly lends itself to such fruitful reconstruction. See eg TRS Allan, 'Dworkin and Dicey: The Rule of Law as Integrity?' (1988) 8 *Oxford Journal of Legal Studies* 266. Allison suggests that these authors propose a normative 'Whig-like' conception of constitutional progress relying on an instrumental use of Dicey: Allison, *The English Historical Constitution* 25.

[22] Dicey, *Law of the Constitution* 73–74.

[23] P Schofield, *Utility and Democracy. The Political Thought of Jeremy Bentham* (Oxford, Oxford University Press, 2006); Postema, *Bentham and the Common Law.*

## II. Dicey's Un-Austinian Concept of Legal Sovereignty

Dicey sets out to develop a distinctly legal conception of the English Constitution which,[24] he claims, rests upon two pillars: the sovereignty of the King-in-Parliament; and the rule of law.[25] The sovereignty of Parliament is nonetheless the 'dominant characteristic' of England's political institutions 'from a legal point of view'.[26] It is an assumption of this chapter that these insights can be discussed in the context of contemporary *British* constitutional law. Throughout the passage of *Law of the Constitution* in which he expounds his concept of sovereignty 'in a legal sense', Dicey discusses John Austin's concept of sovereignty.[27] But whereas Austin's claim is analytic – internal to the logic of legal systems[28] – Dicey brings to light 'an undoubted legal fact'[29] of the British legal Constitution which he sets about trying to 'prove'.[30] This difference in perspective is inconsistent with Austin's thesis, and Dicey's understanding of legal sovereignty turns out to owe relatively little to Austin.

### A. Departing from Austin: A Rule-Based Conception of Law-Making Power

As Maine points out, the logical order of the demonstration in *The Province of Jurisprudence Determined* is unhelpfully reversed.[31] Austin begins with an analysis of legal rules that can only make sense in light of his account of the relation of authority between the sovereign and his subjects which is delayed until the final lecture, by which time the ground has been laid for a reduction of sovereignty to a question of supremacy. As a result, the argument is confused on a crucial issue that came to have influence over Dicey. It is necessary to go into detail here.

Although Austin uses the concept of 'sovereignty', he focuses almost exclusively on the question of supremacy within the legal system. A 'law' is defined as a type of command supported by sanctions issued by a person or body in a position of *superiority*, addressed to persons in a position of *inferiority*, expressing a

[24] Dicey's 'outstanding achievement' (M Loughlin, *The Idea of Public Law* (Oxford, Oxford University Press, 2003) 43) enabled by the jurisprudence of Bentham and Austin (Lobban, *The Common Law and English Jurisprudence* 288).

[25] Dicey, *Law of the Constitution* 183–84. We will come to the third implicit pillar of constitutional conventions in section II below.

[26] ibid 39.

[27] ibid 70–85.

[28] Austin, *Province* (VI) 212, 223. Every state must necessarily contain a body vested both with ultimate and illimitable law-making power.

[29] Dicey, *Law of the Constitution* 68.

[30] ibid 61.

[31] Maine, *Lectures on the Early History of Institutions* 346–50.

desire as to their behaviour and indicating the consequences that will ensue should these commands be disobeyed.[32] This must ultimately refer to the aggregate body of commands issued by 'political superiors' within the relation between sovereign and subject.[33] The force of law itself is examined in factual terms through the social position of superiority of one who can affect others 'with evil and pain' and thus coerce them to adopt a certain course of conduct through the fear of evil.[34] In other words, law-making power is an attribute of the sovereign who enjoys a social position of superiority.[35]

This is not to say that Austin is inattentive to the authority of 'the sovereign' (see section III.A below). The position of superiority is fleshed out in the final lecture. The sovereign is a 'common superior', which is to say a person or body that receives a 'habit of obedience' from the 'bulk' of society (a majority of its members), and does not have a habit of obedience towards any other person or body. This brings into play the concept of an 'independent political society'[36] united by obedience to the common superior, as opposed to the members of a 'natural' society that have frequent and sustained relations but have no common superior, or mere subordinate political societies.[37] It allows Austin to develop the idea that the law-making power of the sovereign can admit of no conceivable legal limitation.[38] This truth is in his view analytic.[39] Indeed, the common superior can issue commands upon all members of the political society and punish acts of disobedience but cannot intelligibly issue binding commands upon himself that he would be powerless to disobey. As such, the concept of sovereignty implies the idea of illimitable law-making power that attaches, not to any form of *justification* – legal or moral – but to the factual reality of the subject's acceptance of the sovereign's position of social superiority.[40] It is this illimitable scope of law-making power as it attaches to the position of supremacy that Austin is interested in.

Dicey, in contrast, does not consider the existence of any internal analytic connection between the supremacy (the rank or position in the hierarchy) of an institution of government, and the illimitable scope of the power to fix decisions of public policy in enacted law. It is enough for his purposes to demonstrate

[32] Austin, *Province* (I) 21–24. Hart has demonstrated that Austin's understanding of laws as commands 'backed by threats' cannot usefully provide an understanding of law as composed of *rules*: Hart, *Concept of Law* chs 1–2. This will play little part in the present chapter.

[33] Austin, *Province* (I) 19.

[34] ibid (I) 30.

[35] Law is a variety of command, and the power to issue commands implies superiority: ibid (I) 30–31. This understanding of law underpins Austin's legal positivist distinction between law as it actually is and law as it ought to be: ibid (V) 157. Austin traces this conception of the sovereign as legislator and of positive law as the will of the sovereign to T Hobbes, *Leviathan* (Oxford, Oxford University Press, 1996 [1651]) 176–77. See eg Austin, *Province* (VI) 165.

[36] Austin, *Province* (VI) 172 ff.

[37] ibid (VI) 176–78.

[38] ibid (VI) 212. It would be a 'flat contradiction in terms'.

[39] ibid (VI) 212: 'the position … will hold universally or without exception'.

[40] As highlighted by LL Fuller, *The Law in Quest of Itself* (Boston, Beacon Press, 1966) 31–33.

that there happens to be a particular institution of government – the King-in-Parliament – that is both supreme and illimitable as a matter of 'legal fact'.[41] Dicey thus sets about trying to 'prove' the principle of parliamentary sovereignty.[42] Contrary to Austin, this *legal* proof does not rely on the extent to which legislative enactments happen to be obeyed empirically by the bulk of the subjects. His focus, rather, is on the recognition of the supremacy of Parliament by other institutions of government – mainly the courts of law:

> The principle of Parliamentary sovereignty means neither more nor less than this, namely, that Parliament thus defined has, under the English constitution, the right to make or unmake any law whatever; and, further, that no person or body is recognized by the law of England as having a right to override or set aside the legislation of Parliament.[43]

This brings about three remarks. First, it follows implicitly from Dicey's attempt to prove the principle of parliamentary sovereignty that *other* constitutional systems must exist (and be intelligible) that contain no institution of government that is both supreme and illimitable 'from a strictly legal point of view'. Thus, the relation between the supremacy of a given institution of government and the illimitable nature of its power is contingent (empirical), not necessary (analytic). Second, the answer to the question whether the legal system does (or does not) contain such an institution depends entirely on the content of the *rules* – of constitutional law – that distribute and condition the exercise of law-making powers: there is a 'law of Parliamentary sovereignty'.[44] In this respect, Dicey's understanding of sovereignty from a specifically 'legal point of view' owes very little to Austin.[45] This is not to say that the law effectively bounds the exercise of the British Parliament's law-making power. The content of the rules highlighted clearly does not.[46] However, Parliament is limited politically to a great extent.[47]

Third, under the British Constitution, these rules involve essentially the relation between Parliament and the courts of law. The 'positive' dimension of the principle of parliamentary sovereignty does not refer merely to the illimited scope of the content of legislation,[48] but to the fact that the courts recognise that Parliament retains full legislative authority to repeal the Acts of a previous legislature.[49]

[41] Dicey, *Law of the Constitution* 39.
[42] ibid 61.
[43] ibid 39–40.
[44] As elegantly put by Walters, *Dicey and the Common Law* 162.
[45] Mark Walters is no doubt correct here: ibid 165.
[46] See *R v Home Secretary, ex p Simms* [2000] 2 AC 115, 131, per Lord Hoffmann: 'The constraints upon [parliamentary sovereignty] are ultimately political, not legal'.
[47] See section III.A below. I thus differ here from Walters' interpretation.
[48] Legislation is both 'constitutive' and 'abrogative': Salmond, *Jurisprudence* 122.
[49] Parliament cannot in principle impose any particular formality on the future reform of legislation: *Vauxhall Estates Ltd v Liverpool Corpn* [1932] 1 KB 733; *Ellen Street Estates Ltd v Minister of Health* [1934] 1 KB 590. See Dicey's discussion in *Law of the Constitution* 64–66. The principle in its positive dimension has undergone some change at the initiative of the courts with the identification

The principle in its 'negative' dimension records the fact that the courts decline their authority to exercise constitutional review (substantive or procedural) of an Act of Parliament that has received royal assent and has been recorded on the Parliamentary Roll.[50] Dicey offers no precedent to support his views here which might have followed at the time from the internal coherence of parliamentary sovereignty as he understood it.[51] However, it might also be a consequence of the fact that no precedent offered an authoritative statement of a principle of parliamentary *sovereignty* as such, which would openly reveal the courts' control of its content.[52]

It is disconcerting that, having conceded so much, Dicey does not make more explicit the principle of statutory interpretation according to which, as 'the will of Parliament can only be expressed through an Act of Parliament', it is subject to practices of narrow statutory interpretation by the courts that 'preven[t] … inroads upon the law of the land'.[53] Indeed, although the courts do recognise the supremacy and the illimited character of Parliament's law-making power, they have also imposed a strong assumption – although not irrebuttable – that Parliament is not legislating contrary to the rule of law. Thus, an Act of Parliament will not be construed so as to overturn settled common law principles and rights if any alternative interpretation is available or unless Parliament has made it clear, in express terms, that it intended to do so.[54]

## B. Some Scepticism Concerning the Interpretivist Reading

This goes some way toward highlighting a 'spirit of legality'[55] under the British Constitution that Mark Walters relies on in his interpretivist reconstruction of

of a category of 'constitutional' statutes that cannot be repealed by implication by an 'ordinary' statute (*Thoburn v Sunderland City Council* [2003] QB 151 para 62) and a hierarchy among constitutional instruments, some being more 'fundamental to the rule of law' than others (*R (Buckinghamshire County Council) v Secretary of State for Transport* [2014] 1 WLR 324 para 207). In light of such evolutions, one cannot but sympathise with Walters' attempt to redeploy Dicey's intuitions on the rule of law to fruitfully engage in contemporary jurisprudential debate: Walters, *Dicey and the Common Law* 8.

[50] *Edinburgh and Dalkeith Railway Co v Wauchope* (1842) 8 Cl & F 710, 725; *Lee v Bude & Torrington Junction Railway Co* [1871] LR 6 CP 576, 582; *British Railways Board v Pickin* [1974] AC 765, 782; *M v Home Office* [1994] 1 AC 377, 395.

[51] ECS Wade, 'Introduction' in Dicey, *Law of the Constitution* xlviii.

[52] D Baranger, *Écrire la constitution non écrite* (Paris, Presses Universitaires de France, 2008) 161.

[53] Dicey, *Law of the Constitution* 407–408.

[54] See passim: ibid 413. It is expressed clearly in *Minet v Leman* [1855] 20 Beav 269, 278, referred to throughout the case law. The principle is relied on in striking fashion in *R v Secretary of State for the Home Department, ex p Pierson* [1997] 3 WLR 492, 518 (per Steyn LJ), and *R v Home Secretary, ex p Simms* [2000] 2 AC 115, 131 (per Hoffmann LJ). Similarly, it has been suggested that Coke's dictum in *Dr Bonham's Case* [1610] 8 Co Rep 113, 118, would have been understood as a rule of construction in the seventeenth century: Allen, *Law in the Making* 450; JW Gough, *Fundamental Law in English Constitutional History* (Oxford, Clarendon, 1955) 35. However, the case has been invoked in the United States as authority for the judicial power to strike down unconstitutional law: TFT Plucknett, '*Bonham's Case* and Judicial Review' (1926) 40 *Harvard Law Review* 30, 61–68.

[55] Dicey, *Law of the Constitution* 184, 201.

the Vinerian Professor's jurisprudential trajectory.[56] Trevor Allan has argued convincingly that Dicey's outwardly 'formal expository method' veils an abstraction of constitutional first principles from an implicit understanding of moral and political principles of constitutional history that weigh down on the exercise of parliamentary sovereignty,[57] thus resulting in a continuity between the judicially enforced elements of the Constitution and the 'constitutional morality' that pervades political practices that would be judged extra-legal in the strict sense.[58] This line of enquiry certainly shows that a form of contemporary interpretivist reconstruction is available. However, Dicey might also be borrowing the expression 'constitutional morality'[59] from Austin (see section III.A below). That he remained unclear here is indicative of the fact that his views on the question were not clear-cut.[60]

Moreover, it would distort Dicey's view to assert that the supreme and illimitable law-making power of Parliament depends entirely on its recognition by the courts, or that sovereignty lies with the courts.[61] It would be closer to the truth to say that the principles of the Constitution are the result of a complex arrangement of institutions vying with one another for influence, and coordinated in their action by the understanding that such principles cannot be revised without overhauling the Constitution.[62] One the one hand, if the sovereignty of Parliament is but 'a construct of the common law', then it can be adjusted by the courts where necessary.[63] On the other, however, to claim that 'the general principles of the

[56] Walters, *Dicey and the Common Law* 91, 160, 328–29.

[57] Allan, *The Sovereignty of Law* 54.

[58] ibid ch 2. This would not make Dicey an interpretivist in the more radical sense developed in RM Dworkin, *Law's Empire* (Oxford, Hart Publishing, 1998 [1986]) that Allan himself seems to reject (TRS Allan, 'Justice and Fairness in *Law's Empire*' (1993) 52 *Cambridge Law Journal* 64, 64–65) in favour of the softer version of interpretivism in Ronald Dworkin's earliest work in *Taking Rights Seriously* (Cambridge, Harvard University Press, 1977) 81 ff. We would argue that Mark Walters' is a stronger form of interpretivism in the idea that the sovereignty of Parliament is 'conditioned', not only by the effect of principles of 'legality' weighing on the reasoning of the judge, but in itself as a morally coherent endeavour: Walters, *Dicey and the Common* Law 165, 188.

[59] Dicey, *Law of the Constitution* 24; Austin, *Province* (VI) 222.

[60] Dicey's hesitations are highlighted by Allison, *The English Historical Constitution* 13–14. In fairness to Walters, he makes it clear that evidence of Dicey's 'unconscious' interpretivist approach is 'fragmentary': Walters, *Dicey and the Common Law* 91.

[61] As, for instance, in JC Gray's attempt to redeploy the Austinian framework by redefining 'the law' as the body of rules laid down by the courts, that is to say the institutions with the last word that, in turn, depend on no other institution, thus reducing parliamentary legislation to a *source* of law: Gray, *The Nature and Sources of Law* 82, 92.

[62] Baranger, *Écrire la constitution non écrite* 160. This complex relation between Parliament and the courts is captured by HWR Wade, 'The Basis of Legal Sovereignty' (1955) *Cambridge Law Journal* 172, 188–89. On sovereignty as a function of institutional arrangements see Loughlin, *The Idea of Public Law* 80.

[63] See Lord Steyn in *R (Jackson) v Attorney General* [2006] 1 AC 262 para 102: 'The supremacy of Parliament … is a construct of the common law. The judges created this principle. If that is so, it is not unthinkable that circumstances could arise where the courts may have to qualify a principle established on a different hypothesis of constitutionalism'. Indeed, the courts *have* made such adjustments in the *Thoburn* and *Buckinghamshire County Council* cases (see above n 49).

constitution … are the result of judicial decisions determining the rights of private persons in particular cases'[64] does not prevent Parliament from overturning such principles.[65] It does mean, as put elegantly by Lord Hoffmann, that 'Parliament must squarely confront what it is doing and accept the *political cost*' (emphasis added).[66]

As a result, the British political Constitution is consistent with the idea that the policy decision of the legislator must prevail over the principled decision of the judge. And in the final analysis, the legislator is limited, not by any legal limitation inherent in a proper understanding of the law's internal coherence, but by the relation of *authority* between those who govern and those who are governed. The 'spirit of legality' is at bottom the judges' role in alerting the political sovereign that the legal sovereign is to be held to account – there is a political cost to be paid – just as the function of the conventions of the Constitution is to ensure that the political sovereign may have the last word.[67] This is to say that any legal limit on Parliament's action due to the nature of its relation with other institutions of government (first and foremost, the courts) is intricately intertwined with external checks that have to do with how parliamentary enactments are received and obeyed by the governed.[68] It would seem that despite Dicey's obvious commitment to a conception of the law-making powers of Parliament as conferred by rules, both the problem of the habit of obedience of the subjects and the final word of the supreme law-maker remain. The Austinian framework holds sway.

Thus, although the line may seem thin between two conceptions of the political nature of constitutional law – the first arguing that it is the body of principles of political morality underpinning the actual institutional functioning of our democracies,[69] the second holding that it is a particular mode of political dispute that cannot be reduced to any legal rationale –[70] there does not seem to be a compelling reason to believe that Dicey himself would have adhered to an interpretivist understanding of constitutional law.

The true mystery is no doubt why Dicey was not steered towards other forms of legal positivism that might have seemed more congenial to his rule-based conception of legal sovereignty. It is surprising that Dicey did not over time incorporate John Salmond's conception of the legal system as founded on 'ultimate legal principles', which do not rest on any further rule of law, and the existence

[64] Dicey, *Law of the Constitution* 195.

[65] *R v Home Secretary, ex p Simms* [2000] 2 AC 115, 131: 'Parliamentary sovereignty means that Parliament can, if it chooses, legislate contrary to fundamental principles of human rights' (per Lord Hoffmann).

[66] ibid. Parliament has done so recently in times of 'moral panic': V Bogdanor, *The New British Constitution* (Oxford, Hart Publishing, 2009) 55–56.

[67] Dicey, *Law of the Constitution* 438.

[68] I find Allan's discussion of constitutional conventions utterly convincing. I simply do not believe it could have been Dicey's view.

[69] Allan, *The Sovereignty of Law* ch 2.

[70] See eg Loughlin, *The Idea of Public Law* 44. I rely on Loughlin a great deal in this passage. To be clear, he does not claim any form of Diceyan heritage.

of which is a matter of historical fact.[71] His argument would have been greatly strengthened by it.[72] In any event, one has to wait for Herbert Hart to build on these insights, developing an account of the legal system as 'a system of *rules within rules*' (emphasis added), thus turning away from the Austinian 'general habit of obedience to the sovereign', focusing instead on 'the general acceptance of a constitutional rule, simple or complex, defining the manner in which the ordinary rules of the system are to be identified'.[73] The Austinian framework nevertheless remains in the background of Hart's study of the complex distribution of the social acceptance of different types of legal rules (primary rules prescribing conduct and secondary rules conferring powers)[74] by different segments of the population (namely, officials and private citizens)[75] reflecting the social fracture between those who govern and those who are governed.[76] This is

[71] Salmond, *Jurisprudence* 124. Salmond dealt with, and revised, the Austinian position: Morison, *John Austin* 153–58.

[72] HWR Wade initially draws this parallel: Wade, 'The Basis of Legal Sovereignty' 187–89. The first edition of *Jurisprudence* was published in 1902 and could therefore have been built into subsequent editions of *Law of the Constitution*. However, Salmond's position simply seems not to have been a part of Dicey's intellectual outlook. There are no references to Salmond in Cosgrove, *Albert Venn Dicey*. Mark Walters notes in passing the congeniality of Salmond's jurisprudence to Dicey's claims in *Dicey and the Common Law* 149.

[73] HLA Hart, 'Introduction' in J Austin, *The Province of Jurisprudence Determined* (London, Weidenfeld & Nicholson, 1954) xii. Like Dicey, Hart developed his positions through his critical understanding of Austin: HLA Hart, 'Answers to Eight Questions' in L Duarte d'Almeida et al (eds), *Reading HLA Hart's The Concept of Law* (Oxford, Hart Publishing, 2013) 282. Hart points expressly to the resources provided by Salmond, rather than Kelsen, in his reappropriation of the Austinian tradition: Hart, *Concept of Law* 292. On Salmond's influence over Hart, see GJ Postema, *Legal Philosophy in the Twentieth Century. The Common Law World* (Dordrecht, Springer, 2011) 24–26, 309–10; G Bligh, *Les bases philosophiques du positivisme juridique de HLA Hart* (Bayonne, Varenne/LGDJ, 2017) 409–13. It is perplexing that Salmond gets no mention in most of the monographs or collected works dedicated to Hart's jurisprudence: Duarte d'Almeida et al (eds), *Reading HLA Hart's The Concept of Law*; N Lacey, *A Life of HLA Hart. The Nightmare and the Noble Dream* (Oxford, Oxford University Press, 2004); M Kramer (ed), *The Legacy of HLA Hart* (Oxford, Oxford University Press, 2008); N MacCormick, *HLA Hart*, 2nd edn (Stanford, Stanford University Press, 2008) 153 *passim*. Postema is thus the exception.

[74] We will not explore further the issue whether secondary rules should be understood as 'parasitic' rather than as rule-conferring. Although the 'rule of recognition' is not power-conferring, the power-conferring rules (the 'rule of adjudication' and the 'rule of change') are necessary *components* of the rule of recognition. Both understandings of secondary rules appear in the same passage: Hart, *Concept of Law* 81. For an exhaustive point of entry into these issues, see G Tusseau, *Les normes d'habilitation* (Paris, Dalloz, 2006) 213–16. See also L Green, 'Notes to the Third Edition' in Hart, *Concept of Law* 314; G Bligh, 'Empirical Complexity as a Conceptual Claim. Reappraising Hart's Account of Law as a Complex Social Practice' in M Carpentier (ed), *Meta-Theory of Law* (London, ISTE/Wiley, 2022) 137.

[75] Hart, *Concept of Law* 112, 116.

[76] This does not appear to have been noted in Rumble's impressive *Doing Austin Justice* ch 9. It is, in our view, the core of truth in Fuller's criticism of Hart's concept of the legal system as a 'one-way projection of authority': LL Fuller, *The Morality of Law* (New Haven, Yale University Press, 1969) 192–93. For a view of Austin and Hart as making the *same kind* of mistake, see P Eleftheriadis, 'Hart on Sovereignty' in Duarte d'Almeida et al (eds), *Reading HLA Hart's The Concept of Law* 75–76. Austin has on occasion been defended against Hart: Moles, *Definition and Rule in Legal Theory* ch 2. It is claimed here simply that Hart criticised and corrected Austin's theory but did not emancipate himself fully from the Austinian framework of investigation. A Continental lawyer will thus perceive Hart's approach as idiosyncratic compared to conceptions of the legal system based on theories of the state (a notion virtually absent in Hart's work).

one way to redirect the Austinian framework towards a rule-based approach to law-making power. Dicey himself did not make any such solution explicit.

## C. Dicey's Austinian Silence Concerning the State

These considerations do reveal, in a roundabout way, a core of Austinian influence in *Law of the Constitution* that is to be found not in the book's claims, but in its silences and omissions. Indeed, neither Austin, nor Dicey after him, have any operative concept of the state.[77] Austin's command theory of law, because it hinges on the problem of supremacy, is restricted to a scheme of concepts presenting the relation of political domination as a direct relation of authority between a governing minority and a general mass of subordinates. The great flaw of this approach is not merely that it calls upon a reductive conception of rules as varieties of commands,[78] but that Austin offers no insight into the *institutionalisation* of power within the state. He may be forgiven for he was writing in a time when the concept of the state had taken little hold in England.[79]

This renders Austin quite unable to adequately identify, and build tension between, the various elements that the concept of the state serves to bring together without contradiction. First, sovereignty within the state relies on implicit lines of tension between: (i) the *unity* (centralisation and monopolisation) of law-making power in the hands of the state (the legal sovereign); (ii) the ultimate symbolic source of the political *legitimacy* of the law (the people as political sovereign); and (iii) the *distribution* among institutions of government of legal powers exercised on behalf of the sovereign – ie in an *official capacity*, not as a matter of private property[80] – according to rules.[81] Second, the relation between sovereign and subject within the state relies on an implicit distinction between: (iv) the citizen

[77] Austin uses the notion of 'state' in passing, eg in Austin, *Province* (I) 35–36. An admirer such as JC Gray refused to follow Austin in reducing 'the state' to 'the sovereign' (and to the problem of supremacy more generally), so problematic appeared to him the evacuation of *legal personality* that this brought about: Gray, *The Nature and Sources of Law* 63.

[78] Hart, *Concept of Law* chs 2–3. Having reversed the logical sequence of his demonstration (as pointed out by Maine, *Lectures on the Early History of Institutions* 346–50), it is possible that Austin's original emphasis on the concept of a single command-rule – rather than the concept of sovereignty – made the institutional nature of law seem a distant concern.

[79] Allison, *The English Historical Constitution* 61, 71.

[80] Loughlin, *The Idea of Public Law* 79–80. Allison suggests that Loughlin's view of the political Constitution is overly 'theoretical': Allison, *The English Historical Constitution* 36. This theoretical framework nevertheless offers a crucial reference point for comparative jurisprudence between Continental European and British constitutional approaches.

[81] This is to insist upon the modern distinction between state and government. See O Beaud, *La puissance de l'État* (Paris, Presses Universitaires de France, 1994) 131; Loughlin, *The Idea of Public Law* 20. This does not necessarily require a concept of the state as a legal person. It is only necessary that the distinction between state and organs of the state is maintained. See, for instance, Hans Kelsen's conception of the state as a 'personification' of the national legal order in 'Aperçu d'une théorie générale de l'État', C Eisenmann (transl) (1926) 43 *Revue du droit public* 561, 573 ff; *General Theory of Law and State*, A Wedberg (transl) (Cambridge, Harvard University Press, 1945) 181 ff, 192–93.

as a member of the political sovereign; and (v) the private person subjected to the exercise of government.[82] Reasoning through the framework of the modern state allows one to rearrange the various elements of these distinctions. For instance, it brings into sharp focus the fact that political power is exercised through legal form, that the sovereign does not typically act directly but through agents, and that the individual person, as a member of the body politic, is both a governed subject and a member of the sovereign people. Moreover, it highlights the predicament of the private citizen in a 'representative' democracy as a member of the political sovereign who, however, does not participate directly in the exercise of government, and is subjected, as an individual, to the exercise of powers of government by agents of the state. These are the constitutive tensions of the exercise of power within the state that modern political philosophy has attempted to resolve.[83]

It is therefore problematic that Austin's notions of 'state', 'sovereign', and 'supreme government' remain confused: the governing group exercising effective powers of domination over the rest of society is the *same* as the body in the hands of which law-making power is centralised.[84] The two problems are treated as alternative statements of the same question. The three distinctions highlighted above collapse into a relation between 'sovereign' and 'subjects'.

The Diceyan conception of the rule of law as 'supremacy *of the law of the land*' cannot adequately stand in for the unity of the law as distinguished from the exercise of the law, because it fully incorporates the idea that the law of the land is made up of rules, any of which can be made or unmade by Parliament.[85] Following Austin on this point, Dicey also falls into a confused description of Parliament as both centralising law-making power (as the legal sovereign) *and* exercising such power as an institution of government. Thus, law-making power is not exercised on behalf of any distinct sovereign entity. In the same way, political sovereignty is a direct social force acting as an external check on the exercise of powers of government. At best it is possible (no doubt necessary) for 'harmony'[86] to be produced between the legal and political sovereigns. Neither Austin nor Dicey have a concept of the state. The paradoxical consequence is that Austin did not have a specifically legal concept of sovereignty within the state that Dicey could have relied on. His doctrine of 'the sovereignty of Parliament' in Austinian terms of

[82] The concept of sovereignty is 'relational', structured as it is by separate relations – the state and the people; government and citizens – that must be considered simultaneously: Loughlin, *The Idea of Public Law* 65–67.

[83] For a more thorough perspective than these summary indications, see M Loughlin, *Foundations of Public Law* (Oxford, Oxford University Press, 2010) ch 7; Beaud, *La puissance de l'État* 27 ff.

[84] The state is treated as synonymous with 'the individual person, or the body of individual persons, which bears the supreme powers in an independent political society': Austin, *Province* (VI) 190 n. This gives a curious liberal-conservative orientation to what is essentially a patrimonial conception of political power developed around the same time in Germany by reactionary lawyers see: O Jouanjan, *Une histoire de la pensée juridique en Allemagne (1800–1918)* (Paris, PUF, 2005) 202–24.

[85] Dicey, *Law of the Constitution* 406 ff. Parliamentary sovereignty and the supremacy of law mutually support one another: ibid 406, 411.

[86] ibid 438.

*supremacy* led him to focus on the legally illimitable legislative powers of *the* sovereign – Parliament – and diverted his attention away from other dimensions of constitutional law. Yet, these dimensions were crucial to the question of the institutionalisation of power within the state, such as the distinction between the King and the office of the Crown.[87]

The concepts of sovereignty and of the state being historically intertwined, it is not clear how any intelligible argument can be developed regarding the former that has no recourse to the latter.[88] Understanding the centralisation of legal powers of domination within the state does not remove the difficulties involved in the relations between the legal and the political aspects of sovereignty.[89] However, it does give some inkling as to what could intelligibly be meant by a 'strictly legal' understanding of sovereignty. Had Dicey been drawn to the German jurisprudence of the time, he might have gravitated naturally towards the controversies surrounding the articulation of the concepts of sovereignty and of the legal personhood of the state that were in full swing at the time *Law of the Constitution* was first published.[90] One finds a surprising lack of clarity on Dicey's part at an important point in his line of reasoning.

***

To summarise so far, Dicey's use of the Austinian framework is paradoxical. His rule-based conception of Parliament's legally illimited law-making power is un-Austinian in that it ultimately ruins the claim that legislative power is *logically* illimitable. However, Austin's influence is evidenced – counterintuitively – in Dicey's inability to escape the way in which the concept of *the* sovereign was framed principally in terms of supremacy in *The Province of Jurisprudence Determined*. As a result, although Dicey's lasting contribution is his account of the British Constitution in legal terms as opposed to political practice, he cannot

[87] Walters, *Dicey and the Common Law* 214–15: 'the entire question of executive power was treated as a kind of afterthought in *Law of the Constitution*'. On the importance of the distinction between the King and the office of the Crown for the concept of sovereignty: Loughlin, *The Idea of Public Law* 20–25; M Loughlin, 'The State: *conditio sine qua non*' (2018) 16 *International Journal of Constitutional Law* 1156, 1157–60. See also JG Allen, 'The Office of the Crown' (2018) 77 *Cambridge Law Journal* 298, 299–300; Baranger, *Écrire la constitution non écrite* ch 4.

[88] Loughlin, *The Idea of Public Law* 73–75. By way of comparison, Léon Duguit jettisons the concept of the state along with the concept of sovereignty in order to focus on the social fracture between a governing minority and a governed mass: L Duguit, *L'État, le droit objectif et la loi positive* (Paris, Dalloz, 2003 [1901]) 1.

[89] As Maurice Hauriou tackled, for instance, in his *Principes de droit public*, 2nd edn (Paris, Sirey, 1916 [1910]) with the theory of the state as the legal incorporation of the political community.

[90] Although he drew benefit from the study of Rudolf von Gneist in particular (Walters, *Dicey and the Common Law*, 304–306), he seemed averse to the influence of foreign jurisprudential thought more generally: Cosgrove, *Albert Venn Dicey* 28; Allison, *The English Historical Constitution* 63. He did not rely on the ongoing debates surrounding the legal personality of the state and public law subjective rights. See Jouanjan, *Une histoire de la pensée juridique en Allemagne* 187–281.

adequately identify a distinct legal aspect of sovereignty (for his lack of any way to distinguish the unity of law-making power in the hands of the state and the distribution and exercise of these powers by determinate institutions of government).[91] This argument need not presuppose a wavering of Dicey's Austinian faith over the course of his lifetime. Rather, it points to an original flaw. The Austinian framework could not adequately have provided Dicey with a doctrine of 'legal sovereignty' even in the first edition of *Law of the Constitution*, regardless of any subsequent change of heart.

## III. Closer to Austin? Dicey's Conception of Political Sovereignty

The main criticism that Dicey levels openly at Austin is that he ignores a crucial distinction between the sovereign in a strictly 'legal sense' and the sovereign in a 'political sense' designating the body ultimately obeyed, or with the final word, on matters of public policy.[92] We may view this criticism in a comical light once we realise that no conception of legal sovereignty can be both Austinian and rule-based. Moreover, whereas Dicey in fact distances himself from Austin in his legal conception of sovereignty, his 'political aspect' of sovereignty seems quite consistent, as will be demonstrated, with certain passages of *The Province of Jurisprudence Determined*. There is a distinctly Austinian flavour to the idea that the exercise of illimitable law-making power must run into some form of extra-legal limitation. This suggests conflicting influences and orientations between the two Diceyan dimensions of sovereignty. His views on political sovereignty can be seen to sit comfortably with his rule-based conception of legal sovereignty once his important work on *Law and Public Opinion* is examined. However, this brings the Austinian framework to breaking point and raises the possibility of other sources of influence, namely Bentham's later work on the 'Public Opinion Tribunal' as set forth in his *Constitutional Code*.[93] This would indeed allow for a coherent reading of Dicey's work while remaining aligned with the overall tenor of his analytical jurisprudence. Nevertheless, it is a moot question just how far the *Constitutional Code* did 'secretly impregnate' the thought of subsequent lawyers,[94] and it remains unclear whether Dicey was aware of it to any relevant extent. My own view is that caution is required here, and that too much ought not to be made of Bentham's influence.

[91] There are signs of this problematic merging of the concepts of 'sovereign' and 'sovereignty' in Walters, *Dicey and the Common Law* 165: 'the sovereignty of parliament is legislative sovereignty only'.

[92] Dicey, *Law of the Constitution* 72–74.

[93] J Bentham, *Constitutional Code*, vol 1 (Oxford, Clarendon, 1983) 36.

[94] Baranger, *Écrire la constitution non écrite* 140.

## A. A Core of Austinian Influence: Political Sovereignty and Voluntary Servitude

Just as the sovereignty of Parliament is a matter of 'legal fact', the sovereignty of the electors is a question of 'political fact'. This political sense 'is fully as important as the legal sense *or more so*' (emphasis added).[95] Ignorance of this distinction leads Austin to an unsatisfying hybrid account of the sovereignty of the King-in-Parliament as composed of the King, the peers of the House of Lords, and the *electorate body* imposing an implicit 'trust' upon the House of Commons.[96] In Dicey's view, this confuses the legal and political aspects of sovereignty and fails to choose which portion of the body politic sovereignty ought to be ascribed to.[97] Seeking to resolve this confusion, *Law of the Constitution* distinguishes the legal sovereignty of the King in Parliament and the political sovereignty of the 'electoral body'.[98] Although Dicey's position on the locus of political sovereignty shifted subsequently (see section III.B below), the distinction remains crucial. The sovereign may be legally illimited, but cannot be illimited de facto (ie politically): 'there are many enactments … which Parliament never *would* and (to speak plainly) never *could* pass' (emphasis added).[99] The King-in-Parliament is certainly not 'an omnipotent body'.[100]

Dicey is in fact more deeply influenced by Austin here than he acknowledges. His analysis of political sovereignty is consistent with lengthy passages of the sixth lecture of *The Province of Jurisprudence Determined*, expounding the idea that the sovereign, although 'incapable of legal limitation',[101] can encounter political limitations.[102] These reside in the principles and maxims of 'constitutional morality'[103] which the sovereign habitually obeys, and which are guaranteed by the feelings of approbation with which they are regarded by the bulk of the population so that any deviation on the part of the sovereign would generate great resistance on the part of the subjects – maybe greater resistance than a government could overcome. These are maxims and principles of *positive morality* which, as such, are set and enforced by 'opinion'[104] and 'imposed' upon the sovereign.[105] It is a matter of political fact, not law.

[95] ibid 74.
[96] Austin, *Province* (VI) 194.
[97] Dicey, *Law of the Constitution* 71.
[98] ibid 73, 430, 432.
[99] ibid 71.
[100] ibid 76.
[101] Austin, *Province* (VI) 212.
[102] The discussion of sovereignty in the sixth lecture covers over a third of *The Province of Jurisprudence Determined* (164–293), the explanation of the political limitation of sovereign power making up the greater part of the lecture 213 ff.
[103] Austin, *Province* (VI) 221–22. Dicey uses the expression to refer to conventions of the Constitution in *Law of the Constitution* 24, 418, 431.
[104] Austin, *Province* (I) 15, 20.
[105] ibid (VI) 214–15. See Morison, *John Austin* 81, 84; I Turégabo Mansilla, 'Reconstructing Austin's Intuitions: Positive Morality and Law' in Freeman and Mindus (eds), *The Legacy of John Austin's*

Austin's hard-nosed focus on the social position of superiority of the sovereign allows him to drive home three important truths concerning the relation between those who govern and those who are governed that any positivist must keep in mind.[106]

First, Austin is attentive to the great *structural weakness* of the position of a supreme body of government that is constituted by nothing more than the sheer habit of obedience of those that are governed. Although subjects may have no real opportunity to disobey their sovereign with impunity, the latter's authority depends entirely on maintaining in the former a habit of obedience. This is strongly reminiscent of Hume's observation that 'force is always on the side of the governed'.[107] It is the great value of Austin's work to have perceived and built into a positivist theory of law the fact that a hierarchical relation between sovereign and subject coexists with the structural dependence of the superior on the inferior, such that sovereign power would disappear along with the collapse of the habit of obedience of the subjects.[108]

Second, the stability of this relation of structural dependence relies on a great *inertia* that works to the advantage of an established sovereign. A mere popular judgment of immorality is not in itself an effective limit on what the sovereign may do legally.[109] In every actual society, habitual obedience is not rationally considered ('enlightened'), but the 'result of custom and the consequence of prejudice'.[110] Indeed, there is both a 'general perception' of the utility of any form of government compared to anarchy, and a 'special inclination' towards the particular form of government that receives habitual obedience within a given society.[111] This is reminiscent of Hume's assertion that 'custom and habit', not reflection, are the foundations of our judgements and actions.[112] To say that the 'authority of the few over the many' relies on the opinion of the governed – their fear of anarchy ('opinion of interest') and their recognition of the right to govern of the ruling minority ('opinion of right')[113] – is not to say that political authority is founded on rational judgement. Over time, habit and mores gradually 'consolidate' both the attachment to public order under a particular government, and the

*Jurisprudence* 308–309; M Lobban, 'John Austin' in T Spaak and P Mindus, *Cambridge Companion to Legal Positivism* (Cambridge, Cambridge University Press, 2021) 233–35.

[106] We would draw a different conclusion from the elements that led Postema to observe that 'it is Austin, not Bentham, who introduced Hobbesian authoritarianism into classical legal positivism': Postema, *Bentham and the Common Law* 319.

[107] Hume, 'First Principles of Government' 16.

[108] Hart is thus unfair in his reading of Austin: Hart, *Concept of Law* 7 ff. As argued above, Hart remains deeply influenced by the Austinian framework.

[109] Austin, *Province* (VI) 283.

[110] ibid (VI) 244–45.

[111] ibid.

[112] D Hume, *A Treatise of Human Nature – A Critical Edition*, vol 1 (Oxford, Clarendon, 2007 [1739]), (SB 118) 81, (SB 148–49) 100–101. Austin speaks of our 'moral instincts' as 'inscrutable facts' in Austin, *Province* (IV) 82. This need not mean that habit excludes a critical reflective stance: M Rodney, 'What Is in Habit?' in Freeman and Mindus (eds), *The Legacy of John Austin's Jurisprudence* 212.

[113] Hume, 'First Principles of Government' 17.

customary principles of legitimacy that develop within a given political system.[114] Habit and opinion are thus closely intertwined in the path-dependent nature of obedience.

This leads Austin to a third idea. A sovereign can deal with isolated acts of disobedience, but must be careful never to provoke resistance beyond a certain threshold, or tipping point, by offending the feelings and sentiments of the 'mass of the subjects'.[115] Thus, the principles and maxims of constitutional morality are imposed upon the sovereign 'by opinions prevalent in the community'.[116] This is the specific intuition that Dicey builds upon in *Law of the Constitution* in his discussion of the strictly political (non-legal) limitations on what a sovereign (even illimited) can do in fact. Although Dicey quotes a passage of the essay *Of the First Principles of Government*, the argument he deploys is found in this third observation drawn from Austin. It fits comfortably with the thrust of Hume's idea, but Austin is the necessary go-between.

Dicey certainly brings great clarity and contrast to the theme of political limitations weighing on the exercise of legal sovereignty. They are of two kinds. Both are elaborations on the problem of voluntary servitude. The 'external limit' has to do with the availability of force to overcome disobedience. A legal sovereign would do well to bear in mind that his powers of coercion are in no way illimited, and that he is thus dependent on the limited 'readiness to obey' of the subjects.[117] A law must therefore not generate greater resistance than can be managed or overcome physically. Dicey here is making the Austinian point that a sovereign who wishes to maintain the broadest possible scope of power must be careful to preserve intact the subject's habit of obedience. In other words, the sovereign must preserve a certain type of relation between sovereign and subject, and must never allow subjects to find out that well-kept secret: there can be no truly effective governmental response to wide-scale disobedience once a tipping point has been reached.

The 'internal' political limit has to do with the *content* of the laws that can be enacted.[118] Every society has certain mores, values, social rules and shared feelings against which it would be quite pointless to demand subjects to act – should the sovereign wish to do so. Both limits are of course related: if a legal sovereign were to violate an internal limit, he would be at risk of achieving nothing more than generating more physical (external) resistance than he would have the actual

[114] D Hume, 'Of the Origin of Government' *Political Essays* (Cambridge, Cambridge University Press, 1994) 22.

[115] Austin, *Province* (VI) 263. Not only would individual members disobey sporadically, but 'influential members' or a 'majority' would begin to actively shirk their legal obligations, thus gradually eroding the habit of obedience upon which the sovereign's authority rests. This Austinian framework is revealed in Hart's elaboration on the theme that the relative stability of legal systems depends on the degree of 'voluntary co-operation within a coercive system': Hart, *Concept of Law* 198.

[116] Austin, *Province* (VI) 214–15.

[117] Dicey, *Law of the Constitution* 78.

[118] ibid 80.

means to overcome. Whenever a ruler is legislating against the feelings, habits, and values, not only of a minority (the resistance of which can be overcome), but of a majority, the internal limit is tested. Just how far a ruler can go will be revealed by the external limit which a sovereign must be careful never to reach.[119]

Thus, it is important not to overlook the possibility that the true core of Austinian influence in *Law of the Constitution* is to be found in certain key intuitions concerning political sovereignty – rather than in Dicey's understanding of legal sovereignty. That Austin has systematically received a rather reductive reading has no doubt not helped to clarify this point.

## B. 'Opinion Controls Legislation': Leaving Austin Behind

Dicey introduces a strong line of tension into his concept of political sovereignty in the final part of *Law of the Constitution* dedicated to 'conventions of the constitution'. The specific function of these principles of 'constitutional morality'[120] (Austin's expression)[121] is to ensure that the final word belongs to the political sovereign, thus introducing 'harmony between the legal and the sovereign political power'.[122] Although undisputed in practice, these conventions are unenforceable in courts of law and are therefore not legal rules strictly speaking. All Austinian so far. However, Dicey asserts that these conventions are *not* only supported 'by the force of public opinion' acting as an external check on the legal sovereign.[123] They are in fact embedded in ('supported by') the law of the land,[124] thus resting on 'the force of law' 'in *addition* to public approval' (emphasis added),[125] insofar as the situations ruled by convention cannot be prised apart from the circumstances that give rise to enforceable claims before the courts.[126] As soon as conventions of the Constitution are taken into consideration, political sovereignty is no longer utterly independent from the law. This line of tension dates back to the first edition of *Law of the Constitution* and is therefore original.[127] Just like the ambiguity of the Austinian influence in Dicey's conception of legal sovereignty (see section II.A above), his position on conventions does not mark any late ebb in the Austinian faith.

[119] ibid 82. Dicey speaks of potential 'divergence' between the two limits.
[120] ibid 24, 418, 431.
[121] Austin, *Province* (VI) 222.
[122] Dicey, *Law of the Constitution* 438.
[123] ibid 444–46.
[124] ibid 446.
[125] ibid 445.
[126] ibid 447–49. To take but one example, a government refusing to resign, even though a new majority has been appointed following the dissolution of the Commons, would be unable to pass the necessary legislation authorising raising taxes. This would not only bring the machinery of government to a halt for lack of revenue, but were any official to nevertheless go ahead in the attempt to raise taxes without statutory authority to do so, acts of disobedience among the citizenry would be rendered legal and would thus enjoy the *protection of the courts*.
[127] See Allison (ed), *Oxford Edition of Dicey* 198–99.

More significantly still, Dicey's views on the nature and locus of political sovereignty evolved away from positions that could be described as obviously Austinian. *Law of the Constitution* offers a thin conception of political sovereignty, understood not as the people, but as the 'electoral body': 'the *will of the electors* shall by regular and constitutional means always in the end assert itself as the predominant influence in the country' (emphasis added).[128] Although Dicey no longer speaks of political sovereignty (or of a political aspect of sovereignty) in *Law and Public Opinion*, it seems that he has moved on to a thicker conception than he had previously entertained. His core claim is now that 'the public opinion which governs a country is the *opinion of the sovereign*, whether the sovereign be a monarch, an aristocracy, or the *mass of the people*' (emphasis added).[129] Thus, political sovereignty is no longer attributed to the electoral body (expressed through the electoral process), but to the 'mass of the people' (expressed through the dynamics of public opinion). Here, excitingly, Dicey leaves Austin's blind spot exposed.

Dicey's sovereign 'mass of the people' is a complex composite social reality that, on closer inspection, can actually be described as 'the mass of' the *governed*. It comprises, first, the active dimension of 'the majority of those citizens who have … taken an *effective part* in public life' (emphasis added).[130] This is no doubt a rough approximation of the electoral body (ie the political sovereign of *Law of the Constitution*).[131] *Law and Public Opinion* goes on to distinguish, second, a prima facie passive 'habit of submission' of the 'subjects who, though they in general take no active share in public affairs, may raise an insuperable opposition to laws which disturb their habits or shock their moral sentiments'.[132] The habits and feelings of the 'subjects' on this broader understanding need also be heeded if any effective legislative action is to be taken. Dicey is very clear, however, that a habit of submission does not rest merely on the fear of punishment or legal enforcement, which must remain occasional and limited to the repression of rebellion or disobedience. Rather, it is grounded, first, on 'a complicated set of sentiments' and a 'moral atmosphere' (the result of which is that the prevailing attitude towards a ruling class and system of government is seldom entirely negative) and, second, on the general 'opinion' that any conflict with the governor could not be won and would therefore be undesirable.[133]

This seems broadly consistent with Austin's awareness of the inertia of authority that works to the benefit of an established government. Merely bringing together the active and passive dimensions of 'political sovereignty' does not extirpate

[128] Dicey, *Law of the Constitution* 73.
[129] Dicey, *Law and Public Opinion* 10.
[130] ibid 10.
[131] Dicey makes no secret of his view that the scope of *political rights* ought to be limited to active contributing members of the political community: ibid xxxv. He also singles out 'voters' besides the 'people': ibid lxxxvi.
[132] ibid 10.
[133] ibid 2–3.

Dicey from his Austinian predicament: his rich tapestry on the relation between public opinion and the growth of legislation is a struggle and balance between two political *forces* – the King-in-Parliament and the mass of the governed.[134] In other words, he continues to describe Austin's relation between the 'sovereign' and the 'bulk of the subjects'. He is not using sovereignty as a way to hold apart the unity of law-making powers in the hands of the legal sovereign, the ultimate symbolic source of political legitimacy, and the exercise of powers by institutions of government on behalf of the sovereign.

There is a twist, however. In *Law and Public Opinion*, Dicey comes to regard as a 'truism' the idea at the heart of *Law of the Constitution* that *any* system of government, whether despotic or free, must feature certain political constraints resting on the mores and customary expectations of the mass of the governed – ie the internal and external political limits.[135] Beyond that truism, Dicey is now interested in 'the peculiar conditions of [certain] advanced civilisation' in which 'opinion controls legislation'.[136] Here, the growth of legislation not only runs up against the resistance of habit and custom, but is responsive to the 'beliefs' and the 'views held by the mass of the people'.[137] This is no mere programmatic twaddle. The entire series of lectures aims to establish how the evolving 'spirit of [the] age'[138] in England in the nineteenth century – 'the transition from individualistic liberalism to unsystematic collectivism or socialism' – affected the growth of legislation.[139] Crucially, it is through a thicker, more complex, notion of public opinion that Dicey can express the idea that legislation is a '*compromise* resulting from a conflict between the ideas of the government and the feelings or habits of the governed' (emphasis added).[140] Public opinion is no longer an extra-legal point of resistance to law-making power, but can be at the initiative of legislative change. As a result, the supreme law-making body, although no doubt in control of the legislative process, is no longer quite in control of the *growth* of legislation. In other words, the political sovereign of *Law and Public Opinion* is un-Austinian. Although Dicey does not truly escape his analytical positivist framework, some stronger operational link seems to be at play between legal and political sovereignty.

To the extent that Dicey is writing about a specific culture – the relations between law and public opinion in England – his reference to a 'moral atmosphere' is no doubt reminiscent of Bagehot's insistence on the underlying attitude of the 'deferential classes'[141] in an English 'culture of decency'.[142] More significantly,

[134] See Cosgrove, *Albert Venn Dicey* 180.
[135] Dicey, *Law and Public Opinion* 3.
[136] ibid 26, 53, 432.
[137] ibid 3–4.
[138] ibid 465.
[139] ibid 7, 399.
[140] ibid 10.
[141] Bagehot, *The English Constitution* 185.
[142] Focusing on the function of constitutional conventions, Catherine Marshall highlights Bagehot's influence in Dicey's work: Marshall, *Political Deference* 102–18. Where the notion of deference does

in my view, Dicey's argument suggests the influence of Bentham's later developments on the 'Public Opinion Tribunal'.[143] This is crucial if we are to attempt to resolve the tension between Dicey's views on political sovereignty and his rule-based conception of legal sovereignty.

## C. Legal Limitations and Public Opinion. Did Dicey have a Benthamite Conception of Sovereignty?

We can now return, finally, to Dicey's implicit commitment to the view that legal sovereignty is not illimitable in principle, but as a matter of 'legal fact' under the British Constitution (see section II.A above). It seems that Jeremy Bentham's original theory of law as a variety of command of the sovereign receiving a habit of obedience would provide Dicey with a more obvious starting point.[144] It would go some way towards resolving the tension between the proclaimed Austinian thrust of his line of reasoning, and his rule-based account of legal sovereignty implying the *possibility* of legal limitations on law-making power in addition to political limitations. First, whereas Austin asserts that the sovereign is 'incapable of legal limitation',[145] Bentham is more nuanced: 'the authority of the supreme body cannot, *unless where limited by express convention*, be said to have any assignable, any certain bounds'.[146] He is quite clear that, because sovereignty is '*de facto* … constituted' by the very existence of a disposition of the subjects to obey, the law-making power of the sovereign may also be 'bounded' by the fact of a limited disposition to obey conditioned on the sovereign's observing certain customary expectations and conventions.[147] Such limitations are not merely a matter of political fact, but a matter of law.[148] Second, to emphasise the

appear in Dicey's work, it is used in a more generic sense than its precise Bagehotian counterpart. Deference to political principles and doctrines can be 'enforced' (Dicey, *Law and Opinion* lxxxi); the belief in democracy can be characterised – or mischaracterised – as founded on a 'deference to public opinion' (Allison (ed), *Oxford Edition of Dicey* 438); and conservatism in the mid-nineteenth century is defined as 'deference to the prejudices of the clergy' (Dicey, *Law and Opinion* 317). However, his interpretation of the democratisation of England's political institutions insists greatly on an attitude of the people that would be described as deferential in the Bagehotian sense: Dicey, *Law and Public Opinion* 55–58.

[143] Bentham, *Constitutional Code* 36. Beyond the 'censorial' and 'executive' functions that Austin would have focused on through constitutional positive morality.

[144] Bentham, *Fragment* 40–41, 101–102. This is developed further in J Bentham, *Of Laws in General* (London, The Athlone Press, 1970) 1; *Introduction to the Principles of Morals and Legislation* (Oxford, Clarendon, 1996 [1789]) 302–307. Sovereignty is 'de facto constituted' by the 'disposition to obey': Bentham, *Of Laws in General* 66.

[145] Austin, *Province* (VI) 212.

[146] Bentham, *Fragment* 98. See also Bentham, *Of Laws in General* 64–67.

[147] Bentham, *Of Laws in General* 66; *Fragment* 102. Similarly, the constitutional scope of law-making power will evolve along with the people's disposition to obey: Bentham, *Of Laws in General* 19 n b.

[148] Postema, *Bentham and the Common Law* 238–39, 248; Rumble, *Doing Austin Justice* 91. Bentham's position seems to have changed somewhat over the course of his lifetime: Lobban, *A History of Philosophy of Law in the Common Law* 159.

influence of Bentham allows the reader to account comfortably for Dicey's evolving approach to the role of public opinion, as will be explained.

However, great caution is required, for it is difficult to argue that Dicey was a Benthamite in any consistent jurisprudential sense.[149] Although *Law and Public Opinion* dedicates much attention to the period of 'Benthamism or individualism'[150] and 'faith in scientific legislation',[151] none of Bentham's major works are relied on directly – except, fleetingly, the *Fragment on Government*,[152] but not for the passages dealing with the sovereign being bounded by 'express convention'. In fact, Bentham is hailed mainly as the 'prophet' of 'scientific legislation', not as analytical theorist.[153] Moreover, Dicey should have been aware of Bentham's later work on public opinion,[154] but it is not mentioned directly.[155]

We can only speculate as to the reasons. One explanation for Dicey's silence could be that it is an aspect of Bentham's work that was reevaluated in recent scholarship,[156] in the same way that Hart's *Essays on Bentham* were crucial to Bentham's reconsideration as a legal theorist. It is entirely possible that Dicey's admiration for Bentham centred on his law-reforming activity.[157] Another explanation could be that Bentham's theory of a Public Opinion Tribunal was part of a general turn towards democratic reform and the principle of universal suffrage as a check on the influence of 'sinister interest' diverting institutions of government from the search for the greatest happiness.[158] Dicey, to the contrary, sought to defend proper understanding of constitutional principles against what he saw as their perversion due to the harmful rise in influence of political parties *enabled* by the extension of the franchise.[159] In other words, Dicey might have been uncomfortable drawing attention to this aspect of Bentham's work for political

[149] See Walters, *Dicey and the Common Law* 362. But compare Cosgrove, *Albert Venn Dicey* 180 ff.

[150] Dicey, *Law and Public Opinion* (lecture VI) 126 ff.

[151] ibid 136.

[152] Other than Bentham's memoirs and correspondence, Dicey refers twice to the *Fragment on Government* which does not develop Bentham's view of public opinion: Dicey, *Law and Public Opinion* 126, 132. It seems that it was Mill far more than Bentham who impressed him. See Walters, *Dicey and the Common Law* 41. Dicey had dedicated three short articles to Mill's work: ibid 409. Mill's *On Liberty* is cited directly in Dicey, *Law and Public Opinion*, xxvii, 205, 308, 386, 425–30.

[153] Dicey, *Law and Public Opinion* 136; leaving analytical jurisprudential applications to Austin: ibid 412–13. Cosgrove distinguishes Dicey's Austinian heritage and his Whig views in Cosgrove. *Albert Venn Dicey* 70.

[154] Indeed, he cites L Stephen's *English Utilitarians* (1900), E Halévy's *Formation du radicalisme philosophique* (1900), and CBR Kent's *English Radicals* (1899): Dicey, *Law and Opinion* xi, 126, 145, 171–72. Moreover, the *Constitutional Code* was available to Dicey at the time in J Bowring (ed), *Works of Jeremy Bentham*, vol IX (Edinburgh, William Tait, 1843).

[155] Dicey does not credit Bentham, but RK Wilson, *History of Modern English Law* (London, Rivingtons, 1875), with the intuition that 'the growth of English law might be … explained by the course of public opinion', and in particular during 'the Benthamite era of scientific law reform': Dicey, *Law and Opinion* x. No passage of Wilson's book in particular deals with the role of public opinion – it is running theme throughout: eg Wilson, *History of Modern English Law* 253–54.

[156] eg Schofield, *Utility and Democracy*.

[157] See Cosgrove, *Albert Venn Dicey* 182. Wilson returns constantly to Bentham's influence as he deals with legislative reform in each area of the law in his *History of Modern English Law*.

[158] Schofield, *Utility and Democracy* ch 5.

[159] Cosgrove, *Albert Venn Dicey* 104–12; Marshall, *Political Deference* 107–18.

reasons. As long as we tread lightly, however, we may gain much insight from detailed attention to Bentham's conception of sovereignty.

If one is committed to the position that a limitation to sovereign power can be authentically legal, then such a limitation must somehow be viewed as internal to – or as inhering in – the law. This is consistent with Bentham's understanding of the force of law. First, whereas for Austin the force of law attaches to the social position of superiority, Bentham distinguishes, on the one hand, the 'source of a law' which he locates in the will of the sovereign who retains control of the content of valid rules of law,[160] and on the other, the 'force of a law' that lies in the motive for obedience which enables laws to be effective. These motives reside in the 'political sanctions' imposed by the sovereign – the consequences, pleasure, or pain, attached to the enforcement of the rules.[161] This allows his theory of sovereignty to resonate with his theory of utility,[162] and for his explanation of both the content and force of law to remain grounded on elements that are *internal* to the legal system. Moreover, this does not preclude a form of conflict between positive law and conventional social morality which may impede or undermine the enforcement of the law, therefore acting as a force that is *external* to the legal system.[163] Whereas political sanctions are enforced by the sovereign, the sanctions of conventional social (positive) morality are enforced through public opinion.

Second, the line of tension between the sources and the force of law bleeds over into the examination of the 'guarantee' of the limitations of sovereign power. Here, the internal/external distinction becomes problematic. The limitations of sovereign power are 'legal' ('laws *in principem*') in the formal sense that they find their *source* in the will of the sovereign prescribing to himself how he must conduct himself towards his subjects.[164] However, no political sanction (internal to the legal system) can be imposed by an unwilling sovereign upon himself. The *force* of these 'laws' must thus reside in the sanctions of conventional social (positive) morality (external to the legal system).[165] These moral sanctions, enforced

[160] Bentham, *Of Laws in General* 18. In this respect, it is 'an abuse of language', from an analytical standpoint, to speak of any act that a sovereign cannot do as illegal: Bentham, *Fragment* 98.

[161] Bentham, *Of Laws in General* 133, 137–39 n h. The pleasurable or painful consequences attached to the application of the rule are the only factors 'capable of giving a binding force to any law or rule of conduct': Bentham, *Principles of Morals and Legislation* 34. One thus governs by inflicting penalties and awarding rewards: ibid 74. This corresponds to the distinction between the penal branch of law and the branch he proposes to call 'remunerative': ibid 126. Austin expressly rejects this idea: although the reward may motivate the recipient of the command to obey, the *binding force* of the command can only be analysed through the harmful consequences incurred in the event of disobedience. See Austin, *Province* (I) 23. Dicey thus suggests that the Austinian conception of law is modelled on the image of criminal law: Dicey, *Law of the Constitution* 72.

[162] Through pleasure and pain, that are the 'sovereign masters' that 'nature has placed over mankind' (Bentham, *Principles of Morals and Legislation* 11) and, as consequences attached to the enforcement of rules, the two 'instruments [a legislator] has to work with' (ibid 38).

[163] Bentham, *Principles of Morals and Legislation* 37. A legal sanction can run into a conflicting 'moral sanction': ibid 35.

[164] Bentham, *Of Laws in General* 64–65: 'laws *in principem*'.

[165] ibid 67–68. See Schofield, *Utility and Democracy* 227–31.

though *public opinion*, are the 'only check' to the 'pernicious exercise of the power of government'.[166] The sovereign must be mindful of public opinion, for he not only exposes himself to disobedience to a particular law, but to the erosion of his subject's general 'disposition' to obey 'with respect to future [acts]'.[167]

This presents us with two possible conflicting reactions to Bentham's theory of the articulation of public opinion and the force of law. Each lends support to a certain interpretation of Dicey's distinction of the legal and political aspects of sovereignty, depending on how much one wishes to make of the idea that limitations on legal sovereignty are necessarily external to the legal system. A first, straightforward interpretation of Dicey focuses on the passages in which he appears to be distinguishing 'legal sovereignty' and 'political sovereignty' as *kinds* of sovereignty, resulting in a friction between two social forces – two identifiable *sovereigns* – the one operating through the legal system (the legal sovereign), the other acting from without (the political sovereign). Here, there would be no escaping the fact that the normative limitation of law-making power cannot be grounded on an observation of fact (habits of obedience).[168] One might as well draw the frustrating Austinian conclusion that the formally valid rules of a legally illimited sovereign can run into external political and moral resistance, rather than grounding legal limitations of sovereign power ultimately on facts of moral or popular disapprobation – however inescapable the verdict of public opinion. Frustratingly, however, it would leave us where we began – with Dicey's commitments to conflicting positions regarding legal and political sovereignty.

A second interpretation of Bentham's constitutional jurisprudence insists on the 'split' nature of the *concept* of sovereignty.[169] On this reading, sovereignty resides at once 'in the people' acting through the Public Opinion Tribunal,[170] and in the supreme law-making institution of government.[171] He also distinguishes the existence of the sovereign and the existence of the several institutions of government.[172] Bentham's split concept of sovereignty is thus very useful for analysing the relation of authority within democratic institutions. An individual

[166] Bentham, *Constitutional Code* 35.

[167] In contrast with the 'habit' of obedience 'with respect of *past* acts' (emphasis added): Bentham, *Fragment* 102. Acts of the sovereign in particular cases are taken as signs of the way his power is likely to be exercised in the future: Bentham, *Of Laws in General* 153. Bentham does not cultivate a 'mechanical' account of obedience to explain the fact of superiority, but an 'interactional' account of the disposition to obey: Postema, *Bentham and the Common Law* 239–40.

[168] As observed by HLA Hart, 'Sovereignty and Legally Limited Government' in *Essays on Bentham* (Oxford, Clarendon, 1982) 238.

[169] O Ben-Dor, *Constitutional Limits and the Public Sphere. A Critical Study of Bentham's Constitutionalism* (Oxford, Hart Publishing, 2000) 49–58. See also Lobban, *A History of Philosophy of Law in the Common Law* 159–60.

[170] Bentham, *Constitutional Code* 25. Sovereignty would intervene not only through a capacity for resistance (censorial function), but through the punishments and rewards meted out through the electoral system (executive function): ibid 36–37.

[171] Bentham, *Of Laws in General* 64.

[172] Bentham, *Fragment* 97; *Constitutional Code* 25–27. In other words, Bentham has a proto-concept of the state distinguishing, on the one hand, legal and political dimensions of sovereignty, and on the other, the sovereign and the institutions of government.

being both a subject of government and a member of the sovereign people, the moral sanction by the subjects of the law-maker's claim to have made valid law turns out to be, through the action of the Public Opinion Tribunal,[173] a reaction of the political dimension of sovereignty to the legal.[174] The force of the conventions bounding the sovereign in the legal sense are guaranteed by the action of public opinion. Following this lead, one could focus on the passages in which Dicey speaks of the legal and political '*aspects*' of the concept of sovereignty. In Benthamite spirit, he would no longer be interpreted as highlighting distinct kinds of sovereignty, but related (albeit distinct) dimensions of a same concept: sovereignty. This would bring internal coherence to the relation between the political sovereignty of 'the mass of the people' and the sovereignty of Parliament. As a result, the distinction between limitations internal and external to the legal system would simply disappear. This would be to take a step in the direction of the interpretative reconstruction of Dicey's constitutional jurisprudence while preserving its overall analytical – Benthamite rather than Austinian – tone.

This second interpretation certainly makes sense of Dicey's position, but it cannot be attributed to him without the greatest caution. Indeed, he claimed in no uncertain terms that the British Parliament is illimited legally, although constrained extra-legally. Had his conception of the distinction between legal and political sovereignty been inspired by Bentham, it should have cut in the opposite direction: no sovereign can *ever* be illimited legally. There can never be an illimited habit of obedience in fact; an observation from which a consistent Benthamite would be bound to draw legal conclusions. Dicey's hard distinction between the legal and the political realms is Austinian. Second, Bentham has a proto-concept of the state; Austin does not. Before attributing to Dicey the idea of a 'split' concept of the sovereign, we would first need to get past the objections raised above (see section II.C above): Dicey proceeds in Austinian fashion in his lack of precision in distinguishing adequately the state and government. This is an important clue that although Dicey clearly reveals the limits of the Austinian framework in his treatment of public opinion, his position cannot simply be described as Benthamite *instead*. He does not have a single concept of 'the sovereign' with distinct but internally related senses. The safest conclusion to draw, I would submit, is that although he would have been better off relying straightforwardly on Bentham, a sustained attention to *The Province of Jurisprudence Determined* got him onto the right path – a fact that is not easily accessible to us if we accept a reductive, in my view incorrect, reading of Austin.

[173] The 'dictates' of the 'tribunal of public opinion' will 'coincide, on most points, with the greatest happiness principle' (Bentham, *Constitutional Code* 35), and public opinion being ultimately composed of all individual members of society (ibid 35), it is necessary for an ethically minded government to allow the public to be informed and to react freely to public policy.

[174] Schofield, *Utility and Democracy* 252; D Lieberman, 'Bentham's Democracy' (2008) 28 *Oxford Journal of Legal Studies* 605, 609, 614; F Cutler, 'Jeremy Bentham and the Public Opinion Tribunal' (1999) 63 *Public Opinion Quarterly* 321, 324; F Rosen, *Jeremy Bentham and Representative Democracy. A Study of the Constitutional Code* (Oxford, Clarendon, 1983) ch 2.

## IV. Conclusion

To conclude, it is clear that Dicey can in no way be described as Austinian through-and-through. It nevertheless seems difficult to resist the conclusion that his proposed distinction between the legal and political dimensions of sovereignty owes a great deal to Austin's intuitions concerning the relation of authority between sovereign and subjects. It has been argued here that an Austinian approach is developed in Dicey's initial understanding of what it means for the political sovereign to have the final word in case of conflict with the legal sovereign, through the checks that constitutional positive morality place on the laws enacted by the legal sovereign. However, Austin's blind side is left exposed in Dicey's subsequent, seemingly simple idea, that the growth of legislation is *controlled*, to an extent, by public opinion. This is the second, more profound, sense of the last word of the political sovereign. It raises the possibility that greater Benthamite influence is at play than Dicey lets on. Nevertheless, because his concept of sovereignty is not based on any robust concept of the state, it is not clear how it can break free from the Austinian mould. It is certainly safe to say that Dicey's work reveals the limits of Austin's jurisprudential framework. That being said, it can be doubted whether he himself would have consciously disowned Austin, or whether the interpretivist reconstructions of recent years, however useful to contemporary debate, can be safely ascribed to him. Indeed, Dicey does not overlook the fact that, as long as the minority in government adheres to fundamental constitutional rules and remains in line overall with the values and beliefs of the governed, a disaffected minority can be sacrificed with little cost to the stability of the legal system provided a *majority* continues to effectively adhere to a system of government and its laws.[175] Reaching a more complex understanding of the relation between those who govern and a majority of the governed by taking public opinion into account should not mask this reality. There is no legal solution that can do away, once and for all, with this political problem.

[175] Hart, *Concept of Law* 117, 201–202. For a worrying survey, see GL Neumann (ed), *Human Rights in a Time of Populism: Challenges and Responses* (Cambridge, Cambridge University Press, 2020).

# 3

# Dicey and Bagehot: What is Left of the Nineteenth-Century Constitution in Twenty-First Century Britain?

ADAM TOMKINS

## I. Introduction

Returning to full-time academic life in 2021 after a five-year stint as an elected Member of the Scottish Parliament, the first task asked of me by the head of my law school was to take charge of our first-year constitutional law course. It was due an overhaul. I rewrote it substantially – thirty-six new lectures and nine new tutorials to accompany them. More or less all I kept was the basic order in which we tackled the topics on the syllabus. We start with the nature of the British Constitution, introducing the basic written/unwritten and laws/conventions distinctions; then we look at the separation of powers and examine in depth each of main institutions of British government – Parliament, the executive, and the courts. Then we take a deep dive into the law of devolution and, in particular (given where I teach), the law of Scottish devolution. After the mid-winter break, we tackle the ongoing influence of European Union law on the UK's constitutional arrangements before looking in detail at the European Convention on Human Rights and the Human Rights Act 1998, taking a number of civil liberties and human rights as case studies. In this last section of the course, we look in particular at freedom of expression and freedom of assembly.

There is nothing particularly remarkable or unusual about this menu of topics. Law schools in England will spend less time than we do on devolution, perhaps. But, other than that, my sense is that law schools everywhere in the UK teach more or less the same sorts of things as we do to our first-year constitutional law students. Some will cram in more about the law of judicial review, but we have a compulsory second-year course on administrative law, and we leave both judicial review and broader issues of administrative justice to the second year. This gives us more space than we would otherwise have for case studies on civil liberties and human rights law.

As I revised the course and wrote new teaching materials, I was struck numerous times by the enduring influence of the great nineteenth-century writers, Dicey and Bagehot. Whilst we assign to our students no specific readings from either the *English Constitution* or the *Law of the Constitution*, both Bagehot and Dicey are more than once discussed in lectures, and the shape their work gave to our constitutional self-understandings continues to be a strong influence, especially in the first third of the course.

In this short chapter I seek to defend two propositions. The first is that no books – whether written before or since – have exerted or enjoyed the same degree of influence over how we understand the British Constitution as Dicey's *Law of the Constitution* and Bagehot's *English Constitution*. The second is that the core arguments of both books continue to be valid, to offer key (indeed, invaluable) insights into what our Constitution is and what rules it provides for, and that the two books' core arguments are right. Right not just for the mid-nineteenth century, but right today, too.

Of course, neither book any longer offers anything like a complete or adequate account of the British Constitution today (and neither professes to, of course). Neither book says anything about devolution, about European Union law, or even about human rights law as we now understand it. But each of these matters, all of which are core components of any modern syllabus on British constitutional law, has been built on the foundations Dicey and Bagehot laid down. These additions supplement – and do not undermine – the core arguments about what our Constitution is and how it should be understood, which Dicey and Bagehot set out a century and a half ago. Such, albeit with one caveat which we will get to at the end, is my broad argument here.

## II. Dicey

Let me start with Dicey. And by 'Dicey' I mean, specifically, the *Law of the Constitution*.[1] I know, of course, that Dicey wrote a whole series of increasingly desperate and angry polemics against home rule (some of which I have read and none of which I would recommend). I know he wrote textbooks on the conflict of laws and on other areas of legal enquiry.[2] I also know he wrote fascinating lectures on the relation of nineteenth-century legislation to public opinion (which deserve a broader audience, not least because they reveal the significant influence both JS Mill and, even more so, Tocqueville had on Dicey's thinking).[3] For the purposes of this chapter, I am going to put all of that to one side and focus on the two core arguments of the *Law of the Constitution*.

[1] AV Dicey, *Introduction to the Study of the Law of Constitution* (London, Macmillan, 1885).

[2] See generally MD Walters, *Dicey and the Common Law Constitutional Tradition: A Legal Turn of Mind* (Cambridge, Cambridge University Press, 2020) chs 4–5.

[3] AV Dicey, *Lectures on the Relation between Law and Public Opinion in England During the Nineteenth Century* (London, Macmillan, 1905).

Dicey's first argument in the *Law of the Constitution* was that the legal rules of our Constitution form only one part of the constitutional whole. In addition to the legal rules there are non-justiciable rules of constitutional behaviour, which Dicey called conventions. The name has stuck, as has the basic idea. Dicey's second argument was that, within the *law* of the Constitution, two rules dominated. The first governed the relation of common law to statute, and he called it the sovereignty of Parliament; the second governed the relation of common law to executive power, and he called it the rule of law. A century after Dicey's death, we continue to use these terms, these labels, and these ideas to understand how the law treats both statute and executive power. I shall return to all that in a few moments. First, a few words on laws and conventions.

Central questions about the UK's constitutional arrangements are neither addressed nor answered by the law: how the monarch is to exercise his powers; how a government is to be formed in the case of a hung Parliament; and, perhaps most critically, what the constitutional relationship is and should be between government and Parliament. These matters are, all of them, governed by rules. But they are rules whose enforcement, in the main, is not for courts and tribunals. This basic distinction was true in Dicey's day – and it remains true in ours.

Of course, courts may have regard to constitutional conventions when determining the application of legal rules to facts concerning government, or ministers, or even the monarchy. However, courts do not enforce conventions as such. In *Attorney General v Jonathan Cape* the Court of Appeal considered the convention of collective ministerial responsibility when determining the scope and application of the law of breach of confidence to the publication by a former Cabinet minister of his diaries.[4] Likewise, and more recently, in *Evans v Information Commissioner*, the Upper Tribunal considered the conventions pertaining to the monarchy when determining where the public interest lay as regards *The Guardian* newspaper's freedom of information request for disclosure of various items of correspondence between HRH Prince Charles, the heir to the Throne (as he then was), and certain government departments.[5] The conventions were not judicially enforced – it was the law of the Freedom of Information Act 2000 that was enforced – but the latter was interpreted and applied in the light of the former.

These cases show, as do countless other examples of government and parliamentary practice, that the British Constitution cannot be understood if you confine your attention only to matters of strict law. The converse is also true: the Constitution cannot be understood if you fail to take into account what the law has to say about it. We take this for granted now – and perhaps we always did (Sir William Blackstone in the eighteenth century and Sir Edward Coke in the seventeenth would surely have agreed that whatever was meant by 'Constitution' in their day was a peculiar amalgam of law and politics, of judicial process and parliamentary practice). Fine, but the point is this: the language we use to navigate

[4] *Attorney General v Jonathan Cape* [1976] QB 752.
[5] *Evans v Information Commissioner* [2012] UKUT 313 (AAC).

our way through the relation of legal to non-legal aspects of the Constitution is the language Dicey bequeathed to us. He was hardly making an original point when he distinguished laws from conventions, but he put the point more crisply and more compellingly than had any of his predecessors, and his way of putting it has stuck with us.

Perhaps that was his trick. He said that the *Law of the Constitution* was a book 'born under a lucky star'.[6] It ran to no fewer than eight editions in his lifetime. It made his name, and it was a roaring success. There are lots of reasons for this. He told his audience what they wanted to hear. He crystallised what they already felt to be true. He put into words – often very pithily – what people already felt was the case but had perhaps not yet been able so neatly to encapsulate or to express: 'constitutional conventions', the 'sovereignty of Parliament', the 'rule of law'. Dicey was a great wordsmith, a great coiner of phrase. Creating a phrase – a slogan – to capture what people already believe to be true, or needed, or necessary, is a gift, and Dicey struck gold not once but three times in the *Law of the Constitution*. Later, I shall argue that some of Bagehot's success is owed to the same ability – to put one's finger on and to give a name to what people already believe to be true.

Of course, and as its name implies, the bulk of the *Law of the Constitution* is concerned not with conventions but with the *legal* rules of the Constitution. It is no longer (if indeed it ever was) the case that the legal rules of the Constitution can be reduced to two, but the two rules Dicey set out in the *Law of the Constitution* continue to govern their fields and, as I have noted, we continue to use the labels that Dicey affixed to them. In some ways this is unfortunate. When we think of the sovereignty of Parliament, for example, we are not really thinking about sovereignty at all and neither are we thinking about Parliament. What we are really thinking about is supremacy (a legal concept) not sovereignty (a political concept) and we are thinking about the supremacy, specifically, of statute over the common law and not of Parliament as an institution (or, as Bagehot would insist, a pair of institutions, the House of Commons and the House of Lords being deliberately kept quite separate in his account).

Parliament may make or unmake any law whatever, and no body or institution (no court or tribunal) may set aside or overturn a properly enacted Act of Parliament. This was true when Dicey conceived and wrote the *Law of the Constitution* and it remains true now. There has, in recent years, been a lot of noise about how these rules might admit of exceptions, or about how they are not as absolute as you might think, or about how they are relics, even, of a nineteenth-century past, with 'a new legal order' now having replaced them.[7] But that 'different hypothesis of constitutionalism'[8] to which Lord Steyn famously referred in his obiter dicta in the *Jackson* case looks, a decade and a half on,

[6] Walters, *Dicey and the Common Law* 125.
[7] *Jackson v Attorney General* [2005] UKHL 56, [2006] 1 AC 262, para 102 (Lord Steyn).
[8] ibid.

remarkably similar to the Diceyan orthodoxy. I would suggest it is Lord Steyn's heterodoxy that has not withstood the test of time, not Dicey's 'classic account'.[9]

This is not to say that the sovereignty of Parliament – the legal supremacy of statute – has not come under both challenge and scrutiny in recent years. Of course, it has. But as matters stand, it has withstood such challenge and survived such scrutiny intact. The challenge came from four quarters: European Union membership; the common law itself; human rights law; and the law of devolution.

To take each of these briefly in turn. First there was the UK's membership of the European Union. As Lord Bridge made clear in *Factortame*,[10] and as the Supreme Court underscored in the *HS2* case in 2014,[11] to the extent that courts and tribunals in the United Kingdom had the power by virtue of European Union law to order that provisions of statute be disapplied (in effect, overturned or set aside), they had that power because and only because Parliament had legislated for it in the European Communities Act 1972. The House of Lords was clear in *Factortame* that the remedy it granted was commanded by Parliament and in no sense contrary to Parliament's enacted will. In any case, the remedy was one unknown to domestic law, finding its authority only in European Union law – and the House had the authority to enforce European Union law because and only because Parliament had willed it so, in the European Communities Act. Moreover, as the Supreme Court emphasised in *HS2*, such authority (and indeed everything in the European Communities Act) had to be interpreted and applied subject to, and not in contravention of, the fundamental tenets of the British Constitution. On this, the courts and Parliament were in full agreement with one another. There was no tension between the way Parliament understood questions of sovereignty in the European Union Act 2011 and the way the courts understood it in case law.

The second challenge was from the common law itself, not only the obiter in *Jackson*, but the implications of *AXA General Insurance*[12] and of a handful of cases in which loose ideas of an untamed beast called 'constitutional statutes' were let, in my view unwisely, off the leash.[13] Thus, Lord Hope suggested, in both *Jackson* and *AXA*, that legislation abrogating the rule of law could be set aside by the courts. Lord Bingham, however, was having none of it. In *Jackson* itself he reminded his court that:

[9] ibid.

[10] *R v Secretary of State for Transport, ex p Factortame (No 2)* [1991] 1 AC 603.

[11] *R (HS2) v Secretary of State for Transport* [2014] UKSC 3, [2014] 1 WLR 324.

[12] *AXA General Insurance v Lord Advocate* [2011] UKSC 46, [2012] 1 AC 868.

[13] *Robinson v Secretary of State for Northern Ireland* [2002] UKHL 32; *Thoburn v Sunderland City Council* [2002] EWHC 195, [2003] QB 151. In *Robinson* the House of Lords suggested that, as a constitutional statute, the Northern Ireland Act 1998 should be interpreted more generously and purposively than other, ordinary statutes. This misguided and unnecessary approach to the interpretation of devolution legislation was abandoned and reversed by the Supreme Court in *Imperial Tobacco v Lord Advocate* [2012] UKSC 61, 2013 SC (UKSC) 153. In *Thoburn* Laws LJ suggested obiter that, because the European Communities Act 1972 was a constitutional statute, its provisions could not be impliedly repealed. These obiter comments were unhelpful – as well as wrong in law – not least because no question of implied repeal arose on the facts of the case. Neither use of the term 'constitutional statute' is sound in law and neither has been developed.

> the bedrock of the British constitution is, and in 1911 [when the Parliament Act was passed] was, the supremacy of the Crown in Parliament … Then, as now, the Crown in Parliament was unconstrained by any entrenched or codified constitution. It could make or unmake any law it wished. Statutes, formally enacted as Acts of Parliament, properly interpreted, enjoyed the highest legal authority.[14]

Amen. 'Then, as now.' These are positions with which the current Supreme Court, presided over by Lord Reed, would unhesitatingly endorse.[15] To the extent that there are contrary dicta in obiter remarks from Lord Steyn, Lord Hope, Lord Justice Laws, or others, they are to be regarded as just that – obiter dicta.

The third challenge comes from the law of human rights but here again it is a challenge that has amounted to rather little. It is true that there lingers in some quarters a degree of political tension about whether the Human Rights Act 1998 permits – or even requires – courts to interpret legislation in ways that trespass beyond the courts' proper constitutional job of interpretation into territory (of legislating and re-legislating) which is properly Parliament's and Parliament's alone. I am sympathetic to the view that the relevant provision of the Human Rights Act 1998 – section 3 – could usefully be amended to shift the balance between when courts should interpret legislation and when they should simply declare that it cannot be interpreted compatibly with Convention rights.[16] Even those who are of this view, however, struggle to identify very many cases in which the current imbalance points to the courts having strayed impermissibly from their brief.[17] For the truth is there have been mercifully few cases in which the section 3 power to interpret legislation has been so stretched by the courts that, in reality, what they have done is not interpret and apply the words Parliament enacted, but ignored those words and substituted others instead.

It is rare. Yet it does happen. Contrary to what Lord Nicholls said in *Ghaidan v Godin-Mendoza*, I do not consider that our human rights law should permit courts to 'depart from the unambiguous meaning legislation would otherwise bear'.[18] Courts should not be permitted – still less, required – to 'do … violence' to statutory language.[19] Their task is to interpret and to apply statute, not to distort or wilfully to misconstrue it – and, if that cannot be done compatibly with Convention rights, then the remedy lies in granting a declaration of incompatibility under section 4.

The fourth and final challenge came from the law of devolution. But this was always the weakest of the challenges and it has now been summarily dismissed by the Supreme Court in its more recent judgments on the law of devolution in

[14] *Jackson* (n 7) para 9.

[15] See, for example, the protection given to the sovereignty of Parliament in cases such as *Reference re UNCRC Bill* [2021] UKSC 42, [2021] 1 WLR 5106.

[16] See the *Independent Human Rights Act Review*, Report, CP 586 (2021) ch 5.

[17] See A Tomkins, *Written Evidence on Human Rights Reform* (submitted to the UK Parliament's Joint Committee on Human Rights, March 2022; published on the JCHR website at https://committees.parliament.uk/work/6404/human-rights-act-reform/publications/).

[18] *Ghaidan v Godin-Mendoza* [2004] UKHL 30, [2004]1 AC 557, para 30 (Lord Nicholls).

[19] ibid para 67 (Lord Millett).

Scotland, in which the Supreme Court has breathed fresh life – indeed fire – into the apparently innocent provision of the Scotland Act 1998 that nothing in that Act affects 'the power of the Parliament of the United Kingdom to make laws for Scotland' (section 28(7)).[20] Devolved legislation which purports to place obstacles in the way of Westminster legislation – or which purports to impose conditions on the way Westminster legislation takes effect – will be unlawful. As the Supreme Court has put it, Westminster 'has an unlimited power to make laws for Scotland, a power which the legislation of the Scottish Parliament cannot affect'.[21] As such, the Scottish Parliament 'cannot make the effect of Acts of Parliament conditional on decisions taken by other institutions'.[22] In short, 'the Scottish Parliament … cannot qualify the sovereignty of Parliament'.[23]

Despite all these challenges and controversies, what Dicey called the sovereignty of Parliament – what I would prefer to call the legal supremacy of statute – remains intact. This does not mean that Parliament can do or undo anything. Parliament is not a sovereign animal, untamed by any restraint. But it does mean that what Parliament properly enacts into law by way of Act of the Crown in Parliament is the highest source of legal authority known to the British Constitution. Those words, however – 'properly', 'enacts', 'law' – are each pregnant with meaning and, moreover, with legal meaning for the courts to interpret and apply. As Mark Walters has persuasively shown in his masterful study and intellectual history of the *Law of the Constitution*, Dicey's theory of sovereignty was narrowly and sharply focused on *legislative* power.[24] It is a theory of the proper scope of legislation as understood in the common law Constitution. It is not licence to do as Parliament pleases. On top of all of this, of course, sits the great insight that Parliament has to bear the political cost of its enactments. As Lord Sankey crushingly observed nearly a century ago, the abstract theory of an omnipotent Parliament is exactly that – a theory; it 'has no relation to realities'.[25] To take an obvious example: even if there were a parliamentary majority in favour of repealing the Scotland Act, abolishing the Scottish Parliament, and abandoning devolution in Scotland, Parliament could not enact those desires into law without facing the consequences. And the consequences would in all likelihood be dire for Scotland's ongoing place in the Union. Parliament could no more repeal the Scotland Act without consequence than it could repeal the Australia Act and impose direct rule on Canberra. Parliament may enjoy legislative supremacy in theory, but the British Constitution – like, I dare say, all constitutions – relies in the end not on high theory but on ordinary, everyday, low common sense and politics to set limits to what may actually be done with the powers it allocates.

[20] *Reference re UNCRC Bill* (above n 15).
[21] ibid para 7.
[22] ibid para 30.
[23] ibid para 50.
[24] Walters, *Dicey and the Common Law* ch 8.
[25] See *British Coal Corpn v R* [1935] AC 500, 520.

If Dicey's sovereignty of Parliament remains intact, what of his second great rule of constitutional law, the rule of law? In my view it remains every bit as vibrant and vital now as it was when Dicey wrote about it. The rule of law governed then – as it still governs now – the relation between the common law and what we now call executive power (what might simply be called 'government' or 'public administration'). The first thing to notice here is that, when we come to consider this relationship, there is no note of sovereignty to be sounded. The only sovereign power Dicey considered was legislative, as we have seen. Government, by contrast, was a creature whose powers were brought entirely within the domain of law, and subject to that domain. Government has no power to make or unmake any rule – and courts certainly have the power to set aside or to override the unlawful acts or decisions of government. Government is subject to the law – and not the other way around. This, as Dicey well knew, is not something to be taken for granted. In today's world, as much as in any other time, that government should be subject to the law (and not the other way around) is something we who believe in it still have to argue and, where necessary, to fight for.

Of course, Dicey was wrong in one particular. For there is still a whiff of sovereignty about British government, even if it is a whiff well masked now by some carefully engineered and delicately applied perfume. For at the apex of executive power in the United Kingdom stands not the law, but the Crown. It is still His Majesty's Government; the Prime Minister is appointed by His Majesty the King; and only the King may appoint the Prime Minister or, indeed, dissolve Parliament. As regards the exercise of these functions, even after the great prorogation case of 2019,[26] it is not obvious that the writ of the common law runs. Further, in the unthinkable event His Majesty or any of his heirs and successors exercised their constitutional authority unlawfully, *M v Home Office* reminds us that there is little the courts could do about it.[27] A minister of the Crown may be found in contempt of court, the House of Lords ruled in that case, but the Crown itself could not be. *M v Home Office* is a reminder both of the strengths of the rule of law and of its limitations.

Putting that one particular to the side, however, Dicey's core insights about the rule of law are valid. First and foremost, the government requires legal authority for any action it takes which impacts on individual rights or liberty. We are free to act as we please, unless our actions are proscribed by law. And, if the government dislikes our actions, it must ensure that the law prohibits them before it may seek to sanction or punish us. The great case of *Entick v Carrington* is all the authority anyone needs for any of that.[28] More deeply than that, government is a product of law. Everyone in government, from a Cabinet minister to a police constable, must exercise their authority within and according to law. And, where this fails to

[26] *R (Miller) v Prime Minister; Cherry v Advocate General* [2019] UKSC 41, [2020] AC 373.
[27] *M v Home Office* [1994] 1 AC 377.
[28] (1765) 19 St Tr 1029; see A Tomkins and P Scott (eds), *Entick v Carrington: 250 Years of the Rule of Law* (Oxford, Hart Publishing, 2015).

happen, courts can and will step in to rule the offending action – or indeed inaction – unlawful. It is not just the manner of exercise of the government's powers: it is the very identifying of what those powers are in the first place. This is a task for the law – and it is part of the rule of law.

## III. Bagehot

Let me turn now to Bagehot. Bagehot's account of the 'English' Constitution is very different from Dicey's. There is little overlap between the two, yet they complement one another beautifully. The two men's purposes were identical. Both sought to explain the Constitution to those who lived under it, celebrating its virtues, boasting of its aptness of fit for the United Kingdom, and suggesting throughout that it was superior both to the United States Constitution and to the French. Both books were written in a similar style, despite the very different professional backgrounds of the two men (Dicey was a lawyer and a professor; Bagehot was neither). Both were unencumbered by burdensome academic apparatus – footnotes are kept (as they always should be) to a minimum. These were books designed to be read and enjoyed, written with a lightness of touch and a briskness of pace from which modern writers could learn a lot.

Like Dicey, Bagehot was a great coiner of phrase and, as with Dicey's book, it is in large measure because of the success of the phrases he coined that we still remember so much about what Bagehot had to say. His distinction between the dignified and the efficient; his great insight (closely related to this distinction) that, in England, 'a republic has insinuated itself beneath the folds of a monarchy';[29] his remarks about letting 'daylight upon magic';[30] his description of the Cabinet as 'the efficient secret of the … constitution' – it represents the 'close union, the nearly complete fusion of the executive and legislative powers', he said;[31] and the famous account of the constitutional powers of the monarch – he or she has 'the right to be consulted, the right to encourage, and the right to warn', Bagehot wrote.[32] In the *Evans* case to which I referred above – the case *The Guardian* newspaper brought seeking disclosure under the Freedom of Information Act of certain correspondence between government departments and HRH the Prince of Wales – this phrase of Bagehot's was called 'the tripartite convention'.[33] That alone is a sign of Bagehot's enduring legacy and influence – that a journalist writing in the 1860s should shape a legal decision on open government in the first decade of the twenty-first century.

[29] W Bagehot, *The English Constitution* (Oxford, Oxford University Press, [1867] 2001) 48.
[30] ibid 54.
[31] ibid 11.
[32] ibid 64.
[33] *Evans* (above n 5) para 77.

But Bagehot's influence has endured also because of what he did in the *English Constitution*. For what he did in that book has been emulated many times since, not least by those who wrote in the 'functionalist' style, as Martin Loughlin called it, associated in particular with the London School of Economics in the early twentieth century.[34] Bagehot wrote about the institutions of state as he found them. His task was to describe not what some high constitutional theory said they should do, but what the institutions of state actually did in practice. Any theory he ascribed to them grew out of his account of what they did – theory followed practice and not the other way around. Sir Ivor Jennings' long works on *Cabinet Government* and *Parliament* were written very much in this vein.[35] Likewise, WA Robson's account of administrative law.[36] Subsequently, John Griffith picked up the baton and wrote always about what he saw courts and parliaments doing (not about what they were supposed to do according to any preconceived ideal).[37] Griffith did not like Bagehot (he once told me): he thought he was a great mythologiser.[38] But, to my mind, Bagehot was the forerunner of precisely the methodology and style that Griffith made his own. Outside of the legal academy, generations of British political scientists, when they wrote about the Constitution or about the great institutions of state, tried to do what Bagehot had done. First, understand what happens and, only then, draw out from that understanding a sense of the purposes served by an institution, its functions, and tasks.

Rather than examining in this chapter every aspect of Bagehot's argument in the *English Constitution*, I want to pick out just one or two highlights. First, the famous distinction he drew between the dignified and the efficient. This distinction overlaps with, although it is evidently not the same as, Dicey's distinction between laws and conventions. Dicey and Bagehot were both, in different ways, fascinated by the relation of constitutional form to substance. As a matter of law, the monarch may appoint whomsoever he wishes to serve as his Prime Minister and, if he wished, he could appoint no one to the role. As a matter of convention, however, the monarch appoints as his Prime Minister the leader of the political party who can, for the time being, command the confidence of the House of Commons. Likewise, as a matter of law, the monarch may either grant or withhold royal consent to legislation passed by the Houses of Parliament. But as a matter of convention such consent is never withheld, at least not without clear ministerial advice.

The dignified/formal/legal powers of the Crown are extraordinary, conferring wide-ranging discretion on the monarch. The efficient substance of how the

[34] See M Loughlin, *Public Law and Political Theory* (Oxford, Oxford University Press, 1992) especially chs 6–8.

[35] Sir Ivor Jennings, *Cabinet Government* (Cambridge, Cambridge University Press, 1936) and *Parliament* (Cambridge, Cambridge University Press, 1939).

[36] WA Robson, *Justice and Administrative Law* (London, Macmillan, 1928).

[37] JAG Griffith, 'The Political Constitution' (1979) 42 *Modern Law Review* 1.

[38] Personal recollection.

Constitution operates in conventional practice, by contrast, tells a different story. One of the things that holds Bagehot and Dicey together is that they each wanted to tell both sides of this story. As we do now: it is important that we understand and explain to our students where formal legal power lies in the Constitution – but it is even more important that we (and our students) understand that the Constitution does not in fact work like that.

A second theme, which binds Bagehot and Dicey together, is their celebration of the ways in which the British Constitution was able to mutate to meet the changing needs of the nation without cracking or crashing into revolution. It is incredibly important to grasp that both men were trying to explain to their compatriots why it was that Britain, more or less alone in Europe, did not suffer political convulsion in the middle of the nineteenth century. Let us not forget: more or less wherever you looked on the Continent in 1848 you would see turmoil. To explain why and how Britain, uniquely in Europe, managed to avoid regime change, *coup d'état*, or revolution was among the principal tasks Bagehot and Dicey set themselves. Their answer was: adaptability. Britain did not experience revolution in the nineteenth century because its Constitution could and did evolve. For Dicey, it evolved through legislative progress – that is what his lectures on *Law and Public Opinion* are all about.[39] For Bagehot it evolved through this process whereby the efficient had taken hold of the dignified, and had done so to such an extent that the 'efficient secret' of the constitution was the Cabinet. The Cabinet: a body entirely unknown to the law, a body that the law did not even recognise, never mind regulate, but a body accountable as it was to the House of Commons, which forms the effective government of the day. Monarchy was the outward form, the appearance, the clothing of the Constitution. But the inner substance was ministers, drawn from and accountable to the House of Commons, leaving the monarchy itself with but three not very impressive functions – 'the right to be consulted', 'the right to encourage', and 'the right to warn'. A republic, indeed, 'insinuated beneath the folds of monarchy'.

## IV. Legacy

Thinking about the broader legacy which Bagehot and Dicey have bequeathed to us, there are three points I want to make by way of conclusion. First, I just want to notice one or two further aspects of what exactly it is we have inherited from them and, in particular, the gaps that persist in that inheritance. Then, I want to offer a few further remarks about why Bagehot and Dicey have been so enduring in their influence. Finally, I want to close with a criticism because, in writing as they did, Bagehot and Dicey both denied the importance of something which I think they

[39] Dicey, *Lectures on the Relation between Law and Public Opinion*.

were wrong to deny – something which was taken much more seriously in the eighteenth century than in the nineteenth, and something which I think we, today, need to recover. More of that in a moment.

First, what is missing from the accounts of the Constitution handed down to us by Bagehot and Dicey? Two obvious absentees, which continue to haunt us, are the state and what exactly the country is. Not inconsiderable gaps, you might think. The British Constitution does not have a theory of the state. Instead, we have the Crown. With one or two exceptions, this has not hampered us all that much. There was a period in the 1980s when the courts tied themselves in knots trying to figure out what was a judicially reviewable public body and what was not, but eventually a sufficient quantity of fudge was applied to the problem and it melted away. But, to a lawyer trained in the Continental tradition, the absence of the state as a constitutional concept would be striking.[40] It is one of the reasons why, for example, Spanish lawyers find the UK's handling of the Scottish independence question bafflingly generous, just as we find the Spanish constitutional court's rulings on Catalan secession so aggressive and, indeed, alien.

Confusion over the country, by contrast, has cost us rather more. Dicey's account was a treatment of the United Kingdom Constitution from an avowedly English common law point of view. The title of Bagehot's book is so ill-chosen that these days it often has the Latin term '*sic*' appended to it in parentheses. It is, if nothing else, a reminder that the tendency amongst the English simply to overlook and to act in ignorance of the fact that England equals neither Great Britain nor the United Kingdom is nothing new. But it is more perniciously problematic in that it has allowed a misconception to develop, in more nationalistic accounts of Scots law, that Dicey's understanding of the sovereignty of Parliament was somehow a peculiarly English beast that has no counterpart in the law north of the border. Even Lord Hope of Craighead – no nationalist, he – was wont to fall into this trap from time to time.[41] However, even a cursory glance at that leading nineteenth-century case on the sovereignty of Parliament, *Edinburgh and Dalkeith Railway v Wauchope*,[42] would show that to pretend Dicey's account was peculiarly English was always a fallacy, even if it was a fallacy which found deceptively authoritative voice in the obiter dicta of Lord Cooper in *MacCormick's* case.[43] It was, let us not forget, the *Scottish* law lord, Lord Reid, who spoke for a unanimous House in what is still the leading House of Lords authority on the modern law of the sovereignty of Parliament, *British Rail v Pickin*.[44] There is no hint there that there is any difference between English and Scots law on the law of parliamentary sovereignty.

I have already offered two reasons why Bagehot's and Dicey's accounts of the Constitution have endured so impressively: their style and their gift at coining a

[40] The best treatment of this matter, and of the episodes to which it gave rise, is JWF Allison, *A Continental Distinction in the Common Law*, rev edn (Oxford, Oxford University Press, 2000).

[41] See his speech (judgment) in *Jackson* (above n 7).

[42] *Edinburgh and Dalkeith Railway Co v Wauchope* (1842) 8 Cl & Fin 710.

[43] *MacCormick v Lord Advocate* 1953 SC 396.

[44] *British Railways Board v Pickin* [1974] AC 765.

phrase; and their uncanny ability to tell their readers what they wanted to hear – indeed, what they already implicitly believed to be true. These are two of the reasons for Dicey's and Bagehot's immense success. But I think it is also worth pointing out that these two books are evidence of an old truth that lies within the cliché that history is written by winners. The mid-Victorians felt privileged and hugely fortunate. As David Cannadine has pointed out, they felt not only Victorian but victorious. In his account, the nineteenth was Britain's 'victorious century'.[45] You do not have to be a Marxist to think that Eric Hobsbawm was right to identify this period as the time when traditions were invented, including constitutional traditions.[46]

Our Constitution is based on history. It is not based on any one moment when the customs of the time were so forthrightly held – or were so robustly under attack – that they had to be crystallised into a single written text. Rather, our constitutional traditions have evolved (including, sometimes, by invention) over a long span of time. Too long a span of time. So long a span of time that no-one can hope to remember it all. Our Constitution is based on history: yes, but it is based on too much history.

So, what we do, to make up for the fact that there is just too much history to remember, is that we select certain highlights, certain moments, or certain periods and we elevate those moments or periods as if they were the foundations on which all else is based. Now, what is so peculiar is that we do not choose the obvious moments. We do not choose 1707 or 1800 or 1922, years in which momentous events took place which, quite literally, changed the shape and the nature of the country. Iain McLean has written about this compellingly: what is wrong with the British Constitution is that it does not pay anything like sufficient attention to what Britain is.[47] Most law students in the United Kingdom go through their entire constitutional law courses without having to confront or think about this question – and that, as I have noted, is part of what we have inherited from Bagehot and Dicey.

So, if we do not choose 1707 or 1800 or 1922, when do we choose? Well, Magna Carta still gets a look-in, as does the occasional episode from the seventeenth century. Not the Civil War, so much, nor the execution of the King, nor even the restoration of Crown. None of that. But Sir Edward Coke we like to talk about, and certain isolated provisions of the Bill of Rights, if not the reasons why they were enacted. In the eighteenth century it is (astonishingly) as if nothing very much happened, save perhaps *Entick v Carrington*. But then come Bagehot and Dicey. That moment, between the first and second Reform Acts,[48] that mid-Victorian moment when Parliament was at its zenith, after the Crown's power had started to

[45] D Cannadine, *Victorious Century: The United Kingdom 1800–1906* (London, Allen Lane, 2017).

[46] See E Hobsbawm and T Ranger (eds), *The Invention of Tradition* (Cambridge, Cambridge University Press, 1983).

[47] I McLean, *What's Wrong with the British Constitution?* (Oxford, Oxford University Press, 2010).

[48] Of 1832 and 1867.

wane but before the rise of modern political party challenged the independence of the Commons. That moment, which Bagehot and Dicey so grippingly narrated – that is a moment we remember, and valorise, and elevate. I am not sure we should. But we do. And that is why Bagehot and Dicey continue to matter.

Bagehot's and Dicey's accounts of the mid-Victorian Constitution deliberately set out to bury and to replace what – before they wrote – had been received orthodoxy. Eighteenth-century orthodoxy, encapsulated most authoritatively in Blackstone's *Commentaries*,[49] was that the triumph of the Constitution rested on its holding in balance the three estates, or interests, or powers, of the land. Britain (of, if you prefer, England) was stable because each of the three estates – each of the three powers – held each other in check. Neither the King nor the Lords nor the Commons could rule alone. Each required and relied upon the support and collaboration of the others. Such had been the triumph of the Glorious Revolution of 1688, whose genius had been to put to an end the constitutional conflicts of the seventeenth century. So Blackstone believed. So, following Locke, everyone believed. In the seventeenth century the King had tried to rule without Parliament.[50] After that disaster, Parliament then tried to rule without the King.[51] Neither experiment was successful; both were short-lived; and neither has ever been repeated.

For Blackstone, what mattered most about the Constitution was its ability to secure stability. This was achieved through the device and art – the statecraft – of balance. It was a mixed monarchy, or a mixed Constitution, which combined the one, the few, and the many (the King, the Lords, and the Commons), allowing none to dominate over the others. Stability was the paramount virtue because the previous century of history had shown that it could not be taken for granted. By the time Bagehot and Dicey came to write about the Constitution, by contrast, the focus was less on how to secure stability and more on how to locate authority. As I have sought to show in this chapter, what both Dicey and Bagehot were concerned to do was to explain where, how, and by whom constitutional authority was exercised in the United Kingdom. Blackstone presented a Constitution whose strength came from harmony and balance. Bagehot, with his focus on the 'efficient secret' of the Constitution being the 'close union, the nearly complete fusion' of the executive and the legislature, and likewise Dicey, with his focus on the sovereignty of the Crown-in-Parliament, presented a Constitution whose strength came from unity, indeed from indivisibility. It is quite the contrast.

What caused this dramatic change of focus was time. Blackstone wrote when the settlement bequeathed by the Glorious Revolution felt neither long-established nor secure. His England was one still reverberating with the echoes and shocks of seventeenth-century turmoil. Bagehot and Dicey, on the other hand, wrote in a

[49] Sir William Blackstone, *Commentaries on the Laws of England* (Oxford, Clarendon Press, 1765–69).
[50] In the period of the 'Personal Rule' (1630–41).
[51] During the Commonwealth and the Protectorate (1649–60).

period in which the British – or at least the English – had shown that they had at last found a way of delivering political change, evolution, and development without causing the tectonic plates of the Constitution to judder or to quake. Thus were old ideas of the mixed Constitution and, alongside them, newer, Enlightenment ideas of the separation of powers, jettisoned.

In contrast with the arguments set out by my friends and colleagues Vernon Bogdanor and Nick Barber, I do not believe that there was an Old Constitution, represented by Dicey, and that at the turn of the millennium a New Constitution somehow overtook or replaced it, represented by our short membership of the European Union, by the Human Rights Act, and by the devolution statutes.[52] I believe, rather, that there was an Enlightenment Constitution, forged in the time of John Locke and celebrated most famously in Blackstone's *Commentaries*, and that this Constitution was right to herald balance as its core principle. I believe too that, in the middle of the nineteenth century, this Constitution was deliberately obscured from view by the mid-Victorian Whigs. And I believe that, one hundred years on from the death of that greatest of the mid-Victorian lawyers, AV Dicey, we do not know quite where we stand.

Ideas and practices and even an embryonic jurisprudence (or case law) of the mixed Constitution, or its modern cousin the separation of powers, are beginning to emerge. You can see it, for example, in each of the Supreme Court's two *Miller* judgments.[53] From under the covers thrown over it by the ingenuity of Bagehot and Dicey, glimpses of what Locke and Blackstone and Montesquieu and even Sir Edward Coke understood by the mixed Constitution are beginning once again to be sighted. They are, as yet, but glimpses. We are a long way from developing a coherent or even a consistent theory of how powers are separated in the modern Constitution. But it may be that we are stuttering towards such a theory. Even if we are, this does not mean that Dicey's account will have to be abandoned as no longer fit for purpose. However, it would mean that it will have to be supplemented. Supplemented, I think, less by something new than by the recovery of that Enlightenment Constitution of balance that he and Bagehot sought so strenuously to deny.

I am not forecasting a revolution. Still less a new constitutional order. My guess is that in fifty or one hundred years from now our successors will still be gathering essays together to reflect on what, two centuries or more on from its first publication, the *Law of the Constitution* still has to offer. Dicey's account is far from complete. But it remains essential.

[52] See V Bogdanor, *The New British Constitution* (Oxford, Hart Publishing, 2009) and NW Barber, *The United Kingdom Constitution: An Introduction* (Oxford, Oxford University Press, 2021). See also their chapters in this volume.

[53] See *Miller/Cherry* (above n 26) and *R (Miller) v Secretary of State for Exiting the European Union* [2017] UKSC 5, [2018] AC 61.

# 4

# Dicey's *Letters to a Friend on Votes for Women*

FRANÇOISE ORAZI

AV Dicey's lifelong interest in political matters has received less attention than his juristic writings. Yet, during his lifetime, Dicey established a considerable reputation as an intellectual[1] and applied his insights to matters beyond the strict confines of the law. Political thought figured prominently among his interests and permeated his legal commentaries, as evidenced by what Dicey himself considered in his own words his 'best' and most 'mature' book,[2] namely *Lectures on the Relation between Law and Public Opinion in England during the Nineteenth Century*. From his Oxford days – if not from his childhood – Dicey was committed to a form of liberalism he described as Benthamite individualism, drawing inspiration from JS Mill's *Principles of Political Economy* and *On Liberty*. However, his liberalism did not evolve towards the socialist-leaning tendencies of the later Mill, nor did it follow the collectivist turn taken by the Liberal Party in its 'new liberal' line. Rather, he maintained a classical liberal orthodoxy, which he held to be compatible with standard conservative views such as staunch opposition to Irish Home Rule along with, not surprisingly,[3] an equally firm disapproval of women's suffrage. Dicey set out his anti-suffrage stance in *Letters to a Friend on Votes for Women*[4] in 1909, a short book inspired by discussions on the subject with his close friend, James Bryce.[5] Although *Letters* is a minor, almost forgotten,

[1] See RA Cosgrove, *The Rule of Law: Alfred Venn Dicey, Victorian Jurist* (London, Palgrave Macmillan, 1980). For instance, 'Historians write frequently of the neglected figure upon whom posterity bestows a posthumous importance; such was not the case of AV Dicey, whose intellectual reputation stood highest in his own lifetime but has now declined sharply', ii.

[2] See 'Introduction' in AV Dicey, *Lectures on the Relation between Law and Public Opinion* (Indianapolis: Liberty Fund, 2008 [1917]), at https://oll.libertyfund.org/title/vandewetering-lectures-on-the-relation-between-law-and-public-opinion-lf-ed.

[3] Julia Bush highlights the frequent connection between imperialists and anti-suffragists: see J Bush, *Women against the Vote: Female Anti-Suffragism in Britain* (Oxford, Oxford University Press, 2007) 112.

[4] AV Dicey, *Letters to a Friend on Votes for Women* (London, John Murray, 1909) henceforth *Letters*.

[5] JM Balshaw, *Suffrage, Solidarity and Strife: Political Partnerships and the Women's Movement 1880–1930* (PhD thesis, University of Greenwich, 1998) 129.

work, it certainly deserves to be examined, if only as testimony to a lesser-known aspect of Dicey's thought and because it provides insight into his reluctance to embrace political and social change, at least in the later part of his life. This chapter focuses on the polemic, first by placing it within the context of the Edwardian debate over female suffrage. From this perspective, Dicey's book reads as classic anti-feminist discourse as his approach mostly replicates traditional anti-suffragist arguments. However, as will be shown in the section II below, *Letters* should not be reduced to a standard anti-suffragist pamphlet, for its author's voice – namely Dicey's unique legalistic and philosophical approach – can be disentangled from a general anti-suffrage stance to pinpoint the specific rationale of Dicey's opposition to women's suffrage, notably his attempt to draw a parallel between Unionism and anti-suffragism. In this perspective, *Letters* is as much a testament to Dicey's thought as a contribution to the anti-suffragist side in the debate on the enfranchisement of women. Section III below will turn to the intertextual aspects of *Letters*, beginning with the Millian intertextuality. Indeed, as a former admirer of JS Mill, Dicey could not ignore Mill's authoritative advocacy of sexual equality. *Letters* is therefore both a call to oppose women's suffrage as well as a rebuttal of Mill's arguments. Moreover, reflecting the implicit dialogue between *The Subjection of Women* and *Letters*, Dicey's text was also the object of a famous rebuttal, namely Bertrand Russell's notorious attack on *Letters*.

## I. A Classic Anti-Suffragist Statement

The early twentieth century saw the height of both suffragist and suffragette activism, as well as a strong reaction, an anti-suffrage movement that enjoyed widespread support. Those who came to be known as the 'Antis' organised in response to the growing sympathy for women's suffrage, particularly in Parliament:

> The Women's National Anti-Suffrage League was launched in July 1908 to counter a new and highly credible threat of imminent female enfranchisement. … it existed independently for only two years before announcing its prospective merger with the Men's League for Opposing Woman's Suffrage in August 1910',[6]

having run out of funds. The Men's league itself was formed in January 1909 to replace the Men's Committee for Opposing Woman Suffrage, which had been founded in 1908. As suggested here, 1908 to 1910 were particularly critical years that witnessed the culmination of the suffragette struggle, which famously became a thorn in the side of the Liberal government.[7] Conversely, there was a surge

[6] Bush, *Women against the Vote* 163.

[7] See, for instance, G Dangerfield, *The Strange Death of Liberal England* (Stanford, Stanford University Press, 1935) 1997 (Dangerfield's well-known thesis is that the 'women's rebellion' that followed the inconclusive attempt to grant women the vote was one of the four causes of the downfall of the Liberal party).

of anti-suffragism that paralleled the progress of its now better-known counterpart. It was during this short span of time that Dicey himself published his *Letters to a Friend*, in 1909. In January 1909 he also published a long article in the 210th volume of the *Quarterly Review* entitled 'Woman Suffrage', which was reprinted in the first part of his book. His writings were heavily criticised by his opponents. In 1909 alone, *The Common Cause* mentioned Dicey no less than 16 times.[8] As noted above, Dicey's anti-suffrage rhetoric was in tune with the gender conservatism that had prevailed in the previous century and was still a force to be reckoned with in the early twentieth century. It usually contained a strong sexist element maintaining that women were incapable, or less capable than men, of participating in public affairs. The alleged incompetence justified opposition to 'the concession of sovereign power to women'.[9] Anti-suffragism was fundamentally derived from the core belief in a difference in the nature of the sexes. The extent and nature of this difference ranged from a pronounced hierarchisation of the sexes to the recognition of women's equal value in difference. Dicey, it must be said, came down firmly in favour of the latter, praising the reforms that had gradually reduced the legal and social exclusions that women faced as wives, mothers, workers, proprietors, and students. However, he sometimes wondered whether some reforms had not gone too far: 'The one question which an English reformer need now ask himself is, Whether the zeal to relieve a married woman from unjust disabilities may not, as against her creditors, have bestowed upon her unfair privileges?'[10] However, even in its less chauvinistic versions, anti-suffragism remained dependent on a worldview that posited the polarisation of men and women along a clear-cut division between the 'masculine' and the 'feminine'. Whereas women were seen as 'a body [who] are more readily influenced than men by the emotions of the moment',[11] power was construed as masculine, and since the state was the embodiment of power, it too was of masculine essence if only because it 'ha[d] been built up by men; its welfare depend[ing] upon the encouragement of manly qualities'.[12]

Despite his relative support for other reforms of women's legal status, notably women's access to universities, Dicey agreed unreservedly with all the points listed in the Anti-Suffrage League's manifesto.

> [It] presented seven main arguments. Most of these had been familiar to suffragists for decades. First, 'the spheres of men and women, owing to natural causes, are essentially different.' Second, women could not 'take any practical part' in the running of the 'complex modern State,' which relies on 'naval and military power, diplomacy, finance, and the great mining, constructive, shipping and transport industries.' Third, women had already been given sufficient opportunity to be politically active, through the

[8] *The Common Cause* was the newspaper of the National Union of Women's Suffrage Societies, published from 1909 until 1920. See https://britishnewspaperarchive.co.uk/titles/common-cause.

[9] Dicey, *Letters* 10.

[10] ibid 26.

[11] ibid 10.

[12] ibid 43.

> municipal vote and their admission to local councils. Fourth, the influence of women 'in social causes will be diminished rather than increased by the possession of the parliamentary vote.' Lastly, the antis argued that women could not be enfranchised, because to enfranchise women on the same terms as men would 'in practice involve an unjust and invidious limitation,' but enfranchising voters' wives would only introduce political disagreement into the home, while the third alternative, adult suffrage, meant that women voters would outnumber the men. (No one explained why this was such a problem.) And, finally, for those who were not convinced, the Anti-Suffrage Manifesto said, at any rate, women's suffrage was a dangerous experiment not worth the risk.[13]

Other anti-suffrage arguments often included the time-worn notion that political authority ultimately rests on physical force, even if a highly civilised state does not need to resort to force directly. This line of reasoning is one of the five reasons Lord Cromer,[14] President of the League from December 1910 to March 1912, puts forth to 'object to granting the Suffrage to Women':[15] 'because those who make the laws should have physical force to enforce them, and this women do not possess'. Dicey follows his President's suit: 'The basis of all government is force, which means in the last resort physical strength. But predominant force lies in the hands of men'.[16]

Lord Curzon, the next (Co-) President of the League develops a slightly more conciliatory line when he lists 15 reasons for opposing the suffrage,[17] including support for the 'intellectual emancipation' of women, reminiscent of Dicey's own position. Apart from this concession (point 14 in Lord Curzon's list), each of the remaining points is also brought up in *Letters*. Moreover, the resemblance between Dicey's and other anti-suffragist literature also includes a similarity of form. As the two examples (Lord Cromer's and Lord Curzon's pamphlets) show, the favoured presentation of anti-suffragist argument is the list. Dicey is no exception – at least three of the five letters in *Letters* contained lists. Indeed, letters two, three, and four share a common structure based on a list of arguments: letters two and three present arguments in favour of the vote and undermine them in a subsequent commentary, while letter four lists the objections to female suffrage – the first and last letters being an introduction and a the summary of argument.

## II. Dicey's Voice: Distinct Arguments

Despite their similar form and a tendency to rely on predictable commonplace arguments, anti-suffragists writings vary to some extent so that they also contain

[13] SA van Wingerden, *The Women's Suffrage Movement in Britain, 1866–1928* (London, Palgrave Macmillan, 1999) 114.
[14] See Appendix 1 below.
[15] 'Lord Cromer's view against women's suffrage', Anti-Suffrage Campaign Pamphlet in A Butterly, '100 Women: the female protesters against giving women the vote' (BBC, 6 February 2018), at https://www.bbc.com/news/uk-42704341.
[16] Dicey, *Letters* 55.
[17] See Appendix 2 below.

distinctive features such as arguments or style. Even as the debate was raging, Dicey's text was seen as more fair-minded than most dismissals of women's claims to equal representation

> We cannot agree with some critics in dismissing Prof. Dicey's book as insignificant. In general tone, it is far superior to any anti-suffrage literature we have seen, being remarkably free from that sentimentality which has its roots partly in egotism and partly in ignorance. … he may be said to put the case for Women's Suffrage much more fairly than is usual in one who opposes it, and for this and for all the good work he has done for the advancement of women in the past we thank him.[18]

Anti-suffragist writings also reflect their authors' interests or backgrounds. For instance, Lord Curzon's aforementioned 15 points insist on the detrimental effect that women's suffrage would have on foreign policy (point 8) and fear it would weaken British rule in India (point 9), an obvious concern for the former Viceroy of India. Similarly, *Letters* contains more personal views alongside the conventional arguments. Relying on a parallel with his rejection of Home Rule in Ireland, Dicey justifies his opposition to the enfranchisement of women on the grounds of the national interest which he sees as superior to the claims of individuals even if they are in the majority: 'the mere desire of a class, however large, for political power or for national independence affords no conclusive reason why the wish should be granted'.[19] Dicey's parallel is explicit.

> I merely insist upon the simple fact that the grounds on which most Unionists rest their moral right to maintain the Union against the wishes of the majority of the people of Ireland are opposed to some of the reasons and much of the sentiment which tell in favour of the movement for woman suffrage.[20]

Thus, in both cases – the Irish demand for Home Rule and women's claim to the vote – Dicey denies that granting them should be based of the popularity of the claim, asserting on the contrary that it must depend on the benefits to the country.

> Since 1885 I have never doubted that a majority of the inhabitants of Ireland are opposed to the Union with Great Britain. I have also never seen the least reason to doubt that the people of the United Kingdom ought to insist upon the maintenance of the Union. … conviction as to the true nature of a Parliamentary vote led inevitably to the conclusion that the expediency, or what in such a matter is the same thing, the justice, of giving Parliamentary votes to English women depends on the answer to the inquiry, not whether a large number of English women, or English women generally, wish for votes, but whether the establishment of woman suffrage will be a benefit to England? To this question I am unable to return an affirmative answer. I have become, therefore, of necessity an opponent of woman suffrage.[21]

[18] *The Common Cause*, London, 12 August 1909, 230.
[19] Dicey, *Letters* 9.
[20] ibid 10.
[21] ibid 9, 12.

It must be admitted that the argument appears to be at odds with democratic principles. Dicey expresses a strongly conservative view on democracy, which informs his perspective on the constitution.

> On matters of constitutional change, I do not think a small majority has any moral right to act with vigour. The presumption is in favour of the existing state of affairs, because on the whole it may be assumed to be the permanent will of the nation. Add to this that a constitutional change once made is, or ought to be, final, and therefore ought not to be made by any body of men who do not clearly represent the final will of the nation. Till modem times this has been the practice, though not the theory, of English constitutional government, and it is, as I have pointed out, recognised as a democratic principle in every true democracy.[22]

Dicey relies here on the distinction between constitutional reform and political reform. In states where the rule of law prevails, the elected majority may legitimately dictate policy, but any fundamental changes to the constitution must have a stronger, broader basis, such as large consensus among representatives, or specific procedures often involving both houses. However, Dicey is not opposed to such change in principle, though he is certainly more reluctant to constitutional change than he is to political reform. Rather, any reform of a constitutional nature must be handled more cautiously, its pros and cons carefully assessed, especially the balance between increased representativeness versus decreased effectiveness.

> It is at least arguable that the establishment of household suffrage has lowered the legislative capacity of the House of Commons. Bold, indeed, would be the paradox-monger who maintained that in no State belonging to the American Commonwealth has the introduction of universal suffrage lowered the moral or intellectual character of the Legislature. We must always, therefore, in legislation which affects the constitution of Parliament, weigh against one another the different qualities of representativeness and effectiveness.[23]

In short, then, part of Dicey's distinctive argumentation against women's suffrage amounts to a defence of restricted suffrage. In his view any extension should be judged in terms of the gain in representativeness against the loss in effectiveness. In this particular case, however, Dicey does not explicitly state what conditions would have to be met for the gain representativeness to outweigh the alleged loss in effectiveness. What is implied is that the dangers associated with women's votes, the potential damage to the 'welfare of the State',[24] are simply too great to take the risk and that, probably because women's nature is what it is – or is supposed to be – no present or future adjustment will reduce the danger. Unlike all other reforms of the electorate, women's suffrage and an extension of the franchise in Ireland are simply out of the question. It should be noted that this line of reasoning can be contrasted with another widely held view, namely the

[22] Letter to Leo Maxse, 1 January 1895, quoted in Cosgrove, *The Rule of Law* 161.
[23] Dicey, *Letters* 21–22.
[24] Dicey, *Letters* 10.

alternative rationale for excluding women from suffrage put forward by James Mill in his famous 1820 article on government.[25] James Mill of course held what would now be described as a familialist view, as he believes that good government was representative government but argues, like many of his contemporaries, that women are represented via their fathers' and husbands' votes. Dicey also believes that representative government is good government, but he adds that representative government is good because it 'is intended to secure for the people of a given country what I may call the "legislative effectiveness" of Parliament – that is, that Parliament shall consist of some of the best and most judicious members of the community, and shall enact good and wise laws'.[26] Incidentally, the emphasis on effectiveness does not stop Dicey from claiming, like James Mill, that women's interests are represented by men 'Where will you find a body of Englishmen who have legislated of set purpose against the interest of their daughters and in favour of their sons?',[27] but this is not to him the heart of the matter. It should be added that 'effectiveness' remains rather loosely defined. It sometimes appears to be contrasted with an 'emotional' manner of ruling, as opposed to 'firmness of purpose' and 'foresight',[28] which allows the avoidance of reacting on the spur of the moment by giving in to 'sentiment.' Interestingly, Dicey contends that 'an English democracy, in common with all democracies, is too emotional'.[29] As one would expect, the conclusion Dicey draws from this premise is that adding women's suffrage would result in an even more emotional regime, unable to 'repel the onslaught of foreign enemies?'[30]

Furthermore, Dicey insists that the representation of women should be strictly distinguished from any other considerations of women's legal status or social role, rejecting the connection between 'emancipation' and 'enfranchisement',[31] or between freedom and political authority. *Letters* contains 12 mentions of 'authority'. 'Moral authority' is mentioned, as the discourse on female suffrage stresses women's moral authority to justify the vote, and Dicey does not deny 'that the possession of votes would in some instances increase the moral authority of women'.[32] 'Political authority', by far the most frequent usage of authority,

[25] The argument put forward by James Mill rested on his utilitarian premise which considered government as a means to an end, ie the happiness of the individuals and the community. Mill concluded that the only system capable of achieving this goal was representative democracy, since representatives would legislate on behalf of, and in the interest of, their electors. Yet he famously excluded women from the vote, claiming 'One thing is pretty clear, that all those individuals whose interests are indisputably included in those of other individuals, may be struck off without inconvenience. In this light may be viewed all children, up to a certain age, whose interests are involved in those of their parents. In this light, also, women may be regarded, the interest of almost all of whom is involved either in that of their fathers or in that of their husbands': J Mill, *(Essays on Government, Jurisprudence, Liberty of the Press and Law of Nations* (London, J Innes, 1828) 21.

[26] Dicey, *Letters* 19.

[27] ibid 24–25.

[28] ibid 52.

[29] ibid 51–52.

[30] ibid 52.

[31] ibid 29.

[32] ibid 40.

means government or the right to govern, which, at first sight, amounts to suffrage within representative government. However, Dicey's understanding of authority seems to exceed this simple definition when he speaks of 'the authority of the nation', which he holds to be different from a representative government's majority.

> It is I think of immense importance that people should realise that a small & transitory political majority, though it necessarily exercises the powers, has not the authority of the nation. On this point my mind is becoming more and more clear.[33]

The same letter mentions 'the permanent will of the nation' as separate from the will of a small majority. This – typically conservative – reference to the permanence of the nation is an important element of Dicey's approach. Without raising the complicated issue of what a nation is besides the sum of its inhabitants joined together in an imagined community, it must be noted that Dicey is wary of women's suffrage precisely because women outnumber men. Female suffrage would, theoretically at least, allow women to rule over men, leading to – as already hinted above – a situation where political power is in the hands of those who do not have the physical power needed to enforce their authority. Therefore, political authority would be separated from actual sovereignty.

> … for women to rely on physical force for the attainment of political authority calls into play the instrument, and creates the condition of opinion, which, should women obtain votes, might deprive them of any real share in sovereignty.[34]

This distinct approach eventually leads onto a far more common idea, which may be termed 'the physical force argument' and is prominent in *Letters*, giving the reader the impression that it is the most convincing, compelling enough to close the debate. It includes both the force to enforce the law in a domestic context and to defend the country against its enemies. Dicey resorts to it in his conclusion, once again with an allusion to the permanence of the nation:

> Let every elector remember for once the main duty which, independent of party connection, lies upon him. He is bound, on the subject of woman suffrage, to vote with a sole eye to the permanent interest of the United Kingdom and of the British Empire. England is surrounded by perils. Our neighbours are military States, each of which maintains armies larger than we can retain within the bounds of the United Kingdom.[35]

## III. With and against John Stuart Mill: Intertextual Aspects

As the last quotation reminds us, Dicey's polemic is clearly situated within the conservative discourse of the time. Though anti-suffragism – like Home Rule or the

[33] Letter to Leo Maxse, 1 January 1895, quoted in Cosgrove, *The Rule of Law* 161.
[34] Dicey, *Letters* 70.
[35] ibid 72–73.

Boer War – cut across the political spectrum, some anti-suffragist arguments were anchored in a broader political ideology. Thus, the left-wing anti-suffragists' main reason for the political exclusion of women is their proximity with the Church. Dicey himself, pulling out all the stops against women's vote, uses the bigot argument:

> Would any Italian patriot, even though he were a Republican irreconcilable to the Monarchy, admit to the Parliamentary franchise the women of Italy at the risk of handing over the government of the country to priests and reactionists? Everyone can supply the true answer to this question.[36]

However, where the left believes that women's suffrage would mean an increase in the Conservative vote, Dicey suspects women will be prone to lavish social expenditures,

> Our politicians have by the Old Age Pensions Act re-established a gigantic system of outdoor relief without waiting to hear the judgment of a Commission appointed to inquire into the working of the Poor Law. They have committed this act of supreme rashness, … Such leaders will not become wiser or more prudent when they find that their seats depend on the approval of new constituents whose tender-heartedness forbids them to see the evil of any form of charity which, at whatever cost to the State, gives immediate relief to individual distress which excites their sympathies.[37]

This anticipation of women's electoral behaviour opens Dicey's text to an attack he appears eager to avoid, that of downright sexism. To be sure, throughout the book, Dicey is at pains to combine his resolute anti-suffragism and the claim that he supports women's liberty. Here the text falls back on John Stuart Mill's authority on liberty and women. Dicey presents Mill's depiction of women in *the Subjection* as more sexist than his own. He alludes to the famous passage in chapter 4, where Mill writes that women place more value in social consideration and public opinion than men, which implies that 'Whoever has a wife and children has given hostages to Mrs. Grundy',[38] distances himself from Mill's negative judgement, 'You know well that this is not my view of the condition or the influence of women. My words summarise the judgment of Mill',[39] yet retains the – qualified – negative assessment for the sake of his own argumentation, 'Mill's unjust disparagement is assuredly not wholly devoid of truth'.[40]

Of course, this is a dishonest interpretation of Mill's point, taken out of context. Mill was arguing in favour of the intellectual emancipation of women and for husbands to accept educated wives. Thankfully not all 25 references to Mill are as misleading. *Letters* actually begins with a very sincere account of Dicey's conversion to anti-suffragism after having embraced feminism and pays a touching tribute to JS Mill.

> You ask how it has happened that, though I was for many years an advocate, I have now become a convinced opponent of the introduction of woman suffrage into England?

[36] ibid 22.
[37] ibid 46.
[38] ibid 45.
[39] ibid 45–46.
[40] ibid 46.

> The question is a natural one. It is the better worth an answer because my own change of opinion has been shared by many of my contemporaries who began to take an interest in politics some fifty or sixty years ago. We all of us were Liberals; we most of us came under the influence of J.S. Mill, and we could not then have found a wiser, a nobler, and, above all, a more public-spirited teacher of the rights and duties of citizens. Under his guidance we favoured every attempt to extend not only the liberty but also the political rights of women.[41]

The introduction sets the tone for the whole polemic, which, in large part, consists of a refutation of Mill, while retaining most of his defence of individual liberty, the more classic aspects of his liberalism. In keeping with the general stance of *Letters*, the refutation consists of hackneyed arguments against Mill's thought, especially his feminism, along with more distinct analyses, which tend to turn Mill's arguments against women's vote.

Mill's feminist stance was often said to be the result of his infatuation for his wife, and he was accused of having surrendered his critical faculties to his emotions. Dicey's interpretation is no exception, almost fifty years later.

> By degrees, too, the admiration for Mill's extraordinary gift of logical exposition, as well as gratitude for much of his teaching, became in my mind compatible with the admission that with him the reality, though not the form, of logic is often sacrificed to the influence of moral emotion, and that this subordination of his reason to the force of generous passion is nowhere more noticeable than in his 'Subjection of Women'.[42]

In the same way, despite Mill's very clear deconstruction of the notion of women's purported nature as well as of custom, Dicey holds onto both to posit a flaw in Mill's reasoning:

> Mill theoretically grounds all knowledge on experience, but throughout this treatise he minimizes the importance of natural and undisputed facts; he in effect inculcates the neglect of the lessons to be derived from historical experience embodied in the general, if not universal, customs of mankind.[43]

Mill's utilitarianism and rebuttal of the natural rights[44] theory is mobilised to support the idea of effectiveness and reject any a priori claims to suffrage. This implies a piecemeal reading of Mill, a form of cherry-picking of his thought such as claiming to adhere to the principle of utility, yet denying that representative government can be judged by such a standard. Finally, Dicey sometimes describes JS Mill as a man of the past whose observations were valid in his time but no longer apply in a different context. For instance:

> Reformers in the middle of the nineteenth century believed, not unreasonably, as assuredly did Mill, that the wrongs done to women could never be removed without giving them a share in sovereign power.[45]

[41] ibid 7–8.
[42] ibid 11.
[43] ibid 11–12.
[44] ibid 18.
[45] ibid 26.

But 'the change in the law produced by the Married Women's Property Acts, 1870–1892', has proved that a male Parliament can work in favour of women's interests. Such dismissals enable Dicey to retain Mill's vindication of liberty or 'civil rights' in Dicey's words and deny women 'political rights'.[46]

## IV. Further Intertextuality: Russell's Answer to Letters

One is tempted to conclude that what is at stake here, beyond making the anti-suffragist case and therefore proving the suffragist part of Mill's thought false, is the coherence of Dicey's thought trajectory, which clearly consists of a political conservatism mixed with an ethical liberalism, or at least a conservatism which, true to its Burkean origins, displays a concern for continuity and a respect for traditional wisdom and usage. It posits the paramount freedom of Englishmen as a legacy of the past, not the consequence of an abrupt change inspired by an abstract moral ideal. However rational his thought may be, Dicey's criticism of Mill's minimisation of historical experience does not stand. Bertrand Russell makes that point very clear when he writes,

> But there is a special fallacy in speaking of 'lessons to be derived from historical experience'. For the only thing that history teaches is that men, as a rule, have not in fact allowed power to women. This is part of the larger 'teaching', that the strong have almost everywhere been ruthless, and the weak have almost everywhere been oppressed. But how can history teach us that this state of things ought to continue?[47]

Indeed, Russell almost immediately launched a scathing attack on Dicey's *Letters*. In a very powerful pamphlet entitled 'Anti-Suffragist Anxieties', published in 1910,[48] Russell famously manages to demolish every single point of *Letters* in a few pages.[49] Russell's text is so compelling that it can hardly be ignored when writing about Dicey's *Letters*, forming a masterly postface of sorts. As it provides a brilliant rebuttal of every argument studied above, it seems to be a fitting conclusion for this chapter. As for the common arguments described in section I above, Russell begins by taunting their predictability,

> It must be confessed that they [the reasons for opposition to women's suffrage] do not make a very formidable array, and that many of them are old friends which have done duty against every reform since the ancient Britons first ceased to dye themselves with woad.[50]

[46] ibid 31.
[47] The Bertrand Russell Society. All quotes are taken from https://users.drew.edu/~jlenz/br-anti-suffragists.html.
[48] B Russell, 'Anti-Suffragist Anxieties' (Westminster, The People's Suffrage Federation, 1910).
[49] Russell's pamphlet contains just 5,294 words.
[50] Russell, 'Anti-Suffragist Anxieties'.

He dissects their logical shortcomings, in a manner reminiscent of Mill:

> … considered more scientifically, if the custom of keeping women in subjection were in fact 'universal', no inference could be drawn from history as to its good or bad effects. In order to argue inductively as to the good or bad effects of an institution, there must be examples both ways: it must be possible to compare the effects of its presence with the effects of its absence.[51]

Russell also rejects the claim that, recently at least, government has proved that it can address the injustice of the status of women. He argues that it is precisely the pressure of organised women's movements that has forced the concessions.

The title of the pamphlet suggests that, for all their criticism of women's emotions, it is the anti-suffragists themselves that fall prey to irrational fear, if only the 'fear of introducing some undefined quality called 'feminine emotion' into politics'. The fear is clearly irrational because it overlooks the fact that 'wherever women are seen taking part in public life', as poor-law guardians, teachers, etc, 'they show a remarkable absence of any so-called "feminine emotion"'.

As for the distinct arguments studied in section II above, Russell rejects Dicey's distinction between political authority and freedom.

> The Professor makes a distinction between civil and political rights, and states that while women ought to have civil rights, they ought not to have political rights. But the distinction, as he states it, is too subtle to be comprehensible to the lay mind. Civil rights, he says, consist in the right to govern oneself, and political rights consist in the right to govern others. But in that case, men, by the possession of political rights, have the right to govern others, i.e., women, and women therefore cannot govern themselves. This is, of course, the fact at present.[52]

He also dismisses the debunking of natural rights:

> The argument from justice does not require any fallacious foundation in the philosophy of natural rights. To inflict a special disability upon one class in the community is in itself an evil, and is calculated to generate resentment on one side and arrogance on the other.[53]

Finally, Russell tackles the physical force argument that Dicey gives such prominence.

> The argument is, that if all women are enfranchised, they will form a majority of the electorate, and laws may be enacted, by their votes, to which a large majority of men are vehemently opposed – laws, for example, dealing with temperance or with the suppression of vice. Such laws men might refuse to obey; and the majority, being mainly composed of women, would be unable to enforce its will. Hence the government would be unstable, and might be upset by a successful revolution. The only way to avoid this is to confine the vote to those who can fight, i.e. to men.[54]

[51] ibid.
[52] ibid.
[53] ibid.
[54] ibid.

Besides the fact that such a division is extremely unlikely to occur, the possibility of an armed conflict between men and women is preposterous: 'A sex-war might provide material for a farce, but could not be conceived in sober earnest',[55] not to mention that government must function, first and foremost, as a defender of the weak and not exclude them. Government exclusively in the hands of the strong does indeed sound dangerously close to tyranny. Indeed, Russell offers a larger perspective than the legal or political one Dicey clings to. Women are not excluded from suffrage for the sake of effectiveness, but because:

> Men fear that their liberty to act in ways that are injurious to women will be curtailed, and that they will lose that pleasing sense of dominion which at present makes 'no place like home.' The instinct of the master to retain his mastery cannot be met by mere political arguments.[56]

Russell's sagacious reading of *Letters* brings him back, implicitly at least, to Mill's analysis of the position of women, which he hopes will eventually be replaced by a fairer one since to 'substitute cooperation for subjection is everywhere the effort of democracy, and it is one of the strongest arguments in favour of the enfranchisement of women'.[57]

# Appendix 1

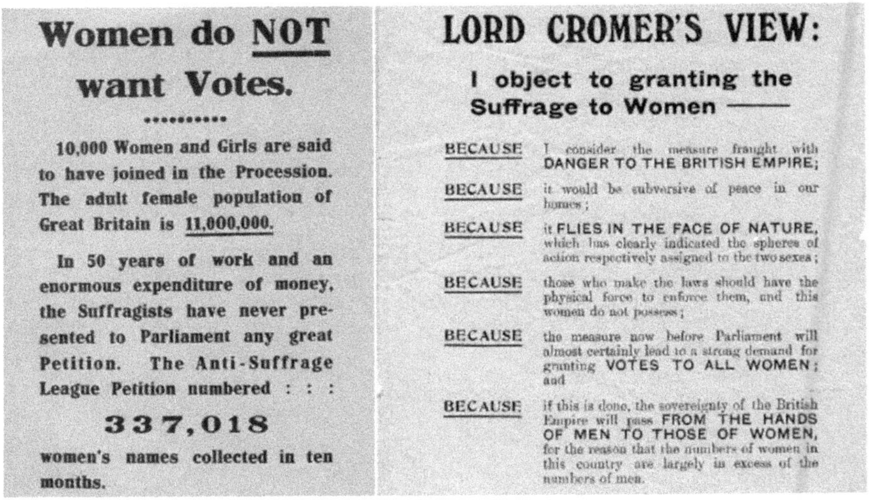


*Source*: The Women's Library at LSE, https://www.bbc.com/news/uk-42704341.

[55] ibid.
[56] ibid.
[57] ibid.

## Appendix 2



***No. 5.***

LORD CURZON'S

# FIFTEEN GOOD REASONS AGAINST THE GRANT OF FEMALE SUFFRAGE.

**LORD CURZON OF KEDLESTON** has said that there are **fifteen sound, valid, and incontrovertible arguments against the Grant of Female Suffrage.** He summarises them as follows :—

(1) Political activity will tend to take away woman from her proper sphere and highest duty, which is maternity.

(2) It will tend by the divisions which it will introduce to break up the harmony of the home.

(3) The grant of votes to women cannot possibly stop short at a restricted franchise on the basis of a property or other qualification. Married women being the women, if any, best qualified to exercise the vote, the suffrage could not be denied to them. Its extension to them would pave the way to Adult Suffrage. There is no permanent or practicable halting-stage before.

(4) Women have not, as a sex, or a class, the calmness of temperament or the balance of mind, nor have they the training, necessary to qualify them to exercise a weighty judgment in political affairs.

(5) The vote is not desired, so far as can be ascertained, by the large majority of women.

(6) Neither is the proposed change approved, so far as can be ascertained, by the large majority of men.

(7) If the vote were granted, it is probable that a very large number of women would not use it at all. But in emergencies or on occasions of emotional excitement, a large, and in the last resort, owing to the numerical majority of women, a preponderant force might suddenly be mobilised, the political effect of which would be wholly uncertain.

(8) The presence of a large female factor in the Constituencies returning a British Government to power would tend to weaken Great Britain in the estimation of foreign Powers.

(9) It would be gravely misunderstood and would become a source of weakness in India.

(10) The vote once given, it would be impossible to stop at this. Women would then demand the right of becoming M.P.'s, Cabinet Ministers, Judges, &c. Nor could the demand be logically refused.

(11) Woman, if placed by the vote on an absolute equality with man, would forfeit much of that respect which the chivalry of man has voluntarily conceded to her, and which has hitherto been her chief protection.

(12) The vote is not required for the removal of hardships or disabilities from which woman is now known to suffer. Where any such exist, they can equally well be removed or alleviated by a legislature elected by men.

(13) Those persons ought not to make laws who cannot join in enforcing them. Women cannot become soldiers, sailors, or policemen, or take an active part in the maintenance of law and order. They are incapacitated from discharging the ultimate obligations of citizenship.

(14) The intellectual emancipation of women is proceeding, and will continue to do so, without the enjoyment of the political franchise. There is no necessary connection between the two.

(15) No precedent exists for giving women as a class an active share in the Government of a great Country or Empire, and it is not for Great Britain, whose stake is the greatest, and in whose case the results of failure would be the most tremendous, to make the experiment. It would not, indeed, be an experiment, since if the suffrage were once granted, it could never be cancelled or withdrawn.

Printed by the National Press Agency Limited, Whitefriars House Carmelite Street; and Published by the NATIONAL LEAGUE FOR OPPOSING WOMAN SUFFRAGE, Caxton House, Tothill Street, Westminster, S.W. Price 2s 6d. per 1,000.

*Source*: National Library of Scotland, https://digital.nls.uk/suffragettes/sources/source-24.html.

# 5

# AV Dicey on English Imperialism

ALEX MIDDLETON

## I. Introduction

This chapter asks how AV Dicey accounted for one of the nineteenth century's most globally consequential revolutions in British political opinion: the growth of pro-imperial sentiment. Modern historiography, arguably, has yet to offer a satisfactory explanation for this late-Victorian intellectual sea change.[1] Dicey's handling of the problem importantly illuminates how he thought about political dynamics, and how he conceptualised the drivers of political change over time.[2] His writing on the subject also opens up wider questions about fin-de-siècle imperial ideas, and political theory. Dicey's analysis of the rise of imperialist conviction reminds us that the phenomenon was not just a background to new currents of imperial political thought, but one of the transformations imperial thinkers aimed to explain.[3] This in turn reveals an even larger, similarly neglected development in

[1] Seminal studies of aspects of the problem include R Price, *An Imperial War and the British Working Class: Working-Class Attitudes and Reactions to the Boer War, 1899–1902* (London, Routledge and Kegan Paul, 1972); HCG Matthew, *The Liberal Imperialists: The Ideas and Politics of a Post-Gladstonian Elite* (Oxford, Oxford University Press, 1973); J MacKenzie, *Propaganda and Empire: The Manipulation of British Public Opinion, 1880–1960* (Manchester, Manchester University Press, 1984); see also MacKenzie's many other relevant publications, including the pioneering comparative J MacKenzie (ed), *European Empires and the People: Popular Responses to Imperialism in France, Britain, The Netherlands, Belgium, Germany and Italy* (Manchester, Manchester University Press, 2011); B Porter, *The Absent-Minded Imperialists: Empire, Society and Culture in Britain* (Oxford, Oxford University Press, 2004); D Bell, *The Idea of Greater Britain: Empire and the Future of World Order, 1860–1900* (Princeton, Princeton University Press, 2007).

[2] These issues lurk in the background in MD Waters, *A. V. Dicey and the Common Law Constitutional Tradition: A Legal Turn of Mind* (Cambridge, Cambridge University Press, 2021); J Kirby, 'A.V. Dicey and English Constitutionalism' (2019) 45 *History of European Ideas* 33; IC Fletcher, '"This Zeal for Lawlessness": A.V. Dicey, The Law Of the Constitution, and the Challenge of Popular Politics, 1885–1915' (1997) 16 *Parliamentary History* 309; J Stapleton, 'Dicey and his Legacy' (1995) 16 *History of Political Thought* 234; S Collini, *Public Moralists: Political Thought and Intellectual Life in Britain, 1850–1930* (Oxford, Oxford University Press, 1993) ch 7; D Sugarman, 'The Legal Boundaries of Liberty: Dicey, Liberalism and Legal Science' (1983) 46 *Modern Law Review* 102; C Harvie, 'Ideology and Home Rule: James Bryce, A.V. Dicey and Ireland, 1880–1887' (1976) 91 *English Historical Review* 1477.

[3] For a recent dissection of the state of the historiography on British imperial political thought see D Bell, *Reordering the World: Essays on Liberalism and Empire* (Princeton, Princeton University Press, 2016) chs 1–2.

the realm of British ideas: the growing preoccupation with the structural explanation of political change in the contemporary world.[4]

Dicey returned repeatedly to the problem of 'English imperialism' after the 1880s. He discussed the subject in most of his major legal and historical tomes, and in his journalism, particularly in articles for the American periodical *The Nation*.[5] This chapter draws on all these sources.[6] It dwells in particular, however, on the analysis outlined in Dicey's *Lectures on the Relation between Law and Public Opinion in England during the Nineteenth Century* (1905/1914).[7] In a volume which was, in significant part, a statement of Dicey's growing alienation from a changing political world, pro-imperial sentiment stands out as almost the only novel current of opinion with which he enthusiastically associated himself.[8] So it is striking to find that Dicey explained its emergence as a (possible) consequence of many of the same forces which had given rise to the rebarbative philosophy of collectivism. His understanding of political dynamics was more materialist, more subtle, and more alive to paradox, than historians have tended to imagine.[9]

The chapter begins by re-reading Dicey's arguments about the drivers of change in modern British politics. It then turns to his analysis of the specific forces behind the growth of imperial sentiment. It concludes by reflecting on the implications of his schemes for our understanding of the shape of contemporary British political thought, imperial and otherwise.

[4] The main synthetic studies of nineteenth-century British political thought touch this theme at best very lightly: see eg HS Jones, *Victorian Political Thought* (Basingstoke, Palgrave Macmillan, 2000); M Francis and J Morrow, *A History of English Political Thought in the Nineteenth Century* (London, Duckworth, 1994); S Collini et al, *That Noble Science of Politics: A Study in Nineteenth-Century Intellectual History* (Cambridge, Cambridge University Press, 1984); C Brinton, *English Political Thought in the Nineteenth Century* (London, Ernest Benn, 1933). But see also the remarks in M Bevir, 'Review Article: English Political Thought in the Nineteenth Century' (1996) 17 *History of Political Thought* 114. By contrast, the scholarship on Victorian historiography has always concerned itself with historians' attempts to account for political change.

[5] For Dicey and *The Nation* see TH Ford, 'Dicey as a Political Journalist' (1970) 18 *Political Studies* 220; and, more broadly, TH Ford, *Albert Venn Dicey: the Man and His Times* (Chichester, Barry Rose, 1985).

[6] Dicey's comments on this chapter's theme in letters to the imperial scholar AB Keith simply restate positions Dicey took in print: RF Shin, Jr, and RA Cosgrove (eds), *Constitutional Reflections: the Correspondence of Albert Venn Dicey and Arthur Berriedale Keith* (Lanham, University Press of America, 1996).

[7] AV Dicey, *Lectures on the Relation between Law and Public Opinion in England during the Nineteenth Century* (London, Macmillan & Co, 1905); AV Dicey, *Lectures on the Relation between Law and Public Opinion in England during the Nineteenth Century*, 2nd edn (London, Macmillan & Co, 1914). All references below are to the second edition, which includes a new introduction but barely changes the original text.

[8] Dylan Lino has ably reconstructed Dicey's wider imperial attitudes in D Lino, 'The Rule of Law and the Rule of Empire: A.V. Dicey in Imperial Context' (2018) 85 *Modern Law Review* 739; D Lino, 'Albert Venn Dicey and the Constitutional Theory of Empire' (2016) 36 *Oxford Journal of Legal Studies* 751.

[9] Since its mid-twentieth-century heyday, the book has attracted only a modest amount of intellectual-historical attention. This is presumably because more recent research on Dicey has tended to prioritise either his role as a jurist, or his career as an opponent of Irish Home Rule, to both of which projects the volume was marginal.

## II. Dicey and Political Dynamics

*Law and Public Opinion* was based on a series of lectures first given at Harvard University in 1898, and finessed in repeat performances back in Oxford. It was the mature statement of an array of arguments Dicey had been developing in his journalism since the 1870s, about the impact of Benthamism and 'collectivist' ideas on the making of public policy, and about shifting currents of public opinion.[10] The book had a long academic afterlife, not least in underpinning classic mid-twentieth-century historical debates about the nature of the so-called 'Victorian revolution in government'.[11] Stefan Collini suggests that it did more to shape later perceptions of Britain's nineteenth-century political development than any other individual work.[12] But historians have always been more interested in testing the book's substantive claims about the influence of particular philosophical schools (or simply in setting them up as straw men) than in understanding the argumentative architecture of the work. Richard A Cosgrove concluded that *Law and Public Opinion* was 'more misleading than informative', and curiously overrated.[13] What attempts there are to capture Dicey's view of political dynamics tend to end up concluding that he was a species of idealist, and typically a rather unsubtle one. Harold Perkin, for instance, claimed that Dicey had a 'naive' view of political change, in which 'a great thinker thinks, and converts disciples, who in turn contrive to turn the master's thought into the dominant wisdom or accepted common sense of the age, which then finds its way onto the Statute Book'.[14]

Dicey's arguments were more complex than this. They were also pioneering. *Law and Public Opinion* was the first attempt by a prominent English intellectual at a sustained, full-dress study of the relations between political theory, the structure of politics, and public policy. Dicey was not, of course, the only turn-of-the-twentieth-century figure to present an ideologically-driven interpretation of recent historical change. In Britain we can point to Edwin Cannan, WEH Lecky, Leslie Stephen, and Graham Wallas, while over the Channel Élie Halévy

[10] For one of Dicey's early discussions of 'opinion' see AV Dicey, 'Louis Napoleon: 1851 and 1873' (1873) 13 *Fortnightly Review* 197. For more developed reflections on opinion and the opinion-forming classes see AV Dicey, 'A Phase of English Opinion' (1885) 41 *The Nation* 319.

[11] RA Cosgrove, *The Rule of Law: Albert Venn Dicey, Victorian Jurist* (Chapel Hill, University of North Carolina Press, 1980) 189–92. See also M Ginsberg (ed), *Law and Opinion in England in the 20th Century* (London, Stevens & Sons, 1959).

[12] Collini, *Public Moralists* 327.

[13] Cosgrove, *The Rule of Law* 183. It is striking, in this context, that the leading modern study of the concept of 'public opinion' in late-nineteenth and early-twentieth-century Britain has almost nothing to say about law and public opinion, or about Dicey more generally: J Thompson, *British Political Culture and the Idea of 'Public Opinion', 1867–1914* (Cambridge, Cambridge University Press, 2013).

[14] H Perkin, 'Individualism versus Collectivism in Nineteenth-Century Britain: a False Antithesis' (1977) 17 *Journal of British Studies* 105, 105. *cf*, however, Morris Ginsberg's observation that it was 'not clear' whether Dicey believed the connection between English law and currents of opinion was causal: Ginsberg, *Law and Opinion* vii.

was engaged on his own comparable studies of philosophic radicalism.[15] In *Law and Public Opinion* itself Dicey acknowledged debts to Stephen and Lecky, and also to the legal historian and political writer Sir Roland K Wilson.[16] He also offered (in the second edition) a warm endorsement of the scholarship of the then President of Harvard, A Lawrence Lowell, who published a weighty analysis of *Public Opinion and Popular Government* in 1913.[17] Dicey's study, however, was distinctive in several ways. It reached up to, and specifically sought to account for, the present; it was based on profound legal learning; and it possessed a breath of conceptual and political vision, and an associated disciplinary agnosticism, which separated it from other comparable contemporary works. This was, after all, a book which ranged between detailed analyses of the Combination Laws and the Married Women's Property Act, to discussions of the philanthropy of Richard Oastler and Lord Shaftesbury, to reflections on Dickens and Gradgrind. It requires its own treatment.

The stated purpose of *Law and Public Opinion* was to connect the changing shape of the law with 'the course of English thought'.[18] What did Dicey think lay behind the emergence and ascendency of new currents of opinion? And how did dominant opinions impact on the organisation of politics?

Dicey's argument about the connections between opinion, law, and politics was not a general or even a generalisable one. The foundation of *Law and Public Opinion's* thesis was the idea that nineteenth-century England was a distinctive political and social arena. England's peculiar constitutional development, the unusual organisation of its public culture, and its incomparable industrial wealth, underpinned a uniquely close connection between 'opinion' and the making of laws.[19] Unlike other countries, in nineteenth-century England changes in opinion were invariably gradual, and, vitally, the opposition between schools of thought was never violent.[20] So while the public opinion of other polities – often France, sometimes Britain's self-governing colonies – could at times be found moving in similar directions to that of England, the structural relation between opinion and law-making was not the same.[21]

Dicey glossed and qualified the concept of 'public opinion' extensively. But the essence of his definition was stable, within and beyond *Law and Public Opinion*. 'Public opinion', for Dicey, meant the dominant ideas about legislation held by

[15] Among the other scholars working at around the same time as Dicey on 'the intellectual underpinnings of the great achievements of the nineteenth century', from a series of different angles, were Edwin Cannan, Graham Wallas, Élie Halévy, and Leslie Stephen: JV Orth, 'On the Relation between the Rule of Law and Public Opinion' (1982) 80 *Michigan Law Review* 753, 759.

[16] Dicey, *Law and Public Opinion*, Roland K Wilson (ix), Leslie Stephen (x), WEH Lecky (178).

[17] ibid lxxii. Dicey described Lowell's book as containing 'the most subtle analysis of public opinion and the best account known to me of its relation to popular government' (lxxii).

[18] ibid vii.

[19] ibid 7.

[20] ibid 27, 36–37.

[21] ibid lxvii, 299–300.

citizens who took an effective part in public life.[22] This was something different from, and larger than, partisan commitment. Dicey's concept of opinion was deliberately hostile to the 'delusion' that English public feeling 'consists in the main of definite and rigid political dogmas'.[23] He argued that the most coherent, and extreme, political and social theories barely affected law.[24] This was not least because citizens often held logically inconsistent social theories together in their minds at once. Dicey at one point mooted the idea that Gladstone's powerful influence over later-Victorian England rested partly on his ability to represent the incoherent sentiments of his age.[25] In practice, the divisions of Dicey's 'opinion' mostly cut across political parties.[26]

Dicey contended that changes in this 'public opinion' were the major influence on changes in legislation. To some extent, they governed politics as well. While Dicey recognised that politics and law were not the same thing, he argued that in England, great changes in political ideas always mirrored changes in legislative opinion.[27] But if dominant currents of opinion were the major factor behind changes in the law, then where did those currents come from? Dicey's answer was not nearly as straightforward as Perkin and others suggest it was, that new ideas were simply conceived by 'great thinkers'.[28] Dicey did not think mechanically about the relation between law, politics, and opinion. He was, in fact, much more concerned with intellectual atmospheres than with individual actors, or the networks they belonged to. He explained that political arguments and philosophical speculations could rarely generate changes in public opinion by themselves. The English were more easily persuaded by ethical convictions than by elaborated ideas.[29] To shift the dial, and therefore to make an impact on law, arguments needed to be articulated within a receptive environment. But it was not the wider tenor of intellectual culture, or the complex interplay between different available views of politics and order, that played the leading role in making those environments receptive. Top billing was reserved for a different entity. This, for Dicey, was 'circumstances'.[30]

'Circumstances', or 'facts', were Dicey's shorthands for the material and external pressures that did more than anything else to shape the progress of opinion. Again and again, in Dicey's analysis, '[o]bvious facts told for more than argument'.[31] So England's 1801 Union with Ireland was not the result of theoretical

[22] ibid 10.
[23] AV Dicey, 'England in 1848' (1920) 234 *Quarterly Review* 221, 224.
[24] Dicey, *Law and Public Opinion* 18.
[25] ibid 273, 360.
[26] ibid 177.
[27] ibid 409.
[28] Though Dicey argued that the clear, programmatic character of Benthamite utilitarianism was among the reasons it gained the legislative hold it did: Dicey, *Law and Public Opinion* 443–44. See also the early passage about the power of single thinkers and schools, which Perkin may have had particularly in mind, at 21–22.
[29] AV Dicey, 'New Jacobinism and Old Morality' (1888) 53 *Contemporary Review* 475, 475.
[30] Dicey, *Law and Public Opinion* 26–27, 301–302.
[31] ibid 451.

advances, but of 'the immediate and irresistible pressure of events'.[32] The legislative flurry of the 1830s arose from the incongruity between England's changing social conditions, especially industrialisation and the growth of wealth in the North, and the country's static legal frameworks.[33] Dicey's explanation for why certain policies (like free trade) became successful often had a sociological bent, centred on the class position of their proponents.[34] The dominance of Benthamism in the middle decades of the nineteenth century, then, was a consequence not of Jeremy Bentham's genius, but of the harmonies of his eponymous philosophy with the political dominance of the middle class, and even more nebulously 'the spirit of the time'.[35] Dicey returned again and again to the determining power of 'patent facts' and 'political facts', insisting that it was often the most glaringly obvious circumstances which mattered the most, and emphasising – perhaps subtly, perhaps circularly – that no category of 'facts' was more important than pre-existing laws.[36] The examples offered by foreign countries invariably had less influence on English social and political movements than the 'logic of facts'.[37] In short, articulate theory had no inherent persuasive power, politically or legally, in the absence of authorising external circumstances.

Dicey commented midway through *Law and Public Opinion*, in one of his many attempts to crystallise his claims, that 'law and speculation, action and thought react upon one another'.[38] The line effectively captures Dicey's argumentative caution, and the indeterminacy of the relationships he wanted to capture. This formula was not precise, but *Law and Public Opinion* did not set out to be precise about the workings of political dynamics. On this front, the book was a provocative, expansive rumination on the driving forces behind political and legal change, not a comprehensive working-through of a distilled, defensible thesis. This was a necessary consequence of the breadth of political and disciplinary vision that separated Dicey from comparable contemporary scholarship. His treatment of political dynamics, then, was as much about circumstances as ideas, and was alive to contradiction and complication.

## III. Dicey and the Growth of English Imperialism

In the final chapter in *Law and Public Opinion*, Dicey invited his readers to '[c]onsider the growth of English imperialism'.[39] This section of the book did not

[32] ibid 104. See also, for Dicey's claim that the pressure of events mattered more than the intentions of the originators of a system of thought, 310.

[33] ibid 111.

[34] ibid 25. See also eg 129.

[35] ibid 170–73, 187.

[36] eg Dicey, *Law and Public Opinion* liii, 47; ibid 42–44, 465.

[37] Dicey, *Law and Public Opinion* lxv. See also AV Dicey, *England's Case against Home Rule* (London, John Murray, 1886) 55–56.

[38] Dicey, *Law and Public Opinion* 255.

[39] ibid 450.

make much impact on contemporary reviewers, nor has it much appealed to later historians of Dicey's politics and thought. In some ways it was a curious subject for him to address in *Law and Public Opinion*, given the volume's primary focus on 'law-making' or 'legislative' opinion.[40] Greater public sympathy towards the British Empire had not – or at least had not in 1905 – had detectable consequences in the realm of domestic law-making. Dicey did take the view that changes in political opinion usually corresponded with alterations in legislative opinion.[41] But it is more relevant to note that the chapter in which the discussion appears – Lecture XII, on the 'Relation between Legislative Opinion and General Public Opinion' – is the most loosely conceived in the book. Here Dicey considers how 'law-making ideas' are reflected in other realms of thought, looking at theological opinion, at attitudes towards peace and economy, at the changing views of individuals including Harriet Martineau, Charles Dickens, and John Stuart Mill, at freedom of discussion, and at the historical method, as well as discussing imperialism.[42] So the attempt to explain the rise of imperial sentiment was not a foundational part of the argument of *Law and Public Opinion*. It was a way to flesh out broader contexts.

The state of public imperial sentiment was a long-standing theme in British imperial political thought. Complaints that public understanding of, and interest in, the empire was defective long pre-dated JR Seeley's diagnosis of a 'fit of absence of mind'.[43] The consequences of this supposed inattention for the soundness of imperial governance, especially in India, were widely discussed among commentators and thinkers from the late eighteenth century on. By the end of the nineteenth century, however, the problem was rather to explain what had driven an apparent surge in imperial patriotism. For most observers, a principal question was how to connect this phenomenon with mass democracy, and the rapidly rising political significance of the working-class electorate. Some proponents of 'Greater Britain'-style visions of imperial unity did their best to claim this new constituency for themselves, imbuing the working classes with a wise and well-founded imperial sympathy, while others argued that the working man needed to be won over to achieve closer imperial unity.[44] Imperial sceptics, like the English positivist Edward Beesly, tended to assert that the new working class voter was indifferent to the empire.[45] A few years before the publication of *Law and Public Opinion*, JA Hobson's classic 1902 *Imperialism: a Study* outlined a catalogue of the forces he perceived to lie behind the rise of imperial patriotism in England, including

[40] ibid 17.

[41] ibid 411.

[42] Parts of the chapter saw Dicey rework material already published elsewhere: *cf* eg AV Dicey, 'The Weak Side of the Historical Method' (1877) 24 *The Nation* 217.

[43] JR Seeley, *The Expansion of England: Two Courses of Lectures* (London, Macmillan and Co) 8, and see eg 177–78.

[44] eg WJ Courthope, 'Problems of Greater Britain' (1890) 15 *National Review* 433; JA Froude, *Oceana: or England and her Colonies* (London, Longmans, Green, and Co, 1886) 337. For a stimulating analysis of Froude's thought on this and other issues see D Bell, 'Republican Imperialism: JA Froude and the Virtue of Empire' (2009) 30 *History of Political Thought* 166.

[45] ES Beesly, 'The Causes of Modern Militarism' (1893) 1 *The Positivist Review* 33, 37–41.

patterns of teaching at schools and universities, newspapers, pulpits, imaginative and travel literature, politicians, and not least, selfish financial interests.[46] So Dicey was contributing to a debate, not identifying a new problem. He sought, moreover, to provide a deliberately partial anatomy of the problem of English imperialism, which he approached neither on its own terms nor with any great polemical purpose, to support wider conclusions.

To the Edwardian reader, the meaning of the phrase 'English imperialism' was not self-evident, having been put to a series of different purposes in recent decades.[47] Dicey made several attempts to pin it down. In 1901 he wrote simply that imperialism (a word he usually capitalised) meant the belief that one of the principal goals of the British government was 'to maintain the power and the authority and the greatness of England'.[48] In 1905, he clarified that the term 'Imperialism', having entered British political language in the 1860s as a shorthand for Napoleonic Caesarism, now meant more precisely 'the wish to maintain the unity and increase the strength of an empire which contains within its limits various more or less independent States'.[49] In the 1915 edition of the *Introduction to the Study of the Law of the Constitution* Dicey specified further that this wish should depend on 'definite and assignable reasons', mainly the conviction that the continued existence of a strong British Empire (usually) secured international peace.[50] In some settings Dicey defined 'imperialism' more narrowly, suggesting that the term signalled a belief that a robust alliance between Britain and its self-governing settler dominions was beneficial to both England and the rest of the world.[51] Dicey associated himself with all these contemporary descriptions of the imperialist agenda. Some other contemporary visions of the term were less sympathetic. He insisted that a healthy Imperialism did not have to dictate support for any kind of formalised imperial federation. This was a project Dicey thought politically, legally, and logically impossible, for reasons which he explained repeatedly, and at length, in his publications.[52] Nor, he insisted, did imperialism have to mean support for preferential tariffs.[53] But Dicey acknowledged that the emergence of

[46] JA Hobson, *Imperialism: A Study* (London, James Nisbet & Co, 1902) pt II, ch 3, esp 228–34.

[47] For the wider concept history of 'imperialism' see R Koebner and HD Schmidt, *Imperialism: the Story and Significance of a Political Word, 1840–1960* (Cambridge, Cambridge University Press, 1964).

[48] An Observer [AV Dicey], 'The Causes of Imperialism in England' (1901) 73 *The Nation* 203, 203. Sometimes Dicey included in his definition the desire to 'increase' the power of the empire: eg An Observer [AV Dicey], 'The Parliamentary Election in England: an English View' (1900) 71 *The Nation* 362, 363.

[49] Dicey, *Law and Public Opinion* 450. In this sense, for Dicey, the term was as applicable to the United States as to England.

[50] AV Dicey, *Introduction to the Study of the Law of the Constitution*, 8th edn (London, Macmillan and Co, 1915) xxxiv–xxxv.

[51] AV Dicey, *A Fool's Paradise: Being A Constitutionalist's Criticism of the Home Rule Bill of 1912* (London, John Murray, 1913) xxxi. For Dicey this alliance would rest on pooling contributions to defence, and on fuller consultation between Britain and its colonies: 25. For the wider intellectual context see Bell, *Greater Britain*.

[52] AV Dicey, *Letters on Unionist Delusions* (London, Macmillan and Co, 1887) 51–58; Dicey, *Law of the Constitution* lxxiv–lxxxxiii.

[53] AV Dicey, 'To Unionists and Imperialists' (1903) 84 *Contemporary Review* 305 esp 311–15.

these less persuasive strands of Imperialist thought belonged to the same wider process of intellectual metamorphosis.

The starting point of this new current of sentiment was not altogether clear in Dicey's mind. He thought its emergence was a historical novelty, rather than a high point in an established cycle, representing 'a new-born sense among Englishmen of their membership in a great imperial state'.[54] He positioned its origin variously in 1850, the 1870s, 1884, 1886, and at one point, in the context of his late-in-life study of the Anglo-Scottish Union, in the mid-eighteenth century.[55] In general, however, Dicey tended to see Imperialist sentiment as taking hold in the 1880s and 1890s. This is certainly when he became aware of its growth. In 1886 Dicey reflected that statesmen were still uncertain whether England's democracy really valued imperial greatness.[56] But by 1901, he was entirely persuaded that imperialism was 'the dominant faith of modern Englishmen', cutting across the age's formal political parties.[57] Unlike many of his fellow proponents of closer imperial unity, Dicey did not seek to press beyond 'modern Englishmen' to divisions of class, and the pressing question of why working class voters seemed to have taken to empire. Broad brushstrokes served Dicey's purposes.

The diffusion of English imperialism rested mainly on a growing sense of unity with the dominions, but Dicey also perceived analogous spikes of interest in parts of the dependent empire. Egypt arrested public attention in the early 1880s, and made him worry about the inconsistency of educated liberal thinking about Britain's proper policy towards the state.[58] This was fleeting, but Dicey detected the emergence of a more robust public interest in India after the Mutiny of 1857. This was driven, he thought, largely by the abolition of the East India Company and the new career opportunities Crown rule offered to the literary classes, by Britain's declining role in Continental politics, and by the (seeming) resolution of the great domestic political questions.[59] Dicey also noted that more general reflection on the facts of Indian civilisation might unsettle the organising ideas around which English law revolved.[60]

[54] Dicey, *Law and Public Opinion* 411. See also Dicey's claim in 1915 that World War I was Britain's 'first great imperial war': AV Dicey, *How We Ought to Feel about the War* (London, Oxford University Press, 1915) 15–16.

[55] For 1850 and 1886 see Dicey, *Fool's Paradise* xxxii; for the 1870s see Dicey, *Law and Public Opinion* 454–55; for 1884 see Dicey, *Law of the Constitution* xxxiii; for the eighteenth century see AV Dicey, *Thoughts on the Union between England & Scotland* (London, Macmillan & Co, 1920) 302–303.

[56] AV Dicey, 'The Permanent Difficulties of English Foreign Policy' (1886) 42 *The Nation* 95, 95.

[57] Dicey, 'Causes of Imperialism' 203. See also Dicey, 'Parliamentary Election' 362.

[58] AV Dicey, 'English Popular Opinion about Egypt' (1882) 35 *The Nation* 418. Dicey's brother wrote extensively about Egypt, and there are overlaps in the two men's thinking about the country. *cf* E Dicey, *England and Egypt* (London, Chapman & Hall, 1881); E Dicey, *The Story of the Khedivate* (London, Rivingtons, 1902); E Dicey, *The Egypt of the Future* (London, William Heinemann, 1907).

[59] [AV Dicey], 'The Influence of India on English Opinion' (1876) 22 *The Nation* 82, 82–83. See also [AV Dicey], 'Thirty Years of European History – I' (1890) 51 *The Nation* 327, 327.

[60] [Dicey], 'Influence of India' 83. See also [AV Dicey], 'Wheeler's Short History of India' (1880) 31 *The Nation* 240; AV Dicey, 'Imperial Rule in India – I' (1899) 83 *The Spectator* 280; AV Dicey, 'Imperial Rule in India – II' (1899) 83 *The Spectator* 312.

But the question is how Dicey accounted for the rise, and triumph, of Imperialist sentiment. The identification of comparative contexts was not the answer.[61] The premise of Dicey's studies of public opinion was that England was a distinctive arena, and moreover Dicey shared the assumption of most of his contemporaries that the British Empire was a political entity of a quite different kind from other empires.[62] Nonetheless, a significant part of Dicey's explanation lay in his preferred bedrock of grand-scale external circumstances and facts. For Dicey 'sane imperialism' was rightly premised on 'the recognition of patent facts'.[63] Here those facts were made to appear even more ineluctable than usual, presumably because Dicey wanted to persuade his audience of the wisdom of the creed. He argued that imperial unity was 'fully defensible on the grounds of good sense and of justice', not least because it harmonised so well with the Unionist cause in relation to Ireland.[64] Imperialism was, Dicey claimed, 'the result of causes so potent and real that it is vain to hope that nations can escape from their influence'.[65] These included the great technological changes of the age – trains, steamships, telegraphs – which had brought the world closer together.[66] More specific to the 1880s and 1890s was the rise of great military states and the growth of great empires, alongside the decline of petty polities. These developments made imperial unity a rational way to defend against foreign aggression, and stimulated the desire for transoceanic imperial expansion.[67]

These facts were reflected, as Dicey claimed all such patent facts of higher significance were, in the writings of contemporary thinkers. In this connection, he liked to cite JR Seeley, JA Froude, and – perhaps less predictably for modern students of imperial political thought – the American Alfred Thayer Mahan, the reviver of Admiral Nelson's reputation, who Dicey strikingly placed first among the group.[68] Dicey claimed that Mahan's writings on Nelson, 'from their great power and from their singular opportuneness', had exerted an influence on English politics as great as that of any leading statesman.[69] But what allowed the ideas of these thinkers to

[61] *cf* AV Dicey, *Comparative Constitutionalism*, JWF Allison (ed) (Oxford, Oxford University Press, 2019).

[62] Dicey, *Law of the Constitution* lxxxi, 346; An Observer [AV Dicey], 'Possible Effects on England of Japan's Triumph' (1905) 81 *The Nation* 315. For some intellectual contexts for the latter article see C Tonooka, 'Reverse Emulation and the Cult of Japanese Efficiency in Edwardian Britain' (2017) 60 *Historical Journal* 95. For an example of Dicey distinguishing between different foreign imperialisms, in this case French and German, see RS Rait, *Memorials of Albert Venn Dicey: Being Chiefly Letters and Diaries* (London, Macmillan and Co, 1925 [1882]) 81.

[63] Dicey, *Fool's Paradise* 30.

[64] Dicey, *Law and Public Opinion* 455; Dicey, *Fool's Paradise* xxxii.

[65] An Observer [AV Dicey], 'The Constitutional Aspects of Mr Chamberlain's Journey' (1902) 75 *The Nation* 477, 478.

[66] Dicey, *Law and Public Opinion* lxv; Dicey, 'Causes of Imperialism' 203. See D Bell, 'Dissolving Distance: Technology, Space, and Empire in British Political Thought, 1770–1900' (2005) 77 *Journal of Modern History* 523.

[67] Dicey, *Law and Public Opinion* 456; Dicey, 'Causes of Imperialism' 203. Dicey also suggested that the shift rested, to some degree, on 'the lessons of history', though Dicey did not develop this point, presumably in part thanks to his scepticism about the historical method: *Law and Public Opinion* 457; and see [Dicey], 'Weak Side of the Historical Method'.

[68] Dicey, 'Causes of Imperialism' 203.

[69] ibid 203.

cut through, Dicey continued, was a particular condition of public sentiment. The decline of fervent democratic ideologies, of utilitarianism, and of nationalism, had created room for new faiths. From this angle Dicey could suggest that 'English Imperialism is, looked at from its good side, a new form of the undying belief in progress'.[70] Admiration for national and imperial bigness, he claimed, also had 'some real connection with what is vulgar in democratic institutions'.[71]

These were the broad strokes of Dicey's explanation for the growth of English imperialism. But his treatment of the theme served two wider argumentative purposes. The first was to buttress his case about how and why individualistic Benthamism had been superseded by collectivist ideas and policies. Dicey proclaimed in an article for *The Nation* in 1900 that the growth of imperialism was 'simply one aspect of the renewed faith in the benefits to be conferred upon the world by the intervention of the state'.[72] He did not explain what he meant, but it is possible to make sense of the point through the lens of Dicey's later works. *Law and Public Opinion* claimed that among all the realms of public life, it was in the field of colonial policy that Utilitarian principles had achieved their most complete hegemony. As *laissez-faire* became 'the order of the day' towards the middle of the nineteenth century, there was no sphere of action in which 'the trouble saved by leaving things alone' was 'more obvious than in England's government of colonies'.[73] George Cornewall Lewis's Austinian *Essay on the Government of Dependencies* of 1841 represented 'the application to our colonial policy … of the tenets propounded by Bentham', arguing that the colonies should be where possible left alone, with the ultimate end being a friendly separation.[74] For Dicey, the (supposedly) separatist views of Cobden and the Manchester School represented the dominant current of mid-Victorian opinion.[75]

But the period since, he said, had seen a thorough change in 'the whole spirit of our colonial policy'.[76] In the 1915 edition of *Law of the Constitution* Dicey insisted that imperialism was 'the natural result of historical circumstances', and more precisely the 'admirable fruit' of the Benthamite policy of *laissez-faire*.[77] Leaving the self-governing colonies to their own devices had drawn the sting from their

[70] ibid 204. For Dicey on the decline of nationalism see also AV Dicey, 'Garibaldi and the Movement of 1848' (1882) 34 *The Nation* 540. For the comparable arguments of Dicey's brother on the trajectories of nationalism see P Towle, 'Edward Dicey, Mass Politics, and International Affairs' (2014) 25 *Diplomacy & Statecraft* 61.

[71] Dicey, 'Causes of Imperialism' 204. Dicey was not certain, however, whether democracy in Britain would ultimately prove compatible with the maintenance of imperial power: AV Dicey, *Letters to a Friend on Votes for Women* (London, John Murray, 1909) 90–91. It might be suggested, further, that since Dicey was aware of the virtues of vagueness in creeds that managed to move large numbers of citizens, the nebulousness of imperial sentiment may have aided its rise: AV Dicey, 'July 14, 1789 – July 14, 1880' (1880) 31 *The Nation* 109, 109.

[72] Dicey, 'Parliamentary Election' 363.

[73] Dicey, *Law and Public Opinion* 451. *cf* JA Froude's more politically-minded analysis of this phenomenon: Froude, *Oceana* 330–36.

[74] Dicey, *Law and Public Opinion* 451–52.

[75] ibid 452–54.

[76] ibid 454–55.

[77] Dicey, *Law of the Constitution* xxxvi.

earlier, understandable discontent, and laid the foundations for the growth of pan-imperial cordiality. So this was a latter-day triumph for Bentham, and Dicey therefore rejected the Prime Minister HH Asquith's idea, outlined at the Imperial Conference of 1911 held to celebrate George V's coronation, that the British Empire had somehow been saved from a meagre mid-nineteenth-century choice between centralisation and disintegration by the inherent political instincts of the race.[78] *Law and Public Opinion* further clarified that the rise of pro-imperial sentiment, and the decline of Cobdenite *laissez-faire* in British colonial policy, had run alongside declining faith in peace and economy as desirable goals.[79] Benthamite liberalism, Dicey went on to claim, could not 'naturally blend' with the sentiments of imperialism and nationalism, because its 'real affinity' was with philanthropy and cosmopolitanism.[80] So it is possible to see why he might have deemed imperialism an ally to collectivism in 1900. But he does not seem to have been sure. Usually wary of making political predictions, Dicey nonetheless suggested in the 1914 edition of *Law and Public Opinion* that novel combinations of patriotism and imperialism might reinforce impatience about excessive taxation, and create new cross-currents of anti-socialist opinion.[81]

The second thesis for which Dicey's discussion of English imperialism was a case-in-point was about the penetration of a politics of feeling into the public culture of the nineteenth century. The later lectures in *Law and Public Opinion* return repeatedly to the nineteenth century's intellectual and moral reaction against the rationalism of the eighteenth.[82] Dicey found this to be the motivating force behind the activities of the High Churchmen of the 1830s, and John Stuart Mill's early manhood, among other things.[83] Dicey posited that a new prioritisation of emotion, which in his words 'has been called the apotheosis of instinct', had ultimately proven to be one of the principal solvents of the Benthamite hegemony.[84] A new conviction that humans could not be studied only as rational actors undermined the basic premises of the Benthamites. Since the middle decades of the nineteenth century, appeals to instinct had taken on new importance in British public life.[85] This was what imperialism illustrated. Dicey argued that resistance to Boer separatism at the turn of the twentieth century was motivated not by the application of a dry utilitarian calculus, but instead by emotional intangibles. It was owed to 'a sense of the greatness, to the memory of the achievements,

[78] tbid xxxiii.
[79] Dicey, *Law and Public Opinion* 411.
[80] ibid 464.
[81] ibid lxxxvii. For his more conventional unwillingness to speculate on the future of imperial sentiment, see eg Dicey, *Law of the Constitution* xxxvi. Dicey argued elsewhere that it was the fear of socialism and its threats to property which had pushed the landowners of France into the arms of the Imperialism of the Second Empire: AV Dicey, *A Leap in the Dark: or Our New Constitution* (London, John Murray, 1893) 150.
[82] For wider context see J Bennett, 'A History of "Rationalism" in Victorian Britain' (2018) 15 *Modern Intellectual History* 63.
[83] Dicey, *Law and Public Opinion* 332, 423.
[84] ibid 433, 448.
[85] ibid 449.

and to faith in the future, of the British Empire'.[86] This pattern of sentiment was fostered by ritual and by literature, including the annual crowning of Nelson on his column, and the writings of Rudyard Kipling, alongside those of Dicey's other favourite imperial authors already cited.[87] Utilitarians could not compute these feelings. Imperialism, Dicey explained, was 'to all who share it a form of passionate feeling; it is a political religion, for it is public spirit touched with emotion'.[88] As he put it elsewhere, '[l]oyalty to the Empire, typified by loyalty to the King, is in short a sentiment developed by the whole course of recent history'.[89]

Dicey's explanation for the rise of imperial sentiment in late-nineteenth-century Britain, then, does not include several of the central dynamics posited by his contemporaries, including ones which have appealed to modern historians. Dicey was not interested in the idea that imperialism was a natural consequence of, or a means of disciplining, a burgeoning British democracy. Indeed, he was at pains to dismiss democratisation as an autonomous driver of legislative or political change in any particular direction.[90] The possibility that individuals might have mattered in fostering imperial enthusiasm, and in particular that Benjamin Disraeli was 'the forerunner of imperialism', was for Dicey 'not quite without reason', but was clearly not very persuasive.[91] Dicey's preferred arguments about the rise of imperial sentiment were, plainly, partial and convenient. The notion, for instance, that the transition to responsible government in the settler colonies was a straightforward application of *laissez-faire* – rather than being driven by a combination of colonial discontent, administrative practicalities, arguments about rights, and a particular phase of political liberalism – was designed to serve a specific argumentative purpose.[92] Precisely because this was the case, however, Dicey's claims neatly demonstrate the need for historians of imperial thought to reflect further on how ideas about shifts in currents of imperial public opinion intersected with broader debates about late-nineteenth and early-twentieth century politics and society.

## IV. Conclusion

Historians have been debating how political ideas and theories shaped the course of nineteenth-century British politics since the 1970s.[93] But they have rarely asked how contemporaries tried to conceptualise the relations between intellectual and

[86] ibid 456.
[87] ibid 456.
[88] ibid 457.
[89] Dicey, *Law of the Constitution* xxxv.
[90] Dicey, *Law and Public Opinion* Lecture III.
[91] ibid 452. See also Dicey, 'Permanent Difficulties' 95.
[92] *cf* eg J Parry, 'The Third Earl Grey, Liberalism, and the British Empire' (2024) *Modern Intellectual History* (First View) 1.
[93] For commentary on some of the relevant historiography see D Craig, '"High Politics" and the "New Political History"' (2010) 53 *Historical Journal* 453; A Middleton, '"High Politics" and its Intellectual Contexts' (2021) 40 *Parliamentary History* 168; A Middleton, 'Ideas in Politics in International Context' (2023) 94 *Political Quarterly* 290.

political change.[94] So it is no surprise that historians of imperial political thought have concentrated on the ways in which sophisticated writers on empire attempted to persuade their audiences into (or out of) imperial enthusiasm, or to frame new schemes of policy, at the expense of asking how they explained changes in public imperial attitudes. Understanding how contemporaries thought about the links between politics, theory, and opinion, and why political writers came to treat the relations between these things as an increasingly important problem in the late nineteenth century, must be an important step towards making sense of questions of political causation. At the least, without exploring how political writers characterised the mechanisms of political change, it is difficult to grasp what they imagined their writing could achieve.

Dicey was among the earliest and most thoughtful British scholarly commentators on the structural relations between politics and ideas. Looking at *Law and Public Opinion* within this framework helps us to grasp what he meant the book to do. Its purpose was not (just) to index phases of public opinion, but to investigate the dynamics driving political and legal change in contemporary Britain. Dicey's vision was much less about the independent power of 'great' thinkers and ideas to drive shifts in law and opinion, than it was about the peculiarities of nineteenth-century England, and the material circumstances and 'facts' which lent particular patterns of thought conviction in the country's very specific political, social, and global contexts. The 'growth of English imperialism' was an important case in point. It could not be understood in isolation from technological developments, and large-scale realignments in international power politics. But it also had something slightly indeterminate to do with local realignments between Benthamite and collectivist ideas, and something more definite to do with the new role of emotion in the politics of the later nineteenth century. The Dicey on display in this realm of *Law and Public Opinion*, then, was not a programmatic thinker. He did not have an inflexible idealist scheme to apply, but was instead a cautious, uncertain, and strikingly materially-minded analyst of political and intellectual change.

In outlining these interlinked analyses, Dicey captured and in some ways heralded a significant new development in British political thought around the turn of the twentieth century. This was the drive to find explanations for recent political change – of which new currents of Imperialist thought and practice were conspicuous elements – in ways that went beyond the 'historical method' and semi-abstract philosophy to the sustained, structural analysis of contemporary political and intellectual processes. Anticipated in many particulars by earlier, less celebrated commentators, Dicey's work helped to inject the theme into the 'high' intellectual culture of his maturity.[95] The contexts and consequences need much more work, but it is clear that Dicey was in this respect – as in so many others – a pivotal figure.

[94] There are important gestures in this direction in C Barrell, *History and Historiography in Classical Utilitarianism, 1800–1865* (Cambridge, Cambridge University Press, 2021).

[95] See eg A Middleton, 'William Rathbone Greg, Scientific Liberalism, and the Second Empire' (2022) 19 *Modern Intellectual History* 681.

# PART II

# Dicey Put to the Test

# 6

# What is Left of Dicey's Constitution?

VERNON BOGDANOR

## I

There is a paradox about Dicey. It is commonly believed that the French, by contrast with the British, have a penchant for abstraction and seek to reduce the phenomena of politics to rules and systems. Life without rules, the French may think, adapting Hobbes, is poor, nasty, British and short! Now Dicey, although, as is well known, he misunderstood the French administrative system, nevertheless had a very French penchant in the sense that he produced a conceptual scheme with which to analyse the British Constitution. He was not a mere empiricist as for example Bagehot was, nor merely a black letter lawyer and that is why he has survived the attacks of his critics – critics as varied as Ivor Jennings, Geoffrey Marshall and Nevil Johnson, thinkers more in accord with what is seen as the British, or perhaps English, tradition of concrete and practical analysis. He produced a scheme which we still argue about. While hardly anyone today would accept Dicey's doctrines in their unvarnished form, no major thinker on the British Constitution has been able to escape his influence; and even his most severe critics are compelled to admit that the lucidity and precision of his analysis have made a massive contribution to our understanding and have yielded insights of permanent value. There cannot be many academic subjects where the modern debate is based on concepts developed by someone who died a hundred years ago, and whose main work was first published nearly 140 years ago. But that is the case with the British Constitution whose principles Dicey sought to codify.

Dicey's Constitution, though uncodified, has, so it seems to me, a philosophical basis. That basis lay in the idea he derived from Hobbes, and somehow instinctive in British thinking, that sovereignty cannot be divided. This idea, some might say, explains the discomfort which the British have always felt when confronted with supranational European institutions. If you drive a nation to adopt procedures which run counter to its instincts, Foreign Secretary Anthony Eden told an American audience at Columbia University in 1952, 'you weaken and may destroy the motive force of its action … You will realise that I am speaking of the frequent suggestions that the United Kingdom should join a federation on the continent of Europe. This is something which we know, in our bones, we

cannot do.' Membership of a European federation, Eden believed, would violate 'the unalterable marrow' of the British nation.[1] British resistance to joining a European federation was not something that could be overcome by argument, by an assessment of costs and benefits; it was an instinctive hostility, something which we knew 'in our bones', we could never do.

But of course France too, so it seems to me, has, since the revolution, viewed sovereignty as something that could not be divided – the sovereignty not of Parliament but of the people – at least until July 1971 when a momentous decision of the Conseil Constitutionnel gave France judicial review of legislation so that the sovereignty of the people would in future be limited by the Constitution.[2] Nevertheless, there is a puzzle as to how France, with her view of undivided sovereignty, found herself at ease with the European Community and the European Union while Britain did not.

If we are to answer the question – what is left of Dicey's Constitution – we must first be clear what that Constitution actually was. As is well known, Dicey argued, in his great work, *Introduction to the Study of the Law of the Constitution*, first published in 1885, that there were three fundamental principles of the British Constitution. The first, and perhaps the most important, was the sovereignty of Parliament, the notion that Parliament had 'the right to make or unmake any law whatever'; and that 'no person or body is recognised by the law … as having a right to override or set aside the legislation of Parliament'. This meant that there could be no entrenched constitutional guarantees to protect civil rights and liberties such as exist in many countries with codified constitutions, and no judicial review of primary legislation. The British Constitution could be summarised in just eight words – whatever the King-in-Parliament enacts is law.

This doctrine – that Parliament can enact any law that it likes except a law to limit its powers – is sometimes misunderstood to mean that Parliament can **justifiably** enact any statute that it likes. That of course was not Dicey's view. He is in no way committed to approving an Act of Parliament which provides that all red-headed men should be executed next Monday. Indeed, he believed that the pre-1914 Liberal government, in seeking to coerce Ulster to join a Home Rule Parliament in Dublin, went beyond its constitutionally legitimate powers. He wrote to *The Times* on 9 March 1914:

> Under a democratic Government there may be no legal limits to the power of a majority among the electors, but every Englishman recognises the fact that there are moral limits to the sovereignty of a majority no less than to the sovereignty of a monarch.

And he had justified the rebellion of the Ulster Unionists in a letter to *The Times* of 27 January 1912 by saying that he was 'too sound a Whig' to deny the right of 'rebellion against a sovereign Parliament', thinking no doubt of the 1640s and 1689.

[1] A Eden, *The Memoirs of Anthony Eden: Full Circle, Facing the Dictators, The Reckoning* (London, Cassell 1960) 36–37.

[2] Décision n 71-44 DC, 16 July 1971, 'loi complétant les dispositions des articles 5 et 7 de la loi du 1er juillet 1901 relative au contrat d'association' (French Conseil constitutionnel).

A statute or action might, then, be lawful without being constitutional. It would, after all, be lawful for the King to refuse assent to government legislation, but it would not be constitutional. Similarly, in Dicey's view, Home Rule legislation was perfectly lawful, but it would not be constitutional. When he declared that the third Government of Ireland Bill of 1912 lacked constitutional authority, he did not mean that it was unlawful. He meant that it lacked moral authority, partly because it did not enjoy popular approval, and partly because, in his view, it would serve to exclude from the kingdom, against their wishes, the Unionists of Ireland, primarily though not exclusively concentrated in the northern counties.

We must distinguish, as not all Dicey's critics have done, between:

1. The legal doctrine that Parliament is sovereign.
2. The political doctrine that the unity of the United Kingdom is best preserved by maintaining the unitary state, federation being unsuited to British conditions.
3. The political doctrine that there is no stable *via media* such as 'Home Rule' or 'devolution' lying between the unitary state and federalism.
4. The moral doctrine that there are certain things which a sovereign Parliament ought not to do and which would therefore be unconstitutional.

Dicey held all of these doctrines. The *Law of the Constitution*, however, is primarily a work of constitutional law devoted to proving the truth of three legal doctrines, the first of which is that Parliament is sovereign. The polemical works on Irish Home Rule are not works of law but are devoted to proving the truth of the second, third and fourth doctrines.

The doctrine of the sovereignty of Parliament, though seemingly straightforward, is far odder than it appears at first sight.

It is, on the face of it, somewhat odd to exemplify the doctrine of the sovereignty of Parliament in terms of something that it **cannot** do, ie bind itself. But if the inability to bind itself is an exception to the doctrine, why should it be the only exception? Why should there not be other exceptions? The alternative is to suggest that a sovereign Parliament can bind itself – the doctrine which HLA Hart labelled 'self-embracing' sovereignty. But, of course, once Parliament has bound itself, it is then no longer sovereign.

Then there is the problem of determining the meaning of the word 'cannot' in the proposition that Parliament 'cannot' pass a law to limit its powers. In 1972, during the parliamentary proceedings on the European Communities Bill, both Lord Hailsham, the Lord Chancellor, and Sir Geoffrey Howe, the Solicitor-General, declared that it was logically impossible for Parliament to limit its powers. Lord Hailsham declared that it was 'abundantly obvious' 'not merely that this bill does nothing to qualify the sovereignty of Parliament but that it could not do so'. Sir Geoffrey Howe declared that 'the ultimate supremacy of Parliament will not be affected, and it will not be affected because it cannot be affected'.[3]

[3] *Hansard*, HL Deb vol 334, col 911, 7 August 1972; *Hansard*, HC Deb vol 840, col 556, 5 July 1972.

It is not clear to me why it is logically impossible for Parliament to pass a statute to limit its powers, nor even why Parliament might find it difficult to do so. Certainly, Dicey did not believe that Parliament was, as a matter either of logic or circumstance, prevented from passing a statute to limit its powers. He says instead, 'the historical reason why Parliament has never succeeded in passing immutable laws … lies deep in the history of the English people and in the peculiar development of the English constitution'. It is in other words merely contingent that Parliament has never passed a statute binding itself. It would, on this view, be perfectly possible for Parliament to bind itself, but, in Dicey's view, there are very good reasons why, as a matter of fact, it has never done so. The 'cannot' is a matter not of logic but of history.

Dicey's second principle was the rule of law. He defined this principle in a rather restricted way. For him, it entailed the supremacy of the ordinary law, the absence of arbitrary or wide discretionary power on the part of the executive, and equality before the law so that all, including government officials, were equally subject to the law of the land adjudicated in the ordinary courts. But rights were to be protected, not by a constitution nor by constitutional courts, but by the ordinary courts and the common law.

For Dicey, there could be no conflict between the two principles of the sovereignty of Parliament and the rule of law, since, on his definition of the rule of law, it did not constrain parliamentary sovereignty. The Human Rights Act 1998 sought to preserve the Diceyan Constitution by ensuring that the two principles do not come into conflict. It did not give judges the power to disapply legislation contravening human rights. Judges were instead under a duty, should they believe that a particular statute or part of a statute could not be construed in accordance with the Human Rights Act, to issue a declaration of incompatibility. Such a declaration has no legal effect. It is merely a statement, and it is up to Parliament, if it so wishes, to amend or repeal the offending statute or part of a statute.

Suppose, however, that Parliament does not wish to amend or repeal the offending statute. Then there would be a conflict between the sovereignty of Parliament and the rule of law, not in terms of Dicey's definition, but in the terms prescribed by the Human Rights Act. When I asked a very senior judge what would happen if there were to be such a conflict, he replied with a smile 'That is a question that ought not to be asked'. The Human Rights Act is a typically British compromise which has, so far at least, worked. Nevertheless, if we regard the rule of law as entailing that there are basic human rights which all governments should acknowledge, then of course it is clear that parliamentary sovereignty and the rule of law are conflicting principles, and that an adherent of parliamentary sovereignty finds it difficult to accommodate the notion of rights against the state, where the enactment of primary legislation conflicts with basic human rights.

The third principle put forward by Dicey was the role of conventions of the Constitution. Conventions were rules regulating the 'conduct of the several members of the sovereign power' which were not enforced by the courts but were parts of constitutional morality. An obvious example is the convention that the

King gives his assent to all government legislation. Conventions, Dicey believed, were designed to uphold the system of representative government; and, if an important convention is breached, the government might take action to put the convention into statute law. That of course was what happened after 1909 when the House of Lords, in rejecting Lloyd George's 'People's Budget', broke the convention that it should not reject financial legislation. The Liberal government responded with the Parliament Act of 1911, putting this convention into statutory form.

Of the three principles, it is the doctrine of the sovereignty of Parliament which has proved most contentious. This doctrine faced a challenge when Britain joined the European Community, precursor of the European Union, in 1973. For the European Community claimed to be a legal order superior to that of Westminster. But how could Britain commit herself to such a legal order if Parliament were sovereign? Was there in 1972, when the European Communities Act was passed, a structural change to the British Constitution? Did Parliament abrogate its sovereignty? Lawyers by skilful drafting tried to show that Community membership could be made perfectly compatible with the sovereignty of Parliament. There was, of course, never any doubt that Parliament could repeal the European Communities Act if it wished – and it duly did so, in the European Union (Withdrawal) Act 2018, following the 2016 Brexit referendum. Indeed, the slogan of those who favoured Brexit in the referendum was 'Take back control', by which they meant restore the sovereignty of Parliament. But had that sovereignty actually been lost while Britain had been in the European Community? For as long as Britain remained in the European Community/European Union, Parliament was in fact restricted by the treaties in what it could do. To take one obvious example, Parliament was unable legally to restrict immigration from the European Union, even though that was probably the wish of the government and of a majority of MPs. At the very least, parliamentary sovereignty had come to mean something different from what it had meant before. It had become, to use Hart's terminology, self-embracing rather than continuous. The rule of recognition was to become, not, as it had been before 1972, that Parliament could enact any law whatever, but, at the very least, that Parliament could enact any law whatever, expect for a law implicitly repealing a European Community law. It remains unclear whether Parliament could, while Britain was in the European Community/European Union, *explicitly* repeal Community law. That question was never tested in the courts. However, as Hart pointed out, once sovereignty had become self-embracing, Parliament was no longer sovereign. It would have exercised its sovereignty to limit its sovereignty.

As is well known, in the second *Factortame* case in 1991,[4] it was established that Community law was the supreme law of the land, and that it could not be implicitly repealed. For the first time, the validity of an Act of Parliament was challenged in the courts, despite Dicey's assurance that 'no person or body is

[4] *R v Secretary of State for Transport, ex p Factortame (No 2)* [1991] 1 AC 603, [1991] 1 All ER 70.

recognised by the law of England as having a right to override or set aside the legislation of Parliament'.[5] In the High Court, Mr Justice Neill spoke of a new

> state of affairs which came into being when the United Kingdom became a Member State of the European Community in January 1973. … the High Court now has a duty … where there is a conflict, to prefer the Community law to national law.

Mr Justice Neill also accepted that Parliament had bound itself in the 1972 Act. The effects of that Act were, 'as I understand it, that directly applicable Community provisions are to prevail not only over existing but also over future Acts of Parliament (that is, Acts subsequent to 1972) in so far as these provisions may be inconsistent with such enactments'. Mr Justice Hodgson declared that it used to be 'unthinkable that there should be in an English court a higher authority than an Act of Parliament, but there is now in English law such a higher authority'.[6] When the *Factortame* case reached the House of Lords, the Law Lords declared that the courts would, for the first time in British history, 'disapply' part of a Westminster statute, the relevant provisions of the Merchant Shipping Act, as being in conflict with Community law.

So, for as long as Britain remained within the European Community/European Union, Westminster was a legislature of limited competence. British courts and tribunals became in effect constitutional courts able to pronounce on the validity of Acts of Parliament. In a later case, *R v Secretary of State for Employment, ex p Equal Opportunities Commission*,[7] after the Law Lords had ruled that parts of a Westminster statute were incompatible with European Community law. *The Times* commented, 'Britain may now have, for the first time in its history, a constitutional court' adding, 'In any other society, such constitutional "revision" would be a subject for heated debate. Its significance must not be lost on Britain's citizens and its Parliament'.[8] There was now in Britain judicial review of primary legislation, a concept hitherto unknown to the British Constitution. 'Most of us', Margaret Thatcher, a former barrister, was to confess in 1995, 'including myself, paid insufficient regard to the issue of sovereignty in consideration of the case for joining the EEC at the beginning of the 1970s … There was a failure to grasp the true nature of the European Court and the relationship that would emerge between British law and Community law'.[9] The legal consequences were perhaps much better understood by the opponents of membership, but in 1975 they were ignored. It is interesting to ask whether, if parliamentarians had appreciated the full consequences of the European Communities Act, as Margaret Thatcher claimed they did not, they would still have passed the legislation.

[5] AV Dicey, *An Introduction to the Study of the Law of the Constitution*, 8th edn (London, Macmillan, 1915) 39–40.

[6] *R v Secretary of State for Transport, ex p Factortame (No 2)* [1989] CMLR 353 at 373, 374 and 381.

[7] *R v Secretary of State for Employment, ex p Equal Opportunities Commission* [1995] 1 AC 1.

[8] *The Times*, 5 March 1994.

[9] M Thatcher, *The Path to Power* (London, Harper-Collins, 1995) 497.

In the words of the majority judgment in the first *Miller* case in 2017,[10] the European Community had provided 'a new constitutional process for making law in the United Kingdom'. So, our entry into the European Community had produced a structural change in the Constitution in relation to Community law. In the words of Lord Bridge in *Factortame*, it was now the 'duty of a United Kingdom court, when delivering final judgment, to override any rule of national law found to be in conflict with any directly enforceable rule of Community law'. The reason for this was that:

> If the supremacy … of Community law over the national law of member states was not always inherent in the EEC Treaty, it was certainly well established in the jurisprudence of the Court of Justice long before the United Kingdom joined the Community.[11]

Parliament, so it seems, had willed a restriction of its sovereignty.

But there is a problem with this proposition. For ministers, as we have seen, argued not only that Parliament was not restricting its sovereignty, but that Parliament was, logically, unable to restrict its sovereignty. Can one have willed something that one does not intend, that one regards indeed as logically impossible? Can one will something when one is convinced that one is doing the opposite? Can one will something that one is not aware of doing?

It might perhaps be argued that it is not the intentions of legislators that are crucial, and that the concept of Parliament willing something is a construct of the courts, who are seeking the true meaning of legislation. On this view, the courts construed the European Communities Act as precluding implied repeal. Yet it is difficult to discover any prominent jurist or constitutional lawyer who believed that this would be the import of the legislation at the time that it was enacted. The truth, surely, is that these judgments were creative decisions made by judges who might, without perhaps causing any great damage to legal logic, have discovered very good reasons for concluding that the European Communities Act had **not** made a fundamental alteration to the British Constitution. For the doctrine of the sovereignty of Parliament would seem to entail that judges should have refused to give effect to legislation which purports to limit that sovereignty. It was therefore the judges who determined the significance of the European Communities Act 1972 by interpreting it as imposing a limitation upon the sovereignty of Parliament. HWR Wade, in a seminal article in the *Cambridge Law Review* in 1955, declared that, 'The seat of sovereign power is not to be discovered by looking at the Acts of any Parliament but by looking at the courts and discovering to whom they give their obedience'.[12] By 1996, he had concluded that, 'Parliament can bind

[10] *R (Miller & others) v Secretary of State for Exiting the European Union* [2017] UKSC 5 § 62.

[11] *R v Secretary of State for Transport, ex p Factortame (No 2)* [1991] 1 AC 659, 643. But, in other parts of his judgment, Lord Bridge declared that the supremacy of European Community law flowed from the 1972 European Communities Act, not from the inherent nature of the Community as a superior legal order. My own view, by contrast, is that the supremacy of Community law was always inherent in the nature of the Treaty of Rome.

[12] HWR Wade, 'The Basis of Legal Sovereignty' (1955) 13 *Cambridge Law Review* 172, 196.

its successors. If that is not revolutionary, constitutional lawyers are Dutchmen'.[13] 'The new doctrine' adumbrated in *Factortame*, Wade believed, 'makes sovereignty a freely adjustable commodity whenever Parliament chooses to accept some limitation'. Sovereignty, however, cannot be freely adjustable. For, just as someone who has lost their virginity can never recover it, so a Parliament which had sacrificed its sovereignty, could never recover that sovereignty. For, like virginity, it is an absolute not a matter of degree. Of course, the view that Parliament had limited its sovereignty in the European Communities Act raises an awkward question. If Parliament could voluntarily limit its sovereignty in the European Communities Act, why might it not also do so with respect to other statutes – the Human Rights Act, for example, or the devolution legislation? What, if anything, was unique about the European Communities Act?

In *Thoburn v Sunderland City Council*,[14] the so-called 'Metric Martyrs Case', Lord Justice Laws went further, arguing that there was a whole category of 'constitutional' statutes and measures which were not subject to implied repeal. He included in this category, in addition to the European Communities Act, Magna Carta, the 1689 Bill of Rights, the Act of Union, the parliamentary Reform Acts, the Human Rights Act and the devolution legislation. In the view of Lord Justice Laws, a constitutional statute could not be repealed by implication as was the case with other statutes, but must be explicitly repealed. Here too, so it was suggested, there was something that a supposedly sovereign Parliament could not do – impliedly repeal a constitutional statute.

But what was the criterion for saying that a statute was 'constitutional' in the absence of a codified Constitution? Lord Justice Laws defined in paragraph 62 of *Thoburn* a 'constitutional statute', as one which '(a) conditions the legal relationship between the citizen and State in some general, overarching manner, or (b) enlarges or diminishes the scope of what we would now regard as fundamental constitutional rights'. But perhaps in a country without a codified constitution, it can never be precisely clear which matters are 'constitutional' and which are not. With an elastic constitution, the definition of what is constitutional must also perhaps be elastic.

Oddly enough, even the British government, when David Cameron was Prime Minister, seems to have come to the view that Parliament could bind itself. In 2011, Parliament passed the European Union Act, intended to guard against further transfers of power to the European Union. It sought to bind future parliaments by providing that no such transfers should take place unless and until validated by a referendum. It is certainly possible that a court, if presented with legislation purporting to transfer powers without a referendum, would have disapplied it. But the Act also declared that Parliament was sovereign. And it had been advocated by a government concerned at the erosion of the principle of parliamentary

[13] ibid; and HRW Wade 'Sovereignty – Revolution or Evolution?' (1996) 112 *Law Quarterly Review* 568, 573.

[14] *Thoburn v Sunderland City Council* [2003] QB 151.

sovereignty. The Act declared that Parliament was sovereign, but proposed to bind a future Parliament by requiring it, if it sought to transfer powers to the European Union, to hold a referendum, whether it wished to do so or not, which would, presumably, also be binding. In Lewis Carroll's *Through the Looking Glass*, the Queen declares that it was possible to believe in six impossible things before breakfast. The European Union Act seemed designed to test that proposition.

The courts have also considered the validity of primary legislation unconnected with the European Union. *R (Jackson) v Attorney-General* dealt with the validity of the 2004 Hunting Act. The Law Lords could have decided, although they did not, that the Act was ultra vires. And in giving judgment, some judges declared, obiter, for the first time, that Parliament's ability to pass primary legislation was subject to substantive limits. Lord Steyn declared, obiter, that the principle of the sovereignty of Parliament, while still being the '*general* principle of our constitution' was:

> a construct of the common law. The judges created this principle. If that is so, it is not unthinkable that circumstances could arise where the courts may have to qualify a principle established on a different hypothesis of constitutionalism.

He then went on to say in words which have been much quoted:

> In exceptional circumstances involving an attempt to abolish judicial review of the ordinary role of the courts, the Appellate Committee of the House of Lords or a new Supreme Court may have to consider whether this is a constitutional fundamental which even a sovereign Parliament acting at the behest of a complaisant House of Commons cannot abolish.[15]

Lord Steyn elaborated on this point by saying that:

> For my part the dicta in *Jackson* are likely to prevail if the government tried to tamper with the fundamental principles of our constitutional democracy, such as five-year Parliaments, the role of the ordinary courts, the rule of law, and other such fundamentals. In such exceptional cases the rule of law may trump parliamentary supremacy.[16]

In another obiter dictum from *Jackson*, Lady Hale of Richmond, later a President of the Supreme Court, said, 'The courts will treat with particular suspicion (and might even reject) any attempt to subvert the rule of law by removing governmental action affecting the rights of the individual from all judicial powers'.[17]

In another obiter dictum in the same case, another Law Lord, Lord Hope of Craighead, declared:

> Parliamentary sovereignty is no longer, if it ever was, absolute. It is not uncontrolled … It is no longer right to say that its freedom to legislate admits of no qualification whatever. Step by step, gradually but surely, the English principle of the absolute legislative sovereignty of Parliament … is being qualified.

[15] *R (Jackson) v Attorney-General* [2005] UKHL 56 § 102.

[16] Lord Steyn, 'Democracy, The Rule of Law and the Role of Judges' (The Attlee Foundation Lecture, 11 April 2006) 20.

[17] *R (Jackson) v Attorney-General* [2005] UKHL 56 § 159.

He then said: 'The rule of law enforced by the courts is the ultimate controlling actor on which our constitution is based'.[18]

Lord Hope, a Scottish Law Lord, spoke significantly of 'the **English** principle' of the sovereignty of Parliament. For the Scots have always been more sceptical than the English of the doctrine of the sovereignty of Parliament, which they find difficult to reconcile with the Acts of Union of 1707.

The implication of these remarks by the three Law Lords is that the sovereignty of Parliament is a doctrine created by the judges which can also be superseded by the judges, indeed that Parliament is itself a creation of law and can only act within the law.

More recently, the High Court and the Appeal Court of Northern Ireland have been prepared to consider the validity of the Northern Ireland Protocol, part of the European Union (Withdrawal) Act 2020 in the case of *In re Jim Allister and others (EU Exit)*.[19] In February 2023, the Supreme Court confirmed the judgment of the lower courts that the Northern Ireland Protocol and the European Union (Withdrawal) Act of 2020 were lawful.

It is not wholly clear to me whether Dicey did or did not believe that Parliament could bind itself. It may be that he was not consistent on this issue. But, on the whole, it appears to me that he thought Parliament could not legally bind itself. In his last book, *Thoughts on the Union between England and Scotland*, written in collaboration with the Scottish historiographer royal, RS Rait, he implied that Parliament could not do so. But Dicey had to confront the conundrum that the Scottish negotiators of the 1707 Treaty of Union believed that they could preserve certain fundamentals of Scottish law even in the new sovereign Parliament of Great Britain. Dicey's answer to the conundrum was that, while Parliament could not bind itself in law, it could bind itself in honour, to preserve certain fundamentals.

> the enactment of laws which are described as unchangeable, immutable, or the like, is not necessarily futile … A sovereign Parliament – although it cannot be logically bound to abstain from changing any given law, may, by the fact that an Act when it was passed had been declared to be unchangeable, receive a warning that it cannot be changed without gave danger to the Constitution of the country.[20]

Dicey did, however, believe that Parliament could, if it wished, abdicate its sovereignty, just as an absolute monarch such as the Czar could abdicate his sovereignty. And of course, Parliament would have to abdicate its sovereignty were Britain to come to enact a codified Constitution.

But little appears to be left of Dicey's doctrine of parliamentary sovereignty, even if the doctrine can be made coherent. Parliament seems no longer sovereign, if it ever was.

[18] ibid § 107 and 120.
[19] [2022] NICA 15.
[20] AV Dicey and RS Rait, *Thoughts on the Union between England and Scotland* (London, Macmillan, 1920) 253.

## II

Dicey's Constitution had no place for devolution or Home Rule as it was then called. His hostility to Home Rule was fierce, but he raised an important constitutional issue, claiming that there was no middle way between the unitary state and separation, apart from federalism which was, he believed, unsuited to British conditions; for in England, there were no provinces and little regional feeling. Home Rule or devolution was, so he believed, an unstable halfway house, bound in the end to lead to separation. Since Irish Home Rule was never in operation, except in loyalist Northern Ireland, where the pressure was centripetal rather than centrifugal, Dicey's proposition could not be tested in relation to Ireland. But it is coming to be tested in Scotland where devolution was implemented in 1998. The main purpose of devolution was to kill separatism. It has certainly not done that in Scotland. Since 2007, the SNP has been the largest party in the Scottish Parliament, and, despite proportional representation, was able to win an overall majority in the 2011 Holyrood election. In consequence, the Prime Minister, David Cameron, felt impelled to offer an independence referendum. This was duly held in 2014; independence was defeated by 55 per cent to 45 per cent. But Brexit, which Scotland voted against, has led to pressure for a second referendum which, so far, British governments have been able to resist. Nevertheless, the question of a second referendum may arise again, if the next election results in a hung parliament in which the Labour Party is dependent on the SNP for a majority at Westminster; independence therefore remains a live issue.

It is of course impossible to know what would have happened in Scotland had devolution been rejected. Arguably devolution has provided a forum for the SNP which would have been weaker without the chance of exercising power in Holyrood. But it is equally arguable that Scots, faced with a stark choice between the unitary state and independence, and no middle way, would have opted for independence. So, on Dicey's contention that devolution cannot be a constitutionally stable resting place, the jury remains out.

## III

Dicey's Constitution did, however, find room for another recent constitutional innovation, the referendum. He was indeed the first to advocate it in an article 'Ought the Referendum to be Introduced into England' [sic] published in the *Contemporary Review* in April 1890. He wrote two further articles on it in the *National Review* 1894 and in the *Quarterly Review* in 1910 in the course of reviewing books on the Swiss political system; and finally, a long introduction on various proposed constitutional reforms which included the referendum in the 8th edition of *Law of the Constitution*, published in 1915, the last edition personally supervised by him.[21]

[21] AV Dicey, 'Ought the Referendum to be Introduced into England (sic)' (1890) 57 *Contemporary Review* 489.

Dicey favoured the referendum because he wanted to defeat proposals for Irish Home Rule which, so he believed, would not be supported by British voters. He regarded the referendum as remedying a crucial weakness in the British system of government: 'The possibility … which no one can dispute of a fundamental change passing into law which the mass of the nation do not desire'. Legally, Parliament was sovereign; but, in a democracy, political sovereignty lay with the people. The referendum, Dicey claimed, offered the only form of constitutional protection possible in a country with a sovereign Parliament. It was, moreover, a form of constitutional protection which was in essence democratic since it gave power to the people, to the electorate. Further, in a referendum, by contrast with a general election under the first-past-the-post system, every vote had an equal weight. So, a referendum could give a better verdict on a specific issue than a general election. The referendum, then, was a democratic check on democracy.

Dicey produced two arguments to buttress his case. The first was that it would do away 'with the strictly speaking absurd system which at present exists, of acting on the presumption that electors can best answer the question raised by e.g. Home Rule, when it is put together with totally different questions'. It was as if a jury were told that it could only convict an accused, X, if it simultaneously also convicted Y and Z, charged with totally different offences.

The second argument was that the referendum was 'an emphatic assertion of the principle that nation stands above party'. Modern democracies were dominated by the party system which, so Dicey believed,

> whatever its advantages, and they are not insignificant, is opposed to the sovereignty of the people, which is the fundamental dogma of modern democracy. That system throws the control of legislation first into the hands of a party, and then into the hands of the most active or the most numerous section of that party.

Dicey dealt with some obvious criticisms of the referendum. The first was that it would weaken Parliament. But it was, Dicey believed, a mistake to regard Parliament as a Burkean body of independently-minded MPs. The whips were as active in the early twentieth century as they are today. Indeed, as AL Lowell, the Harvard political scientist, showed, in his book, *The Government of England* [sic], published in 1908, party cohesion in early twentieth-century Britain was very strong indeed – stronger in fact than today.

Dicey believed that the referendum would actually strengthen Parliament, since it would make parliamentary debates more relevant.

> If it was certain that the ultimate fate of a measure – would finally turn not upon the votes of members in Parliament, but on voters outside who never took part in the hollow and artificial warfare waged at Westminster, it is conceivable that speakers in Parliament. might address themselves to the task of convincing an unseen audience [and] conceivable … that the power of reasoning might become a force of some slight moment even in practical politics.[22]

[22] AV Dicey, 'Ought the Referendum to be Introduced into England' 503.

Dicey sought to counter the argument that the referendum was an appeal from knowledge to ignorance. This argument was to be used in 1974 by Jean Rey, ex-President of the European Commission, who opposed a referendum on the subject of Europe, declaring in London on 17 July, that,

> A referendum on this matter consists of consulting people who don't know the problems instead of consulting people who know them. I would deplore a situation in which the policy of this great country should be left to housewives. It should be decided instead by trained and informed people.[23]

Dicey believed that such a line of attack 'on the principles of an appeal to the people, is an assault upon the foundations of representative government'.[24] The criticism of the referendum went too far. It is, after all, much easier for a voter to make a decision on a specific issue than to weigh in her mind and balance out the host of competing issues on which she has to give a verdict in a general election. If the voter can be trusted with a decision on the latter, why not also the former?

It might seem, at first sight, as if Dicey contradicted himself in supporting both parliamentary sovereignty and the referendum. But that is not so. For, if Parliament can enact any law that it likes, then it can enact a law providing for a referendum. What it cannot do is to enact a law providing for a legally binding referendum. A government can voluntarily agree to be bound by the outcome of a referendum, but a sovereign Parliament, in Dicey's view, could not be so bound – although, of course, MPs would not be expected to go against the wishes of the people. The point was well put by the then Leader of the House, Edward Short, in 1975, when he said that the referendum was 'wholly consistent with parliamentary sovereignty. The Government will be bound by its result, but Parliament, of course, cannot be bound by it'. He then added 'Although one would not expect hon. Members to go against the wishes of the people they will remain free to do so'.[25]

By 1910, Dicey's advocacy of the referendum appeared near to success. The referendum was proposed at the Constitutional Conference held in that year both as a method of resolving deadlocks between the Commons and the Lords, and also as a means of deciding 'constitutional' issues. The conference indeed came near to agreement on drawing up a codified Constitution. In the December 1910 general election, the referendum was the main Conservative counter-proposal to the Liberal policy of replacing the absolute powers of the Lords with a suspensory veto. In addition, the Conservatives agreed that their main economic policy proposal, tariff reform, should be put to referendum. But the referendum did not in fact then become part of the Constitution. The Parliament Act of 1911 yielded an alternative method of resolving conflict between the Lords and the Commons, while the concession after the 1914–1918 war of Irish Home Rule and then independence

[23] *The Times*, 18 July 1974.
[24] Dicey, 'Ought the Referendum to be Introduced into England'.
[25] *Hansard*, HC Deb vol 888, col 293. 11 March 1975.

drove the referendum and indeed constitutional issues in general out of British politics for over 50 years.

The referendum came to be thought as unconstitutional until the 1970s. When, in 1945, Churchill proposed a referendum on whether to maintain the wartime coalition into peacetime, Attlee told him,

> I could not consent to the introduction into our national life of a device so alien to all our traditions as the referendum, which has only too often been the instrument of Nazism and Fascism. Hitler's practices in the field of referenda and plebiscites can hardly have endeared these expedients to the British heart.

This was, however, an absurd argument. One might as well argue that Stalin's misuse of elections discredited elections.

Nevertheless, the referendum remained off the political agenda for nearly 30 years after the war and was little discussed. In 1964, a well-known textbook, *Representative and Responsible Government* by AH Birch, declared, 'It has occasionally been proposed that a referendum might be held on a particular issue, but the proposals do not ever appear to have been taken seriously'.[26]

But Britain was to hold her first national referendum in 1975 on the question of whether she should remain in the European Community which she had joined in 1973. That referendum, by contrast with that of 2016, led to a two to one majority for remaining in the European Community.

A naïve observer might suggest that this referendum resulted from an earnest desire on the part of British political leaders to discover the view of the British people on Europe. That, of course, was not the case. The referendum came about as a result of the vicissitudes of party politics and in particular from the need to paper over divisions in the Labour Party. The referendum enabled Labour to avoid making a commitment on whether or not it favoured Britain's membership of the European Community. Instead it proposed that the people should decide. 'It is singular', Dicey had said in 1909, when it had appeared that the referendum might become part of the Constitution, 'and not perhaps very fortunate that, in accordance with English habits, a reform good in itself, should be proposed by men who probably do not believe in it, and who want to meet a party difficulty. Still, I hail it with satisfaction'.[27]

Harold Wilson, Prime Minister at the time of the 1975 referendum, declared that it was a unique constitutional experiment which could not be repeated since Europe was a unique issue. But of course a precedent had been set and further referendums were held in 1979, on devolution to Scotland and Wales. More referendums have been held since. Dicey indeed had been 'quite certain that, once established the Referendum would never be got rid of by anything short

[26] AH Birch, *Representative and Responsible Government. An Essay on the British Constitution* (London, George Allen and Unwin, 1964) 277.

[27] R Cosgrove, *The Rule of Law. AV Dicey, a Victorian Jurist* (London, Macmillan, 1980) 108.

of a revolution. This is its great merit. It makes the democracy itself a check on party tyranny.'[28]

Although introduced to resolve a problem of internal party politics, there was a principled case for a referendum on Europe. In the 1970 general election, the last before Britain entered the European Community, all three major parties had favoured entry. There was, therefore, no way in which a voter who was opposed to entry could indicate her opposition by her vote. Moreover, neither of the major parties was united on the issue. So the party system was not operating effectively since it is not well adapted to dealing with issues on which parties are divided.

But, even if the party system had been working effectively such that there had been a clear division between two united parties on Europe, there was a case for the referendum on grounds of legitimacy. As Edward Short told the Commons in March 1975, 'The issue continues to divide the country. The decision to go in has not been accepted. That is the essence of the case for having a referendum.'[29] It was said after the referendum that, while the Conservative Prime Minister who negotiated entry, Edward Heath, had taken the British establishment into Europe, it took a Labour Prime Minister, Harold Wilson, to take the British people into Europe. Some issues, it might be suggested, are of such fundamental importance that they cannot be given legitimacy just by Parliament. They also need endorsement by the people.

But what are these issues? Can they be defined in a country without a codified Constitution? Can there be rules for when referendums should be held? Or does a flexible Constitution entail a flexible use of the referendum, so that it can be used at the discretion of the government of the day? We have, however, in a typically unplanned British way been developing rules.

The most fundamental of the issues on which it is agreed that referendums are required is the secession of a part of the United Kingdom. The Belfast or Good Friday Agreement 1998 confirms that Northern Ireland cannot secede without a border poll, while in Scotland, the nationalists have accepted that independence requires a referendum.

The second fundamental issue requiring a referendum is a transfer of the legislative powers of Parliament downwards through devolution. And the now irrelevant European Act 2011 provided that Parliament could not transfer major powers upwards to the European Union without a referendum.

These provisions have a rationale in liberal thought. In his Second *Treatise of Government*, Locke declares, 'The Legislative cannot transfer the power of making laws to any other hands. For it being but a delegated power from the people, they who have it cannot pass it to others.'[30] Voters, it might be suggested, entrust their MPs with legislative powers, but give them no authority to transfer that power; for that, they need a specific mandate – to be obtained through a referendum.

[28] RA Cosgrove, *The Rule of Law: Albert Venn Dicey, Victorian Jurist* (Macmillan, 1980) 107.
[29] *Hansard* HC Deb vol 888, col 292, 11 March 1975.
[30] J Locke, 'Second Treatise' in P Laslett (ed), *Two Treatises of Government* (Cambridge, Cambridge University Press, 1988) 362.

The third fundamental issue on which it is agreed that a referendum is required is a change in the electoral system, such as the alternative vote, the subject of the 2011 referendum. For it is obviously desirable to prevent a government from altering the electoral system for partisan reasons.

The 2016 Brexit referendum was a further and even more important constitutional innovation. Indeed, Takis Tridimas, Professor of European Law at King's College, London, declared at a seminar held shortly afterwards that it was the most significant constitutional event in Britain since the restoration of the monarchy in 1660. For the 2016 referendum showed, or perhaps confirmed, that, on the issue of Europe, the sovereignty of the people trumped the sovereignty of Parliament. Admittedly, the 2015 European Union Referendum Act had provided that the referendum would be advisory, like that of 1975 and not binding, as allegedly was the referendum on the alternative vote held in 2011. Nevertheless, the government, although in favour of Britain's continued membership – as were the majority of MPs and peers – had agreed in advance to be bound by the result. So Brexit came about, not because government or Parliament wanted it, but because the people wanted it. Government and Parliament felt themselves constrained to do something that they did not wish to do. That is a situation quite without precedent in Britain's long constitutional history. The majority of the Cabinet which legislated for Brexit were Remainers; so were the majority in the Commons, and even the majority of Conservative MPs; while the majority in the Lords for Remain was far larger than the majority in the Commons. In the conflict between a supposedly sovereign Parliament and a sovereign people, the sovereign people triumphed. The referendum had become, in effect, a third chamber of Parliament, issuing legislative instructions to the other two chambers. The sovereignty of Parliament was now to be constrained not by Brussels but by the people.

The principle of the sovereignty of the people has often been deplored. Liberals have feared that it would prove a threat to liberties, while conservatives were worried lest it lead to mob rule; and Remainers regarded the 2016 referendum as a triumph of the ignorant. All echoed the fear of the great French reactionary, Joseph de Maistre, who wrote that 'The principle of the sovereignty of the people is so dangerous that, even if it were true, it would be necessary to conceal it'.[31]

The referendum, however, far from bringing about mob rule, has proved an instrument of constitutional protection, providing a safeguard against major constitutional changes which the people do not want. It has become the people's veto. It was, Dicey believed, 'the only check on the predominance of party which is at the same time democratic and conservative'.[32] It has proved a check less on Parliament than on the party system; and whether or not it is favoured will depend on one's view of the efficacy of the party system. 'It is certain', Dicey declared, 'that no man who is really satisfied with the working of our party system will ever

[31] J de Maistre, *Oeuvres Completes*, vol 9 (Geneva, Slatkine Reprints, 1979) 494, https://gallica.bnf.fr/ark:/12148/bpt6k47768/f500.item (author's translation).

[32] Dicey, 'Ought the Referendum to be Introduced into England?' 507.

look with favour on an institution which aims at correcting the vices of party government'.[33]

The referendum, then, is now part of the British Constitution. Not only is the principle now generally accepted. So also, are the conditions for its use, amounting perhaps to a constitutional convention as to when one is required. It has become, as Dicey predicted, a weapon of entrenchment. It has prevented introduction of the alternative vote electoral system and the introduction of regional government in England, while fear of the outcome of a referendum prevented the Blair government from proposing British entry into the eurozone. The referendum has provided a barrier to fundamental change which the people do not want. It may well be, as Dicey believed, the only constitutional weapon of entrenchment in a country which lacks a codified Constitution. And, as Dicey appreciated, used only rarely as it has been in Britain, it **supplements** but does not **replace** representative government.

From this point of view, therefore, Dicey was a prophet.

## IV

The referendum, however, has by no means been the only constitutional innovation in Britain in the last 50 years. But the innovations have been little noticed by the general public, in England at least. We are, after all, very good at hiding change. The monarchy, the House of Lords and the House of Commons have all existed for many hundreds of years. But of course, they function today in a quite different manner from the past. France, by contrast, has known much constitutional change, since 1789, often in the form of revolutions. But, as Tocqueville was but the first to point out, these revolutions changed much less than many fondly imagined.[34] Our revolutions, by contrast, have been quiet ones which nobody notices. When in 1945, the Labour Party won an electoral landslide, enabling it to form its first majority government, American President Truman visiting Britain, said to George VI, 'I see you have had a revolution'. The king replied, 'oh no, we don't have that sort of thing here'. But of course, the Attlee government, Britain's first Labour majority government, did produce a social revolution whose consequences have proved long-lasting.

Our constitutional revolutions are equally masked. Indeed, we have had two recent constitutional revolutions in Britain. The first was the series of reforms initiated by the Blair government after 1997, in particular the Human Rights Act, devolution, and the introduction of directly elected mayors – the first such mayor in British history being elected in London in 2000. No fewer than 40 per cent of us in

[33] Dicey, *Law of the Constitution Introduction* c.
[34] A de Tocqueville, *The Old Regime and the Revolution*, vol 1 (Chicago, University of Chicago Press, 1998).

Britain now live under directly elected mayors and more are in prospect. In addition, there has been the widespread adoption and acceptance of proportional representation for sub-national elections – elections to the devolved bodies, the London Assembly, and for local government in Scotland, Wales, and Northern Ireland. We have also had, as I mentioned earlier, for the first time in our history Parliament legislating for something to which a majority of its members were opposed.

All this has meant the end of Dicey's characterisation of the British Constitution as a 'historic' Constitution. What he meant by that description was not merely that the British Constitution was very old, but that it had evolved by a process of adaptation rather than as a result of conscious planning.[35]

But, as a result of the radical reforms that have taken place since 1997, the British Constitution can no longer be characterised as 'historic'. Instead, it offers a spectacle perhaps unique in the democratic world, of a country gradually transforming its uncodified Constitution in an ad hoc and unplanned way into a codified one, there being neither the political will nor yet sufficient popular consensus to produce such a Constitution in one fell swoop. The new British Constitution, the twenty-first-century Constitution, is marked by two central principles, the first being a diffusion of power away from Parliament to devolved bodies and the courts, the second being, as we have seen, the sovereignty of the people.[36]

But there is an incipient second constitutional revolution occasioned by Brexit which withdraws us from a protected constitution – the treaties of the EU – to an unprotected one. To 'take back control' means, for many of its advocates, a return to the Constitution as it was before 1973, the Constitution of parliamentary sovereignty.

Brexit both disentrenches the British Constitution, and removes Britain from a human rights regime – the European Charter of Fundamental Rights – which offered a much wider and more modern protection of rights than the European Convention on Human Rights, and allowed judges, by contrast with the Convention, to disapply primary legislation as contrary to human rights, as the Supreme Court did in the *Benkharbouche* case of 2017 – as important in my view as *Factortame*. For this was the first occasion in British history that the courts disapplied primary legislation on human rights grounds. The Charter, however, is one of the few parts – perhaps the only part – of EU law not to be incorporated into British law. Andrew Langdon QC, former Chair of the Bar Council, has commented, 'Rights are not being brought home, they are being abolished'. It is rare if not unprecedented for a democracy to exit from a major international human rights regime and no democracy to my knowledge has hitherto moved from a protected to an unprotected constitution. Other Member States of the

[35] Dicey's characterisation of the British Constitution as a 'historical' Constitution is to be found in his unpublished lectures on the Comparative Study of Constitutions, now collected and edited by JWF Allison in A.V. Dicey, *Comparative Constitutionalism* (Oxford, Oxford University Press, 2013) 172–86.

[36] V Bogdanor, *The New British Constitution* (Oxford, Hart Publishing, 2009).

European Union continue, of course, to be bound by the Charter, while countries such as the United States and Canada have their own provisions protecting human rights against a majority in the legislature. So, we have to ask a very un-Diceyan question. Are our MPs so much more sensitive to human rights than legislators in other democracies that they are fit to be entrusted with the protection of human rights? I leave the answer to that question to you.

Brexit has also strained the territorial constitution. Indeed, it is beginning to appear as if Britain, far from having no constitution, has four different constitutions, a different constitution in each of the territories of the United Kingdom. The government, in effect largely an English government, continues to emphasise the sovereignty of Parliament; the Scots regard their Constitution as being based on the sovereignty of the Scottish people, something tacitly recognised in the independence referendum of 2014; the Welsh government seeks a quasi-federal constitutional settlement; while in the divided province of Northern Ireland, the Unionists, as King's rebels, champion – as Dicey did – a Whig and contractual Constitution, allegiance to which is dependent upon the government at Westminster respecting the Union; and the Nationalists believe that the Good Friday Agreement provided a Constitution of shared rule between Britain and the Republic of Ireland. There is an American saying, 'where you stand depends upon where you sit'.

Brexit, then, increases uncertainty as to what our Constitution actually is, more particularly what the conventions of the Constitution actually are, and to what extent they bind. In 1904, at the beginning of the twentieth century, Sidney Low, in his book *The Governance of England*, declared that the Constitution was based not on codified rules but on tacit understandings, although, as he ruefully remarked, 'the understandings are not always understood'.[37] Perhaps these understandings are now even less well understood. The late Lord Bingham, regarded by many as the greatest judge of his generation, declared even before Brexit, that 'constitutionally speaking, we now find ourselves in a trackless desert without any map or compass', and argued for a codified Constitution.[38]

Brexit, precisely because it involves a process of disentrenchment and exit from a major international human rights regime, is an existential moment for the British Constitution. It would be a striking paradoxical consequence if Brexit, which Dicey himself would almost certainly have supported, were to prove a catalyst for a codified British Constitution. But it is just possible that Brexit, by revealing the very nakedness of our unprotected Constitution, could prove Britain's constitutional moment, so enabling her to move out of her Diceyan isolation. Were that to happen, Dicey's Constitution would have become of purely historical interest.

[37] S Low, *The Governance of England* (London, T Fisher Unwin, 1904) 12.

[38] Quoted in *A Constitutional Crossroads: Ways Forward for the United Kingdom: Report of an Independent Commission* (London, Bingham Centre for the Rule of Law, 2015) 18.

# 7

# Dicey in the *Miller 1* and *Miller 2* Judgments

AURÉLIEN ANTOINE

Evaluating an author's influence on the reasoning of a Supreme Court Judge requires an examination of what French jurists identify as two sources of law: doctrine and jurisprudence. This Cartesian categorisation is not necessarily recognised as clearly in studies of British common law. The debate is old and recurrent in French law. It is less common in the United Kingdom and one must admit that previous analyses of the *Miller 1* and *Miller 2*[1] judgments did not specifically focus on the use made (or not made) of Dicey.

The first case was based on the decision by the Prime Minister at the time, Theresa May, to send a letter to the European Council notifying it of the United Kingdom's intent to leave the European Union without Parliament's express agreement.[2] The Supreme Court found that notice by such a letter would not be lawful and required the Government to bring the matter to the legislature. Two years later, in the second case, the highest British jurisdiction rejected Boris Johnson's plan, enacted by royal decree in Privy Council, to suspend Parliament for five weeks.

Despite the absence of academic literature on the links between these two judgments and Dicey, the cardinal principles of the British Constitution relating to them are nevertheless entirely covered in the works by the famous jurist, particularly in his *Introduction to the Study of the Law of the Constitution* (hereafter *Introduction*).[3] In addition, the explicit or implicit reference to Dicey in the 2017 and 2019 decisions is undeniable: simple observation should be sufficient. Beyond this rather offhand remark, this chapter will use the two *Miller* decisions to evaluate the influence and real use by the Supreme Court of an author sometimes called an 'oracle'.[4] This requires the use of a particular methodology.

[1] *R (Miller & others) v Secretary of State for Exiting the European Union* [2017] UKSC 5 (*Miller 1*); *R (Miller & others) v The Prime Minister; Cherry and others v Advocate General for Scotland* [2019] UKSC 41 (*Miller 2*).

[2] Art 50(2) of the Treaty on European Union.

[3] AV Dicey, 'Introduction to the Study of the Law of the Constitution' in *The Law of the Constitution*, vol 1, JWF Allison (ed) (Oxford, Oxford University Press, 2013).

[4] Term given by AWB Simpson, taken up in I Ward, *The English Constitution, Myths and Realities* (Oxford, Hart Publishing, 2004) 24.

To begin, the discussion which follows is neither in the field of philosophy of law nor in the history of political ideas.[5] It is not a question of presenting an historical appreciation or critique of Dicey's thought as such, and is not intended to incite debate on its coherence and how its use may have led to some simplifications, particularly in the case of the debates relating to Brexit.[6] This is also not the place to determine whether the justices' appeal to Dicey was really in conformity with the complexity of his thought – often more subtle than is sometimes presented in contemporary formulations, which are occasionally mythicised, including by the judiciary.[7] The current study can nevertheless help us reflect on the contemporary pertinence of Dicey's analyses in positive law.

Next, the illumination which will be cast on Dicey is based on two external perspectives. The first begins with that of the judge. In this first perspective, the original premise of departure comes down to sharing the conclusion of certain doctrinal discussions: at the risk of a sort of tautology, Dicey remains worthy of interest since he continues to be cited in decisions, not only in relation to his judicial analysis, but also by the fact that he actively participated in the 'historic' construction of the principles of the British Constitution, principles which were (and still are) badly understood or the object of diverging interpretations due to their age.[8] This understanding does not mean, however, that his use must be given too much weight, theorists sometimes having the tendency to do so when working on one of their prestigious ancestors.

This first external view of Dicey is accompanied by a second, related to the author of this chapter. As a Frenchman, educated in a scientific, Cartesian approach to classifying sources of law, influenced by laconic formulations of decisions, and descending from a tradition of the relationship between judges and doctrine, he is necessarily victim of a distorting prism in understanding a question dealing with Dicey and the British Supreme Court. In France, and without attempting to look at the debate in depth, the role of doctrine as a source of law is accepted in principle,[9] but the reality is debatable considering the use which the supreme jurisdictions or

[5] For a recent work which was much cited during this conference, see MD Walters, *A.V. Dicey and the Common Law Constitutional Tradition: A Legal Turn of Mind* (Cambridge, Cambridge University Press, 2020).

[6] R Weill 'Dicey was not Diceyan' (2003) 62(2) *Cambridge Law Journal* 474; against see MD Walters, 'Was Dicey Diceyan?' in Walters, *Dicey and the Common Law* 378. During Brexit, Dicey was frequently cited to promote an absolutist vision of Parliament's sovereignty in order to question the authority of the Supreme Court (see the contributions of the authors participating in the Judicial Power Project, close to the Conservative Party, https://judicialpowerproject.org.uk/). It must be noted here that Dicey's conception has been diluted by judges in the last few decades, not only under the influence of European Union law and the European Convention on Human Rights, but also through United Kingdom laws of a constitutional nature (particularly in the field of devolution).

[7] For such an analysis, see Walters ibid.

[8] V Bogdanor, *The New British Constitution* (Oxford, Hart Publishing, 2009) 18 ff.

[9] P Deumier, *Introduction générale au droit*, 7th edn (Issy-les-Moulineaux, LGDJ-Lextenso, 2023) para 379 ff. Doctrine, as an authority of discovery, explanation, and interpretation of the law occupies

the legislators make of it. While there may well be a dialogue between the Cour de cassation, the Conseil d'Etat, and the Conseil constitutionnel and doctrine, it never appears explicitly in their decisions. Mention of theoretical works will be found officially in the opinions expressed by the Advocate General of the Cour de cassation, the Public Rapporteur of the Conseil d'Etat, in the official commentary on a decision by the Conseil constitutionnel provided by the Secretary General, or on the occasion of consultations undertaken by the Houses of Parliament in the context of their mission of government supervision or for information purposes. In addition, the relationships between doctrine and a judge are increasingly analysed based on a distinction between academic and organic doctrine. We will see in what way this can be used to understand the contemporary relationship between British doctrine and the Supreme Court.

The third series of methodological remarks concerns the scientific material on which this work is based and which reveals a descriptive, formal, and empirical approach while endeavouring to limit the theoretical presuppositions and attempting to remove oneself from the considerable scientific production on the influence and validity of Dicey's theses. Beyond the two *Miller* decisions and the *Introduction*, the effort to contextualise implies expanding the body of references to the jurisprudence on which the justices relied in *Miller 1* and *2*.

To this material distinction must be added the substantial elements which make it possible to know how, and for what purpose, Dicey is used by the justices of the Supreme Court in the *Miller 1* and *2* decisions. The themes which echo those of the *Introduction* are the following:

- parliamentary sovereignty;
- the rule of law principle;
- royal prerogative;
- government responsibility (accountability);
- constitutional conventions;
- the referendum.

For all these subjects, the United Kingdom Supreme Court justices were, a priori, able to refer to *Introduction*, insofar as it is often considered as having clearly, and for the first time, theorised the bases of British constitutional law from a scientific and positivist perspective. What is its real use in the two *Miller* decisions?

a central place in Romano-Germanic judicial systems. As Deumier explained, doctrine's particular role 'plays a historic role' in the Romano-Germanic family, para 383: 'Roman law was a jurisconsultes law, a modified form of doctrine; universities and legislators later worked on the rediscovery of Roman law but also on putting in order customs and the preparation of civil codes. On the other hand, it corresponds to a certain conception of the law, as a rational and consistent body, which requires one to focus on this systematisation and this science of law'.

# I. Parliamentary Sovereignty: Homage to Diceyan Orthodoxy?

Parliamentary sovereignty and its interpretation were at the heart of *Miller 1*. For the justices, it was a question of verifying to what extent the notification of the intent to withdraw from the European Union infringed upon this principle, as a result of the government's exercising prerogatives leading to a modification of domestic law.[10]

The reference to Dicey is explicit in paragraph 43. Lord Neuberger, the author of the majority opinion, highlighted:

> This is because Parliamentary sovereignty is a fundamental principle of the UK Constitution, as was conclusively established in the statutes referred to in para 41 above. It was famously summarised by Professor Dicey as meaning that Parliament has 'the right to make or unmake any law whatsoever; and further, no person or body is recognised by the law as having a right to override or set aside the legislation of Parliament' – *op cit* 38. The legislative power of the Crown is today exercisable only through Parliament. This power is initiated by the laying of a Bill containing a proposed law before Parliament, and the Bill can only become a statute if it is passed (often with amendments) by Parliament (which normally but not always means both Houses of Parliament) and is then formally assented to by HM The Queen. Thus, Parliament, or more precisely the Crown in Parliament, lays down the law through statutes – or primary legislation as it is also known – and not in any other way.[11]

The justices base their reasoning and their interpretation on Dicey's premise. His statement appears rather prescriptive, before the majority of eight justices reveal the more subtle implications.

Faithfulness to Diceyan positivism is also implicitly discernible when the Court develops the argument of the frustration of parliamentary powers using royal prerogative.[12] While not explicitly mentioned by Dicey in his *Introduction*, the principle comes directly from his concept of parliamentary sovereignty though a dynamic vision of the role of common law judges. Dicey underlines that:

[10] 'The extent of ministers' power to effect changes in domestic law through exercise of their prerogative powers', (*Miller 1* para 4); 'The main issue on this appeal concerns the ability of ministers to bring about changes in domestic law by exercising their powers at the international level, and it arises from two features of the United Kingdom's constitutional arrangements' (*Miller 1* para 5).

[11] *Miller 1* para 43.

[12] 'Further, ministers cannot frustrate the purpose of a statute or a statutory provision, for example by emptying it of content or preventing its effectual operation' (*Miller 1* para 51). Robert Craig discerns a frustration principle. He writes: 'the frustration principle means that a prerogative persists and can be exercised by the Crown but not in a way that frustrates the intention of Parliament in any Act' in R Craig, 'A Simple Application of the Frustration Principle: Prerogative, Statute and Miller' (2017) *Public Law, Brexit Special Issue* 33. It should be noted that in *Miller 1*, ten justices think that the principle makes it possible to limit the application of royal prerogative. For Lord Carnwath, it only controls the exercise or abuses. See M Elliott et al, *The UK Constitution after Miller. Brexit and Beyond* (Oxford, Hart Publishing, 2018) 20. The frustration principle will be taken up again in *Miller 2* when identifying the standard of accountability (*Miller 2* para 50).

> The fact that the most arbitrary powers of the English executive must always be exercised under Act of Parliament places the government, even when armed with the widest authority, under the supervision, so to speak, of the Courts. Powers, however extraordinary, which are conferred or sanctioned by statute, are never really unlimited, for they are confined by the words of the Act itself, and what is more, by the interpretation put upon the statute by the judges. Parliament is supreme legislator, but from the moment Parliament has uttered its will as lawgiver, that will becomes subject to the interpretation put upon it by the judges of the land, and the judges, who are influenced by the feelings of magistrates no less than by the general spirit of the common law, are disposed to construe statutory exceptions to common law principles in a mode which would not commend itself either to a body of officials or to the Houses of Parliament, if the Houses were called upon to interpret their own enactments.[13]

His conclusion is thus clear:

> By every path we come round to the same conclusion, that Parliamentary sovereignty has favoured the rule of law, and that the supremacy of the law of the land both calls forth the exertion of Parliamentary sovereignty, and leads to its being exercised in a spirit of legality.[14]

The interpretation of the European Communities Act 1972 in *Miller 1* is based on a relatively similar logic.

This is not the case in *Miller 2*: no direct mention is made of Dicey. Maybe the justices considered that the reference was less useful, as they may have understood *Miller 2* as a kind of diptych with the 2017 decision. The two judgments should be read together, which the references to *Miller 1* in *Miller 2* confirm. It nevertheless remains that the statement 'Two fundamental principles of our constitutional law are relevant to the present case. The first is the principle of Parliamentary sovereignty'[15] could have been taken directly from Dicey.

On the other hand, Dicey's writings are harder to evoke when parliamentary sovereignty is confronted with the European Communities Act, whose constitutional character is recognised.[16] On this subject the Court's approach is unprecedented in *Miller 1*, since the original protection from which the European Communities Act benefited and its specific scope in the normative domestic order serve to preserve parliamentary sovereignty, while, until then, it had rather led to relativising it. It is, in fact, the idea that parliamentary acts may enjoy special protection which is often presented as contrary to Dicey's opinions.

Three years before the new justices of the Supreme Court took office, Lord Steyn's opinion, expressed on the occasion of the *Jackson* judgment, reveals in part the current position of British courts, not without ambiguities with regard to the Diceyan heritage: 'the supremacy of Parliament is still the *general* principle of our

[13] Dicey, *Introduction* 183–84.
[14] ibid 184.
[15] *Miller 2* para 41.
[16] *Miller 1* paras 67 and 68.

constitution', but he specifies in advance that its 'pure and absolute' acceptance as it was constructed by Dicey 'can now be seen to be out of place in the modern United Kingdom'. He does not fail to express an opinion which we know is debatable, that is to say that the principle would be 'a construct of the common law' which the judges created. Lord Steyn deduced from this that 'it is not unthinkable that circumstances could arise where the courts may have to qualify a principle established on a different hypothesis of constitutionalism'.[17]

Between the assumed faithfulness to Dicey in *Miller 1* and its implicit reinforcement in *Miller 2*, it appears that the Diceyan concept was not so 'out of place in the modern United Kingdom'. Further, what appears as one of the bases of its relativisation (European law) proved to be a vector for its reinforcement in *Miller 1* and *2*. In the first judgment, initiating the withdrawal from the EU by a notification letter was an infringement of this particular protection, which occurs through Parliament's intervention given the immediate judicial impact of the decision by the executive on the rights and liberties of individuals. According to Lord Neuberger:

> A complete withdrawal represents a change which is different not just in degree but in kind from the abrogation of particular rights, duties or rules derived from EU law. It will constitute as significant a constitutional change as that which occurred when EU law was first incorporated in domestic law by the 1972 Act.[18]

However, such a constitutional change can only be initiated by Parliament.[19]

Finally, it is not even certain that invoking the fundamentality or the particularity of certain acts of Parliament in the domestic judicial order completely contradicts Dicey's thought on parliamentary sovereignty. Often judges (and not only judges) refer to one of the passages of *Introduction* in which Dicey clearly states the absence of distinction between fundamental laws and those which are not.[20] However, the categorical appearance of Dicey's proposals is balanced in other parts of his text, since he affirms:

> In England we have laws which may be called fundamental or constitutional because they deal with important principles (as, for example, the descent of the Crown or the terms of union with Scotland) lying at the basis of our institutions, but with us there is no such thing as a supreme law, or law which tests the validity of other laws.[21]

[17] *R (Jackson) v Attorney General* [2005] UKHL 56, [2006] 1 AC 262 at para 103. It is on this occasion that Lord Steyn hypothesised that Parliament's sovereignty could be set aside in the exceptional case of an attempt to suppress judicial review (para 102).

[18] *Miller 1* para 81.

[19] ibid para 82: 'We cannot accept that a major change to UK constitutional arrangements can be achieved by ministers alone; it must be effected in the only way that the UK Constitution recognises, namely by parliamentary legislation. This conclusion appears to us to follow from the ordinary application of basic concepts of constitutional law to the present issue'.

[20] Dicey affirms that 'There is under the English constitution no marked or clear distinction between laws which are not fundamental or constitutional and laws which are fundamental or constitutional. The very language therefore, expressing the difference between a "legislative" assembly which can change ordinary laws and a "constituent" assembly which can change not only ordi nary but also constitutional and fundamental laws, has to be borrowed from the political phraseology of foreign countries': *Introduction* 52.

[21] ibid 78.

The contemporary jurist specialising in the British Constitution cannot make much objection to this statement, given that the notion of a supreme and unique law, on which the constitutionality of other laws depends, does not exist.[22]

It is thus possible to consider that *Miller 1* and *Miller 2* contribute to reinforcing parliamentary sovereignty based on a prior interpretation which seemed to relativise it. The paradox is only apparent because the jurisprudence which was deployed to reduce parliamentary sovereignty was only aiming to better oversee the government texts, with regard to which Parliament's role had weakened over time. To the extent that the *Miller* decisions reduce the power of the executive, they are consistent with the framework of a sovereignty which hides the legislative dominance of the executive. In this respect, the *Miller* jurisprudence is, in part, dependent on the history of the British Constitution as it was presented by Dicey, and, more broadly, by contemporary common law constitutionalism.

In spite of Dicey's essential contribution to the construction of the principle of parliamentary sovereignty, it is on the subject of royal prerogative that the justices refer to him more freely, or at least develop a case based on Diceyan assumptions.

## II. Royal Prerogative: A Consecration of Dicey's Dynamic Approach?

As Robert Craig clearly states in his commentary on *Miller 1*, 'the literature contains two principal definitions of the Royal Prerogative. Dicey's definition is fairly straightforward and has been consistently preferred by the judiciary'.[23] Keith Ewing shares this finding: 'Although powerfully restating and applying Dicey's first principle in relation to the 1972 Act, it was with Dicey's second limb that *Miller* was principally concerned, that is to say the power of the Government by the use of the prerogative to trigger Article 50'.[24]

In *Miller 1*, the Supreme Court retained Dicey's definition without citing it but while clarifying it. According to the justices, 'the Royal prerogative encompasses the residue of powers which remain vested in the Crown, and they are exercisable by ministers, provided that the exercise is consistent with Parliamentary legislation'.[25] Remember that for Dicey 'the discretionary authority of the Crown originates generally, not in Act of Parliament, but in the "prerogative"'.[26] As with

[22] If Dicey's vision has been jeopardised, it is on the political nature he attributes to these texts which would prevent a real judicial sanction. For Dicey, the fundamentality comes from a form of protection of a political nature. In other words, the fundamentality is conceived in political and conventional terms rather than in strict judicial terms.

[23] R Craig, 'A Simple Application of the Frustration Principle' (2017) *Public Law, Brexit Special Issue* 28.

[24] K Ewing, 'Brexit and Parliamentary Sovereignty' (2017) 80 *Modern Law Review* 711, 715.

[25] *Miller 1* para 47.

[26] Dicey *Introduction* 188.

the principle of parliamentary sovereignty, the Supreme Court does not innovate by mentioning Dicey, and uses him as a premise that it is completing, interpreting, or criticising – as with any source of law. Before *Miller 1*, the Court had based itself on Dicey's analyses in relation to prerogatives, particularly the famous *Burmah Oil* dispute, cited in *Miller 1* and *2*.[27] In *Burmah Oil*, Lord Reid added two elements: the limits of Dicey's definition, nevertheless retained; and, subsequently, a more precise approach. According to him 'The definition of Dicey always quoted with approval – "the residue of discretionary or arbitrary authority, which at any given time is legally left in the hands of the Crown" does not take us very far'.[28]

In 2017, the Supreme Court's judgment in fact refers to Lord Reid, then *expressis verbis*, to the definition of prerogative given by Wade (Dicey's faithful heir) in 1961:

> [T]he residual prerogative is now confined to such matters as summoning and dissolving Parliament, declaring war and peace, regulating the armed forces in some respects, governing certain colonial territories, making treaties (though as such they cannot affect the rights of subjects), and conferring honours. The one drastic internal power of an administrative kind is the power to intern enemy aliens in time of war.[29]

Wade's support also allowed the Supreme Court to insist in *Miller 1* on the increasingly residual character of prerogative, confirming that Dicey's dynamic understanding was correct: Parliament can deliberately make it disappear, but its eclipse can also result from a necessary implication of an act of Parliament.

The continuity between *Miller 1* and Dicey is settled by the mention of passages on prerogative in *Introduction*. Dicey underlines the perplexity provoked by this residual power and the difficulties it causes in a judicial system which gives pre-eminence to the law. Prerogative is perceived as the original form of power, because what remains of 'the residue of discretionary or arbitrary authority, which at any given time is legally left in the hands of the Crown'.[30] Conscious of the gap

[27] *Burmah Oil Co v Lord Advocate* [1965] AC 75, cited in *Miller 1* paras 47, 49, and 52; and in *Miller 2* para 40.

[28] 'The definition of Dicey always quoted with approval in *Burmah*': para 21. In this same judgment, other judges, while taking up Dicey, partially criticise his presentation. Lord Radcliffe indicates: 'there is relevance in quoting Dicey's definition of the prerogative as "the residue of discretionary or arbitrary authority which at any given time is legally left in the hands of the Crown". But in Dicey's terminology every executive action not cognisable in a court of law tended to be categorised as arbitrary or irresponsible, and generations of English lawyers have since found salvation in this faith. Where we are dealing, as here, with executive acts of the Crown under the war prerogative, I should have thought that they are conspicuously not discretionary or arbitrary in any typical sense. On the contrary, they are acts of necessity, performed in sudden and extreme emergency, when there is, in effect, only one thing to be done for the public safety' (*Burmah*). His reading calls into question Dicey's overly sharp view of prerogative. While recognising the interest of the Vinerian Professor's analysis, Lord Radcliffe limits Dicey's definition of arbitrary power to exceptional circumstances. It should be noted that, to define prerogative, Lord Upjohn and Lord quote the same passage from *Introduction* to define prerogative (*Burmah*).

[29] *Miller 1* para 47.

[30] Dicey *Introduction* 188.

between this first state of the exercise of power and the rule of law, Dicey attempts to exclude it from the field of law by linking the regime of prerogative to constitutional conventions, themselves based on ethics, morals, and political deference which prevail between institutional actors. He underlines:

> that the conventions of the constitution are in the main precepts for determining the mode and spirit in which the prerogative is to be exercised, or (what is really the same thing) for fixing the manner in which any transaction which can legally be done in virtue of the Royal prerogative.[31]

This concept, described as orthodox by Lord Roskill in the *Council of Civil Service Unions v Minister for the Civil Service* decision,[32] refers on the one hand to the way the Supreme Court justices 'depoliticised' the exercise of prerogative relating to international relations[33] in *Miller 1* and *2*, and on the other to the relations between Parliament and the government regarding prorogation. By turning prerogatives into legal questions through taking into account even their indirect effects on the rights and liberties of citizens and the sovereignty of Parliament, the justices set aside in these instances the idea that prerogatives would be regulated only by constitutional conventions. In *Miller 1*, the justices make prerogative an adversely affecting act basing notification on a specific foundation: that of European Union law which is an area of domestic law.

As a result, reasoning based on the treaty making or unmaking power[34] to determine the competent body would not hold. By not making prerogative a political question based on Dicey's orthodox thought, the judge is able to extract notification from the domain of international relations. A similar conclusion can be drawn in *Miller 2*, when the Court admits the justiciability of prorogation which in principle results from the purely political relations between the executive and Parliament.

Dicey's definition thus situates itself within the descriptive statement of prerogative, but appears, despite the criticisms of the justices previously cited in *Burmah*

[31] And also 'Constitutional conventions are mainly rules for governing exercise of prerogative': Dicey *Introduction* 189.

[32] *Council of Civil Service Unions v Minister for the Civil Service* [1985] AC 374 per Lord Roskill: 'In short the orthodox view was at that time that the remedy for abuse of the prerogative lay in the political and not in the judicial field'.

[33] It should be noted that Dicey discusses conventions in the matter of treaty-making powers: 'To this it must be added that imperial treaties legally bind the colonies, and that the "treaty-making power", to use an American expression, resides in the Crown, and is therefore exercised by the home Government in accordance with the wishes of the Houses of Parliament, or more strictly of the House of Commons, whilst the authority to make treaties is, except where expressly allowed by Act of Parliament, not possessed by any colonial government': Dicey, *Introduction* 65. Dicey treats this rule as a convention. It would have been interesting had he pushed this argument further by asking about the potential role of the judge if a violation of the convention had led to an infringement of the rights and liberties of individuals.

[34] The intellectual construction is very clear: 'the Royal prerogative to make and unmake treaties, which operates wholly on the international plane, cannot be exercised in relation to the EU Treaties, at least in the absence of domestic sanction in appropriate statutory form': *Miller 1* para 86 (see also paras 87, 90, and 92).

*Oil*, as a negative presumption insofar as it allows the judge to make a constructive interpretation of the scope of prerogative, notably through its depoliticisation, turning the issue into a judicial question – which makes it possible for the judge to classify it. Prerogative evolves but is certainly not a 'relic of past age'[35] which the Supreme Court confirms by stating that it is not 'anomalous or anachronistic'.[36] It cannot be excluded from Anglo-British sources of common law. Finally, for the Court, the anomaly lies in the inability to legally decide about a measure with major impacts on the normal functioning of a parliamentary democracy governed by the rule of law. Cases that are beyond legal consideration must be reduced as much as possible, as illustrated in *Miller 2*.

In this judgment, the merits of Dicey's definition are no longer discussed and *Burmah Oil* is cited only to once again shed light on the relationship between the exercise of power of the executive and legislative authorisation.[37]

Indirect reference to Dicey on the subject can be found using jurisprudence of the House of Lords, *Council of Civil Service Unions v Minister for Civil Service* (the *CCSU* case).[38] The reference to this case makes it possible for the Supreme Court to explain what is covered by the justiciability of certain prerogatives in relation to their nature and their purpose (justifying, in 1984, explicitly excluding the decision to dissolve Parliament from all action before the judge). The *CCSU* case provides the opportunity to note a particularly rich mobilisation of doctrine beyond Dicey and a presentation of the 'orthodox' doctrine worthy of interest.

Nevertheless, it is again in the *Miller 1* judgment that indirect reference to Dicey by the intermediary of prior jurisprudence on the question of prerogative abounds. The *De Keyser*[39] case is cited several times in *Miller 1*,[40] unlike in *Miller 2* (where there is only a single occurrence).[41] Essentially, mentioning this decision has the aim of reinforcing the fact that a government cannot argue about its discretionary power linked to prerogative in order to remove itself from Parliament's control. This famous dispute from the period just after the war is probably the first leading case from the House of Lords which makes use of Dicey, Lord Dunedin proceeding by allusion.[42]

In terms of identifying direct or indirect references to Dicey to determine the judicial regime of prerogative, it must be admitted that, not only is the author essential, but also the continuity with which he is used by the judge allows one to say that his approach is a veritable source of law about prerogative. This conclusion is not without calling into question an appreciation of Dicey's work as an element

[35] Lord Reid's expression, taken up in *Miller 1* para 49.
[36] ibid.
[37] *Miller 2* para 40.
[38] See previous reference, and also *Miller 2* para 35, cited also in *Miller 1* para 52.
[39] *Attorney General v De Keyser's Royal Hotel Ltd* [1920] AC 508.
[40] *Miller 1* paras 48, 168, 170, 85, 231–36, 203, and 257.
[41] *Miller 2* para 41.
[42] 'The prerogative is defined by a learned constitutional writer as "The residue of discretionary or arbitrary authority which at any given time is legally left in the hands of the Crown"', a citation which we have seen was taken up again in *Burmah Oil*, but also in *Laker Airways Ltd v Department of Trade* [1976] EWCA Civ 10 per Lord Roskill, cited in *Miller 1* at paras 51, 168 and 235.

of the 'Old Constitution' which would be superseded by the contemporary 'New Constitution'.[43]

However, beyond the two cardinal principles of the British Constitution, Dicey does not appear explicitly, though this does not signify that his shadow does not hover over the justices' reasoning, notably relating to constitutional conventions and the referendum.

## III. Constitutional Conventions and the Referendum: A Political Dimension in Accordance with Dicey's Conclusions

On these two subjects, the Supreme Court does not embark on long discussions. The nature and the reach of conventions and the referendum decision are purely political, according to Court.[44] No judicial consequence is drawn as to the possible lack of respect for the Sewel convention (which requires that a Westminster Parliament which wants to legislate on a subject concerning the competence of devolved authorities must obtain the express agreement of the Parliaments of Scotland, Wales, or Northern Ireland).[45] This is even less the case when the argument on the particular nature of the referendum of 23 June 2016 is put forward by the lawyers for the government in *Miller 1*.[46] According to them, the referendum – because of its popular dimension – authorised the government to dispense with Parliament in order to notify the intention to withdraw,[47] because only the government should bear all the consequences of the results of an election authorised by Westminster.[48]

[43] V Bogdanor, *The New British Constitution* (Oxford, Hart Publishing, 2009) 2. Dicey and Bagehot here are the commentators on an ancient Constitution which would no longer really conform to contemporary realities, while Bogdanor supports the emergence of a new Constitution.

[44] Concerning the conventions, the political nature 'outclasses' all conclusions which could have been drawn from an organic and formal approach. In fact, the Sewel convention, having been consecrated by Parliament in an act of Parliament, the only application of a formal and organic criteria, would have led to the conclusion that the convention had become hard law, which the Supreme Court refused to admit. In the present case the origin, nature, and spirit of the relevant rule is required. For the referendum, the Supreme Court seems to limit itself to analysis of only judicial sovereignty and its protection (that of Parliament) and not to the constraint born from the expression of political sovereignty (that of the people by referendum). It should be noted that Dicey's position, rather favourable to a referendum, was to make this latter compatible with the principle of parliamentary sovereignty: see MD Walters, 'Was Dicey Diceyan?' in MD Walters, *Constitutional Tradition: A Legal Turn of Mind* (Cambridge, Cambridge University Press, 2020) 380 ff.

[45] 'Judges therefore are neither the parents nor the guardians of political conventions; they are merely observers' *Miller 1* para 146.

[46] Such as binding Parliament, for example *Miller 1* para 119 ff.

[47] *Miller 1* para 116.

[48] This interpretation is not without reference to the Referendal theory pronounced by Lord Salisbury at the end of the nineteenth century from which comes the Salisbury doctrine. According to an interpretation *a contrario* of this constitutional convention, the House of Lords cannot permanently oppose a proposed law which comes directly from the electoral program of the party which has won the general elections.

The Supreme Court did not accept this reasoning, which opposes parliamentary and popular sovereignties on the distribution of the proper competences between Cabinet and Parliament. The referendum merely indicated a political choice whose judicial effects could only result from parliamentary action.[49]

The absence of reference to Dicey does not prevent his ghost from haunting the decision of the Court in *Miller 1*. As emphasised by Mark Elliott on the conventions,

> the Court's view of the role of constitutional conventions – and of their relationship with law – is notably conservative. Judicial reticence in respect of convention chimes, of course, with Diceyan orthodoxy, and the notion that courts cannot enforce conventions is generally, albeit not universally, accepted.[50]

Beyond fidelity to the basic concept of conventions, the reference to Dicey is also indirect, through a judgment by the Supreme Court of Canada, *Resolution to Amend the Constitution*,[51] in order to characterise the nature of constitutional conventions. The Canadian jurisdiction leans rather heavily on Dicey's analyses to define conventions as political and not judicial objects.[52] In this decision, the Court indicated that the federal government's choice not to obtain the consent of the Canadian provinces with regard to modifying the Constitution was legally possible, but politically unconstitutional in light of a breach of custom. The decision of the Court led the federal executive to embark on negotiations with the provinces.[53]

The United Kingdom Supreme Court holds to the Diceyan analysis, which refers to 'other set of rules' which:

> consist of conventions, understandings, habits, or practices which, though they may regulate the conduct of the several members of the sovereign power, of the Ministry, or of other officials, are not in reality laws at all since they are not enforced by the Courts.[54]

[49] 'Where … implementation of a referendum result requires a change in the law of the land, and statute has not provided for that change, the change in the law must be made in the only way in which the UK Constitution permits, namely through Parliamentary legislation': *Miller 1* para 121.

[50] M Elliott, 'The Supreme Court's Judgment in Miller. In Search of Constitutional Principle' (2017) 76 *Cambridge Law Journal* 276–77: 'The Court's view of the role of constitutional conventions – and of their relationship with law – is notably conservative. Judicial reticence in respect of convention chimes, of course, with Diceyan orthodoxy, and the notion that courts cannot enforce conventions is generally, albeit not universally, accepted'.

[51] *Resolution to Amend the Constitution* [1981] 1 SCR 753, cited in *Miller 1* para 141.

[52] ibid 858 ff.

[53] This argument was raised again by the Lord Advocate in relation to a draft law before the Scottish Parliament aiming to organise a new referendum on independence. According to the Scottish government's representative, the British executive was acting unconstitutionally by refusing to organise a new referendum: *Reference by the Lord Advocate of devolution issues under paragraph 34 of Schedule 6 to the Scotland Act 1998* [2022] UKSC 31. The Lord Advocate explicitly cites Dicey in his argument.

[54] Dicey *Introduction* 20. See also 18: 'What is the principle on which a Cabinet may allow of open questions; these and the like are the kind of enquiries raised and solved by writers whom, as being occupied with the conventional understandings of the constitution, we may term conventionalists. These enquiries are, many of them, great and weighty; but they are not enquiries which will ever be debated in the law courts.'

In contrast, contrary to the Canadian jurisdiction, the Court refuses to discuss the infringement of convention which might lead it to distinguish between illegality (judicial) and unconstitutionality (political). Excluding such a distinction allows the United Kingdom Supreme Court to avoid recognising a purely political obligation weighing on the executive to include the devolved authorities in the process of negotiating the withdrawal from the European Union, or making the referendum of 23 July 2016 a prescriptive decision.

Notably exploited by the Supreme Court when parliamentary sovereignty and prerogative are at issue, very much present in the terms employed to characterise the Constitution's conventions, Dicey is absent from the other subjects of analysis, most prominent of which is the rule of law principle.

## IV. The Principles of the Rule of Law and Accountability: Beyond Dicey

As surprising as it may appear, Dicey is never cited on the rule of law principle, despite the latter running through the *Miller 1* judgment. There is no explicit, implicit, or indirect reference. Several reasons explain this. Without doubt the rule of law is considered by the judge as his goal, 'his thing', conformable to Dicey's thinking (the principle 'means, in the first place, the absolute supremacy or predominance of regular law as opposed to the influence of arbitrary power, and excludes the existence of arbitrariness, of prerogative, or even of wide discretionary authority on the part of the government',[55] which implies the power of the judge). However, this principle is raised in *Miller 1* as a mantra on the same basis as democracy, without precise judicial consequences having been drawn.[56] The rule of law is much more than a concept of positive law. It is not a question of pretending that the principle would not make sense – quite the contrary – but that it embraces, in some way, all the problematics and the action of the justices. The rule of law provides the framework for the judge's opinion. In this sense it is possible to consider once again that *Miller 1* is dependent on Dicey, who always thought that the relationship between parliamentary sovereignty and the rule of law was complementary. The opposite analysis is often pertinently sustained, particularly after the jurisprudence relativised parliamentary sovereignty and the identification of statutes benefiting from specific protection in the domestic judicial order. On the other hand, what is more surprising is the silence in *Miller 2* on this principle, which is not mentioned a single time, thus marking the great particularity of the decision. This characteristic is confirmed when recognising the standard of accountability.

Accountability is one of the aspects of *Miller 1* and *2* which is not dependent on a Diceyan point of departure. Only Wade is cited in this field, through the opinion

[55] Dicey *Introduction* 119.
[56] The principle is cited in *Miller 1* paras 41, 43, 53, and 151.

of Lord Lloyd of Berwick in the *Fire Brigades* case,[57] but in a sense which does not seem favourable to the justiciability of prorogation:

> No court would ever depreciate or call in question ministerial responsibility to Parliament. But as Professor Sir William Wade points out in *Wade and Forsyth, Administrative Law*, 7th ed (1994), 34, ministerial responsibility is no substitute for judicial review.

We will not attempt to artificially connect Dicey with this new standard of the British Constitution, for the moment hardly operational beyond the case being studied.[58] However it could be useful to show that this creation of the Supreme Court is not incompatible with the thought of the author of the *Introduction*. In his work, Dicey recalls that:

> The fictions of the Courts have in the hands of lawyers such as Coke served the cause both of justice and of freedom, and served it when it could have been defended by no other weapons. For there are social conditions under which legal fictions or subtleties afford the sole means of establishing that rule of equal and settled law which is the true basis of English civilisation.[59]

Is this not what the judge bound himself to in *Miller 2*, by intervening to defend the liberty of parliamentarians who 'could be defended by other means'? Without providing an appreciation of the reality of an absence of other means, or of the fact that they would not have been implemented, Dicey remains a defender of the creative power of a judge, who would not perhaps have denied the identification of accountability, even if one should always refrain from putting words into the mouths of the dead. In this respect Dicey's concept of the notion of precedent is enlightening. For him 'the appeal to precedent is in the law courts merely a useful fiction by which judicial decision conceals its transformation into judicial legislation'.[60] Common law is, for the judge, 'instrumental to some extent'.[61] Denis Baranger also emphasises that 'the Constitution is not inscribed in history, but in a proactive right',[62] a positivist nature whose emergence was sustained by Dicey's work.

* * *

Four conclusions can be drawn from this chapter. In the first place, Dicey is incontestably present in the two judgments, even if the Supreme Court's attachment

[57] *Miller 2* para 33.

[58] Notably in the context of the Covid-19 pandemic, which could have led to new applications of this principle (for an example, A Duffy, 'L'état d'exception, nouveau régime de droit commun des droits et libertés. Du terrorisme à l'urgence sanitaire. Royaume-Uni' (2021) XXXVI *Annuaire international de justice constitutionnelle* 553).

[59] Dicey *Introduction* 16.

[60] ibid 17–18.

[61] K Bouchard, *Constitutionnalisme et common law dans la pensée juridique anglo-américaine* (Paris, Classiques Garnier, 2021) 111.

[62] D Baranger, *Écrire la constitution non-écrite. Une introduction au droit politique britannique* (Paris, Presses Universitaires de France, Léviathan Collection, 2008) 185.

is more easily discerned in *Miller 1*. *Miller 2*'s originality is thus represented by the absence of explanation of a Diceyan framework which echoes the circumscribed body of jurisprudence on which the justices rely. This self-limitation is rather unprecedented, since the Court discovers a standard of constitutional law (accountability) which would have merited a more explicit doctrinal and jurisprudential foundation.

In the second place, to start with, the Court positions itself in relation to Dicey for the sole purpose of building a framework on which to deploy an evolving vision of the cardinal principles of the British Constitution, as they were presented in *Introduction*.[63] For Paul Daly, *Miller 1* joins the ancient and the new Constitutions,[64] taking into account contemporary realities which, under the influence of continental constitutionalism, the Europeanisation of law, and the major domestic constitutional changes such as devolution, no longer have much to do with Dicey.[65]

In the third place, Dicey does not escape from a form of instrumentalisation in the sense that the Supreme Court only refers to him when it suits its arguments. Dicey's pronouncements are thus prescriptive only when the Court so decides, and this is indeed what distinguishes doctrine from legislative regulatory actions as sources of law. Beyond the two decisions discussed in this chapter, the judgments of the Supreme Court pay little attention to Dicey, including when they discuss their relationship with doctrine.[66]

Finally, it is important to underline that Dicey is not the only scholar used by the justices. The influence of Paul Craig is certain, for example, but he is not explicitly cited, along with the rest of the academics whose work the Court welcomes in *Miller 1*.[67] Amongst contemporary authors, Campbell McLahlan is taken up

[63] *Miller 1* para 40: 'Our constitutional arrangements have developed over time in a pragmatic as much as in a principled way, through a combination of statutes, events, conventions, academic writings and judicial decisions. Reflecting its development and its contents, the UK Constitution was described by the constitutional scholar, Professor AV Dicey, as "the most flexible polity in existence". *Introduction to the Study of the Law of the Constitution* (8th ed, 1915) 87.'

[64] P Daly, 'Miller: Legal and Political Fault Lines' (2017) *Public Law, Brexit Special Issue* 80.

[65] Devolution led the court to interest itself in the consequences of the legislative power which the devolved parliaments disposed of over the sovereignty of the British Parliament. The Sewel convention also was subject to interpretation in light of parliamentary sovereignty which is described as 'unqualified': *The UK Withdrawal From The European Union (Legal Continuity) (Scotland) Bill* [2018] UKSC 64 para 53. This leads to just as unconditional a legislative power recognised by the British Parliament to legislate for Scotland References (Bills) by the Attorney General and the Advocate General for Scotland: *United Nations Convention on the Rights of the Child (Incorporation) (Scotland) Bill and European Charter of Local Self-Government (Incorporation) (Scotland) Bill* [2021] UKSC 42, paras 21 and 40 in particular.

[66] See, notably, Lord Reed, 'Triremes and Steamships: Scholars, Judges, and the Use of the Past' (The Scrymgeour Lecture, University of Dundee, 30 October 2015).

[67] *Miller 1* para 11: 'We have also been much assisted by a number of illuminating articles written by academics following the handing down of the judgment of the Divisional Court. It is a tribute to those articles that they have resulted in the arguments advanced before this Court being somewhat different from, and more refined than, those before that court.'

in *Miller 1* on the dualism of the British judicial order.[68] Finally, other classic authors are present. The Court uses Wade[69] twice, takes up Munro on constitutional conventions,[70] and the opinions formulated on the rule of recognition are implicitly linked to Hart.[71]

Highlighting the two *Miller* cases from Dicey's perspective reveals a certain and sincere interaction of the justices with the doctrine constituting an accessory source of law whose scope is partially prescriptive.[72] Most frequently, Dicey's work makes it possible to elaborate on a judicial statement or a discussion which can be described as academic, classic enough for judges of common law. Taking *Introduction* as a point of departure, the justices develop clear opinions, particularly on the distinction between law and politics. Invoking Dicey plays a role also, along with those of other often positivist authors,[73] in constructing public law as common law, marked by the extension of constitutionalism protecting rights and liberties and searching for a better balance of powers. Recognising the standard of accountability is an illustration of common law constitutionalism.

However, confronting the two *Miller* judgments does not make it possible to identify a clear approach to parliamentary sovereignty and the rule of law, nor to affirm that the Supreme Court confirms this or that academic theory.[74] The debate via opinions and discussions between the justices on the principle of parliamentary sovereignty as defined by Dicey is an illustration of the difficulty of envisioning the existence of an organic doctrine as coherent as that of the French Conseil d'Etat, for example. It is one more illustration of the original nature of the role of the judge in the United Kingdom who is, first, an individual authority who does not express himself in the name of the people or of any other collective authority. This results in a form of pluralism when expressing opinions which most frequently prevents debates from being decided, such as the origin of the principle of parliamentary sovereignty (the work of the judge, Parliament, constitutional and age-old political arrangements, or even doctrine?).

If Dicey remains pertinent through the fact that his work is the manifestation of a judicial culture of which the judge is the product, and sometimes the guardian, the question of his use must be approached with caution and relativism in a British

[68] ibid para 57.

[69] ibid paras 47, 48, and 50.

[70] ibid para 146. On the other hand, Jennings is not mentioned, despite his precise definition (perhaps too much so for the Court) of the constitutional conventions (see Ewing (n 23) 713).

[71] *Miller 1* para 22 Lord Neuberger and para 224 ff Lord Reed.

[72] For Marie Padilla, Dicey 'also gave the Justice a vocabulary and a grammar to pronounce and to sanction infringements of the British Constitution': M Padilla, *Droit public et doctrine publiciste au Royaume-Uni. Regard critique sur un objet à (re)construire* (PhD thesis, Université de Bordeaux, 2021) 834.

[73] Which does not prevent the Supreme Court from citing authors such as John Finnis in other disputes, even though that author instead belongs to the school of natural law constitutionalism: *R (on the application of Barclay and others) v Secretary of State for Justice and others* [2009] UKSC 9 paras 52–53 per Lady Hale.

[74] Padilla, *Droit public et doctrine publiciste* 843, 901.

constitutional law which has always been marked by change within continuity and, in the contemporary period, by the dynamic, pragmatic and creative role of the judge. In the matter of judicial review, judges continue to oscillate between the self-restraint linked to common law of the classic period and the extension of his role which Dicey envisaged with the first positivism of public law across the Channel. The tension inherent in British common law between the role of the judge, parliamentary sovereignty, and the discretionary power of the executive (which prerogative conceals) remains in part indebted to Dicey but does not offer the reader of Supreme Court decisions an appropriate analytical framework. Dicey's presentation at the end of the nineteenth century is deeply marked by his period and by Whig liberalism, even though the personal evolution and convictions of the famous author cannot confine him within the liberal mythology of the British Constitution.[75] Despite his paradoxes, his complexity and his evolutions, his thinking continues to be indispensable to the comprehension of constitutional culture. Diceyan orthodoxy favoured the success of a certain positivism and a scientific approach to law, promoting the expansion of the power of the judge. It nevertheless remains that, in the daily work of the supreme British jurisdiction, Dicey is more of a reminiscence than an oracle.

[75] Dicey finished his career at the London School of Economics whose member jurists opposed the Diceyan concept of the Constitution. He was, furthermore, resolutely opposed to Home Rule for Ireland, as were a large number of conservatives.

# 8

# The Parliamentary Executive

TIMOTHY ENDICOTT

## I. The Beekeeper

At the outset of his book on the law of the Constitution, Dicey said that earlier generations had thought of the Constitution as something that the English had constructed by instinct, 'much as bees construct a honeycomb, without undergoing the degradation of understanding the principles on which they raise a fabric more subtly wrought than any work of conscious art'.[1]

Dicey was fascinated by what the bees do – he was an observer of their conduct, and his work was distinguished by his shrewd and novel focus on 'understanding the principles'. He was not a historian, and in fact he was wary of history. He concluded the preface to the first edition of his book by saying that the historical method, universally admired at the time, 'may induce men to think so much of the way in which an institution has come to be what it is, that they cease to consider with sufficient care what it is that an institution has become'.[2] The huge success of Dicey's book has a moral for any legal academic: give a statement of the principles that everyone will want to disagree with, and your work will be famous.

Contrast Dicey's title – *Introduction to the Study of the Law of the Constitution* – with the title of the very fine book published at about the same time by his friend and close colleague William Anson, the Warden of All Souls: *The Law and Custom of the Constitution*. In his preface, Anson wrote concerning Dicey that, 'He has done the work of an artist. I have tried to do the work of a surveyor'.[3] He said that he had tried 'to state the law relating to existing institutions, with so much of history as is necessary to explain how they have come to be what they are'.[4]

That was precisely the approach that Dicey had rejected. Anson's book sparkles with intelligent insights. For a law student in the 1880s, I think that it would

[1] AV Dicey, *Introduction to the Study of the Law of the Constitution*, 8th edn (London, MacMillan and Co, 1915) 3.
[2] ibid viii.
[3] W Anson, *The Law and Custom of the Constitution* (Oxford, Clarendon Press,1886) vi.
[4] ibid v.

have been just as good an introduction to the Constitution as Dicey's book, or better. Right from his title, Anson showed good sense by setting the constitutional significance of law and custom on a par, where Dicey distorted his account of the constitution by insisting that his subject was 'the Law of the Constitution'.[5] But Anson's excellent book is forgotten these days because it sprawled into two volumes, heavily laden with history, and he largely left it to his readers to identify the principles of the Constitution. It is a book with which is it not easy to disagree. Dicey's book, by contrast, is being read today; it exerts influence by giving other people something to disagree with.

Dicey's book also survives because the Constitution itself has survived. I will not focus on the two 'principles' that he identified: the rule of law and the sovereignty of Parliament. I want to focus on the surprisingly sustainable central structural element in the Constitution, which Dicey called 'the parliamentary executive'.[6] Dicey discerned the central features of the British scheme of executive governance. But in my attempt to articulate those features in this essay, I will follow in the long tradition of disagreeing with Dicey. I will be engaged in the same enterprise he undertook, trying to point out what is salient and worthwhile in the Constitution of the United Kingdom – what law students ought to grasp about it.

Then, I will outline how the parliamentary executive has survived the vicissitudes of the century since Dicey – a century in which the executive functions of the British government and their legal and political and constitutional context have changed fundamentally. Like Dicey, I am not actually aiming to do history, but to understand what the bees have constructed – what it is that the institution of executive government has become.

Here is the gist of my argument: the resilience and the usefulness of the parliamentary executive are demonstrated by the fact that the *very same constitutional device* serves the United Kingdom well in the changed conditions of the twenty-first century. It is a controversial argument to make, when so many people think that the way in which the United Kingdom Constitution institutes executive government is defective. In my conclusion, I will try to support my upbeat assessment through a discussion of Dicey's conjecture in 1915: in the future as he contemplated it – in our present day – he speculated that the parliamentary executive might evolve into a non-parliamentary executive, in which the House of Commons would function as an electoral college for a presidential government. I think it is very revealing that we have not moved in that direction, in spite of what anyone will tell you. That fact supports my conclusion about the sustainable usefulness of the parliamentary executive in changing political circumstances.

[5] In 'Dicey and Analytical Jurisprudence' in A Dickinson et al (eds), *Dicey + 100* (Cambridge, Intersentia, 2024) I argue that his focus on the law knocked his presentation of the Constitution somewhat off kilter, as if the structure of executive power were peripheral to the concerns of a constitutional lawyer.

[6] It is only the political leadership of the executive branch of government that is parliamentary (and not, eg, the military or the police or the National Health Service), but I will follow Dicey in using the term 'executive' for that leadership – ie in the United Kingdom case, the Ministers of the Crown.

There is something valuable in the parliamentary executive; it belongs with parliamentary sovereignty and the rule of law, right in the foreground of a clear picture of the United Kingdom Constitution.

## II. The Structure of Executive Government

From the first edition of his book, Dicey addressed the executive rather obliquely in the discussion of the conventions of the Constitution in chapters XIV and XV. But starting with his fourth edition in 1893, you will also find it described in Note III in the Appendix, 'Distinction between a Parliamentary Executive and a Non-Parliamentary Executive'.[7] Dicey wrote in the preface to his fourth edition that the subject of Note III 'is of some novelty, and will be found to possess considerable importance'.[8] By the phrase 'parliamentary executive', he meant a form of representative government in which the legislature 'appoints and dismisses the executive'. The members of the executive are 'chosen from among the members of the legislative body',[9] and they 'hold office at the pleasure of parliament'.[10] He distinguished it from non-parliamentary regimes in which the executive is 'not appointed by the legislature';[11] he had in mind the United States in particular. In sum:

> The Cabinet is, in reality and in fact, a parliamentary executive, for it is in truth chosen, though by a very indirect process, and may be dismissed by the House of Commons, and its members are invariably selected from among the members of one or other House of Parliament.[12]

The influence of Walter Bagehot is evident here, in the insight about the significance of the Cabinet and also in the distinction between reality and appearance:

> in appearance and in name, the Cabinet is now what it originally was, a non-parliamentary executive; every Minister is the servant of the Crown, and is in form appointed and dismissible, not by the House of Commons, nor by the Houses of Parliament, but by the King.[13]

[7] AV Dicey, *Introduction to the Study of the Law of the Constitution*, 4th edn (London, MacMillan and Co, 1893); I will refer to Note III as it appeared in Dicey 1915, 480 ff.

[8] Dicey 1893, *Introduction to the Study of the Law of the Constitution* iv.

[9] Dicey 1915, *Introduction to the Study of the Law of the Constitution* 480–81.

[10] ibid 482.

[11] ibid 481.

[12] ibid 483. Consider also this remark in the discussion of conventions in ch 14: 'the elective portion of the legislature in effect, though by an indirect process, appoints the executive government': 426.

[13] ibid 483. Dicey's debt to Bagehot is very significant; in the preface to his first edition, he mentioned 'works like Bagehot's incomparable *English Constitution*, which analyse the practical working of our complicated system of modern Parliamentary government', and said that he had a different purpose, because his book was 'a treatise on the principles of the law of the constitution': vi.

I think that there is great insight in describing the evolution of the Constitution from the 1660s to the 1880s as a movement from a non-parliamentary to a parliamentary executive. By the time of Dicey and Bagehot, relations between the ministry and the House of Commons had been transformed from what they were under Charles II, or even under George III. And Dicey appreciated the value of the new device. Executive government had become accountable to MPs in the House of Commons, in a form of responsible government – by which I mean that the executive was not free to act in whatever self-interested way it saw fit, but had to respond to the views of representatives of the electors. Dicey explained that 'a rule which gives the appointment and control of the government mainly to the House of Commons is at bottom a rule which gives the election and ultimate control of the executive to the nation'.[14]

Yet it seems to me that both Dicey and Bagehot misdescribed those relations. It is true that the members of the executive are 'chosen from among the members of the legislative body', and also that the executive holds office at the pleasure of the House of Commons, since (by a convention that was relatively new in Dicey's day) the Prime Minister and the whole government must resign after a vote of no confidence. But the legislature does not appoint the executive, and it did not do so in Dicey's day. It is not even the case that the executive is 'chosen, though by a very indirect process' by the House of Commons.[15] Perhaps Dicey got the idea from Bagehot, who made the same misstatement of the case: 'A cabinet government is the government of a committee elected by the legislature'.[16] Appointing, choosing, electing – these are intentional actions that an agent or an agency undertakes. But the House of Commons *does nothing* to make a person Prime Minister, or to fill any of the positions in the Cabinet. I think that it is an important aspect of the Constitution that a Prime Minister is not chosen by the House of Commons.

It may seem to make no difference, since the Prime Minister is chosen by the monarch on the basis of the number of MPs from each party in the House of Commons. You can, of course, see how Dicey came to say that the House of Commons appoints or elects a Prime Minister. But the best we can say for it is that he was speaking figuratively, perhaps as a way of emphasising the importance of executive accountability to the House of Commons. And as a figure of speech, this one is misleading.

After Lord Salisbury's coalition won 393 out of 670 seats in House of Commons in the general election of July 1886, Queen Victoria invited him to form a government; after Boris Johnson's party won 365 out of 650 seats in the general election of December 2019, Queen Elizabeth invited him to form a government. Perhaps in 1886, Victoria still thought of it as a matter of prudence on her part, to choose as her Prime Minister a man who could command the confidence of the House of

[14] ibid 426–27.

[15] *cf*: '... indirectly appointed by Parliament' (ibid 424), and Dicey's reference to Parliament's 'ability to appoint and dismiss the executive' (ibid 481). He held tenaciously to this idea.

[16] W Bagehot, *The English Constitution*, 2nd edn (Boston, Little, Brown, and Co, 1873) 191.

Commons. By 2019, Queen Elizabeth undoubtedly viewed it, instead, as her iron-clad constitutional duty (whatever she might think about the person in question). But still under Elizabeth II and under Charles III, it has remained constitutionally significant that it is the monarch, and not the House of Commons, who appoints the Prime Minister. In the appointment of a Prime Minister, there was in Dicey's time and there is today *no decision* for the House of Commons to take, *no business* for it to conduct. MPs have no power to decide. When a Prime Minister is appointed, they may well hear about it on the BBC. Likewise, when the Prime Minister advises the monarch on the appointment of ministers.

Dicey mentioned the election of a head of the executive by the National Assembly in the French Third Republic,[17] and the difference between that arrangement and the British parliamentary executive ought to have been in the front of his mind. It mattered that the National Assembly had to deliberate over the appointment, and that it was the responsibility of its members to make the appointment. The imaginary world in which the House of Commons elects a Prime Minister would be significantly different from the actual world. First of all, the symbolism that such arrangements carry would differ, making the Prime Minister beholden to the House for his or her appointment, and severing the symbolically significant notion of obligation to the Crown. In the real world, the Prime Minister is appointed by the monarch, and is at the mercy of a House of Commons that can force a resignation. In the imaginary world, the Prime Minister would owe his or her position to a decision of the House of Commons.

The difference is not only symbolic. Suppose that after each general election (or when a Prime Minister resigns), in the imaginary world, the House of Commons needed to meet to elect a new Prime Minister. After a general election like those in 1886 or 2019, everyone would know perfectly well who would be about to win the election in the House. But what about the 2010 general election (resulting in 306 seats for the Conservatives, 258 for Labour, and 57 for the Liberal Democrats)? In the real world, the allocation of executive power in 2010 was worked out through a negotiation behind closed doors among parties, until the discussions reached the point at which David Cameron had a coalition with the Liberal Democrats, so that it was clear to the Queen that he could command the confidence of the House. In the imaginary world, there would no doubt still be negotiations behind the scenes, but the *scene* itself would be a debate or a series of debates in the House of Commons. In the imaginary world, Gordon Brown's speech in the House of Commons in a debate on a resolution to elect David Cameron as Prime Minister would itself have been a significant political event.

Or consider the 2017 election, in which Theresa May's deeply divided Conservative Party lost its majority: in the imaginary world, the choice of Prime Minister in such a case would not be determined simply by party membership but by unpredictable ad hoc politicking, in which party divisions would create

[17] Dicey 1915, *Introduction to the Study of the Law of the Constitution* 483.

the possibility that rebellion or the crossing of the floor by a small number of MPs might bring down the leader of the party with the most seats.

If you want to picture an imaginary world in which the House of Commons elects a Prime Minister, consider the election of a Speaker in the United States House of Representatives: an appointment process decided by a vote of the House, the results of which can usually be predicted with confidence by counting party membership in the House. Usually, but not necessarily. When the Republican Party was divided in 2023, the election proceedings after the ousting of Speaker Kevin McCarthy became disruptive and unpredictable, and the very fact that the election ordinarily proceeds on party lines gave a particular political tenor and significance to radical politicking. In the appointment of a Prime Minister in the UK, it is significant that there is no such proceeding. If a Speaker of the US House of Representatives were appointed by a third party on the basis of the number of registered Republicans and Democrats in the House, then the 2023 opposition to McCarthy would have played out within the Republican conference, controlled by the party machine. It would not be business for the House, and McCarthy's position would have been solid.

So, I think it was a mistake for Bagehot and Dicey to say that the legislature elects the executive. I also think that Dicey misstated the implications of the vulnerability of a government to being thrown out on a vote of no confidence. He said that once the tenure in office of the executive is at the pleasure of the House of Commons, 'parliamentary government has reached its full development and been transformed into government by parliament'.[18] To be charitable, we might say that this was a figurative way of speaking by which Dicey was presumably trying to point out the importance of Parliament to the executive. However charitably we put it, though, we should see that the central functions of the House of Commons are not as a government agency, but as a legislative chamber, which serves as a *forum* in which the actual government – the ministers of the Crown – can be held to account or can be forced out of office.

The Cabinet is not an instrumentality by which the House of Commons carries out its policies. The House of Commons does not even have policies; the parties with seats in the House have policies. The House does not conduct the executive business of government – not even indirectly. And the government does not form or implement policy on behalf of the House of Commons. As a body, the House of Commons can throw a government out. But it cannot tell the government what to do. The House of Commons has no power of review over executive action. It cannot countermand an executive decision. Executive government in the United Kingdom is not government by Parliament. It is government by a ministry that is accountable to Parliament, and that is formed on the basis of party representation in the House of Commons.

[18] ibid 483.

The nature of the parliamentary executive is determined not only by the appointment of a Prime Minister, but also by the ways in which people stop being Prime Minister. Prime Ministers tender their resignation to the monarch, not to the House of Commons.[19] When, as Lord Rosebery did in 1895, a Prime Minister decides to resign after losing a vote in the House of Commons, the notion is that they owe it to their monarch to resign, because without the support of the House of Commons, they cannot carry out the service they owe to the monarch. They owe nothing similar to the House of Commons. To that House, they owe the duties of any MP, plus leadership in the deliberations of the House, plus readiness to answer questions in the House candidly and honestly on behalf of the government. Their executive duties are owed to the nation, and to the Crown, and to particular persons or groups affected by their decisions, and do not involve any duty to carry out the will of the House of Commons; they simply face the predicament that the House can force them to resign, any day, for any reason that a majority of MPs may consider sufficient.

Prime Ministerial resignations offer a poignant reminder of the character of the parliamentary executive. Consider a very dramatic difference between heads of government in the UK and in the non-parliamentary executive of the United States. In the United States, of 45 Presidents since 1789, only one – Richard Nixon – has resigned for political reasons during the four-year term of office. Three have been impeached, none of whom was removed from office. In the United Kingdom, just since 1945, *ten out of sixteen* British Prime Ministers have resigned while holding a majority in the House of Commons, without losing a vote of confidence or an election: Winston Churchill. Anthony Eden. Harold MacMillan. Harold Wilson. Margaret Thatcher. Tony Blair. David Cameron. Theresa May. Boris Johnson. Liz Truss. Each resigned the powerful office of Prime Minister for political reasons, while holding a majority that would not or could not help them; the list includes every Prime Minister in this century except Gordon Brown (who lost a general election) and Rishi Sunak. A majority in the House of Commons makes a person Prime Minister but does not give a Prime Minister tenure in power.

Think of two Prime Ministers who won large majorities in the House of Commons: Margaret Thatcher and Boris Johnson. The Constitution gave them extraordinary power as head of the government, and their party's majority gave them excellent prospects in securing passage of legislation, and the magnitude of their electoral successes made them seem invincible. But their power vanished when they undermined their own MPs' sense that their leadership would bring success at the next election. And when their ministers started resigning, each moved out of Downing Street into other accommodation. As for Johnson's successor, Liz Truss, it took less than two months for her premiership to be destroyed by

[19] That is still the case today: after losing a general election, the government stays in office until 'the Prime Minister tenders his or her resignation and the Government's resignation to the Sovereign': Cabinet Office, *The Cabinet Manual* (2011) 14.

the same mechanism: ordinary politics, focused by the Prime Minister's constitutional need for support in the House of Commons. Once more, a vote of no confidence was not needed; she had to go when her ministers started resigning. In her resignation statement on 20 October 2022, she said,

> I came into office at a time of great economic and international instability. Families and businesses were worried about how to pay their bills. Putin's illegal war in Ukraine threatens the security of our whole continent. And our country has been held back by for too long by low economic growth. I was elected by the Conservative Party with a mandate to change this.[20]

Notice that Liz Truss was only elected as *party leader* by the Conservative Party. She came into office as Prime Minister because Queen Elizabeth dutifully appointed the new leader of a party that had a majority in the House of Commons. I propose that in the best interpretation of the parliamentary executive, it is a structure of governance that confers *no personal mandate whatsoever*. Unlike the American presidency, it does not confer a term of office. The rules expose the Prime Minister to the arbitrary say-so of MPs who can throw out any government at any time. Anything that could be well described as a 'mandate' comes only from whatever dispositions the MPs of the Prime Minister's party may have to support the Prime Minister. The associated political pressure on the Prime Minister is intense and irresistible. When things are going well, as they did for Thatcher for years, for Johnson for months, and for Truss for a few days, that is because their MPs are content.

The executive is indeed parliamentary, as Dicey put it, but not in the sense that Parliament elects the executive, or that Parliament makes executive decisions. It does neither. The executive is parliamentary in the sense that a Prime Minister is appointed on the basis of a presumed capacity to command the confidence of the House of Commons, and in the sense that the Prime Minister and all the ministers are accountable in Parliament, and in the sense that they can be forced to resign in Parliament.

## III. Flux in the Structure

The functions and operations of executive government were changing in Dicey's time and have changed since. I want to point out some of the changes, to set the scene for an argument as to the ongoing value of the parliamentary executive for the present and the future.

The first change to notice since Dicey is that the British Empire has been dismantled, and the Cabinet has lost its executive and legislative powers over some

[20] See 'Liz Truss Resignation Speech in Full' (*The Guardian*, 20 October 2022), https://www.theguardian.com/politics/2022/oct/20/liz-truss-resignation-speech-in-full.

aspects of government for a quarter of the world. The Empire was never static, and the dismantling process had already started before Dicey wrote his book, with Canadian self-government in 1867. It was largely completed by the wave of Caribbean and African decolonisation a century later.

Just before Dicey's death, the United Kingdom itself had been torn apart when the Anglo-Irish Treaty created the Irish Free State in 1921. Dicey had been right to foresee that Irish Home Rule, introduced by the Government of Ireland Act 1914 (the first statute passed via the Parliament Act 1911), would lead to independence. He had been vehemently opposed to Home Rule for any part of the United Kingdom (notice the tone of voice in his discussion of it).[21] In the twenty-first century, we have ended up with Home Rule in Scotland and Wales and Northern Ireland, and Dicey would no doubt have been averse to those devolutions, too. I think that those arrangements have not actually deprived Parliament in Westminster of its sovereignty (I cannot defend that view here; perhaps Dicey would have disagreed). But the establishment of devolved executives in Scotland, Wales, and Northern Ireland has very materially changed the role of the parliamentary executive in Westminster.

The democratisation of Parliament had been largely attained in Dicey's lifetime by the advent of votes for women and the removal of property requirements for men in the Representation of the People Act 1918. But it was only after Dicey that the Representation of the People Act 1928 gave women the vote on the same basis as men. Since then, democracy has changed the background to executive government, because of a feature of the parliamentary executive that is precisely the same today as it was in 1885: the parliamentary executive is very acutely subject to the power of the electors. So universal adult suffrage has changed the power dynamics of the executive. The electoral reforms of 1832 and 1867 were important in principle and substance, and so was the advent of the secret ballot in 1872. But when Dicey wrote his first edition in 1885, the parties' prospects at a general election – and therefore the prospects for forming or sustaining a ministry – were in the hands of a male franchise that was still very deliberately designed to exclude men without property. Those men were presumed not to have the stake in good government that men of property had, or to be vulnerable to undue influence because of their poverty, or both. When Dicey wrote that the parliamentary executive 'gives the election and ultimate control of the executive to the nation',[22] he was going along with those presumptions, counting decisions of the men with property as the decisions of the nation. Today, the adult franchise means that the parliamentary executive is democratic, and a successful government never forgets it.

[21] Dicey 1915, *Introduction to the Study of the Law* civ–cviii; see also Dicey 1887, *Introduction to the Study of the Law* and M Mulholland 'Revolution and the Rule of Law: Dicey on Irish Home Rule' in Dickinson et al (eds), *Dicey + 100* (Cambridge, Intersentia, 2024).

[22] Dicey 1915, *Introduction to the Study of the Law of the Constitution* 426–27.

Since 1945, the burgeoning welfare-and-regulatory-and-administrative state has also changed the executive, which now presides over a dramatically broadened range of governmental functions involving a more complex assemblage of institutions. Many of the new institutions have forms of independence in making government policy and in oversight (just think of the Monetary Policy Committee of the Bank of England), and some of them constrain the executive in new ways, and some of them carry out executive functions. I expect that the increased complexity of contemporary governance must have, to some extent, driven the growth in the parliamentary leadership of the executive itself: Rishi Sunak's government had 109 ministers, 23 of them in the Cabinet. In 1874, Disraeli's cabinet of 12 men ruled an empire. But I wonder if such populous ministries have also been a technique of management of the parliamentary executive, since they offer opportunities for giving incentives, and a way of getting 109 MPs to commit themselves to support government policy. Perhaps Dicey would count the bloated ministries of the twenty-first century as another increase in party government.

The forms of accountability of the executive outside the House of Commons have been transformed since Dicey's day; they include judicial review that is in some ways much more wide-ranging and more intrusive than in 1885, and also ombudsmen and tribunals, and public consultations on policy making, and freedom of information, and data protection. And processes within the House of Commons have changed since 1885, particularly through changes to the committee structures.

The operation of the parliamentary executive has been transformed through the progressive ascendancy of the House of Commons over the House of Lords since 1885. The great landmark in that ascendancy was the Parliament Act 1911; in his eighth edition in 1915 Dicey copied it into the appendix and said 'The Parliament Act is the last and greatest triumph of party government'.[23] That was a lament.

The ascendancy of the House of Commons has not only changed the legislature; it has changed executive government. When Lord Salisbury resigned (after a split in his Cabinet) in 1902, it would not have been obvious that he would be the last Prime Minister to run a government from the House of Lords. But some had already considered that the Prime Minister should be in the House of Commons. By 1940, Lord Halifax thought that he could not lead a government from the House of Lords after Chamberlain's resignation, because of 'the difficult position of a Prime Minister unable to make contact with the centre of gravity in the House of Commons'.[24] Things have changed further since then: it is not just a difficult position, it is unthinkable. And whereas Disraeli's Cabinet had six peers and six commoners, the only Cabinet ministers from the House of Lords in Rishi Sunak's government were the government's representative to the peers (the Leader

[23] ibid cx, 557.
[24] See https://history.blog.gov.uk/2013/04/24/prime-ministers-in-the-house-of-lords/.

of the House of Lords), and the very exceptional case of David Cameron as Foreign Secretary; 25 of the 86 junior ministers were in the House of Lords, the rest were in the House of Commons.

This list of changes since Dicey's time in the role and operation of the parliamentary executive is only meant to be illustrative; other significant changes could be added (I have not even mentioned the decline of the Liberals and the rise of Labour, or the ways in which 47 years in the EU changed British governance, or the transformation of communications media ...). I think the changes I have jotted down support a striking conclusion: that the basic structure of the parliamentary executive is *just the same today* as in 1885, and has the same constitutional value, even though political and constitutional circumstances have changed dramatically.

Let me explain by outlining two changes in the rules of the parliamentary executive itself, both of which have further reduced the vestigial role of the monarch since Dicey's day: change in the way in which the monarch decides whom to appoint as Prime Minister; and the new convention that the monarch must not dismiss a Prime Minister who has the confidence of the House of Commons.

## A. Choice of a Prime Minister

How is the monarch to choose whom to appoint as Prime Minister? Dicey said that 'The party who for the time being command a majority in the House of Commons, have (in general) a right to have their leaders placed in office', and, 'The most influential of these leaders ought (generally speaking) to be the Premier, or head of the Cabinet'.[25] It is a reminder that in Dicey's day, as now, it would be utterly impossible for the monarch to work out who could command the confidence of the House of Commons without the parties. Say what you like about them, we could not have a parliamentary executive without political parties.

Today, the *Cabinet Manual* offers a straightforward doctrine that the ability to command the confidence of the House of Commons is the defining qualification for a Prime Minister.[26] The crucial change since Dicey's day is that the main political parties have taken over the decision as to which person is to form a ministry, if the party has a majority. In Dicey's day, if a party won a majority, the question of which of its leaders was 'the most influential' could only be answered by an open-ended assessment of the political situation. It might be entirely obvious, but then again it might call for a sensitive grasp of the mood of a party, and the tendencies and expectations and allegiances and divisions of party members, and it might call for good judgement as to how things were likely to develop. The need for such an assessment gave Queen Victoria a significant resulting discretion.

[25] Dicey 1915, *Introduction to the Study of the Law of the Constitution* 417.
[26] Cabinet Office, *The Cabinet Manual* (2011) 14.

But Queen Elizabeth II was dutifully committed to exercising no such discretion. To avoid having to do so, she needed the parties to resolve the matter, and they have all developed selection processes for a party leader, settling the matter for the monarch. This change represents a further step since Dicey's day in the removal of the monarch's power over the executive.

The change really began with Edward Heath's 1965 election by Conservative MPs under new rules; since then, that party's rules have changed further, and Liz Truss's election as party leader and her 49 days in office as Prime Minister of the United Kingdom were due to the system of electing a party leader by vote of all party members. Conservative MPs would have chosen Rishi Sunak, but the rules put the decision in the hands of a constituency that was evidently swayed by Truss's dramatic plan to cut their taxes.[27] When Truss was forced to resign, the party carefully ensured that its party members would not get another choice of that kind, by modifying the rules so that there would only be one candidate. The fiasco shows a distinct drawback of the twenty-first-century parliamentary executive: selection of a Prime Minister may result not from a general election, but from a vote by members of a political club. The leading parties (Conservatives, Labour, Liberal Democrats, Scottish National Party) all have one-member-one-vote processes (with various requirements of support for nominations from the party's MPs or members). It is easy for a party to pretend that a vote by party members is democratic, but their members are not the *demos*. Their processes would be more democratic if a leader were chosen in such a situation by the parliamentary party, ie by the party's MPs. They, at least, were elected by actual voters, and are answerable in a general election.

## B. Dismissing a Ministry

Dicey thought that 'there are certainly combinations of circumstances under which the Crown has a right to dismiss a Ministry who command a Parliamentary majority'.[28] He viewed it as protection against representatives who pursue policies that the voters do not actually support: 'A dissolution is allowable, or necessary, whenever the wishes of the legislature are, or may fairly be presumed to be, different from the wishes of the nation'.[29]

Today, by contrast, 'Prime Ministers hold office unless and until they resign'.[30] That pithy proclamation is in the *Cabinet Manual* – a statement of the rules of the parliamentary executive that was prepared by the Cabinet Secretary in 2011

[27] For a description of the process, see 'How Liz Truss Won the Conservative Leadership Race' (*BBC*, 5 September 2022), https://www.bbc.com/news/uk-politics-60037657.

[28] Dicey 1915, *Introduction to the Study of the Law of the Constitution* 428.

[29] ibid 429.

[30] Cabinet Office, *The Cabinet Manual* (2011) 14. This document, drafted by the Cabinet Secretary, Sir Gus O'Donnell, 'records rules and practices, but is not intended to be the source of any rule': iv.

at the request of Prime Minister David Cameron, in an initiative started by his predecessor, Gordon Brown. The *Manual* goes on to comment that 'Historically, the Sovereign has made use of reserve powers to dismiss a Prime Minister or to make a personal choice of successor, although this was last used in 1834 and was regarded as having undermined the Sovereign'.[31]

I think that it is patently sound to say that it is now a constitutional convention that the monarch cannot dismiss a Prime Minister who has the confidence of the House of Commons. I say so not only because of the regular practice since 1834, but because of a crucial matter of impression: that the sense of the role of the monarch today, in political circles, includes a shared opinion that he or she must not interfere with the democratic, representative executive.

Yet Dicey thought that in his time, the monarch's power to dismiss a ministry because of its policies was not only accepted by the political classes as constitutional, but was also supported by constitutional principle. As Dicey said with his accustomed candour, 'This looks at first sight like saying that in certain cases the prerogative can be so used as to set at nought the will of the nation'.[32] But he argued that it is, on the contrary, a protection against a problem with representative democracy: that 'the wishes of the legislature' might diverge from 'the wishes of the nation'.[33] The principle at stake was 'the fundamental principle of our existing Constitution that not Parliament but the nation is, politically speaking, the supreme power in the State'.[34] And he saw the authority of the House of Commons to be entirely derivative from the authority of its electors. Dicey thought that Queen Victoria could remove a government with a majority in the House of Commons (in fact, he thought that it was her duty to do so), if she could see that its policies were adverse to the will of the people.

A constitutional mechanism that would allow King Charles III to dismiss a misbehaving Prime Minister has an obvious advantage: it would authorise the King to solve a perennial problem with political representation. How are the current representatives to be forced to represent the people faithfully? Dicey thought that a parliamentary executive 'is likely to become the creature of the parliament by which it is created, and to share, though in a modified form, the weaknesses which are inherent in the rule of an elective assembly'.[35] If we had an authority that could decree that the government should face the electorate forthwith instead of years later, that might give the electorate the actual say just when it needs to have a say. And the mere possibility would structure the government's operations, incentivising the government not to act so as give the monarch cause, or even ostensible cause, to bring about such a crisis.

[31] ibid 14.
[32] Dicey 1915, *Introduction to the Study of the Law of the Constitution* 428.
[33] ibid 429.
[34] ibid 431.
[35] ibid 484.

But you see the drawback – the reason why it is constitutionally unthinkable for the Crown to exercise such authority today: the putatively democratic device would be a monarchical power of government. The idea that a monarch might legitimately do what William IV did in 1834 is the clearest survival of the institutional power of the monarch in Dicey's work. In 1834, the King did not trust the radical reformers among Lord Melbourne's Whig majority. The King dismissed Melbourne and his ministry and appointed Sir Robert Peel, a conservative. Peel formed a ministry, but failed to put together enough support to govern, and had to ask the King to dissolve Parliament to make way for a new general election. The Whigs won the election convincingly by 385 seats to 273, and after that it was obviously politically necessary for the King to put up with Melbourne as Prime Minister. Dicey wrote that whether the King's decision had been compatible with the principles of the constitution depended on 'the still disputable question of fact, whether the King and his advisers had reasonable ground for supposing that the reformed House of Commons had lost the confidence of the nation'.[36] You see what a dramatic monarchical power Dicey attributed to the monarch: it was the same power of dismissal of a government that the House of Commons wields in a vote of no confidence, with the proviso that the King was meant to exercise it on the basis of his sense of the mind of the voters. Dicey had inherited the mid-Victorian liberal picture of a mixed constitution in which the democratic element was on the one hand balanced and on the other hand protected by non-democratic structures of authority that were familiar to William Blackstone.

If Dicey's sense of things was behind the times, I do not think it was very far behind the times. But Queen Elizabeth II, with her well-informed and sensitive instinct for the requirements of the Constitution, knew that she had no authority to dismiss a government that was supported by a majority in the House of Commons. Today, the Constitution has given up the protection for democracy that, in Dicey's view, a monarch might provide by acting on his or her own assessment of a 'disputable question of fact': whether the House of Commons has lost the confidence of the nation.

## IV. Conclusion: Dicey's Conjecture

Dicey thought the Parliament Act was 'the last and greatest triumph of party government'. What would he have thought of events in 2022? Party members selected Liz Truss as Prime Minister; she thought she had a mandate from the Conservative Party. The parties' own processes have taken over from the monarch in deciding who should be selected as Prime Minister if the party attains a majority in a general election. And the monarch cannot protect the electors against a party with a majority by forcing a general election.

[36] ibid 432.

Some, indeed, have thought that we have abandoned the parliamentary executive for a presidential system. Take Jacob Rees-Mogg, who served as a Cabinet minister under Boris Johnson and Liz Truss. In the early days of the trouble that led to Boris Johnson's resignation, while Rees-Mogg was Leader of the House of Commons, he told the BBC that 'we have moved, for better or worse, to an essentially presidential system. Therefore the mandate is personal rather than entirely party … any prime minister would be very well advised to seek a fresh mandate'.[37] Rees-Mogg was suggesting that if Boris Johnson were forced to resign, there ought to be a general election to secure a new, personal mandate for a new, presidential Prime Minister (presumably, he was offering his colleagues friendly advice against opposing Johnson). There is that word 'mandate' again. I propose that Boris Johnson, like any Prime Minister in the parliamentary executive, *had no mandate*: he was holding power at the pleasure of his party's MPs, and he only held it until he displeased them. If you want to call it a 'mandate', it is a mandate that is revocable at the drop of a hat.

The leader of a party may well have personal support among the voters that leads decisively to that party's securing a majority (I am sure that was the case in the December 2019 general election). That makes no change in our Constitution, which has simply preserved the parliamentary executive that had emerged by the 1880s. And indeed, the downfall of Johnson and then of Truss illustrates it in action. The head of government is radically dependent on the political judgement and sensibilities and action of Members of Parliament.

Dicey himself, in Note III on the parliamentary executive in his final edition, had said that already in 1915, 'a general election may be in effect, though not in name, a popular election of a particular statesman to the Premiership',[38] and he engaged in a conjecture about the future – that is, about our days:

> It is a matter of curious speculation, whether the English Cabinet may not at this moment be undergoing a gradual and, as yet, scarcely noticed change of character, under which it may be transformed from a parliamentary into a non-parliamentary executive. … the time may come when, though all the forms of the English constitution remain unchanged, an English Prime Minister will be as truly elected to office by a popular vote as is an American President.[39]

He was thinking of the Electoral College system in the US: a body of representatives of the people, elected to choose a president. A conventional rule had very swiftly developed (certainly by the 1830s) that ran just contrary to the design of the founders: a rule that those sent to the Electoral College were not free to use their own judgement, but had a duty to vote in favour of the candidate they had been

[37] K Nicholson, 'Jacob Rees-Mogg Now Thinks the UK is "Essentially" a Presidency' (*Huffington Post*, 26 January 2022) https://www.huffingtonpost.co.uk/entry/jacob-rees-mogg-partygate-presidency_uk_61f1210ae4b04f9a12b68d00.

[38] Dicey 1915, *Introduction to the Study of the Law of the Constitution* 483.

[39] ibid 483.

elected to support. I want to conclude by pointing out how deeply different the role of an MP in the House of Commons is today, from the role of an elector sent to the Electoral College in the US.

It is crucial that MPs are legislators, each with a vote on every Bill presented before Parliament. It is crucial that they are constituency representatives, in a political culture in which each is expected to attend to concerns and complaints of constituents (or, at least, to assemble a team that will do it). I have argued that they do not select a Prime Minister; the monarch does that on the basis of the mere fact that a particular number were elected as a party's candidates. It is crucial that, unlike the members of the US Electoral College, they can vote a government out of office. And that role – reflecting the requirement of the confidence of the House of Commons – is embedded in their general political role as constituency representatives in a legislature. But they do not generally need to hold a vote of no confidence in order to force a Prime Minister out. Votes of no confidence brought down ministries more than a dozen times in the nineteenth century; since then, they have only succeeded in 1924 (twice) and in 1979. In another significant development of party government, the destruction of a premiership ordinarily takes place not by a vote of no confidence, but through irresistible pressures within the governing party. The Cabinet itself serves an accountability function, because the ministers are still (just as much as in Dicey's day) leaders in the party, with the opportunity to catalyse the downfall of a Prime Minister.

So – for good and ill – we have party government in a *stronger* form than in Dicey's day. But we still have a parliamentary executive. It still gives the UK responsible executive government. Does it yield good government? Yes, of course it does, if the Prime Minister and the Cabinet respond well to the inescapable forces to which it subjects them.

# 9

# What Dicey Forgot

NW BARBER

For over a century, Dicey's account of the rule of law dominated constitutional scholarship and, like any successful academic exercise, has not lacked critics. Recently, that criticism has focused on the relationship between the rule of law and empire. Within the United Kingdom, or, more precisely, within Britain, the eulogisation of Dicey's rule of law was understandable, after all, the principle served as a guarantor of liberty. It ensured that limits on liberty were grounded in law and, crucially, those limits were knowable; people were free to act as they pleased, save in those areas in which the law proscribed conduct. Outside of Britain, within the British Empire, the rule of law played a very different role, justifying both the imperial project and particular acts of coercion by the imperial powers. Rather than protecting liberty, the rule of law became a tool of domination and oppression. This chapter argues that the imperial critique of Dicey is correct, but that the remedy can be found in Dicey's own work, in his discussion of sovereignty and in the hints he dropped about the social basis of the rule of law. In each case, a link is drawn between the community and the law that regulates it, a link that renders the rule of law morally defensible and efficacious. This chapter argues that Dicey's rule of law becomes radically less attractive when it is divided from the community the law governs, and that a fuller understanding of the rule of law shows that the principle weighs against the imperial project.

The chapter starts by outlining Dicey's principle of the rule of law, looking at its contents and at the understanding of law on which it rests. It argues that the concept of law and liberty that underpins Dicey's rule of law is drawn from the work of John Austin and JS Mill. The second section of the chapter examines the imperial critique of Dicey, and contends that it is Dicey's inheritance from Austin and Mill that validates this critique. The third section of the chapter argues that there is a richer, post-Austinian, understanding of law within Dicey's work, and that once the rule of law is interpreted in this light it can no longer be relied upon as a defence of imperial rule.

# I. Dicey's Inheritance

Dicey divides his account of the rule of law into three parts.[1] The first two parts embody the demands of the rule of law, whilst the third sets out the benefits brought by the principle. The first part of Dicey's rule of law requires that individuals not be punished unless they have committed a distinct breach of the law.[2] Part of this requirement relates to the form laws should take: laws should be expressed in a manner that enables people to predict the actions that will lead to punishment. Dicey warns against laws that give people in positions of power 'wide, arbitrary, or discretionary powers of constraint'.[3] Individuals should not be subjected to the caprice of officials, even if that caprice had received legal sanction. But this part of Dicey's rule of law is not merely concerned with the mode of expression of legal rules; it also engages the application of those rules within the community. The rule of law does not just require that people can determine when the law permits or requires the infliction of a punishment; it also requires that people only suffer punishment when it has been mandated by the law. So, when Dicey recounts the story of Voltaire being beaten by the servants of the Duc de Rohan – or, as Dicey puts it, 'thrashed by lackeys in the presence of their noble master' – he is drawing attention to the failure of French law to constrain Rohan's capacity to inflict harm.[4] The legal rules did not permit the Duke to punish the author, but the punishment went ahead all the same; the social context in which the law operated allowed Voltaire to be punished even though the law did not permit this act. There is a pair of intertwined demands in Dicey's first element of the rule of law which combine to render the exercise of force predictable. The rules mandating punishment are expressed in a manner that allows people to predict the infliction of legally sanctioned punishment and, in addition, people can be confident that they will not be exposed to non-legally sanctioned punishment.

The second part of Dicey's rule of law is the mirror image of the first. It requires that everyone, including state officials, be bound by the 'ordinary law of the land and amenable to the jurisdiction of the ordinary tribunals'.[5] Once again, there is a formal aspect to this requirement: the rule of law is set in opposition to the grant of arbitrary legal immunities.[6] This does not mean that the same law applies, or should apply, to everyone: people who occupy specific legal offices have different legal duties and rights. Most obviously, state officials have special legal duties and special legal rights, but these legal offices also exist in the private sphere:

[1] AV Dicey, *Introduction to the Study of the Law of the Constitution*, 10th edn (London, MacMillan, 1959) ch 4. The following four paragraphs are modified from NW Barber, *The United Kingdom Constitution: An Introduction* (Oxford, Oxford University Press, 2021) ch 20.

[2] Dicey, *Introduction to the Study of the Law* 188–93, 202.

[3] ibid 188.

[4] ibid 190.

[5] ibid 194.

[6] ibid 195, 204.

company directors, trustees, landlords, spouses – all take on distinct legal duties and rights when they take on their roles. Though Dicey does not make this explicit, it seems that the rule of law requires that these special rights and duties be justified and explained by the legal role occupied by an individual; when they can be so explained, these variations in legal rights and duties are not arbitrary.[7]

As well as not including arbitrary exceptions within the substance of the law, the rule of law further requires that there not be any practical immunities from the ordinary operation of the law; that the law is, in reality, applied to those who break its demands. Once again, there is a social dimension to this aspect of Dicey's rule of law. Returning to Voltaire, the Duke's capacity to inflict punishment stemmed from his practical immunity from the ordinary operation of the law. As Dicey puts it, the rule of law is imperilled where certain people can 'defy the law';[8] they enjoy immunities based on power, even though not recognised by law.

Dicey's two aspects of the rule of law are complementary, amounting to a broad demand that power be exercised through law. Dicey's third element of the rule of law is not a further requirement of the principle, but, instead, a conclusion: the benefits conferred by the rule of law. According to Dicey, the rule of law protects liberty by requiring the state to make explicit the limitations on people's allowed area of action; the legal order is structured such that whatever is not forbidden is permitted. The chapters that followed Dicey's account of the rule of law go on to discuss freedoms of the person, of discussion, and assembly, and, in each case, liberty is presented as the space left to the individual after the encroachments of the law.

Dicey's rule of law is a product of his time and shaped by the intellectual environment of his day. Perhaps the most important influence on Dicey's account of the rule of law is the work of John Austin.[9] Though Dicey's intellectual relationship with Austin is not simple and, as we shall see, Dicey departs from it in other parts of his work,[10] it seems that it is Austin's model of law that underpins Dicey's account of the rule of law, both in terms of the structure of the law and in its understanding of law's function.

In terms of the structure of law, in Austin's account, law is understood as the commands issued by a sovereign to their subjects, backed by sanctions.[11] We can identify the sovereign by looking at the behaviour of its subjects, as the sovereign's subjects are in a 'habit of obedience' towards it, following the

[7] TRS Allan, *Constitutional Justice: A Liberal Theory of the Rule of Law* (Oxford, Oxford University Press, 2001) 21–25.

[8] Dicey, *Introduction to the Study of the Law* 194.

[9] RA Cosgrove, *The Rule of Law: Albert Venn Dicey, Victorian Jurist* (Chapel Hill, University of North Carolina Press, 1980) 23–29.

[10] MD Walters, *A.V. Dicey and the Common Law Constitutional Tradition* (Cambridge, Cambridge University Press, 2020) 88–90.

[11] J Austin, *The Province of Jurisprudence Determined* (London, Weidenfeld and Nicolson, 1954) 13–16.

sovereign's commands.[12] Though the sovereign and subject are tied together in Austin's account, with each side needing the other for its existence, the model of law that this relationship generates is vertical and unidirectional. It is vertical, in that law is located within the interactions of sovereign and subject. Though laws are normally addressed to a wide group of people, the legal connection between the subject and sovereign is a personal one, and each individual encounters the law by themselves. This contrasts with a model of law in which the law is understood to regulate interactions within the community, where law has both a vertical aspect, between the institutions of the state and the recipients of law, and a horizontal aspect, between members of that community. Additionally, under Austin's model, law moves in one direction, it is unidirectional, flowing from the sovereign down to the subject. Law is then seen as something that happens to the people it addresses, something they experience and navigate. This contrasts with a model of law in which law is understood as bidirectional, where those who are the 'subjects' of the law also engage in its creation, interpretation, and application. Although Austin's account of law embeds law within a group, it does not embed law within a community: the group is defined solely by their shared submission to a political superior; how they relate to each other is, for the purposes of Austin's account of law, irrelevant.

In terms of the function of law, Austin's account is avowedly scientific, and seeks to move away from accounts of law that are tied to morality or divine will.[13] As such, Austin provides a 'positivist' account of law, in that his account purports to be morally inert. The reasons why we should want law within our society are excluded, and the moral evaluation of the law decoupled from questions of its existence. Whilst this is how Austin presents his account of law, it is impossible, when reading Austin, not to see Thomas Hobbes' shadow in his work.[14] Austin's sovereign is, essentially, that of Hobbes, and Hobbes' reasons for wanting a sovereign, Hobbes' moral arguments for the state, shape and inform Austin's work.[15] For Hobbes, we have a choice between the state of nature, where life is 'solitary, poore, nasty, brutish, and short', and living in the state, a polity characterised by order and comparative security.[16] And if we want to live in a state, we must accept the authority of a sovereign: the type of relationship that Austin presents as key to understanding law must be established. Though Austin sets aside the normative aspect of Hobbes' sovereign, his account of law is not morally inert. The moral basis of Hobbes' state is smuggled into Austin's work through the concept of the sovereign – it is the supposed moral value of order that enables Hobbes to identify and pick out the important features of law, like its commands and sanctions, and

[12] ibid 193–200.

[13] ibid 126–30; Cosgrove, *The Rule of Law* 25–25, 69–71; Walters, *A.V. Dicey and the Common Law* 60–61.

[14] Austin, *The Province of Jurisprudence* esp 260 n 23, 276 n 25.

[15] D Dyzenhaus, 'Austin, Hobbes, and Dicey' (2011) 24 *Canadian Journal of Law and Jurisprudence* 411, 415–17.

[16] T Hobbes, *Leviathan*, R Tuck (ed) (Cambridge, Cambridge University Press, 1991) 89.

enables Austin to make the same selection.[17] The suppression of moral evaluation in Austin's work, and, indeed, in that of many of his successors, permits controversial assumptions about law to remain unchallenged. When the significance of order within Austin's account is addressed directly, questions about its role emerge. Is order intrinsically valuable or instrumentally valuable? And, if it is instrumentally valuable, what is it instrumentally valuable for?[18] The answers to these questions have implications for the way we understand the purpose and nature of law.

A second figure standing behind Dicey is John Stuart Mill.[19] Mill's account of liberty is echoed both in Dicey's rule of law and in his discussion of the freedoms found within the Constitution.[20] Mill's liberty is a form of negative liberty, that is, liberty is present where a person is free to act without the interference of others; it consists in freedom from constraint rather than freedom to act.[21] The merit of liberty, for Mill, is that individuals are given space to decide for themselves how they want to live, they get some degree of control over their lives. Though this approach to liberty dominates Victorian discourse, work since that time has become more concerned with liberty as a capacity to act, whether that is being able to choose from a valuable range of options, or being free from the domination of others.

Drawing the preceding paragraphs together, there are four elements from the work of Austin and Mill which appear to have shaped Dicey's concept of the rule of law. First, within the confines of the principle of the rule of law, we are presented with an issuer of the law and a receiver of the law, and the two remain distinct. Dicey's rule of law does not speak to the ways in which the law is produced. Second, law is something that people navigate rather than engage. Dicey's rule of law rests on a model of law as a set of prohibitions and permissions, not as a tool they may utilise. Third, there is an unexplored assumption that the animating purpose of law is to establish order, and further questions over the purpose of establishing order are not explored. Dicey clearly thinks the rule of law is an attractive principle, one which those with power over the law should follow. Following Austin, the unarticulated assumption seems to be that the establishment of order is a good in itself. Finally, and building on these three elements, liberty is understood as the space between constraints, what is left over after the state has issued its demands. Liberty is presented as a side-effect of the rule of law, a feature that is an implication of the establishment of order.

[17] Dyzenhaus, 'Austin, Hobbes, and Dicey' 419–20; J Finnis, *Natural Law and Natural Rights*, 2nd edn (Oxford, Oxford University Press, 2011) 6–18.

[18] Jennings levels this charge against Dicey: I Jennings, *The Law and the Constitution*, 5th edn (London, University of London Press, 1959) 60; Cosgrove, *The Rule of Law* 82–84.

[19] Cosgrove, *The Rule of Law* 12–13; Walters, *A V. Dicey and the Common Law* 40–44.

[20] D Lino, 'The Rule of Law and the Rule of Empire: A.V. Dicey in Imperial Context' (2018) 81 *Modern Law Review* 739, 740.

[21] JS Mill, 'On Liberty' in JS Mill, *On Liberty and Other Essays* (Oxford, Oxford University Press, 2008); I Berlin, 'Two Concepts of Liberty' in I Berlin, *Four Essays on Liberty* (Oxford, Oxford University Press, 1969) 169–70.

## II. The Rule of Law as a Tool of Empire

It is this conceptual framework, inherited from Austin and Mill, that permitted the rule of law to be used as a defence of imperial rule. As Caroline Elkins argues, Dicey's rule of law played two justificatory roles within the British Empire. First, it provided an overarching justification for the imperial project. The application of imperial law within the territories brought order and, within the confines of Dicey's account, this order was, in and of itself, a benefit for which those subject to British rule ought to be grateful.[22] Through their control of a territory, the British were providing something of value to its people, a service, indeed. Allied to this, the creation of order created liberty.[23] By channelling power through law, the imperial structures left space to those subject to British rule; paradoxically, the domination of empire could be seen as a prerequisite to the creation of liberty. Second, breaching the law provided a justification for punishment within the territories.[24] One way of rationalising this through the rule of law would have been that the value of order justified the imposition of coercion, those who broke the law deserved to be punished because of their decision to undermine the efficacy of the law. But arguments about the moral purpose of law were deeply buried in the rule of law, and often the assumption may have been a far cruder claim, a caricature of legal positivism, that the only valid assessment of a sanction was legal – that is, if the sanction was legally justified no further assessment of its propriety was necessary or, indeed, acceptable.[25] Looked at squarely, such an argument is implausible, but it is a tempting one, a way of bringing quick closure to questions about the morality of state power. Once the assumption that breach of the law warrants punishment was permitted, this assumption then reflected back on the conduct that had been proscribed. If the sanction was warranted, the conduct must have been immoral: liberation struggles were transformed into mutinies, and campaigners for freedom became seditious rebels. Opposition to imperial rule was framed as opposition to the rule of law and, as such, conceptualised in morally negative terms.

Elkins' claim that Dicey's rule of law acted as a justification for, and facilitator of, empire is well made, and raises a worry about the principle. If the rule of law does provide such a broad defence of the imperial project and the violence used to realise it, the attractions of the principle are called into question. The rule of law, including Dicey's version of the principle, is presented as a moral principle, one which engages the question of how the state ought to exercise power and how its citizens should respond to this. If it generates immoral outcomes, this suggests that something has gone wrong further back in the account, either that the whole

[22] C Elkins, *Legacy of Violence: A History of the British Empire* (London, Bodley Head, 2022) 13, 100–101.

[23] Lino, 'The Rule of Law and the Rule of Empire' 20, 748–49, 758–59.

[24] Elkins, *Legacy of Violence* 50–51, 144.

[25] For a remarkable example of such reasoning, see N Biggar, *Colonialism* (London, William Collins, 2023) 223.

principle rests on a mistake, or something has gone wrong in our reasoning at some point. In the case of Dicey's model of the rule of law, the problems stem from the understandings of law he inherited from Austin and the model of liberty bequeathed by Mill discussed in the previous section. Drawing on this inheritance, law is seen as distinct from the society it serves. In his discussion of the rule of law, Dicey presents it as a tool of power rather than as a feature of a community. The manner in which the law is created or how it is developed is not directly relevant to the principle. Relatedly, law is understood in simple mandatory terms, it requires or forbids activities, and it is not presented as an institution that empowers and supports those it addresses. It is this division between law and community that permits the rule of law to be used as a defence of empire. In an empire, law is, ultimately, controlled by the metropole and applied to the imperial territories. Whilst those territories may be given some latitude in the creation of law, they only have limited and provisional control over it. By treating law as simply commands issued over a people, commands that bring the benefit of order and the possibility of a form of negative liberty, Dicey avoided engaging with questions about the creation and development of the law.

## III. What Dicey Forgot

Although Dicey's rule of law may have been formulated in terms which split law from the community it regulated, there are elements of his work that point towards a richer understanding of law which links these together. Dicey's discussion of parliamentary sovereignty and his discussion of the social base of the rule of law move his work beyond the Austinian model of law.

Turning to Dicey's account of sovereignty, there are two elements in this part of his work which pull away from the simple command theory of law and push towards a concept of law, or at least of state law, in which law is tied to the community it serves. First, Dicey recognised, in a way which Austin did not, that sovereignty was a legal construction rather than simply a political fact; the law-making power of Parliament was created through the existence of legal rules, rather than existing separate from those legal rules.[26] Law had the capacity to create and empower, as well as to mandate and prohibit.[27] As Dicey noted, Austin's paradigm of law was essentially that of a rule found in a criminal law statute, one which forbade or required a given action, and was far removed from the type of law that established the law-making power of institutions.[28] In contrast to criminal law, parliamentary sovereignty was a facilitative legal structure, one which

[26] Dicey, *Introduction to the Study of the Law* 39–50; Walters, *A.V. Dicey and the Common Law* ch 8.

[27] Indeed, this can be seen in Dicey's wider discussion of the nature of law: Walters, *A.V. Dicey and the Common Law* 148–59.

[28] Dicey, *Introduction to the Study of the Law* 72.

enabled Parliament to legislate. Second, though Dicey's principal focus was on legal sovereignty, he linked legal sovereignty to popular sovereignty, contending that, ultimately, it was the people, the nation, that provided political legitimation to the system.[29] Indeed, as Rivka Weill has shown, Dicey believed that some legal changes were so significant that before they were undertaken this popular sovereignty ought to be re-accessed through referendum.[30] For most questions, though, Parliament acted as a medium through which the people were able to set the contents of the law, and parliamentary sovereignty provided a legal structure through which the popular will could determine the exercise of state power within the United Kingdom.[31] Negative liberty, of the type expounded by Mill, was valuable, but so too was the capacity of the law to create and facilitate, bringing opportunities to the community it served. Though Dicey's understanding of democracy was radically flawed, and his embrace of it was qualified,[32] his work on sovereignty established a connection between democracy and the law through the medium of parliamentary sovereignty.

In the *Law of the Constitution* sovereignty and the rule of law are kept distinct. But it is easy to spot the connections between the two, lying just under the surface of Dicey's work. It is parliamentary sovereignty, with its tie to democratic governance, that provides the justification for the rule of law, and it is a justification which extends beyond the mere establishment of Hobbesian order. In Dicey's account of the United Kingdom's Constitution, the assertions of authority made by the state, embodied in the law, have a democratic grounding. The law is not simply the commands of a sovereign but consists of the commands of a community mediated through a representative institution. The rule of law should be understood as located within this broader constitutional context. Within the United Kingdom's constitutional order, part of the legitimating narrative of the state is its vindication of democracy: people should support and obey the law because the law is underpinned by a democratic mandate, and because flouting those laws would undermine the democratic process. Given that all states should be democratic, or be in the process of becoming democratic, the justificatory link between democracy and the rule of law extends beyond the United Kingdom and is a general feature of the rule of law. Dicey's principle of the rule of law is attractive because it establishes a form of social control that is vindicated by, and which is necessary for, democratic government. The function of the rule of law is not simply to condition the exercise of power and, by so doing, to establish order and leave space for liberty; it also facilitates the establishment of democratic structures within the state. The relationship goes both ways. The rule of law needs democratic government to render the law legitimate and so justify the demands of the principle. Democratic government, on the other hand, requires the rule of law to enable

[29] ibid 75–77; Walters, *A.V. Dicey and the Common Law* 221–25.
[30] R Weill, 'Dicey was not Diceyean' (2003) 62 *Cambridge Law Journal* 474.
[31] Dicey, *Introduction to the Study of the Law* 59, 73–74.
[32] AV Dicey, *Letters to a Friend on Votes for Women* (London, John Murray, 1909).

a people, through elected institutions, to govern effectively. The two principles, democracy and the rule of law, are intimately connected.[33]

The first connection between the rule of law and the community advances a pair of normative arguments, contending that the rule of law is both necessary for, and partly legitimated by, the principle of democracy. A second link in Dicey's work is empirical in nature, contending that community support is necessary for the successful operation of the rule of law.[34] At various points in his writings, Dicey emphasises that the rule of law is tied to a particular community, the English people.[35] According to Dicey, it was their national character and habits that made the rule of law possible.[36] One way of reading this, and perhaps the way that Dicey intended, is as a piece of parochialism, a claim that only the English have the virtue and fortitude to create the rule of law.[37] Such a claim would be easy to disprove, as effective legal orders have developed in many countries at many points in time. But an alternative, perhaps charitable, reading would take this as recognition that law is not simply a top-down institution. To a degree, law's existence depends on the support of the community in which it operates. Whilst Austin and many of his successors in the legal positivist tradition sought to shut down the question of why people obey law, Dicey is willing to entertain the issue.[38] After all, the answers inform our understanding of law: there are limits to what can be accomplished with threats and force, and in a society where people decline to use legal institutions to resolve disputes and refuse to cooperate with state officials, the institution of law would swiftly collapse.[39] This minimum necessary level of support can be quite low, but to have a flourishing legal system, a legal system in which the rule of law is more fully realised, requires deep and broad community support. Tom Tyler has examined the reasons that lead to community support for law and has picked out two important factors about why people are more likely to obey rules: when they have been made in a manner they believe to be procedurally fair;[40] and when the contents of the law are seen as generally just.[41] These will often be connected: a process of law creation that the community regards as procedurally fair is likely to produce rules that track the values of the community – and, on the other hand, a process that produces laws that track the values of the community is likely to be regarded as procedurally fair.

[33] See further, NW Barber, *The Principles of Constitutionalism* (Oxford, Oxford University Press, 2018) esp chs 2 and 4.

[34] Dyzenhaus, 'Austin, Hobbes, and Dicey' 427–28.

[35] Dicey, *Introduction to the Study of the Law* 187; Cosgrove, *The Rule of Law* 78–80; Walters, *A.V. Dicey and the Common Law* 231–32.

[36] Walters, *A.V. Dicey and the Common Law* 95–96, 228–29.

[37] Dicey, *Introduction to the Study of the Law* 188; Lino, 'The Rule of Law and the Rule of Empire' 474.

[38] Dyzenhaus, 'Austin, Hobbes, and Dicey' 427–28.

[39] Dicey, *Introduction to the Study of the Law* 78–80; D Lino, 'Albert Venn Dicey and the Constitutional Theory of Empire' (2016) 36 *Oxford Journal of Legal Studies* 751, 766–67.

[40] T Tyler, *Why People Obey the Law* (New Jersey, Princeton University Press, 2006) ch 12.

[41] J Jackson et al, 'Why Do People Comply with the Law?' (2012) 52 *British Journal of Criminology* 1051.

In the United Kingdom, Dicey's constitution, the two most important modes of law-making are through the legislatures and the courts. Each of these sets of institutions provides a legitimating narrative which grounds their development of the law in the community. The legitimating narrative of the legislature is obvious enough: as an elected institution, Parliament possesses a democratic mandate from the community to make law and, because of the connection established between the legislature and its people through elections, it is likely to be responsive to their values and concerns. Within the courts, the classic legitimating narrative of the common law is that the judges develop the common law out of the moral beliefs of the community in which they operate, articulating the values of the community within the legal order. The extent to which these legitimating narratives track reality can, and should, be disputed – Parliament is imperfectly representative, the courts are often far removed from those they regulate – but the narratives are important in themselves and, moreover, within the United Kingdom probably possess enough credibility to shape the way those subject to the legal orders of that state see the law. It could be that Dicey's claims about the empirical base of the rule of law are correct: the rule of law flourished within the United Kingdom because the law was grounded, and was seen to be grounded, in the community it served. Its institutions presented the law to their people in this way, these were the stories the state told about the law, and this legitimating story was sufficiently close to reality to be persuasive.

There are powerful criticisms that could be made of these legitimating narratives within the United Kingdom, especially at the time Dicey is writing, but outside of the United Kingdom, within imperial territories, these narratives are stripped of all plausibility. The essence of imperial rule is that one state, the metropole, controls territory outside of its borders. In the context of the British Empire, this means that laws which depend for their legitimacy and efficacy in their grounding in one community, the British community, are applied outside of that community to other peoples. To an extent, this was mitigated by the facilitation of some self-government within imperial territories, either by enabling local democratic structures to emerge or by the validation of local laws, but it is of the nature of imperial control that it impairs the governed community's engagement with its laws.[42] Whatever accommodations are made, the overarching structure is one of domination, control of one community by another.

## IV. Conclusion: The Rule of Law and the Rule of Empire

Dicey's rule of law has rightly been criticised as a tool of empire, one which provided justifications both for the imperial project and for the punishment of

[42] Lino, 'The Rule of Law and the Rule of Empire' 770–73.

those who resisted imperial rule. That Dicey's rule of law was capable of being used in this way was due to the assumptions he inherited from other scholars about the nature of law and liberty, assumptions that are present in his discussion of the rule of law but absent from other parts of his work, in particular from his discussion of sovereignty. The seeds of an answer to the imperial critique made by Elkins and others can be found buried in Dicey's work. It is a defence which rests upon a more sophisticated understanding of the rule of law, one in which the rule of law, as a principle of constitutionalism, sits alongside other principles, such as state sovereignty and democracy, informing and being informed by these other principles. The links between the rule of law and self-government are then exposed. One of the reasons we have for valuing the rule of law, and, indeed, supporting the operation of the law, is that it makes democracy possible within a community. Severed from self-rule and democracy, the defensibility of the rule of law is impaired, and it cannot be fully realised within the state. Additionally, Dicey recognised the importance of community support for the flourishing of the rule of law. Some level of community support is necessary for law to function at all, but for the rule of law to flourish, people must support legal institutions. It is hard to see how imperial rule, based on the domination of one group by another, could ever establish the attitudes conducive to the flourishing of the rule of law within the dominated group. Those subject to imperial rule will argue, almost invariably correctly, that the process by which those laws that are applied to them were created is unfair, and that these laws are not responsive to their values and needs. That the rule of law was seen as a justification of empire was Dicey's fault, and one he did not seek to correct, but when the principle is interpreted in the wider context of his work, it is shown to require a connection between the law and the community it regulates, a connection antithetical to imperial rule. Properly understood, Dicey's rule of law stands in opposition to empire.

# PART III

# Dicey Beyond Borders

# 10

# Dicey's Theory of the British Constitution in the Light of the Home Rule Question

THIBAULT GUILLUY

> There is no living writer whom I read more gladly and with more profit than Mr. Dicey. I am a Home Ruler, he is an unionist. But I know that in his writings I shall always find the case for the other side as clearly and powerfully put as it can be.[1]

If Dicey's *Law of the Constitution* and *Conflict of Laws* contributed, among others, to the academic authority gained by the Vinerian Professor, his more polemic writings[2] on the reforms involving autonomy in Ireland, known as 'Home Rule' tend to be relegated to his work as a 'political journalist'.[3] However, such an assessment undermines the importance of these writings in understanding Dicey's theory of the British Constitution and, more generally, his approach to constitutional law. Proposals for Home Rule in Ireland were, after all, one of the main constitutional issues throughout Dicey's whole career.

The Home Government Association, later known as the Home Rule League, was founded in 1870 by Isaac Butt in order to offer an institutional and thus peaceful solution to the growing hostility expressed by Ireland during the second half of the nineteenth century. Dubious about the chances of achieving independence, Butt sought a more pragmatic solution to the nationalist crisis and found in federalism – or, at least, in a particularly unitary interpretation of the federal

[1] EA Freeman, 'The Physical and Political Bases of National Unity' (1892) *Britannic Confederation* 33.

[2] AV Dicey, *England's Case against Home Rule* (London, J Murray, 1886); AV Dicey, *Letters on Unionist Delusions* (London, MacMillan, 1887); AV Dicey, *A Leap in the Dark* or *Our New Constitution* (London, J Murray, 1893) 19; AV Dicey, *A Fool's Paradise. Being A Constitutionalist's Criticism of the Home Rule Bill of 1912* (London, J Murray, 1913). For articles, see his 'Home Rule from an English Point of View' (1882) 42 *The Contemporary Review* 66; 'The Defence of the Union' (1892) 61 *The Contemporary Review* 314.

[3] This expression was used to present Dicey's contribution to the newspaper *The New York Nation* (or *The Nation*). See TH Ford, 'Dicey as a Political Journalist' (1970) 18 *Political Studies* 220.

idea – a way of guaranteeing Irish autonomy within the United Kingdom. The Home Rule League had its first electoral success in 1874, winning 60 seats in the British Parliament. But it was only under the leadership of the 'uncrowned King of Ireland', Charles Stewart Parnell, that the movement really took off. Parnell's obstructionist policy in the British Parliament led to his expulsion from the House of Commons in 1881. After transforming Butt's movement into the Irish Parliamentary Party in 1882, Parnell achieved a major victory in the 1885 elections, with the nationalist party winning 86 seats. William E Gladstone, doubtful that the Irish crisis could be resolved by force, realised the electoral benefits of devolution in Ireland. As early as 1886, the Liberal Prime Minister therefore proposed a first Home Rule proposal, the Irish Government Bill, which did not pass the House of Commons. Gladstone saw his own party split over the issue, with the Home Rulers opposing the Unionists. The conflict ultimately led to his resignation and defeat at the 1886 elections, when Joseph Chamberlain's new Liberal Unionist Party joined forces with the Conservative party to prevent Gladstone's victory. Gladstone had to wait until 1892 to return to government and work on a new Home Rule Bill,[4] which passed the Commons in 1893 but was vetoed by the House of Lords. The Conservative party's new policy, 'kill Home Rule by kindness',[5] proved to be fairly effective, as the idea did not reappear until 1912. The adoption of the Parliament Act in 1911 removed any risk of obstruction by the Upper House, so Asquith's Liberal government proposed a third Bill, which was finally passed in September 1914[6] but was never implemented because of the war. The fourth and final devolution Bill for Ireland was passed in 1920,[7] approved for the first time by both Houses, but again proved unworkable in the midst of the Anglo-Irish War.

In 1886, with the publication of his *England's Case against Home Rule*,[8] Dicey was fiercely opposed to Gladstonian devolution, unlike his friends and colleagues James Bryce and Edward Freeman. He took an active part in Unionist campaigns against those reforms, writing committed articles during this period.[9] His activism also led him to publish two essays, one in 1893 which criticised Gladstone's new proposal, *A Leap in the Dark*,[10] and another in 1913 against the third Home Rule Bill, *A Fool's Paradise*.[11] Dicey was therefore an important figure in the anti-devolution movement and, throughout his life, served the Unionist cause. The purpose of this chapter is not, however, to try to elucidate the political motivations behind Dicey's commitment to the Unionist cause. His biography by Richard Cosgrove[12]

[4] Irish Government Bill 1893.

[5] Lord Salisbury's government was behind the Local Government (Ireland) Act of 1897, which introduced a policy of administrative decentralisation in Ireland.

[6] Government of Ireland Act 1914 (c 90).

[7] Government of Ireland Act 1920 (c 67).

[8] Dicey, *England's Case against Home Rule*.

[9] Dicey, 'The Defence of the Union'.

[10] Dicey, *Leap in the Dark*.

[11] Dicey, *A Fool's Paradise*.

[12] RA Cosgrove, *The Rule of Law: Albert Venn Dicey, Victorian Jurist* (London, Macmillan, 1980).

and his more recent intellectual biography by Mark Walters[13] are both remarkable and authoritative studies on Dicey that would prove more resourceful on the subject that anything I could write. This chapter aims rather at taking seriously those polemic works relating to Home Rule, and trying to assess what they reveal of Dicey's idiosyncratic theory of the British Constitution.

Of course, Dicey's writings on Home Rule reveal his visceral opposition to these reforms. It is probably both his attachment to English constitutionalism and his instinctive hostility, as a conservative, towards constitutional modernism, that appear to be the most prominent and visible reasons for his staunch criticism of Home Rule reforms. But it is also the naivety which, in his view, characterises those proposals, inspired by an overly angelic vision of federalism, that seems to exacerbate his suspicion. Indeed, the core basis of Dicey's argument may be summed up in the following syllogism: (a) Home Rule means federalism; (b) federalism means written constitutionalism; (c) therefore Home Rule implies a perversion of the British Constitution. In order to prove his case, Dicey first draws a theory of federalism (see section I below) before demonstrating the inadaptability and undesirability of a federal reform of the British Constitution (see section II below). But, as we will see subsequently (in section III below), in order to assert the federal nature of the Home Rule arrangement, Dicey is forced to depart from the somehow rigid and orthodox legal positivism that characterises his theory of the British Constitution as presented in the *Law of the Constitution*, shedding a different light on his theory of constitutional law.

## I. Dicey's Theory of Federalism

In all his writings on Irish Home Rule, Dicey makes it very clear that the proposed reforms establishing Irish institutional autonomy, which make up a 'new constitution' for the United Kingdom, will lead to the 'federalisation' of the country. In *A Leap in the Dark* (1893), Dicey writes that 'the new constitution is at bottom a federalist or semi-federalist constitution; it introduces into English institutions many of the forms of federalism and still more of its spirit'.[14] And also:

> The Home Rule Bill is a new constitution; it subverts the bases of the English constitution as we now know it, for it destroys throughout Ireland the effective authority of the Imperial Parliament, and turns the United Kingdom into a federal government of a new and untried form.[15]

No one should thus be fooled: the Home Rule arrangement is nothing other than federalism in disguise. And Dicey is no stranger to the theory of federalism; on the

[13] MD Walters, *A.V. Dicey and the Common Law Constitutional Tradition. A Legal Turn of Mind* (Cambridge, Cambridge University Press, 2020).

[14] Dicey, *A Leap in the Dark* 14.

[15] ibid 19.

contrary. His article on federal government, published in 1885 in the *Law Quarterly Review*,[16] sees Dicey developing a genuine theory of federalism, something that was not so common in British academia. If the political context surrounding this work, and especially the Home Rule debate, may, to a certain extent, have interfered with his perception of federalism and explained some of his rather dogmatic positions, Dicey offers a fairly detailed, though admittedly fragmentary, analysis of the federal phenomenon which is worthy of interest. Twenty-five years after Dicey's death, KC Wheare, author of the remarkable *Federal Government*, wrote:

> There is no adequate book in English on the working of federal government. The most illuminating discussion of the subject is to be found in [*The Law of the Constitution*], first published in 1885. In successive editions Dicey devoted an increasing space to federalism and all that he says is lucid and penetrating?[17]

Dicey's account of federalism therefore deserves to be presented.

Federalism and sovereignty: Dicey places great emphasis on the role of the Constitution in federal systems. The federal organisation of power is characterised by three principles which tend to present federalism as the quintessence of legal constitutionalism: 'the supremacy of the constitution – the distribution among bodies with limited and co-ordinate authority of the different powers of government – the authority of the Courts to act as interpreters of the constitution'.[18] These principles could of course be said to be more characteristic of constitutionalism than federalism, but Dicey understands that the latter calls for the former. Federal theory implies a certain legal formalism, in particular the drafting of a written constitution to distribute powers, and, correlatively, a hierarchised system of norms. This leads him to analyse the federal constitutional framework along three main lines: (A) the sovereignty of constituent power; (B) the distribution of powers; and (C) the authority of the courts.

## A. The Sovereignty of Constituent Power

Federalism being based on the coexistence, within a single body, of different autonomous political entities, it therefore creates two levels of political power, one federal, relating to the union created, and the other local, relating to the different members of this union. Of course, such a distribution of power challenges the traditional theory of the state, built upon the concept of sovereignty by Bodin, Hobbes, and their successors. What distinguishes the state is that it embodies a supreme power, the expression of a single irresistible will. The indivisible nature of sovereignty therefore poses a problem when it comes to comparing the federal

[16] AV Dicey, 'Federal Government' (1885) 1 *The Law Quarterly Review* 80. This is the main draft for the chapter on federalism in *The Law of the Constitution*.

[17] KC Wheare, *Federal Government* (Oxford, Oxford University Press, 1946) 261.

[18] Dicey, *Introduction to the Study of the Law of the Constitution* 74.

structure with the classical theory of the state. The question arises of where to locate sovereignty in a federation, which is characterised precisely by the dualism of its political system. The dualistic nature of the American Constitution of 1787 was thoroughly discussed by James Madison in the *Federalist Papers*:

> the proposed government cannot be deemed a national one; since its jurisdiction extends to certain enumerated objects only, and leaves to the several States a residuary and inviolable sovereignty over all other objects … The proposed Constitution, therefore, is, in strictness, neither a national nor a federal Constitution, but a composition of both.[19]

The American States and the Union were therefore jointly sovereign, ie sovereign in their respective spheres. John Austin, whose influence on Dicey does not need to be restated, defends such an interpretation of federal constitutionalism when he writes:

> In the case of a composite state, or a supreme federal government, the several united governments of the several united societies, together with a government common to those several societies, are jointly sovereign in each of those several societies, and also in the larger society arising from the federal union.[20]

Refusing this middle path, Dicey solves the problem of locating sovereignty in the American federal system by postulating first that 'behind all the mechanism and artifices of the constitution there lies, however artfully concealed, some sovereign power which must have the means both to support the principles of the constitution and, when occasion requires, to modify its terms'.[21] If such a sovereign power exists, it is not to be found in the union or the several states, but in the Constitution itself, or more precisely in the constituent power:

> one may say, with sufficient accuracy for our present purpose, that the legal sovereignty of the United States resides in the States' governments as forming one aggregate body represented by three-fourths of the several States at any time belonging to the Union.[22]

If this recognition of the sovereignty of the constituent power could appear disappointing at first, as a similar conclusion could be drawn for any legal system with a rigid Constitution, it might, however, reveal itself to be quite astute when applied to a federal system, as it prevents Dicey from allocating sovereignty either in the union or the several states and thus hurting the very idea of a federal balance. As Carl Friedrich later wrote: 'No one has "the last word". The idea of a compact is inherent in federalism, and the "constituent power", which makes the compact, takes the place of the sovereign'.[23]

[19] J Madison, *The Federalist*, vol 2 (New York, McLean, 1788) 27–28.

[20] J Austin, *The Province of Jurisprudence Determined* (Cambridge, Cambridge University Press, 1995) 206.

[21] Dicey, 'Home Rule from an English Point of View' 74.

[22] AV Dicey, *Introduction to the Study of the Law of the Constitution*, 8th edn (London, Macmillan, 1915) 81.

[23] CJ Friedrich, *Trends of Federalism in Theory and Practice* (London, Praeger, 1968) 8.

But if Dicey insists on the supremacy of the Constitution and the sovereignty of the constituent power, it is precisely because he wants to demonstrate that federalism and, more generally, modern constitutionalism carry with them a weakened conception of political power, mainly because constituent power manifests itself quite rarely and on an ad hoc basis. As Dicey coins it, it is a 'despot hard to rouse'[24] and he easily infers from this a tendency towards conservatism that is inherent in federalism. The rigidity of the federal constitutional framework, which places the constituent power 'outside' the constitution itself, and therefore makes constitutional amendments complex, entrenches constitutional provisions, therefore fostering the emergence of a 'conservative sentiment'.[25] Of course, such a conclusion is influenced by the comparative approach adopted by Dicey. Asserting the sovereignty of the constituent power in federal systems enables him to contrast the vitality and strength of sovereign power in the United Kingdom, that 'ever-wakeful legislator' that is the British Parliament, with the torpor and timidity of its American counterpart, a 'monarch that slumbers and sleeps'.[26] The inherent superiority and vigour of the British Constitution therefore appears all the more striking.

## B. Federalism and Distribution of Powers

As Dicey explains,

> a federal state is a political contrivance intended to reconcile national unity and power with the maintenance of 'state rights'. The end aimed at fixes the essential character of federalism. For the method by which Federalism attempts to reconcile the apparently inconsistent claims of national sovereignty and of state sovereignty consists of the formation of a constitution under which the ordinary powers of sovereignty are elaborately divided between the common or national government and the separate states.[27]

Dicey's vision of the federalism is therefore highly mechanical. Federalism aims at achieving a particularly difficult objective: to organise state power while preserving the federal balance between the two levels of authority. This objective could only be achieved by a certain constitutional mechanism, which made the federal model particularly 'artificial'[28] in Dicey's eyes. This mechanism is constitutionalism and, correlatively, the distribution of powers between two levels of authority. To maintain the federal balance, a rigid written constitution is thus required to regulate this vertical distribution of powers between both levels of government.

In a more horizontal perspective, the American Constitution establishes a 'distribution of limited, executive, legislative, and judicial authority among bodies

[24] Dicey, *Introduction to the Study of the Law of the Constitution* 81.
[25] ibid 99.
[26] ibid 81.
[27] ibid 76–77.
[28] Dicey, 'Home Rule from an English Point of View' 79.

each co-ordinate with and independent of the other'.[29] In a way that is very representative of his mechanical approach to federalism, which he sees as a rigid and fixed system, or, to use Carl Friedrich's phrase, as a 'static pattern',[30] Dicey describes the federal constitution as a work of meticulous and systematic division of power between non-sovereign authorities. He can thus easily conclude: 'The distribution of all the powers of the state among co-ordinate authorities necessarily leads to the result that no one authority can wield the same amount of power as under a unitarian constitution as possessed by the sovereign'.[31] In the United States and in federal systems, therefore, all political bodies have limited powers, delegated to them by the Constitution and by the constituent power, which alone is sovereign. Dicey is particularly critical of this obsession of modern constitutionalism, and particularly federalism, with limiting power. He sees it as an unnecessary complication and 'a certain waste of energy'.[32] On this point, the American Constitution is the exact opposite of the English Constitution, which is characterised by its flexibility. For Dicey, the balance of powers established in the English Constitution is not at all rigid, since the powers are in fact codependent. The British executive needs parliamentary support in order to exist and govern, and Parliament does not hesitate to intervene in the executive or administrative sphere. But this balance of powers, inherent in parliamentary systems, is only made possible by the domination of one authority over the other constitutional bodies. Therefore, the keystone[33] of British constitutionalism is obviously the doctrine of an absolute sovereignty of Parliament. In the United Kingdom, all state or sovereign power is therefore in the hands of the King-in-Parliament, and the authority of any of the bodies constituted by the Constitution of 1787 cannot rival that of Parliament in the British Constitution.

Therefore, for Dicey, dividing power means diluting power, and this idea serves as the basis of his criticism of federalism. The reconciliation of the principles of national unity and state autonomy, which underpins the entire federal theory, comes at this price. Political power is thus doubly fragmented in a federal system: first distributed between the federal and state spheres, it is again divided between the different organs of government. This is also the case at state level, since, as Dicey points out,[34] the various constitutions of the American states reaffirm the principle of the separation of powers in their constitutional organisation. As a result of this dual separation of powers, there is little left of the political power which, for Dicey, makes the greatness of a state governed by a sovereign power. He can therefore conclude, like Tocqueville before him,[35] that the federal theory

[29] Dicey, *Introduction to the Study of the Law of the Constitution* 74.
[30] Friedrich, *Trends of Federalism* 8.
[31] Dicey, *Introduction to the Study of the Law of the Constitution* 97–98.
[32] ibid 98.
[33] ibid 25.
[34] AV Dicey, 'Bryce's American Commonwealth' (1889) 169 *The Edinburgh Review* 497: 'It is, like the Federal Constitution which it imitates, pervaded by the belief in the balance of powers'.
[35] A de Tocqueville, *Democracy in America*, vol 1 (Indianapolis, Liberty Fund, 2012) 263–76.

is tainted by a certain weakness of the federal government.[36] And the conclusion comes logically: the superiority of unitary states, which alone can combine greatness and power under the reign of unity: 'a federation therefore will always be at a disadvantage in a contest with unitarian states of equal resources'.[37]

There is, therefore, a logic in the theories of modern constitutionalism and federalism that is deeply disturbing to British constitutional theory. The asserted omnipotence of the Constitution implies that the ordinary powers of government, and in particular the legislative power, are merely powers subordinate to the legal order of the Constitution. But all of this is only true if the Constitution is indeed supreme. In order to guarantee this supremacy, the intervention of the judiciary is necessary.

## C. Federalism and the Judicial System

The important role given to the American judiciary is, according to Dicey, the corollary of the supremacy of the Constitution. For it is necessary to guarantee this supremacy and make it effective. The judiciary is therefore competent to interpret the Constitution and to sanction it. However, as Dicey rightly points out,[38] this is not enough to really guarantee this supremacy, as there is a risk that federal judges will interpret the Constitution in a way favourable to the federal government, and that state judges, on the other hand, will favour a more state-centered interpretation. It was therefore necessary to entrust a single body with the final interpretation of the Constitution, namely the Supreme Court through its appellate jurisdiction. It is only the guardianship given to the Supreme Court that made the 1787 Constitution the supreme law of the United States, since it was binding on all authorities, federal and state alike. Dicey himself recognises the merit of the Founding Fathers in the meticulous construction of American constitutionalism, writing that 'the glory of the founders of the United States is to have devised or adopted arrangements under which the Constitution became in reality as well as name the supreme law of the land'.[39] Dicey thus acknowledges the ingenuity of federal construction, even if he deplores the fact that it was used in the service of a theory of constrained power.

The Federal Supreme Court is therefore the guardian of the supremacy of the Constitution throughout the union. But it is all the more necessary in a federal system because the Constitution establishes a vertical division of power between two levels of authority. This division creates a permanent tension in the federation between local and national power. The institution of an arbiter, an impartial third party, is therefore necessary to guarantee the federal balance, as Dicey clearly

[36] Dicey, *Introduction to the Study of the Law of the Constitution* 97: 'Federal government means weak government'.
[37] ibid 98.
[38] ibid 88–90.
[39] ibid 87.

states: 'under every federal system there must almost of necessity exist some body of persons who can decide whether the terms of the federal compact have been observed'.[40] It ensures the viability of the federation: 'the Supreme Court and institutions like it are the protectors of the federal compact, and the validity of that compact is, in the long run, the guarantee for the rights of the separate States'.[41] Dicey does not forget, however, that the Swiss Confederation does not have such a judicial authority. Yet, he attributes this central role of arbiter to the Federal Council, as guarantor of the prevalence of the Constitution.[42] This incidentally illustrates the confusion of executive and judicial powers in Switzerland, which Dicey describes as a 'serious flaw'.[43]

But while Dicey recognises the need for judicial review in federal systems, he deplores its drawbacks. First and foremost, it means that a law, whether federal or at the state level, can be considered null and void and inapplicable simply by the decision of a judicial body. Congress is therefore not entirely in control of the legislative process, since it can see its own rules invalidated by the judiciary. The courts are consequently 'the pivot on which the constitutional arrangements of the country turn'[44] to the extent of a hypothetical judicial supremacy. But such a supremacy of the judiciary is justified, according to Dicey, by the 'legal spirit'[45] that dominates the American people, characterised by their particular reverence for the ideas of law and justice. Only this spirit of legality can give force of law to a judicial decision and make judicial power effective, and for Dicey it is a prerequisite for the viability of federalism. The predominance of the judiciary and the spirit of legality are thus the two manifestations of the 'legalism'[46] that characterises the federal constitutional model. While he deplores this 'judicialisation' of federal constitutional law, he nonetheless recognises its necessity for the proper functioning of the federation and the maintenance of the federal balance.

Federal constitutionalism therefore implies that the powers are subordinate not only to the Constitution itself, but to the judiciary as a whole. Comparing the Westminster Parliament to the American Congress is meaningless, since in a federal system the legislative power itself is subordinate to the judiciary, as Dicey stresses. To illustrate his point, he compares the American Congress to the English railway companies which, in the nineteenth century, had regulatory power delegated by the British Parliament to manage and organise the railway network by the means of bye-laws. As the question soon arose as to the extent of the companies' powers, the doctrine of ultra vires emerged in the British courts, asserting that the legal acts of these companies are valid only within the limits of the delegation

[40] ibid xcvi.
[41] ibid 102.
[42] ibid 374–77.
[43] ibid 96.
[44] ibid 100: 'That in a confederation like the United States the Courts become the pivot on which the constitutional arrangements of the country turn is obvious'.
[45] ibid 103.
[46] ibid 100.

of power granted by the British Parliament. The judge therefore declares himself competent to review the conformity of these acts with the parent act, and to declare them invalid if they fall outside the scope of the law. There is no doubt that such a comparison reflects an educational effort by Dicey for his British readers, and that he in no way intends to compare, in terms of importance, the American Congress to the English railway companies. But it is a particularly good illustration of Dicey's conception of American legislative power, which is merely a delegated, subordinate, 'powerless' power.[47]

However biased and influenced by Dicey's desire to prove the superiority of the unitary state model, his theory of federalism offers an interesting outlook on federal systems, and especially American federalism. But the insight of his reading of federal constitutionalism is apparent precisely because Dicey does not stop there. He sets out to show that federalism cannot be reduced to a constitutional or legal model and that, in order to emerge and prosper, it needs certain extra-legal conditions to come together. For Dicey, federalism is then also a work of compromise. It is a compromise which, in his view, could not and should not be adopted in the United Kingdom.

## II. 'Federal' Home Rule or the Perversion of the British Constitution

Dicey astutely understands that, being a compromise between unity and diversity, federalism is fragile by nature and needs specific and favourable conditions to flourish. Or, as Alexis de Tocqueville put it: 'in order to succeed, the federal system needs not only good laws, but also favourable circumstances'.[48] A reader of Tocqueville, Dicey is well aware of the existence of these 'natural causes of union'.[49] It is these that motivate his opposition to any form of federalisation of United Kingdom or, to the simultaneous idea, of the British Empire ('Home Rule all around'). For Dicey, the conditions conducive to the development of a federal system, whether legal or extra-legal, are not present. But his main focus is to demonstrate that a 'British federalism' would come up against the constitutional and legal tradition of the United Kingdom.

### A. A Constitutional Revolution

In Dicey's view, the various Home Rule Bills could not be ordinary Acts of Parliament. They are genuine draft constitutions for the United Kingdom as

[47] Dicey, *England's Case against Home Rule* 170.
[48] *Democracy in America* 270.
[49] ibid 263.

they substantially modify the organisation and operation of British institutions even though they are formally legislative acts. But because Home Rule means the implementation of federalism in the United Kingdom, there is no doubt that such a reform would pave the way for a 'rigidification' of the British Constitution and would appeal for a conversion to modern constitutionalism, that 'artificial constitutionalism'[50] which implies, in particular, a legal formalism perceived as restrictive. Dicey could not, of course, accept this idea. He sees the British Constitution as a political and institutional equilibrium produced by the history of the English people – as an inheritance that has been passed down from one generation to the next since time immemorial. To adopt a written constitution would therefore be to turn one's back on British tradition and forsake the wisdom, ingenuity and flexibility of the British Constitution. Moreover, he is convinced of its superiority, since it offers British people 'the greatest and freest and best governed state of the modern world'.[51] The constitutional status quo is therefore self-evident.

Similarly, the conversion of the United Kingdom or the British Empire to modern constitutionalism would seriously and profoundly undermine the most fundamental principle of British constitutional law, namely the sovereignty of the King-in-Parliament. Criticising the 1886 Home Rule Bill, Dicey writes:

> It revolutionizes the whole Constitution of the United Kingdom; by undermining the sovereignty of Parliament, it deprives English institutions of their elasticity, their strength, and their life; it weakens the Executive at home, and lessens the power of the country to resist foreign attack.[52]

As we have seen, for Dicey, federalism implies the distribution of powers, whereas the very essence of the British Constitution is to keep power unified. Moreover, if the adoption of a rigid and written Constitution would definitively undermine the absolute sovereignty of Parliament, this would also be the case with the various Home Rule projects. For, according to Dicey, even if the preserved sovereignty of the British Parliament is explicitly restated in the various Home Rule Bills, this would really only be a 'reserved sovereignty',[53] ie limited to a certain sphere. The Westminster Parliament would thus lose some of its power of domination over Irish territory, through the delegation granted to the new Irish government. Yet nominally the British Parliament would still remain the legal sovereign, retaining the power to amend or withdraw the delegation granted by the Home Rule Bill, but political power is no less weakened.

For Dicey, these various devolution projects are nothing more than clumsy compromises, attempting to reconcile the irreconcilable. He defines the 1893 draft as 'an attempt – its admirers may think an original and ingenious attempt – to

[50] Dicey, *England's Case against Home Rule* 169.
[51] AV Dicey, 'The Causes of Imperialism in England' (1901) 73 *The Nation* 204.
[52] Dicey, *England's Case against Home Rule* 196.
[53] Dicey, *A Leap in the Dark* 25. He also describes this sovereignty as 'nominal sovereignty': ibid 49.

combine the sovereignty of an Imperial Parliament with the elaborate limitation and distribution of powers which distinguish federal government'.[54] For Dicey, this compromise is impossible, since Parliament's sovereignty would necessarily be limited. But by attacking this 'keystone' of the British Constitution, it would bring down the whole edifice. Therefore, it would not only be the Constitution that would be undermined, but also the greatness and prestige of the British state as a whole. For the classical theory of the state sees unity of power as synonymous with strength and power.

Of course, Dicey's stance also reveals the expression of a genuine English nationalist sentiment as much as the fear of seeing England assimilated to a mere state within a British confederation, losing its dominant position within the United Kingdom. England would no longer be anything more than an authority subordinate to an outside power, merged into a higher political body over which it would not have sole control. The historian EA Freeman expresses this 'nationalist' position with verve:

> Does every one who talks about federation, 'Imperial', 'Britannic', or any other, always think what any kind of federation means as regards the Parliament of Great Britain? We are used to boasting that Parliament knows no superior on Earth, that its powers are limited only by the physical powers of nature. Make Great Britain a member, make England and Scotland separate members, of a Britannic Confederation, and all this greatness passes away. The powers of the British, English, Scottish, Parliament will at once cease to be boundless; they will be cut down to the measure of such powers as the Federal Constitution may leave to each of the several states. The British, English, Scottish, Parliament will sink to the level of the Legislature of Delaware or the Grand Council of Zug. Are we ready for this? I can speak for one man only. I am no lover of 'empire'; I am not anxious for my country to exercise lordship over other lands, English-speaking or otherwise. But I will not, so far as one man can hinder it, have my country ruled over by any other power, even by a power in which my country itself has a voice.[55]

The adoption of a federal scheme of any kind in the United Kingdom would thus have at least two harmful consequences: 'First, the sovereignty of the Imperial Parliament would be destroyed and all English constitutional arrangements would be dislocated; secondly, the power of Great Britain would be diminished'.[56] Therefore, and especially because it would deprive the British Parliament of its sovereignty that was instituted 'by the nature of things',[57] the implementation of Home Rule would mean one thing: a constitutional revolution in the United Kingdom.

[54] ibid 20.
[55] EA Freeman, 'The Physical and Political Bases of National Unity' 56.
[56] Dicey, *England's Case against Home Rule* 168.
[57] Dicey, *Introduction to the Study of the Law of the Constitution* cviii.

## B. Institutional Reform

'The whole thing is an experiment and an experiment without precedent'.[58] This is how Dicey describes the Home Rule Bill of 1893, which appeared, however, to be a compromise, an adaptation of federal theory to the British unitary system. Of course, the several Home Rule schemes did not intend to completely transform the United Kingdom into a federation; they merely injected certain federal mechanisms into the British Constitution that had to be integrated into the institutional framework provided by the Constitution. Nevertheless these various projects still required substantial reform of British institutions, and particularly of the most important of them, the Parliament of Westminster.

From the very beginning, the question of maintaining Irish representation at Westminster had arisen and had been at the centre of the debates surrounding all Home Rule proposals. The question was especially sensitive as all Home Rule Bills denied full fiscal power to Ireland. This resulted in an issue, which had already arisen with the American colonies at the eve of the Revolution. Since the Magna Carta of 1215, the English Constitution established the principle of 'no taxation without representation'. If the British Parliament still had fiscal power over Ireland, then Ireland had to be represented at Westminster. However, Gladstone opted for the opposite solution in 1886, perhaps seeing this as an opportunity to counter Parnell's obstructionist policy. The 1886 draft provided for the exclusion of Irish representatives from both Houses of Parliament, in defiance of the historical and fundamental constitutional principle. The hybrid nature of Gladstone's 'federal' project was particularly apparent. Indeed, one cannot really speak of federalism since Ireland was not associated with the exercise of general, or federal, legislative power. The Irish Parliament was, however, involved in the procedure to revise the Home Rule Act. The first 'Gladstonian constitution' remained a compromise rather favourable to the United Kingdom. Dicey himself notes the contradiction, which placed Ireland in the position of a colony but maintained the imperial tax. But he does not advocate maintaining Irish representation in the Westminster Parliament. On the contrary, he thinks it preferable to free Ireland from imperial taxation:

> Let me not be misunderstood. I do not recommend Home Rule under any form whatever: what I do assert is that of all its forms the Colonial form is the least injurious to British interests, and that the experiment of placing Ireland in the situation of Victoria can be carried out neither with fairness nor with any chance of success, unless Englishmen let Ireland, like Victoria, be exempt from Imperial taxation.[59]

This position may seem surprising at first sight from a staunch Unionist like Dicey. He would rather see Ireland acquire true Dominion status, even if it means

[58] Dicey, *A Leap in the Dark* 20.
[59] Dicey, *England's Case against Home Rule* 217.

limiting the United Kingdom's fiscal power, than accept Irish representation at Westminster. Nonetheless it also shows Dicey's true attachment to constitutional principles, even if they go against his personal opinions as a Unionist. We might even extrapolate and suggest that Dicey would have preferred to see an independent Ireland more than a constitutional revolution, as he writes: 'We are rightly proud of our connection with our colonies, but no one would seriously propose to retain nominal sovereignty in Canada at the price of a perilous and injurious change in the constitution of England'.[60] The constitutional revolution to which the Home Rulers aspired was therefore far too high a price to pay to preserve such 'nominal' sovereignty for the United Kingdom, a *minimal* sovereignty that did not correspond to effective power.

In the 1893 draft, however, Gladstone reversed his initial position. The second Home Rule Bill provided for the presence of 80 Irish representatives in the House of Commons but introduced an 'in and out' clause. Under this clause, the Irish were only allowed to take part in discussions and vote when the common interests of Great Britain and Ireland were at stake. In *A Leap in the Dark*, Dicey railed against the reinstatement of Irish representation, despite the fact that it was a symbol of a degree of sovereignty preserved in the British Parliament. On the contrary, he saw it as a great injustice to the British people, especially the English, since the Irish representatives would have been involved in appointing the Prime Minister. Conversely, British representatives would have not been able to intervene in the choice of the Irish executive. In Dicey's view, the 1893 draft was therefore rather favourable to Ireland, and he almost regretted the loss of the 1886 Home Rule Bill: 'The withdrawal of the Irish members from Westminster might give Ireland the chance of obtaining some of the benefits, and compensate England for some of the evils, of Home Rule'.[61] The conditional maintenance of Irish representation at Westminster therefore posed serious constitutional problems. For example, it could have been conceivable that the Irish delegation in Parliament alone could determine the government majority, in which case the majority would depend on whether or not the Irish representatives participated. It was perhaps the fear of such a constitutional crisis that encouraged the Liberal Party to remove the 'in and out' clause from the 1914 Devolution Act, while maintaining Irish representation.

Yet this clause is ultimately indicative of the institutional issues that arose from Home Rule schemes and this so-called 'federalisation' of the United Kingdom. For, by providing for the participation of Irish representatives in common affairs only, the 1893 draft in reality duplicated the British Parliament. Depending on the presence or absence of the Irish, the latter would have acted as the Parliament of the United Kingdom or as the Parliament of Great Britain alone. This clearly showed the compromising nature of Home Rule schemes, and the ambition to adapt federalist features to the existing framework of British institutions. In the same way, it was for the Judicial Committee of the Privy Council to check that an act of the

[60] Dicey, *A Leap in the Dark* 51.
[61] ibid 65.

Irish government did not exceed the terms of the delegation of power thus granted by Parliament, assuming the role of the US Supreme Court, as Dicey points out.[62] But the hybrid nature of those schemes, both federal and unitary, also showed its limits, as the duplication of the Westminster Parliament would have caused insurmountable practical difficulties. The exclusion of the Irish representatives appeared unacceptable from a constitutional point of view. On the other hand, the permanent representation of Ireland in the Westminster Parliament would not have been acceptable either from a substantive point of view, leading to a confusion between the two mandates that the Parliament would hold, representing Great Britain alone and the United Kingdom as a whole. For such a federal system to work, two separate legislative bodies would have to be created to represent the two levels of authority established by the Home Rule Act. This would mean that the Imperial Parliament would become federal and that a Parliament of Great Britain would be created, or at least reconstituted, as it existed before the Union of 1801. This would therefore require genuine constitutional and institutional reform. Part of Dicey's criticism of Home Rule schemes is aimed, not without reason, at the proponents of Home Rule for not raising those questions and for failing to appreciate the scale of the constitutional revolution they were advocating.[63] But in his pessimistic view, Home Rule would cause such difficulties that, if it was to function properly, it would lead to the ruin of the British Constitution.

## III. Dicey and the Law of the 'New' Constitution

In order to reach that conclusion, grounded on the idea that Home Rule would mean the end of parliamentary sovereignty, Dicey is nevertheless forced to adopt a perspective on the British Constitution that is, to a certain extent, different from the one in *The Law of the Constitution*.

When the first edition of *The Law of the Constitution* was published in 1885, Dicey's objective is clearly stated: the law professor, who has recently arrived at Oxford, conceives of this work as a manual for his students:

> It deals only with two or three guiding principles which pervade the modern constitution of England. My object in publishing the work is to provide students with a manual which may impress these leading principles on their minds, and thus may enable them to study with benefit in Blackstone's Commentaries and other treaties of the like nature those legal topics which, taken together, make up the constitutional law of England.[64]

This educational ambition, which leads him to clarify, reorganise, and thus rationalise the English Constitution, should not be underestimated. It is as such that Dicey can be presented as a 'codifier' of the English Constitution, bringing

[62] Dicey, *Introduction to the Study of the Law of the Constitution* 92.
[63] ibid ci.
[64] Dicey, *Introduction to the Study of the Law of the Constitution* xxv.

together diverse materials and sources in a coherent and comprehensive manner. But Dicey's work of rationalisation and codification, while 'it ossified or encapsulated a moving constitution'[65] (the Constitution of the nineteenth century, that of Bentham and Austin), is carried out through a theoretical and legal prism, that of legal positivism. One of Dicey's most faithful heirs and an advocate of his doctrine of parliamentary sovereignty, Sir William Wade, acknowledged that Dicey's theory 'crystallised the past rather than foreshadowed the future'.[66]

Influenced by the positivist theory of law developed by John Austin, Dicey reconstructs, for the didactic purposes previously evoked, British constitutional law in a system in which the principle of parliamentary sovereignty occupies an overwhelming place. Dicey, from his own positivist perspective, proposes a version that sometimes appears excessively rigid and tends to give precedence to the logic of legal reasoning over British institutional reality, which nevertheless reappears in his work under the heading of 'conventions of the Constitution', this 'more doubtful and speculative ground'.[67] Dicey interestingly refers to this in the introduction of the *The Law of the Constitution*. This process of 'purifying' the law to identify the rules that are sanctioned by the courts leads him to exclude important elements of the British Constitution from the legal sphere in order to deploy the implacable logic of sovereignty. If Austin provided for the theoretical ground for British legal positivism, Dicey's contribution on this point is more specific: it formulates, from the perspective of a constitutional law conceived as autonomous, the legal precepts stemming from a logic, that of the organic sovereignty of Parliament.

The irony, however, is that the legal theory developed by Dicey in these more polemic writings on Home Rule shows a slight shift in the way he approaches law. If, in the *The Law of the Constitution*, legal logic seems to prevail over political reality or constitutional morality, it is quite the opposite in his analysis of the Home Rule Bills. For example, Dicey writes in *A Leap in the Dark* that:

> the powers of the Imperial Parliament, it may be said, are under the new constitution subject to no limitations. In words this assertion is true, in substance it is false. If the constitution works properly the Imperial Parliament will clearly be subject to the terms of the Government of Ireland Act, 1893, or, in other words, of the Federal Constitution. This subjection is not absolute; it is moral, not legal, still it exists. A breach of the federal compact will be no light matter.[68]

Indeed, as previously mentioned, all Home Rule Bills explicitly[69] (whereas it may be deemed superfluous under the traditional doctrine of parliamentary sovereignty

[65] JWF Allison, *The English Historical Constitution: Continuity, Change and European Effects* (Cambridge, Cambridge University Press, 2007) 9.

[66] HWR Wade, 'Law, Opinion and Administration' (1962) 78 *Law Quarterly Review* 189: 'Yet it crystallised the past rather than heralded the future'.

[67] Dicey, *Introduction to the Study of the Law of the Constitution* cxlviii.

[68] Dicey, *A Leap in the Dark* 15.

[69] Although, as Dicey rightly points out (ibid 24), clause 33 of the 1893 Bill is ambiguous and its drafting may be described as flawed.

as expounded in *The Law of the Constitution*) provided for the preserved sovereignty of the British Parliament, that could still legislate for Ireland on any matter, as, nowadays, it can still legislate for Scotland in devolved matters by virtue of section 28(7) of the Scotland Act 1998.[70] But Dicey here deliberately chooses to insist upon the political reality established by Home Rule more than the strictly legal and positive provisions of the acts. Drawing a comparison with the position of the Dominions towards imperial parliamentary authority, Dicey describes the authority retained by Westminster as 'shadowy' or 'nominal':[71]

> As a matter of legal theory Parliament has the right to legislate for any part of the Crown's dominions .... The Imperial Parliament is supreme in the United Kingdom, it is also supreme in Victoria. But the supremacy of the Imperial Parliament is a misleading expression; it means one thing in the United Kingdom, and another thing in Victoria or in Canada. In the United Kingdom it means the exercise of real, actual, effective, and absolute authority. In Victoria it means little more than the claim to regulate matters of a distinctly and exclusively Imperial character.[72]

Of course, such a distinction between law and morality is not unfamiliar to Austinian positivism, which is built upon the opposition between 'positive law' and 'positive morality'. Dicey himself, when describing the provisions of the 1707 Act(s) of Union between England and Scotland that were declared to be 'perpetual' and unchangeable, clearly accounts for their dual meaning, in terms of positive law or constitutional morality:

> A sovereign Parliament, in short, though it cannot be logically bound to abstain from changing any given law, may, by the fact that an Act when it was passed had been declared to be unchangeable, receive a warning that it cannot be changed without grave danger to the Constitution of the country.[73]

Nevertheless what must be noted here is the prevalence of one account (legal or moral) over the other. It is clear that, whereas the orthodox theory of the British Constitution, as expounded in the *The Law of the Constitution*, tends to make legal theory prevail over constitutional morality, the outlook is reversed in the Home Rule context.

Such a shift in the way Dicey apprehends constitutional law is of course easily understandable. These polemic writings are politically motivated, as Dicey is arguing against Home Rule. As previously said, he needs to prove the federal nature of the new institutional arrangement set out by those reforms, which would lead in his view to the decline and decay of British constitutionalism. A federal interpretation of Home Rule could not stem from a literal, strictly positivist analysis of the provisions of the Bills, but only from a broader, more political understanding of

[70] 1998 c 46.
[71] Dicey, *A Leap in the Dark* 59.
[72] ibid 4–5.
[73] AV Dicey and RS Rait, *Thoughts on the Union between England and Scotland* (London, Macmillan, 1920) 253–54.

the process at work. In other words, Dicey here focuses on the 'spirit' of the reform more than on its technical implementations. Whether this is done by necessity in order to build his case against Home Rule is of course relevant, but it should not be overlooked that those works shed an interesting light on Dicey's understanding of constitutional law. In a way that may be deemed ironic, Dicey, as a positivist lawyer, appears less dogmatic or rigid in his legal analysis of Home Rule. And we might even go as far as to discern something 'Burkean' in his battle against Home Rule for the sake of the British Constitution, endangered, in the Diceyan narrative, by hazardous adventurers. For, as Ian Ward suggested it, 'in many ways, his political affinities mirrored those of one of his greatest intellectual heroes, Edmund Burke; intellectually libertarian, sentimentally conservative'.[74]

[74] I Ward, *The English Constitution, Myths and Realities* (Oxford, Hart Publishing, 2004) 25.

# 11

# Dicey in America: The Rule of (Administrative) Law, a Century Later[1]

MICHAEL GREVE

## I. Introduction

Liberal government, AV Dicey famously insisted, is fundamentally inconsistent with royal prerogative – that is, executive authority to act, with binding force, outside, or above, or without the law. That was the central point of Dicey's initially bold and, later, increasingly petulant and implausible pronouncements to the effect that there had never been, and that there could not be, anything like France's *droit administratif* in England. That legal regime, Dicey insisted, embodied royal pretensions that had been rejected in England, supposedly once and for all, in 1688–89.[2]

America's Founders, one might say, were pre-Diceyans in this crucial respect. Their written Constitution conspicuously vests in an elected Congress, powers once claimed by the Crown – to declare and wage war, and to raise armies; to raise, spend, and borrow money without legislative approval; to establish tribunals; to corrupt the legislature by way of dangling lucrative appointments; to suspend the law.[3] The President commands the armed forces, but may not declare war. He may veto legislative enactments, but only subject to a Congressional override. He may appoint officers, but only with the advice and consent of the Senate. And far from being able to suspend the ordinary operation of the law, the President has an affirmative constitutional duty to see to the faithful execution of the law.

[1] Thanks to Natalia Castro for exceptional research and editorial assistance, and to Joseph Postell and especially Jeremy Rabkin for helpful comments on earlier drafts.

[2] MD Walters, *A.V. Dicey and the Common Law Constitutional Tradition: A Legal Turn of Mind* (Cambridge, Cambridge University Press, 2020) 216. 'Dicey never flinched from his Whig ideals: any remaining notion of a broad prerogative power to act above or outside the law had been put to rest in 1688–1689'.

[3] See generally MW McConnell, *The President Who Would Not Be King* (Princeton, Princeton University Press, 2020).

Contemporary American government differs dramatically from the picture of a modest, hemmed-in presidency. Congress has yielded immense powers and discretion to executive and administrative agencies, which produce most of the federal law that governs United States citizens. Courts as well as legal scholars and pundits have raised alarm over a poorly controlled, imperial executive. It is in this context that AV Dicey, whose once luminous star had faded after America's embrace of administrative government, has experienced a striking resurgence. Learned scholars have reinvigorated his averments to the effect that administrative law (not this or that arcane doctrine, but all of it) has no place under the English Constitution – let alone, American neo-Diceyans contend, the United States Constitution.[4] On the other side of a vibrant, ideologically charged and occasionally vituperative legal and political debate, defenders of the administrative state and its law have dismissed critics as near-hysterical 'anti-administrativist'[5] peddlers of 'The New Coke'[6] who would lay waste to administrative government as we have known it for well over a century or perhaps much longer. 'Diceyan' is a conventional adjective in the debate.[7]

This chapter sketches the trajectory of AV Dicey's reception in the United States, from profound to nil to resurgent. I write at the peril of not being able to explain, terribly well, American administrative law to Europeans, nor Dicey and his notions of *droit administratif* to contemporary Americans. I consider myself excused by two incontrovertible facts: Dicey himself was not all that good at comparative administrative law. And though a Whig at heart, I am not AV Dicey.

## II. In the Beginning

In the United States, administrative law has always been problematic. Administrative agencies that make, adjudicate, and enforce the law under a single institutional roof fit poorly (if at all) into the constitutional system of separated powers, and to many minds there is something illegitimate and lawless about them.[8] Partly to dispel that unease and abiding distrust of centralised power, Yale Professor Jerry

[4] The most sustained (nay, ferocious) argument along these lines is P Hamburger, *Is Administrative Law Unlawful?* (Chicago, University of Chicago Press, 2014) (discussed in Part V below).

[5] GE Metzger, 'Foreword: 1930s Redux: The Administrative State under Siege' (2017) 131 *Harvard Law Review* 1, 4 and passim.

[6] CR Sunstein and A Vermeule, 'The New Coke: On the Plural Aims of Administrative Law' (2015) *Supreme Court Review* 41.

[7] See eg J Pojanowski, 'Neo-Classical Administrative Law' (2020) 133 *Harvard Law Review* 852, 859–60.

[8] Attempts to 'legitimate' the administrative state in an atmosphere of pervasive distrust fill library shelves. The titles of leading scholarly contributions suggest the theme. See eg JO Freedman, *Crisis and Legitimacy: The Administrative Process and American Government* (Cambridge, Cambridge University Press, 1980); P Verkuil, *Valuing Bureaucracy: The Case for Professional Government* (Cambridge, Cambridge University Press, 2017); CR Sunstein and A Vermeule, 'The Morality of Administrative Law' (2018) 131 *Harvard Law Review* 1924.

Mashaw has argued that we have had an administrative state – and accompanying legal instruments – ever since the Founding.[9] In a very limited, technical sense, that is surely right: there have always been administrative and executive agencies, as well as statutes to organise their operations. However, it is widely recognised (and Professor Mashaw readily acknowledges) that at the time of the first edition of Dicey's *Law of the Constitution* in 1885, American law still conformed to his understanding of the rule of law, which famously blocks any 'administrative law' at variance with common-law precepts.

There were of course signal differences between England and America at the time, sufficiently glaring to make one puzzle in retrospect over Dicey's enthusiastic stateside reception. Foremost, his encomia to parliamentary sovereignty were bound to fall on deaf ears in a country, with a written Constitution and Bill of Rights, that knows only one sovereign ('We the People') and then parcels out powers among branches and levels of government. Constitutional due process guarantees, the separation of powers, federalism: all that pushes hard against Dicey's understanding of the English Constitution. Massive differences in constitutional traditions and design, one might think, should preclude any easy transposition of one rule of law model into another setting. Eventually they did, as we shall see anon. At the outset, though, those difficulties were blurred by the fact that America's judicial system still operated on Diceyan premises.

In nineteenth-century America, as in Dicey's England, the term 'administrative law' was practically unknown before the turn of the twentieth century.[10] Here as there, it could justly be said that 'the want of a name arises at bottom from non-recognition of the thing itself'.[11] Claims against government actors were brought in ordinary courts, and administrative tribunals were virtually unheard of. There was next to no direct constitutional or statutory review of agency action. Overwhelmingly, legal challenges to government action rested on claims at common law (such as trespass or assumpsit), an extraordinary writ such as *mandamus*, or in equity (for example, anti-suit injunctions). Those cases generally sought relief from individual officers. They differed from wholly private lawsuits in that the official had a defence not available to a private defendant: I acted on the lawful authority of the United States. To which the plaintiff would respond: no, you did not – either because you acted ultra vires or else because Congress, for constitutional reasons, had no business conferring that authority. In the event, officers

[9] J Mashaw, *Creating the Administrative Constitution: The Lost One Hundred Years of American Administrative Law* (New Haven, Yale University Press, 2012).

[10] As late as 1938, Felix Frankfurter lamented that 'To this day administrative law has no rubric in the ordinary digests, and flickering cross-references to the subject first begin to appear in 220 United States Reports [ie 1911]. Not until 280 United States reports does the term appear to have established itself in the index': F Frankfurter, 'Foreword' (1938) 47 *Yale Law Journal* 515, 518.

[11] AV Dicey, *Introduction to the Study of the Law of the Constitution* (Indianapolis, Liberty Fund, 1982, reprint of the 1915 8th edn published by Macmillan). All cites and quotations in this chapter are to this edition.

were held *personally* liable for ultra vires actions.[12] The common law, one might say by way of inverting Justice Oliver Wendell Holmes's dreadful aphorism, was no 'brooding omnipresence in the sky'.[13] In cases against government officials, as in wholly private cases, it was 'a benevolent omnipresence on the ground'.[14]

Administrative law, in the sense in which we now understand it, began to take shape in the immediately following decades – the decades between the first edition of Dicey's *Law of the Constitution* and its final (eighth) edition in 1915.[15] The Interstate Commerce Commission (ICC), established in 1887 for the regulation of railroad rates, is uniformly viewed as the first administrative agency. In a long-running controversy over railroad regulation by independent commission, American administrative law developed an 'appellate review' model quite at odds with Diceyan premises.[16] It postulates that administrative agencies may regulate and adjudicate with binding legal force, subject (at least ordinarily) to judicial review – *re*-view of a legal decision that has been made at least once before. The adoption of that model progressed in fits and starts over the ensuing decades, amid a grim debate between defenders of the traditional understanding of the rule of law and Progressive and, later, New Deal advocates of flexible and expert administration. A compromise between the contending forces was eventually enshrined in the Administrative Procedure Act (APA) in 1946.

AV Dicey's shadow loomed very large in those decades. Harvard Professor Joseph Beale, the principal author of the American Law Institute's *First Restatement of Conflict* (1934), wholeheartedly embraced Dicey's theory of 'vested rights'. By that direct route, Dicey profoundly shaped what Americans call 'Conflicts Law' and continental lawyers, 'private international law'.[17] Dicey's *Lectures on the Relation between the Law and Public Opinion* met with a somewhat diffident reaction at their delivery at Harvard Law School in 1898[18] – unsurprisingly, given the author's preoccupation with 'collectivist' English sentiments and social welfare programmes that had no American equivalent at the time. Still, *Law and Public Opinion* did find American admirers, at the time and even in much later decades.[19]

[12] Under American as under English law, *respondeat superior* liability was effectively unknown. In a celebrated case, the United States Supreme Court held that even a *military* officer could be held personally liable for trespass committed pursuant to his direct orders but beyond the scope of the authorising statute: *Little v Barreme*, 6 US 170, 179 (1804).

[13] *Southern Pacific Co v Jensen*, 244 US 205, 222 (1917). 'The common law is not a brooding omnipresence in the sky, but the articulate voice of some sovereign or quasi sovereign that can be identified'.

[14] RR Gasaway and A Parrish, 'In Praise of Erie – And Its Eventual Demise' (2013) 10 *Journal of Law Economics & Policy* 225, 244.

[15] A ninth edition appeared in 1939, long after Dicey's death, with an Introduction by ECS Wade.

[16] T Merrill, 'Article III, Agency Adjudication, and the Origins of the Appellate Review Model of Administrative Law' (2011) 111 *Columbia Law Review* 940, 943. See also TW Merrill and K Tongue Watts, 'Agency Regulations with the Force of Law' (2002) 116 *Harvard Law Review* 467.

[17] AV Dicey's treatise was first published in 1896 under the title *A Digest of the Laws of England with Reference to the Conflict of Laws* (London, Stevens & Sons, 1896). In later editions, it has remained a standard reference to this day.

[18] TH Ford, *Albert Venn Dicey: The Man and His Times* (Chichester, Barry Rose Publishers, 1985) 246–47.

[19] eg R Pound, 'The Rule of Law and the Modern Welfare State' (1953) 7 *Vanderbilt Law Review* 1.

None of that oeuvre, however, was formative in the way the *Law of the Constitution* proved formative. Its first edition and its sharp juxtaposition of the 'rule of law' and its foil and negation, the French *droit administratif*, was eagerly received by American scholars and legal luminaries who sought to defend the 'supremacy of law' against Progressive and New Deal innovations.

Dicey stated his rule of law convictions in a few familiar passages. 'The supremacy or rule of law' means, first, 'that no man is punishable or can be lawfully made to suffer in body or goods except for a distinct breach of law established in the ordinary legal manner before the ordinary Courts of the land'.[20] It means, second, that 'every man, whatever be his rank or condition, is subject to the law of the realm and amenable to the jurisdiction of the ordinary tribunals'.[21] It 'excludes the idea of any exemption of officials or others from the duty of obedience to the law which governs other citizens or from the jurisdiction of the ordinary tribunals'.[22] The rule of law means, third, that 'the general principles of the constitution … are with us the result of judicial decisions determining the rights of private persons in particular cases brought before the Courts'.[23] In contrast, France's *droit administrative*, as Dicey initially understood it, clothed government officials with expansive immunities and made their actions reviewable by specialised administrative tribunals rather than ordinary courts. Moreover, 'the security (such as it is) given to the rights of individuals results, or appears to result, from the general principles of the constitution'.[24] All those features, Dicey insisted, were alien and antithetical to the English Constitution. They all smacked of 'despotism'.

This understanding, and especially Dicey's singular emphasis on the central role of ordinary courts, profoundly shaped the administrative law debate in the United States. Morton J Horwitz's widely read volume on *The Transformation of American Law*, for example, credits Dicey's 'enormously influential pronouncements' on the rule of law and identifies him as the leading exponent of a 'legalist' tradition, an 'entirely judge – and court-centered system of thought'.[25] Dicey's pull was evident in the legal literature, legislative records, and professional debates.[26] It was loudly

[20] Dicey, *Law of the Constitution* 110. The point of this principle, Dicey explained, is to minimise government discretion, for 'wherever there is discretion there is room for arbitrariness': ibid 111.

[21] ibid 114.

[22] ibid 120. Accordingly, Dicey proudly noted, 'The Reports abound with these cases in which officials have been brought before the Courts, and made, in their personal capacity, liable to punishment, or to the payment of damages, for acts done in their official character but in excess of their legal authority': ibid 114.

[23] ibid 115. 'Parliamentary declarations of the law such as the Petition of Right and the Bill of Rights', Dicey added in a slightly curious footnote, 'have a certain affinity to judicial decisions'.

[24] ibid 115.

[25] MJ Horwitz, *The Transformation of American Law, 1870–1960* (Oxford, Oxford University Press, 1992) 221, 225–30.

[26] A single example shall suffice to convey the intellectual atmosphere. In 1911, responding to early proposals to establish an administrative Federal Trade Commission to regulate and adjudicate anti-competitive practices, an eminent lawyer (the aptly named HB Hornblower) trumpeted his Diceyan convictions to the American Bar Association and denounced the proposed scheme as 'repugnant to our American traditions and principles. It has always been our boast that no one should be condemned

lamented by Progressive and New Deal proponents. For them, Dicey embodied an appallingly pre-modern ideal of law – a fantasy world of 'moribund unrealities' about administrative law, in the words of Harvard Professor Felix Frankfurter, a principal theorist and architect of the emerging administrative state and, after 1939, a Supreme Court Justice.[27] Frankfurter acknowledged Dicey's influence with a tone of exasperation. 'Generations of judges and lawyers', he wrote, 'were brought up in the mental climate of Dicey'.[28] Dicey's 'influence "long threw a chilly shadow over administrative law" and for the next fifty years managed to persuade Anglo-American lawyers that administrative law was "simply a misfortune inflicted upon the benighted folks across the channel"'.[29]

Horwitz contrasts the 'legalist' tradition with a 'scientific' tradition that informed Progressive and New Deal champions of the administrative state.[30] Some of its exponents, prominently Ernst Freund at The University of Chicago Law School and Frank J Goodnow (a non-lawyer) at Columbia University, drew on Continental ideas, especially German theories of the *Rechtsstaat*. Freund, the most Teutonic of those theorists, had no patience for administrative discretion and advocated a rigid, rule-based regime. Other Progressives, foremost Felix Frankfurter and his student James Landis (later Chairman of the Securities Exchange Commission), held very different views. They and their followers exalted administrative specialisation, flexibility, and expertise, and they were deeply suspicious of generalist courts and common law adjudication.[31]

The debate between the legalist and scientific camps accompanied the growth of administrative agencies and the evolution of the appellate review model over the first four decades of the twentieth century. It became increasingly fierce in the 1930s, as the Roosevelt Administration created 'vast congeries of agencies',[32] as New Deal theorists propounded ever-bolder theories to unleash administrators from legal strictures,[33] and as Germany and Italy succumbed to fascism. In 1937, the American Bar Association (ABA) appointed Roscoe Pound, an eminent jurist and long-time Dean of the Harvard Law School, as head of its Special Committee on Administrative Law. In a legendary Report, Pound rang the alarm bells. He inveighed against the spread of 'administrative absolutism', meaning 'a highly centralised administration set up under complete control of the executive for the

except by the courts after an opportunity to be heard, and upon competent testimony. … If this is to become a government by executive edict or by bureaucratic domination, the days of our republican institutions are certainly numbered': quoted in J Dickinson, *Administrative Justice and the Supremacy of Law* (Oxford, Oxford University Press, 1927) 236.

[27] F Frankfurter, 'Foreword' (1938) 47 *Yale Law Journal* 515, 517.

[28] DE Ernst, *Tocqueville's Nightmare: The Administrative State Emerges in America, 1900–1940* (Oxford, Oxford University Press, 2014) 30, quoting Frankfurter, ibid 517.

[29] Horwitz, *Transformation* 226 (quoting and citing several authors).

[30] ibid 220–30.

[31] See Ernst, *Tocqueville's Nightmare* 9–26.

[32] F Frankfurter, 'The Task of Administrative Law' (1927) 75 *University of Pennsylvania Law Review* 614, 614.

[33] See eg JM Landis, *The Administrative Process* (New Haven, Yale University Press, 1938).

time being, relieved of judicial review and making its own rules'.[34] Pound implored the Bar to act, otherwise 'there is nothing to check the tendency of administrative bureaus to extend their operations indefinitely even to the extent of supplanting our traditional judicial regime by an administrative regime'.[35]

That certainly sounds like AV Dicey in near despair. There are reasons to doubt whether Pound, let alone the ABA at large, actually held those convictions to the point of questioning the legitimacy of administrative law in general.[36] In any event, it was far too late in the day to mount those ramparts. America had already fumbled her way to a compromise between rule of law precepts and the demands of prompt, expert administration, in response to pressures and problems about which Dicey had not much useful to say.

## III. The Appellate Review Model Takes Shape

The improvised path of American administrative law in its early stages becomes intelligible in juxtaposition to three of Dicey's writings, all dating to the year 1915. Two of them – a new Introduction to the *Law of the Constitution*, and a brief law review essay tellingly entitled *The Development of Administrative Law in England*[37] – famously reflect Dicey's acknowledgements that England had in fact acquired something very much like *droit administratif*, while France had made great strides towards a juridical system under which increasingly independent tribunals afforded substantial legal protection for citizens. The third writing, a cantankerous Introduction to the second edition of *Law and Public Opinion*, describes a number of statutes enacted after 1905 that 'most directly illustrate the progress of collectivism' in England.[38] Among them was the 1911 National Insurance Act, governing unemployment insurance. Here as with respect to other enactments, Dicey inveighed against the 'collectivist' and 'socialist' aims of the statute. He further argued that the Act's 'administrative methods' likewise 'illustrate the influence of collectivism or socialism on English legislation'.[39] The Act 'greatly increases both the legislative and the judicial authority of the Government or of

[34] *Report of the Special Committee on Administrative Law* (1938) 63 *Annual Reports of the American Bar Association* 336, 343.

[35] ibid 339.

[36] Daniel Ernst, for one, argues that for all the 'absolutism' bluster, Pound in fact accepted basic administrative law precepts and that his chief objectives were to simplify and speed up judicial review and to ensure a fair process within agencies. 'Had Pound stated his views dispassionately', Ernst argues, 'he would be seen today as what he in fact was: another sign of an emerging consensus that the structural and procedural reforms of agencies would keep Tocqueville's nightmare at bay': Ernst, *Tocqueville's Nightmare* 125.

[37] AV Dicey, 'The Development of Administrative Law in England' (1915) 31 *Law Quarterly Review* 148.

[38] Dicey, *Law and Public Opinion* 365.

[39] ibid 367.

officials closely connected with the Government of the day'.[40] At the legislative front, government officials 'have the power to make regulations for the carrying out of the Act which, if not annulled by the King in Council, become part of the Act itself'.[41] The government of the day, it appeared, could 'at any moment, without the need for any Act of Parliament, extend the statute's reach "to every trade throughout the United Kingdom"'.[42]

'The Insurance Commissioners', Dicey continued, 'have judicial authority'.[43] The statute created a complex internal appeals process, terminating in the decision of an 'umpire' appointed by the government of the day. 'The decision of the umpire is final and conclusive, *ie* the jurisdiction of the law courts is apparently excluded',[44] Dicey complained. And the officials lacked 'the security of tenure conferred on every judge of the High Court under the Act of Settlement'.[45]

The scope of legislative and judicial authority afforded to administrators, Dicey concluded, was 'enough to prove that the Insurance Act creates in England a system bearing a marked resemblance to the administrative law of France'.[46] Dicey conceded that administrative law in that configuration had 'some distinct merits' – foremost, speed and low cost. 'But administrative law has two defects which have till very recent years forbidden its existence in England'. 'Administrative tribunals always tend to exclude the jurisdiction of the ordinary law Courts'. Moreover, 'Administrative Courts are always more or less connected with the Government of the day. Their decisions are apt to be influenced by political considerations. Government officials cannot have the thorough independence of judges'.[47]

Quite clearly, Dicey recognised two problems that would soon dominate the administrative law debate in the United States: the delegation of legislative and judicial powers to executive-administrative agencies, and the related danger of politicised or abusive administrative decisions – the fear of the 'unscrupulous administrator', as Chief Justice Charles Evans Hughes put it in a memorable 1931 speech to the ABA.[48] Having seen the problems, though, Dicey apparently despaired of answers.

In the *Development of Administrative Law* essay, celebrated among Progressive American jurists at the time as evidence that even Dicey himself had at last seen the

[40] ibid 368–69.

[41] ibid 369. Quoting and commenting on the statutory language, Dicey writes that 'This power to make regulations [with the force of law] is probably the widest power of subordinate legislation ever conferred by Parliament upon any body of officials'.

[42] ibid 370.

[43] ibid. Apparently, appeal to regular courts could be had; but it had 'been made little or no use of'.

[44] ibid 371.

[45] ibid.

[46] ibid, citing Dicey, *Law of the Constitution* ch xii.

[47] ibid 370.

[48] 'An unscrupulous administrator might be tempted to say, "Let me find the facts for the people of my country and I care little who lays down the general principles"': L Bell, '"Let Me Find the Facts …"' (1940) 26 *American Bar Association Journal* 552, 552.

light of day,[49] Dicey acknowledged that Parliament may grant quasi-judicial power to administrators. What else, then, may Parliament confer? Little, if anything, in Dicey's writings suggests any limit to parliamentary grants of effectively unlimited powers, of a quasi-legislative as well as a quasi-judicial nature, to the executive. That grim inference may come naturally to a resolute defender of parliamentary sovereignty, but it is hard to reconcile with Dicey's earlier averments that 'wherever there is discretion there is room for arbitrariness'.[50] Administrators, Dicey wrote, need not follow ordinary court procedures so long as they treat affected parties in a 'spirit of judicial fairness and equity'.[51] What if they act in some other spirit – the agency's mission, for example; or the demands of the government of the day? Why, Dicey responded rather insouciantly,

> the fact that the ordinary courts can deal with any actual and provable breach of the law committed by any servant of the Crown still preserves that rule of law which is fatal to the existence of true *droit administratif*.[52]

That begs the rule of law question in more than one way. How can ordinary courts effectively check the monumental volume of executive decisions? And if, per Dicey, ordinary courts are supposed to take the whole case *de novo*, why have agency adjudication in the first place?

Dicey's 1915 writings all revolve around unchecked or poorly checked executive power. Yet, they fail to engage the vexing topic. 'The entire question of executive power was treated as a sort of afterthought in the *Law of the Constitution*',[53] including the final edition; and the same is true of the second edition of *Law and Public Opinion*. That might make a modicum of sense if one believes that the executive prerogative to act above or outside the law was affirmatively buried in the Glorious Revolution; or that ministerial responsibility – in the conventional sense, responsibility to Parliament, not the King – would act as a check on a run-away executive;[54] or that the ordinary courts would continue to do so after all. Finally, one might think (although Dicey did not say so with any clarity) that concerns over the displacement of ordinary courts are at a nadir when government agencies – pursuant to the National Insurance Act, say – dispense benefits, as distinct from issuing coercive rules and verdicts.[55] But none of those answers could do in

[49] See eg Frankfurter, 'The Task of Administrative Law' 615.

[50] Dicey, *Law of the Constitution* 111.

[51] Dicey, 'The Development of Administrative Law' 151.

[52] ibid 152.

[53] Walters, *A.V. Dicey and the Common Law Constitutional Tradition* 215.

[54] See Dicey, *Law of the Constitution* ch xi. Ministerial responsibility in the conventional sense, Dicey explains, is a matter of – well, convention, rather than law: ibid 215. In a 'strict' legal sense, it means that any minister is 'legally responsible for the legality of the act in which he takes part. Hence, indirectly but surely, the action of every servant of the Crown, and therefore in effect the Crown itself, is brought under the supremacy of the law of the land'.

[55] Few propositions have been more intuitive to American jurists than the notion that government decisions over public benefits – 'privileges' as distinct from rights, in nineteenth century parlance – pose minimal (if any) constitutional or rule of law issues. Dickinson's *Administrative Justice* 6–7,

America, under its regime of separated powers and a skeletal system of ordinary federal courts; and not when administrative law develops, as it did at the time in America, in the context of regulatory rather than benefit-granting agencies. American lawyers had to think differently and more creatively about both problems: the delegation of legislative and judicial authority to executive agencies, and the abuse of discretion and judicial control.[56]

Over time, the law settled on the same two-part answer in both domains: administrative procedures, and appellate judicial review. As noted, that regime initially developed in the battle over railroad regulation. Landmark cases, decided later in the 1930s, illustrate the trajectory.

## A. Delegation

In two momentous 1935 decisions, *Panama Refining* and *ALA Schechter Poultry*, the Supreme Court invalidated key provisions of the National Industrial Recovery Act (NIRA).[57] That Act, a centrepiece of the Roosevelt Administration's agenda, purported to authorise the President and his subordinates, in concert with trade associations, to establish 'codes of fair competition' for every American industry. The two decisions – to this day, the only Supreme Court cases to invalidate a federal statute on nondelegation grounds – were not entirely unexpected at the time, but still required explanation. After all, the Court had routinely sustained regulatory statutes against nondelegation challenges. That included the ICC and the Federal Trade Commission (FTC), charged with policing 'unfair methods of competition'. In distinguishing those statutes from the NIRA, the Court struck distinctly Diceyan notes. The FTC's orders, it observed, required judicial enforcement.

305–306 sounds the theme: government need not provide such benefits in the first place. Thus, it may commit their determination to administrative adjudication without raising due process or anti-delegation concerns, at least so long as some kind of hearing remains available. Through various twists and turns, that has remained the law: *Mathews v Eldridge*, 424 US 319, 333 (1976). In contrast, due process problems and concerns over the delegation of adjudicatory and rulemaking powers to administrative agencies arise with full force in the context of coercive government interference with private right. See eg *Gundy v United States*, 139 S Ct 2116, 2140 (2019) (Gorsuch J dissenting) (explicating the principle in the context of a delegation case). While the question of what exactly qualifies as a 'private right' is among the messiest in all American public law, the general principle that such matters must be committed to Article III courts – to the exclusion of administrative tribunals – has gained increased judicial acceptance. See *Securities and Exch comm v Jarkesy*, 603 US (2024); *Oil States Energy v Greene's Energy*, 138 S Ct 1365, 1373 (2018); *Stern v Marshall*, 564 US 462, 492 (2011).

[56] The single most impressive contribution to the debate, still worth close study a century later, is John Dickinson's aptly titled *Administrative Justice and the Supremacy of Law in the United States*. The author – a distinguished professor at the University of Pennsylvania Law School and an accomplished litigator in private practice and, during the early Roosevelt Administration, at the Department of Justice – straddled the divide between the 'legalist' and 'scientific' camps. Fully acknowledging the force of Dicey's supremacy-of-law convictions (ibid 32–37), he undertook the project Dicey himself never contemplated: the preservation of those commitments under changed institutional and economic conditions.

[57] *Panama Refining Co v Ryan*, 293 US 388 (1935); *ALA Schechter Poultry Corp v United States*, 295 US 495 (1935).

In contrast, NIRA codes were immediately binding and could be contested only in a criminal defence proceeding. The FTC's determinations of 'unfair methods' were of course not identical to common law rules (why else have an agency?), but they could be readily analogised by ordinary judicial reasoning. Finally, the Court noted that the FTC and its sister agencies had to follow regularised procedures for factual determinations, adjudication, and rulemaking (to the limited extent that agencies had that authority). The NIRA, in contrast, contained no such mechanisms.

The Court's insistence on procedural regularity, on display not only in *Schechter* and *Panama Refining* but in numerous cases of the era, proved formative. At a legislative level, the New Dealers understood the Court's message very well and wrote statutes accordingly. For a prominent example, the National Labor Relations Act, enacted shortly after *Schechter*, provided the procedural and judicial safeguards that the NIRA so obviously lacked. In that form, the Act easily survived a nondelegation challenge.[58] At a doctrinal level, some of *Schechter*'s constitutional precepts morphed into administrative law doctrine. In earlier cases, the Court had consistently held that Congress could delegate to the executive fact-finding tasks, precedent to the enforcement of a legislatively determined rule or standard. The NIRA was found wanting in that regard, too. (It merely required the President's general statement of opinion.) The constitutional fact-finding requirement quickly migrated into administrative law: the so-called *Chenery* doctrine, firmly entrenched in jurisprudence and a rock-bottom presumption of the APA, holds that agencies must give reasons and supply evidence for their decisions.[59] Under APA law as it has developed over the decades, agencies must build an adequate record in rulemaking as in adjudication.[60] They must rest their decisions on that record, and they may not supplement it after the fact and for purposes of litigation.

## B. Appellate Review

The scope and standard of judicial review, on questions of law and fact, was a central theme of administrative law from the beginning and has remained central to this day. The basic, obvious tension is between the need for bureaucratic speed, expertise, and economy of decision-making on one side and rule of law concerns over excessive discretion and abuse on the other. It appears in glaring light in the Supreme Court's foundational, notoriously ambiguous decision in *Crowell v Benson* (1932).[61] At issue was a routine injury dispute between a maritime employer and

[58] *NLRB v Jones & Laughlin Steel Corp*, 301 US 1, 30 (1937).

[59] See KM Stack, 'The Constitutional Foundations of Chenery' (2007) 116 *Yale Law Journal* 952, 974–75.

[60] For the great majority of rulemaking proceedings, the record is subject to judicial 'hard look' review: *Motor Vehicle Mfrs Ass'n v State Farm*, 463 US 29, 38–39 (1983).

[61] *Crowell v Benson*, 285 US 22 (1932).

employee. Congress had by statute committed the adjudication of such disputes to a federal agency with opportunity for judicial review, but under what standard? A lower court went 'all Dicey' and exercised *de novo* review on all questions of law and fact, lest the statute transgress the Constitution. Congress might have left private disputes of the kind at issue entirely to ordinary *state* courts (which would adjudicate such cases either under common tort law or state statutory law). However, the conferral of jurisdiction on an administrative agency rather than ordinary *federal* courts posed a separation of powers problem – to wit, the transfer of what looked like a quintessentially judicial power to an administrative body.

The *Crowell* Court struggled. Part of Chief Justice Hughes' opinion is fairly described as a paean to virtues even Dicey had acknowledged in the *droit administratif*: speed, and institutional capacity to handle a large volume of cases. Thus, the Court concluded that the determination of ordinary facts – the extent of the injury, the level of responsibility – should be left to the administrator, subject to very deferential review. Questions of law, in contrast, would remain subject to judicial determination. So, too, with questions of 'constitutional fact' and 'jurisdictional fact': the Court would exercise Dicey-style ultra vires review.

What then, of the 'unscrupulous administrator' whose factual findings would principally serve to advance the agency's agenda and set judicial review to naught? The Court supplied an answer, of sorts, by describing agency adjudicators as 'adjuncts' to ordinary courts, akin to juries or special masters. That, though, was not much more than polite fiction even at the time, when agencies operated principally through adjudication. It became wholly untenable in later decades, when agencies acquired expansive, quasi-legislative rulemaking powers.

Of even greater consequence, the Court's insistence on the de novo review of questions of constitutional and jurisdictional fact – a remnant of Dicey's world of ultra vires review – soon eroded. It is often difficult to identify subsets of such facts apart from all the other facts within the agency's purview.[62] And if courts exercise judicial deference with respect to one set of (ordinary) facts, why not the others? The natural tendency for courts was to defer to agencies and to migrate from the review of poorly understood factual disputes and confusing statutory terms to the thing courts can understand: the review of agency procedures.

## IV. The APA, and Beyond

After a long, hard-fought political contest, the compromises just sketched became enshrined in the APA. It gestures in a Diceyan direction, except when it does the

[62] Arguably, the distinction between 'jurisdiction' and 'substance' is questionable in an administrative context. It makes sense to say that a court had jurisdiction but got the merits wrong. In contrast, an administrator who mangles the facts or the law has made a decision outside his authority – his 'jurisdiction', one might say. See *City of Arlington v FCC*, 569 US 290, 301 (2013). The *Crowell* Court acknowledged the difficulty in an unconvincing footnote: *Crowell v Benson*, 285 US 22, 55 n 17 (1932).

opposite. The reviewing court 'shall set aside' agency actions that are 'contrary to law'.[63] Then again, the APA instructs courts to exercise deference with respect to reviewing questions of fact.[64] It commands courts to set aside agency actions that are 'arbitrary, capricious, or an abuse of discretion';[65] then again, it precludes judicial review of decisions that are 'committed to agency discretion by law'.[66] The APA's principal focus is on administrative *procedure*, which is to serve as a kind of substitute for the constitutional 'due process of law' that can be had only in regular courts. The APA seeks to mimic the separation of powers by functionally insulating agency adjudicators from direct political control. Even so, the adjudicators' rulings remain reversible by politically appointed agency heads, lest the agency lose control over its agenda.

The APA has been described as a 'fierce compromise' between Diceyan defenders of 'legal supremacy' and Progressive and New Deal proponents of flexible, expert administration.[67] The Act, to repeat, does contain Diceyan elements. Final administrative decisions remain subject to review by ordinary courts, and the system is heavily court-centred. Then again, the APA contains profoundly anti-Diceyan elements, such various forms of judicial 'deference' to administrative decisions. And it sports features on which Dicey had nothing interesting to say, especially the expansive rulemaking powers of administrative agencies.

Of late, the question of whether the APA compromise is fish or fowl, fair or just foul, Diceyan or not, has re-emerged as a bone of scholarly contention. That should not come as a surprise: American administrative law has never been stable for extended periods of time. Even after the APA, it continued to vacillate between 'crisis and legitimacy'.[68] Contrary to a famous judicial pronouncement, the APA has never proven a formula on which 'the contending forces of society have come to rest'.[69] Its 'fierce compromise' may be better understood as an under-theorised agreement to keep fighting.

The APA worked reasonably well for some two decades, so long as agencies served the purpose for which they had been designed in the New Deal era: administer, in a moderate, bipartisan political environment, cosy cartels of broadcasters, airlines, truckers, stock exchanges, or agricultural producers. In the 1960s and 1970s, however, a sense that agencies had been 'captured' by the industries they were supposed to regulate produced a 'reformation of American administrative law' that effectively doubled down on the appellate review model.[70] Administrative

[63] Administrative Procedure Act, 5 USC § 706(2).

[64] ibid § 706(2)(E).

[65] ibid § 706(2)(A).

[66] ibid § 701(a)(2).

[67] See GB Shepherd, 'Fierce Compromise: The Administrative Procedure Act Emerges from New Deal Politics' (1996) 90 *Northwestern University Law Review* 1557, 1680–81.

[68] See Freedman, *Crisis and Legitimacy.*

[69] *Vermont Yankee Nuclear Power Corp v Natural Resources Defense Council, Inc*, 435 US 519, 523 (1978) (citing and quoting *Wong Yang Sung v McGrath*, 339 US 33 (1950) (Jackson J)).

[70] RB Stewart, 'The Reformation of American Administrative Law' (1975) 88 *Harvard Law Review* 1669, 1685.

procedures became much more involved, and private litigants with statutory 'public interest' claims ('private attorneys-general', in American parlance) gained much easier access to courts. Moreover, while the Supreme Court precluded lower courts from imposing on agencies procedural requirements in excess of statutory law, courts – including the High Court itself – subjected the agencies' reasoning process, from fact-finding to rulemaking and inferences in-between, to a 'hard look' review. At the same time, it transpired that supposedly 'legal' determinations under broadly worded statutes are often policy decisions admitting of one or another plausible answer. So, the Court held, in its most-cited case ever, that legal ambiguity requires judicial deference: presumptively, ambiguity means that Congress intended those kinds of decisions to be made by expert administrators, rather than unaccountable laypersons on the Bench.[71] In that crucial regard – probe the administrators' reasoning and good sense; cut them slack on the law – American administrative law circa 1990 had become almost comically non-Diceyan.

Decades thence, that model, too, has come under heavy fire. Critics, prominently including Justices of the United States Supreme Court, have denounced it as wholly inadequate to controlling a lawless, overbearing, oppressive, illegitimate administrative state that has leapt constitutional bounds.[72] And in this context, Diceyan rule of law tropes have resurfaced in the legal literature and in judicial opinions. The United States Supreme Court has held that agency adjudicators are *executive* officials who must at all times be appointed in the constitutionally envisioned fashion, either by the President or one of his direct subordinates.[73] It may follow that the adjudicators must also be *removable* at will. Were the Court to arrive at that conclusion, the APA's enterprise of mimicking the constitutional separation of powers through a separation of functions within agencies will have come to an end.[74] In the same vein, the Court has held that disputes over private rights always require an ordinary court and may not ever be committed to an administrative tribunal.[75] In a momentous case, the Court explicitly overruled its 1984 decision

[71] *Chevron Inc v Natural Resources Defense Council, Inc*, 467 US 837, 843–44 (1984).

[72] See eg *Perez v Mortgage Bankers Ass'n*, 575 US 92, 124 (2015) (Thomas J, concurring). '[D]eference amounts to a transfer of the judge's exercise of interpretive judgment to the agency. But the agency, as part of the Executive Branch, lacks the structural protections for independent judgment adopted by the Framers, including the life tenure and salary protections of Article III. Because the agency is thus not properly constituted to exercise the judicial power under the Constitution, the transfer of interpretive judgment raises serious separation-of-powers concerns'; see also *City of Arlington v FCC*, 569 US 290, 312–13 (2013) (Roberts J, dissenting), 'Although modern administrative agencies fit most comfortably within the Executive Branch, as a practical matter they exercise legislative power, by promulgating regulations with the force of law; executive power, by policing compliance with those regulations; and judicial power, by adjudicating enforcement actions and imposing sanctions on those found to have violated their rules'; *Gundy v United States*, 139 S Ct 2116, 2137 (2019); '[W]hile Congress can enlist considerable assistance from the executive branch in filling up details and finding facts, it may never hand off to the nation's chief prosecutor the power to write his own criminal code. That "is delegation running riot"' (internal citations omitted).

[73] *Lucia v SEC*, 138 S Ct 2044, 2050–51 (2018).

[74] *Lucia v SEC*, 138 S Ct 2044, 2060 (2018) (Breyer J, concurring). See also CJ Walker, 'Constitutional Tensions in Agency Adjudication' (2019) 104 *Iowa Law Review* 2679, 2680.

[75] *Securities Exch comm v Jarkesy* 603 US (2024).

in Chevron v. NRDC, which for four decades commanded judicial deference to agencies' legal determination in a great number of administrative law cases.[76] And there is no shortage of scholarly, judicial, and even legislative suggestions that just perhaps, we should rethink and revamp the law of official immunities, the better to hold rogue officers to account.[77]

Much of the agitation is driven by grim formalism about the constitutional separation of powers. That orientation, in turn, reflects the dominance of an 'originalist' jurisprudence which, in its more positivist versions, is much at odds with Dicey's common law convictions and in fact deeply suspicious of courts that purport to 'find' law. Even so, Dicey's contentions resonate; and now, as a century ago, they lend themselves readily to wholesale rhetorical attacks on a despotic 'administrative state'. It is worth asking, though, whether and to what extent they will aid 'anti-administrativist' proponents of the rule of law, as those jurists understand it; or whether Dicey's errors and blind spots on the subject of administrative law will again impede the fiendish task of elaborating a more lawful framework for an administrative state that will be with us for the foreseeable future.

## V. A Blind Spot – And Dicey's Nightmare?

The contention that Dicey fundamentally misunderstood France's evolving *droit administratif* and that he misrepresented and misapprehended the 'administrative' elements of English law at the time is common currency. Even Dicey's most eloquent defenders concede that administrative law was the most glaring of his 'blind spots'.[78] From there, it is but a short hop to laments or polemics over Dicey's baneful influence. His overwrought pronouncements on the glories of the English courts and the despotic nature of *droit administratif*, the storyline goes, impeded and delayed the arrival of a sensible administrative-legal system in common law countries.

For the most part, that has been the refrain of Progressive jurists. It was also articulated, however, by FA Hayek – under no suspicion of having advocated an unchecked administrative state and on his own account an 'unrepentant Old Whig'.[79] In an important chapter in *The Constitution of Liberty* – like much of Hayek's oeuvre, widely read in the United States – Hayek celebrated the evolution

[76] *Loper Bright Enter v Raimondo*, 603 US (2024) overruling *Chevron Inc v Natural Resources Defense Council* 467 US 837 (1984).

[77] See eg W Baude, 'Is Qualified Immunity Unlawful?' (2018) 106 *California Law Review* 45 (the author's answer is 'yes'). See also D Zaring, 'Personal Liability as Administrative Law' (2009) 66 *Washington & Lee Law Review* 313.

[78] Walters, *A.V. Dicey and the Common Law Constitutional Tradition* 299, 'Dicey had a number of intellectual blind spots. Administrative law was the biggest one'.

[79] FA Hayek, *The Constitution of Liberty: The Definitive Edition* (Chicago, University of Chicago Press, 2011) 531.

of the German idea of the *Rechtsstaat* as a massive advance for the rule of law. The advance, as Hayek saw it, was the institutional solution of subjecting administrative acts to control and adjudication by independent (albeit specialised) administrative courts. That solution, Hayek argued, was missed among Dicey's obsession with the Conseil d'Etat and its offspring. '[B]y his attempt to vindicate the rule of law as he saw it', Hayek wrote,

> Dicey in effect blocked the development which would have offered the best chance of preserving it. He could not stop the growth in the Anglo-Saxon world of an administrative apparatus similar to that which existed on the Continent. But he did contribute much to prevent or delay the growth of institutions which could subject the new bureaucratic machinery to effective control.[80]

There is a great deal to this indictment, especially vis-à-vis the United States. The option of establishing independent administrative courts was considered in the 1930s.[81] The ABA advanced proposals to that effect for much of the decade, and Congressional committees considered Bills to establish such courts in one form or another. However, nothing came of it. In part, the proposals foundered on account of interest group politics. Lawyers who practised in then-existing specialised courts – the Court of Customs and Patent Appeals, and the Board of Tax Appeals (now the United States Tax Court) – apprehended that those favourable tribunals might be merged into a general administrative court of unknown quality and composition.[82] Clearly, however, Diceyan suspicions of administrative tribunals played a large role.[83] The ABA abandoned the idea in 1937 and instead mobilised to judicialise the process *within* administrative agencies.[84]

Was that a mistake? Perhaps. 'Ordinary courts', to Dicey, meant common law courts. In the United States, with its federal and separation-of-powers system, it had to mean *federal* courts established pursuant to Article III of the Constitution. Of those, there are few. Depending on one's count, the number of federal agencies alone, to say nothing of their myriad rules and decisions, may exceed the number of Article III judges – fewer than 900 at all levels, in a country of some 340 million administered citizens.

The obvious absurdity of trying to exercise effective judicial control under those institutional arrangements has prompted renewed calls, here and there, to establish independent administrative courts in America after all, in one form

[80] ibid 307.

[81] See RM Cooper, 'The Proposed United States Administrative Court' (1936) 35 *Michigan Law Review* 193, 196.

[82] Ernst, *Tocqueville's Nightmare* 120.

[83] ibid 120, citing and quoting a leading member of the ABA Special Committee on Administrative law to the effect that the ABA should be loath to transgress 'the basic Anglo-American concept of the supremacy of law administered in one court, the same court, over public official and private citizen alike'.

[84] Ernst, *Tocqueville's Nightmare* 120–21.

or another.[85] Such, proposals, however, plainly exceed the bandwidth of a Congress that has never meaningfully amended the core provisions of the APA since 1946. Moreover, they meet with firm resistance not only from mainstream administrative law scholars who would rather tinker with the existing machinery but also from sworn enemies of the administrative state.

The most thoroughgoing assault on that state is Columbia Law Professor Philip Hamburger's influential book, *Is Administrative Law Unlawful?*[86] The author's answer is, yes. As the book title suggests, Professor Hamburger is an unreconstructed Diceyan – but only up to a point. Like Dicey, he insists that there was constitutionalism before and without a written Constitution, in the United States as in England. In long chapters, he identifies constitutionalism with common law institutions and jurisprudence and with the rejection, way back in the seventeenth century, of any kind of royal prerogative. Like Dicey (and for that matter Lord Hewart or James Beck),[87] Professor Hamburger denounces administrative law as a resurrection of absolutist pretensions.

Even so, Professor Hamburger parts company with Dicey. The 'dual principle of government through the law and its courts', he writes, was 'astonishingly … most severely weakened by its most prominent defender' – ie AV Dicey.[88] Dicey, Professor Hamburger laments, 'focused on the significance of the courts at the cost of understating the more basic point that the government could constrain subjects only through the law'.[89] Dicey, the passage continues, 'did not clearly foreclose the possibility that the breach [of law] might consist of violating a statute giving effect to administrative regulations'.[90]

The point of these somewhat cryptic sentences is the delegation of rulemaking authority to administrative bodies. Dicey, as noted, recognised the problem, but it did not trouble him overly much. For Professor Hamburger, it looms front and centre. Only Congress or ordinary courts, he insists time and again, may bind citizens with legal force. Any subdelegation of that authority is 'despotic'.

More vehemently than even Dicey, Professor Hamburger traces the resurrection of prerogative in administrative form to the nefarious influence of continental, civilian jurists – in Hamburger's telling, German jurists who powerfully influenced Progressive thinkers and strategists in America around the turn of the twentieth century. In a book chapter that uncannily resembles Dicey's 1915

[85] See eg SG Calabresi and G Lawson, 'The Depravity of the 1930s and the Modern Administrative State' (2018) 94 *Notre Dame Law Review* 821, 864–65; MB Rappaport, 'Replacing Administrative Adjudication with Independent Administrative Courts' (2019) 26 *George Mason Law Review* 811; M Greve, 'Why We Need Federal Administrative Courts' (2021) 28 *George Mason Law Review* 765.

[86] Hamburger, *Is Administrative Law Unlawful?*

[87] *cf* Lord Gordon Hewart, *The New Despotism* (London, Ernest Benn Ltd, 1929); JM Beck, *Our Wonderland of Bureaucracy* (London, Macmillan, 1932). Beck served as United States Solicitor General under the Coolidge administration.

[88] Hamburger, *Is Administrative Law Unlawful?* 280.

[89] ibid.

[90] ibid 280–81.

writings, Professor Hamburger grudgingly concedes that German states had made great strides in establishing a *Rechtsstaat* that mimicked lawful forms. Nothing, however, can free that construct from the odour of top-down government control. And America's Progressives, besotted as they were with the supposed demands of speedy, expert administration, could not even bring themselves to embrace the law-like safeguards, especially including independent administrative courts, that the Germans had established so arduously.[91]

Professor Hamburger will have no truck with the *Rechtsstaat*. He wants AV Dicey's rule of law, coupled with a grim rule against the subdelegation of legislative or judicial powers to the executive. Again, though, one wonders whether that agenda is much more than a gesture without institutions equipped to handle the task, lest Professor Hamburger's project collapse back into what he deems to be Dicey's fateful error. Who, pray tell, will answer to the task of saving America from recrudescent prerogative? Surely not the Congress that built the administrative state in the first place. The federal courts, then? Numerous non-profit law firms – including one established by Professor Hamburger himself – are committed to that project. Whatever its prospects, it is far more court-centred than anything AV Dicey ever envisioned.

All those contentions revolve, in one way or another, around the first of Dicey's rule of law criteria: breaches of the law must be established in ordinary courts, in the ordinary way. Perhaps, though, Dicey's second and third criteria merit renewed consideration in the contemporary American context. The second precept, as noted, was the personal liability of executive officers for violating the law and the rights of citizens. Dicey suspected that the obvious substitute – governmental compensation, or 'waivers of sovereign immunity' in United States parlance – would provide a 'new protection' to officers and invite them to lord it over citizens.[92] That was not and is not obviously right. After all, the same corrosive effect would occur if government indemnified officers, as is the practice in virtually all United States jurisdictions. But it hangs together with Dicey's third precept – to wit, the notion that 'the general principles of the constitution … are with us the result of judicial decisions determining the rights of private persons in particular cases brought before the Courts'.

The well-known sentence reflects Dicey's remedial conception of 'law' – his insistence on providing citizens with the same common law rights against public officers that they would be able to enforce in private litigation; and his corresponding, deep suspicion of airy assurances of rights. He deemed such rights part and parcel of a 'rigid' continental Constitution. He questioned whether such constitutions could be stable,[93] and he questioned their bite and reliability. 'In many foreign countries', Dicey wrote, 'the rights of individuals, eg to personal freedom, depend on the constitution, whilst in England the constitution is little else than the

[91] ibid 471–75.
[92] Dicey, *Law of the Constitution* lxiii–lxiv.
[93] ibid 66–68.

generalisation of the rights which the Courts secure to individuals'.[94] Alas, 'foreign constitutionalists have, while occupied in defining rights, given insufficient attention to the absolute necessity for the provision of adequate remedies by which the rights they proclaimed might be enforced'.[95] 'Under favourable circumstances', Dicey conceded, 'formal declarations of right may, from their influence on popular feeling, possess greater weight than is generally attributed to them in England'.[96] But reliance on 'moral or political sentiment' is perilous, inasmuch or at least so long as 'an overestimate of the effect to be produced by general declarations of rights' goes together with 'a settled jealousy of any intervention by the judges in the sphere of politics'.[97]

Dicey conspicuously exempted the United States Constitution and the Bill of Rights from his indictment. 'The statesmen of America', he wrote, 'have shown unrivalled skill in providing means for giving legal security to the rights declared by American constitutions'.[98] For that reason, 'The rule of law is as marked a feature of the United States as of England'.[99]

That, one is tempted to say, was then. At the end of the nineteenth century, we have seen, American legal practice still conformed to Dicey's common law-based, remedy-oriented jurisprudence. However, 'rights' in the United States became constitutionalised even in Dicey's lifetime, and progressively thereafter.[100] At the same time, common law rights – such as the right to go about your productive business as you see fit and without harming others – contracted as state legislatures, Congress, and the Supreme Court struggled with the regulation of large, powerful industries. Such industries, the Court determined, could be regulated and governed administratively so long as they were 'affected with a public interest'. Over the course of the New Deal, just about every private productive activity, including retail sales of milk or beef, became so 'affected'.[101] Ordinary private pursuits thus became a matter of public rather than private right. Congress may subject such rights to comprehensive regulation, and it may provide for their adjudication in any number of ways, prominently including administrative adjudication.[102]

During the first decades of the twentieth century, this move was accompanied by intermittent judicial interventions to protect 'economic' rights directly

[94] ibid 119.
[95] ibid 117–18.
[96] ibid 71.
[97] ibid.
[98] ibid 118–19.
[99] ibid 119.
[100] JE Pfander, 'Dicey's Nightmare: An Essay on the Rule of Law' (2019) 107 *California Law Review* 737, 740, 'Over the course of some 230 years of constitutional experience, moreover, the United States has switched from a system of government remediation that relied heavily on the common-law forms to one that features far greater reliance on statutes and constitutional norms.'
[101] *Nebbia v New York*, 291 US 502 (1934); *Yakus v United States*, 321 US 414 (1944).
[102] In a weird judicial inversion, formerly private rights may become public *because* Congress has subjected them to a pervasive scheme of regulation. See *Thomas v Union Carbide Agr Products Co*, 473 US 568 (1985); *Atlas Roofing Co v Occupational Safety and Health Review Comr*, 430 US 442 (1977).

under the Constitution – for example, a 'liberty of contract' inferred somewhat loosely from the Due Process Clause.[103] However, after the New Deal, those rights became anathema. In later decades, the Court embarked on a 'rights revolution' aimed at protecting personal, 'non-economic' constitutional rights against government infringements. Judicial decisions establishing such rights in the broad penumbras of the Bill of Rights abound with lofty declarations to the effect that ours is a government of laws, committed at all times to protecting liberty. In numerous settings, however, rights expansion has been accompanied by remedy contraction.

Contemporary American administrative law is almost entirely declaratory. With only slight exaggeration, one can call it the law of meaningless remedies. Even and especially in cases that redraw the constitutional boundaries, nominally prevailing private plaintiffs obtain nothing more than a remand to the agency – that is, an administrative second chance.[104] One observes the same dialectic – rights expansion, remedy contraction – more directly in closely related settings. In landmark cases decided in the 1960s and 1970s, the Court held that common law protections were inadequate to protect citizens against unlawful and oppressive conduct by law enforcement agents.[105] Under certain conditions, the Court ruled, citizens could obtain damages from the responsible officers directly under the Constitution or federal rights-granting statutes.[106] It likewise held that constitutional due process guarantees applied to administrative deprivations of 'new property' entitlements, such as welfare benefits.[107] In relatively short order, however, the Court compensated for the rights explosion with off-setting moves. It greatly expanded states' sovereign immunities against suits for monetary relief.[108] It developed an expansive set of official immunities from suit.[109] It held that so-called *Bivens* actions, brought for damages against individual federal officers for constitutional violations, are available only if Congress has provided for absolutely no alternative remedy.[110] It held that 'due process' in agency proceedings means such process as the agency can reasonably afford, given the circumstances.[111] And as if to provide a showpiece for Diceyan apprehensions, the Supreme Court held that that over-all

[103] *Lochner v New York*, 198 US 45, 63–65 (1905).

[104] eg *Free Enterprise Fund v Public Co Accounting Oversight Board*, 561 US 477, 508 (2010); *Collins v Yellen*, 141 S Ct 1761, 1787–88 (2021). See D Zaring, 'Towards Separation of Powers Realism' (2020) 37 *Yale Journal on Regulation* 708, 728–36.

[105] See *Bivens v Six Unknown Named Agents*, 403 US 388 (1971); *Monroe v Pape*, 365 US 167 (1961).

[106] See 42 United States Code § 1983. The provision is the principal means of enforcing federally protected rights against state and local governments and their officers.

[107] *Goldberg v Kelly*, 397 US 254, 266 (1970).

[108] See *Seminole Tribe v Florida*, 517 US 44 (1996); *Alden v Maine*, 527 US 706 (1999).

[109] As a general rule, officers may be held personally liable only if they knew or should have known that their actions violated the plaintiffs' well-established rights: *Harlow v Fitzgerald*, 457 US 800, 818–19 (1982).

[110] *Egbert v Boule*, 596 US 482, 493 (2022) (citing and quoting *Ziglar v Abbassi*, 582 US 120, 136 (2017)).

[111] *Matthews v Eldridge*, 4224 US 319, 330–32 (1976).

calculus applies not only to the denial of food stamps and such but also and of all things to military detentions and the detainees' habeas petitions.[112]

France's declarations of rights, Dicey noted, ran up against her insistence that courts must never interfere with the operation of the state. That, he fairly snarled, is how Voltaire ended up in prison.[113] However overwrought, there are reasons to think that Dicey's critique has some bearing on America's much less 'statist' experiment, as it has evolved over the past century. Exuberance over lofty rights that are supposedly much better and certainly more copious than humdrum common law actions for trespass and such soon runs up against the harsh necessity of maintaining a workable government. Officer liability (*sans* indemnification), for example, is a plausible regime so long as it is tied to a limited set of common law actions and ultra vires review. Once the rights doors are thrown wide open, and especially once rights become a sword rather than a shield against government, the calculus looks very different. And 'calculus' seems just the right word. The 'rights of individuals' Dicey had in mind were a matter of ancient, well-established legal practice. In contrast, rights 'from above' – from statutes, even constitutions, or for that matter judicial *ex cathedra* declarations – will often look like contestable and perhaps transient policy commitments. 'Rights' of that sort ought to be balanced against rival commitments that shift over time; and that task is much more plausibly committed to legislatures than to courts.

The dynamic may not be irresistible. By 1915, Dicey observed – a bit grudgingly, but candidly – that the Conseil d'Etat had over time developed institutional habits and legal practices that approximated, in real life though perhaps not in spirit, the protections afforded to English citizens.[114] Conversely, though, an understanding of rights that are grounded in ordinary social practice and common law jurisprudence may erode. Once that happens, the earlier understanding is not easily recovered.

## VI. Conclusion

A rock-bottom proposition of American law, firmly enshrined in federal law and taught to every law student, is that *we must not have* nineteenth-century common law in federal courts. The common law may 'brood', so long as state legislatures let it, in state courts of general jurisdiction. Federal courts, in contrast, are supposedly prohibited – *constitutionally* prohibited, no less – from recognising any 'federal general common law'.[115] Originally, that proposition was a key tenet among

[112] *Hamdan v Rumsfeld*, 548 US 557 (2006).

[113] Dicey, *Law of the Constitution* 111–12.

[114] ibid lxi–lxvi.

[115] Recognition and enforcement of such law would be unconstitutional, the Supreme Court held in its most-cited case ever: *Erie Rly v Tompkins*, 304 US 64 (1938). To be sure, American public law teems with federal common law rules. But under current doctrine they must be derived, however artfully,

Progressive and New Deal proponents of administrative law. In later decades, and a bit ironically, it became the clarion call of conservative jurists who inveighed against the federal courts' rights enthusiasms.

Of late, it has begun to dawn in quarters of the American legal profession that this cannot be quite right. A handful of scholars have attempted to rehabilitate and refine a Diceyan understanding of the common law.[116] And in decisions on core administrative law problems, from administrative adjudication to the delegation of legislative authority to private parties' 'standing to sue', some Justices have come to recognise (or so it seems) that the rule of law problems that afflict the administrative state are, at the end of the day, unanswerable without a grasp of the common law freedoms that lie below the written Constitution.[117] It is a long way from such glimmers of recognition to a Diceyan jurisprudence for this day and age. If the Whiggish, Victorian embers still throw off light, that may be because they contain a truth that merits remembrance.

from constitutional or statutory norms or grants of jurisdiction. Common law rules cannot flow from 'the Judicial Power of the United States' that the Constitution confers on the federal courts.

[116] eg SE Sachs, 'Finding Law' (2019) 107 *California Law Review* 527; W Baude, 'Adjudication outside Article III' (2019) 133 *Harvard Law Review* 1511; J Harrison, 'Public Rights, Private Privileges, and Article III' (2019) 54 *Georgia Law Review* 143; C Nelson, 'Adjudication in the Political Branches' (2007) 107 *Columbia Law Review* 559; Nelson, 'The Persistence of General Law' (2006) 106 *Columbia Law Review* 503; Gasaway and Parrish, 'In Praise of Erie'.

[117] eg *Oil States Energy v Greene's Energy*, 138 S Ct 1374 (2018); *Gundy v United States*, 139 S Ct 2116, 2137 (2019) (Gorsuch J, dissenting); *TransUnion v Ramirez*, 594 US 413, 454 (2021) (Thomas J, dissenting).

# 12

# Resolving Dicey's Contradictions? Rights, Freedoms, and Parliamentary Sovereignty in Canada

NICHOLAS S DICKINSON

## I. Introduction

This chapter addresses the influence of AV Dicey on the Canadian Constitution and constitutional thought. The initial sections lay out Canada's constitutional framework, emphasising the dual logics of local and universal principles that shape it. Next, the resilience of Canada's dualist democracy, the complexities of amending the Canadian Constitution, and controversies surrounding the judicialisation of politics are discussed. The chapter then outlines the impact of patriation, detailing the process by which Canada gained full sovereignty over its Constitution from the United Kingdom, and its implications for Canadian constitutional law and governance, as well as the 1982 Charter of Rights and Freedoms, its impact on the Supreme Court, and the accommodationist approach modern Canada takes towards its federal structure and the rights of First Nations.

With this foundation AV Dicey's influence on Canadian constitutionalism is assessed, focusing particularly on his contributions to understanding of the rule of law and parliamentary sovereignty. Dicey's classical definition of the rule of law, anchored in powerful but simple fundamental principles is examined: the absence of arbitrary power, equality before the law, and the Constitution working in harmony with the ordinary law of the land. Dicey's views are critiqued for failing to fully articulate how these constitutional principles can co-exist with parliamentary sovereignty, and also explores Dicey's broader thoughts on federalism, legal collectivism, and executive power, noting that these themes find resonances in Canada to a much broader degree than the modern United Kingdom. However, the Canadian case clearly demonstrates Dicey's limitations in addressing issues like the legacy of colonial genocide against Indigenous peoples, rooted in the nature of his historical method. Dicey's principles are seen to be inherently contradictory, especially in the context of rights-restricting mechanisms like section 33

of the Charter.[1] It will be argued that Dicey's model may not be an adequate framework to understand executive power during an emergency in which public officials might find themselves compelled to act outside the law. Dicey's views on this topic are contrasted with the Canadian experience, particularly the invocation of the Emergencies Act in 2022 during the 'Freedom Convoy' protests. Unlike Dicey's approach, the Emergencies Act mandates parliamentary review of Cabinet orders and regulations, ensuring democratic oversight during crises.

In conclusion, the enduring relevance of AV Dicey's constitutional principles in the context of Canada's jurisprudential and political landscape will be discussed. Despite Canada's ongoing constitutional journey post-Confederation and post-patriation, Canada's constitutional framework is still reflective of the United Kingdom's constitutional principles. Thus, Dicey's principles continue to have relevance to Canada, contingent only upon the broad retention of this constitutional semblance. Through various crises and challenges since 1867, Canada's constitutional resilience and development can be seen to have both resolved many of Dicey's contradictions while also transcending his work entirely where it provides little helpful guidance.

## A. Canada's Constitutional Framework

Canadian constitutional culture has been defined as a complex interplay between two distinct but complementary logics: the local and the universal.[2] The local logic is deeply rooted in the specificities of Canada's diverse communities, emphasising the role of local traditions, customs, and norms in shaping the constitutional framework. This facet is most evident in the federal structure of Canada, where provinces enjoy a degree of autonomy to govern in accordance with local needs and preferences. On the other hand, the universal logic is anchored in abstract legal principles that transcend local particularities. These principles often come to the fore in matters concerning human rights and freedoms, which are viewed as universal values. This dualistic approach allows for a nuanced interpretation and application of the Constitution, balancing the unique historical and social contexts of different regions with overarching legal norms.

The implications of these dual logics for Canadian constitutionalism are manifold. In the realm of federal-provincial relations, the tension and harmony between local and universal logics provide a conceptual framework for understanding the intricate balance that must be struck between local autonomy and national

[1] Section 33 of the Canadian Charter of Rights and Freedoms, commonly referred to as the 'notwithstanding clause', allows federal or provincial parliaments to enact legislation that may operate notwithstanding certain provisions of the Charter. Specifically, it permits such legislation to override ss 2 and 7–15 of the Charter, which cover fundamental freedoms, legal and equality rights.

[2] BL Berger, 'Children of Two Logics: A Way into Canadian Constitutional Culture' (2013) 11 *International Journal of Constitutional Law* 319.

interests. Judicial interpretation of constitutional provisions also reflects this duality, as courts must navigate between the specific historical and social contexts of a case and the universal principles that underpin the legal system. Similarly, policymakers are tasked with crafting laws that are both locally relevant and universally justifiable, a challenge that requires a deep understanding of these dual logics. Such dualism allows for local variations in law and governance while simultaneously upholding universal principles that bind the nation together.[3]

Canada's dualist democracy has shown remarkable resilience in the face of a global decline in democratic governance. This is attributed to three key institutional factors. The first is the concept of 'constrained parliamentarism', a middle ground between presidentialism and pure parliamentary systems.[4] This model has been seen as crucial in maintaining democratic stability by preventing unhealthy concentrations of power and providing a durable framework for new or transitional democracies. The second factor is Canada's robust 'democracy branch', which serves as both a source and a driver of democratic resilience by offering checks and balances within the system.[5] The third factor contributing to Canada's democratic resilience is the unique role of the Supreme Court of Canada, described as 'political but not politicized'.[6] The Court has the capacity to issue decisions that are highly political in nature while remaining largely non-partisan, thereby reinforcing the nation's democratic resilience.

On the other hand, Albert[7] notes that the Canadian Constitution, particularly since the enactment of the Constitution Act of 1982, presents a complex and challenging landscape for amendments. This complexity is not merely a result of the textual provisions of the Constitution itself but is further complicated by extra-textual factors. These include Supreme Court rulings, parliamentary and provincial statutes, and constitutional conventions, all of which add layers of intricacy that make formal amendments exceedingly difficult. The structure established by the 1982 Constitution Act has created a labyrinthine set of formal amendment rules that make significant changes nearly impossible to enact. This rigidity in the Canadian Constitution has implications that extend beyond the mere difficulty of amendment. It also raises questions about the democratic legitimacy of the Constitution itself. The extra-textual factors not only contribute to the Constitution's rigidity but also undermine the democratic ethos and the very purpose of having a written constitution. Major constitutional amendments, which are defined as those that significantly impact the framework and identity of the state, have been achieved only once since the 1982 Constitution Act came into force. This is further complicated by the empirical challenges in measuring the

[3] ibid.

[4] RN Albert and M Pal, *The Democratic Resilience of the Canadian Constitution* (Oxford, Oxford University Press, 2017).

[5] ibid.

[6] ibid.

[7] RN Albert, 'The Difficulty of Constitutional Amendment in Canada' (2015) 53 *Alberta Law Review* 85.

difficulty of constitutional amendments. Both the voting thresholds required for amendments and the national culture surrounding them are significant yet hard-to-measure variables that contribute to this complexity.[8]

## B. Judicialisation of Politics

Perhaps surprisingly, Canada's adoption of a Charter of Rights and Freedoms as part of the 1982 constitutional settlement led to only a limited judicialisation, primarily affecting the field of criminal justice rather than significantly shifting power from the legislative or executive branches to the judiciary.[9] While the Charter expanded the judiciary's sphere of activity, this expansion did not come at the expense of other branches of government. Instead, the Charter has transformed the nature of political discourse, saturating divisive moral and constitutional issues with 'rights talk'. While section 33 of the Charter allows legislatures to pass laws notwithstanding certain specific rights, this override is rarely used. Moreover, at least 80 per cent of court cases involving Charter-based judicial review fall within the realm of criminal justice, suggesting that key economic and social policy areas have not been significantly impacted by the Charter.[10]

Legislative amendments in 1975 and the introduction of the Charter of Rights and Freedoms in 1982 have nonetheless had a profound impact on the Court's docket.[11] Prior to 1975, the Court primarily focused on private economic disputes; however, after these pivotal years, the Court increasingly dealt with criminal and civil liberties appeals. Political, ideological, and policy-related attitudes of justices also play a role in decision-making. Justices appointed by Liberal Party Prime Ministers for example, tend to render more liberal opinions, and regional factors, such as the justice's place of origin, further influence voting patterns.[12] Despite these ideological influences, it is noteworthy that 75 per cent of Supreme Court decisions are unanimous, indicating that legal criteria continue to be a significant driver in the Court's decision-making process.[13]

Yet the Charter's influence extends beyond the judiciary to the broader political culture. It has the potential to shape public opinion and shift the political spectrum, especially if its rights are considered more fundamental than other societal interests. However, the Supreme Court of Canada has exercised judicial restraint in its interpretation of the Charter, thereby limiting its scope and the extent of judicialisation. This cautious approach has kept the Court in line with mainstream

[8] ibid.

[9] PH Russell, 'Canadian Constraints on Judicialization from Without' (1994) 15 *International Political Science Review* 165.

[10] ibid.

[11] DR Songer, *The Transformation of the Supreme Court of Canada: An Empirical Examination* (Toronto, Univeristy of Toronto Press, 2008).

[12] ibid.

[13] ibid.

political opinion. Thus, while the Charter may not have led to a significant judicialisation of politics in terms of power dynamics, it has had a profound impact on the nature of political discourse and could potentially influence long-term policy directions, a point explored further below.[14]

## C. Accommodationism and the First Nations

As a result of its unique multinational and multiethnic structure, Canada's constitutional model holds a prominent place in political theory concerning minority.[15] This prominence is noteworthy given Canada's own constitutional crisis in the 1990s when Quebec nearly seceded. The model has been significantly shaped by Canadian political theorists like Joseph Carens and Will Kymlicka, who have influenced the discourse on minority nationalism.[16] Kymlicka, in particular, celebrates the 'Canadian model' of ethnocultural relations. However, the model's rise to prominence coincided with a period of constitutional crisis in Canada, specifically the accommodation of Quebec nationalism.[17]

The debate on managing diversity often centres around two approaches: accommodationist and integrationist.[18] Canada adopts an accommodationist stance through its system of multinational federalism. However, this approach comes with its own set of complexities and limitations. Brian Barry's critique of Canadian multiculturalism, for instance, questions the universal applicability of the Canadian experience to other contexts. This critique specifically targets the work of Will Kymlicka and suggests that a nuanced understanding of constitutional politics in multinational states is necessary. Thus, the Canadian model serves as a cautionary tale for some, highlighting the limitations of constitutional design in addressing minority nationalism and questioning its universal applicability.[19]

Beyond Quebec's distinctive position within federation, Aboriginal Constitutions in Canada are distinctively shaped by Indigenous traditions, customs, values, and structures, setting them apart from non-Aboriginal constitutions.[20] These constitutions recognise local Indigenous traditions to varying degrees, falling on a continuum between purely Western and traditional Indigenous systems. The roles of elders and elders' councils are particularly noteworthy; while some Aboriginal groups assign them purely advisory roles, others give them more

[14] Russell, 'Canadian Constraints'.

[15] S Choudhry, 'Does the World Need More Canada? The Politics of the Canadian Model in Constitutional Politics and Political Theory' (2007) 5 *International Journal of Constitutional Law* 606.

[16] ibid.

[17] ibid.

[18] ibid.

[19] Choudhry, 'Does the World Need More Canada?'.

[20] C Alcantara and G Whitfield, 'Aboriginal Self-Government through Constitutional Design: A Survey of Fourteen Aboriginal Constitutions in Canada' (2010) 44 *Journal of Canadian Studies/Revue d'études canadiennes* 122.

extensive judicial and/or legislative powers based on local customs. Additionally, some Aboriginal Constitutions establish youth councils and hereditary chieftain positions, reflecting the significance of youth and traditional leadership within these communities.[21]

Community rights are another salient feature of Aboriginal Constitutions. For instance, the Huu-ay-aht First Nations Constitution guarantees rights such as the right to participate in cultural life, speak the traditional language, and live in a healthy environment. They incorporate Indigenous legal traditions, serving as a lens through which one can understand how First Nations are navigating principles of Indigenous tradition, democracy, human rights, and the prevention of tyranny. These constitutions address the protection, repatriation, and control of cultural heritage and identify environmental concerns as central to the resurgence of Aboriginal legal traditions. They aim to function at the intersection of colonialism and decolonisation, striving to find a balance between Western and Indigenous.[22]

# II. Patriation and the Charter of Rights and Freedoms

## A. The Patriation Reference

The term 'patriation' refers to the process by which Canada gained full sovereignty over its Constitution from the United Kingdom. Prior to patriation, amendments to the Canadian Constitution had to be made by the British Parliament. The process culminated in 1982 with the passage of the Constitution Act, which included the new Constitution of Canada and the Charter of Rights and Freedoms. This act allowed Canada to amend its own Constitution without requiring approval from Britain, effectively making Canada fully sovereign in constitutional matters.

However, as a result of opposition from federal Conservatives, as well as from the provinces of Quebec, British Columbia, Prince Edward Island, Alberta, and Newfoundland, the Liberal government of Pierre Trudeau was forced to seek a decision on the right of the federal government to pursue patriation in spite of provincial objections. This gave rise in the Patriation Reference, officially known as *Re: Resolution to Amend the Constitution*, decided by the Supreme Court of Canada on 28 September 1981.[23] The case addressed the legality of the federal government's ability to patriate and amend Canada's Constitution without the consent of the provincial governments. The court ruled that, from a strictly legal standpoint, the federal government had the authority to unilaterally patriate and amend the Constitution. However, the court also emphasised the importance of

[21] ibid.
[22] ibid.
[23] Supreme Court of Canada, *Re: Resolution to Amend the Constitution* [1981] 1 SCR 753.

constitutional conventions, stating that unilateral federal action in areas affecting provincial powers would constitute a breach of these conventions.

The court's decision underscored the complex interplay between constitutional law and constitutional conventions in shaping the governance of Canada. It highlighted that while the federal government may have the legal authority to act unilaterally, doing so without provincial consent in matters affecting provincial jurisdiction would violate established norms and practices that have been integral to Canadian federalism. The court encapsulated this nuanced understanding by stating, 'Constitutional convention plus constitutional law equal the total constitution of the country'.[24] This statement underscores the dual nature of Canada's constitutional framework, where both written laws and unwritten conventions play a pivotal role in defining the rules of governance and intergovernmental relations.

The meaning and legacy of the Patriation Reference is thus a central topic in the realm of Canadian constitutional law and has been the subject of extensive scholarly analysis. The constitutional patriation project has been seen by some as an incomplete exercise that left the main institutions and processes of Canadian government largely undisturbed. It was thus frequently characterised as a flawed operation that would require re-examination in the future.[25] Nonetheless, the Patriation Reference was an indication of the direction of the modern constitutional method in Canada. It has been seen as predictive of broad patterns in constitutional litigation and jurisprudence and presaged the modern approach to constitutional interpretation.[26] In particular, patriation has been argued to have favoured the reinforcement of the state's archival authority in relation to Aboriginal peoples' claims. Berger sees the reference as seminal in the development of a domestic Canadian constitutional culture, along the dualist universal-local lines described, as well a key juncture in the history of modern Canadian politics.[27]

Trudeau himself had mixed feelings on the reference. In a convocation speech delivered at the opening of the Bora Laskin Law Library in the summer of 1991, and in the context of renewed constitutional debates in Canada, Trudeau argued that the *dissenting* opinion in the Patriation Reference, formulated by Justices Estey, McIntyre, and Chief Justice Bora Laskin, was not 'not only the better law but the better common sense, and consequently it was also wiser politically'.[28] Trudeau argued that the majority judgment in the Patriation Reference shifted the locus of sovereignty from the 'people' to the 'governments'. In other words, the judgment seemed to endorse the idea that ultimate authority in constitutional matters

[24] ibid.

[25] E McWhinney, 'The Constitutional Patriation Project, 1980–82' (1984) 32 *American Journal of Comparative Law* 241.

[26] C Mathen, 'The Question Calls for an Answer, and I Propose to Answer it: The Patriation Reference as Constitutional Method' (2011) *The Supreme Court Law Review: Osgoode's Annual Constitutional Cases Conference* 54.

[27] Berger, 'Children of Two Logics'.

[28] PE Trudeau, 'Convocation Speech at the Opening of the Bora Laskin Law Library' (1991) 41 *The University of Toronto Law Journal* 295.

resides not with the collective will of the Canadian people but rather with the various provincial and federal governments. Trudeau further also criticised the majority judges for their handling of conventions, stating that they chose to ignore legal arguments that could have led them in a different direction.[29]

## B. The Charter of Rights and Freedoms

Through patriation, Trudeau sought to entrench a stronger set of rights in the Canadian Constitution via the inclusion of a Charter of Rights and Freedoms in the Constitution Act 1982. The Charter guarantees a range of civil liberties and human rights to all individuals in Canada, including freedom of expression, religion, and assembly; the right to a fair trial; and equality rights, among others. It acts as a higher law and serves as a cornerstone for the protection of individual rights and freedoms against actions of government institutions.

Importantly, however, Trudeau viewed the Charter as a means to weaken the power of provincial governments to infringe on Canadians' fundamental rights. This emphasis was informed by Trudeau's background in Quebec politics after the Quiet Revolution. The Quiet Revolution was a period of intense social, political, and cultural change in Quebec, from roughly 1960 to 1966. Initiated by the election of a Liberal government led by Jean Lesage, the Quiet Revolution marked a departure from the conservative, church-dominated society that had characterised Quebec for decades. Trudeau became an influential intellectual and political actor in the period that followed, particularly in shaping the discourse around federalism and Quebec's place within Canada. A strong advocate for a united Canada and a critic of Quebec nationalism, Trudeau argued against the idea that Quebec should have a special status within the Canadian federation.

In practice, however, the Supreme Court of Canada's approach to Charter review has been to seek reconciliation between Charter rights and federalism, diminishing the importance of the centralising vision represented by Trudeau and the federal Liberals.[30] Rather than promoting conflict between judicial and legislative branches, the Charter frequently promotes unique forms of institutional interaction and dialogue between courts and legislatures on the meaning of the rights it contains.[31] This is facilitated in part by the Charter's open-ended and expansive wording, along with its careful balancing of individual rights and collective values.[32]

[29] ibid.

[30] JB Kelly, 'Reconciling Rights and Federalism during Review of the Charter of Rights and Freedoms: The Supreme Court of Canada and the Centralization Thesis, 1982 to 1999' (2001) 34 *Canadian Journal of Political Science/Revue canadienne de science politique* 321.

[31] S Stephenson, 'Constitutional Reengineering: Dialogue's Migration from Canada to Australia' (2013) 11 *International Journal of Constitutional Law* 870.

[32] M Jackman and B Porter, 'Socio-Economic Rights under the Canadian Charter' in M Langford (ed), *Social Rights Jurisprudence: Emerging Trends in International and Comparative Law* (New York, Cambridge University Press, 2008).

This is not to say that the Charter has not expanded the scope of judicial involvement in traditionally political topics. It has implications for cultural diversity and the equality of Canada's many ethnic communities, particularly in the context of religious freedom.[33] The debate over whether the Charter should protect positive socio-economic rights, such as access to healthcare, also presents an ongoing conundrum for both courts and legislators.[34]

## C. Meech Lake and Charlottetown Accords

The contested nature of the patriation process and the Charter inevitably resulted in attempts to revise and refine the constitutional settlement after 1982. The Meech Lake Accord was a set of proposed amendments to the Constitution of Canada, negotiated in 1987. The Accord aimed to persuade the province of Quebec to endorse the 1982 Canadian Constitution, which it had not ratified. The primary architect of the Accord was then-Prime Minister Brian Mulroney, whose federal Conservatives had also contested the Liberal-led process of codification in the early 1980s.

The Accord sought to address several key objectives aimed at restructuring the Canadian federation. Among these were the recognition of Quebec as a 'distinct society' with its unique language, culture, and legal system; the provision of a constitutional veto to all provinces, including Quebec, over future constitutional changes that would directly affect them; reforms to the Senate appointment process to give provinces greater influence; granting Quebec more control over its immigration policies; and involving provinces in the appointment of judges to the Supreme Court of Canada. Despite its ambitious goals, the Accord was mired in controversy and ultimately failed to gain the necessary support for ratification. Critics pointed to the lack of public consultation, arguing that the Accord was negotiated behind closed doors. Regional tensions also flared, as some provinces felt that the Accord disproportionately favoured Quebec. Indigenous groups also opposed the Accord, citing the absence of consultation and the failure to address their rights and claims. The Accord's ratification process required unanimous approval from all ten provinces within a three-year window, a condition it failed to meet. Neither Manitoba nor Newfoundland ratified the Accord by the 1990 deadline, leading to its failure.

The Meech Lake Accord has been seen to symbolise that traditional forces would continue to play a significant role in defining Canadian values, despite demographic and economic changes and the transformation of Canadian federalism

[33] SI Smithey, 'Religious Freedom and Equality Concerns under the Canadian Charter of Rights and Freedoms' (2001) 34 *Canadian Journal of Political Science/Revue canadienne de science politique* 85.

[34] E MacFarlane, 'The Dilemma of Positive Rights: Access to Health Care and the Canadian Charter of Rights and Freedoms' (2014) 48 *Journal of Canadian Studies* 49.

through patriation.[35] However, the course of negotiations from 1987 to 1990 reveal that partisan motives offer more plausible rationales for decisions, with political affiliations and agendas the key drivers in the process.[36] The failure of the Meech Lake Accord had significant implications for Canadian politics, including the rise of the Bloc Québécois, a federal political party advocating for Quebec sovereignty, and the negotiation of another set of constitutional amendments known as the Charlottetown Accord, which also failed to gain approval.

The Charlottetown Accord was a further attempt at constitutional reform in Canada, coming after the failure of the Meech Lake Accord. Negotiated in 1992, the Charlottetown Accord sought to address some of the criticisms and shortcomings of the Meech Lake Accord, while also expanding its scope to include a broader range of issues and stakeholders. The Accord aimed to build upon the objectives of the Meech Lake Accord, but with several key differences and additions. Like its predecessor, it sought to recognise Quebec as a distinct society within Canada. However, it went further by acknowledging the inherent right of Aboriginal self-government, a significant departure from Meech Lake. The Charlottetown Accord also proposed a more democratic, elected Senate with equal representation from each province, as opposed to the appointed Senate in Meech Lake. It aimed to clarify the division of powers between federal and provincial governments, granting provinces jurisdiction over areas like fisheries and tourism. Additionally, it maintained the concept of a constitutional veto for all provinces. Unique to Charlottetown was the decision to put the Accord to a public referendum, allowing Canadians to have a direct say in its ratification.

The Accord was rejected in a national referendum in 1992 for different reasons across various parts of Canada. The rejection indicated a divided national sentiment and suggested that political developments in Quebec might bring these constitutional questions back onto the agenda.[37] The Accord failed in part because it expanded the agenda to include the demands of multiple groups without fostering any greater consensus on the way forward.[38] Some political figures, including Pierre Trudeau, took pride in their contribution to the Accord's failure, indicating the contentious nature of the agreement and the polarised opinions it generated.[39]

[35] RA Macdonald, '… Meech Lake to the Contrary Notwithstanding (Part I)' (1991) 29 *Osgoode Hall Law Journal* 253.

[36] AL Esselment, 'A Little Help from My Friends: The Partisan Factor and Intergovernmental Negotiations in Canada' (2013) 43 *Publius – the Journal of Federalism* 701.

[37] RC Vipond, 'Seeing Canada through the Referendum: Still a House Divided' (1993) 23 *Publius – the Journal of Federalism* 39.

[38] M Lusztig and C Knox, 'Good Things and Small Packages: Lessons from Canada for the Northern Irish Constitutional Settlement' (1999) 5 *Nations and Nationalism* 543.

[39] GJ Inwood, 'Review of *The Politics and Economics of Eric Kierans: A Man for All Canadas* 1994 John N McDougall (Montreal, McGill-Queen's University Press, 1993) xvi, 302' (1994) 27 *Canadian Journal of Political Science* 623.

## III. Dicey and Canada

Canadian constitutional culture balances local traditions and universal legal principles. This dualism has significant implications for federal-provincial relations, judicial interpretation, and policymaking. It also contributes to Canada's democratic resilience, which is further bolstered by key institutional factors such as 'constrained parliamentarism' and the unique role of the Supreme Court. However, the rigidity and complexity of the Canadian Constitution, particularly since the 1982 Constitution Act, raised questions about its democratic legitimacy.

The Charter of Rights and Freedoms has led to some judicialisation of politics, though its impact is primarily in the realm of criminal justice and political discourse rather than a significant shift of power to the judiciary. On the other hand, Canada's accommodationist approach to diversity, focusing on First Nations and Quebec nationalism, both questions its straightforward universal applicability and inevitably involves the courts in adjudicating the limits of accomodation. Patriation is thus a pivotal moment in Canadian constitutional history, but one which has only emphasised the complex relationship between issues of sovereignty, governmental authority, and individual and collective rights in Canada.

The invocation of AV Dicey's constitutional theories by Canadian scholars, jurists, and politicians serves as a lens through which to understand the complexities of Canadian constitutional culture. Dicey's emphasis on the rule of law and constitutional conventions provides a framework for navigating the dualistic nature of Canadian constitutionalism, which balances local traditions with universal legal principles. His ideas resonate with the Canadian concept of 'constrained parliamentarism', a middle ground between presidentialism and pure parliamentary systems, as well as the unique role of the Supreme Court in upholding democratic resilience. Dicey's theories also offer a way to grapple with the rigidity and complexity of the Canadian Constitution, particularly since the enactment of the 1982 Constitution Act, by focusing on the importance of constitutional conventions in maintaining democratic legitimacy.

Similarly, Dicey's work on the separation of powers and the role of the judiciary can be applied to understand the limited judicialisation of politics in Canada, particularly in the wake of the Charter of Rights and Freedoms. His ideas offer a nuanced understanding of how the Charter has influenced political discourse without significantly shifting power away from the legislative and executive branches. Furthermore, Dicey's theories on federalism and minority rights can be employed to scrutinise Canada's accommodationist approach to diversity, especially concerning First Nations and Quebec nationalism. In this context, Dicey's work serves as a foundational text for dissecting the complexities arising from the patriation of the Canadian Constitution, emphasising the intricate relationship between these issues in modern Canadian politics.

## A. Dicey and Colonial Canada

The late nineteenth-century Canadian constitutional settlement has been seen as primarily preoccupied with the delineation of legislative powers between federal and provincial governments, rather than safeguarding individual rights.[40] This focus allowed Canada to sidestep the ideological clash between individualism and collectivism that marked Lochner-era jurisprudence in the United States. However, an alternative vision of federalism was also articulated by provincial politicians like Oliver Mowat, the premier of Ontario, who envisioned the provinces as autonomous and sovereign entities within the Canadian federation.[41]

In this environment, Dicey has been viewed by some as a surprising advocate for limitations on the power of Parliament to exercise the broadly unlimited jurisdiction which he argued characterised the 'mother' Parliament in Westminster. A notable example was *Ontario (AG) v Canada (AG)*, also known as the *Local Prohibition Case* (1896),[42] which restricted the federal government's authority to regulate trade. Dicey's *Introduction to the Study of the Law of the Constitution* provided the ideological framework of the Privy Council's decision in the *Local Prohibition* case.[43] This framework was deeply rooted in a distrust of legislative power and a fear of democratic 'tyranny'. The court's ruling was faithful to Dicey's interpretation of federalism, which emphasised limited government and was predicated on the idea that federal laws should be tested against the same standards as those of a delegated authority under British constitutionalism.[44] This perspective was also evident in the economic ideology that favoured property and individual rights over legislative regulation, a stance reflected in Lord Watson's decision to limit the federal government's power to regulate but not prohibit commerce.[45] Dicey likened the legislative power in a federal regime, a description which he applied to Canada without qualification,[46] to the powers afforded to a municipality or a railway company, a view that guided the Privy Council to treat federal power over trade and commerce as limited akin to that of any subordinate agency.[47]

However, while Schneiderman[48] offers an argument about Dicey's support for federalism in the context of early Canadian constitutional law, this influence was clearly rooted in the subordinate nature of the Canadian federal parliament at the time: a colonial legislature under the British Empire. Another perspective

[40] D Schneiderman, 'A.V. Dicey, Lord Watson, and the Law of the Canadian Constitution in the Late Nineteenth Century' (1998) 16 *Law and History Review* 495.
[41] ibid.
[42] *Attorney General of Ontario v Attorney General of Canada* (*Local Prohibition Case*) (1896).
[43] ibid.
[44] ibid.
[45] ibid.
[46] AV Dicey, 'Parliamentary Sovereignty and Federalism' in AV Dicey (ed), *Introduction to the Study of the Law of the Constitution* (London, Palgrave Macmillan, 1979).
[47] Schneiderman, 'A.V. Dicey, Lord Watson, and the Law of the Canadian Constitution'.
[48] ibid.

is provided by Walters[49] based on the later pivotal case of *Roncarelli v Duplessis* (1959).[50] The case is a cornerstone in the understanding of the rule of law in Canadian jurisprudence. Frank Roncarelli, a restaurant owner, sued Quebec Prime Minister Maurice Duplessis after his liquor licence was revoked, allegedly as retribution for his support of Jehovah's Witnesses. The case reached the Supreme Court of Canada, where Justice Ivan Rand delivered a landmark judgment. He affirmed the rule of law as a 'fundamental postulate of our constitutional structure', marking a pivotal moment in Canadian legal history. This case became an integral part of legal discourse among judges and lawyers in Canada and is considered a classical application of the Diceyan concept of equality and the rule of law.[51]

*Roncarelli v Duplessis* was not an isolated legal event but part of a broader discourse on constitutionalism that had been unfolding in Canada during the previous decade. It was seen as part of a package of cases that affirmed a 'judicial Bill of Rights' and the potential for a common law-based protection of civil liberties.[52]

Walters contends that *Roncarelli v Duplessis* serves as a critical example of the 'legality as reason' approach to the rule of law. Contrary to the standard reading, Walters portrays Dicey as a proponent of 'legality as reason' rather than 'legality as order', an approach to the rule of law that emphasises the importance of reasoned judgement and interpretive engagement in the application and understanding of legal principles. Unlike 'legality as order', which focuses on the autonomous structure of rules and their enforcement, 'legality as reason' is concerned with the underlying rationale, principles, and moral commitments that inform legal rules and decisions. Justice Rand's judgment in the case is seen as an integral part of a larger contribution to a common law discourse on constitutionalism in Canada. His reasons in *Roncarelli* effectively integrated both doctrinal and conceptual approaches to legality.[53]

Dicey's influence on Canadian constitutional law prior to patriation can thus be seen as consistently in support of the rule of law and individual rights, albeit filtered through a conception of the latter as primarily the personal liberty of business owners in the free commercial economy which Dicey and his Victorian contemporaries strongly favoured. However, the origin of this support can be alternatively depicted as a top-down conception stemming from Dicey's conception of the British Empire as a unified legal structure[54] or as a bottom-up conception stemming from his equally fervent support for common law as a source of individual rights.[55]

[49] MD Walters, 'Legality as Reason: Dicey, Rand, and the Rule of Law' (2010) 55 *McGill Law Journal / Revue de droit de McGill* 563.

[50] *Roncarelli v Duplessis* [1959] SCR 121.

[51] ibid.

[52] Walters, 'Legality as Reason'.

[53] ibid.

[54] D Lino, 'Albert Venn Dicey and the Constitutional Theory of Empire' (2016) 36 *Oxford Journal of Legal Studies* 751.

[55] JE Pfander, 'Dicey's Nightmare: An Essay on the Rule of Law' (2019) 107 *California Law Review* 737.

Specifying Dicey's contributions to modern Canada as a sovereign constitutional state thus relies on clarifying his position, not so much in relation to the origins and nature of the Canadian state, but to the sovereign constitutional states resembling modern Canada which were present in his own time, and on which he wrote extensively, primarily the United Kingdom's parliamentary democracy at the turn of the nineteenth century. However, given the important differences between Canada and the historic British Constitution, Dicey's broader thoughts on federalism, legal collectivism, and executive power also find resonances in Canada to a much broader degree than even the modern United Kingdom. These themes will be explored in the remainder of this chapter.

# IV. Dicey and the Modern Canadian Constitution

## A. Canada and the Rule of Law

Dicey's classical definition of the rule of law is anchored in three fundamental principles: the absence of arbitrary power; equality before the law; and the constitution working in harmony with the ordinary law of the land.[56] Dicey posited that no individual can be punished or made to suffer except for a breach of law proven in an ordinary court. However, he was particularly sceptical about the necessity of a strict separation of powers, especially within the British constitutional framework, arguing that the British Constitution did not require such a separation.[57]

While Dicey's contributions to the understanding of the rule of law are seminal, they are not without limitations. One significant critique is that Dicey failed to fully articulate how these constitutional principles could co-exist with parliamentary sovereignty, let alone mutually reinforce each other.[58] This has led to a rich body of legal and political theory that both accepts and challenges the notion that the primary function of the rule of law is to limit the arbitrary exercise of legislative as well as executive power.[59]

The issues of parliamentary sovereignty will be dealt with further below. However, issues with Dicey's conception of the rule of law do not begin or end with the riddle of parliamentary sovereignty. As Burgess[60] points out, the concept of the rule of law has undergone significant changes over time, affecting its contemporary understanding and necessitating 'identification of the change mechanism' that drives this process. Dawson further suggests that the rule of law also depends

[56] R Bellamy, *The Rule of Law and the Separation of Powers* (London, Routledge, 2017).
[57] ibid.
[58] ibid.
[59] ibid.
[60] P Burgess, 'The Rule of Lore in the Rule of Law: Putting the Problem of the Rule of Law in Context' (2020) 12 *Hague Journal on the Rule of Law* 333.

on characteristics of society, not just the state.[61] Thus, the rule of law takes various forms across states and over time, challenging the notion of it being a uniform concept.[62]

While a degree of flexibility may be seen as a positive feature of the idea, sweeping reformulations of the rule of law may also impair the concept by weakening principles of sovereignty and non-intervention.[63] Rajkovic argues that the concept of the 'rule of law' is often employed without adequate inquiry into its practical political meaning.[64] Holcombe and Rodet[65] point out that better enforcement of the rule of law can also enhance the ability of incumbent governments to remain in power through controlling corruption, thus serving political stability but raising questions about the effects on democratic choice.

Where does the Canadian interpretation of the rule of law stand in relation to these complexities? In some ways Canada may be seen as a worst-case scenario for Dicey's parsimonious universalist definition of the rule of law. As outlined above, Canada's constitutional development has been defined by repeated revisions of core principles in response to the emergence of an independent sovereign state, and has been repeatedly confronted by issues of geographical, ethnic, and national diversity deeply woven into the fabric of Canadian society. Dicey's assumptions around uniformity in core political philosophy and the nature of a good society thus receive a severe challenge in the Canadian case. Nonetheless, Canadian scholars, jurists, and politicians have found Dicey consistently useful in parsing these challenges.

These issues arose even prior to the Charter, as a result of the earlier attempt to clarify the rights of citizens in the 1960 Canadian Bill of Rights. This resulted in the 1970 case of *R v Drybones*,[66] in which the Supreme Court of Canada declared a specific clause of the Indian Act to be 'inoperative'. The court determined that the provision contravened section 1(b) of the Canadian Bill of Rights, which assured equality under the law. However, later jurisprudence significantly muddied the waters. In *Lavell*,[67] the issue was whether section 12(1)(b) of the Indian Act, which discriminates between Indian men and women, was rendered inoperative by section 1(b) of the Canadian Bill of Rights. The Supreme Court, in a 5 to 4 decision, held that the Indian women involved were not denied equality before the law.[68] In

[61] AJ Dawson, 'The Social Determinants of the Rule of Law: A Comparison of Jamaica and Barbados' (2013) 45 *World Development* 314.

[62] RE Carlin, 'Rule-of-Law Typologies in Contemporary Societies' (2012) 33 *Justice System Journal* 154.

[63] B Delcourt, 'The Rule of Law as a Vehicle for Intervention' (2015) 9 *Journal of Intervention and Statebuilding* 471.

[64] NM Rajkovic, '"Global Law" and Governmentality: Reconceptualizing the "Rule of Law" as Rule "Through" Law' (2012) 18 *European Journal of International Relations* 29.

[65] RG Holcombe and CS Rodet, 'Rule of Law and the Size of Government' (2011) 8 *Journal of Institutional Economics* 49.

[66] *R v Drybones* [1970] SCR 282.

[67] *Attorney General of Canada v Lavell* [1974] SCR 1349.

[68] W Tarnopolsky, 'The Canadian Bill of Rights and the Supreme Court Decisions in Lavell and Burnshine: A Retreat from Drybones to Dicey' (1975) 7 *Ottawa Law Review* 1.

*Burnshine*,[69] the focus was on section 150 of the Prisons and Reformatories Act. The Court allowed the appeal by a majority of 6 to 3, suggesting that the Canadian Bill of Rights did not render the section inoperative.[70]

Tarnopolsky[71] invokes Dicey as a point of comparison, suggesting a retreat from the *Drybones* case to a Diceyan understanding of law, which he views as emphasising legal equality and the absence of arbitrary power and also a black letter understanding of the law. He argues that the majority judgments in *Lavell* and *Burnshine* could result in a 'drastic and unjustifiable limitation on the effectiveness of the Bill of Rights', potentially aligning more with Dicey's traditionalist views. He nonetheless also criticises the majority judgments in both cases for their broad declarations and lack of concise analysis, arguing that the Court could have been more precise in its reasoning and should not have engaged with irrelevant arguments, such as the claim that the Canadian Bill of Rights invalidated the whole Indian Act.[72]

This illustrates the 'Dicey Dilemma'[73] still frequently faced by Canadian courts. The tension between Parliament and the judiciary in Canada has been exacerbated by the introduction of the Canadian Charter of Rights and Freedoms. Prior to this, in spite of the contradictions Tarnopolsky noted over federal law, the principles of 'parliamentary supremacy' and 'the federal principle' coexisted relatively unproblematically within Canada's political system.[74] Yet Dicey had warned against the fusion of these two principles, cautioning that it could lead to inherent tensions. The Charter fundamentally altered the dynamics by establishing constitutional supremacy and entrenching personal freedoms, thereby elevating the judiciary's role in reviewing government legislation.[75] This shift has had significant implications for the concept of 'responsible' government, limiting Parliament's ability to hold the government accountable. The Charter also entrenched the practice of judicial review, enabling Canadians to bypass Parliament and directly challenge government legislation in the courts.[76]

Garver[77] argues that the response of Canadian jurisprudence has been to interpret the rule of law as serving primarily to limit the arbitrary exercise of power, a concept that aligns more easily with both legal literature and case law across federalism, criminal law, and administrative law. This understanding is deeply rooted in Dicey's conceptualisation, which posits requirements for the rule

[69] *R v Burnshine* [1975] 1 SCR 693.
[70] Tarnopolsky, 'The Canadian Bill of Rights'.
[71] ibid.
[72] ibid.
[73] AB Lennox, *Parliament Versus the Judiciary: The Unrelenting Dicey Dilemma* (Ottawa, National Library of Canada / Bibliothèque nationale du Canada, 2001).
[74] ibid.
[75] ibid.
[76] ibid.
[77] N Garver, 'The Canadian Approach to Rule of Law' (2022) available at https://papers.ssrn.com/sol3/papers.cfm?abstract_id=4130539.

of including that punishment can only occur under a legal mechanism, no individual is above the law, and that any special rights are constitutionally afforded.[78]

At the same time, this view does not require limited or narrow judgments by Canadian courts. St-Hilaire et al[79] examine the challenges of judicial interpretation of constitutional provisions on the constitutional amendment process. Using Dicey as a framework for the discussion, the authors identify a shift from substantive to procedural criteria in constitutional law, outlining how this shift has implications for constitutional amendments. They nonetheless critique the Supreme Court's approach to interpreting Part V of the Constitution Act, suggesting that the Court's interpretation gives it enormous power to determine fundamental questions.[80]

The discourse on the rule of law encompasses debates over its 'thickness' or 'thinness'. While scholars like Joseph Raz focus on a 'thin' rule of law that emphasises formal procedural aspects, others like Lord Bingham advocate for a 'thick' rule of law that incorporates moral principles. Overall, scholars suggest that the Canadian interpretation of the rule of law leans towards a 'thick' conception.[81] It emphasises that the rule of law in Canada is not just about procedural or formal aspects but also incorporates moral values and principles. The unanimous Court in *Reference re Quebec Secession*, for example, acknowledges that the legitimacy of the law comes from its capability to reflect the aspirations of the people and from its moral authority.[82]

## B. Canada and Parliamentary Sovereignty

Dicey's concept of parliamentary sovereignty finds clear resonance in the Canadian context given the country's Westminster-style parliamentary system. However, the judicialisation of politics in Canada presents a counterpoint to Dicey's emphasis on legislative supremacy. Dicey contends that the principles of parliamentary sovereignty and the rule of law in the Westminster system are mutually reinforcing, asserting that individual rights are secure only when a parliament's legislative powers are unlimited. This perspective has been increasingly scrutinised in the context of Canadian political thought, particularly in relation to section 33 of the Canadian Charter of Rights and Freedoms, commonly known as the 'notwithstanding clause'.[83]

[78] ibid.

[79] M St-Hilaire et al, 'The Constitution of Canada as Supreme Law: A New Definition' (2019) 28 *Constitutional Forum* 7.

[80] ibid.

[81] Garver, 'The Canadian Approach to Rule of Law'.

[82] ibid.

[83] J Ajzenstat, 'Reconciling Parliament and Rights: A.V. Dicey Reads the Canadian Charter of Rights and Freedoms' (1997) 30 *Canadian Journal of Political Science/Revue canadienne de science politique* 645.

This clause of the Canadian Charter of Rights and Freedoms is a provision that allows federal, provincial, or territorial governments in Canada to temporarily override certain Charter rights and freedoms. Specifically, section 33 permits governments to enact legislation that overrides the rights and freedoms protected under sections 2 and 7–15 of the Charter for a period of up to five years, after which the legislation must be renewed, or it will expire. The clause is designed to strike a balance between parliamentary sovereignty and protecting individual rights. It is thus viewed as a concession to parliamentary sovereignty but has garnered criticism for its potential to undermine individual rights.

The existence of the notwithstanding clause brings into sharp focus the contradictions of Dicey's arguments on parliamentary sovereignty. Dicey associated the guarantee of individual rights with the partisan debates within legislatures, but this raises questions about why such a clause need exist in the Charter.[84] Various intellectual critiques, including those by Paul Romney and David Sugarman, argue that Dicey's principles are inherently contradictory. Michael Foley offers another perspective, suggesting that Dicey intentionally avoids discussing these contradictions to maintain the system's legitimacy. These debates serve as a benchmark for understanding the evolving perceptions of parliament and parliamentary debate in Canada, especially in the era of the Charter. This focus is particularly relevant given the growing loss of confidence in parliamentary deliberation, including in Canada, leading to questions about the very viability of parliamentary democracy.[85]

Debeljak[86] argues that rights-restricting mechanisms like section 33 can go beyond what is needed to establish an institutional dialogue and tend to unnecessarily promote parliamentary sovereignty at the expense of human rights. Likewise, Tolley,[87] writing on the United Kingdom, argues that the effectiveness of parliaments in safeguarding rights depends on informed parliamentary debate and on preventing Bills with rights problems from becoming law. This may not be incentivised by a mechanism like the notwithstanding clause, which facilitates – and thus goes some way to legitimating – explicit violations of rights otherwise understood to be fundamental.

One particularly Diceyan method to sidestep this critique is to view parliamentary sovereignty as subject to the principles of legality internal to common law.[88] However, even in the United Kingdom the common law basis of large parts

[84] ibid.

[85] Ajzenstat, 'Reconciling Parliament and Rights'.

[86] J Debeljak, 'Balancing Rights in a Democracy: The Problems with Limitations and Overrides of Rights under the Victorian Charter of Human Rights and Responsibilities Act 2006' (2009) 32 *Melbourne University Law Review* 422.

[87] MC Tolley, 'Parliamentary Scrutiny of Rights in the United Kingdom: Assessing the Work of the Joint Committee on Human Rights' (2009) 44 *Australian Journal of Political Science* 41.

[88] TRS Allan, 'Questions of Legality and Legitimacy: Form and Substance in British Constitutionalism' (2011) 9 *International Journal of Constitutional Law* 155.

of the Constitution and criminal law have been superseded by legislation, a trend which seems likely to continue. Similarly, Eleftheriadis[89] suggests that the doctrine of parliamentary sovereignty should not be seen as a unique legal arrangement but rather a set of related and mutually supporting principles by which courts and Parliament should operate. Yet the disparity between a Parliament whose powers are formally unlimited but increasingly constrained by norms based on fundamental rights must therefore be accommodated by means of well-defined constitutional conventions.[90]

## C. Judicial Behaviour and Constitutional Conventions

The American or Marshallian model of constitutionalism, rooted in Chief Justice Marshall's reasoning in *Marbury v Madison*,[91] posits that a written constitution gains its legal foundation and moral legitimacy from an original act of will or consent by a sovereign people. In this framework, the Constitution serves as the 'supreme law of the land,' providing the criteria for the legal validity of all political actions and decisions. Judicial review is upheld as a morally legitimate mechanism to enforce the will of the people.[92] In contrast, the British or Diceyan model contends that the law of the Constitution arises from the rights of private persons as determined by courts in specific cases. In this view, the Constitution is 'judge-made', evolving from judicial decisions that establish the rights of private individuals. The Diceyan model suggests that the law of the constitution should be conceived as the consequence of what is accepted as legitimate governmental action and decision.[93]

Dicey's work on constitutional conventions can be applied to understand the 'unwritten' aspects of the Canadian Constitution. Dicey's legal flexible approach to legal formalism, which emphasised the role of courts in interpreting the constitution, can be seen as complementary with the Canadian approach that seeks political compromise and judicial restraint. As Walters[94] puts it, 'Dicey thought that the law of the constitution can only be understood if a legal rather than an historical point of view is adopted'. At the same time 'the legal viewpoint must not be formalistic but rather must be contextualised by (amongst other things) history'.[95] This model

[89] P Eleftheriadis, 'Parliamentary Sovereignty and the Constitution' (2009) 22 *Canadian Journal of Law & Jurisprudence* 267.

[90] MC Elliott, 'Parliamentary Sovereignty and the New Constitutional Order: Legislative Freedom, Political Reality and Convention' (2002) 22 *Legal Studies* 340.

[91] *Marbury v Madison*, 5 US 137.

[92] LB Tremblay, 'Two Models of Constitutionalism and The Legitimacy of Law: Dicey or Marshall?' (2006) 6 *Oxford University Commonwealth Law Journal* 77.

[93] ibid.

[94] MD Walters 'Dicey's Legal Constitution' in MD Walters (ed), *A.V. Dicey and the Common Law Constitutional Tradition: A Legal Turn of Mind* (Cambridge: Cambridge University Press, 2020).

[95] ibid.

is particularly relevant to the contemporary practice of constitutional adjudication in many Commonwealth countries, including Canada.[96]

In the Canadian legal context, the rule of law has been repeatedly recognised as one such principle. It is mentioned in the preambles of both the Canadian Charter of Rights and Freedoms, and the 1867 Constitution Act. The Supreme Court of Canada has invoked these preambles when relying on the rule of law, as seen in specific cases like the Manitoba Language Reference (1985), where the Court acknowledged the rule of law as a foundational postulate of Canada's constitutional order.[97] Moreover, the Court explicitly stated that the rule of law was an 'unwritten constitutional principle,' a stance that was evident in the 1997 Provincial Judges Reference.[98] In this case, which involved a challenge to legislation in three provinces that reduced the salaries of provincial court judges, the Supreme Court suggested that a breach of the rule of law could invalidate a duly enacted law.

This arguably goes further than Dicey, who tended to insist on a rigid separation between the law and the conventions of the Constitution, despite the importance of the former. The Canadian Supreme Court's use of the term 'constitutional architecture' has been critiqued for its vagueness and for incorporating constitutional conventions without sufficient transparency.[99] This lack of clarity was evident in the Court's recent handling of the Senate reform proposal which would have disrupted established constitutional conventions. Instead of addressing this directly, the Court invoked the notion of 'constitutional architecture', a move that had the effect of entrenching some constitutional conventions and blurring the line Dicey sought to draw between convention and law.[100]

The Supreme Court's approach to constitutional interpretation also diverges from Dicey's more absolutist stance on conventions surrounding parliamentary sovereignty.[101] In *Babcock*,[102] the Court held that the unwritten principle of the rule of law had to be balanced against the principle of parliamentary sovereignty. Similarly, the Federal Court of Appeal in *Singh*[103] upheld that parliamentary sovereignty remains a significant principle in Canada, despite the emergence of unwritten constitutional principles. Moreover, the Court has expanded the scope of the rule of law to create positive constitutional obligations, as in *BCGEU v British Columbia*,[104] where it considered the issue of physical access to the courts and issued an injunction against a picketing union of civil servants. This judicial

[96] Tremblay 'Two Models of Constitutionalism and The Legitimacy of Law'.
[97] PW Hogg and FZ Cara, 'The Rule of Law in the Supreme Court of Canada' (2005) 55 *The University of Toronto Law Journal* 715.
[98] ibid.
[99] L Sirota, 'Immuring Dicey's Ghost: The Senate Reform Reference and Constitutional Conventions' (2019) 51 *Ottawa Law Review* 325.
[100] ibid.
[101] F Ahmed et al, 'Judging Constitutional Conventions' (2019) 17 *International Journal of Constitutional Law* 787.
[102] *Babcock v Canada (Attorney General)* [2002] 3 SCR 3.
[103] *Singh v Minister of Employment and Immigration* [1985] 1 SCR 177.
[104] *BCGEU v British Columbia (Attorney General)* [1988] 2 SCR 214.

behaviour represents a partial departure from Dicey's limited view of the rule of law as merely a safeguard against arbitrary power.

## D. Federalism and the First Nations

Dicey's *Introduction to the Study of The Law of the Constitution* illustrates the nature of parliamentary sovereignty in the United Kingdom by comparing it with the system of federalism, particularly as it exists in the United States of America, but also other examples of federal government including the Swiss Confederation, the German Empire, and the Dominion of Canada.[105] Dicey suggested that while each of these states (including Canada) could offer insights into the subject matter, the focus was primarily on the United States for its more completely developed type of federalism. Nonetheless, Dicey stated that the Dominion of Canada served as one of the noteworthy examples of federal government without qualification based on its institutions at the time.[106]

Dicey went on to elaborate on the conditions and aims of federalism, stating that a federal state requires a body of countries closely connected by factors such as locality, history, or race. He mentioned that the provinces of Canada fit this description, being closely connected and capable of bearing an 'impress of common nationality'. In a federal state, he argued, every power – executive, legislative, or judicial – was subordinate to, and controlled by, the Constitution, which must be immutable or changeable only by an authority beyond ordinary legislative bodies.[107] While the latter broadly describes the modern Canadian Constitution, caveats around section 33 aside, the former emphatically does not describe the social or historical reality of Canada's multinational polity.

AV Dicey's views have thus been invoked to highlight some of the deficiencies of Canadian federalism.[108] Dicey argued that federalism involves a balance between two somewhat inconsistent feelings: 'the desire for national unity and the determination to maintain the independence of each man's separate State'.[109] LaSelva suggests that if Canadians are to rethink federalism, they will have to take Dicey's insight seriously and consider discarding some of their most cherished self-images. He argues that Canadian federalism should be understood as a 'way of life' and a 'moral value,' rather than merely a political or constitutional arrangement. The adoption of the Charter in 1982 without sufficient attention to these points led to a crisis in federalism, undermining the legitimacy of what he calls 'executive federalism' or 'federalism by elites'.[110] The Confederation failed Canadians by not

[105] Dicey, 'Parliamentary Sovereignty and Federalism'.
[106] ibid.
[107] ibid.
[108] SV Laselva, 'Federalism as a Way of Life: Reflections on the Canadian Experiment' (1993) 26 *Canadian Journal of Political Science / Revue canadienne de science politique* 219.
[109] Dicey, 'Parliamentary Sovereignty and Federalism'.
[110] Laselva, 'Federalism as a Way of Life'.

providing them with a foundation myth or moral ideal that could sustain them during times of trouble.[111]

LaSelva[112] suggests that Canadians seek alternative foundations for federalism, given that the Charter has forced a rethinking of its moral dimensions, introducing the concept of 'federalism as fraternity'. Yet replacing Dicey's more ethnonationalist formulation of the foundations of federalism with a vague modernised version may fail to confront the unsavoury origins of his original concepts. This can be clarified by a closer examination of Dicey's inconsistent approach to history and to the issues of colonialism in an era of constitutional government. Drevikovsky[113] critically examines Dicey's approach to legal history, particularly focusing on his methodological choices and their implications for understanding constitutional law. Dicey divided history into 'legal history' and 'non-legal history', often using this division to advance his more contentious arguments, particularly against Irish Home Rule. Dicey's historical method, which has been described as 'analytical jurisprudence', incorporated elements of Whig history, which viewed the past as a progression towards the present. This approach is selective and served specific political ends.

In a Canadian context, Drevikovsky[114] raises the *Case of the Canadian Prisoners* as an example. Dicey used this case to argue for the right to personal freedom under the rule of law, yet omitted the vital political and social context, focusing solely on the legal aspects to support his argument. The case involved Canadian 'rebels' who were found guilty of treason in Canada and were being transported. They were brought before the Exchequer on a writ of habeas corpus. These 'rebels' were in fact Upper Canadian (Quebecois) radicals who opposed the colonial administration in their province.[115] They rose up between 1837 and 1838 with demands that sound reasonable from a modern constitutional standpoint, such as legal primacy for local assemblies and control over the executive. The Upper Canadian legislature had passed an 'Act to enable the government of this province to extend a conditional pardon in certain cases to persons who have been concerned in the late insurrection'. The Act allowed the Lieutenant-Governor to grant a pardon with conditions, including penal transportation, wholly within the Lieutenant-Governor's discretion. This concentration of unfettered executive power contradicted Dicey's own principles about the rule of law, which aimed to prevent the 'exercise by persons in authority of wide, arbitrary or discretionary powers'. Yet by omitting these details, Dicey's account becomes a narrow legal narrative that supports his argument but lacks the broader context that might challenge it.[116]

[111] ibid.
[112] ibid.
[113] JO Drevikovsky, 'From Pseudochrony to Diachrony: A.V. Dicey, Home Rule and the Invention of Legal History' (Venour V Nathan Prize Essay, University of Sydney, 2023).
[114] ibid.
[115] ibid.
[116] ibid.

Likewise, Dicey's pronouncements on the structure and prerequisites for successful federalism elide social and historical context. The omission of such context from constitutional theory has nonetheless become increasingly untenable in modern Canada. The recent discovery of over 1,300 unmarked graves at former residential schools in western Canada has reignited a national conversation over the country's colonial legacy. Canada's Indian residential school system, which operated from 1883 to 1997 aimed at cultural 'assimilation' and separated more than 150,000 Indigenous children from their families, subjecting them to harsh conditions, including inadequate medical care and malnutrition. Contrary to claims that attribute the high mortality rates to diseases like tuberculosis, historical records reveal that the schools themselves were the primary contributors. These subpar conditions extended to racially segregated Indian hospitals and TB sanatoria, where Indigenous patients received inferior care and were often isolated for extended periods. Increasing awareness of chronic and intentional underfunding and neglect by federal officials challenges the narrative that seeks to downplay the schools' role in what many now characterise as genocide.

Dicey's view of federalism is fatally contaminated by nationalist and imperialist assumptions which run parallel to the imperatives which established the residential school system. Canada's Aboriginal Constitutions, with their distinct local Indigenous structures falling on a continuum between purely Western and traditional Indigenous systems, and the political drive in Canadian politics to go further in recognising First Nations sovereignty, cannot be separated from the Canadian state and British Empire's history of colonial genocide against Indigenous peoples. Dicey did not and could not provide adequate answers to these problems, as his historical method took little account of these concerns.

## E. Legal Collectivism

Two less explored areas about Dicey are his views on legal collectivism and executive and emergency powers. *Dicey's Lectures on the Relation between Law and Public Opinion in England during the Nineteenth Century* explores the intricate relationship between the evolution of English law and public opinion during the early twentieth century.[117] In tracing this development, he contrasted the Benthamite liberalism rooted in *laissez-faire* principles that dominated the mid-Victorian era with the legislative landscape at the close of the nineteenth century.[118] By 1900, the doctrine of *laissez-faire* had waned significantly, giving way to emerging collectivist ideologies. This ideological shift, associated with the so-called 'New Liberalism', is exemplified by several key Acts of Parliament in the early twentieth century,

[117] AV Dicey, *Lectures on the Relation between Law and Public Opinion in England during the Nineteenth Century* (London, Routledge, 2017).
[118] ibid.

such as the Old Age Pensions Act 1908, the National Insurance Act 1911, and the Trade Disputes Act 1906.[119] These legislative measures signified a growing acceptance of state intervention in individual lives. He concluded that this transition from individualism to collectivism was not merely a legislative phenomenon but also a broader change in public opinion and intellectual climate that he anticipated would persist into the future.[120]

While Dicey's thoughts in this area have received less attention than concepts such as the rule of law and parliamentary sovereignty, they find strong resonance in one particular contribution to contemporary Canadian constitutional debates. As part of his opposition to the Charlottetown Accord, Pierre Elliott Trudeau delivered a speech in October 1992 in Montreal. The speech was an in-depth analysis and critique of the Charlottetown Accord, focusing on its implications for individual and collective rights in Canada and exploring distinctly Diceyan concerns about the constitutional theory behind the accord.[121] Trudeau identified six categories of Canadian citizens, as per the Charlottetown Accord's 'Canada Clause', suggesting that were intended to place citizens in a hierarchy based on various criteria.[122]

First, Quebec was identified in the Accord as a distinct society within Canada, characterised by a French-speaking majority, unique culture, and a civil law tradition, and it fell upon the Quebec legislature and government to preserve this distinctiveness. Aboriginal peoples constituted the second category, possessing the right to promote their culture and traditions. The third category encompassed Canadians, and their governments, committed to the vitality and development of official language minorities. The fourth category consisted of Canadians committed to gender equality, although this commitment was not as robust as those for Quebec and Aboriginal peoples. The fifth category confirmed the principle of equality among provinces while acknowledging their diverse characteristics, noting that new provinces did not enjoy the same rights as existing ones. The sixth category included citizens who did not fit into any of the aforementioned categories and thus lacked special rights per the Charlottetown Accord. Trudeau criticised this hierarchical categorisation, contending that it eroded the principle of equality among citizens and weakened the protections on individual rights offered by the Charter of Rights and Freedoms.[123]

Trudeau underscored that the referendum's outcome would determine whether individual rights took precedence over collective rights and whether all citizens were treated as equals before the law. He warned against the perils of prioritising collective rights, citing historical and contemporary instances where this had led

[119] ibid.
[120] ibid.
[121] PE Trudeau, *Trudeau: A Mess that Deserves a Big No: Pierre Elliott Trudeau's Historic Speech at the Eleventh Cité Libre Dinner* (Toronto, Robert Davis Publishing, 1992).
[122] ibid.
[123] ibid.

to dictatorships and inequality. Trudeau scrutinised the 'Canada Clause' in the Charlottetown Accord, arguing that it created a hierarchy of citizens that undermined the principle of equality. He criticised the Accord's ambiguous language, particularly the use of the term 'commitment', which he believed weakened existing protections under the Charter of Rights and Freedoms. He also pointed out contradictions in the Accord, such as the simultaneous assertion of provincial equality and the designation of Quebec as a distinct society, and noted that new provinces would not enjoy the same rights as existing ones. He further argued that the Accord failed to adequately protect minority communities and could erode services in both official languages when federal jurisdictions were transferred to the provinces.[124]

While these concerns are recognisable from Dicey's writing, with which Trudeau as Canadian a lawyer trained in the 1940s would have been familiar, his position was significantly more nuanced and cannot be so easily dismissed. Trudeau questioned the continuing inclusion of the 'notwithstanding clause', warning that it could be misused by various levels of government, including Aboriginal governments as well as those of the provinces. In spite of the failure of the Accord, aspects of these concerns have proven prophetic, in particular the recent transformation of Quebec nationalism from a focus on separatism to aggressive secularism premised on Quebec's distinct collective identity.

Brahm argues that the decline of separatism in Quebec since the 1990s does not signify a decrease in nationalist issues; rather, it indicates an evolution led by Premier François Legault and the right-wing populist Coalition Avenir Québec (CAQ).[125] The CAQ is highlighted as a key player in this transformation, particularly through the implementation of Bill 21 (An Act respecting the Laicity of the State). Passed into law in 2019, Bill 21 aimed to ban wearing religious symbols by public sector employees in positions of authority, including judges, Crown attorneys, police officers, prison guards, and teachers.[126] As Trudeau predicted, the Quebec government asserted that the application of section 33, the 'notwithstanding clause', which received one of its rare uses in the Bill, rendered Bill 21 impervious to challenges based on Charter rights, including the freedom of religion. The CAQ's implementation of Bill 21 is seen as a strategic move to consolidate its leadership in Quebec nationalism, and a cornerstone in the CAQ's efforts to satisfy public demands for change and establish a new paradigm on nationalism.[127]

However, the Bill and the CAQs rhetoric concerning it have been seen as an attack on religious freedom and on Muslim Canadians in particular.[128] Bill 21 built on the previously enacted Bill 62 (2017), which banned individuals from covering

[124] ibid.
[125] A Brahm, 'Quebec's Evolving Nationalism: Tipping from Separatism to Secularism' (Research Paper, University of Ottawa, 2021).
[126] ibid.
[127] ibid.
[128] A Hmimssa, 'Citizenship under Pressure: Mapping Debates over Religious Freedom in the Second Decade in Quebec' (2023) 57 *Journal of Canadian Studies* 114.

their faces while receiving or providing public services. As a result, some Muslim women who wear the hijab or niqab in Quebec argue that such policies not only limit their career opportunities but also create an environment of hostility towards Muslims, affecting their public self-presentation.[129] The laws are seen to carry extra-legal messages that signal societal disapproval of Islam, thereby curtailing the freedom of Muslim women to wear religious clothing at work or in public spaces. This legislative landscape exacerbates existing discrimination and the hostile interpersonal confrontations that these women face.[130]

## F. Emergencies and Executive Power

AV Dicey's conceptual framework categorised executive authorities into two main types: statutory and 'prerogative'.[131] This bifurcation has been criticised for generating analytical confusion and for missing an opportunity to bring clarity to the relatively understudied area of contemporary Canadian governance and constitutionalism. Dicey's original framework was not intended to serve as an analytical tool for understanding executive authorities; rather, it was focused on constitutional conventions. Dicey's framework also does not account for the modern legal landscape where judicial review plays a significant role. Courts now have the ability to annul exercises of prerogative powers, a development that Dicey's original conceptualisation did not anticipate.[132]

To address the limitations of Dicey's framework, Bolt and Lagasse suggest a more nuanced taxonomy for understanding executive authorities in Canada. This taxonomy identifies six categories of executive power: statute-based authorities, constitutional authorities, Crown prerogatives, authorities from exercises of the Crown prerogative, common law police powers, and authorities of the Crown as a person. The authors highlight the confusion surrounding executive authorities in Canada, citing the example of *Conacher v Canada (Prime Minister)*,[133] which dealt with the issue of judicial review of the Prime Minister's advice to the Governor General. In this case, the applicant, Duff Conacher, sought judicial review of the Prime Minister's advice to prorogue Parliament in 2008. They argued that the Diceyan approach led to analytical confusion and that it was imperative to be more precise about the source of a particular executive authority.[134]

The conception of the rule of law as articulated by Dicey has also been employed to critique the Supreme Court of Canada's approach to expanding

[129] J Doering and E Peker, 'How Muslims Respond to Secularist Restrictions: Reactive Ethnicity, Adjustment, and Acceptance' (2022) 45 *Ethnic and Racial Studies* 2956.

[130] ibid.

[131] A Bolt and P Lagasse, 'Beyond Dicey: Executive Authorities in Canada. (2021) 3 *The Journal of Commonwealth Law* 1.

[132] ibid.

[133] *Conacher v Canada (Prime Minister)* 2009 FC 920.

[134] ibid.

police powers.[135] Dicey's doctrine emphasised that all executive actors, including police officers, should be subject to the ordinary law of the land unless there was an express legislative grant of authority. This perspective rests on the premise that the rule of law should be understood in terms set out by Dicey, advocating for a strict constructionist approach. Dicey also argued for the narrow interpretation of grants of authority to administrative actors, positing that if Parliament was to be truly supreme, courts had ensure that these actors did not overstep their statutory boundaries.[136]

However, Dicey's model may not be an adequate framework through which to understand police powers in modern Canada. Plaxton ultimately proposes an alternative administrative model which allows for police discretion and offers a more nuanced understanding of the issue. This is premised on the idea that police officers, as administrative actors, have the discretion to determine the extent to which Charter rights may be infringed. This administrative model suggests that the strict constructionist approach advocated by Dicey may not be the most effective way to ensure the balance between state authority and individual liberties.[137]

Figures like Carl Schmitt and Adrian Vermeule argue that the rule of law encounters fundamental limitations, especially in times of crisis.[138] Despite these critiques, the prevailing view in both Canadian case law and philosophical literature remains that the rule of law serves as a crucial mechanism for protecting citizens from arbitrary executive actions even in extremis.[139] Dyzenhaus delves into the complexities surrounding Dicey's view on responses to such states of emergency. Dicey argued that during an emergency, public officials might find themselves compelled to act outside the law. Parliament might then indemnify them, but this did not make their actions legal. Instead, it placed them in a 'zone uncontrolled by law – a legal black hole, to use the current term'.[140]

Nonetheless, Dicey distinguished between two legal responses to an emergency. In the first, the response was after-the-fact recognition that officials acted outside of the law because it was necessary. In the second, Parliament gave officials resources to deal with emergencies in advance, in accordance with the rule of law. Dicey preferred the second option, although he acknowledged that officials might have to react to an emergency situation before Parliament could respond. Thus, while political power could always be exercised in a brute fashion, it would be far better if Parliament were to delegate in advance the resources to public officials to deal with an emergency. Dicey was thus not only enthusiastic about taming the prerogative by subjecting it to statutory control, but he also maintained it would be

[135] M Plaxton, 'Police Powers after Dicey' (2012) 38 *Queen's Law Journal* 99.
[136] ibid.
[137] ibid.
[138] Garver, 'The Canadian Approach to Rule of Law'.
[139] ibid.
[140] D Dyzenhaus, 'The State of Emergency in Legal Theory' in K Roach et al (eds), *Global Anti-Terrorism Law and Policy* (Cambridge, Cambridge University Press, 2005).

wrong to suppose that a prospective legislative grant of emergency powers merely substituted the 'despotism of Parliament for the prerogative of the Crown'.[141]

Recent Canadian experience demonstrates the potential problem with this approach. The Canadian 'Freedom Convoy' protests of early 2022 were a grassroots movement that initially focused on opposing vaccine mandates for cross-border truckers but soon expanded to contest broader COVID-19 restrictions. Utilising tactics such as road blockades and public demonstrations, particularly a prolonged sit-in in Ottawa, the protesters claimed that the mandates infringed upon civil liberties. The movement elicited a polarised public and governmental response, leading to the unprecedented invocation of the 1988 Emergencies Act by the Canadian government. The Emergencies Act resulted from an overhaul of the War Powers Act in the aftermath of the latter's use by Pierre Trudeau during the October Crisis of 1970. Justin Trudeau's invocation of the Act marked the first use of the Act since its inception, expanding governmental and law enforcement powers to manage the protests. It facilitated the seizure of assets, like towing trucks, and financial measures against protesters.

Several premiers nonetheless opposed the Trudeau government's actions. In particular, Premier Legault expressed disapproval over the invocation of the Emergencies Act, arguing that it was unwarranted in Quebec as the province had not faced significant issues with the protests, and implementing the Act could detrimentally affect the social climate. Legault explicitly acknowledged the historical resonance with the War Measures Act's invocation by the elder Trudeau during the 1970 October Crisis in Quebec.[142] The former act, though invoked in response to clear acts of terrorism by the Front de libération du Québec, including the kidnapping of a minister and a British official, had enabled extensive police powers, leading to unwarranted searches, arrests, and indefinite detentions of numerous Quebecers later determined to be unjustified.

Unlike the War Measures Act, however, the Emergencies Act drew on the experience of 1970 and followed a markedly less Diceyan approach to the problem.[143] Rather than simply granting, and thus in effect constitutionalising, otherwise extra-legal action by the executive, the Act mandated parliamentary review of Cabinet orders and regulations, ensuring a democratic oversight during crises, and forced the government to demonstrate sufficient cause for its actions, something Pierre Trudeau failed to do in 1970.[144] It stipulated compensation for those affected by government actions and adhered to the Canadian Charter of Rights and Freedoms and the Canadian Bill of Rights, establishing a framework of rights protection during national exigencies.

[141] ibid.

[142] S Rukavina, 'François Legault Says Trudeau's Invoking of Emergencies Act "Not Necessary" in Quebec' (*CBC*, 14 February 2022).

[143] R Alford, 'Emergency Powers and the Rule of Law: Why Inquiries Matter' (Macdonald-Laurier Institute, 2022).

[144] ibid.

Though this framework could be read as concordant with Dicey's concern over pre-parliamentary approval of emergency action, his version was both broader and less specific about constitutional and rights-based remedies after a crisis ended, seeing the distinction between the 'despotism of Parliament' and the despotism of the raw prerogative as essentially sufficient.[145] In Canada, by contrast, the debate over the use of the Emergencies Act in 2022 had, by virtue of its non-Diceyan structure, not been restricted to questions of its simple legality. The legally mandated Public Order Emergency Commission reviewing the decision, chaired by Justice Paul Rouleau of the Court of Appeal for Ontario, heard from residents, police, politicians and the protesters themselves.[146] It also included an extensive 'policy phase' hearing from numerous legal experts who study the Charter of Rights and Freedoms.[147] The resulting 2,000-page report, though ultimately approving of Trudeau's actions, has been described as a 'deep dive' into questions of the rule of law in relation to emergencies, and made 56 recommendations to better manage future large-scale protests and regulate the use of the Emergencies Act.[148] It was notably even-handed, with observers noting its analysis ultimately demonstrated that 'nearly everyone fell short' in upholding the rule of law during the crisis.[149]

## V. Conclusion

At Confederation, the preamble of the British North America Act promised a 'Constitution similar in Principle to that of the United Kingdom'.[150] In spite of Canada's ongoing constitutional journey post-Confederation and post-patriation, the preamble of the British North America Act germinated a framework still reflective of the United Kingdom's constitutional principles. AV Dicey, as a seminal figure in elucidating the principles of the United Kingdom Constitution, thus has perennial relevance to Canada's jurisprudential landscape, contingent only upon the broad retention of this constitutional structure. Even through the crucible of myriad crises and challenges since 1867, Canada's constitutional resilience and development can still be viewed through lens of the doctrines propagated by Dicey, particularly in the realms of the rule of law and parliamentary sovereignty. Indeed, Canada has often navigated through the ideological paradoxes of these doctrines with a degree of finesse surpassing that of the United Kingdom,

[145] Dyzenhaus, 'The State of Emergency in Legal Theory'.

[146] L McQuillan, 'Explainer: Emergencies Act Inquiry – What's Been Said, What Happens Next' (*CBC*, 23 November 2022).

[147] L Osman, 'Emergencies Act Inquiry Studies Fundamental Rights and Rreedoms at Stake in Protests' (*CBC*, 28 November 2022).

[148] JP Tasker, 'Four Highlights from the Emergencies Act Inquiry's Final Report' (*CBC*, 17 February 2023).

[149] J Stacey and NC Lazar, 'Emergencies Act Inquiry Final Report is a Reminder that We All Have a Role in Upholding the Rule of Law' (*The Conversation*, 21 February 2023).

[150] Constitution Act 1867, Preamble.

substantially attributable to the Canadian judiciary's interpretive pragmatism and its nuanced adherence to constitutional conventions.

Nevertheless, the intricacies of Canada's modern social and political fabric encapsulate some of the key limitations inherent in Dicey's work, thereby necessitating that Canadian politicians and jurists transcend beyond the purview of his theories on a regular basis. The salient doctrines of the rule of law and parliamentary sovereignty have found robust expression in Canada's legal and political architecture. Yet, conversely, in the realms of federalism, legal collectivism, and executive power, Dicey's theories encounter limits to their applicability. The demands of Canada's federal structure in particular have engendered a trajectory of constitutionalism that navigates beyond the orthodoxies delineated by Dicey. The ascendancy of modern Canadian executive power, often a point of legal and political contention, further underscores the imperative for a more expansive constitutional vista than Dicey provided.

Through addressing these problems head on, Canada has not only transcended the Diceyan paradigm but has also embarked on a path of constitutional innovation, thereby juxtaposing the United Kingdom's continuing and often frustrating constitutional conservatism. This juxtaposition elucidates a Canadian constitutional narrative that, while rooted in Diceyan orthodoxy, has long since burgeoned beyond it to foster a jurisprudential and political ecosystem that is both reflective and anticipatory of the multifaceted challenges encapsulated within its modern governance paradigm.

# 13

# Dicey in Hong Kong

RICHARD CULLEN

## I. Introduction[1]

For 150 years, the British ran Hong Kong with no directly elected representation within the Legislative Council. From 1842 to 1997 the all-powerful Governor was simply appointed (and replaced, as needs be) by London. Especially after the Second World War, however, the British visibly improved on what was already a successful governance structure based on authoritarian legality.[2] As one looks more closely at the British Hong Kong political-legal experience, it becomes clear these governance achievements, which both served the Imperial project and fostered stability and prosperity in Hong Kong, were built on British constitutional foundations forged over many centuries. Britain does not have a single, codified written Constitution but an unwritten one which is an evolved (rather than revolutionary) creation. This central feature of the British Constitution left the way open for Professor AV Dicey to analyse and describe – indeed, reveal – the essence of this historically tempered set of resilient governance principles.

It is now over 180 years since Hong Kong's authoritarian legality governance model was first put in place. Over the last decade it has, once again, held firm, as that model has been tested significantly and repeatedly, arising from a delayed, though potent and disturbing, post-colonial experience. In 2014, we saw hugely disruptive, mass political reform protests which ran for almost three months. In February 2016, the worst political rioting in Hong Kong since the 1960s unfolded

[1] This chapter draws on and repeats arguments from certain chapters in R Cullen, *Hong Kong Constitutionalism: The British Legacy and the Chinese Future* (Abingdon, Routledge, 2020) and other works by Richard Cullen.

[2] Authoritarian is a key term used in this chapter. The literature on the typology of authoritarianism is extensive. In this chapter, by *authoritarian*, I mean: a governance regime where the ruling authority enjoys ostensible plenary power (which takes priority over personal freedoms) combined with indefinite political tenure. By (modern) constitutionalism I mean: the principle that the authority of government derives from and is limited by a body of fundamental law and embedded, political behaviour norms. Authoritarian Legality, as it is deployed in this chapter, refers to authoritarian government which is operationally committed to a measurable, continuing degree of constitutionalism. See further Cullen, ibid 237–38.

over the course of one evening. In 2019, massive peaceful political protests gave rise to a sustained political insurrection, which lasted for over seven months. These developments are comprehensively explored in a new book by Daniel Vukovich, described by one reviewer as: '[A] blistering critique of Hong Kong's troubled decolonization since 1997'.[3] The way in which Diceyan principles have shaped Hong Kong's governance model for well over a century is explained below in Part II.

This chapter argues that 'Diceyan Constitutionalism' was fundamental (within the pivotal context of 'Chinese Familism') in shaping the development of governance institutions and pivotal operational procedures within this British colony. It explains how Hong Kong's Diceyan authoritarian legality system came to pass; the essence of that system; and how it has made the transition as British Hong Kong became the Hong Kong Special Administrative Region within the People's Republic of China under the One Country Two Systems governing principle. It also discusses how that system has coped with the most recent, radical, political structure reforms imposed on Hong Kong by Beijing, as Hong Kong actively comprehends its future as an inalienable part of China.

## II. Constitutional Evolution

Dicey is on record as saying that Edmund Burke was one of the writers he 'read with perpetual profit and enjoyment'. He also regarded Burke as an 'adventurer' – though one with principles. Ultimately, he felt that Burke was 'not a just man'. He explained that 'Not a single weak point in the position of the French Revolutionists escaped his glance … but to the good or better side of the revolutionary movement [in France] he was as blind as the stupidest of Tory squires'.[4]

These views are informing. They indicate Dicey's joint concern about abuses of power arising from unrestrained power in the hands of either rulers or the mass of people within any modern jurisdiction.

Most of Dicey's primary research and writing took place in the midst of brutal nineteenth century poverty in a United Kingdom by then replete with countless 'dark satanic mills'[5] crammed into numerous cities hugely enlarged in terms of population by the Industrial Revolution.[6] Moreover, the darkest side of the British Empire, during its peak period, included terrible famines. Shocking examples included repeated deadly food crises in India, and right within the (then) United Kingdom, in Ireland. Millions perished from starvation. Despite (and, to a degree,

[3] DF Vukovich, *After Autonomy: A Post-Mortem for Hong Kong's First Handover, 1997–2019* (London, Palgrave Macmillan, 2022).

[4] D Maciag, *Edmund Burke in America: The Contested Career of the Father of Modern Conservatism* (Ithaca, Cornell University Press, 2013) 112 ff.

[5] W Blake, 'Jerusalem' (BBC Poetry), https://www.bbc.co.uk/poetryseason/poems/jerusalem.shtml.

[6] The documentation of this harsh and dismal reality is extensive. See for example, EP Thompson *Whigs and Hunters* (New York, Pantheon Books, 1975) (and his other work).

because of) this reality, the concept of the modern 'free and lawful' citizen was still reinforced as a central norm of the common law.[7]

Limited monarchy and the emergence of Cabinet government by the early eighteenth century had, by 1837, irrevocably become constitutional monarchy, under Queen Victoria.[8] This was when parliamentary (or representative) government was developed, consolidated, and confirmed within the United Kingdom. All ultimate political power (according to the doctrine of parliamentary sovereignty explained by Dicey) was placed within the Parliament at Westminster, where regular elections (for the House of Commons) were mandated to select new governments or to confirm sitting governments. Each government had to be composed, according to constitutional convention, of members of the Westminster Parliament.[9]

Around 100 years after Victoria came to the throne, George Orwell wrote his 1941 essay, 'England Your England', which is the first part of a longer work, *The Lion and the Unicorn: Socialism and the English Genius*. The essay, written during the German Blitz unleashed on England and especially London, famously begins, 'As I write, highly civilized human beings are flying overhead trying to kill me'.[10]

In the course of the essay, Orwell did not use the term *social ontology*.[11] His insightful study of what, at that time, made England, England can be aptly so characterised, however. He canvassed the powerful and complex connecting forces within a highly class-based, hierarchical society. The hatred of war, militarism, and power worship all existed alongside acceptance, indeed, pride, in the then still vast British Empire. The binding nature of the shared experience of the weather, the continual dampness, bad teeth, bitter beer, heavy coins, gentle manners, suet puddings, red pillar boxes – and more – all helped forge the deep sense of national loyalty and bottom-up, potent (though mainly non-demonstrative) patriotism.

One passage may be quoted with benefit:

> Here one comes upon an all-important English trait: the respect for constitutionalism and legality, the belief in 'the law' as something above the State and above the individual,

[7] These examples of terrible, vast poverty and mass human ruination were matters of intense political debate in the United Kingdom (especially with respect to Ireland) in the nineteenth century, which saw the government in Westminster change hands between Conservatives (led by Benjamin Disraeli) and Liberals (led by William Gladstone). These debates prompted a series of statutory reforms over several decades aimed at relieving poverty, preventing famine, improving education, and widening the franchise. See *BBC History*, 'Victorian Britain', https://www.bbc.co.uk/history/british/victorians/.

[8] DM Walker, *The Oxford Companion to Law* (Oxford, Oxford University Press, 1980). 'Monarchy', 'Parliamentary government', 'Parliament of England', 'Parliament of Great Britain' and 'Parliament of The United Kingdom'.

[9] ibid.

[10] G Orwell, 'England Your England' in *The Lion and the Unicorn: Socialism and the English Genius* (London, Secker and Warburg, 1941), https://www.orwell.ru/library/essays/lion/english/.

[11] Theodore Schatzki defines 'social ontology' as 'I mean ideas about, including the self-conscious study of, the nature, character, or basic features, structures, or elements-constituents of social life. A social ontology, accordingly, is a statement or understanding of the nature, character, or basic features, structures, or constituents of this. It is an explication or understanding of the basal "what there is" to social existence': Cullen, *Hong Kong Constitutionalism* 238.

> something which is cruel and stupid, of course, but at any rate incorruptible. It is not that anyone imagines the law to be just. Everyone knows that there is one law for the rich and another for the poor. But no one accepts the implications of this, everyone takes it for granted that the law, such as it is, will be respected, and feels a sense of outrage when it is not.[12]

Putting aside the contrast between Dicey's faith in 'justice' (generally, and within the law) and Orwell's manifest lack of a similar level of confidence, one can see a continuity in the shared understanding of the essential nature of law – and the way in which the law stands not shamelessly-beneficially hand-in-glove with centralised power but at a very clear distance therefrom. This central political-legal phenomenon was a product of several centuries of often fractious but continuous and evolved, shared (elite-mass) interactive experience.

The system of parliamentary government, based on regular elections (outlined above) was incorporated into the largely white components of the British Empire, including Canada, Australia, and New Zealand from the mid-nineteenth century.[13]

However, the new colony of Hong Kong, like many other similarly ranked jurisdictions within the Empire, took a form of government structurally-based on the established (pre-parliamentary) government model such as applied during the reign of George III (1760–1820), where a strong executive government, headed by the Governor, operated essentially outside of the legislature. The Legislative Council within British Hong Kong, was, in keeping with this model, fully appointed by the Governor (this remained the case for almost 150 years). Combined with these two institutions was the independent judiciary – with its equally independent legal profession.

Incorporated within this formally authoritarian governance structure, however, were powerful governance principles derived from Diceyan constitutionalism. Included within this framework were the independent judicial-legal system just noted – and a commitment to a 'single-track' system of regulating state-citizen relationship. That is, the same courts applied the common law (and Legislative Council Ordinances) in interactions between state and citizen and in citizen-citizen disputes. Dicey stressed this British common law advantage in comparison to the French system of maintaining a separate court regime for state-citizen disputes.

An argument can be made that Dicey's influence on the development of governance structures in Hong Kong (and numbers of other similar, smaller jurisdictions within the British Empire) was not significant because the United Kingdom, even in Dicey's time, was gradually transforming itself into a modern, pluralistic, representative democracy. This is so, but it remains the case that British colonial-constitutional thinking was fundamentally influenced by British constitutional thinking – as seminally explained by Dicey. One would hardly expect otherwise.

[12] ibid.

[13] DM Walker, *The Oxford Companion to Law* (Oxford, Oxford University Press, 1980). These were given 'dominion status'.

It is true that the British chose not to introduce any sort of elected legislatures and thus parliamentary government across many of the colonies within the British Empire – but this did not inhibit the application of fundamental Diceyan protocols in framing colonial governance institutions. The rule of law paradigm, with its stress on judicial independence, is pivotal to Dicey's constitutional standpoint and these aspects of his thinking have been crucially relevant in Hong Kong since the inception of British Hong Kong until the present day.

# III. British Hong Kong

## A. Foundational Developments

Prior to the British acquiring Hong Kong Island in 1842 under the Treaty of Nanking (now Nanjing)[14] it was an outpost within Imperial China and home to a number of small fishing communities.[15] The Treaty of Nanking, along with almost all other treaties signed by the Chinese under (mainly) European pressure, particularly during the nineteenth century, was regarded as *unequal* and therefore not recognised by China as a proper treaty.[16]

The British took possession of Hong Kong Island after what is known as the First Opium War (1837–1842). The British, as a result of their success in this war, were able to force Imperial China to open its doors to much increased trade and, especially, to substantial trade in opium.[17]

Hong Kong became a Crown colony within the British Empire with a Constitution provided in the Letters Patent and Royal Instructions,[18] issued through the Privy Council in London. This was the customary method the British used for providing constitutional underpinnings to colonies like Hong Kong.[19] Such colonies remained subject to the direct application of United Kingdom law in certain circumstances, and their own law-making powers were limited, normally, to laws having effect within the specific colony. The Letters Patent for Hong Kong,

[14] The romanised versions of Chinese place names vary in their spelling. This is the result of historical practice.

[15] S Tsang, *A Modern History of Hong Kong* (London, IB Tauris, 2007) ch 1.

[16] See P Wesley-Smith, *Unequal Treaty 1898–1997: China, Great Britain and Hong Kong's New Territories* (Oxford, Oxford University Press, 1983); Y Ghai, *Hong Kong's New Constitutional Order*, 2nd edn (Hong Kong, Hong Kong University Press, 1999) ch 1.

[17] Initially, the opium trade was, officially, mainly from India, through Hong Kong, to North America, Europe, and Australia, at a time when such trade was quite legal and opium was used extensively as a primary painkiller (pre-aspirin). Unofficially, there was very substantial trade into China using smuggling methods. Eventually, that trade with China was legalised about 20 years after the establishment of British Hong Kong. See further R Cullen and K Tso, 'Using Opium as a Public Revenue Resource – Not as Easy as it Looks: The British Hong Kong Experience' (2012) 2 *British Tax Review* 226.

[18] Ghai, *Hong Kong's New Constitutional Order* ch 1.

[19] 'Legislative Council in Brief' (Legislative Council, January 2022), https://www.legco.gov.hk/en/education/understand/brief/factsheet11.html.

which were subject to a number of amendments, remained Hong Kong's primary constitutional document until the change of sovereignty in 1997.[20]

The Second Opium War was fought by the British (and French) from 1858 to 1860 after further Chinese resistance to the opium trade. In 1860 the British took possession of the Kowloon Peninsula and Stonecutters Island, directly north of Hong Kong Island, under the First Convention of Peking. As in the case of Hong Kong Island, under this new Treaty, the area was ceded to the United Kingdom in perpetuity.

In 1894–1895, modernising, highly militarised Japan inflicted another defeat on China. Japan took control of Taiwan at this time and various European powers (including the United Kingdom) moved in to obtain further concessions from China. In 1898, the British obtained a 99-year lease of the New Territories under the Second Convention of Peking. This added to the existing Crown colony a large area north of the Kowloon Peninsula plus a number of nearby islands. The land area of Hong Kong was increased to around 1,100 square kilometres. The population at this time was about 250,000.[21]

In 1912, the decaying Qing dynasty finally collapsed and the Republic of China was established under its new President and pre-eminent founding father, Sun Yat-sen. Overall, British Hong Kong continued to prosper, though it endured difficult periods during the 1920s and 1930s.[22] Over the same period, the Japanese dramatically extended their control and influence in Mainland China. Almost at the same time as the Japanese bombed Pearl Harbour on 7 December 1941, they attacked Hong Kong from their base in Guangdong Province, directly to the north. They overran the colony with ruthless speed. By Christmas Day 1941 all of Hong Kong was in Japanese hands.

After the defeat of Japan in 1945, the Civil War in China resumed between Chiang Kai-Shek's Kuomintang (KMT) and the Communist Party of China, led by Mao Zedong. By 1949, the defeated KMT had retreated to the island of Taiwan. The new People's Republic of China was proclaimed on 1 October 1949.

Although the People's Liberation Army (of the Communist Party of China) was on the border with Hong Kong by 1949, no attempt was made to invade. By 1950, China had entered the war on the Korean Peninsula on the side of North Korea. This made any near-term invasion of Hong Kong unlikely for several reasons. First, the limited resources of the new People's Republic of China were already stretched by the war in the north-east. Also, the British were, by now, well dug in, in Hong Kong. Next, the Korean War demonstrated, to Beijing, the advantage of having this British enclave in the south-west. Following the outbreak of the Korean War, the western powers placed an embargo on the export of strategic goods to

[20] Ghai, *Hong Kong's New Constitutional Order* ch 1.

[21] J Morris, *Hong Kong: Epilogue to an Empire* (London, Penguin, 1990) 35.

[22] N Miners and J Tuck-Hong Tang, *The Government and Politics of Hong Kong*, 5th edn (Oxford, Oxford University Press, 1991) 4.

the People's Republic of China. China was, nonetheless, able to obtain important supplies through Hong Kong.[23]

Out of this experience grew a largely unspoken, mutual understanding between Beijing and London. The essence of this understanding was that, provided Hong Kong did not become any sort of strategic threat to the People's Republic of China, the British presence there would be tolerated *pro tempore*. The key elements of this *modus vivendi*, according to Norman Miners, included no significant moves towards democracy in Hong Kong; no operational Taiwanese (that is, KMT) political presence in Hong Kong; and no impediments to China participating in and profiting from the Hong Kong economy.[24]

Under this arrangement, Hong Kong enjoyed a near continuous, significant growth in prosperity for a period of five decades following the end of the Second World War. In 1945, Hong Kong's per capita Gross Domestic Product (GDP) was, by some estimates, lower than that of India and Kenya.[25] By 1992, Hong Kong's per capita GDP had overtaken that of the United Kingdom. By 2004, Hong Kong was ranked 23 in a global, 'highest GDP per head' table, ahead of Canada and Australia.[26] Wealth distribution in Hong Kong remains very uneven; significant poverty persists. Nevertheless, Hong Kong materially transformed itself in the decades after 1945 from a war-ravaged colony of fewer than 800,000 to a leading international finance and service centre with a population of over seven million. Hong Kong also became one of the world's busiest container ports and the most popular tourist destination in Asia after the People's Republic of China.

Over the period from 1945 to 1997, Hong Kong experienced (or was caught up in to some degree) various regional crises including the Korean War; the upheaval and famine associated with Mao's infamous 'Great Leap Forward' (1958–1961);[27] Mao's even more ill-famed, 'Great Proletarian Cultural Revolution' (1966–1976);[28] and the Vietnamese War, followed by the military crushing massive protests in Beijing in June 1989. In all these and other cases, Hong Kong absorbed the impact, recovered and, usually with remarkable swiftness, returned to a path of strong growth.

## B. Influential Values

### *i. Diceyan Constitutionalism*

I outlined above how Diceyan constitutionalism shaped the creation and maintenance of a strong, largely constructive, and consistent public institutional

[23] ibid 4.
[24] ibid 6.
[25] J Bartholomew, *The Welfare State Made Britain Poor* (Hull, Biteback Publishing, 2013).
[26] *Pocket World in Figures 2005* (Economist Books, 2004) 28.
[27] *Cambridge Paperback Encyclopedia*, 3rd edn (Cambridge, Cambridge University Press, 1999) 365.
[28] ibid 228. See also J Chen, *Chinese Law: Context and Transformation* (Leyde, Brill, 2015) ch 2.

framework in Hong Kong. It also powerfully influenced operational procedures for the officers of these institutions.

Many defects remained within this scheme. The British governance system during this era has been portrayed, as, 'systematically biased against Chinese and other non-European defendants'.[29] Peter Wesley-Smith describes the rule of law as being, throughout this period, '[a British] ideal more dramatically subverted than any other'.[30]

Although the record is clear that the colonial rule of law in Hong Kong steadily fell short of working in accordance with its better foundational principles, two high-profile cases – one from the nineteenth century and another from the twentieth – show how well, when put to the test, it could live up to those values.

First, the outbreak of the Second Opium War in 1856 war prompted strong reactions, conspicuously from a British Hong Kong baker: Cheong Ah-lum was the principal of a business supplying bread to expatriates in British Hong Kong. It is widely believed that in 1857 he laced bread with arsenic in a bid to decimate a significant section of leading members of the British population in Hong Kong. In almost all cases, those who ate the bread vomited soon after and failed to ingest much arsenic. Attorney-General Anstey favoured a 'drumhead court martial'. As the United Kingdom was at war with China by then, this was a legally available option. Anstey favoured such a trial the better to secure a swift verdict of death by hanging. The Governor rejected this option and insisted on a civilian trial by jury (some of whose members had been poisoned). Chief Justice Hulme advised the jury that no matter how angry they felt, 'hanging the wrong man will not further the ends of justice'. Based on the evidence presented, Cheong was acquitted by the jury. He swiftly relocated to Macau and then to Vietnam and died, aged 70, in 1900.[31]

The next case concerns the paramount leader of the Vietnamese revolution against French occupation, Ho Chi Minh. In 1929 he was sentenced to death, by the French in Indochina, in absentia. He went to British Hong Kong in 1930 to escape the French, to spread his belief in communism, and to work to overthrow French rule in Indochina. The French discovered his presence in Hong Kong and alerted the British authorities. Ho was detained in Victoria Gaol in 1931. He refused to admit his real identity. The British nevertheless made ready to deport him to Indochina on a French ship.[32]

[29] C Munn, *Anglo-China: Chinese People and British Rule in Hong Kong, 1841–1880* (London, Curzon Press, 2001) 251.

[30] P Wesley-Smith, review of Christopher Munn's *Anglo-China: Chinese People and British Rule in Hong Kong – 1841–1880* (2003) Jan–Feb *China Perspectives* 74.

[31] See B Schoonakker, 'Racial Tensions Mixed with a Dash of Arsenic and Yeast' (15 January 2007) *South China Morning Post*, https://www.scmp.com/article/578666/racial-tensions-mixed-dash-arsenic-and-yeast; and K Tso, 'Fundamental Political and Constitutional Norms: Hong Kong and Macau Compared' (2012) 13 *Australian Journal of Asian Law* 25.

[32] S Chan, 'Ho Chi Minh in Victoria Gaol' (Hong Kong Memory, 2011), https://www.hkmemory.hk/MHK/collections/victoria_prison/Ho_Chi_Minh_in_Victoria_Gaol/index.html.

Francis Loseby, Ho's lawyer in Hong Kong, successfully prevented this with a writ of habeas corpus. After the High Court in Hong Kong subsequently ordered Ho's deportation, Loseby lodged an appeal with the Privy Council in London. In 1932, the matter was settled outside of the Privy Council.[33] It is understood that the British Colonial Office had an internal rule that a prisoner of the British should not be deported to face a death penalty (especially one handed down in absentia).

Ho suffered from both tuberculosis and dysentery. A cover story was leaked, to deflect the French, that he had died in Hong Kong of tuberculosis. In the meantime, Ho was eventually put on a ship out of Hong Kong to Amoy (now Xiamen) in China. Ho retained a friendship with Loseby, who visited him (as President of North Vietnam) in Hanoi in 1960.[34]

The governance system which, shaped by Diceyan principles, evolved within British Hong Kong was, taken as a whole, rational, predictable, coherent and, for the time, primarily measured rather than arbitrary. It was also resilient and successful. Its enduring merits were more central than its continuing drawbacks and those merits stood up well, comparatively. Hong Kong came to experience an operational governance system of qualified integrity.[35]

### *ii. Chinese Familism*[36]

The population of Hong Kong is predominantly Chinese (over 95 per cent). The Chinese have created and maintained the largest, most enduring civilization on the planet. This is a culture of immense depth and, despite its complexity, a culture which has displayed a set of clear hallmarks over many centuries, deeply influenced, above all and for over 2,000 years, by the critical teaching of the venerated philosopher Confucius (551–479 BC).[37]

The Belgian-Australian sinologist, Simon Leys, argued that:

> It is only when we contemplate China that we can become exactly aware of our own identity and that we begin to perceive which part of our heritage truly pertains to universal humanity, and which part merely reflects Indo-European idiosyncrasies.[38]

[33] ibid.

[34] Y Kwok, 'Liberating the Past' (*South China Morning Post*, 13 May 2008), https://www.scmp.com/article/637331/liberating-past.

[35] Tso, 'Fundamental Political and Constitutional Norms'. This article evaluates the core values, continuity of policy development, and relative autonomy established within British Hong Kong, and compares this to the notably more changeable governance patterns evident over the comparable period in Portuguese-run Macau.

[36] This term is explored and developed in an influential 1981 article by SK Lau, 'Chinese Familism in an Urban-Industrial Setting: The Case of Hong Kong' (1981) 43 *Journal of Marriage and Family* 997.

[37] H Smith, *The Religions of Man* (New York, Harper & Row, 1964) ch 4. For discussions of the influence and impact of Confucian thinking on Chinese culture through modern times, see GW Wang, *China and the Overseas Chinese* (Singapore, Times Academic Press, 1991); GW Wang, *Bind Us in Time: Nation and Civilization in Asia* (Singapore, Times Academic Press, 2002). (*Confucius* is the (Jesuit) latinised version of the Chinese name, *Kong Fuzi*.)

[38] S Leys, *The Burning Forest: Essays on Chinese Culture and Politics* (London, Paladin, 1988) 42.

Professor Allinson explained how Confucius placed the family at the centre of the system of human values, concluding that:

> For the Chinese mind, the value of the family is self evident. It is not simply an ingredient in an overall [Hegelian] proof structure such that the entire world can be seen as fitting into an overall organic whole. What makes for this difference between East and West? If my general theory of at-homeness is correct, then, for the Chinese mind, the family represents a natural extension of oneself. There is no need to prove the priority of the family. It is accepted as a given fact.[39]

The process of socialisation of Chinese children typically involves much loving care but also: (a) early restrictions on movement; (b) early schooling commencement; and (c) a firm corrective regime.[40] The crucial socio-economic role of the family is as deeply embedded in Hong Kong as in other Chinese societies.[41] Another historical, abiding concern in Chinese societies is the maintenance of social order. The family rather than the state is seen (and experienced) as the most important hedge against chaos.[42]

Leo Goodstadt provided penetrating criticism of the governance of British Hong Kong (and the Hong Kong Special Administrative Region) in his book, *Uneasy Partners*, published in 2005.[43] He noted that:

> There was never any need for the rulers to keep the people of Hong Kong at a distance or to exclude them from participation from government .... It would have been hard to find anywhere a society more socially responsible and tolerant, more politically mature and self-reliant, or a people easier to serve and rule. They were ideal constituents, the secure foundations on which Hong Kong's success had been built despite the economic turbulence and political uncertainty.[44]

There is a reflection, here, of the way in which the collectively self-reliant and self-regulating aspects of Chinese familism engaged so productively with the predictable, essentially rational, colonial governance institutions shaped by Diceyan constitutional thinking. Fundamental concepts, arising from that thinking, such as the free and lawful citizen (whose status was institutionally protected), had, it transpired, remarkable potential to mesh with the entrenched, positive, collectivist aspects of Chinese familism.

Goodstadt also observed the way in which Hong Kong emerged so swiftly from the terrible post-war poverty arising from the brutal, often horrific, Japanese

[39] RE Allinson, *Understanding the Chinese Mind: The Philosophical Roots* (Oxford, Oxford University Press, 1995) 19.

[40] M Harris Bond, *Beyond the Chinese Face: Insights from Psychology* (Oxford, Oxford University Press, 1992) ch 2.

[41] SK Lau, *Society and Politics in Hong Kong* (Hong Kong, Chinese University Press, 1991) ch 3.

[42] SY Han, *The Crippled Tree: Story of War and Revolution in China* (New York, Triad/Panther, 1984) 71.

[43] LF Goodstadt, *Uneasy Partners: The Conflict between Public Interest and Private Profit in Hong Kong* (Hong Kong, Hong Kong University Press, 2005) 'Conclusions, The Ideal Constituents'.

[44] ibid.

occupation from 1941–1945, adding that, 'the British came close to matching the standards of acceptable government set by Chinese traditional norms'.[45]

## C. The *Single-Track* Mode of Civil Society Regulation

A pivotal aspect of Diceyan constitutionalism was the belief in, and the requirement for, a single set of courts to adjudicate all legal disputes. Specialist courts mediating the relationship between state and citizen, such as existed in France in Dicey's time, were reviewed comparatively and adversely as a way of demonstrating the benefits – to the citizen above all – of the British approach.[46] A concurrent understanding was that the law regulating the state-citizen relationship should be the product of transparent (normally non-retrospective) law made by the legislature.

Furthermore, in the case of enforcing institutions, even when there was a perceived need for clandestine surveillance, the general rule was that such operations should be housed within primary institutions, notwithstanding their covert role. Thus, the first Special Branch responsible for assuring national security and controlling political violence was formed in London in 1883 as a unit *within* the London Metropolitan Police Force.[47] When British Hong Kong acquired its own Special Branch by 1933, it was housed within the Hong Kong Police Force, in conformity with the United Kingdom example.

## D. Political-Legal Developments – After the Second World War

Despite the lack of democracy, Hong Kong was allowed, after the Second World War, to develop, under British rule, into arguably the freest society in East Asia. The press and the media generally were able to flourish[48] and the rule of law, implemented primarily through an independent judiciary, put down deep roots.[49] Meanwhile the task of governing Hong Kong remained in the hands of a London-appointed Governor working with a Civil Service notable for its very high level of political engagement.

[45] ibid.

[46] B Schwartz, *French Administrative Law and the Common-law World* (New York, New York University Press, 1954) ch 2. The author argues that Dicey ultimately backed away from the level of severity of his original criticism of the *droit administratif*.

[47] J Steele, 'End for Special Branch after 122 Years' (*The Telegraph*, 9 September 2005), https://www.telegraph.co.uk/news/uknews/1497979/End-for-Special-Branch-after-122-years.html.

[48] M Bonnin, 'The Press in Hong Kong – Flourishing but under Threat' (1 September 1995) *China Perspectives* 48.

[49] See Y Ghai, 'Praise is Not Enough' (*South China Morning Post*, 22 March 1998); and C Jones, 'Politics Postponed' in K Jayasuriya (ed), *Law, Capitalism and Power in Asia* (Abingdon, Routledge, 1999).

One factor rarely highlighted but, in fact, of central importance in underpinning the strength of governance institutions in Hong Kong has been Hong Kong's long-term, extraordinary fiscal health. Within around 40 years of the establishment of British Hong Kong, the government had already amassed over a year's total public expenditure, in fiscal reserves. Public financial reserves remain similarly robust today.[50]

Politically, British Hong Kong remained mainly stable during the decades after the Second World War. But there were periods of violent political disruption during this time, with the worst of these arising in 1967, after the Cultural Revolution began in the People's Republic of China in 1966.[51]

The British actively – and successfully – discouraged mass interest in greater politicisation of Hong Kong.[52] This complied with the unwritten provisions in their 'pact' with Beijing, which endured until the early 1990s.[53] It also suited Hong Kong's Chinese and non-Chinese business elites. They typically felt that the lack of electoral politics was good for trade and business. And they were, throughout this period, highly influential with the government.[54]

The regular, mainstream of the population remained largely apolitical. Elite views had some influence in this regard. But other factors were also important in explaining this comparative lack of interest in politics. The vast majority of the post-war population had migrated from – mostly fled – the People's Republic of China. Many of them saw Hong Kong as a staging post – their aim was to migrate (or at least see their children migrate), usually to a range of western, English-speaking countries.

The government also helped deflect community disaffection and agitation by moving to address many key problems on its own initiative.[55] The government also instituted comprehensive programs (particularly from the 1970s) dealing with: housing (building one of the world's most massive public housing systems within a single city); education; health; and infrastructure.[56]

[50] Cullen, *Hong Kong Constitutionalism* ch 5 'Revenue and the Rule of Law'.

[51] ibid 37.

[52] M Sing, *Hong Kong's Tortuous Democratization* (Abingdon, Routledge-Curzon, 2004) chs 3 and 4.

[53] The United Kingdom appointed a professional politician, Chris Patten (rather than a Foreign Office China specialist), as the last Governor of Hong Kong in 1992. Patten attempted, rashly and without durable impact, to introduce greater democratisation over the period 1992–1997. Beijing reacted strongly and adversely to these political initiatives. Beijing replaced the 1995 Legislative Council with a Provisional Legislative Council which operated for a year after 1 July 1997. Despite these tensions, the handover ultimately proceeded fairly smoothly. See further Y Ghai, *Hong Kong's New Constitutional Order*; R Cullen, 'Revenue Law in Hong Kong: The Future' in R Wacks (ed), *The New Legal Order in Hong Kong* (Hong Kong, Hong Kong University Press, 1999) ch 12; and G Cross, 'Chris Patten's Folly: Doomed Legacy Foretold in Westminster' (*China Daily*, 1 February 2024), https://english.dotdotnews.com/a/202402/03/AP65bcbefbe4b07371379fbeb1.html.

[54] LF Goodstadt, *Uneasy Partners* (Hong Kong, Hong Kong University Press, 2005). See also M Littlewood, 'Taxation without Representation: The History of Hong Kong's Troublingly Successful Tax System' (2002) 3 *British Tax Review* 212.

[55] SNM Young and R Cullen, *Electing Hong Kong's Chief Executive* (Hong Kong, Hong Kong University Press, 2010) ch 3.

[56] R Cullen, 'Hong Kong's Housing Crisis – an Underlying Factor in the 2019 Riots' (18 April 2021) *Pearls and Irritations*, https://johnmenadue.com/hong-kongs-housing-crisis-an-underlying-factor-in-the-2019-riots/.

It was the approaching expiry of the 99-year, New Territories Lease-Treaty which prompted the United Kingdom to initiate discussions with the People's Republic of China in the late 1970s on the future of Hong Kong. Beijing made it clear, early on in the negotiations, that Hong Kong was to revert to People's Republic of China sovereignty on 1 July 1997 – the day after the expiry of the New Territories Lease-Treaty.

These negotiations led to the signing of the Joint Declaration between London and Beijing in 1984, which set out the agreement for the return of full sovereignty over British Hong Kong to the People's Republic of China from 1 July 1997.[57] The Joint Declaration provided that the essence of the economic, social and political systems which had developed and been applied in British Hong Kong were to be retained for 50 years (in the sense of *at least* – no change after the 50 years is mandated by the Joint Declaration). The Joint Declaration also promised that a Basic Law would be established for the new Hong Kong Special Administrative Region, to take effect on 1 July 1997. This Basic Law, founded significantly on the Joint Declaration, was passed by the National People's Congress (NPC) in Beijing in April 1990.[58] The Basic Law, according to Article 5, is worded to apply for a minimum of 50 years and, on the face of it, to apply indefinitely.

## IV. Recent Radical Developments

In 1989, the Group of Seven (G7) nations set up the Financial Action Task Force (FATF) to combat serious, organised cross-border crime. Various other jurisdictions were invited to join, including British Hong Kong.[59] The *FATF 40 Recommendations* published in October 2004 highlighted the need for strengthened extradition facilities across all relevant jurisdictions, including British Hong Kong.[60] In fact, the extradition provisions, such as they were, created during the British Hong Kong era were minimal. As Grenville Cross explained, the Hong Kong Special Administrative Region, in 2019, still lacked extradition agreements with over 170 countries and the other parts of China,

[57] Joint Declaration of the Government of the United Kingdom and Northern Island and the Government of the People's Republic of China on the Question of Hong Kong (1984). The People's Republic of China declared in the Joint Declaration that it had decided to resume the exercise of sovereignty over Hong Kong (the leased territories, together with Hong Kong Island and Kowloon) effective 1 July 1997. The United Kingdom declared that it would restore Hong Kong to the People's Republic of China effective 1 July 1997. The Joint Declaration came into force on 27 May 1985, when the two governments exchanged instruments of ratification. It was registered as a treaty at the United Nations by the Chinese and British governments on 12 June 1985. See further CL Lim, *Treaty for a Lost City: The Sino-British Joint Declaration* (Cambridge, Cambridge University Press, 2022).

[58] The Basic Law of the Hong Kong Special Administrative Region of the People's Republic of China.

[59] House of Lords, 'The Fora for International Cooperation' in European Union Committee 19th report, *Money Laundering and the Financing of Terrorism*, https://publications.parliament.uk/pa/ld200809/ldselect/ldeucom/132/13205.htm.

[60] FATF, *FATF 40 Recommendations*, https://www.fatf-gafi.org/en/publications/Fatfrecommendations/The40recommendationspublishedoctober2004.html.

namely Macau, Mainland China and Taiwan.[61] The Reuters news agency also highlighted, in 2019, how the FATF had flagged that the lack of extradition provisions to other parts of China presented 'an obstacle to tackling money laundering and terrorism financing'.[62]

This was part of the important proximate context, prompting the introduction by the Hong Kong Special Administrative Region government of a new, comprehensive Extradition Bill in early 2019. However, this legislative initiative provoked a highly influential, critical media campaign and a series of very large, mass protest marches.

Professor Lim noted how the violent, multi-month political upheaval, which arose out of that series of peaceful protests (mainly directed against the Extradition Bill) has been variously labelled as 'anti-government protests', 'radical uprising' and 'revolt'.[63] The retired permanent judge of the Court of Final Appeal, Henry Litton, best captured the essence of what ultimately unfolded, when he explained that: 'What Hong Kong faced was an insurgency, the overthrow of the government, nothing less'.[64]

The city-wide damage done during the insurrection in Hong Kong vastly exceeded that done during Washington's one-day insurrection on 6 January 2021. The repair bills for businesses, public facilities, universities and shopping malls were colossal.[65] This highly destructive rioting was followed, in turn, by radical legal reforms applied in the Hong Kong Special Administrative Region by Beijing, including the new National Security Law. The National Security Law, which was drafted in Beijing and then gazetted to apply in the Hong Kong Special Administrative Region from late on 30 June 2020, in accordance with the procedure laid down in Article 18 of the Basic Law, was needed, in Beijing's view, 'to quell further unrest, indeed what bordered on an insurrection', according to Professor Lim.[66]

## A. The Geopolitical Standoff

The ill-tempered geopolitical context surrounding the 2019 insurrection and the far-reaching, subsequent, political-legal responses remain significant. Briefly,

[61] G Cross, 'Fugitive Surrender: Rights and Responsibilities' (*China Daily*, 12 June 2019), https://www.chinadaily.com.cn/hkedition/2019-06/12/content_37479723.htm.

[62] A John, 'Lack of Extradition Process from Hong Kong to Mainland China Flagged by Anti-Money Laundering Body' (*Reuters*, 4 September 2019), https://www.reuters.com/article/idUSKCN1VP261/.

[63] Lim, *Treaty for a Lost City* 200–201.

[64] H Litton, 'A Close Run Thing in Hong Kong in 2019' (9 July 2021) *Pearls and Irritations*, https://johnmenadue.com/a-close-run-thing-in-hong-kong-in-2019/.

[65] See C Zhong, 'Hong Kong Protests Cost Embattled MTR Operator $204 Million' (*Bloomberg*, 5 December 2019) https://www.bloomberg.com/news/articles/2019-12-05/hong-kong-protests-cost-embattled-mtr-operator-204-million; and JJ Zou and EB Logan, 'Key Facts to Know about the Jan 6 Insurrection' (*Los Angeles Times*, 5 January 2022), https://www.latimes.com/politics/story/2022-01-05/by-the-numbers-jan-6-anniversary.

[66] Lim, *Treaty for a Lost City* 201.

as the Joint Declaration was signed in 1984, the basic GDP of the United States was, according to World Bank and International Monetary Fund figures, 15 times larger than that of the People's Republic of China. In 2023, United States GDP was estimated to be about 1.4 times larger than that of the People's Republic of China.[67] The population of China is around four times that of the United States, which is one factor signalling the potential for a continuing lift in China's GDP compared to that of the United States.[68]

A leading American political commentator, Fareed Zakaria, openly called, in March 2023, for the United States to step firmly away from a China-related foreign policy 'forged out of paranoia, hysteria and above all, fears of being branded as soft'.[69] He went on to compare today's severe policy-making dysfunctionality and panic-driven decisions in America to the worst of the McCarthy era in the 1950s.[70]

A fundamental factor underpinning this confrontational American geopolitical viewpoint is the astounding rise of China outlined above. Washington finds this extraordinary uplift very difficult to accept.[71] The 'China Threat' story, driven by the rise of China, has been transformed into a profoundly dominant narrative across the western world, which, in turn, is promoting this viewpoint globally.[72] This move, over the last decade, towards an emphatic marketing of a negative western appraisal of what China has become, reminds one of Professor AV Dicey's view of Edmund Burke (see above).

This is the context within which the Hong Kong Special Administrative Region has, as Professor Lim says, 'become one of the focal points in a continued deterioration of the Sino-US relationship spanning territorial, trade, and human rights controversies'.[73]

## V. Conclusion

The narrative and analysis above explain how the development of Hong Kong's modern political-legal structure began with the establishment of British Hong

[67] 'Comparing the United States and China by Economy' (*Statistics Times*, 8 December 2023), https://statisticstimes.com/economy/united-states-vs-china-economy.php.

[68] Cullen, *Hong Kong Constitutionalism* 200. See also R Cullen, 'Review Essay: Treaty for a Lost City – The Sino-British Joint Declaration' (2023) 53 *Hong Kong Law Journal* 797.

[69] F Zakaria, 'Washington has Succumbed to Dangerous Groupthink on China' (*Washington Post*, 2 March 2023), https://www.washingtonpost.com/opinions/2023/03/02/china-hearings-bipartisan-hysteria/.

[70] ibid.

[71] J Ganesh, 'The US is Not Responsible for China's Rise' (*Financial Times*, 14 December 2021), https://www.ft.com/content/917596e5-66e1-4bd4-88da-42d4d3bf5b3a.

[72] C Nair, 'Anti-China Rhetoric is off the Charts: What Explains the Mass Hysteria in the West?' (24 February 2023) *Pearls and Irritations*, https://johnmenadue.com/anti-china-rhetoric-is-off-the-charts-what-explains-the-mass-hysteria-in-the-west/. In a significant way, the China Threat narrative has become a primary 'ace in the hole' for the mainstream western media. See R Cullen, 'The Wisdom of Billy Wilder and Western Media Collusion' (21 August 2022) *Pearls and Irritations*, https://johnmenadue.com/the-wisdom-of-billy-wilder/.

[73] Lim, *Treaty for a Lost City* 256.

Kong in 1842. This extended process drew, from the outset, on certain settled principles of British constitutional ordering. Those tenets were, by the nineteenth century, most convincingly argued, organised and related in a seminal fashion in the deeply influential work of Professor Dicey.

Although Hong Kong's political-legal framework has undergone significant adaptation since 1842, one can still clearly see how these Diceyan precepts have been relied on consistently and significantly for over 180 years, both during the British Hong Kong era and since 1997, when the Hong Kong Special Administrative Region was established.

Hong Kong's basic governance regime has been stress-tested many times. Major political insurgencies erupted in the 1950s and 1960s, for example, which challenged the essential stability of British Hong Kong. Remedies were sought, and especially after 1967, radical remedies were developed and applied in ways which ultimately strengthened the enduring system of authoritarian legality, which the British fostered so successfully in Hong Kong.

Since 1 July 1997, however, the Constitution of the People's Republic of China (1982) and especially the Basic Law, have provided the fundamental *legal* framework for the Hong Kong Special Administrative Region. The Basic Law has continued to do this within a broad social-political context. In more recent times, that context has been exceptionally challenging.

First, the extraordinary rise of China has drastically altered the political-economic circumstances within which the Hong Kong Special Administrative Region now finds itself situated in the People's Republic of China. Compared to 1997, when the Mainland economy was only around four times larger, today Mainland China has an economy that is at least 40 times larger than that of Hong Kong. This astounding rise has had an immense geopolitical impact on the Sino-US relationship. The United States' hostility to the rise of China has intensified at a remarkable rate over the last decade, and especially following the election of President Trump in 2016. That essential antipathy has been maintained ever since by President Biden. Since 2018, a number of United States commentators have spoken of a new Cold War with China.[74] More recently, the rancour has been likened to a paranoia recalling the worst of the United States anti-communist hysteria of the early 1950s. The hostile United States containing response to the unprecedented and continuing rise of China is a central part of the contemporary context within which Hong Kong's British-legacy, authoritarian legality governance system operated today. That adverse context has influenced and distorted the United States' and western responses to the 2019 insurrection – and has continued to shape commentary on the Hong Kong Special Administrative Region since.

[74] See WR Mead, 'Mike Pence Announces Cold War II' (*Hudson Institute*, 8 October 2018), https://www.hudson.org/foreign-policy/mike-pence-announces-cold-war-ii; and J Mearsheimer, 'There's No Question We're in a New Cold War' (*China Global Television Network*, 11 February 2023), https://news.cgtn.com/news/2023-02-11/Mearsheimer-There-s-no-question-we-re-in-a-new-cold-war-1hl9ZgHvQUE/index.html.

Next, the prolonged, exceptionally destructive insurrection, which steadily spun off in the Hong Kong Special Administrative Region, from a series of large, nonviolent protest marches in 2019, profoundly jolted the socio-political landscape to a degree not seen in over 50 years.[75] For months on end, Hong Kong faced a terrifying breakdown in the sort of law-abiding order that had made it one of the safest big cities in the world for many decades. It swiftly sank from being an exemplar jurisdiction, where Franklin Roosevelt's esteemed, *freedom from fear* had applied to a remarkable degree.[76] This was when the basic freedoms of millions in Hong Kong were crushed for an extended period.

In sum, Hong Kong found itself sitting right across a geopolitical fault-line.[77] This remains the case today. Radical political-legal structural adjustments have been applied by Beijing in the Hong Kong Special Administrative Region, in response to the extraordinary and endangering political circumstances. These changes have not been cost free. Restrictions on high volume and inflammatory politicking are now measurably greater than they were. However, given the extended, intensely destabilising circumstances, the argument that these remedies were badly needed is robustly grounded.

The serious case challenging this view typically stresses the singular importance of maintaining conceptual individual rights in Hong Kong within a western liberal framework.[78] The more extravagant challenges are actively shaped to fit within the extensive, censorious western media campaign arguing that China is failing to meet geopolitical behaviour standards stipulated by the West, which are embodied in that narrative.[79]

This western-shaped, critical perspective will likely strengthen for some years to come. Yet when you square the ledger, following the radical upheaval and response thereto seen over the last several years, what stands out is the way that Hong Kong's crucial British-shaped governance systems, anchored by the precepts of the common law, have, once more, firmly re-asserted themselves – reckless claims to the contrary notwithstanding.[80] More than 25 years after the establishment of the

[75] Vukovich, *After Autonomy* ch 2.

[76] FDR Library, 'FDR and the Four Freedoms Speech', https://www.fdrlibrary.org/four-freedoms.

[77] C Loh, 'Hong Kong Living on a Fault Line' (11 June 2023) *Pearls and Irritations*, https://johnmenadue.com/hong-kong-living-on-the-fault-line/.

[78] See for example H Zhu, 'A Chinese Law Wedge into the Hong Kong Common Law System: A Legal Appraisal of the Hong Kong National Security Law' (2023) 21 *Northwestern Journal of Human Rights* 43.

[79] 'The World Should Study China's Crushing of Hong Kong's Freedoms' (*The Economist*, 24 August 2023), https://www.economist.com/china/2023/08/24/the-world-should-study-chinas-crushing-of-hong-kongs-freedoms.

[80] D Abate, 'Shout from the Rooftops for Hong Kong' (*South China Morning Post*, 29 September 2023), https://www.mayerbrown.com/en/news/2023/09/shout-from-the-rooftops-for-hong-kong; G Cross, 'Targeting HK Judiciary Should be Condemned' (*China Daily*, 29 May 2023), https://www.chinadaily.com.cn/a/202305/29/WS6473fb55a310b6054fad57df.html. Recent cases from the Court of Final Appeal in the Hong Kong Special Administrative Region confirm this position. See for example *Sham Tsz Kit v Sectary for Justice* [2023] HKCFA 28 (limited legal recognition of same-sex marriage supported); and *HKSAR v Lui Sai Yu* [2023] HKCFA (interpreting the National Security Law).

Hong Kong Special Administrative Region the deep roots of Diceyan constitutionalism remain distinctly influential. Ongoing structural examples include: the independent judiciary; the independent legal profession – from which judges are drawn; the single court regime governing all disputes; and rights of appeal established within this legal regime. The operation of this system is governed by rule of law principles: including the presumption of innocence; the right of defence; the right to counsel; the right to give, call and challenge evidence and the right not to be compelled to testify against oneself or to confess. Since 1997, the Hong Kong Special Administrative Region has also retained a panel of senior, offshore judges who sit as Non-Permanent Judges on the highest court, the Court of Final Appeal.

# PART IV

# Dicey vs Dicey

# 14

# Between *Traces* and *Aura*, Dicey's Many Lives in Contemporary Public Law Scholarship

MARIE PADILLA

'When I use a word,' Humpty Dumpty said in rather a scornful tone, 'it means just what I choose it to mean – neither more nor less.'

'The question is,' said Alice, 'whether you can make words mean so many different things.'

'The question is,' said Humpty Dumpty, 'which is to be master – that's all.'[1]

## I. Introduction

What do we call Dicey in public law? What does the name 'Dicey' stand for? The question seems provocative for its answer sounds obvious. Dicey is a person. A man, born in Lutterworth in 1835, who died in Oxford in 1922.[2] He was a law professor at the University of Oxford, an All Souls College Fellow who was appointed as the seventh Vinerian Professor in 1882.[3] This rather concise portrait could be refined by the addition of some adjectives: English, liberal, mid-Victorian,[4] Austinian, analytical, Unionist. Each one of these words opens a new perspective to be explored for anyone who would like to meet Dicey. Yet more than that, and maybe more critically, Dicey is an author. He wrote *Introduction to the Study of The Law of the Constitution*, first published in 1885, and *Conflict of Laws*

[1] L Carroll, *Through the Looking Glass, and What Alice Found There* (London, Macmillan, 1872) 124.

[2] R Cosgrove, *The Rule of Law. Albert Venn Dicey, Victorian Jurist* (Chapel Hill, University of North Carolina Press, 1980) 4.

[3] M Lewans, 'Interpreting Dicey' (2023) 73 *University of Toronto Law Journal* 499.

[4] M Loughlin, 'Dicey and the Making of Common Law Constitutionalism' (2022) 42 *Oxford Journal of Legal Studies* 366.

in 1896, or 'Can English Law be Taught at the University?'[5] However, Dicey's figure is maybe better captured through the words of others. According to Harold Laski, member of the Fabian Society, professor of political science at the London School of Economics, who was one of Dicey's students, 'it was Dicey who captivated me most – a kind of mellow wisdom that was really masterly. I didn't always agree and I sometimes doubted accuracy, but I never stopped admiring – a very big achievement'.[6] In the same way, his peer and colleague James Bryce wrote to Gladstone 'Mr. Dicey's book, *The Law of the Constitution*, which some of us here are disposed to think the most valuable contribution made to the scientific study of the British Constitution since the publication of Mr. Bagehot's brilliant essay'.[7] The quotations could be multiplied to paint a more personal portrait. But still, a first-year student could answer such a simple question about Dicey's identity after a few weeks of constitutional law lectures.[8] Indeed, and as reminded by Mark Walters in his challenging book *A.V. Dicey and the Common Law Constitutional Tradition: A Legal Turn of Mind*, 'Law students from around the common law world [have] been reading Dicey for more than a century'.[9]

However, does one say everything Dicey is by reciting his identity? Can the question of Dicey's importance for public law be settled so easily? There is room for doubt, as the diversity of the contributions gathered in this book seems to crack the apparent simplicity of the previous answer. They all tell the story of a different Dicey. Maybe one could articulate Dicey's many lives by explaining the role Dicey's oeuvre has played for British legal thought and more critically for constitutional law. But even in this attempt to conciliate the many portraits previously painted, the multiplicity of Dicey's too many lives will not disappear. Neither will the discomfort coming from the complexity expressed by Dicey's name. How to explain that Dicey appears to be at the same time more and less than himself? More than himself as the continuous process of reinterpretation of his work creates an always renewed connection between texts, between authors, between norms and theories, between past and present. But, at the same time, he is less than himself, as the mainstream approach to Dicey seems to limit his thought to the first edition of *Law of the Constitution*, sacrificing the complexity of the man behind the unity of the author.

Taking a step sideways may be necessary here in order to change our perspective. From the tension between the – at least – two 'Diceys' a new perspective can be adopted. Dicey's name is more than a proper name. The never-ending work to

[5] AV Dicey, 'Can English Law be Taught at the University?' in AV Dicey, *The Law of the Constitution*, JWF Allison (ed) (Oxford, Oxford University Press, 2013) 489.

[6] H Laski, 'Holmes-Laski Letters' in Cosgrove, *The Rule of Law* 67.

[7] ibid 68.

[8] JWF Allison, 'Editor's Introduction to Volume One' in Dicey, *Law of the Constitution* xi, 'Generations of first-year law students have learnt about Dicey when they have learnt about parliamentary sovereignty, the rule of law, and constitutional convention in their first few weeks of legal study'.

[9] MD Walters, *A. V. Dicey and the Common Law Constitutional Tradition. A Legal Turn of Mind.* (Cambridge, Cambridge University Press, 2020) ix.

elucidate what Dicey's actual legacy is to public law, can neither be fully answered nor solved by the question of his identity as a person. This is because Dicey's name is more than just an indication or a description of a person. The nature of Dicey's name is different. It is a space for interpretation, identification and ultimately appropriation of concepts and discourses in public law. The passing from 'Dicey' as a surname to the adjective 'Diceyan' as used in Rivka Weill's paper 'Dicey was not Diceyan'[10] is a significant trace of this evolution. It unveils the transformation Dicey's name underwent during the past hundred years, from a mere designation function to a discursive function. During this time, Dicey's name has become a discursive space for competitive discourses in public law. Then, one should return to our first question and ask again: What do we call Dicey in public law?

This chapter aims to discuss the use of Dicey's name in contemporary public law scholarship, assuming that its contemporary use refers rather to a discursive function than to a historical figure or to an actual person. This approach intends to provide new perspective on Dicey's writings and their use by public law scholars. To do so, section II below will suggest adopting a method inspired by the French historian Patrick Boucheron[11] and his use of Walter Benjamin concepts of '*trace*' and '*aura*'[12] to better identify the different layers of discourses we call Dicey. Following the divide between *traces* and *aura*, section III below will argue that contemporary public law writings focusing on Dicey's traces – ie Dicey's name understood as a designation function and his historical reality – are less important for public law scholarship than writings focusing on his aura – ie Dicey's name understood as a specific discursive function within public law scholarship. The fourth part of the paper will analyse Dicey's aura in order to highlight how Dicey's name is used to justify and legitimate different readings of the Anglo-British Constitution in a context of theoretical competition between at least two readings of the Anglo-British Constitution – namely legal constitutionalism and common law constitutionalism. Finally, chapter will conclude by advocating in favour of legal epistemology as a necessary tool for a deeper understanding of the role and importance played by academic authors in the development of legal disciplines and legal culture.

## II. Traces and Aura: A Method for Reading Academic Authors in Public Law

Dicey's name exists between two distinct functions: a designation function, that is the common function for all proper names; and a discursive function that is

[10] R Weill, 'Dicey was Not Diceyan' (2003) 62 *Cambridge Law Journal* 474.

[11] P Boucheron, *Traces and Aura. The Recuring Lives of Ambrose of Milan* (New York, Other Press, 2022).

[12] W Benjamin, *The Arcades Project*, transl H Eilin and K McLaughlin (Cambridge, The Belknap Press of Harvard University Press, 1999) 447.

not attached to all proper names but only to a very few.[13] This second function is the consequence of a particular aspect of Dicey's identity as an author. Saying that Dicey is an author is a clear and simple affirmation. However, one should be careful when faced with what looks like evidence. Indeed, within such a simple statement lies a first difficulty: what do we actually understand or refer to when we use the word 'author'? The question is not secondary and comes with two methodological problems to be solved. The first methodological problem is (i) of the definitions of the author's nature; and (ii) the definition of the author's function. Following this divide in his paper 'What is an Author?'[14] the French philosopher Michel Foucault observes that more than a person, the notion of author is a specific way to connect texts together, to bind them into a same corpus identified under a specific proper name.[15] From this perspective an author appears to be a specific discursive tool allowing one to attribute texts or groups of texts to a same discursive mode identified by an author's name. Ultimately, the author's name, 'establishes a relationship among the texts … a relationship of homogeneity, filiation, authentication … reciprocal explication, or concomitant utilization'.[16]

Understood in this way, the statement 'Dicey is an author' adds a new layer of complexity to our initial question about what Dicey's name means. It attempts to determine what corpus of texts we refer to when saying 'Dicey said this …' or 'Dicey thought that …'. Additionally, it forces us to ask whether we are always referring to the same texts or if there is anything like a consensus among public law scholars to identify a limited and closed corpus of texts when using the name Dicey. On the surface, public law literature seems to favour at least three ways of using Dicey's name as an author's name. Some scholars use the name Dicey as a common and shared reference, a static unit 'producing a detached and "smooth-surfaced entity known as 'Dicey'"'.[17] They usually write without giving any precisions about the texts they are considering under the name. Others will make clear that behind Dicey's name, his seminal work *Law of the Constitution* is the one concerned. However, it is not always clear whether scholars referring to *Law of the Constitution* are considering the text as a single unit or not. *Law of the Constitution* is rarely portrayed as an evolutive text, despite the successive editions of the book that largely amended Dicey's initial approach to English public law. The evolution of his treatment of French administrative law through the different editions[18] and the defence of the referendum in the introduction of the eighth edition are illustrations of the moving and evolving nature of *Law of the Constitution*.[19] In this way and as highlighted by John Allison, *Law of the Constitution*'s 'multiple texts

[13] M Foucault, 'What is an Author?' in M Foucault, *Aesthetics, Method, and Epistemology*, JD Faubion (ed) (New York, The New Press, 1998) 210.
[14] ibid 209.
[15] ibid 210.
[16] ibid 211.
[17] Allison, 'Editor's Introduction to Volume One' vi.
[18] Dicey, *Law of the Constitution* 368.
[19] Allison, 'Editor's Introduction to Volume One' vi.

are in contrast with Dicey as known or commonly understood'.[20] Thus, and just like Dicey's name, the use of the same title to identify a plurality of texts tends to blur their diversity. In other words, just like the name of an author, the title of a work tends to dissolve the object's inner dynamics and complexity under a false and on-surface unity. Finally, some scholars openly use Dicey's name to refer to broader corpuses than the unitarian vision of *Law of the Constitution*.[21] Usually they develop in their own writings a discourse about the ruptures, the inconsistencies and evolutions between the texts forming the corpus and use them to justify a new interpretation of Dicey's legacy for public law.[22]

From this observation, Dicey's name as a corpus of texts can be approached from two perspectives. First, a 'small-Dicey' approach can be adopted, where the corpus identified under Dicey's name is very limited and where, beyond the actual texts and their connections, what matters is a general and shared representation of Dicey. Second, one can prefer 'a large-Dicey approach' where the corpus is broader, usually contextualised and where the degree of unity between the texts is of less importance, as what matters is the spaces and breaches between the texts. Of course, these two ideal categories come with nuances and a deeper analysis of the corpuses used under Dicey's name – especially a quantitative analysis – could confront them with reality and ultimately could refine them. But at least they capture two main types of attitudes when using Dicey's name as an author and prove that there is no clear consensus on the texts connected and identified under Dicey's name. This lack of consensus is maybe better illustrated by Mark Walters' method. Through his proposal for an 'intellectual biography',[23] Walters broaden the corpus of texts he ascribes to Dicey's name as an author. He includes types of sources as letters and private correspondence that are usually not identified as part of the oeuvre of an academic author.[24] The question of the author's nature then appears as a never-closed question which is not a methodological deadlock as soon as this question is opened and discussed to better understand the perspective from where the various Diceys are speaking.

This first methodological difficulty is to be completed by an additional level of complexity. Dicey's name as an author is not only defined by the existing connections between texts identified as being part of a Diceyan entity. Dicey's name as an author refers to more than just texts. As observed by Foucault, 'one can be the author of much more than a book – one can be the author of a theory, tradition or discipline in which other books and authors will in their turn find a place'.[25] This category of authors performs a specific discursive function as 'they have

[20] ibid xvi.

[21] For example J Bell, *Contemporary French Administrative Law* (Cambridge, Cambridge University Press, 2022) 1, I Mclean and A McMillan, 'Professor Dicey's Contradictions' (2007) *Public Law* 435.

[22] Walters, *Dicey and the Common Law.*

[23] ibid 6.

[24] Foucault, 'What is an Author?' 214.

[25] ibid 216–17.

produced something else: the possibilities and the rules for the formation of other texts'.[26] They are, according to Foucault, 'founders of discursivity'.[27] Regarding the long-lasting influence of his thought, Dicey certainly belongs to this last category. When publishing for the first time his constitutional law lectures in *Law of the Constitution*, Dicey created the conditions for the emergence of a legal discourse about the Anglo-British Constitution and more broadly about public law in England. Through his clear and pedagogic style – which was celebrated[28] – Dicey systematised, within the language of legal positivism, all the concepts and structures necessary for the formation and study of legal discourses about the Anglo-British Constitution. He created a legal vocabulary and a legal grammar for public law discourse as a different and autonomous discourse from history and political theory. The sovereignty of Parliament, the rule of law, the constitutional conventions, all these concepts are still the main language units of public law discourses in the United Kingdom. Thus, after 1885, more than the author of a text, Dicey became the author of an academic discipline.

Dicey's main success was maybe only contextual,[29] by filling an existing gap in the English legal scholarship and by giving it the means to say, think, and represent public law, but still, the social reproduction of his public law vocabulary and grammar through legal education, its incorporation within court's decisions, the recurrence, the criticisms, and its disciplinary crisis show that his legacy is broader. The public law implementation as an academic discipline in the aftermath of *Law of the Constitution* acts as a confirmation: Dicey's name is attached to more than just some texts about the Anglo-British Constitution. As an author, Dicey is the source of a discipline. Thus, Dicey's name not only refers to a corpus of texts but also designates the disciplinary matrix for public law discourses in the United Kingdom and a number of former countries of the Empire. Therefore, using Dicey's name means ascribing oneself within the disciplinary matrix built by Dicey. It is also speaking the disciplinary language he built, using as one's own words the words Dicey created to say, to think, and to reflect about public law. Yet using Dicey's name as a discipline is more than that. Being the name of a disciplinary tradition, Dicey's name offers the always-opened possibility to side with or against Dicey. Put differently, being a disciplinary matrix, Dicey's name offers a discursive space for a plurality of interpretations, rewritings of the founding concepts such as the sovereignty of Parliament[30] or the rule of law.[31] The disciplinary language created by Dicey, being seized by others, is an always open process

[26] ibid.
[27] ibid.
[28] Allison, 'Editor's Introduction to Volume One' xxiv.
[29] Lewans, 'Interpreting Dicey' 500.
[30] TRS Allan, *The Sovereignty of Law: Freedom, Constitution and Common Law* (Oxford, Oxford University Press, 2013).
[31] TRS Allan, 'Dworkin and Dicey: The Rule of Law as Integrity' (1988) 8 *Oxford Journal of Legal Studies* 266; T Bingham, *The Rule of Law* (London, Penguin Books, 2010).

of writing. Dicey's name can be reduced or enlarged depending on what those acting and speaking in lieu of Dicey attach to his name and to the public law discipline.

As with other academic discourses, public law scholars define 'a proposition's theoretical validity in relation to the work of the founde[r]'.[32] Thus, Dicey's name is at the same time the map helping one navigate the concepts included within the public law discursive world, but also the horizon of this discursive world, always to be overtaken, always to be reimagined. Passing from the author as a corpus of texts to the author as a disciplinary tradition, Dicey's name is no longer his own. Dicey's name has become a common good, a shared discursive space inhabited by all those who are encultured in English public law. It has become the vessel of a disciplinary identity. Then, it does not matter whether one agrees or rejects Dicey's theory because Dicey's name – considered as a disciplinary matrix – has a discursive function deeper than formulating a valid or invalid proposition about public law. It refers to a mode of recognition between public lawyers. By becoming the source of such a common identity, Dicey becomes 'one of those patched-together rememberings through which a society invents a common past, picking out the traces of what remains available. Not every trace: this legacy is, by nature, selective'.[33] Thus it is not surprising that every period of public law scholarship invents its own Dicey, using in Dicey's name the 'scraps of the past useful in supporting the invention of a collective identity'.[34] Finally, once it is acknowledged that Dicey's name also refers to a disciplinary matrix for public law, speaking in lieu of Dicey suddenly reveals a strategic dimension. As a disciplinary tradition, Dicey's name is a continuous discursive process that discriminates between what can be said about public law in England and what cannot be said about it without being an invalid theory. Developing a new interpretation of Dicey's work that will become the main interpretation of Dicey's thought is a way to capture the key of the disciplinary matrix and to rearticulate it along the structure of one's own theory. In this way, speaking in lieu of Dicey is a way to legitimate one's own theory of English public law and to reject all other attempts to form new propositions about it.

The presentation of the different dimensions of Dicey's name as an author does not solve the problem of the polysemous nature of Dicey's name. The use of an author's name creates a principle of unity that makes unclear what objects one designates by using it. It is even more obscure once one agrees that 'in the ordinary language, we rely on a simple similarity between two different objects coming after one another at the same place to say they are one and a same object'.[35] Then, how can one be sure to properly distinguish between the different discursive functions and objects coming at the same place, under the use of Dicey's name within the public law discourse? How can one excavate, within the aggregation and accumulation through times of discourses said to be Dicey's words, the discourses of

[32] Foucault, 'What is an Author?' 219.
[33] Boucheron, *Traces and Aura* 12.
[34] ibid.
[35] V Descombes, *Les embarras de l'identité* (Paris, Gallimard, 2013) 191.

those acting *under the veil of* Dicey's name and the discourses that are actually Dicey's words? There is no definitive or absolute answer to such a methodological question. However, the historical method developed by Patrick Boucheron in his study of Ambrose of Milan's 'recuring lives'[36] offers an interesting path to explore. Trying to untie the intertwined layers of discourses between the symbolic rewritings of Ambrose's work and life, Boucheron exposes the continuous writing process between past and present, relying on two concepts developed by Walter Benjamin in *The Arcades Project*:[37] the *trace* and the *aura*. These two notions, which Benjamin develops later in his study of reproducing art works, are captured by the following:

> trace and aura. The trace is appearance of a nearness, however far removed the thing that left it behind may be. The aura is appearance of a distance, however close the thing that calls it forth. In the trace, we gain possession of the thing, in the aura it takes possession of us.[38]

Interpreting the aphorism, Boucheron reveals the dialectic between the trace and the aura allowing one to enter into a specific space of the construction of an identity. The trace is a return to the remains of an historical object, to the print it left upon the contemporary understanding and representation of the world and the studied object. The aura, by opposition, is a more evasive notion. Complex and plural under Benjamin's writings, it develops a more functional dimension within Boucheron's approach. Thus, the aura appears to be the total of meanings and symbols invested by a community within historical reality. It is what is added to historical facts, what nourishes them, blurs them, writes, and rewrites them. Consequently, with Dicey's trace, it is the reality and the history of an author and his thought that is sketched in the distance, remaining available for the contemporary reader. With Dicey's aura, something else appears. We meet with all the posthumous and contemporary Dicey lives, those that mask under the apparent identity of a complex and elusive name everything that is usefully added or forgotten about Dicey's name. The aura is, then, everything that updates and renews, over time and academic necessities, what one can say within the public law discourse, and everything that Dicey is as a disciplinary function.

## III. The Traces: Dicey's Past and Reality

The trace is the 'appearance of a nearness, however far removed the thing that left it behind may be'.[39] It is what is coming from a past that still marks our present, the

[36] Boucheron, *Traces and Aura.*
[37] Benjamin, *The Arcades Project* 447.
[38] ibid.
[39] ibid.

remains of a forgotten historical object that still haunts our contemporary representations.[40] Taking such a definition as a starting point, searching for Dicey's trace is searching for what remains of him despite or beyond his death. Nonetheless, searching for the appearance of a removed Dicey it must first be ascertained which Dicey we are searching for. In this inquiry, one can follow two different, although intertwined, paths. The first is searching for the trace of Dicey as a historical and actual person. The second is searching for the trace of Dicey's name as an author. Both inquiries are by nature historical processes and require a specific methodology that is not usual for legal scholars. The first approach is maybe better pursued through biographical research whereas the second one, involving research about the texts connected under Dicey's name, seems to relate more to the legal historian. However, and as observed by Mark Walters, 'to tell the story of Dicey's book' is deeply connected with 'tell[ing] the story of Dicey'.[41] In the same way, John McEldowney highlights the interest of legal biography for the understanding of legal thought, observing that: 'the biographies of prominent lawyers can uncover many aspects of legal history that would otherwise remain hidden'.[42] Thus, the two inquiries may be different in nature, but they are dependent on one another.

Despite this inherent connection, biographical research is not the main path used by lawyers when searching for the trace of a legal author. If papers and books engaging with Dicey's entity (as an author or as a disciplinary matrix) usually give some biographical elements, few of them engage with a true biographical inquiry. John McEldowney identifies only two main biographers for Dicey: Richard A Cosgrove and Trowbridge H Ford. Cosgrove's book, *The Rule of Law: Albert Venn Dicey, Victorian Jurist*, published in 1980, has gained recognition among law academics. Subsequent works about Dicey's past, such as those by Mark Walters[43] or John Allison,[44] make references to Cosgrove's biography. The same cannot be said for Ford's biography published in 1985 and whose original approach – mainly based on a polarised political reading of Dicey's life and work – seems to not have been incorporated with the same success within the sources used by public law academics when referring to biographical elements about Dicey. The interest of such biographies is to unveil 'The various influences that affected Dicey's development of the constitutional principles'.[45] In this regard, Cosgrove's work deploys a rich contextualisation of how Dicey's concepts such as the sovereignty of Parliament[46] or the rule of law[47] were constructed.

[40] P Boucheron, *Faire profession d'historien* (Paris, Points, 2018).
[41] Walters, *Dicey and the Common Law* 4.
[42] J McEldowney, 'Challenges in Legal Bibliography: The Role of Biography in Legal History' (2004) 39 *Irish Jurist* 215, 216.
[43] Walters, *Dicey and the Common Law.*
[44] Dicey, *Law of the Constitution.*
[45] McEldowney, 'Challenges' 237.
[46] Cosgrove, *The Rule of Law* 72.
[47] ibid 67.

However, and despite the narrative qualities and the force of the historical and personal contextualisations of Dicey's works, Cosgrove's biography does not disperse all aura's veil that surrounds Dicey's figures. His work does not allow one to encounter Dicey's traces directly but only through the mediation of Cosgrove's own reading of Dicey's life and Dicey's name as an author. Said differently, if the biographical work and its contextualisation help clarify the picture of Dicey's one too many lives, they do not pierce the thickness of the symbolic and identity-forming rewritings of Dicey's entity. They help burst the superficial layers of the aura, but they cannot make one seize the trace.

Whereas the biographical approach to Dicey fails to excavate his trace, the legal historical approach seems to offer the necessary tool to unveil the author's trace. At least, it does in John Allison's editorial tour de force with the publication of *Law of the Constitution* and *Comparative Constitutionalism* in 2013. Offering a new edition to the different versions of Dicey's *Law of the Constitution* and a first publication to some of Dicey's unpublished lectures, John Allison introduces directly and without any mediation – except for some contextual notes and comments – Dicey's texts to his reader. In other words, John Allison seizes the trace of Dicey's name as an author and exposes it, making clear that 'the central task of an editor is neither that of a critic, nor that of an apologist, and even less that of an eulogist. It is to enable access to what is being edited and explain why and how'.[48] Of course, one could retort that the selection process of Dicey's texts and the discrimination between those deserving to be published and those that are not, is the result of the editor's personal choice which blurs the trace of Dicey's name as an author behind individual interpretation. Yet, as already explained, the discursive function of an author's name as a connection between texts is never settled for good. New texts can be added, others can be ruled out. Still, the validity of such a process would be for the one connecting texts under a same author's name to present the reason behind his selective operation. This is precisely what John Allison does, clearly exposing his text selection method and giving arguments to justify his choices.[49] The purpose of his work is simply to offer 'sources [to] understand *The Law of the Constitution*'s textual history'[50] and by doing so, 'to facilitate reconsideration of Dicey's exposition and of its authority'.[51] In this regard, John Allison acts as a cautious historian. He deploys a clear and precise methodology that allows him to disperse the aura and to seize the trace of Dicey's name as an author, through contextualisation of the texts but by always paying attention to never speaking in lieu of Dicey. Such a reflexive scientific posture finds some explanations in Allison's vision of legal history and, more critically, constitutional history. Quoting Quentin Skinner, he describes legal 'history as offering "a kind of exorcism" from

[48] Allison, 'Editor's Introduction to Volume One' xliii.
[49] ibid vi.
[50] ibid xii.
[51] ibid.

bewitchment in our believing the inevitability of "ways of thinking" … bequeathed to us by the mainstream of our intellectual tradition'.[52] According to him:

> Legal history might … seek to expose and illuminate legal cultural prejudices and assumptions by explaining their historical development, thus bringing them into deliberation and open debate where, subject to rational and normative assessment, they might more readily change or be adapted.[53]

John Allison's anxious defence of legal history and its method in contemporary public law scholarship also comes with the following observation: the contemporary use of legal history by public lawyers too often looks like cherry-picking, rewriting the past to justify contemporary answers to legal question.[54] On the contrary, and away from this kind of utilitarian use of history, Allison's treatment of Dicey's name as an author acts as an exorcism of Dicey's myth and aura. Through the implementation of his legal historical method, his editorial work unveils Dicey's trace. However, in the context of the historical study of an author, such a methodological approach implies, for the contemporary writer, retreating behind the late author's words. It requires the living to accept that the past cannot always look like the present and that sometimes it must remain silent so they may hear what has been left behind. Silence is not easy and the recurrence of Dicey's name in contemporary public law scholarship seems to highlight that, beyond what Dicey's words may actually say, in the end, what appears to matter most is rather what one can make them say.

## IV. The Aura: Dicey's Present and Reinterpretations

The aura is the 'appearance of a distance, however close the thing that calls it forth'.[55] It is a 'strange weave of time and space' where the present takes the mask of the past to better recompose the common memory of a shared object produced for a community. It is what is coming from a present that still marks our past, the memory of a contemporary object that still haunts our past representations. Searching for the aura is no longer searching for the light that pierces through the fog, but rather sinking into the fog to spend time with the shadows inhabiting it. The specific space that Dicey's aura occupies appears through all the constant additions and subtractions to Dicey's entity that public law scholarship produces. It is the permanent rewritings that always renew the usefulness of Dicey's discursive function for public law as an academic discipline. Such rewriting is necessary for this community's construction because all the different versions of Dicey

[52] JWF Allison, 'History to Understand, and History to Reform, English Public Law' (2013) 72 *Cambridge Law Journal* 526, 544.
[53] ibid.
[54] ibid.
[55] Benjamin, *The Arcades Project* 447.

superimposed upon one another make Dicey's name constantly relevant for the disciplinary function at the heart of the public law discourse. In this blur between past and present, one of the last versions of Dicey added to the discursive structure of public law scholarship is the one depicted by Mark Walters.

Adopting an approach that seems to open a median path between biography and legal history, Mark Walters contemplates the writing of an 'intellectual biography'[56] for Dicey. In appearance, such a project sounds close to the ones achieved by Cosgrove or Allison. In truth, Walters adopts a method that relies mainly on archival sources of Dicey's writings.[57] Yet, unlike John Allison, who made clear why he only used Dicey's academic writings,[58] Walters suggests that private papers (private letters, drafts, notes) can help to 'improve our own interpretative engagement with that text'.[59] Walters completes this methodological statement, observing that 'unpublished materials that provide context are texts in their own right and must also be interpreted contextually'. Thus, Walters integrates new texts in the filiation and connecting process performed by Dicey's name as an author. But whereas Cosgrove used these texts for writing a version of Dicey's life, Walters uses the same sources to open a new interpretation of Dicey's works. This last point is made clear when Walters writes 'where a canonical text is open to different interpretations, reference to materials in the author's private domain may shed a light on whether an interpretation that has become dominant should give way to alternative interpretations'.[60] The result is simple: by adding new texts to the corpus called 'Dicey', Walters opens a discursive space where he tries to justify how and why his interpretation of Dicey's concepts – the ones that form the disciplinary matrix for public law – is more valid and legitimate than the already existing and orthodox readings of the rule of law or the sovereignty of Parliament. Such a move has been highlighted by some reviewers of the book like Martin Loughlin[61] or Peter Cane.[62] According to Loughlin it is:

> [the] recent rejuvenation of Dicey's ideas and the reordering of his framework that drives Walters' project. In his methodically researched and forcefully argued book, Walters challenges the orthodox interpretation of Dicey as a legal positivist and reveals that he had 'a far subtler, more nuanced understanding of the relationship between sovereignty and legality'.[63]

Similarly, Peter Cane observes that:

> In a nutshell, Walter's argument in *Dicey and the Common Law Tradition* is that Dicey's 'intellectual life involved a sort of journey from a conception of legality as ordered rules

[56] Walters, *Dicey and the Common Law* 6.
[57] ibid.
[58] Allison, 'Editor's Introduction to Volume One' vi.
[59] Walters, *Dicey and the Common Law* 8.
[60] ibid.
[61] Loughlin, 'Dicey and the Making of Common Law' 366–82.
[62] P Cane, 'AV Dicey as Legal Theorist' (2022) 85 *Modern Law Review* 247, 248.
[63] Loughlin, 'Dicey and the Making of Common Law Constitutionalism' 7.

> towards a conception of legality as reasoned discourse'. In effect, Walters reimagines Dicey as a participant in twentieth-century, post-Hartian, theoretical and philosophical debates about the nature of law ….[64]

Of course, Walters is not the first person to use Dicey's name and words. The Dicey created by Sir Ivor Jennings and against which he built his own reading of the Anglo-British Constitution is well known. In the same way, one could discuss the democratic interpretation of Dicey built by Paul Craig in his paper 'Dicey: Unitary, Self-Correcting Democracy and Public Law'.[65] However, what is particular to Walters' interpretation is that it articulates clearly Dicey's discursive function for the public law discourse with a contemporary political and academic project. In this regard, Martin Loughlin wonders:

> Why is so much intellectual energy now invested in revealing the 'true' meaning of the lecture notes of this mid-Victorian professor? This is no antiquarian exercise. Presented as intellectual history, Walters' book is intended as an intervention in contemporary political debate. He seeks to reinterpret the meaning of *The Law of the Constitution* precisely because it has lingered on as the canonical text of British constitutional law.[66]

Mark Walters makes clear that his project is to follow the reinterpretation Trevor Allan gave to Dicey's works and reinforces the legitimacy of this interpretation by placing the words and concepts of contemporary common law constitutionalists in Dicey's mouth. To put it differently, Walters covers Dicey's trace under the veil of an aura marked by the political and theoretical project of common law constitutionalism. His interpretation, presented as Dicey's own conception of constitutional law, creates a continuous narrative that makes it possible to connect common law constitutionalism, Dicey and other important figures such as Edward Coke, in the same spectrum of intellectual and disciplinary legitimacy. This strategic use of Dicey's aura helps in understanding the main discursive function played by Dicey's name. As demonstrated by Carol Harlow and Richard Rawlings in their classification of public law scholarship,[67] Dicey's disciplinary function articulates the identities that fracture public law scholarship. The one mastering the most accepted interpretation of Dicey's work has mastery over the disciplinary matrix for which Dicey's name stands. Mastering Dicey's interpretation is then mastering Dicey's disciplinary function at the core of the public law discourse and opens the possibility of rejecting all interpretations that are not consistent with one theoretical framework as non-dominant models for public law. Far from being in search of Dicey's traces, contemporary public law scholarship mainly relies on the disciplinary functions that Dicey plays within public law discourses. It comes

[64] For an additional example see Lewans, 'Interpreting Dicey'.

[65] P Craig, 'Dicey: Unitary, Self-Correcting Democracy and Public Law' (1990) 106 *Law Quarterly Review* 105.

[66] Loughlin, 'Dicey and the Making of Common Law Constitutionalism' 376.

[67] C Harlow and R Rawlings, *Law and Administration* (Cambridge, Cambridge University Press, 2009) 22.

as no surprise that in a period of disciplinary crisis, Dicey becomes the name of a renewed place for discursive competition.

## V. Conclusion: The Need for Epistemology in Public Law Scholarship

Between *traces* and *aura*, Dicey's contemporary lives within public law scholarship appear to be diverse and complex. Where the search for the trace of Dicey's name tends to fix Dicey's identity in a past always looking at our present, the multiplication of the various 'Diceys', through the continuous process of rewriting by public law scholars, is a reminder that identity of a discourse relies on the reader's interpretation rather than on the author's intent.

Epistemic tools such as the notions of *trace* and *aura*, therefore, offer an important input for the study of public law scholarship. They help to highlight the diversity of objects too often veiled behind the apparent unity of a name. Understanding the discursive function of an author's name is important because it allows one to exorcise the layers of myths and prejudices that blur the signification of a simple proper name such as Dicey's. Then, the question is no longer 'What do we call *Dicey* in public law?' but rather 'which is to be master – that's all'.[68]

[68] Carroll, *Through the Looking Glass* 124.

# 15

# Dicey and the History of Liberalism

ALAN S KAHAN

It is a curious fact that today John Locke is considered a central figure in the history of liberalism, while AV Dicey is at best regarded as a marginal player of parochial importance. While Dicey has never faded from view for students of the British Constitution, he has been a dim shadow in accounts of liberalism. More often, indeed, he is simply forgotten. Yet for much of the history of liberalism, Dicey's direct influence was great and Locke's minimal. Indeed, at the time Dicey wrote, Locke's political philosophy was regarded as just the sort of learned footnote of purely antiquarian interest that, for historians of political thought, Dicey's work has since become – wrongly, as this essay will show.

Dicey's influence on liberalism and how liberalism was perceived by both its friends and its foes was central during many decades in which Locke's influence was minimal, and this has been generally overlooked. Building on the pioneering work of Donald Lutz, Gail Arcena has described the long period of hibernation Locke's thought underwent in the United States before Louis Hartz (indirectly assisted by Friedrich Hayek and Harold Laski) gave it new life in the 1950s. On the Continent, as Duncan Bell and Timothy Stanton have shown, the situation was much the same. Ironically, without Dicey, Locke might never have been considered an important part of the liberal tradition, because he can only play such a role in the context of a Diceyan understanding of liberalism. Not that Dicey, in this a good representative of nineteenth-century liberalism, bothered to discuss Locke himself, but Dicey's influential understanding of liberalism in terms of individualism created the intellectual space that Locke later came to occupy. The above statements about Locke may strike some readers as outrageous, or at least, as sufficiently unusual to be dismissed out of hand, and yet they are the common conclusions of the scholarly literature of the early twenty-first century with regard to Locke's reputation on both sides of the Atlantic.[1]

In his own time, Dicey was clearly the main discussion partner for the New Liberal LT Hobhouse, whose rival history of liberalism had the not inconsiderable

[1] See the discussion in AS Kahan, *Freedom from Fear: An Incomplete History of Liberalism* (Princeton, Princeton University Press, 2023) 23–28.

merit of being titled *Liberalism* rather than concealing its light under the umbrella title *Lectures on Law and Public Opinion*.[2] But if Hobhouse's New Liberal interpretation of liberal thought was equally – if not more – celebrated than Dicey's book at the time, it has had far less impact on posterity. Dicey was, if not the inventor of the term 'classical liberalism', then the person who did most within English-language liberalism to cement the classical liberal historical account of liberalism and make it the foundation for much of the historical discussion of liberalism since.

Dicey's influence on the view that future generations took of liberalism has been enormous, whether acknowledged or not. Friedrich Hayek frequently referred to Dicey but did not choose to mention that the chronology of liberal decline he used in *The Road to Serfdom* derived from him, perhaps via Walter Lippmann, himself a key figure in 1930s liberalism. Lippmann adopted not only Dicey's chronology but his vocabulary in *The Good Society*, and duly acknowledged his source. Dicey's influence extends down to Judith Shklar in the late twentieth century. On the negative side, the caricature often drawn of 'neoliberalism' looks a lot like the highly schematic and often inaccurate construct that Dicey called classical liberalism.[3]

'Classical liberalism', a term often used without reflection, was invented or popularised by Dicey in the service of a polemic. During the *fin de siecle*, British liberalism witnessed a dispute that was typical of the internecine conflicts taking place throughout the liberal world at the time. It was a contest between those who in Britain were known as New Liberals (in the United States, Progressives; in France, Solidarists; in Germany, Social Liberals; in general, I call them 'modern liberals') and those who then began to call themselves classical liberals. The issue was over the meaning and very soul of what it meant to be a liberal.

Modern liberals believed that *fin de siecle* liberalism was called upon to confront the problem of poverty, and that the only way to do this effectively was through a massive expansion of the role of the state. Of course, poverty was not invented in the *fin de siecle*. Indeed, by the 1870s the most extreme form of poverty, mass famine, had disappeared from the West. Yet, if absolute poverty had not increased, and perhaps even decreased (the subject is controversial), many people were experiencing new kinds of poverty, and their poverty, concentrated in urban centres rather than hidden away in the countryside, was more visible. The boom-and-bust cycles of nineteenth-century industrial life were frightening. The new discipline of sociology cut its teeth on studies of the urban poor, while mass-distribution newspapers brought their readers a new consciousness of social ills – as Dicey himself pointed out.[4] Fear of poverty and the desire to do something about it was stimulated by growing urban blight, by the supposed immorality of the urban

[2] This is a little unfair to Dicey, as writing about liberalism was not the ostensible purpose of *Law and Public Opinion*, but from the perspective of the history of political thought it is accurate.

[3] W Lippmann, *The Good Society* (New York, Routledge, 2017) 46 n 8.

[4] As did the American Progressive Jane Addams. See J Addams, *Democracy and Social Ethics*, Kindle edition 3; AV Dicey, *Lectures on the Relation between Law and Public Opinion in England during the Nineteenth Century* (Indianapolis, Liberty Fund, 2008), R VandeWetering (ed) 156 ff. This edition contains both the original 1905 text and the 1914 revisions.

poor, and perhaps most important, by increasing, and increasingly violent, labour strife. Strikes and the growth of socialist political parties reinforced the old liberal fear of revolution, even if most fin-de-siecle socialist parties were more reformist than revolutionary. At the same time, the vastly increased wealth of nations such as Britain in 1880 as compared to 1800 meant that the resources to do something about the problem of poverty appeared to be available on a new scale.

These phenomena combined to put poverty at the top of the agenda for many liberals in a way it had never been before. As Raymond Aron put it, in a view which echoed that of Dicey, 'the ambition to eliminate [poverty] was new and testified to a pride that neither the Founding Fathers nor Tocqueville would have shared or approved of'. In the Aron/Dicey view, since the *fin de siecle*, public opinion had equated subjection to impersonal economic forces with despotic coercion, and thus was born the duty of liberal governments to do something about it.[5]

In support of this view, modern liberals argued that liberalism had always recognised the need for considerable social intervention in social and economic questions. LT Hobhouse's 1911 book *Liberalism* argued that this position was largely in continuity with historical liberalism, and that where it represented a deviation, it was a natural evolution in response to changing circumstances. Thus, liberal anti-poverty efforts ultimately fulfilled rather than contradicted liberalism's ultimate goal, a solution to the 'problem of realising liberty'.[6]

By contrast, classical liberals identified historical liberalism with a strict *laissez-faire* attitude in order to bolster their case for minimising the role of government. They feared modern liberals more than they feared poverty because, from their perspective, the fight against modern liberalism was the old struggle against despotism and arbitrary authority. The modern liberals' fight against poverty might seem superficially attractive but to classical liberals it was just another scheme of state-sponsored salvation, doomed to failure. Unlike in the past, this scheme would be carried out by bureaucrats rather than clergy, and if no longer accompanied by burnings at the stake, it was all the more suffocating in its gentle and all-pervasive fiscal and regulatory pressure, a form of the soft democratic despotism that Tocqueville had feared. The contemporary Inquisitor worked for the tax office, and the preferred instrument of torture was the audit. If modern liberals maintained the traditional liberal optimism that history was on their side, classical liberals felt beleaguered, not merely by the usual sources of liberal fear, revolutionary and counter-revolutionary despotisms, but also by the desertion of modern liberals from their cause. As a result, their mood often oscillated between pessimism and outrage. At any point after the 1870s, classical liberals throughout the western world could be found lamenting the decline of liberalism and the rise of socialism.[7] Dicey was no exception.

[5] R Aron, *Essai sur les libertés* (Paris, Fayard, 2014) 64, 213.
[6] LT Hobhouse, *Liberalism and Other Writings* (Cambridge, Cambridge University Press, 1994) 120.
[7] This trend extends to the time of writing.

Hobhouse's and Dicey's works are examples of how modern and classical liberals wrote histories of liberalism to bolster their genealogical claim to be the only legitimate heirs of nineteenth-century liberalism. Both distorted the facts to suit their case, and the dispute has resulted in a good deal of polemical distortion of the history of liberalism, then and since. But it is Dicey's work that in the long run exerted the most intellectual influence, even if, paradoxically, it was modern liberalism of the sort Hobhouse affirmed that dominated politically in the *fin de siecle* and afterwards.

Dicey's *Lectures on the Relation between Law and Public Opinion in England during the Nineteenth Century*, published in 1905 and revised in 1914, confronted the new challenges faced by fin-de-siecle liberalism. The book was considered a major contribution when first published, but fell into obscurity thereafter, only to be revived after the Second World War by classical liberals and libertarians who found its history of liberalism congenial, and therefore convincing. When Hobhouse constructed his modern liberal genealogy of liberalism in 1911, it was a counter-history to the story told by Dicey: Hobhouse attempted to show that almost no liberal worthy of the name had ever embraced *laissez-faire*. But the curious thing is that *Law and Public Opinion* was actually not intended to be history at all – Dicey had no use for history. But if *Law and Public Opinion* was bad history – frequently inaccurate and contradictory – it was highly influential and remains an excellent introduction to classical liberalism in the *fin de siecle*. Both for its role at the time, and its enormous, if sometimes subterranean, influence thereafter, it merits an extended account.[8]

In an important sense Dicey was not only typical of classical liberalism, but correct in his understanding of modern liberalism, or Collectivism, as he called it (Dicey either popularised or invented the highly influential distinction between 'Collectivism' and 'Individualism'). He put his finger on what was at stake in the battle between modern and classical liberals: the problem of poverty and the role of the state in dealing with it. Because he was right about this, his historical errors and textual misreading have been overlooked or minimised. Dicey's vision of liberalism influenced contemporary and later liberals, especially but not only, those on the right of the liberal spectrum, as much or more than the twentieth-century revival of Locke.

*Law and Public Opinion* was a lawyer's attempt to discover the laws of liberalism based on selected precedents abstracted from historical context and reduced to rational principles. Dicey reduced classical liberalism to a single principle, 'Individualism', which he identified with negative freedom (freedom from coercion) as embodied in a *laissez-faire* state and a *laissez-faire* society. Dicey impoverished the history of British liberalism by leaving out most of what had

[8] RA Cosgrove, *The Rule of Law: Albert Venn Dicey, Victorian Jurist* (Chapel Hill, University of North Carolina Press, 1980) xiii, 79, 189, 191–92. In Dicey's view the purpose of history was 'to deduce from past events the general principles on which their course has depended'. But historians had completely failed in this task, and it is 'extremely doubtful whether a single principle has yet been ascertained which can even metaphorically be termed a historical law': cited in Cosgrove 172–73.

passed for liberalism before the 1870s. The Whigs were barely mentioned, and their rare appearances were in purely supporting roles to the dominant Benthamites. That he omitted or distorted contradictory elements even in the thought and action of figures he cited extensively (notably Bentham and Macaulay), was of little concern to Dicey. What mattered was elucidating the lawlike principles behind Individualism and its rival, 'Collectivism'.

In Dicey's view, liberalism started out around 1830 with a consensus in favour of Individualism/*laissez-faire*, but in the *fin de siecle* it divided into two. Those here described as modern liberals left the true path, preferring 'the road to serfdom', to adopt another latter-day phrase; Dicey called it Collectivism. Dicey preferred to use Collectivism rather than 'Socialism' because he thought Collectivism was the broader term, even though he did 'on occasion use the more popular and current expression socialism as equivalent to collectivism'. Meanwhile, classical liberals remained on the path of freedom, which Dicey called Individualism. The history of the two divergent principles formed the framework for Dicey's defence of classical liberalism. Dicey's vocabulary and its history were thus conceived as a weapon in the battle between modern liberalism (New Liberalism in England) and classical liberalism. Interestingly, in the twentieth century, for different reasons classical liberals, modern liberals and even socialists preferred Dicey's classical liberal history to Hobhouse's modern liberal history. They preferred it because each, for their own reasons, wanted to emphasise the *laissez-faire* elements in the liberal past, as Dicey had, rather than the departures from *laissez-faire*, as Hobhouse had.

During what Dicey called 'the period of Benthamism or Individualism (1825–1870)', Individualism backed by public opinion, swept 'away restraints on individual energy, and … exhibit[ed] a deliberate hostility to every historical anomaly or survival, which appear[ed] to … in any way place a check on individual freedom'. Benthamism was 'little else than the logical and systematic development of those individual rights, and especially that of individual freedom which has always been dear to the common law of England'. The restraints removed were primarily legal in nature. For Dicey the lawyer, liberalism was about law reform.[9]

Dicey identified liberalism in its heyday with Jeremy Bentham, a somewhat idiosyncratic choice. Bentham in Dicey's view was a legal philosopher and law reformer, not a 'utilitarian moralist' or a 'philanthropist'. At first glance, this would seem to be a very narrow view of liberalism as well as of Bentham, but because Dicey identified law with the protection of individual freedom, legal reform translated into the creation of a *laissez-faire* state. It was the principle of *laissez-faire* which, according to Dicey, 'really governed Benthamite legislation'. 'Faith in laissez faire … was in practice the most potent and vital principle of Benthamite reform'. That this was not an accurate description of Bentham did not disturb Dicey in the least, even though he was conscious of the problem.[10]

[9] Dicey, *Law and Public Opinion* 46.

[10] *Law and Public Opinion* 92, 105 n 22, 104. See 368 n 8, where Dicey recognised that Bentham himself might have been prone to violate *laissez-faire* dogma.

Bentham was only a convenient shorthand for Dicey, who was aware that most of the reforms of the Benthamite period were carried out by people who did not look to Bentham as their inspiration, and that 'some of them would have certainly repudiated the name of utilitarians'. Indeed, he went on to include among his Individualist reformers Macaulay, who was neither a Benthamite, nor a utilitarian, nor a supporter of *laissez-faire*. And just as he was aware that most liberals were neither Benthamites nor even utilitarians, Dicey recognised that 'this dogma of laissez-faire is not from a logical view an essential article of the utilitarian creed', a creed which allowed for benevolent despotism – Dicey cited Mill's passage about how an ignorant people could hope for no better than dictatorship by an Akbar or a Charlemagne. But during the period of Individualism this did not matter, since public opinion supported Individualism. All the reformers, Dicey claimed, were firm believers in 'common-sense utilitarianism', which is to say they supported a limited, *laissez-faire* state. They accepted 'that Benthamism of common sense which, *under the name of liberalism*, was to be for thirty or forty years a main factor in the development of English law' (emphasis added).[11]

What mattered to Dicey was boiling down the varied historical precedents to the legal principle that lurked behind them, which according to him was *laissez-faire*, and thus discovering the correct principle on which to reach a legal judgement about who was a liberal. For Dicey, true liberalism meant Individualism, both historically and in the *fin de siecle*, with the difference that in the *fin de siecle*, unlike in the past, classical liberal Individualists had to add modern liberal Collectivists to their list of enemies.[12]

Dicey saw Collectivism, the 'hope of social regeneration' brought about by the state, as Individualism's rival. Dicey's description of the heresy of Collectivism, ie modern liberalism, was just as influential, if not more so, than his 'history' of liberalism's *laissez-faire* and utilitarian origins. In his view, Individualism had opened the way for Collectivism through the 'dogma' of utility, to which both appealed; through the idea of parliamentary sovereignty, which both made their instrument and could be a powerful tool of democratic despotism; and through the improved efficiency of government administration, engineered by Benthamite legal reforms, which made Collectivist government intervention possible. The Collectivist possibilities of these elements had remained latent before 1870 or so because the current of public opinion was strongly Individualist, fearful of state-sponsored coercion. Once that changed, and social regeneration, motivated by the fear of poverty, became the order of the day, Collectivism found little to oppose it. Collectivist law-making and legal interpretation became the new rule: hence the title of Dicey's book, *Law and Public Opinion*.[13]

[11] *Law and Public Opinion* 120, 121, 128, 126, 121. See also 49: '... Benthamite individualism, which in accordance with popular phraseology, may often be conveniently called liberalism'.

[12] *Law and Public Opinion* 104, 105 n 23.

[13] ibid 50, 215, 217, 218.

Collectivism, Dicey acknowledged, had a less clear meaning than Individualism. He cited a dictionary to the effect that the word was only invented in 1880 and meant state ownership of the means of production. Yet Dicey intended it in a much broader sense: 'Collectivism … favours the intervention of the State, even at some sacrifice of individual freedom, for the purpose of conferring benefit upon the mass of the people'. There was no parallel to the attachment of Bentham's name to Individualism; no one person served Dicey as the eponymous hero of Collectivism. Since 1865, according to Dicey, the Collectivist current of opinion had been growing, to such an extent that by 1900 'the doctrine of *laissez faire*, in spite of the large element of truth which it contains, had more or less lost its hold upon the English people'. Even though many of the actions taken by British governments in 1865–1900 might individually be justified with *laissez-faire* arguments, taken as a whole, they showed that hostility to state interference had, at the very least, much diminished.[14]

The reasons Dicey gave for the sea-change in public opinion varied over time, but in the end he emphasised that it was the question of poverty and how to deal with it that had brought about the fin-de-siecle split between classical and modern/New Liberals, or in his terms Individualists and Collectivists. It is interesting to see how his understanding changed as he came to recognise the central role poverty played for liberals in this period.

Even his earlier analyses are suggestive. In Dicey's original 1905 account, three things were behind the change in public opinion from Individualism to Collectivism: First, 'faith in laissez faire suffered an eclipse'. Second, the broadening of the suffrage in 1867 and 1884 meant greater political pressure for state intervention (after the 1867 reform roughly 40 per cent of adult British males could vote, while post-1884 it was about 60 per cent).[15] Finally, improved administrative machinery made Collectivism possible. Later Dicey gave reasons *why* faith in *laissez-faire* declined. Perhaps the most interesting was the revival of nationalism: for Dicey, 'the opposition between Benthamism and nationalism is obvious'. The fashion for historical studies had aggravated nationalist sentiments and had 'produced racial divisions and animosities, which are not only in themselves a gigantic evil and an impediment to all true progress' but could not be assuaged by any kind of rational reform. Dicey recognised the increasing tensions between liberalism and nationalism in the *fin de siecle*. There is something to be said for Dicey's linkage of modern liberalism and nationalism or imperialism, as can be seen in such figures as Joseph Chamberlain in Britain and Friedrich Naumann in Germany.[16]

Elsewhere, Dicey added a different reason for the declining belief in *laissez-faire*. He pointed out that the growth of trade and commerce had been

[14] ibid 46–47, 47 n 5, 364.

[15] Dicey hesitated over which suffrage reform was fatal. See R Weill, 'Dicey was not Diceyan' (2003) 62 *The Cambridge Law Journal* 485–86.

[16] *Law and Public Opinion* 220, 307–29, 328–29; Cosgrove, *The Rule of Law* 178–79. On the relationship between modern liberalism and nationalism, see Kahan, *Freedom from Fear* 280–307.

the backbone of faith in the benefits of unlimited competition, that is, of the free market pillar of liberalism. But the growth of large corporations owned by myriad shareholders 'has gradually become the soul of modern commercial systems'. This 'has in more ways than one fostered the growth of collectivist ideas'. Anticipating some later Ordoliberal analyses, Dicey suggested that 'every large business may become a monopoly, and that trades which are monopolies may wisely be brought under the management of the State. The characteristics of modern commerce … make for socialism'. From a modern liberal perspective, this would be an argument about the *need* for 'socialism' to counter oppression by private monopolies; for the Ordoliberals it was cause for an aggressive campaign of state regulation to prevent the formation of cartels, but for Dicey neither was the case.[17]

By 1914, however, Dicey had decided that the only thing that mattered for the rise of Collectivism was the fear of poverty: 'Now, for the last sixty years and more, the needs and sufferings of the poor have been thrust upon the knowledge of middle-class Englishmen'. Consciousness of poverty had led to a desire to do something about it:

> Against this evil of poverty the State ought, it is felt by collectivists, to protect the wage-earning class, and … must go a good way towards securing for every citizen something like the same advantages, in the form of education, or of physical well-being, as the rich can obtain by their own efforts.

Dicey was conscious that poverty was the issue of the day, and that the moral status of poverty had changed. Modern liberal policies implemented by the state in the *fin de siecle* (Dicey dated the rise of Collectivist policy from 1870) had deliberately removed the stigma attached to poor relief, for example by giving pensions to all elderly poor people, regardless of their character, thus negating the idea that it was 'the duty of every citizen to provide for his own needs, not only in youth, but in old age …'. Laws to protect women and children from working long hours, or to protect society against the adulteration of food, were based on the idea 'that the State is a better judge than a man himself of his own interest, or at any rate of the right way to pursue it'. Dicey was as perceptive about what motivated his contemporaries as he was blind to the deviations from *laissez-faire* individualism that had been common among liberals during the earlier part of the nineteenth century.[18]

Understanding did not bring agreement. For Dicey and for classical liberals in general, modern liberals had perverted liberalism and justified coercion. Creeping despotism was revealed by rising taxation. During the period of Individualism, liberals had thought lowering taxes was good in principle. But since 1870, in the period of Collectivism, this was no longer true. 'Indifference to the mere lightening of taxation, as an end absolutely desirable in itself' was characteristic of a period in which people 'expect far more benefit for the mass of the people from

[17] *Law and Public Opinion* 174, 176.
[18] ibid 378–82, 383, 195, see also 383, 386, 198.

the extension of the power of the State than from the energy of individual action'. Progressive taxation, introduced in 1910, set the precedent of taxation for the sake of redistributing wealth and with 'the aim of promoting social or political objects'.

> Such taxation may easily become the instrument of tyranny .... Revolution is not the more entitled to respect because it is carried through not by violence, but under the specious though delusive appearance of taxation imposed to meet the financial needs of the State.

The laudable desire to help the poor had turned into an illiberal revolution quietly led by the British Inland Revenue Service.[19]

From Dicey's perspective, modern liberals' attempt to address poverty with the help of the state had only had illiberal consequences. Dicey presented classical liberals' characteristic slippery slope argument: first free elementary education for the poor, supported by Adam Smith and many mainstream liberals during the period of Individualism before 1865; then free elementary education for everyone; then free school lunches for the poor; then free secondary education to offer equal opportunity; then progressive and confiscatory taxation to pay for it all and bring about real equality and an illiberal revolution: the slow descent leading to the socialist abyss – very much the argument Hayek, a prominent twentieth-century reader of Dicey, would later make in *The Road to Serfdom*. Dicey and his fellow classical liberals then and later were not alone in this view: around the same time as Dicey was writing, the revisionist Marxist Eduard Bernstein was arguing that revolution was unnecessary because liberalism was evolving into socialism anyway. Like Bernstein, if from a very different perspective, the classical liberal response to modern liberalism represented by Dicey looked ahead to the twentieth century, but regarded with horror the trends that filled Bernstein with hope.[20]

The fear of poverty motivated modern liberals, and the fear of modern liberals helped motivate classical liberals to hew ever more closely to *laissez-faire*. The overall result was a refoundation of liberalism in the *fin de siecle* based on new fears and above all a new hope, that of ending poverty. In Dicey's terms, 'Benthamism is a doctrine of law reform; collectivism is a hope of social regeneration'. Once poverty became the central question confronting liberals, the story of liberalism in the *fin de siecle* became a battle about the role of the state. There was always a temptation for modern liberals to put so much trust in the state as an instrument to fight poverty that the growth of the State would end up becoming the end rather than the means. This led more than one modern liberal to abandon liberalism in favour of socialism, just as Dicey had predicted.[21]

In this battle, both in his own time and thereafter, Dicey's thought, for all its historical flaws and its schematic legalism, played a crucial role. Dicey represented

[19] ibid 209, 186, 292, 377.

[20] Cosgrove, *The Rule of Law* 184; on Bernstein, see H Rosenblatt, *The Lost History of Liberalism* (Princeton, Princeton University Press, 2018) 232.

[21] *Law and Public Opinion* 50.

a classical liberalism predominantly interested in the fears of individuals, not of groups (like the poor), and resolutely opposed to any expansion of the role of government. He illustrated how classical liberals imagined themselves the true heirs of a *laissez-faire* economic tradition of liberalism, a tradition to a large extent invented by Dicey himself, and enthusiastically endorsed by his fellow classical liberals. One reason classical liberals liked to stress their orthodoxy and adopted the label 'classical' was that the word implied that they were the only authentic liberals, the true majority. The strategy is reminiscent of Lenin's describing his faction of the Russian Social Democratic Party as the 'Bolsheviks' – which means 'majority' in Russian. The Bolsheviks were really the minority faction, and classical liberals too rapidly found themselves in a minority when faced by the local modern liberals. Nevertheless, classical liberals have continued to be an important strand of liberal thought throughout the twentieth century, thanks in part to the convincing story of liberal history told by Dicey.

Dicey's distinction between Collectivism and Individualism, and the peculiar history which supported it, has played a key role in the conceptualisation of liberalism by both friends and enemies. Arguably, Dicey's work was the single most influential contribution of its period. Herbert Spencer was far more widely read at the time, and in the twentieth century Locke was anointed the patriarch of liberalism, but in the anglophone liberal tradition perhaps the only figure who can really rival Dicey's influence, from the *fin de siecle* to the present, is John Stuart Mill. Not bad for a lawyer.

# 16

# Dicey's Influence on English Administrative Law

NICOLAS GABAYET

This chapter intends to complement a previous paper in which I tried to assess the influence in France of Dicey's criticism of French administrative law. First, I set the French context that inspired Dicey's distrust of *droit administratif*; second, I studied the reception of Dicey's doctrine by French and foreign scholars; finally, I assessed what remained of Dicey's critics in French contemporary debates on administrative law.[1] The paper was oriented towards French law and legal thought[2] and I was eager to explore the influence Dicey had on administrative law in his own country.

However, this issue seems quite well known on the British side of the Channel, and even beyond, throughout the whole common law world. Every English administrative law textbook has extensive developments on Dicey's thought on administrative law, numerous papers have been written on the subject, and Mark Walters' landmark book on Dicey's thought includes a whole chapter dedicated to 'Dicey's Administrative Law Blind Spot'.[3] Therefore, one might wonder what is left to write on such an issue. I must confess that I have wondered this myself, when writing for English-speaking readers on a subject on which brilliant scholars, born and raised within the common law legal tradition, have already written so much. I can only hope that at least, as a continental European scholar (very interested in the common law legal tradition and especially in English administrative law), the outsider's perspective and understanding I have on Dicey's influence on English administrative law might be of interest for those who read the following pages. Moreover, since this book celebrates Dicey's thought, with its strengths

[1] N Gabayet, 'Une page de l'histoire de la pensée du droit administratif: le "moment Dicey"' (2018) 21 *Jus Politicum* 415.

[2] For this reason, this chapter focuses on the influence of Dicey's ideas on English administrative law only, and I do not discuss the way French scholars received and discussed Dicey's ideas in the early twentieth century as the issue was addressed in the paper cited above.

[3] MD Walters, *A.V. Dicey and the Common Law Constitutional Tradition: A Legal Turn of Mind* (Cambridge, Cambridge University Press, 2020) 299.

and weaknesses, there might have been a 'blind spot' – to paraphrase Walters – in the picture should Dicey's ideas on administrative law and their posterity not have been considered.

The first section of this chapter briefly restates the reasons for Dicey's aversion to administrative law, while the second and third sections aim to assess the influence of Dicey's doctrine on legal scholars who specialise in administrative law on the one hand, and on contemporary administrative law, on the other.

# I. Dicey's Denial of the Existence of English Administrative Law

Dicey's theory that there cannot be any administrative law in England is founded on the allegation that administrative law is averse to the rule of law. Such a view seems ideological, with Dicey fearing the development of Collectivism in the United Kingdom.

## A. Administrative Law as Averse to Rule of Law

The bulk of Dicey's writings on administrative law lies in Part II of *Introduction to the Study of the Law of the Constitution* (hereafter *Law of the Constitution*), on 'The Rule of Law'. The section includes a chapter devoted to a comparison between rule of law and French administrative law: 'Chapter XII: Rule of Law Contrasted with Droit Administratif'.[4]

The declared purpose of the comparison is to highlight the rule of law as a constitutional principle that protects individual rights, by seeking to contrast it with French administrative law. The latter is said to be a vector of arbitrariness and to serve the *raison d'Etat*: the Administration claiming its own cases and civil servants being protected from actions in tort.

It has been well established that Dicey's sources were authors such as Tocqueville, who wrote about the state of French administrative law in the middle of the nineteenth century,[5] whereas the decisive reforms modernising French administrative law occurred around the last quarter of the century. Still, despite foreign scholars drawing Dicey's attention to the fact that French

[4] AV Dicey, *Introduction to the Study of the Law of the Constitution*, 3rd edn (London, Macmillan, 1889) 303–30.

[5] On Tocqueville's critical views on French administrative law, see A de Tocqueville, *De la démocratie en Amérique*, vol 1, 12th edn (Paris, Pagnère, 1848) 167–68; *L'Ancien Régime et la Révolution* (Paris, Michel Lévy frères, 1856) 86; S Gilbert, 'Rapport de M. de Tocqueville sur le Cours de droit administratif de M. Macarel' (1846) (2007) *Revue Française de Droit Administratif* 1115, 1121. On French liberal criticism of administrative justice prior to the late nineteenth century reforms, see also Gabayet, 'Le "moment Dicey"' 417–23.

administrative law at the end of the nineteenth century was significatively different from Napoleonic administrative law as it existed in the mid-nineteenth century and was much more consistent with the rule of law[6] – which he acknowledged[7] – Dicey did not modify Chapter XII, 'Rule of Law Contrasted with Droit Administratif',[8] of the *Law of the Constitution*. He persisted instead in keeping the chapter unchanged and never changed his views regarding the impossibility of administrative law developing in England.

Dicey's rejection of the core idea of any development of administrative law in England was therefore irrational in two ways. On the one hand, it was based on an error regarding French administrative law that he could not possibly ignore. On the other, it was based on the idea that there could only be one model of administrative law, this model being the French one. Therefore, it seems that in Dicey's mind, if there was to be an English administrative law, it would necessarily derive from the French model.

The reasons for this apparent irrational rejection of administrative law are probably not to be found in legal – and should we say *rational* – arguments, but rather in ideological ones.

[6] See JW Garner, 'La conception anglo-américaine du droit administratif' in *Mélanges M Hauriou* (Paris, Sirey, 1929) 337–85; G Jèze, *Les principes généraux du droit administratif*, vol 1, 3rd edn (Paris, Giard, 1925) 1–2.

[7] AV Dicey, *Introduction à l'étude du droit constitutionnel* (Paris, Giard et Brière, 1902) XXXI–XXXII: 'Je tiens à affirmer tout particulièrement qu'une étude attentive de la Juridiction administrative de Laferrière et d'autres ouvrages récents et autorisés, m'a convaincu non seulement que je suis tombé dans quelques erreurs de détail qui sont peut-être pardonnables à un anglais qui écrit sur le Droit français, mais encore que le Droit administratif a subi en France, pendant les cinquante ou soixante dernières années, une évolution remarquable dont, en 1885, je ne m'étais pas rendu un compte suffisant' ['I wish to insist on the fact that a careful study of Laferrière's *Juridiction administrative* and other recent and authoritative works has convinced me not only that I have fallen into a few errors of detail which are perhaps forgivable to an Englishman writing about French law, but also that administrative law has undergone an important development in France over the last fifty or sixty years, of which, in 1885, I had not been sufficiently aware' – translated with DeepL.com (free version): 'Droit Administratif in Modern French Law' (1901) 17 *Law Quarterly Review* 302, 307–308. This also emerges from Dicey's private correspondence with Bryse and MacMillan & Co. These archives are quoted by Walters in *Dicey and the Common Law* 324–25.

[8] AV Dicey, *Introduction à l'étude du droit constitutionnel*, ibid: 'Il importe d'ajouter ici que, pour une comparaison avec le Droit anglais, le Droit administratif français, tel qu'il existait au milieu du XIX$^{e}$ siècle, convient tout autant que le Droit administratif plus développé de nos jours. À la vérité, mon exposé du Droit français fondé, comme il l'était sur bien des points, sur les écrits d'Alexis de Tocqueville ne correspond pas complètement, ainsi que me l'ont fait remarquer plusieurs critiques estimables, avec le Droit administratif actuel ; mais le Droit français, tel qu'il existait, par exemple, en 1850, est une illustration admirable, par voie d'opposition, du Droit Constitutionnel anglais. C'est pourquoi j'ai pensé qu'il n'y avait pas lieu de modifier matériellement les pages publiées pour la première fois en 1885' ['It is important to add here that, for the purposes of comparison with English law, French administrative law, as it existed in the mid-nineteenth century, is just as appropriate as the more developed administrative law of today. In fact, my account of French law as it was based, in many respects, on the writings of Alexis de Tocqueville, does not fully correspond with present-day administrative law, as several estimable critics have pointed out to me; but French law, as it existed, for example, in 1850, is an admirable illustration, by way of contrast, of English constitutional law. This is why I thought that there was no need to materially modify the pages first published in 1885'– translated with DeepL.com (free version)].

## B. Administrative Law as a Tool for Collectivism?

One possible answer to explain Dicey's absolute rejection of administrative law lies in his hostility to the development of public services.[9] In the famous article 'The Development of Administrative Law in England' published in 1915, Dicey seems to deplore the development of a New Liberal state, writing that:

> during the last fifty years, and notably since the beginning of the twentieth century, the nation as represented in Parliament has undertaken to perform a large number of duties with which before the Reform Act of 1832 no English Government had any concern whatever.[10]

As Carol Harlow noted, Dicey was concerned that collectivism and socialism were gaining influence in Britain

> Dicey condemned wide administrative powers because of their collectivist connotation. Because he viewed the constitution primarily as 'an instrument for protecting the fundamental rights of the citizens, and not an instrument for enabling the community to provide services to the benefit of the citizens' … he came to confuse 'discretionary' with 'arbitrary' powers.[11]

Indeed, Dicey's writings show clear apprehension regarding the development of public services in the early twentieth century. He called them 'new duties' imposed upon the government by Parliament. The focus of Dicey's argument against the development of such 'new duties' is based on the incompatibility of the rule of law with the management of a 'business', as he explained in 'The Development of Administrative Law in England':

> [W]e must remember that when the State undertakes the management of business properly so called, and business which hitherto has been carried on by each individual citizen simply with a view to his own interest, the Government, or, in the language of English law, the servants of the Crown, will be found to need that freedom of action necessarily possessed by every private person in the management of his own personal concerns. If a man of business were to try to conduct his own affairs in accordance with the rules which, quite properly, guide our judges in the administration of justice, he would discover that at the end of the year he had realized no profits and had come near to bankruptcy. How could any trade prosper if it were in the hands of a man who could not dismiss a clerk until the employer had obtained conclusive proof of fraud or misconduct by the servant, or if no evidence were allowed to tell against the alleged delinquent unless it were what lawyers consider the very 'best evidence'?

[9] But see MD Walters, 'Public Law and Ordinary Legal Method: Revisiting Dicey's Approach to "Droit Administratif"' (2016) 66 *University of Toronto Law Journal* 52, 57.

[10] AV Dicey, 'The Development of Administrative Law in England' (1915) 31 *Law Quarterly Review* 148, 149.

[11] C Harlow and R Rawlings, *Law and Administration*, 4th edn (Cambridge, Cambridge University Press, 2022) 22; see also their article 'Administrative Law in Context: Restoring a Lost Connection' (2014) *Public Law* 28, 30: 'Dicey also deplored the growth of collectivism, which he saw as inimical to the common law tradition'.

> The management of business, in short, is not the same thing as the conduct of a trial. The two things must in many respects be governed by totally different rules.[12]

In short, according to Dicey, the conduct of what we would now call public service would be inefficient if the public authority empowered to discharge it were to be strictly limited by law in its freedom to perform its statutory duty. The need for a certain freedom implies that public authorities are not only empowered with a duty to discharge, but also with discretionary powers to enable this mission. Dicey's reasoning was that the growth of public services would be accompanied by a backlash to the rule of law and a risk of arbitrariness.

Yet, in a less sophisticated reasoning, Dicey also wrote in the introduction of the eighth edition of *The Law of the Constitution* (1915) that 'it may not be an exaggeration to say that in some directions the law of England is being "officialised" ... by statutes passed under the influence of socialistic ideas'.[13] According to Jennings, this 'doctrine ... most obviously exhibits Dicey's Whiggism',[14] that is a mid-nineteenth-century Whiggism, that could probably be labelled as 'conservative' in the beginning of the twentieth century.[15] On that account, Walters, after Lawson, emphasises an apparent time-lag between the late Dicey and the turn of the new century.[16]

## II. Dicey's Views on Administrative Law: A Lukewarm Reception from Legal Scholars

Notwithstanding the tremendous influence *The Law of the Constitution* had over generations of British lawyers,[17] it seems – at least from what might be perceived as a French perspective – that legal scholars mostly rejected his theory upon which English law would be averse to administrative law.[18]

The rebuttal of Dicey's ideas on administrative law was probably partly ideological (as were Dicey's ideas themselves). Indeed, functionalism, the main school of thought criticising the Vinerian professor's lack of vision on administrative law, emerged from the Fabian socialist context of the early years of the London

[12] ibid 150.

[13] AV Dicey, *Introduction to the Study of the Law of the Constitution*, 8th edn (London, Macmillan, 1915) lxi.

[14] WI Jennings, 'In Praise of Dicey (1885–1935)' (1935) 13 *Public Administration* 123, 130.

[15] Walters tries to define Dicey's political inclinations in Walters, *Dicey and the Common Law* 24–27.

[16] ibid 249–50; FH Lawson, 'Dicey Revisited' (1959) 7 *Political Studies* 109, calling Dicey an 'angry old man'.

[17] Editor's Introduction to vol 1 of *A.V. Dicey, Law of the Constitution*, JWF Allison (ed) (Oxford, Oxford University Press, 2013); Harlow and Rawlings, *Law and Administration* 11–12; WI Jennings, 'In Praise of Dicey' 133; 'Administrative Law and Administrative Jurisdiction' (1939) 20 *Journal of Comparative Legislation and International Law* 99; W Robson, 'Dicey's Law of the Constitution: A Review' (1939) 38 *Modern Law Review* 205; Walters, *Dicey and the Common Law* 358.

[18] Gabayet, 'le "moment Dicey"' 431–33.

School of Economics,[19] and was therefore 'tied with new liberalism, social democracy, progressivism, or democratic socialism'.[20] Although Loughlin identifies ten characteristics of functionalism, the main feature of this school of legal thought is that public law is distinguishable from private law and based on the political will to act for fulfilling social solidarity.[21] The three major functionalist authors emerging from the London School of Economics in the inter-war period, Griffith, Jennings, and Laski, opposed Dicey's theory regarding the absence of administrative law in England. For instance, Jennings explained that Dicey remained blind to the existence of English administrative law because he failed to consider powers delegated by Parliament to public authorities, 'even the peculiar powers and immunities of the Crown', which amounted to a failure to 'consider the substance of administrative law'.[22]

Dicey's ideas on administrative law were also confronted by scholars who studied the use of prerogative writs in the history of common law. They deduced from the existence of special judicial forms of actions applicable only to disputes with officials that there were special proceedings and special remedies applicable only to litigation involving public authorities. In other words, a scheme of administrative justice. After the seminal and decisive researches on that matter from foreign scholars contemporary with Dicey, in particular Gneist (who also identified schemes of regulation by local authorities, or what would be considered under French law '*police administrative*'),[23] and Goodnow,[24] English scholars built upon the theory under which a scheme of administrative law has existed through prerogative writs since the eighteenth century. This is especially the case with de Smiths's famous paper in the early 1950s.[25] The idea that Dicey failed to consider the historical existing form of English administrative law seems now unchallenged. Craig makes it clear that the Vinerian professor did not take into account the 'UK administrative law [that] existed for over 300 years prior to Dicey'[26] before establishing the significant volume of prerogative remedies cited in UK case law between 1220 and 1827 (and mostly 'from the late sixteenth century onward'): '6637 citations to certiorari, 5563 to prohibition, 7111 to mandamus, 2512 to quo warranto'.[27] In his book, Walters emphasises the oddity of Dicey's 'blind spot' on that matter in stating Dicey's activities as a Counsel to the Commissioners of the

[19] Harlow, and Rawlings, 'Administrative Law in Context' 32.

[20] M Loughlin, 'The Functionalist Style in Public Law' (2005) 55 *University of Toronto Law Journal* 361, 363.

[21] ibid.

[22] Jennings, 'In Praise of Dicey' 131.

[23] R von Gneist, *Das englische Verwaltungsrecht der Gegenwart* (Berlin, Springer 1867).

[24] FJ Goodnow, 'The Writ of Certiorari' (1891) 6 *Political Science Quarterly* 493.

[25] SA de Smith, 'The Prerogative Writs' (1951) 11 *Cambridge Law Journal* 40.

[26] P Craig, *Administrative Law*, 9th edn (London, Sweet & Maxwell, 2021) 2. See also 2–4.

[27] ibid 42. For a more detailed study, see P Craig, *UK, EU and Global Administrative Law. Foundations and Challenges* (The Hamlyn Lectures, Oxford University Press, 2015) 25–62. See also FW Maitland, *The Constitutional History of England: A Course of Lectures Delivered* (Cambridge, Cambridge University Press, 1908) 505.

Inland Revenue, and especially the several cases he argued in which *mandamus* was involved.[28]

Dicey's ideas on administrative law seem, however, to still have influence on contemporary scholars. The influence is not in denying the existence of English administrative law per se, but rather on some scepticism regarding the idea of a public-private divide within the English legal system. The public-private divide is sometimes regarded as foreign to the English legal tradition, resulting from a legal transplant of a continental European concept,[29] and even sometimes as something that does not have an actual existence or utility.[30] This is linked to Dicey's ideas on the 'ordinary law of the land'.

More generally, one may wonder to what extent Dicey's chauvinistic approach to administrative law might have contributed, if only marginally, to shaping the representation of their own legal culture by some British legal scholars. The perception of its uniqueness in relation to civil law tradition might have been reinforced by Dicey's approach. Consistently with the Brexit phenomenon, since the end of last century several British authors and judges have expressed concerns about the continentalisation of English law, particularly under the influence of European law.[31]

## III. An Indirect Influence of Dicey's Doctrine on Contemporary English Administrative Law

As emphasised above, Dicey ignored – or pretended to ignore – English administrative law. Therefore, contemplating the idea that he might have had an influence on the current state of English administrative law sounds highly paradoxical.

Indeed, as it has been noted in the previous section, Dicey already failed, first, in considering that the use of prerogative writs over the previous 300 years shaped English administrative law. Secondly, he failed to acknowledge the growth of the administrative state and the discretionary powers of public authorities.

[28] Walters, *Dicey and the Common Law* 306–19.

[29] JWF Allison, *A Continental Distinction in The Common Law* (Oxford, Oxford University Press, 1996) 3–33; C Harlow '"Public" and "Private" Law: Definition without Distinction' (1980) 43 *Modern Law Review* 241.

[30] D Oliver, *Common Values and the Public-Private Divide* (Cambridge, Cambridge University Press 1999); 'Public Law Procedures and Remedies. Do We Need Them?' (2002) *Public Law* 91; 'What, if any, Public-Private Divide Exists in English Law' in M Ruffert (ed), *The Public-Private Divide: Potential for Transformation* (London, BIICL, 2009) 1; M Taggart, 'The Peculiarities of the English Law: Resisting the Public/Private Law Distinction' in P Craig and R Rawlings (eds), *Law and Administration in Europe, Essays in Honor of Carol Harlow* (Oxford, Oxford University Press, 2009) 107.

[31] eg HWR Wade, 'Sovereignty – Revolution or Evolution?' (1996) 112 *Law Quarterly Review* 568. Regarding the scepticism expressed by judges on the Europeanisation of UK law see S Boyron, 'The Judiciary's Self-Determination, the Common Law and Constitutional Change' (2016) 22 *European Public Law* 149.

Considering how blind this spot was, Dicey's thought on that subject had little to do with the current state of administrative law. In that respect, it would even be fair to say that English administrative law rose *despite of* his influence.

Setting aside the social and economic context and the New Liberal policies, the increased development of administrative law in the second half of the twentieth century is particularly related to two decisive legal factors unquestionably foreign to the realm of Dicey's thought. First, the 1977 reform of Order 53 of the Rules of the Supreme Court aggregating the fragmented available remedies in litigating administrative law (quashing orders, mandatory orders, and prohibiting orders, deriving from the prerogative remedies of *certiorari*, *mandamus*, and prohibition, plus injunctions, declarations, and damages) in the single procedure of judicial review.[32] This reform greatly simplified the application for judicial review and therefore contributed to increasing the applications for public law remedies and ultimately the number of administrative law cases settled by courts. Second, the *O'Reilly v Mackman* case in the early 1980s, in which the House of Lords filled the gaps in the revised Order 53, determining that judicial review is the exclusive procedure by which to challenge the decision of a public authority in the field of public law.[33] The 1977 reform had brought together prerogative remedies and ordinary remedies of injunction and declaration in a single judicial review procedure. However, the redaction of the rules was not clear as to whether the claimants had a choice between seeking injunction and declaration through judicial review or through an ordinary procedure. Several prisoners involved in prison riots were punished with a forfeiture of remission of sentence by the Board of Visitors of Hull Prison. Although the Board had disciplinary jurisdiction on that matter under Rule 51 of the Prison Rules [1964], it nonetheless acted in breach of the rules of natural justice and fairness (in this case, bias and failure to grant a fair hearing). The punished prisoners sought to have the disciplinary award declared null and void but they did so outside the scope of the judicial review procedure. The House of Lords, led by Lord Diplock's judgment, followed the Board counsels in holding that this was an abuse of the court process. This was because judicial review procedure was created to enable the challenge of public authorities' decision when a question of public law was at stake. In *O'Reilly*, the Board was exercising a disciplinary power deriving from statute law (Rule 51 of the Prison Rules 1964) and, therefore, the prisoners' legitimate expectation that the Board would observe the rules of natural justice in the decision-making process emerged from a public law right to a fair hearing (as opposed to a private law right). There is probably no need to go any further in the course of the development of contemporary English administrative law to emphasise how averse to Dicey's ideas is the judgment dismissing a case because the specific *public law*

[32] Rules of the Supreme Court (Amendment No 3) 1977, SI 1977/1955. Now Part 54 of the Civil Procedure Rules.

[33] *O'Reilly v Mackman* [1983] 2 AC 237.

procedure has not been used. It is also difficult to imagine the reaction Dicey would have had to the creation of the Administrative Court,[34] as a special division of the King's Bench Division of the High Court in charge of adjudicating the cases on application for judicial review.

A more indirect influence of Dicey's ideas on contemporary administrative law might yet be found in the way administrative law is conceived in the United Kingdom. The idea of administrative law and the procedure of judicial review seem to merge with each other (at least from a continental perspective). To this extent, studying English administrative law is equivalent to studying judicial review. English textbooks on administrative law are indeed much oriented towards administrative justice (the other chapters of the textbooks dealing with institutions). For example, a classic textbook such as Wade & Forsyth's *Administrative Law* has 24 sections, 12 of which are directly linked to judicial review, and six indirectly, being powers of legal authorities (that give rise to decisions subject to review) and their foundations, three sections present the public authorities, one the influence of European Union law, and one the liability of public authorities.[35] By contrast, any textbook on French *droit administratif général* (that is the basics of French administrative law, studied in the second year of any French LLB), would probably only have one chapter on remedies against decisions made by public authorities (that would mostly be about *recours pour excès de pouvoir*), and one chapter on the legal norms applicable to the judicial review, but all the rest of the book would deal with substantive administrative law: administrative activities, that is public services (*services publics*) and regulation (*police administrative*), the legal means public authorities may use to fulfil their action, which are a wide range of decisions (*les actes administratifs unilatéraux*) and public contracts (*les contrats administratifs*), public liability (*la responsabilité administrative*), and sometimes also a presentation on the different types of public authorities.[36] In addition, there is a wide range of textbooks on specific subjects related to administrative law (*droit administratif special*) which are taught in every French law school: public contracts and procurements (*droit des contrats publics/administratifs*),[37] planning law (*droit de l'urbanisme*),[38] public property law (*droit administratif des biens*),[39] public employment law

[34] Civil Procedure (Amendment No 4) Rules 2000, SI 2000/2092, which inserted Part 54 into the Civil Procedure Rules 1998, SI 1998/3132.

[35] HWR Wade and CF Forsyth, *Administrative Law*, 11th edn (Oxford, Oxford University Press, 2014). But see P Craig, *Administrative Law*, 9th edn (Oxford, Oxford University Press, 2021); Harlow and Rawlings, *Law and Administration* for a more extensive approach to administrative law.

[36] Eg R Chapus, *Droit administratif général*, 15th edn, vol 1 (Paris, LGDJ, Précis Domat, 2001); D Truchet, *Droit administratif*, 7th edn (Paris, Presses Universitaires de France, Thémis, 2017), P-L Frier and J Petit, *Droit administratif*, 17th edn (Paris, LGDJ, Précis Domat, 2023). The same research may be done with most textbooks on *droit administrative général*.

[37] eg L Richer and F Lichère, *Droit des contrats administratifs*, 12th edn (Paris, LGDJ, Manuel, 2021).

[38] eg P Soler-Couteaux and E Carpentier, *Droit de l'urbanisme*, 8th edn (Paris, Dalloz, Hypercours, 2022).

[39] eg J-F Giacuzzo, *Droit administratif des biens*, 1st edn (Paris, Dalloz, Cours, 2023).

(*droit de la fonction publique*),[40] public law applicable to economics (*droit public économique*).[41] This brief comparison of the scope of English and French administrative law tends to show that in the English conception, administrative law appears essentially procedural, as opposed to substantive.[42] This leads us to identify two possible links with Dicey. On the one hand, his concept of administrative law deriving from his understanding of French administrative law was rather procedural:

> *Droit administratif* … may, for our present purpose, be best described as that portion of French law which determines, (i) the position and liabilities of all State officials, (ii) the civil rights and liabilities of private individuals in their dealings with officials as representatives of the State, and (iii) the procedure by which these rights and liabilities are enforced.[43]

There is nothing in Dicey's definition of '*droit administratif*' about the activities carried out by public authorities nor about the means to carry out these activities (decision-making process, contracts, corporations). By contrast the notions of administrative activities and administrative means (*l'activité et les moyens de l'Administration*) are the core of French administrative law. As Jennings put it

> Dicey was concerned with two aspects of constitutional and administrative law only[:] [that] fundamental liberties … do not arise out of constitutional guarantees but out of civil law; and … that the English law of *contentieux administratif* is applied by the civil courts.[44]

Yet, the idea that the purpose of administrative law would only exist to make sure that public authorities do not exceed what they have been statutorily authorised to do (ultra vires doctrine) is very relevant to Dicey's commitment to the *laissez-faire* doctrine under which the State should interfere as little as possible in peoples' everyday life, as opposed to providing for a range of public services. Considering that controlling the intra vires character of decisions made by public authorities is the purpose of administrative law is what Harlow and Rawlings call the 'Red-light' theory or approach of administrative law, as opposed to the welfare-State-oriented 'Green-light' theory.[45]

To conclude, although it is well established that Dicey was mistaken and lacked vision about the development of an English administrative law consistent with the rule of law, it seems possible to identify an influence, in at least two respects. First, the substance of English administrative law, forged by the ultra

[40] eg E Aubin-Kanezuka, *Droit de la fonction publique*, 1st edn (Paris, LGDJ, Précis Domat, 2023).

[41] eg P Delvolvé, *Droit public de l'économie*, 2nd edn (Paris, Dalloz, Précis, 2022).

[42] With regard to how European Union law has contributed to enhance the substance of English administrative law, see N Gabayet, 'Les mutations du droit administratif anglais sous l'influence du droit de l'Union européenne' (2017) 2 *Revue du droit public et de la science politique* 295.

[43] Dicey, *Introduction*, 8th edn (1908) 216–17. See also Jennings, 'In Praise of Dicey' 131.

[44] Jennings, ibid.

[45] Harlow and Rawlings, *Law and Administration* 7–11.

vires doctrine, remains mostly procedural, in line with the 'Red-light' theory. Second, a number of English academics remain sceptical regarding the idea of a public-private divide within English law.

It is also possible to consider that to some extent Dicey's negation of the existence of English administrative law had some influence on the perception of English administrative law outside the United Kingdom, and particularly in France. Indeed, whereas the most eminent scholars, including Goodnow, Gneist, Jennings, and de Smith have proven Dicey wrong, the French perception of English administrative law has long been that it did not exist. A certain level of ignorance by French scholars on English legal culture may certainly explain Dicey's undue influence on French scholars' perceptions of English administrative law. But beyond that, it seems that the most famous French specialist of administrative law, Hauriou, who was a contemporary of Dicey's, played a part in spreading Dicey's ideas in France.[46] In his landmark textbook, he presents French administrative law as fundamentally exorbitant regarding private law and classifies England among the countries 'without an administrative law regime'.[47] The idea remained firmly established among French public law scholars.

[46] S Cassese, *La construction du droit administratif. France et Royaume-Uni* (Paris, Montchrestien, 2000) 57–58.

[47] M Hauriou, *Précis de droit administratif et de droit public*, 12th edn (Paris, Dalloz, 2002 [1933]) 1–2. See also Hauriou's position regarding English administrative law in N Gabayet, 'le "moment Dicey"' 433–34.

# 17

# No, Really, Dicey Was Not Diceyan

IAIN McLEAN AND SCOT PETERSON

## I. Introduction

Several authors have pointed to AV Dicey's inconsistent positions on parliamentary supremacy.[1] However, Mark Walters, who calls McLean's account 'particularly extreme', maintains, 'Dicey never relented in his insistence that the *English or British* constitution embodied the two principles, parliamentary sovereignty and the rule of law, as he expounded them in the *first edition* of his book *Law of the Constitution*' (emphasis added).[2]

The following facts are, we think, not in dispute:

(1) According to Dicey, 'parliamentary sovereignty' implies that:
   — no parliament may bind its successor;[3] hence that
   — sections of statutes which purport to entrench the statute have no legal force;[4] and hence that: 'Should the Dentists Act, 1878, unfortunately contradict the terms of the Act of Union [Union with Scotland Act 1707], the Act of Union would be *pro tanto* repealed.'[5] This statement remained in all editions of *Law of the Constitution* published in Dicey's lifetime.

(2) In 1884, Dicey deplored the House of Lords' obstruction of the Liberal government's franchise Bill: 'Their one plea for rejecting a measure passed by overwhelming majorities in the House of Commons is that the House does not represent the country. But the validity of this plea can be tested only by a General Election .... Are the English people prepared to introduce into

[1] RFV Heuston, *Essays in Constitutional Law* (London, Stevens, 1961) 1–3; R Weill, 'Dicey was not a Diceyan' (2003) 62 *Cambridge Law Review* 474; I McLean, *What's Wrong with the British Constitution?* 2nd edn (Oxford, Oxford University Press, 2012).

[2] MD Walters, *A.V. Dicey and the Common Law Constitutional Tradition: A Legal Turn of Mind* (Cambridge, Cambridge University Press, 2020) 389–90.

[3] AV Dicey, *Lectures Introductory to the Study of the Law of the Constitution*, 1st edn (1885) 51, reprinted in AV Dicey *The Law of the Constitution*, JWF Allison (ed) (Oxford, Oxford University Press, 2013).

[4] ibid 78.

[5] ibid.

the practice of the Constitution one of the most dubious devices of Swiss Democracy – namely the so-called "Referendum"[?]'.[6]

(3) The House of Lords rejected the Budget of 1909 on the grounds that 'this House is not justified in giving its assent to the Bill until it has been submitted to the judgment of the country'.[7] That judgement took the form of the General Election of January 1910, forced by the Lords' first rejection of supply since the English Civil War. It returned a Liberal government with Irish Party support.

(4) Dicey changed his mind about referendums. In several tracts[8] and in his introduction to the eighth edition of *Law and the Constitution*,[9] he demanded a referendum, on the grounds that Home Rule for Ireland was an example of fundamental constitutional change that should be subject to a 'people's veto'. Indeed, he mused whether Parliament could adopt a Referendum Act protecting important statutes, which might be binding on future parliaments: a rejection of the doctrine of parliamentary supremacy.[10] While still demanding an appeal to the people (as he had in 1884), he now rejected the idea that a general election settled the appeal. Evidently three Liberal General Election victories in a row (1906 and two in 1910) did not represent the judgement of the country. He expressed confidence that the people, if asked, would reject Home Rule in a referendum.

(5) He recanted his earlier support for women's suffrage, saying: '[but] history exemplifies the futility of giving to any class, whether of men or women, political rights in excess of genuine political power'.[11]

(6) Like many English public intellectuals of his day, he was hostile to Irish Catholics and nationalists, and supportive of Irish Protestants and Unionists. But he supported Italian nationalists.[12]

(7) He almost always referred to the *English* Constitution. However, in his last book, he and his Scottish co-author stated that the drafters of the Scottish Act of Union intended to entrench some clauses, an effort which they called 'not unmeaning'.[13] The Scottish Act was endorsed unaltered by the English Parliament, creating the final Act of Union.

Facts such as these have led Weill, McLean and McMillan, and McLean to claim that Dicey was radically inconsistent and that he abandoned support for both

[6] [AV Dicey], 'Notes on the Crisis' *Northampton Mercury*, 5 July 1884, 5A, ascribed to Dicey by AV Dicey and RS Rait, *Memorials of A.V. Dicey* (London, Macmillan, 1925) 122.

[7] *Hansard*, HL Dec (series 5) vol 4, col 731, 22 November 1909 (Lord Lansdowne).

[8] See eg AV Dicey, *A Leap in the Dark, or Our New Constitution* (London, J Murray, 1893) 198.

[9] AV Dicey, *Introduction to the Study of the Law of the Constitution*, 8th edn (1915) Introduction, xci–c, reprinted in JWF Allison, *Laws of the Constitution* 415, 474.

[10] Walters, *Dicey and the Common Law Tradition* 383–85.

[11] AV Dicey, *Letters to a Friend on Votes for Women* (London, J Murray, 1909) 73.

[12] eg [AV Dicey] Untitled Article, *Northampton Mercury*, 19 May 1860, 2G–H (ascribed to Dicey by AV Dicey and RS Rait, *Memorials of A.V. Dicey* (London, Macmillan, 1925) 50).

[13] AV Dicey and RS Rait, *Thoughts on the Scottish Union* (London, Macmillan, 1920) 253.

parliamentary sovereignty and the rule of law from 1885 to 1921, while engaged in his campaign against Home Rule.[14] Walters avers that 'Dicey remained steadfastly Diceyan to the end'.[15] We find Walters' arguments unconvincing.

## II. Dicey and Diceyanism

AV Dicey (1835–1922) was born at Claybrooke Hall, near the border between Leicestershire and Northamptonshire, where his family owned the *Northampton Mercury*. He attended Balliol College, Oxford. After two unsuccessful tries, he became a fellow of Trinity College, Oxford, where he taught law until he forfeited his fellowship by marrying in 1872. He lived in London from 1861, where he practised law and wrote articles and legal treatises. He returned to Oxford in 1882, when he became Vinerian Professor of Law, a position he held for 27 years.[16]

Dicey had a disability, from 'an obstetrical error', which made him unable to control physical movements or to write legibly.[17] He dictated everything he wrote, including nearly all his correspondence. He was unable to tie his tie before his Oxford examinations; the Master of Balliol tied it for him.[18] He also had difficulty attending to what was happening around him.[19] He seems to have coped with these constraints by adopting a forceful style of exposition. 'For Dicey, real *writing* was, in effect *speaking*'.[20]

Diceyanism comprises two central principles and a set of facts about governance. The principles are the sovereignty (or supremacy) of Parliament and the rule of law. Parliament comprises the monarch, the House of Commons, and the House of Lords. Parliamentary sovereignty means that:

> Parliament thus defined has, under the *English* constitution, the right to make or unmake any law whatever; and … no person or body is recognised by the law of *England* as having a right to override or set aside the legislation of Parliament.[21] (emphasis added)

The rule of law means, first, that no one can be punished except for a breach of law proven in court; second, that everyone is subject to the law and to the courts' jurisdiction; and third, that general principles of the Constitution come from judicial decisions about the people's rights in particular cases.[22] Alongside these

[14] Weill, 'Dicey'; I McLean and A McMillan, 'Professor Dicey's Contradictions' (2007) *Public Law* 435; McLean, *What's Wrong*.

[15] Walters, *Dicey and the Common Law Tradition* 404.

[16] RA Cosgrove, *Rule of Law: Albert Venn Dicey, Victorian Jurist* (Chapel Hill, University of North Carolina Press, 1980).

[17] ibid 4; Walters, *Dicey and the Common Law Tradition* 30–31.

[18] Cosgrove, *Rule of Law* 10–11.

[19] Dicey and Rait, *Memorials* 289.

[20] Walters, *Dicey and the Common Law Tradition* 31.

[21] Dicey, *Lectures Introductory* 27.

[22] ibid 97, 100, 115.

two legal principles sit the facts now known as constitutional conventions, which are not enforced by courts, but also constrain law and politics.[23] However, Dicey did not consistently believe in the sovereignty of parliament. His position on parliamentary supremacy changed twice.

In December 1885 Liberal leader WE Gladstone announced his support for Home Rule in Ireland. The large majority of Irish MPs already supported Home Rule, but neither party in Great Britain previously had. From then until 1921, Home Rule became the defining cleavage in United Kingdom politics. Gladstone's conversion split his party. Those Liberals who could not accept Home Rule became known as Liberal Unionists, and they campaigned with the Conservatives against Home Rule, agreeing on a single Unionist candidate in (almost) every seat from 1892, and formally merging in 1912. The Labour Party emerged as a separate party supporting Home Rule (for Scotland as well as for Ireland). The Irish Party already controlled every seat in Ireland outside the majority-Protestant areas in the north-east. It split more than once in the period, especially in 1890 when most followers of its dictatorial leader CS Parnell rejected him. Contested elections in Catholic Ireland were fought (often bitterly) between supporters and opponents of Parnell, and later of other politicians who split from the main Irish Party. But every MP elected from Catholic Ireland (about 85 of the 105 Irish seats) supported Home Rule. Many seats were uncontested.

Dicey's changing views on referendums tracked successive Liberal Home Rule Bills. In 1890, '[T]here is much more to be said for, no less than against, the popular veto than English thinkers are generally ready to admit'.[24] By 1893, following the Unionists' electoral defeat in 1892, this had become, 'a direct appeal to the electors in the nature of a Referendum' might be necessary, following the Lords' certain rejection of the second Home Rule Bill. The Lords should demand that the Bill should receive assent in a referendum before becoming law:

> This course, it may be said, is unconstitutional. This word has no terrors for me; it means no more than unusual, and the institution of a Referendum would simply mean the formal acknowledgement of the doctrine which lies at the basis of English democracy – that a law depends at bottom for its enactment on the assent of the nation as represented by the electors.[25]

The Lords rejected the Bill outright in September 1893 by 419 votes to 41 without inserting a referendum provision.

By 1910, following the Unionists' electoral loss after the Lords had rejected the 1909 Budget, Dicey advocated a Referendum Act, mandating protection for 'statutes of the highest importance'.[26] He had come a long way from 1884.

[23] ibid 186–88.

[24] AV Dicey, 'Ought the Referendum be Introduced into England?' (1890) 57 *The Contemporary Review* 489, 511.

[25] Dicey, *A Leap in the Dark* 198.

[26] AV Dicey, 'The Referendum and Its Critics' (1910) 212 *The Quarterly Review* 538, 554.

## III. Who Would Have Won a Referendum on Home Rule?

The electoral qualification in the United Kingdom, and the number and distribution of seats in the House of Commons, remained unchanged for the whole of the period covered by our analysis, from 1886–1918. Adult male householders had the vote, as did some men who were not householders. The latter found it easier to register if they were rich.[27] Therefore, in the poorest part of the United Kingdom, Ireland, the enfranchised proportion of the population was probably lower than in Great Britain. On the other hand, the 1885 redistribution of seats led Ireland to be over-represented, and as Ireland's relative population continued to decline, its overrepresentation increased, from about 20 per cent in 1891 to over 50 per cent in 1911 (see Appendix 2, Table 1).

Even given these distortions of representation, support for Home Rule was far stronger than Dicey made it out to be. Table 2 shows the seat and vote shares for the pro- and anti-Home Rule coalitions in the seven general elections in the period (see Appendix 3, Table 2).

Because of the United Kingdom's single-member district electoral system, the seat shares in Table 2 swing around violently. The Unionists had a majority in the Commons from 1886 to 1892 and from 1895 to 1905. They resigned from government, hopelessly split, in December 1905, and in the ensuing 1906 general election their seat share plummeted from 60 per cent to less than a quarter. This volatility is shown in the standard deviation of the seat shares for the two factions (of nearly 14 per cent). But a referendum would have counted votes, not seats. Therefore, the popular vote, not membership of the House of Commons, best predicts the outcome of a hypothetical referendum on Home Rule.

Table 2 shows that the vote share for the two factions was much more stable than the seat share. The Unionist (anti-Home Rule) vote share was never more than 51.42 per cent (in 1886) and never less than 43.05 per cent (in 1906). Disregarding a tiny number of unclassifiable candidates, the pro-Home Rule coalition's vote share was just the converse. As is to be expected in a polarised polity where Home Rule was the dominant issue, these vote shares were stable, as shown in the low standard deviations in Table 2.

Table 2 shows that the anti-Home Rule coalition won the popular vote just twice, in 1886 and 1900. But most seats in Ireland were uncontested, thus suppressing turnout there. Irish nationalists, and indeed Irish Unionists, cast few election votes. But they would have voted in Dicey's referendum. How do the numbers in Table 2 change if we allow for this? We extrapolated from contested seats (where there were any), and imputed by other means where there were none,

[27] N Blewett, *The Peers, the Parties and the People: The General Elections of 1910* (London, Macmillan, 1972) 362.

to get hypothetical vote totals for the pro- and anti-Home Rule coalitions, in both nationalist and unionist Ireland. Details of our imputation method are in Appendix 1. The result is shown in Table 3 (see Table 3, Appendix 4).

The rightmost columns of Table 3 show two things. One is that the standard deviation of vote share is still lower than before the imputation process, confirming that opinions were both polarised and stable. The other is that the pro-Home Rule parties would have received a majority of votes in all seven elections.

There were also uncontested seats in Great Britain (ie the United Kingdom minus Ireland). These often roughly cancelled out, but in 1886 and 1900 Unionist uncontested seats considerably outnumbered Liberal ones because of collapses in Liberal organisation – in 1886 because of the split, and in 1900 because of vast popular enthusiasm for the Boer War, which at the time was going well for Britain. In a later paper we will extend our modelling to allow for this factor. But at a minimum, for the five other parliaments in our series, Home Rule would prima facie have won any referendum. Why then were Dicey and other Unionists so confident of the opposite outcome? We suggest several overlapping explanations.

## A. Seat-Vote Illusion

Unionists may have failed to look beyond their control of the Commons from 1886–92 and 1895–1905 (and of the Lords and the monarchy for the entire period).[28] They were therefore more shocked than they should have been when the electoral majority for Home Rule parties translated into a Commons majority.

## B. England, Great Britain, and the United Kingdom

Any referendum would have been held in the same territory that elected the House of Commons – including, for the avoidance of doubt, Ireland. Did Unionists manage to forget that Ireland was part of the United Kingdom when totting up votes, while at the same time insisting that it must forever remain part of the United Kingdom when resisting Home Rule?

In a pamphlet entitled *A Fool's Paradise* Dicey observed that there are 40 million people in Great Britain and 4 million in Ireland, of whom a million are Unionists.[29] (These numbers are very roughly right, according to the 1911 census). As an 'old … Benthamite', Dicey declared that he prefered the welfare of the 40 million to that of the 3 million.[30] So: his referendum was not to take place in Ireland, or at

[28] McLean, *What's Wrong.*

[29] AV Dicey, *A Fool's Paradise: Being a Constitutionalist's Criticism on the Home Rule Bill of 1912* (London, J Murray, 1913) viii–ix.

[30] ibid.

least if the United Kingdom majority in such a referendum was in favour of Home Rule while the Great Britain majority was against, the latter should prevail.

## C. Racism and Othering

Racist and/or religious disparagement of the Catholic Irish population of the United Kingdom was prevalent in this period.[31] It was a frequent component of Unionist appeals to working-class voters.[32] Dicey was a case in point:

> There have been … cases in which every one of *us* would hold that rebels risking their own lives for the freedom of *their country* were performing a high duty …. If in a moment of disgrace and weakness England should place *Ulster* in subjection to a Parliament in Dublin, it would be easier to adduce than to confute the reasons which in the eyes of many Englishmen and Scotchmen would justify Ulster in resisting a power to whom Ulstermen owed no moral allegiance.[33] (emphasis added)

*Us:* who were we? Apparently, everyone who supported 'rebels risking their own lives for the freedom of *their country*'. Were those the Irish nationalists? Certainly not; they were the people of *Ulster* who were resisting Home Rule. But who were the people of Dicey's Ulster? Ulster is one of the four historic provinces of Ireland. In terms of seats, Ulster had been a dead heat in the most recent elections (1885: 16 U, 17 N; 1886: 17 U, 16 N). 'Ulster' here does not mean 'the people of Ulster'. It means 'the Protestant people of Ulster'. The passage, typical of Unionist writing of its time, displays clear 'othering' of the Catholics/ nationalists (the terms had become essentially interchangeable) who comprised the large majority of the population of Ireland, and almost half the population of Ulster.

Dicey was far from alone. For instance, in his poem 'Ulster' (1912) Rudyard Kipling similarly mistook Protestant Ulster for Ulster and expressed visceral hatred of Catholicism:

> We know the war prepared
> On every peaceful home,
> We know the hells declared
> For such as serve not Rome –
> The terror, threats, and dread
> In market, hearth, and field –
> We know, when all is said.
> We perish if we yield.[34]

[31] M Pugh, *The Tories and the People 1880–1935* (Oxford, Blackwell, 1985) 84–85; RF Foster, *Paddy and Mr Punch: Connections in Irish and English History* (Harmondsworth, Penguin, 1993).

[32] RT McKenzie and A Silver, *Angels in Marble: Working-Class Conservatives in Urban England* (London, Heinemann, 1968) 54–61.

[33] AV Dicey, *The Verdict: A Tract on the Political Significance of the Report of the Parnell Commission* (London, Cassell, 1890) 119.

[34] R Kipling, *Poems, 1886–1929*, vol 3 (London, Macmillan, 1929) 22, 23.

However, Dicey had supported Giuseppe Garibaldi's campaign for Italian unification: 'The contest will doubtless aid in establishing the personal freedom of every Italian, but it is not primarily a struggle to obtain political liberty so much as to gain national independence'.[35] What is the difference?

## D. Belief that Voters for Pro-Home Rule Parties Did Not Support Home Rule

Party manifestoes are multidimensional. It is perfectly possible that people in Great Britain who voted for pro-Home Rule parties did not support their party's policy on Home Rule but supported it for other reasons. For Dicey and other fervent Unionists, this was an article of faith. There is no opinion polling in this period. Evidence from election results does not show any notable effect. The Unionists had been insisting since 1885 that 'Home Rule is Rome Rule'. No one could be in any doubt about their position, or that of the Irish Party. The Liberal and Labour parties were less forthright, but such evidence as we have suggests that Home Rule was not a salient issue for many of their voters. In 1913, the Prime Minister, Herbert Asquith (admittedly an interested party) responded to the King, who had been pressing Dicey's and others' Unionist arguments, arguing that opposition to Home Rule was weak:

> All the most trustworthy observers agree that, even when the bye-elections have gone against the Government, the attempt (wherever made) to arouse interest and resentment by pushing to the forefront the case against Home Rule and the supposed wrongs of Ulster, has met with no success.[36]

Passionate opposition to Home Rule was already baked into Unionist vote totals. By, at latest, 1910, it was obvious that voting Liberal, Irish Party, or Labour was voting for Home Rule. As more than half of the vote went to the Home Rule parties three times in a row, there is no evidence for the fervent Unionist belief that the people did not support Home Rule.

# IV. From a Contradiction Anything Follows

In 1885 Dicey argued for what HLA Hart labels 'continuing omnipotence':[37] the Dentists Act 1878 could impliedly repeal the Treaty and Acts of Union between Scotland and England.[38] We label this position 'Dicey 1'. In his polemics against

[35] [Dicey], Untitled Article.
[36] HH Asquith to George V, [19] September 1913, quoted in McLean, *What's Wrong* 277.
[37] HLA Hart, *The Concept of Law*, 3rd edn (Oxford, Oxford University Press, 2012) 149.
[38] Dicey, *Lectures Introductory* 78.

Home Rule, Dicey abandoned parliamentary sovereignty for any straw in the wind, including a referendum that he thought the Unionists would win. We label this 'Dicey 2'. Finally in 1920 he and his Scottish co-author adopted something akin to Hart's 'self-embracing omnipotence': viz, that Parliament could, at least once, bind itself by 'exercising an even larger sphere of legislative competence than [continuing omnipotence] allows to it'.[39] We label this 'Dicey 3'. Dicey 3 contradicts Dicey 1, and Dicey 2 contradicts both.

Introducing his Home Rule Bill in 1886, Gladstone argued that *Law of the Constitution* showed 'the absolute supremacy of Parliament' in its most 'distinct and emphatic manner' and Parliament's illimitable power to pass Home Rule for Ireland.[40] That Bill failed in the Commons and never reached the Lords. The Second (1893) and Third (1912) Home Rule Bills were carried in the Commons but defeated in the Lords. Under the provisions of the Parliament Act 1911, the 1912 Bill became the Government of Ireland Act 1914 without Lords' consent after passing three times in the Commons. Dicey argued that the increased strength of party discipline devalued parliamentary sovereignty. Party discipline had, according to Dicey, permitted the alliance of a true party (ie the Liberals) with a mere 'faction' (Irish Nationalists) to make passage of Irish Home Rule possible.[41] However, he did not define party or faction. The iron discipline of Parnell over his party was already obvious when *Law of the Constitution* was first published in 1885, and Dicey's appeal to a golden age was to Palmerston's governments of 1855 and 1859.[42]

Dicey 2 wrote that there might be 'acts of oppression on the part of a democracy, no less than of a king, which justify resistance to the law, or, in other words, rebellion',[43] and that the 1912 Bill lacked 'constitutional authority' because it had not been confirmed in a general election. However, the governing Liberals had won three successive general elections. Dicey's claim that the government lacked constitutional authority for the Government of Ireland Act 1914 makes no Diceyan 1 sense. He argued in 1910, 'The People's Budget [of 1909] has been rejected by the people' because 'every [MP] from Ireland, whether a Unionist or a Nationalist, detested the Budget'.[44] But the people elected a government that enacted the People's Budget in April 1910. He claimed in 1911 that the 'hereditary House of Lords, and not the newly elected House of Commons, truly represented the will of the nation'[45] when it rejected Irish Home Rule in 1893. By then Dicey was demanding a referendum or a dissolution to prove that the will of the nation

[39] Hart, *Concept of Law* 149; *cf* Dicey and Rait, *Thoughts* 252–54.

[40] *Hansard*, HC Deb (series 3) vol 304, col 1048, 8 April 1886.

[41] AV Dicey, 'The Parliament Act 1911 and the Destruction of All Constitutional Safeguards' in WR Anson (ed), *Rights of Citizenship: A Survey of Safeguards for the People* (London, Warne, 1912) 102.

[42] ibid 101.

[43] Dicey, *A Fool's Paradise* 114.

[44] Dicey, *The Referendum and its Critics* 548.

[45] Dicey, *A Leap in the Dark*, 2nd edn (London, J Murray, 1911) xvii.

was what he said it was, and hoped that King George V would veto the Home Rule Bill. He claimed the Third Home Rule Bill was illegitimate:

> A combination of discordant parties is attempting to drive through Parliament, without an appeal to the electors, a policy which has been twice deliberately rejected by the electorate of the United Kingdom …. Every loyal citizen of the United Kingdom ought in general, and as a paramount duty, to obey the law of the land, or, *in other words, the clearly and indubitably expressed will of the nation. But … such obedience can be due only when a law is the clear and undoubted expression of the will of the nation.*[46] (emphasis added)

When Dicey said that Home Rule had been 'twice deliberately rejected by the electorate of the United Kingdom', he seemed to refer to the general elections of 1886 and 1895.[47] But only 1886 was fought on Home Rule. In 1895 the overt issues of the election were elsewhere, including the government's alleged failure to equip the Army. The overwhelming issue in 1900 was the Boer War. Even then, the Unionists won a bare majority of votes cast (Table 2). But if every seat had been contested, the Home Rule coalition would probably have won a majority of votes in 1895.

Dicey celebrated 'the old Whig doctrine that oppression, and especially resistance to the will of the nation, might justify what was technically conspiracy or rebellion'.[48] This echoed his party leader, Bonar Law, who said, 'I can imagine no length of resistance to which Ulster can go in which I should not be prepared to support them'.[49] In 1914 Dicey wrote,

> Unionists must applaud every word of one of the noblest utterances of Sir Edward Carson: '… The first time the Government tries by means of the Army to enforce the Bill, that moment will the manhood of England rise and declare "You shall not do this terrible thing"'.[50]

All of these positions contravene parliamentary supremacy, but also the rule of law.

English and other common law public lawyers are still strangely protective of Dicey. They often do not regard his polemics as 'really' part of Dicey's writings. But he wrote them; he called his opponents delusional in the title of one of them and fools in another.[51] Why is it inappropriate to read them together, and thence to argue that his oeuvre is contradictory? The most recent attempt to defend

[46] Dicey, *A Fool's Paradise* 112–14.
[47] ibid 112; see also Dicey, *The Parliament Act 1911* 86.
[48] Dicey, *A Fool's Paradise* 125.
[49] A Bonar Law, speech delivered 27 July 1912, reprinted in R Blake, *The Unknown Prime Minister: The Life and Times of Andrew Bonar Law, 1858–1923* (London, Eyre & Spottiswoode, 1955) 130. See also 'Mr. Law on Ulster's Resistance' *The Times*, 29 July 1912, 7F.
[50] AV Dicey, 'The Enigma Still Unsolved? (II) Facts and Thoughts for Unionists' (1914) 75 *The Nineteenth Century* 717, 718.
[51] AV Dicey, *Letters on Unionist Delusions* (London, Macmillan, 1887); Dicey, *A Fool's Paradise*.

Dicey does review several of the polemics (not all of them),[52] but has considerable difficulty with his racism, misogyny, and abandonment of sovereignty.

## V. Scotland, Nationalism and Constitutional Statutes

Dicey's attitude towards Scotland was initially dismissive. In 1882, in an article entitled 'Why do people hate Mr Gladstone?' Dicey offered four explanations, one being that 'Mr Gladstone is by descent a Scotchman', and that 'educated Englishmen' were both put off by the 'vehemence, the warmth, the hortatory morality of the pulpit' but also found them 'dull'.[53] Nearly all references to Scotland in *Law of the Constitution* are examples of continuing parliamentary supremacy, denying any Scottish institutional autonomy. In addition to implied repeal and the Dentists Act, Dicey argued that efforts to entrench the Treaty and Acts of Union 1706–7 failed because Parliament abolished the requirement that professors at Scottish universities subscribe to the Westminster Confession of Faith.[54] The theory behind Dicey 1 incorporates a single, central source of political power, to the exclusion of any real delegation of governmental authority. Scottish national identity presented a threat to that position. It still does, as does the status of Northern Ireland under the Good Friday (Belfast) Agreement of 1998.

In 1886 Dicey claimed, in anti-Catholic mode, that 'from the commencement of their ill-starred connection' Ireland and England had 'been countries standing on different levels or at different stages of civilization' and that the 'passion of Irish peasants for the possession of land' was somehow evidence for this,[55] whereas the passion of dukes for the possession of land was apparently not. He deplored the:

> monstrosity of imposing Anglican Protestantism upon a people who had not reached the stage of development which is essential for even the understanding of Protestant dogma, and who if left to themselves would have adhered to Catholicism.[56]

Dicey had supported Italian unification, but he rejected Irish Home Rule on the basis that the Irish had not yet reached a level of development suited to a self-governing people. His approach to Scottish (but not Irish) nationalism became more sympathetic in old age. Scotland was a Protestant-majority country. Dicey started visiting Scotland every year, and befriended Robert Rait, the Historiographer Royal for Scotland.[57] In 1920 they published *Thoughts on the*

[52] Walters, *Dicey and the Common Law Tradition* 378–404.
[53] AV Dicey, 'Why Do People Hate Mr Gladstone?' (1883) XXXV *The Nation* 218.
[54] Dicey, *Lectures Introductory* 40.
[55] AV Dicey, *England's Case against Home Rule* (London, J Murray, 1886) 79–80.
[56] ibid 89.
[57] Dicey and Rait, *Memorials* 197; Cosgrove, *Rule of Law* 289.

*Union between England & Scotland.* There they emphasised the importance of the statutory protection of the Church of Scotland in the union of 1707. They described that settlement as 'a real treaty or contract between England and Scotland, [having] the leading characteristic of a contract between individual persons'.[58] The special virtue of such a contract was that it provided benefits to both parties. This is a historically accurate view of the negotiations of 1706–7. They admitted that 'The extension to Scotland of the supreme authority of Parliament is not recorded by a single word in the Act of Union. It may well be doubted whether, either in England or in Scotland, it was clearly realised or perceived'.[59] On Dicey's contractual theory of the union, parliamentary supremacy could hardly be binding on Scotland.

Although Dicey and Rait continued to refer incorrectly to a single 'Act of Union', they contradicted Dicey's earlier dismissal of the second, English, Act of Union as an ordinary statute. The Scots Parliament, moving first, put entrenchment of safeguards for the Church of Scotland into its Act, and made it a condition of Union that the English Parliament should carry over the Scottish entrenchment, while being free to add an entrenchment of its own church. The [English] Union with Scotland Act 1706, recited and incorporated at Article 25 the following from the prior Act of the Scottish Parliament:

> [T]he … true Protestant religion and the worship, discipline and government of this church [shall] continue without any alteration to the people of this land in all succeeding generations.[60]

Dicey and Rait called the Patronage Act 1711, which undermined the 1707 settlement, 'the chief and almost the only example' of a law 'passed in violation of the Act of Union',[61] which was 'the work of Tories meditating the restoration of the [Catholic] Stewarts'.[62] They explained:

> Englishmen … have … an intellectual difficulty derived really from their being accustomed to the sovereignty of Parliament, in admitting the possibility of any division of sovereignty between Church and State.[63]

Well, one Englishman did, apparently, until enlightened by his Scottish co-author.

Later judicial remarks also challenged Dicey 1. In 1953, Lord-President Cooper (the senior judge in the highest domestic Scottish court), citing Dicey and Rait, said:

> The principle of the unlimited sovereignty of Parliament is a distinctively English principle which has no counterpart in Scottish constitutional law …. [T]he Treaty and

[58] Dicey and Rait, *Thoughts* 182.
[59] ibid 242-43.
[60] Union with Scotland Act 1706 (6 Ann c 11).
[61] Dicey and Rait, *Thoughts* 280.
[62] ibid 283.
[63] ibid 244.

> the associated legislation, by which the Parliament of Great Britain was brought into being as the successor of the separate Parliaments of Scotland and England, contains some clauses … which emphatically exclude subsequent alteration …. I have never been able to understand how it is possible to reconcile with canons of construction the adoption by the English constitutional theorists of the same attitude to these markedly different types of provisions.[64]

In *Thoburn v Sunderland City Council*,[65] the lawyers for Thoburn, who had displayed weights in pounds and ounces on his market stall, argued, consistently with Dicey 1, that the Weights and Measures Act 1985 (which permitted imperial measurements) *pro tanto* implicitly repealed the European Communities Act 1972. Lord Justice Laws ruled against them (and Dicey 1) by distinguishing between 'ordinary' and 'constitutional' statutes, just as Dicey 3 did. He included in the latter class, which he said were immune from implied repeal by later, non-constitutional statutes, nearly all those that Dicey 3 wanted to protect with a referendum requirement: the Act of Settlement, the Acts of Union with Scotland, and the various Reform Acts, but not the Union with Ireland Act 1800.[66]

The tension between Dicey 1 and Dicey 3 has been evident in judgments about the United Kingdom's departure from the European Union. Dicey 1's parliamentary sovereignty appears in the judgment of the Supreme Court in the first *Miller* case, that the process giving rise to the United Kingdom's withdrawal could not be initiated by ministerial fiat.[67] Instead, parliamentary authority was necessary to give notice under Article 50 of the Treaty on European Union, that the United Kingdom was leaving the EU. Getting there, however, required consideration of 'seminal events', including the enactment of constitutional statutes that gave the government its current structure, including the Acts of Union of 1706 and 1707.[68] At the same time, the court rejected the argument of devolved administrations that their consent to withdrawal was required, including a claim that section 28(8) of the Scotland Act 1998 required legislative consent to trigger Article 50.[69] The court did so while still allowing, in an echo of Dicey 3, that 'the purpose of the legislative recognition' of the convention in the Scotland Act 2016, was 'to entrench it as a convention'.[70]

[64] *MacCormick* v *Lord Advocate* [1953] SC 396 at 411.
[65] *Thoburn v Sunderland City Council* [2003] QB 151.
[66] ibid 186; *cf* Dicey, *The Referendum and Its Critics* 554.
[67] *Miller v Secretary of State for Exiting the European Union* (*Miller 1*) [2017] UKSC 5, [2018] AC 61, [121].
[68] *Miller 1* at [41].
[69] *Miller 1* at [148]–[150].
[70] *Miller 1* at [149]; see also M Elliott, 'The Supreme Court's Judgment in Miller: In Search of Constitutional Principle' (2017) 76 *Cambridge Law Journal* 257; JEK Murkens, 'Mixed Messages in Bottles: The European Union, Devolution, and the Future of the Constitution' (2017) 80 *Modern Law Review* 685.

## VI. Conclusion

Conor Gearty has argued that Lord Reed, a Scottish judge who serves as the current President of the United Kingdom Supreme Court, has:

> a very un-Scottish veneration of parliamentary sovereignty .... Many judges over the years have realised that parliamentary sovereignty is an empty shell, that Parliament is a creature of the executive, and never has this been truer than after the Brexit landslide election of December 2019.[71]

He fears that the Supreme Court under its current President may retreat into formalism, factual particularism, and history. Dicey 1 absolutism seems currently in the ascendant in both the United Kingdom courts and the United Kingdom government, where it has been labelled as 'muscular unionism'.[72]

Dicey refused to see any analogy between the preservation of Scottish identity in 1706/7 and the demand for Irish Home Rule. Dicey 1 assumed a unitary United Kingdom, which he called 'England'. Dicey 2 attempted to prioritise the 'will of the nation,' as expressed in the hereditary House of Lords or even by his circle of friends there, and demonstrated the poverty of absolutism to solve real-world problems, which involve politics. But by the 1920s Dicey 3 and his co-author bemoaned the absence of English legal imagination and its inability to conceive of constitutional protections that might be stronger than any particular parliament.

Ivor Jennings dismissed Dicey's *Introduction to the Law of the Constitution* as 'a book of profound historical significance which need no longer be read'.[73] He is still being read, and so he should be read, warts and all. This is currently important because some politicians and lawyers take a strongly Diceyan (Dicey 1) line on Dicey's favourite subject – the Union of the United Kingdom. In the Northern Ireland case *Allister v Secretary of State for Northern Ireland*, the Unionist appellants made a Dicey 3 argument that the Acts of Union 1800 were constitutional statutes not subject to implied repeal.[74] The Supreme Court, however, held,

> The debate as to whether Article VI created fundamental rights ... whether the Acts of Union are statutes of constitutional character ... is academic. ... The most fundamental rule of UK constitutional law is that ... the Crown in Parliament, is sovereign and that legislation enacted by Parliament is supreme.[75]

[71] C Gearty, 'In the Shallow End' *London Review of Books*, 27 January 2022, https://www.lrb.co.uk/the-paper/v44/n02/conor-gearty/in-the-shallow-end.

[72] A Henderson and R Wyn Jones, *The Ambivalent Union: Findings from the State of the Union Survey* (London, Institute for Public Policy Research, 2023) 30, https://www.ippr.org/articles/the-ambivalent-union-findings-from-the-state-of-the-union-survey.

[73] I Jennings, 'Review of Dicey, Introduction to the Law of the Constitution (9th ed)' (1940) 3 *Modern Law Review* 321, 322.

[74] *Re Allister's Application for Judicial Review* [2023] UKSC 5, [2023] 2 WLR 457, [58].

[75] ibid [66].

To the appellants' 'Dicey 3', the court retorted 'Dicey 1'. Exactly like Dicey in 1914, the *Allister* appellants wished to retain the historic constitutional status of Northern Ireland. Dicey 3 can help them; Dicey 1 cannot.

In Scotland, the current Conservative United Kingdom government supports Dicey 1, and Scottish legal nationalists support Dicey 3. Legal nationalism is not the same as political nationalism. The pre-eminent Scottish legal nationalists were professor Neil MacCormick (1941–2009), son of the petitioner in *MacCormick* v *Lord Advocate*, and the Scots judge Lord Rodger of Earlsferry (1944–2011). The Scots negotiators of the Treaty of Union, as Dicey and Rait as well as Lord Cooper acknowledged, meant their protections of the Scottish church and Scots law to be perpetual. This is recognised in the text of the Accession Oath that King Charles III has recently sworn.[76] Furthermore, the church disruption controversies of the 1830s and 1840s, and some unhelpful legal judgments in the 1900s[77] were put to rest by the Church of Scotland Act 1921.[78] This Act flies in the face of Dicey 1. It enacts that the doctrine of the Church of Scotland is as determined by its General Assembly and may not be altered by Parliament (except by explicit repeal). Scottish legal nationalists therefore welcome *Thoburn*'s distinction between constitutional and other statutes and the suggestion that a constitutional statute may only be modified explicitly and by a later constitutional statute.

However, Dicey 1 hovers over the current constitutional settlement in Scotland. The Scotland Act 1998 states in section 28(7) that the creation of the Scottish Parliament 'does not affect the power of the Parliament of the United Kingdom to make laws for Scotland'.[79] In 2016 a more Dicey 3-ish subsection (8) was added: 'But it is recognised that the Parliament of the United Kingdom will not normally legislate with regard to devolved matters without the consent of the Scottish Parliament'. But that section has been drawn into question by withdrawal from the European Union and the enactment of the United Kingdom Internal Market Act 2020 without the consent of the Scottish Parliament. As noted above, *Miller 1* rejected the Scottish government's claim that it should have been consulted, holding that the word 'normally' is to be interpreted by politicians, not courts.

Dicey 1's absolutism aspired to solve constitutional problems of the mid-1880s. However, he became involved in politics, endorsing Garibaldi's unification of Italy, supporting, then opposing, votes for women, as well as with his bugbear, Irish Home Rule. That forced him into political realism. Reconciling all the Diceys we have discussed here provides an interesting problem for intellectual

[76] 'His Majesty The King's Oath Relating to the Security of the Church of Scotland' (Royal Website, 10 September 2022), https://www.royal.uk/his-majesty-kings-oath-relating-security-church-scotland.

[77] *General Assembly of Free Church of Scotland v Overtoun* [1904] AC 515 (HL).

[78] A Rodger, *The Courts, the Church and the Constitution: Aspects of the Disruption of 1843* (Edinburgh, Edinburgh University Press, 2008).

[79] Scotland Act 1998, s 28(7).

historians. However, 'Dicey' as a unitary actor offers little to those concerned with the pressing problems of the twenty-first century, nor does it to constitutional lawyers. He need no longer be read.

# Appendix 1: Irish Election Results 1885–1910 and Imputation for Missing Values

The pattern of contests is that minority politicians often stood once or twice, got derisory vote shares, and did not contest later elections. In nationalist Ireland, numerous seats were also contested in 1892 between pro- and anti-Parnell nationalists, even though Parnell had died in 1891. Their joint vote total gives what may be a lower bound on the imputed nationalist vote in other, uncontested, elections. (A lower bound because it is reasonable to suppose that some nationalist voters sat out the internecine feud.)

We therefore estimate what the vote shares would have been if all seats in Ireland had been contested. Almost the only contests were intra-communal, among varieties of unionist in Unionist seats, and varieties of nationalist in Nationalist seats. After 1886, inter-communal contests occurred only in the few seats where Unionists (≈Protestants) and Nationalists (≈Catholics) voted in comparable numbers. In just three seats (Dublin St Stephen's Green, Tyrone N, and Tyrone S) no imputation is required as every election was contested by at least one Unionist and one Nationalist.

Candidates labelled 'Liberal' in the data source are deemed to be Unionist in 1885–86 and Nationalist thereafter.[80] The justification for this is that the formal split of the Liberal Party took place in 1887, after which Liberal Unionists are labelled LU in the data source. As some Liberal candidates in 1885 and 1886 were probably Gladstonians, this slightly depresses the N imputation and increases the U imputation.

Our complete spreadsheet is available on request.

## A. The Imputation Method

(1) Seat with no contests at all (Donegal West). U vote share imputed at 2.5 per cent in line with U share in comparable seats in 1885. Turnout imputed at 75 per cent in line with comparable seats.

[80] FWS Craig, *British Electoral Facts 1832–1987* (Dartmouth, Parliamentary Research Services, 1989); BM Walker, *Parliamentary Election Results in Ireland, 1801–1922* (Dublin, Royal Irish Academy, 1978).

(2) Unionist seats with only intra-communal contests (Antrim Mid, Antrim East, Belfast East). U vote extrapolated from contested intra-U elections. N vote imputed at 2.5 per cent of U vote.
(3) Nationalist seats with only intra-communal contests (Cork N, Cork NE, Galway Connemara, Galway N, Galway S, Kerry N, Kildare S, Kilkenny City, Limerick W, Limerick E, Louth N, Louth S, Mayo N, Mayo E, Meath N, Meath S). N vote extrapolated from contested intra-N elections. U vote imputed at 2.5 per cent of N vote.
(4) Unionist seats where Nationalist candidates contested three or fewer elections (Antrim N, Antrim S, Armagh N, Armagh Mid, Belfast S, Down N, Down E, Down W). N and U votes extrapolated from mean in contested elections.
(5) Nationalist seats where Unionist candidates contested three or fewer elections (Carlow, Cavan W, Cavan E, Clare W, Clare E, Cork City, Cork Mid, Cork E, Cork W, Cork S, Cork SE, Donegal N, Dublin College Green, Dublin Harbour, Dublin St Patrick's, Dublin Co. N, Kerry W, Kerry S, Kerry E, Kildare N, Kilkenny N, Kilkenny S, King's County (Birr), King's County (Tullamore), Leitrim N, Leitrim S, Limerick City, Longford N, Longford S, Mayo W, Mayo S, Queen's County (Ossory), Queen's County (Leix), Roscommon N, Roscommon S, Sligo N, Sligo S, Tipperary N, Tipperary Mid, Tipperary S, Tipperary E, Waterford City, Waterford W, Waterford E, Westmeath N, Westmeath S, Wexford N, Wexford S, Wicklow W). N and U votes extrapolated from mean in contested elections.
(6) Competitive seats (all other seats). Missing U and N votes in uncontested elections supplied by interpolation.

## B. Results

Uncontested seats lead to an undercount of both Unionist and Nationalist support in Ireland. But because Ireland was predominantly Nationalist, the undercount of Nationalist support is greater in every election except that of 1892, when most Nationalist seats were contested because of the Parnell split (even though Parnell was dead). The full matrix of imputations is available for those who wish to check our maths and assumptions. We estimate that the underlying Nationalist vote in Ireland was between 300,000 and 400,000, and the underlying Unionist vote was between 80,000 and 100,000. Splits between Nationalist factions tended to depress the Nationalist vote.

What happens when we plug these 'missing' votes back into the actual election results is shown in Table 3, viz, that if every seat in Ireland had been contested, the Home Rule coalition would have won all seven elections in the series.

# Appendix 2

**Table 1** Nominal Vote Shares and Seat Shares, General Elections 1886–1910

| Election | Con (and LU) | | Lib | | Lab | | Irish nationalist | | Other | | Pro Home Rule | | Anti Home Rule | |
|---|---|---|---|---|---|---|---|---|---|---|---|---|---|---|
| | Vote share | Seat share | Vote share | Seat share | Vote share | Seat share | Vote share | Seat share | Vote share | Seat share | Vote share | Seat share | Vote share | Seat share |
| 1886 | 51.42 | 58.66 | 45.18 | 28.66 | | | 3.41 | 12.69 | | | 48.59 | 41.35 | 51.42 | 58.66 |
| 1892 | 46.99 | 46.72 | 46.72 | 40.75 | 0.51 | 0.45 | 6.75 | 12.09 | 0.38 | 0.00 | 53.98 | 53.29 | 46.99 | 46.72 |
| 1895 | 49.25 | 61.34 | 45.58 | 26.42 | 0.96 | 0.00 | 3.93 | 12.24 | 0.28 | 0.00 | 50.47 | 38.66 | 49.25 | 61.34 |
| 1900 | 50.22 | 60 | 45.07 | 27.31 | 1.29 | 0.3 | 1.77 | 11.34 | 1.66 | 1.04 | 48.13 | 39.99 | 50.22 | 60.00 |
| 1906 | 43.05 | 23.43 | 48.98 | 59.70 | 5.86 | 4.48 | 0.62 | 12.39 | | | 55.46 | 76.57 | 43.05 | 23.43 |
| 1910J | 46.75 | 40.75 | 43.03 | 41.04 | 7.58 | 5.97 | 1.90 | 12.24 | | | 52.51 | 59.25 | 46.75 | 40.75 |
| 1910D | 46.26 | 40.60 | 43.82 | 40.60 | 7.10 | 6.27 | 2.52 | 12.54 | | | 53.44 | 59.41 | 46.26 | 40.60 |
| | | | | | | | | | | Mean | 51.80 | 52.65 | 47.71 | 47.36 |
| | | | | | | | | | | Standard Deviation | 2.80 | 13.82 | 2.82 | 13.82 |

*Source*: FWS Craig, British Electoral Facts 1832–1987 (Dartmouth, Parliamentary Research Services, 1989).

# Appendix 3

**Table 2** Vote Shares for Elections, 1886–1910

| Election | Unionist | Liberal | Labour | Irish | Other | Unionist | Home Rule |
|---|---|---|---|---|---|---|---|
| 1886 | 51.42 | 45.18 | | 3.41 | | 51.42 | 48.59 |
| 1892 | 46.99 | 46.72 | 0.51 | 6.75 | 0.38 | 46.99 | 53.98 |
| 1895 | 49.25 | 45.58 | 0.96 | 3.93 | 0.28 | 49.25 | 50.47 |
| 1900 | 50.22 | 45.07 | 1.29 | 1.77 | 1.66 | 50.22 | 48.13 |
| 1906 | 43.05 | 48.98 | 5.86 | 0.62 | | 43.05 | 55.46 |
| 1910J | 46.75 | 43.03 | 7.58 | 1.90 | | 46.75 | 52.51 |
| 1910D | 46.26 | 43.82 | 7.10 | 2.52 | | 46.26 | 53.44 |

# Appendix 4

**Table 3** Imputed Vote Shares and Seat Shares, General Elections 1886–1910

| Election | Con (and LU) | | | Lib | | | Lab | | | Irish nationalist | | | Other | | | Pro Home Rule | | Anti Home Rule | |
|---|---|---|---|---|---|---|---|---|---|---|---|---|---|---|---|---|---|---|---|
| | Votes | Vote share | Seat share | Votes | Vote share | Seat share | Votes | Vote share | Seat share | Votes | Vote share | Seat share | Votes | Vote share | Seat share | Vote share | Seat share | Vote share | Seat share |
| 1886 | 1462863 | 47.37 | 58.66 | 1245930 | 40.35 | 28.66 | 0 | | | 379165 | 12.28 | 12.69 | 0 | | | **52.63** | 41.35 | **47.37** | 58.66 |
| 1892 | 2103145 | 47.40 | 46.72 | 1962170 | 44.22 | 40.75 | 27036 | 0.61 | 0.45 | 344472 | 7.76 | 12.09 | 137 | 0.00 | 0.00 | **52.60** | 53.29 | **47.40** | 46.72 |
| 1895 | 1855055 | 47.92 | 61.34 | 1632138 | 42.16 | 26.42 | 40511 | 1.05 | 0.00 | 343188 | 8.87 | 12.24 | 52 | 0.00 | 0.00 | **52.08** | 38.66 | **47.92** | 61.34 |
| 1900 | 1748822 | 48.61 | 60.00 | 1475923 | 41.03 | 27.31 | 45440 | 1.26 | 0.3 | 322345 | 8.96 | 11.34 | 4800 | 0.13 | 0.00 | **51.39** | 38.95 | **48.61** | 60.00 |
| 1906 | 2393991 | 42.58 | 23.43 | 2567225 | 45.66 | 59.70 | 311252 | 5.54 | 4.48 | 336706 | 5.99 | 12.39 | 12780 | 0.23 | 0.00 | **57.32** | 76.57 | **42.58** | 23.43 |
| 1910J | 3009349 | 46.15 | 40.75 | 2717748 | 41.68 | 41.04 | 459185 | 7.04 | 5.97 | 321944 | 4.94 | 12.24 | 12309 | 0.19 | 0.00 | **53.79** | 59.25 | **46.15** | 40.75 |
| 1910D | 2357610 | 45.66 | 40.60 | 2159202 | 41.82 | 40.60 | 315696 | 6.11 | 6.27 | 330212 | 6.39 | 12.54 | 970 | 0.02 | 0.00 | **54.46** | 59.41 | **45.66** | 40.60 |
| Mean | | | | | | | | | | | | | | | | 51.80 | 52.65 | 47.71 | 47.36 |
| Standard Deviation | | | | | | | | | | | | | | | | 2.80 | 13.82 | 2.82 | 13.82 |

*Sources*: FWS Craig, *British Electoral Facts 1832–1987* (Dartmouth, Parliamentary Research Services, 1989); BM Walker, *Parliamentary Election Results in Ireland, 1801–1922* (Dublin, Royal Irish Academy, 1978).

# Conclusion: The High Priest of Orthodox Constitutional Theory: AV Dicey Revisited

MARK D WALTERS

Albert Venn Dicey was appointed to the Vinerian Professorship of English Law and fellow of All Souls, Oxford, in late 1882, and his friend Frederick Pollock was appointed Professor of Jurisprudence and fellow of Corpus Christi College soon after. Both now held famous chairs in law. Yet Dicey enjoyed something Pollock did not: access to the extensive collection of legal books held in the All Souls Codrington Library. Dicey saw no sense in this and went to bat for Pollock. In October of 1883, he wrote to the Warden of All Souls, Sir William Anson, to argue that Pollock should be offered a key to the Codrington Library. 'I am convinced', he wrote, 'that such an offer would do a great deal to promote the study of law'.[1]

The Codrington Library was not just the best repository of law books in Oxford, but it was and remains a kind of shrine to the inaugural Vinerian professor of English law, Sir William Blackstone, whose marble statue dominates the main room. Dicey did not see eye to eye with Blackstone on all aspects of constitutional law. However, in his final lecture as Vinerian professor in 1909, Dicey celebrated the connection between Blackstone and law books, and in doing so intimated that the values of legality prized in English law are ultimately manifested through 'the union between law and letters', that is, through a distinctive style of legal writing.[2]

Over a century later, we now see leaders of the past and the statues and libraries built in their honour in a more complicated way. Today there is a plaque at the entrance to the All Souls Library which reads: 'In the memory of those who worked in slavery on the Codrington plantations in the West Indies'. This is a reminder, if one is needed, of the problematic reality of law's empire. I think Dicey might have appreciated the sentiments behind this plaque. His family

[1] AV Dicey to Sir W Anson, 5 October 1883, Anson Papers, All Souls College, Oxford, ff 51–53.

[2] AV Dicey, 'Blackstone's Commentaries' (December 1909) 65 *National Review* 653–75, reprinted (1932) 4 *Cambridge Law Journal* 286, 302.

played a significant part in the campaign to end the slave trade in the British Empire, and as a young lawyer he contributed to efforts to hold a colonial governor to account for crimes committed against former slaves in the West Indies.

Yet Dicey was also a committed imperialist who believed in extending English civilisation, especially legal values, to peoples across the seas. His obsession with imperial unity led him to troubling positions on Ireland. He was also, one might say, imperialistic at home too, at least in his later years, arguing against political equality for women and against the establishment of the modern welfare state. Dicey was a complex person. We are all products of our times and Dicey was and remained, as he liked to remind people, a 'mid-Victorian'.[3]

The essays collected in this volume are a testament to both the promise and problems of Dicey's contributions to constitutionalism. There are other collections of essays on Dicey. The 1985 collection in the journal *Public Law* celebrated the centenary of the first edition of Dicey's book, *Law of the Constitution*,[4] but with the exception of one essay written from a French perspective they focused on the law of the United Kingdom.[5] The recent collection that marks the centenary of Dicey's death, *Dicey + 100*, covers Dicey's contributions in a broader sense, including essays on legal education, the conflict of laws, and Ireland.[6] However, the volume for which I am now writing these closing remarks is distinctive in its own way. It focuses on Dicey's work relating to constitutionalism, but it includes, in addition to common law perspectives, contributions from legal and political theorists and historians from France.

It has been said that Dicey's work was based upon a 'xenophobic antipathy to France'.[7] Indeed, Dicey was hard on France – or at least French *droit administratif*. Still, Dicey was fascinated by France and was treated with respect by some French scholars. His work resonated with that of Émile Boutmy, whose book Dicey's wife, Elinor (Bonham-Carter) translated into English.[8] Dicey was a constitutional comparativist. It was reading his (then) unpublished manuscripts on comparative constitutionalism in the Codrington Library that led me to write about Dicey in the first place.[9] Nicolas Gabayet may be right in saying that Dicey's portrayal of

[3] AV Dicey to James Bryce, 4 August 1911, James Bryce Papers, Bodleian Library, Oxford University, 3: 100–108 (hereafter *Bryce Papers*).

[4] AV Dicey, *Introduction to the Study of the Law of the Constitution* [1st edn 1885], 8th edn (London, Macmillan, 1915).

[5] R Errera, 'Dicey and French Administrative Law: A Missed Encounter?' (1985) *Public Law* 695.

[6] A Dickinson et al (eds), *Dicey + 100: Albert Venn Dicey: A Centennial Commemoration* (Cambridge, Intersentia, 2024).

[7] S Sedley, *Lions under the Throne: Essays on the History of English Public Law* (Cambridge, Cambridge University Press, 2015) 270.

[8] E Boutmy, *Études de droit constitutionnel : France – Angleterre – États-Unis* (Paris, E Plon, Nourrit et Cie, 1885); E Boutmy, *Studies in Constitutional Law France – England – United States*, EM Dicey, trans (London, Macmillan & Co, 1891).

[9] See JWF Allison (ed), *The Oxford Edition of Dicey*, vol II: *Comparative Constitutionalism* (Oxford, Oxford University Press, 2013).

French and English public law as opposing ideal-types discouraged comparative law scholarship in the field.[10] But perhaps this might change. For now, however, we may surmise that Dicey would have been pleased by the cross-Channel aspect to the present collection of essays.

It is an honour to be asked by the editors to write a conclusion for this volume. They suggested that I might see the task as an opportunity to reflect critically upon my own book on Dicey, *A.V. Dicey and the Common Law Constitutional Tradition: A Legal Turn of Mind*.[11] As I read the essays, I realised that their range and richness would made this task both daunting and rewarding. In my remarks, I will not try to engage with each chapter in detail. I will instead identify some broad themes about Dicey's work that are covered in this volume that I did not cover, or cover well, in my own book, and provide some observations. My comments will be suggestive and incomplete, but perhaps will provide avenues for further consideration. The themes I have in mind are: Dicey and law today – the Brexit cases (I); Dicey, sovereignty, and state (II); Dicey, liberalism, and administrative law (III); Dicey, women, race, and empire (IV); and, Dicey and the morality of legal biography (V).

## I. Dicey and Law Today – The Brexit Cases

A number of chapters in this book consider Dicey's impact on public law in different jurisdictions historically and today. The present status of Dicey's ideas is contested. In his chapter, Vernon Bogdanor (who also contributed an essay to the *Public Law* collection some 40 years ago[12]) argues there is very little left of Dicey's constitution in the United Kingdom. Adam Tomkins says most of it is still left. As I was intent upon assessing Dicey's work on its own terms, this topic was not one I considered in my book on Dicey. I therefore left the momentous decisions of the United Kingdom Supreme Court on Brexit, *Miller 1*[13] and *Miller 2*,[14] unaddressed (though I did suggest that Dicey would have been shocked by the conclusion in *Miller 2*, which held a decision to prorogue Parliament to be unlawful, and might have needed, as a colleague suggested to me, a large Scotch to settle his nerves).[15]

[10] N Gabayet, 'Une page de l'histoire de la pensée du droit administratif : le "moment Dicey"' (2018) 21 *Jus Politicum* 415.

[11] M Walters, *A.V. Dicey and the Common Law Constitutional Tradition: A Legal Turn of Mind* (Cambridge, Cambridge University Press, 2020).

[12] V Bogdanor, 'Dicey and the Reform of the Constitution' (1985) *Public Law* 652.

[13] *R (Miller) v Secretary of State for Exiting the European Union* [2017] UKSC 5, [2018] AC 61 (*Miller 1*).

[14] *R (Miller) v Prime Minister; Cherry v Advocate General for Scotland* [2019] UKSC 41, [2020] AC 373 (*Miller 2*).

[15] Walters, *AV Dicey and the Common Law Constitutional Tradition* 359.

Aurélien Antoine takes on Dicey and the Brexit cases in his chapter, approaching the question from a French legal perspective in which the relationship between judicial and academic writing is less direct than it is in common law jurisdictions. Dicey himself thought law professors 'can influence far more than is generally believed not the form only but the substance of the law',[16] and one reason he thought the Conseil d'État in France was becoming a real court of law (I leave to the side why he thought it was not one already) was because it was increasingly influenced by 'the writers of text-books and commentaries'.[17] In light of Antoine's essay, I wonder whether this last point is entirely accurate. I do agree, however, that Dicey's claim – academic work that brings unity and coherence to a body of rules and principles assists the judge's work in doing the same – is worthy of investigation.

Considering Dicey and Brexit may also tell us something about Dicey and the constitutional tradition he sought to explain. A few comments on *Miller 1* may be illustrative. In this case, the United Kingdom Supreme Court held that the British government did not have authority under the royal prerogative to trigger Britain's exit from the European Union after a referendum victory in favour of (so-called) Brexit, because Brexit would affect legal rights established in domestic law by the European Communities Act 1972 and the royal prerogative – the inherent powers of the executive – cannot be used by the Crown or its ministers to change, abrogate, or frustrate statute law. The case hinged on a technical question, whether the European Communities Act had overtaken or displaced the prerogative power of the Crown and its ministers to make and unmake international treaties relating to the European Union – but larger principles were at stake.

On one side of the equation was the power of the legislature. Here, the majority in *Miller 1* dutifully cited Dicey's famous account of parliamentary sovereignty.[18] On the other side was the question of executive power. Dicey was not expressly mentioned on this point, but he was here too. The majority defined the royal prerogative as 'the residue of powers which remain vested in the Crown' and cited two cases that, in turn, cited Dicey when adopting the same definition.[19] True, in one of those cases it was stated that Dicey's definition of the prerogative 'does not take us very far'.[20] But in *Miller 1* this definition provided a starting point that arguably coloured the entire analysis that followed.

Writing before the Supreme Court decided *Miller 1*, Dicey's successor as Vinerian professor, Timothy Endicott, observed that the royal prerogative is often

[16] AV Dicey, *Can English Law Be Taught At The Universities? An Inaugural Lecture, Delivered At All Souls College, 21st April 1883* (London, Macmillan, 1883) 24.

[17] AV Dicey, '*Droit Administratif* in Modern French Law' (1901) 17 *Law Quarterly Review* 302, 312.

[18] *Miller 1*, [43].

[19] *Miller 1*, [47], [48], citing *Burmah Oil Co Ltd v Lord Advocate* [1965] AC 75 (Lord Reid) and *Attorney-General v De Keyser's Royal Hotel* [1920] AC 508 (Lord Dunedin).

[20] *Burmah Oil*, Lord Reid at 99.

seen as an 'unprincipled holdover of autocracy', a 'remnant of arbitrary power', or a 'stubborn stain' on the law to be removed, an attitude that the Diceyan residue theory encourages, and this attitude may well leave one predisposed to think that, in this case, an ancient prerogative power had been overtaken by a modern statute and withdrawal from the EU therefore required another statute.[21] But a different starting point might justify a different outcome. Endicott argued that we should start with a more robust account of executive power, one that, in the words of the first Vinerian professor, secures for the executive 'unanimity, strength and dispatch' when addressing 'the exigencies of state'.[22] This robust executive power cannot be so easily displaced by statute. Endicott's analysis was influential. The Blackstonian starting point for the prerogative seemed to produce a different result for at least one judge: in his dissenting reasons in *Miller 1*, Lord Reed quoted the same passage from Blackstone that Endicott did and concluded that the prerogative power to withdraw from the European Union remained intact.[23]

Endicott's argument about Brexit resonates with his contribution to this volume on Dicey's understanding of the 'parliamentary executive'. Endicott is concerned that Dicey's focus on parliamentary sovereignty (legislative power) and the rule of law (judicial power) fails to account for the central and enduring role of the executive as an independent and distinctive source of power. From this perspective, the prerogative is not a dispensable relic but is inherent and integral to the good government of the state. 'Many things there are', wrote John Locke in a passage quoted by Endicott, 'which the law can by no means provide for; and those must necessarily be left to the discretion of him that has the executive power in his hands, to be ordered by him as the public good and advantage shall require'.[24] Locke goes on to say in this passage that 'it is fit that the laws themselves should in some cases give way to the executive power, or rather to this fundamental law of nature and government'.[25] Returning to Blackstone, although he located legislative sovereignty with the King-in-Parliament, he also insisted that 'the supreme executive power' or the 'prerogatives of sovereign power' or the 'attribute of sovereignty' which consists of the 'executive part of government', lies with the King alone.[26] Indeed, Blackstone's definition of the royal prerogative, as 'that

[21] T Endicott, 'This Ancient, Secretive Royal Prerogative' (*UK Constitutional Law Blog*, 11 November 2016), https://ukconstitutionallaw.org/. Also, T Endicott, *The Stubborn Stain Theory of Executive Power: From Magna Carta to Miller* (London, Policy Exchange, 2017) 13.

[22] Endicott, 'This Ancient, Secretive Royal Prerogative' (quoting W Blackstone, *Commentaries on the Laws of England 1765–69* (Oxford, Oxford University Press, 2016) Book 1, 162.

[23] *Miller 1* [160].

[24] T Endicott, *The Stubborn Stain Theory of Executive Power: From Magna Carta to Miller* (London, Policy Exchange, 2017), 12, quoting J Locke, *Second Treatise on Government* (1690) ch xiv, para 159.

[25] For forceful criticism of Endicott for his use of Locke, see T Poole, 'Losing our Religion? Public Law and Brexit' (*UK Constitutional Law Blog*, 2 December 2016), https://ukconstitutionallaw.org/, and T Poole, 'The Strange Death of Prerogative in England' (2018) 43 *University of Western Australia Law Review* 42.

[26] 1 *Bl. Comm.* 190, 241, 250.

especial pre-eminence, which the king hath, over and above all other persons, and out of the ordinary course of the common law, in right of his regal dignity', was lifted from the work of John Cowell, the controversial civilian who put the King above both common law and statute law in the early seventeenth century.[27] This is a strong version of executive power. Blackstone's reliance upon Cowell when defining the prerogative led to the charge that he had not fully escaped Roman absolutism.[28]

Whether *Miller 1* was really a contest between Diceyan and Blackstonian visions of executive power is open to debate.[29] But framing the case in this way helps us to understand the central questions about constitutionalism in the common law tradition. Others in Dicey's day accepted the Blackstonian conception of sovereign 'dualism' whereby state sovereignty is divided into legislative sovereignty and executive sovereignty.[30] But Dicey did not. He located legal sovereignty in the King-in-Parliament, leaving the King or King-in-Council without any sovereign powers at all. Once we attend to this fundamental point, many of the confusing or concerning parts of Dicey's account of the Constitution begin to make sense – including his distinctive approach to states of emergency, his attachment to the concept of ordinary law, his concerns about the French civilian tradition, his scepticism of constituent power, and his challenging argument that parliamentary sovereignty and the rule of law are intimately linked and reconcilable legal principles – or at least so I have tried to argue.[31]

By objecting to a concept of executive power that is 'out of the ordinary course of the common law' (Blackstone) or defined by a 'fundamental law of nature and government' different from rest of 'the law' (Locke), Dicey rejects the long juridical tradition explained eloquently by Martin Loughlin that conceives of an extraordinary law of state that both generates ordinary law and authorises executive exceptions to ordinary law.[32] He insists instead upon a common law tradition that sees ordinary law as enveloping and conditioning all state institutions all the time, including (especially) executive power in both mundane and exceptional

[27] 1 *Bl. Comm.* 232. *cf* J Cowell, *The Interpreter: or Booke containing the signification of words … mentioned in the lawe writers, or statutes* (Cambridge, Iohn Legate, 1607), entry for 'Prerogative' [no pagination] (prerogative is 'that especial power, pre-eminence, or privilege that the King has in any kind, over and above the ordinary course of the common law, in the right of his Crown').

[28] CK Allen, *Law in the Making* (Oxford, Clarendon Press, 1927) 9, 12.

[29] R Craig, 'Casting Aside Clanking Medieval Chains: Prerogative, Statute and Article 50 after the EU Referendum' (2016) 79 *Modern Law Review* 1041, 1043. Despite using Dicey's definition of prerogative, the majority insisted that the characterisation of the prerogative as a 'relic of a past age' should not be understood as implying that it is 'anomalous or anachronistic': *Miller 1* [49].

[30] Sir WR Anson, *The Law and Custom of the Constitution. Part I Parliament* (Oxford, Clarendon Press, 1886) 4, 37, 39; JW Salmond, *Jurisprudence, or The Theory of the Law* (London, Stevens & Haynes, 1902) 630.

[31] Walters, *AV Dicey and the Common Law Constitutional Tradition*. Also, M Walters, 'Public Law and Ordinary Legal Method: Revisiting Dicey's Approach to *Droit Administratif*' (2016) 66 *University of Toronto Law Journal* 53.

[32] M Loughlin, *Foundations of Public Law* (Oxford, Oxford University Press, 2010); M Walters, 'Is Public Law Ordinary?' (2012) 75 *Modern Law Review* 899.

circumstances. In my book, I argued that understanding this compelling account of constitutionalism is one reason to reread Dicey today. But I acknowledge that this version of the common law constitutional tradition, and of Dicey, was and remains contested, as the work on the executive by the present Vinerian professor illustrates.

## II. Dicey, Sovereignty, and State

The basic structure of Dicey's constitutional thought that I have just summarised is not at first obvious from his writings. My own Dicey project has been, as Gregory Bligh in his contribution to this volume describes it, one of 'reconstruction'. The challenge for this task is that it seeks answers about the common law constitutional tradition from someone who, despite all of his celebrated analytical powers, worked within a distinctively common law mindset. History and theory were important to Dicey, but they were ancillary to the pragmatic objective he set for himself of expounding the constitution from the internal perspective of the common lawyer. The task is further complicated by the fact when Dicey turned to historians or theorists, he went to those close at hand for the mid-Victorian jurist, Bagehot, Hearn, Maine, and (especially) Austin, and on the big questions of sovereignty and state we are left wondering how Dicey's views fit within the grand theories of Bodin and Hobbes.

It is not surprising, then, to find contributors to this volume grappling with Dicey's distinction between political and legal sovereignty (chapters by Michael Lobban, Gregory Bligh, and Adam Tomkins) and his failure to offer a theory of state (Bligh, Tomkins), and suggesting that by 'legal sovereignty' or 'parliamentary sovereignty' perhaps Dicey used the wrong word and did not mean 'sovereignty' at all (Lobban, Tomkins). We want to see a linear and rational progression of power and principle, from the exercise of sovereign constituent power by the nation, to the establishment of a state and constitution, to the exercise by institutions thus constituted of powers to make, interpret, and execute ordinary laws – only to find Dicey upsetting logic by claiming that there is no difference between fundamental and ordinary law, between constitutive and constituted powers. If you wish to use 'the political phraseology of foreign countries', he says, then you can find the 'constituent' power lodged in the very institution that makes ordinary law – Parliament.[33]

Upon reflection, I do not think that this non-linear constitutionalism is peculiar to Dicey. Sometimes it takes an outsider to notice the essential features of a practice or tradition, and the striking language used by Émile Boutmy (as translated by Elinor Dicey) to describe the English constitution is telling: 'The nation'– the

[33] Dicey, *Law of the Constitution* 1885, 81–82; Dicey, *Law of the Constitution* 1915, 84–85.

English people who designed the constitutional settlement of 1688–89 – 'reminds us not of a theorist discussing his reasons, but of a proprietor with an old title going into court with his title-deeds', '[t]he great political powers in England are in no way the creations of a constitution (*pouvoir constituant*), for their existence is anterior to any fundamental law whatever'.[34] We could try to fix Dicey and say that when he refers to political sovereignty he means sovereign constituent power and when he refers to legal sovereignty he means legally constituted authority not sovereignty. But I continue to think that he really meant that legal sovereignty is *sovereignty* because, in the common law tradition, ordinary law folds back upon, explains, even conditions sovereign power and the difference between constitutive and constituted power, so important to other legal traditions, simply never applies.[35]

## III. Dicey, Liberalism, and the Administrative State

A message linking several contributions to this volume is that we should return to Dicey's 1905 book *Law and Public Opinion* if we are interested in understanding Dicey's legal and political thought fully. *Law and Opinion* is a sprawling account of the impact of the currents and cross-currents of public opinion in England on law reform over the course of the nineteenth century, moving through phases that Dicey identified as Tory Quiescence, Benthamite Individualism, and Collectivism. The relationship between Dicey and the central figure in this story, Jeremy Bentham, emerges from the essays as a curious, even mysterious one.

Doubts are raised about just how much Bentham Dicey read. In his essay, Michael Lobban wonders whether Dicey's knowledge of Bentham came from his reading Leslie Stephen's *English Utilitrarians*.[36] In fact, Dicey conceded that Stephen's knowledge of Benthamism was 'infinitely greater than I could pretend to'.[37] 'I am glad I lectured [referring to his 1898 lectures at Harvard that led to *Law and Opinion*] before my cousin published & before I read his book', Dicey wrote privately, otherwise everyone (himself included) would have thought that 'whatever merit there was in the lectures was the result of petty larceny'.[38] Lobban and Gregory Bligh suggest that Dicey would have benefited from a deeper reading of Bentham, both pointing to the advantages of Bentham's

[34] E Boutmy, *Studies in Constitutional Law France – England – United States*, EM Dicey (transl) (London, Macmillan & Co, 1891) 40, 148–519.

[35] Walters, *AV Dicey and the Common Law Constitutional Tradition* 178–87.

[36] L Stephen, *The English Utilitarians* (London, Duckworth & Co, 1900).

[37] AV Dicey to Charles Eliot, 5 December 1898, Charles W Eliot Papers, UAI 5.150, Box 36, Harvard University Archives.

[38] AV Dicey to Charles E Norton, 19 March 1901, Charles Eliot Norton Papers, MS Am 1088.14, no 1747, Houghton Library Harvard.

complex reflections on the relationship between people, sovereigns, and limitations on sovereign power over Austin's simple model. I think the same could be said of Bentham and the rule of law.[39]

In *Law and Opinion*, Dicey was less concerned about Bentham's ideas as such and more interested in the way he says they came to dominate political discourse in a 'loose' and 'common sense' way 'under the name of liberalism', by which he meant *laissez-faire* individualism.[40] An anonymous reviewer of *Law and Opinion* observed that although Dicey 'in many phrases here and there makes one suspect that his sympathies took a bias in the earlier period when individualism was triumphant, he is strictly the impartial historian and his book is not in any sense controversial'.[41] In his contribution to this volume, Alex Middleton states that Dicey in *Law and Opinion* 'was not a programmatic thinker … [with] an inflexible idealist scheme to apply, but was instead a cautious, uncertain, and strikingly materially-minded analyst of political and intellectual change'. Alan Kahan, however, reads the book very differently. In his contribution to this volume, Kahan argues that Dicey's book was never intended to be a history of ideas, but was rather a reconstruction of the genealogy of liberal thought meant to advance his own distinctive vision of classical liberalism. Dicey emerges as one of the most important influences on liberal political thought of the twentieth century.

Kahan's reading of *Law and Opinion* raises again the question about how to read Dicey's account of the rule of law in *Law of the Constitution*. His argument reinforces a view perhaps most famously made by Ivor Jennings, that the rule of law as articulated in *Law of the Constitution* is 'the subconscious reaction of Dicey's Whig mind against the intervention of the State in economic life'[42] and thus his rule of law is nothing but 'a rule of action for Whigs and may be ignored by others', especially those interested in building modern administrative law.[43] Dicey's classical liberalism may have had a 'subconscious' impact on how he explained the rule of law, but I continue to think that his liberal fear of collectivism was not the driving motive. In 1885, Dicey simply had yet to fear the regulatory state in the way that he later would. In *Law and Opinion*, he says the influence of collectivism on legislation did not become perceptible until 1868 or 1870, or dominant until about 1880.[44] Dicey's writings on social policy from the early 1880s are less overtly ideological than they would later become. I argued in my book that the principal

[39] Walters, *AV Dicey and the Common Law Constitutional Tradition* 92–93.

[40] Dicey, *Law and Public Opinion* 169–70, 171.

[41] 'Professor Dicey on Legislation', *Saturday Review of Politics, Literature, Science and Art*, 100:2594 (15 July 1905) 86–87.

[42] WI Jennings, 'Courts and Administrative Law: The Experience of English Housing Legislation' (1936) 49 *Harvard Law Review* 426, 430.

[43] WI Jennings, *The Law and the Constitution* (London, University of London Press, 1933) 256. For a similar claim, see W Burnett Harvey, 'The Rule of Law in Historical Perspective' (1961) 59 *Michigan Law Review* 487, 493. Of course, Jennings' view of the constitution was informed by his political viewpoint: KD Ewing, 'The Law and the Constitution: Manifesto of the Progressive Party' (2004) 67 *Modern Law Review* 734.

[44] Dicey, *Law and Public Opinion* 66.

concerns Dicey then had can be characterised as the 'existential challenge' rather than the 'regulatory challenge for executive power and the state.[45]

We know how Dicey's rule of law can be read to support the classical, individualist liberal state – to obstruct the 'new despotism' that Dicey's arch-conservative admirers feared so much.[46] That is easy. I think the more interesting question is how can Dicey's work offer a productive way of imaging legality in the modern, regulatory liberal state? Dicey may have objected to the emergence of such a state, but, returning *Law and Opinion*, I think we can say his ideological preferences were coupled with a basic sense of pragmatism. He saw the inevitability of the administrative state, and offered a few fragmentary hints of how a 'Diceyan' might respond in a positive way.[47] Reading Dicey as a unifier rather than divider may help us to work through this ongoing challenge.

Indeed, the contributions to this volume by Nicolas Gabayet, Michael Greve, and Nicholas Dickinson show how the denier of administrative law shapes debates about modern administrative law in the United Kingdom, the United States, and Canada in this way. Only in the United States, it seems, is Dicey being invoked in support of a 'ferocious' anti-administrative state agenda by certain scholars.[48] In all three common law jurisdictions, Dicey's main role is to serve as a kind of compass pointing in general directions on general questions without giving specific directions. The general directions on the Diceyan administrative law compass are now familiar: administrators should generally be subject to review by independent courts; reviewing courts should generally be generalist courts or administrative law branches thereof; legislative attempts to restrict or oust judicial review should be narrowly interpreted; judges should review administrators on a deferential standard on points of fact, policy, and specialised law but a less deferential standard on important or general points of law; common law principles of reasonableness and procedural fairness are either implicit in or imposed upon most statutorily delegated powers; that, in short, there should be a balance between administrative fairness and administrative efficiency.

## IV. Dicey, Women, Race, and Empire

In their contribution to this volume, Iain McLean and Scot Peterson raise the concern that my book on Dicey is an apologetic defence of a jurist who held morally offensive views. I will address this concern in this and the next section of

[45] Walters, *AV Dicey and the Common Law Constitutional Tradition* 248–49.

[46] Lord Hewart, *The New Despotism* (London, Ernest Benn, 1929); FA Hayek, *The Road to Serfdom* (London, George Routledge & Sons, 1944).

[47] AV Dicey, 'The Development of Administrative Law in England' (1915) 31 *Law Quarterly Review* 148.

[48] Greve cites P Hamburger, *Is Administrative Law Unlawful?* (Chicago, University of Chicago Press, 2014).

my comments. In this section, I will comment on their claim that I fail to address Dicey's 'misogyny' and 'racism'. In doing so, it will be necessary to consider the question of Dicey and empire, which is the subject of Nick Barber and Alex Middleton's chapters and is also addressed in the chapters by Richard Cullen and Nicholas Dickinson.

The concern that McLean and Peterson raise is not wholly unfounded. In the final editing phase, I left out draft chapters that addressed Dicey's views on women, race, federalism, and empire and the book may have an unbalanced feel as a result. I did address Dicey's arguments on female suffrage, and a racist statement Dicey made in the course of developing those arguments, but only briefly.[49] Much more needs to be said about Dicey's views about women. Françoise Orazi's chapter in this volume is therefore an important contribution, providing a careful analysis of Dicey's tortured arguments in his 1909 book *Letters to a Friend on Votes for Women*.[50] This is one topic on which Dicey did change his mind due to his obsession with Ireland. As he informed a friend, 'It has been no pleasure to me to oppose a movement in wh[ich] I at one time believed'.[51] He was remarkably candid in *Letters to a Friend* about one reason for his change of heart: his opposition to Irish Home Rule 'told in several respects upon the way in which I gradually came to look upon the movement in favour of woman suffrage'.[52]

In her essay, Orazi draws to our attention to Dicey's strained distinction between civil and political rights and Bertrand Russell's devastating response. The progress toward 'human freedom' has been, Dicey wrote, the result of extending 'civil or private rights' or 'personal freedom'.[53] Here Dicey purported to follow John Stuart Mill. He explained that the individual must be free to decide upon his (or her) own concerns, for 'his own concerns are his private or civil rights' subject only to 'the equal rights of his neighbours'.[54] He thought women already had equal civil rights. But, he continued, the rights of the individual in relation to 'matters which primarily concern the State' are 'public or political rights', or, in other words, 'duties or functions to be exercised … with a view to the interest of the State, and therefore may, even according to Mill's doctrine, be limited or extended in any way which conduces to the welfare of the community'.[55] Women, he thought, should be excluded from these rights. Dicey was blunt: 'personal freedom has little or nothing to do with participation in sovereign authority'.[56]

[49] Walters, *AV Dicey and the Common Law Constitutional Tradition* 378.
[50] AV Dicey, *Letters to a Friend on Votes for Women* (London, John Murray, 1909).
[51] AV Dicey to John St Loe Strachey, 30 May 1910, Papers of John St Loe, 5/5/19, Parliamentary Archives, United Kingdom Parliament.
[52] Dicey, *Letters to a Friend* 3.
[53] ibid 31–32.
[54] ibid 33–34.
[55] ibid.
[56] ibid 31.

Having defended the idea that equality in civil rights is consistent with inequality in political rights, Dicey concluded:

> Our constitution, resting as it does on the unquestionable supremacy of the civil power and the universal rule of equal law, is, with all its defects, the strongest, the freest, the most pacific, we may venture to say the most humane, form of government which has ever existed in any great State or Empire.[57]

The analysis is troubling on so many different levels it is hard to know where to begin. One thing is clear: as Orazi observes, Mill did not see liberty in this way. On the contrary, Mill argued that personal freedom implies a right to participate within the political life of the community, or the need to recognise 'political rights', for personal freedom is impossible to cultivate in any meaningful sense for those people who are 'left out of the constitution … [and] reduced to plead from outside the door to the arbiters of their destiny'.[58]

*Letters to a Friend* is concerning for theories of rights, democracy, and representation. As Michael Lobban and Gregory Bligh explain in their chapters, Dicey rejected the view of John Austin that the sovereign in Britain is the King, Lords, and the people who vote for representatives sitting in the Commons, and insisted instead that the King-in-Parliament, ie the King, Lords, and the elected representatives in the Commons, constitutes the legal sovereign whilst the electorate constitutes the political sovereign. In discussing this part of Dicey's work in my book, I explained how he overlooked an older common law discourse that defined Parliament as a corporate body politic embracing Crown, Lords, the Commons – *all* of them not just their elected representatives.[59] In part of the draft manuscript that did not find its way into my book, I sought to develop a link between Dicey's views on political rights in *Letters to a Friend* and his conclusion in *Law of the Constitution* that the electorate does not form part of the legal sovereign. The common law theory of Parliament as a single juridical entity that includes the electorate involves a special understanding of representation and thus of voting (which does not rely on Austin's idea of trusteeship and is consistent with Dicey's point that laws can only be made by the King, Lords, and representatives in the Commons). Closely connected to this understanding is the idea, articulated in *Ashby v White* by the Lord Chief Justice, Sir John Holt, that the right to vote was originally a common law right enforceable in a common law action 'on the case', or, in other words, a private law tort action.[60] Said Holt, 'every man, that is to give his vote on the election of members to serve in Parliament, has a several and particular right in his private capacity'; a man's right to vote for a representative to serve in Parliament who will 'concur to the making of laws, which are to bind his liberty and property' is 'a most transcendent thing'.[61] The line of logic here

[57] ibid 90.
[58] JS Mill, *Considerations on Representative Government* (London, Parker, Son & Bourn, 1861) 66, 177.
[59] Walters, *AV Dicey and the Common Law Constitutional Tradition* 165–75.
[60] *Ashby v White* (1703) 2 Ld Raym 938.
[61] ibid 953.

overlaps with Mill's arguments about political rights and voting, but is opposed to Dicey's. I am not suggesting that an eighteenth-century analysis of voting by property-owning men should be accepted today. My point, rather, is that had Dicey confronted the older common law understanding of Parliament, representation, and voting, he would not have been able to declare with such confidence in *Law of the Constitution* that the electorate is not part of part of the legal sovereign, or, later in *Letters to a Friend*, that there is no right to participate in the exercise of sovereign authority.

Gregory Bligh argues in his chapter that Dicey appeared to shift from defining the political sovereign as the electorate in *Law of the Constitution* to defining it in more amorphous terms as the mass of the people in *Law and Public Opinion*. Thinking about this point together with Orazi's chapter leads me to a thought I had not considered before. The electorate – the people with a right to vote – is a legal concept that by Dicey's day had long been defined by statute. Dicey's insistence that the legal sovereign, the King-in-Parliament, is constrained by the political sovereign, the electorate, looks rather strange once we recall that the electorate is a body constituted by Act of Parliament. Given Dicey's equation of the political sovereign with the electorate, we must say that, in his scheme, the legal sovereign creates the political sovereign; indeed, we may go so far as saying that the legal sovereign confers upon certain people a legal right (the right to vote) that then gives them the opportunity to exercise political sovereignty. The idea that political sovereignty is constituted by legal sovereignty seems a long way from Dicey's intended understanding of legal and political sovereignty. Or does it? Perhaps the line between political and legal sovereigns is permeable, that their relationship is reflexive or non-linear. Or perhaps using a legal concept, the electorate, to define the political sovereign is a problem avoided if, as Bligh suggests, Dicey moved to a non-legal body, the 'mass of the people', instead.

Turning now to Dicey and race, my book alludes to evidence of Dicey's progressive approach to racial relations and a racist comment found in his arguments about female suffrage and leaves the contradiction unresolved.[62] I intended to return to this question and I have recently made a start in an essay that confronts Dicey's ideas about race and equality.[63] I suggest in this essay that Dicey considered the idea of 'equality before the law' that forms an integral part of the rule of law as embracing a substantive understanding of racial (and religious) equality. Yet Dicey's ideas about racial equality and the rule of law cannot be separated from his views about empire, and as Dylan Lino has established, in his groundbreaking research, the imperial legacy of the rule of law is deeply problematic.[64]

[62] Walters, *AV Dicey and the Common Law Constitutional Tradition* 11, 56–57, 378.

[63] Walters, 'Dicey on Legality and Equality' in *Dicey + 100* 75–88.

[64] D Lino, 'Albert Venn Dicey and the Constitutional Theory of Empire' (2016) 36 *Oxford Journal of Legal Studies* 751; D Lino, 'The Rule of Law and the Rule of Empire: A.V. Dicey in Imperial Context' (2018) 81 *The Modern Law Review* 739.

Wrote Dicey in 1914: 'I yield to no man in my passion for the greatness, the strength, the glory, and the moral unity of the British Empire'.[65] This enthusiasm was tested, however, by the socially, culturally, racially, and legally pluralistic nature of the imperial order. On one hand, Dicey expressed concern that discriminatory laws in the colonies were threatening the prospect for 'equal citizenship of all British subjects ... which Englishmen in the middle of the nineteenth century' – ie mid-Victorians like him – 'hoped to see established through the length and breadth of the Empire'.[66] On the other hand, the remedy that seemed necessary, that imperial authorities needed to intervene within colonies to act as 'protector of the rights of natives of Eastern and of more or less uncivilised countries',[67] and that special measures were needed 'for raising backward races of the world ... to a position of freedom and equality',[68] not only appeared to require the very kind of paternalistic discretionary power his rule of law denied, but also involved an insidious form of cultural superiority that insisted on assimilation and denied distinctive national, ethnic, cultural identities. Alex Middleton observes in his chapter that Dicey the imperialist saw tensions between imperialism, nationalism, and Benthamite individualism and acknowledged that imperial policy often meant state intervention associated with collectivism.

Drawing upon Lino's work, Nick Barber in his chapter claims that in the hands of officials tasked with extending imperial power over conquered and colonised peoples around the globe, Dicey's rule of law was nothing but a tool of oppression. Viewed in a thin or procedural sense, the rule of law simply sharpened the edge of the imperial legal knife. Viewed in a thicker sense, however, the imperial legacy of the rule of law may be more complicated – a point Barber pushes us toward. This complexity is illustrated by Richard Cullen's chapter on the legacy of the rule of law in the dynamic cross-cultural setting of Hong Kong. Cullen reminds us of EP Thompson's controversial claim that even within unjust legal orders the rule of law may be an unqualified human good.[69] The applicability of this insight to the understanding of legality in colonial settings deserves much greater consideration.[70] To take just one example, when a colonial judge ruled that it would be 'monstrous' to interpret legislation introducing English law into a territory as extending to marriages between Indigenous peoples who yet 'adhere to their own peculiar marriage custom and usages', was the judge trying to administer justice equally or was he wielding a tool of empire (or both)?[71]

[65] Dicey, *Law of the Constitution* 1915 lxxxv.

[66] ibid xxxvii.

[67] AV Dicey to AB Keith, 27 June 1914, in RA Shinn and RA Cosgrove (eds), *Constitutional Reflections: The Correspondence of Albert Venn Dicey and Arthur Berriedale Keith* (New York, University Press of America, Inc, 1996) 25–26, 131–32.

[68] Dicey, *Law and Public Opinion* lvii–lviii.

[69] EP Thompson, *Whigs and Hunters: The Origins of the Black Act* (London, Penguin, 1977) 266.

[70] M Walters, 'Histories of Colonialism, Legality, and Aboriginality' (2007) 57 *University of Toronto Law Journal* 819, 827–28.

[71] *The Queen v Nan-E-Quis-A-Ka* (1889) 1 Terr LR 211 (NWT Sup Ct) 215; MD Walters, 'The Judicial Recognition of Indigenous Legal Traditions: *Connolly v. Woolrich* at 150' (2017) 22 *Review of Constitutional Studies* 347.

## V. Dicey and the Morality of Legal Biography

In his contribution on Dicey and federalism, Thibault Guilluy suggests that it is odd that Dicey, the positivist lawyer who focused on law in *Law of the Constitution*, would argue against Irish Home Rule on the grounds that once powers were devolved parliamentary sovereignty would become constrained in a political sense, producing de facto federalism. The short answer is that this did not represent a change in tack for Dicey, since from the beginning he acknowledged that political realities, including the growing autonomy of political units within the Empire, could, 'whatever lawyers may say', render the 'dogma' of parliamentary sovereignty 'no better than a legal fiction'.[72] But does this technical point miss a broader point Guilluy is making?

In their chapter, McLean and Peterson make an even stronger claim than Guilluy does, arguing that Dicey abandoned parliamentary sovereignty even in its more technical, nominal, or fictional sense, and so I am wrong to say, in the Appendix to my book, that Dicey remained 'Diceyan'. I am not certain that I can add anything more to what I did say on this point in the Appendix. However, it is important to acknowledge that in the closing pages of his 1913 book, *Fool's Paradise*, Dicey cuts very close to the line, including in the passage that McLean and Peterson quote in their chapter, when arguing against a Home Rule statute enacted without the prior sanction of the United Kingdom electorate. Having read these pages again, however, I think it is clear that he did not cross the line to argue that a Home Rule statute would be unlawful – immoral and unconstitutional, yes, but not unlawful.[73] It is worth noting that Dicey completed *Fool's Paradise* in January of 1913.[74] He was at this time already planning an eighth edition of *Law of the Constitution*.[75] Dicey was not the kind of scholar to repudiate one of the central legal positions articulated in a book that he was about to reissue.

Yet, stepping back to survey Dicey's writing over time, it must be said that in a broader sense the closing pages of *Fool's Paradise* are probably the most un-Diceyan pages Dicey ever wrote. My insistence that Dicey remained in technical compliance with his earlier views on parliamentary sovereignty may therefore seem oddly formalistic. In fact, my objective in the Appendix was to respond to certain claims made about Dicey that were put on a formal legal level and I felt that it was important to respond on that same level. I endeavoured to ensure, however, that the arguments were framed by an acknowledgement that Dicey advanced views that were politically and morally problematic.

I think it is evident that there is a sort of morality of legal biography at play here – that a history of the ideas of a legal scholar will have to be true,

[72] Dicey, *Law of the Constitution* 1885 63, 65, 73.

[73] AV Dicey, *A Fool's Paradise: Being a Constitutionalist's Criticism on the Home Rule Bill of 1912* (London, John Murray, 1913) 110–30.

[74] Dicey, *Fool's Paradise*, preface dated January 1913.

[75] Dicey informed his publisher of his plan in July of 1912: AV Dicey to Sir Frederick Macmillan, 1 July 1912, British Library, Macmillan Archive 55085, ff 25–30.

and therefore precise, about the legal views that the scholar held, but true as well as to the other parts of their intellectual lives. The biographer will need to be careful about striking a morally defensive balance in this respect. The challenge for me is that, as I stated in the introductory chapter to my book, my objective was not just 'intellectual biography and the history of legal ideas' but also 'normative legal analysis'– 'an interpretation of constitutionalism within the common law tradition framed by the story of Dicey and his book *Law of the Constitution*'– and I appreciated that I was 'running together styles of legal writing that for reasons of academic integrity are usually kept apart'.[76] I wanted to find Dicey the person behind the image he had acquired as 'the high priest of orthodox constitutional theory'.[77] This involved interpretation of historical facts. I also sought to find in his work a compelling version of constitutionalism, and this involved normative legal interpretation which took me past – but not too far past! – what Dicey himself thought and wrote. What I did not wish to engage in was a normative reconstruction of Dicey the person who, as a mid-Victorian scholar of a certain class and education, was who he was. I hope the resulting account of Dicey and his work will take its place, along with the essays in this volume, within the larger discourse about the fundamental values of legality necessary for peaceful, sustainable, equitable, and flourishing societies.

The test of good scholarship is that it forces the reader to examine their own views critically and with a sense of intellectual humility. After reading these essays, I have learned much I did not know before about Albert Venn Dicey and his legacy for constitutionalism. I have learned not just about the history of legal ideas but also about the importance of attending to the different ways that we can write about the history of legal ideas.

[76] Walters, *AV Dicey and the Common Law Constitutional Tradition* 4.
[77] M Loughlin, *Public Law and Political Theory* (Oxford, Clarendon Press, 1992) 140.

# BIBLIOGRAPHY


Addams, J, *Democracy and Social Ethics* (University of Illinois Press, 2001).

Ahmed, F, Albert, R and Perry, A 'Judging Constitutional Conventions' (2019) 17 *International Journal of Constitutional Law* 787.

Ajzenstat, J, 'Reconciling Parliament and Rights: A.V. Dicey Reads the Canadian Charter of Rights and Freedoms' (1997) 30 *Canadian Journal of Political Science/Revue canadienne de science politique* 645.

Albert, RN, 'The Difficulty of Constitutional Amendment in Canada' (2015) 53 *Alberta Law Review*.

Albert, RN and Pal, M, *The Democratic Resilience of the Canadian Constitution* (Oxford, Oxford University Press, 2017).

Alcantara, C and Whitfield, G, 'Aboriginal Self-Government through Constitutional Design: A Survey of Fourteen Aboriginal Constitutions in Canada' (2010) 44 *Journal of Canadian Studies/Revue d'études canadiennes* 122.

Alford, R, 'Emergency Powers and the Rule of Law: Why Inquiries Matter' (Macdonald-Laurier Institute, 2022).

Allan, TRS, 'Dworkin and Dicey: The Rule of Law as Integrity?' (1988) 8 *Oxford Journal of Legal Studies* 266.

—— 'Justice and Fairness in *Law's Empire*' (1993) 52 *Cambridge Law Journal* 64.

—— *Constitutional Justice: A Liberal Theory of the Rule of Law* (Oxford, Oxford University Press, 2001).

—— 'Questions of Legality and Legitimacy: Form and Substance in British Constitutionalism' (2011) 9 *International Journal of Constitutional Law* 155.

—— *The Sovereignty of Law. Freedom, Constitution, and Common Law* (Oxford, Oxford University Press, 2013).

Allen, CK, *Law in the Making*, 1st edn (Oxford, Clarendon Press, 1927).

—— *Law in the Making*, 7th edn (Oxford, Clarendon Press, 1963 [1927]).

Allen, JG, 'The Office of the Crown' (2018) 77 *Cambridge Law Journal* 298.

Allison, JWF, *A Continental Distinction in the Common Law* (Oxford, Oxford University Press, 1996).

—— *The English Historical Constitution. Continuity, Changes and European Effects*, (Cambridge, Cambridge University Press, 2007).

—— (ed), *The Oxford Edition of Dicey* (Oxford, Oxford University Press, 2013) vols 1 & 2.

Allinson, RE, *Understanding the Chinese Mind: The Philosophical Roots* (Oxford, Oxford University Press, 1995).

American Bar Association, 'Report of the Special Committee on Administrative Law' (1938) 63 *Annual Reports of the American Bar Association* 336.

Amos, S, *Fifty Years of the English Constitution, 1830–1880* (London, Longmans Green and Co, 1880).

Anon, 'Professor Dicey on Legislation', *Saturday Review of Politics, Literature, Science and Art*, 100:2594 (15 July 1905) 86–87.

Anson, WR, *The Law and Custom of the Constitution* (Oxford, Clarendon Press, 1886).

Arendt, H, 'What is Authority?' *Between Past and Future* (New York, Viking Press, 1961) 91.

—— *On Revolution* (London, Penguin Books, 1963).

Aron, R, *Essai sur les libertés* (Paris, Fayard, 2014).

Aroney, N and Leigh, I, *Christianity and Constitutionalism* (Oxford, Oxford University Press, 2022).

Austin, J, *Lectures on Jurisprudence, or, The Philosophy of Positive Law*, 4th edn (London, John Murray, 1873).

—— *The Province of Jurisprudence Determined* (Cambridge, Cambridge University Press, 1995 [1885]).

Bagehot, W, *The English Constitution*, 2nd edn (Boston, Little, Brown, and Co, 1873).

—— *The English Constitution*, M Taylor (ed) (Oxford, Oxford University Press, 2001 [1867]).
Baker, JH, *An Introduction to English Legal History*, 4th edn (Oxford, Oxford University Press, 2007).
Balshaw, JM, *Suffrage, Solidarity and Strife: Political Partnerships and the Women's Movement 1880–1930* (PhD thesis, University of Greenwich, 1998).
Baranger, Denis, 'Angleterre' (Culture juridique)' in S Rials and D Alland (eds), *Dictionnaire de la culture juridique* (Paris, Presses Universitaires de France, 2003) 52–59.
—— *Écrire la constitution non-écrite. Une introduction au droit politique britannique*, (Paris, Presses Universitaire de France, 2008), coll. Léviathan.
—— 'Brexit as a Constitutional Decision' (2018) 21 *Jus Politicum* 287.
Barber, NW, *The Principles of Constitutionalism* (Oxford, Oxford University Press, 2018).
—— *The United Kingdom Constitution: An Introduction* (Oxford, Oxford University Press, 2021).
Bartholomew, J, 'The Welfare State Made Britain Poor' (Hull, Biteback Publishing, 2013).
Baude, W, 'Is Qualified Immunity Unlawful?' (2018) 106 *California Law Review* 45.
—— 'Adjudication Outside Article III' (2019) 133 *Harvard Law Review* 1511.
Beaud, O, *La puissance de l'État* (Paris, Presses Universitaires de France, 1994).
Beck, JM, *Our Wonderland of Bureaucracy*, 1st edn (London, Macmillan, 1932).
Bell, D, *Reordering the World: Essays on Liberalism and Empire* (Princeton, Princeton University Press, 2016).
Bell, L, '"Let Me Find the Facts …"' (1940) 26 *American Bar Association Journal* 552.
Bellamy, R, *The Rule of Law and the Separation of Powers* (London, Routledge 2017).
Ben-Dor, O, *Constitutional Limits and the Public Sphere. A Critical Study of Bentham's Constitutionalism* (Oxford, Hart Publishing, 2000).
Bentham, J, *A Fragment on Government* [1776] in JH Burns and HLA Hart (eds), *A Comment on the Commentaries and a Fragment on Government* (Oxford, Oxford University Press, 1977).
—— *Introduction to the Principles of Morals and Legislation*, HLA Hart and JH Burns (eds) (Oxford, Clarendon Press, 1996 [1789]).
—— *Traités de Législation Civile et Pénale* (Paris, Bossange, Masson et Besson, 1802).
—— *Constitutional Code*, in *The Works of Jeremy Bentham*, vol 10, J Bowring (ed) (Edinburgh, William Tait, 1843).
—— *Of Laws in General* (London, The Athlone Press, 1970).
—— *First Principles Preparatory to Constitutional Code*, P Schofield (ed) (Oxford, Oxford University Press, 1989).
—— *Of the Limits of the Penal Branch of Jurisprudence*, P Schofield (ed) (Oxford, Clarendon, 2010).
Berger, BL, 'Children of Two Logics: A Way into Canadian Constitutional Culture' (2013) 11 *International Journal of Constitutional Law* 319.
Berlin, I, 'Two Concepts of Liberty' in I Berlin, *Four Essays on Liberty* (Oxford, Oxford University Press, 1969).
Bermann, HJ, *Law and Revolution II. The Impact of Protestant Reformation on the Western Legal Tradition* (Cambridge, Belknap Press of Harvard University, 2003).
Biggar, N, *Colonialism* (London, William Collins, 2023).
Bingham Centre for the Rule of Law, *A Constitutional Crossroads: Ways Forward for the United Kingdom: Report of an Independent Commission* (2015).
Birch, AH, *Representative and Responsible Government. An Essay on the British Constitution* (London, George Allen and Unwin, 1964).
Blackstone, W, *Commentaries on the Laws of England* (Oxford, Clarendon Press, 1765–69).
Blick, A and Hennessy, P, *The Bonfires of the Decencies. Repairing and Restoring the British Constitution* (London, Haus Publishing, 2022).
Bligh, G, *Les bases philosophiques du positivisme juridique de H.L.A. Hart* (Bayonne, Varenne, 2017).
—— 'Empirical Complexity as a Conceptual Claim. Reappraising Hart's Account of Law as a Complex Social Practice' in M Carpentier (ed), *Meta-Theory of Law* (London, ISTE/Wiley, 2022) 93.
Bogdanor, V, 'Dicey and the Reform of the Constitution' (1985) *Public Law* 652.
—— *The New British Constitution* (Oxford, Hart Publishing, 2009).

—— *Beyond Brexit: Towards a British Constitution* (London, Tauris 2019).

Bold, A and Lagasse, P, 'Beyond Dicey: Executive Authorities in Canada' (2021) 3 *The Journal of Commonwealth Law.*

Bond, MH, *Beyond the Chinese Face: Insights from Psychology* (Oxford, Oxford University Press, 1992).

Bonnin, M, 'The Press in Hong Kong – Flourishing but Under Threat' (1 September 1995) *China Perspectives.*

Bouchard, K, *Constitutionnalisme et common law dans la pensée juridique anglo-américaine* (Paris, Classiques Garnier, 2021).

Boucheron, P, *Traces and Aura. The Recuring Lives of Ambrose of Milan* (New York, Other Press, 2022).

Boutmy, Émile, *Études de droit constitutionnel : France – Angleterre – États-Unis* (Paris, E Plon, Nourrit et Cie, 1885)

—— *Studies in Constitutional Law France – England – United States*, EM Dicey, trans (London, Macmillan & Co, 1891).

Bowers, J, 'Conventions, the Rule of Law and Declining Standards: What Happens when Good Chaps do not Behave' in *Downward Spiral. Collapsing Public Standards and how to Restore Them* (Manchester, Manchester University Press, 2024) ch 15.

Boyron, S, 'The Judiciary's Self-Determination, the Common Law and Constitutional Change' (2016) 22 *European Public Law* 149.

Brahm, A, 'Quebec's Evolving Nationalism: Tipping From Separatism to Secularism' (Research Paper, University of Ottawa, 2021).

Brebner, JB, 'Laissez Faire and State Intervention in Nineteenth-Century Britain' (1948) 8 *Journal of Economic History* 59.

Bryce, J, 'Flexible and Rigid Constitutions', *Studies in History and Jurisprudence*, vol 1 (New York, Oxford University Press, 1901).

—— 'The Nature of Sovereignty', *Studies in History and Jurisprudence*, vol 2 (Oxford, Oxford University Press, 1901).

Burgess, P, 'The Rule of Lore in the Rule of Law: Putting the Problem of the Rule of Law in Context' (2020) 12 *Hague Journal on the Rule of Law* 333.

Burrow, JW, *A Liberal Descent* (Cambridge, Cambridge University Press, 1981).

Bush, J, *Women against the Vote: Female Anti-Suffragism in Britain* (Oxford University Press, 2007).

Cabinet Office, 'The Cabinet Manual: A Guide to Laws, Conventions and Rules on the Operation of Government' (2011).

Calabresi, SG and Lawson, G, 'The Depravity of the 1930s and the Modern Administrative State' (2018) 94 *Notre Dame Law Review* 821.

Cane, P, 'AV Dicey as Legal Theorist' (2022) 85 *Modern Law Review* 247.

Cannadine, D, *Victorious Century: The United Kingdom 1800–1906* (London, Allen Lane, 2017).

Carlin, RE, 'Rule-of-Law Typologies in Contemporary Societies' (2012) 33 *Justice System Journal* 154.

Cassese, S, *La construction du droit administratif. France et Royaume-Uni* (Paris, Montchrestien, 2000).

Chan, S, 'Ho Chi Minh in Victoria Gao' (Hong Kong Memory, 2011) https://www.hkmemory.hk/MHK/collections/victoria_prison/Ho_Chi_Minh_in_Victoria_Gaol/index.html.

Chen, J, *Chinese Law: Context and Transformation* (Leyde, Brill, 2015).

Choudhry, S, 'Does the World Need More Canada? The Politics of the Canadian Model in Constitutional Politics and Political Theory' (2007) 5 *International Journal of Constitutional Law* 606.

Collini, C, *Public Moralists: Political Thought and Intellectual Life in Britain, 1850–1930* (Oxford, Oxford University Press, 1993).

Cooper, RM, 'The Proposed United States Administrative Court' (1936) 35 *Michigan Law Review* 193.

Cosgrove, RA, *The Rule of Law: Albert Venn Dicey, Victorian Jurist* (London, Macmillan, 1980).

Cowell, J, *The Interpreter: or Booke containing the signification of words … mentioned in the lawe writers, or statutes* (Cambridge, Iohn Legate, 1607).

Craig, P, *UK, EU and Global Administrative Law. Foundations and Challenges* (The Hamlyn Lectures, Oxford University Press, 2015).

—— 'Six Dimensions of Public Law. Pressure-Testing the UK and EU Systems' in E Fischer, J King, AL Young (eds), *The Foundations and Future of Public Law* (Oxford, Oxford University Press, 2020).
—— *Administrative Law*, 9th edn (Oxford, Oxford University Press, 2021).
Craig, P and Rawlings, R (eds), *Law and Administration in Europe, Essays in Honor of Carol Harlow* (Oxford, Oxford University Press, 2009).
Craig, R, 'Casting Aside Clanking Medieval Chains: Prerogative, Statute and Article 50 after the EU Referendum' (2016) 79 *Modern Law Review* 1041.
—— 'A Simple Application of the Frustration Principle: Prerogative, Statute and *Miller*' (2017) *Public Law, Brexit Special Issue* 33.
Creasy, ES, *The Rise and Progress of the English Constitution*, 3rd edn (London, Richard Bentley, 1856).
Cullen, Richard, 'Revenue Law in Hong Kong: The Future' in R Wacks (ed), *The New Legal Order in Hong Kong* (Hong Kong, Hong Kong University Press, 1999).
—— *Hong Kong Constitutionalism: The British Legacy and the Chinese Future* (Abingdon, Routledge, 2020).
—— 'Hong Kong's Housing Crisis – an Underlying Factor in the 2019 Riots' (18 April 2021) *Pearls and Irritations* (John Menadue's Public Policy Journal).
—— 'The Wisdom of Billy Wilder and Western Media Collusion' (21 August 2022) *Pearls and Irritations* (John Menadue's Public Policy Journal).
—— 'Review Essay: Treaty for a Lost City – The Sino-British Joint Declaration' (2023) 53 *Hong Kong Law Journal* 797.
Cullen, Richard and Tso, Kevin, 'Using Opium as a Public Revenue Resource – Not as Easy as it Looks: The British Hong Kong Experience' (2012) *British Tax Review* 226.
Cutler, F, 'Jeremy Bentham and the Public Opinion Tribunal' (1999) 63 *Public Opinion Quarterly* 321.
Daly, P, 'Miller: Legal and Political Fault Lines' (2017) *Public Law, Brexit Special Issue*.
Dangerfield, G, *The Strange Death of Liberal England* (Stanford, Stanford University Press, 1997 [1935])
Dawson, AJ, 'The Social Determinants of the Rule of Law: A Comparison of Jamaica and Barbados' (2013) 45 *World Development* 314.
Debeljak, J, 'Balancing Rights in a Democracy: The Problems with Limitations and Overrides of Rights under the Victorian Charter of Human Rights and Responsibilities Act 2006' (2008) 32 *Melbourne University Law Review* 422.
Delcourt, B, 'The Rule of Law as a Vehicle for Intervention' (2015) 9 *Journal of Intervention and Statebuilding* 471.
Deumier, Pe, *Introduction générale au droit*, 7th edn (Issy-les-Moulineaux, LGDJ-Lextenso, 2023).
Dicey, AV, *A Treatise on the Rules for the Selection of the Parties to an Action* (London, W Maxwell, 1870).
—— 'The Development of the Common Law' (1871) 21 *Macmillan's Magazine*.
—— 'Freeman's Growth of the English Constitution' (1872) 15: 376 *The Nation*.
—— 'Stubbs's Constitutional History of England' (1875) 20: 505 *The Nation*.
—— 'Maine's Early History of Institutions' (1875) 20: 509 *The Nation*.
—— 'Digby on the History of English Law' (1875) 21: 545 *The Nation*.
—— *The Law of Domicil as a Branch of the Law of England, Stated in the Form of Rules* (London, Stevens and Sons, 1879).
—— 'The Study of Jurisprudence' (1880) 5 (5th ser) *Law Magazine and Review*.
—— 'Home Rule from an English point of view' (1882) 42 *The Contemporary Review*.
—— 'Can English Law Be Taught At The Universities? An Inaugural Lecture, Delivered At All Souls College', 21 April 1883 (London, Macmillan, 1883).
—— to Sir W Anson, 5 October 1883, Anson Papers, All Souls College, Oxford.
—— 'Federal Government' (1885) 1 *The Law Quarterly Review*.
—— *Introduction to the Study of the Law of Constitution* (London, Macmillan, 1885).
—— 'Gneist's History of the English Constitution' (1886) 42: 1095 *The Nation*.
—— *Letters on Unionist Delusions* (London, MacMillan, 1887).

—— *England's Case against Home Rule*, 3rd edn (London, John Murray, 1887).
—— 'Bryce's American Commonwealth' (1889) 169 *The Edinburgh Review*.
—— *Introduction to the Study of the Law of the Constitution*, 3rd edn (London, Macmillan, 1889).
—— 'Ought the Referendum to be Introduced into England?' (1890) 57 *Contemporary Review* 489.
—— 'The Defence of the Union' (1892) 61 *The Contemporary Review*.
—— *Introduction to the Study of the Law of the Constitution*, 4th edn (London, MacMillan and Co, 1893).
—— *A Leap in the Dark* or *Our New Constitution* (London, J Murray, 1893).
—— *A Digest of the Law of England with Reference to the Conflict of Laws* (London, Stevens and Sons, 1897).
—— to Charles Eliot, 5 December 1898, Charles W Eliot Papers, UAI 5.150, Box 36, Harvard University Archives.
—— to Charles E Norton, 19 March 1901, Charles Eliot Norton Papers, MS Am 1088.14, no 1747, Houghton Library Harvard.
—— An Observer 'The Causes of Imperialism in England' (1901) 73 *The Nation* 203.
—— *Introduction to the Law of the Constitution*, 6th edn (London, MacMillan and Co, 1902).
—— *Introduction à létude du droit constitutionnel* (Paris, Giard et Brière, 1902).
—— *Lectures on the Relation between Law and Public Opinion in England during the Nineteenth Century* (London, Macmillan, 1905).
—— *Letters to a Friend on Votes for Women* (London, John Murray, 1909).
—— to John St Loe Strachey, 30 May 1910, STR 5/5/19.
—— to James Bryce, 4 August 1911, James Bryce Papers, Bodleian Library, Oxford University, 3: 100–108.
—— to Sir Frederick Macmillan, 1 July 1912, British Library, Macmillan Archive 55085.
—— *A Fool's Paradise: Being a Constitutionalist's Criticism on the Home Rule Bill of 1912* (London, John Murray, 1913).
—— *Lectures on the relation between Law and Opinion in England during the Nineteenth Century*, 2nd edn (London, MacMillan and Co, 1914).
—— *Introduction to the Study of the Law of the Constitution*, 8th edn (London, Macmillan and Co, 1915).
—— 'The Development of Administrative Law in England' (1915) 31 *Law Quarterly Review* 148.
—— *Lectures on the Relation between Law and Public Opinion* (1917, Liberty Fund, Online Source).
—— 'Blackstone's Commentaries' (December 1909) 65 *National Review* 653, reprinted (1932) 4 *Cambridge Law Journal* 286.
—— *Introduction to the Study of the Law of the Constitution*, 10th edn (London, Macmillan, 1959).
—— 'Parliamentary Sovereignty and Federalism' in AV Dicey (ed), *Introduction to the Study of the Law of the Constitution* (London, Palgrave Macmillan, 1979).
—— *Introduction to the Study of the Law of the Constitution* (Indianapolis, Liberty Fund, 1982, reprint of the 1915 8th edn published by Macmillan).
—— *Lectures on the Relation between Law and Public Opinion in England during the Nineteenth Century*, 2nd edn (Indianapolis, Liberty Fund, 2008 [1917]).
—— *Lectures Introductory to the Study of the Law of the Constitution. The Oxford Edition of Dicey*, vol 1, JWF Allisson (ed) (Oxford, Oxford University Press, 2013).
—— *The Law of the Constitution*, (Oxford, Oxford University Press, 2013) vol 1 in JWF Allison, *The Oxford Edition of Dicey*.
—— *Lectures on Comparative Constitutionalism*, JWF Allison (ed) (Oxford, Oxford University Press, 2013).
—— *Lectures on the Relation between Law and Public in England during the Nineteenth Century* (London, Routledge, 2017).
Dicey, AV, Morris, and Collins, *The Conflict of Laws*, 16th edn (London, Sweet and Maxwell, 2022).
Dicey, AV and Rait, RS, *Thoughts on the Union between England and Scotland* (London, Macmillan, 1920).

Dickinson, A, Endicott, T and Ernst, W (eds), *Dicey + 100: Albert Venn Dicey: A Centennial Commemoration* (Cambridge, Intersentia, 2024).

Dickinson, J, *Administrative Justice and the Supremacy of Law* (Oxford, Oxford University Press, 1927).

Doering, J and Peker, E, 'How Muslims Respond to Secularist Restrictions: Reactive Ethnicity, Adjustment, and Acceptance' (2022) 45 *Ethnic and Racial Studies* 2956.

Douglas-Scott, Sionaidh, 'Brexit and the Challenges of a Post-Sovereign Legal Landscape' in *The Foundations and Future of Public Law* (Oxford, Oxford University Press, 2020).

—— *Brexit, Union, and Disunion. The Evolution of British Constitutional Unsettlement* (Cambridge, Cambridge University Press, 2023).

Drevikovsky, JO, 'From Pseudochrony to Diachrony: A.V. Dicey, Home Rule and the Invention of Legal History' (University of Sydney, 2023).

Duarte d'Almeida, L et al (eds), *Reading HLA Hart's The Concept of Law* (Oxford, Hart Publishing, 2013).

Duffy, A, 'L'état d'exception, nouveau régime de droit commun des droits et libertés. Du terrorisme à l'urgence sanitaire. Royaume-Uni' (2021) 36 *Annuaire international de justice constitutionnelle.*

Duguit, L, *L'État, le droit objectif et la loi positive* (Paris, Dalloz, 2003 [1901]).

Duxbury, N, *Frederick Pollock and the English Juristic Tradition* (Oxford, Oxford University Press, 2004).

Dworkin, RM, *Taking Rights Seriously* (Cambridge, Harvard University Press, 1977).

—— *Law's Empire* (Oxford, Hart Publishing, 1998 [1986]).

Dyzenhaus, D, 'The State of Emergency in Legal Theory' in K Roach, M Hor and VV Ramraj (eds), *Global Anti-Terrorism Law and Policy* (Cambridge, Cambridge University Press, 2005).

—— 'Austin, Hobbes, and Dicey' (2011) 24 *Canadian Journal of Law and Jurisprudence* 411.

Eleftheriadis, P, 'Parliamentary Sovereignty and the Constitution' (2009) 22 *Canadian Journal of Law & Jurisprudence* 267.

—— 'Hart on Sovereignty' in L Duarte d'Almeida et al (eds), *Reading HLA Hart's The Concept of Law* (Oxford, Hart Publishing, 2013) 59.

Elkins, C, *Legacy of Violence: A History of the British Empire* (London, Bodley Head, 2022).

Elliott, M, 'Parliamentary Sovereignty and the New Constitutional Order: Legislative Freedom, Political Reality and Convention' (2002) 22 *Legal Studies* 340.

—— 'The Supreme Court's Judgment in *Miller*. In Search of Constitutional Principle' (2017) 76 *Cambridge Law Journal* 257.

Elliott, M, Williams, J, Young, A, *The UK Constitution after Miller. Brexit and Beyond* (Oxford, Hart Publishing, 2018).

Endicott, T, 'This Ancient, Secretive Royal Prerogative', *UK Constitutional Law Blog* (11 Nov 2016) (available at https://ukconstitutionallaw.org/).

—— *The Stubborn Stain Theory of Executive Power: From Magna Carta to Miller* (London, Policy Exchange, 2017).

—— 'Dicey and Analytical Jurisprudence' in A Dickinson, T Endicott, and W Ernst (eds), *Dicey + 100* (Cambridge, Intersentia, 2024).

Ernst, DE, *Tocqueville's Nightmare: The Administrative State Emerges in America, 1900–1940* (Oxford, Oxford University Press, 2014).

Errera, R, 'Dicey and French Administrative Law: A Missed Encounter?' (1985) *Public Law* 695.

Esselment, AL, 'A Little Help from My Friends: The Partisan Factor and Intergovernmental Negotiations in Canada' (2013) 43 *Publius – the Journal of Federalism* 701.

Ewing, K, 'The Law and the Constitution: Manifesto of the Progressive Party' (2004) 67 *Modern Law Review* 734.

—— 'Brexit and Parliamentary Sovereignty' (2017) 80 *Modern Law Review* 711.

Ford, TH, 'Dicey as a Political Journalist' (1970) 18 *Political Studies* 220.

—— *Albert Venn Dicey: The Man and His Times* (Barry Rose Publishers, 1985).

Fortescue, J, *De Laudibus Legum Angliae*, SB Chrimes (ed) (Cambridge, Cambridge University Press, 1942).

Frankfurter, F, 'The Task of Administrative Law' (1927) *University of Pennsylvania Law Review* 614.
—— 'Foreword' (1938) 47 *Yale Law Journal* 515.
Freedman, JO, *Crisis and Legitimacy: The Administrative Process and American Government* (Cambridge, Cambridge University Press, 1980).
Freeman, EA, *The Growth of the English Constitution from the Earliest Times* (London, MacMillan, 1872).
—— 'The Continuity of English History' in *Historical Essays*, first ser, 3rd edn (London, MacMillan and Co, 1875).
—— 'The Physical and Political Bases of National Unity' (1892) *Britannic Confederation* (London, G Philip & Son, 1892).
Freeman, M and Mindus, P (eds), *The Legacy of John Austin's Jurisprudence* (Dordrecht, Springer, 2013).
Friedrich, CJ, *Trends of Federalism in Theory and Practice* (London, Praeger, 1968).
Fuller, LL, *The Law in Quest of Itself* (Boston, Beacon Press, 1966).
—— *The Morality of Law*, 2nd edn (New Haven, Yale University Press, 1969).
Gabayet, N, 'Les mutations du droit administratif anglais sous l'influence du droit de l'Union européenne' (2017) 2 *Revue du droit public et de la science politique* 295.
—— 'Une page de l'histoire de la pensée du droit administratif : le "moment Dicey"' (2018) 21 *Jus Politicum* 415.
Garner, JW, 'La conception anglo-américaine du droit administratif', in *Mélanges M. Hauriou* (Paris, Sirey, 1929) 337.
Garver, N, 'The Canadian Approach to Rule of Law' (2022), available at https://papers.ssrn.com/sol3/papers.cfm?abstract_id=4130539.
Gasaway, RR and Parrish, A, 'In Praise of Erie – And Its Eventual Demise' (2013) 10 *Journal of Law Economics & Policy* 225.
Ghai, Y, *Hong Kong's New Constitutional Order*, 2nd edn (Hong Kong, Hong Kong University Press, 1999).
Gladstone, WE, *Gleanings of Past Years* (London, John Murray, 1879) vol 1.
Gneist, R von, *Das englische Verwaltungsrecht der Gegenwart* (Berlin, Springer 1867).
Goodnow, FJ, 'The Writ of Certiorari' (1891) 6 *Political Science Quarterly* 493.
Goodstadt, LF, *Uneasy Partners: The Conflict Between Public Interest and Private Profit in Hong Kong* (Hong Kong, Hong Kong University Press, 2005).
Gough, JW, *Fundamental Law in English Constitutional History* (Oxford, Clarendon, 1955).
Gramsci, A, *Selections from the Prison Notebooks*, Q Hoare and G Nowell Smith (eds and trans) (New York, International Publishers, 1971).
Gray, JC, *The Nature and Sources of Law* (New York, Columbia University Press, 1909).
Green, L, 'Notes to the Third Edition' in HLA Hart, *The Concept of Law*, 3rd edn (Oxford, Oxford University Press, 2012) 309.
Greve, MS, 'Why We Need Federal Administrative Courts' (2021) 28 *George Mason Law Review* 765.
Griffith, JAG, 'The Political Constitution' (1979) 42 *Modern Law Review* 1.
Gungwu, W, *China and the Overseas Chinese* (Singapore, Times Academic Press, 1991).
—— *Bind Us in Time: Nation and Civilization in Asia* (Singapore, Times Academic Press, 2002).
Halévy, E, *La Formation du Radicalisme Philosophique* (Paris, F Alcan, 1901–04).
Hamburger, P, *Is Administrative Law Unlawful?* (Chicago, University of Chicago Press, 2014).
Harlow, C, '"Public" and "Private" Law: Definition without Distinction' (1980) 43 *MLR* 241.
—— *Disposing of Dicey: From Legal Autonomy to Political Discourse* (2002) 48 *Political Studies* 356.
Harlow, C and Rawlings, R, 'Administrative Law in Context: Restoring a Lost Connection' (2014) *Public Law* 28.
—— *Law and Administration*, 4th edn (Cambridge, Cambridge University Press, 2022).
Harrison, J, 'Public Rights, Private Privileges, and Article III' (2019) 54 *Georgia Law Review* 143.
Hart, HLA, 'Introduction' in J Austin, *The Province of Jurisprudence Determined* (London, Weidenfeld & Nicholson, 1954) vii.

—— 'Sovereignty and Legally Limited Government' *Essays on Bentham* (Oxford, Clarendon, 1982) 220–42.
—— *The Concept of Law*, 3rd edn (Oxford, Oxford University Press, 2012).
—— 'Answers to Eight Questions', in L Duarte d'Almeida et al (eds), *Reading HLA Hart's The Concept of Law* (Oxford, Hart Publishing, 2013) 279–97.
Harvey, WB, 'The Rule of Law in Historical Perspective' (1961) 59 *Michigan Law Review* 487.
Hauriou, M, *Principes de droit public*, 2nd edn (Paris, Sirey, 1916 [1910]).
Hauriou, M, *Précis de droit administratif et de droit public*, 12th edn (Paris, Dalloz, 2002 [1933]).
Hayek, FA, *The Road to Serfdom* (London, George Routledge & Sons, 1944).
—— *The Constitution of Liberty: The Definitive Edition* (Chicago, University of Chicago Press, 2011).
Hewart, G, *The New Despotism* (London, Ernest Benn Ltd, 1929).
Hmimssa, A, 'Citizenship under Pressure: Mapping Debates Over Religious Freedom in the Second Decade in Quebec' (2023) 57 *Journal of Canadian Studies* 114.
Hobbes, T, *Leviathan* (Oxford, Oxford University Press, 1996 [1651]).
Hobhouse, LT, *Liberalism and Other Writings* (Cambridge, Cambridge University Press, 1994).
Hobsbawm, E and Ranger, T (eds), *The Invention of Tradition* (Cambridge, Cambridge University Press, 1983).
Hogg, PW and Cara, FZ, 'The Rule of Law in the Supreme Court of Canada' (2005) 55 *The University of Toronto Law Journal* 715.
Holcombe, RG and Rodet, CS, 'Rule of Law and the Size of Government' (2011) 8 *Journal of Institutional Economics* 49.
Holland, TE, *Elements of Jurisprudence*, 11th edn (Oxford, Clarendon, 1910).
Holmes, OW, 'The Path of the Law' (1897) 10 *Harvard Law Review* 457.
Horwitz, MJ, *The Transformation of American Law, 1870–1960* (Oxford, Oxford University Press, 1992).
Hume, D, 'Of the First Principles of Government'in *Political Essays*, K Haakonssen (ed) (Cambridge, Cambridge University Press, 1994) 16.
—— 'Of the Origin of Government' *Political Essays*, K Haakonssen (ed) (Cambridge, Cambridge University Press, 1994) 20.
—— *A Treatise of Human Nature – A Critical Edition* Vol 1 (Oxford, Clarendon, 2007 [1739]).
Hume, LJ, 'Bentham and the Nineteenth-Century Revolution in Government' (1967) 10 *Historical Journal* 361.
Inwood, GJ, 'Review of *The Politics and Economics of Eric Kierans: A Man for All Canadas* 1994 John N McDougall' (1994) 27 *Canadian Journal of Political Science* 623.
Jackson, J B Bradford, H Hough, A Myhill, P Quinton, and T Tyler, 'Why Do People Comply With the Law?' (2012) 52 *British Journal of Criminology* 1051.
Jackman, M and Porter, B, 'Socio-Economic Rights under the Canadian Charter' in M Langford (ed), *Social Rights Jurisprudence: Emerging Trends in International and Comparative Law* (New York, Cambridge University Press, 2008).
Jennings, WI, *The Law and the Constitution* (London, University of London Press, 1933).
—— 'In Praise of Dicey (1885–1935)' (1935) 13 *Public Administration* 123.
—— *Cabinet Government* (Cambridge, Cambridge University Press, 1936).
—— 'Courts and Administrative Law: The Experience of English Housing Legislation' (1936) 49 *Harvard Law Review* 426.
—— *Parliament* (Cambridge, Cambridge University Press, 1939).
—— *The Law and the Constitution*, 5th edn (London, University of London Press, 1959).
Jones, C, 'Politics Postponed' in K Jayasuriya (ed), *Law, Capitalism and Power in Asia* (London, Routledge, 1999).
Jouanjan, O, *Une histoire de la pensée juridique en Allemagne (1800–1918)* (Paris, PUF, 2005).
Kahan, AS, *Freedom from Fear: An Incomplete History of Liberalism* (Princeton, Princeton University Press, 2023).
Kelly, JB, 'Reconciling Rights and Federalism during Review of the Charter of Rights and Freedoms: The Supreme Court of Canada and the Centralization Thesis, 1982 to 1999' (2001) 34 *Canadian Journal of Political Science/Revue canadienne de science politique* 321.

Kelly, PJ, *Utilitarianism and Distributive Justice: Jeremy Bentham and the Civil Law* (Oxford, Clarendon, 1990).
Kelsen, H, 'Aperçu d'une théorie générale de l'État' C Eisenmann (trans) (1926) 43 *Revue du droit public* 561.
—— *General Theory of Law and State*, A Wedberg (trans) (Cambridge, Harvard University Press, 1945).
Kendle, J, *Ireland and the Federal Solution: The Debate over the United Kingdom Constitution, 1870–1920* (Montreal, McGill-Queen's University Press, 1989).
—— *Federal Britain: A History* (London, Routledge, 1997).
Kirby, J, 'A.V. Dicey and English Constitutionalism' (2019) 45 *History of European Ideas* 33.
Koebner, R and Schmidt, HD, *Imperialism: the Story and Significance of a Political Word, 1840–1960* (Cambridge, Cambridge University Press, 1964).
Kojève, A, *La notion de l'autorité* (Paris, Gallimard, 2004).
Kramer, M (ed) *The Legacy of HLA Hart* (Oxford, Oxford University Press, 2008).
La Boétie E de, 'Discours de la servitude volontaire' *Œuvres complètes*, P Bonnefon (ed) (Paris, J Rouam & Cie, 1892) 1.
Lacey, N, *A Life of HLA Hart. The Nightmare and the Noble Dream* (Oxford, Oxford University Press, 2004).
Landis, JM, *The Administrative Process* (New Haven, Yale University Press, 1938).
LaSelva, SV, 'Federalism as a Way of Life: Reflections on the Canadian Experiment' (1993) 26 *Canadian Journal of Political Science / Revue canadienne de science politique* 219.
Lawson, FH, 'Dicey Revisited' (1959) 7 *Political Studies* 109.
Lennox, AB, *Parliament Versus the Judiciary: The Unrelenting Dicey Dilemma* (Ottawa, National Library of Canada= Bibliothèque nationale du Canada, 2001).
Leys, S, *The Burning Forest: Essays on Chinese Culture and Politics* (London, Paladin, 1988).
Lieberman, D, *The Province of Legislation Determined: Legal Theory in Eighteenth-Century Britain* (Cambridge, Cambridge University Press, 1989).
Lieberman, N, 'Bentham's Democracy' (2008) 28 *Oxford Journal of Legal Studies* 605.
Lim, CL, *Treaty for a Lost City: The Sino-British Joint Declaration* (Cambridge, Cambridge University Press, 2022).
Lino, D, 'Albert Venn Dicey and the Constitutional Theory of Empire' (2016) 36 *Oxford Journal of Legal Studies* 751.
—— 'The Rule of Law and the Rule of Empire: A.V. Dicey in Imperial Context' (2018) 85 *Modern Law Review* 739.
Lippmann, W, *The Good Society* (New York, Routledge, 2017).
Littlewood, M, 'Taxation without Representation: The History of Hong Kong's Troublingly Successful Tax System' (2002) 3 *British Tax Review* 212.
Litton, H, 'A Close Run Thing in Hong Kong in 2019' (9 July 2021) *Pearls and Irritations* (John Menadue Public Policy Journal).
Lobban, M, *The Common Law and English Jurisprudence, 1760–1850* (Oxford, Clarendon, 1991).
—— *A History of Philosophy of Law in the Common Law World, 1600–1900* (Dordrecht, Springer, 2007).
—— 'John Austin' in T Spaak and P Mindus (eds), *Cambridge Companion to Legal Positivism* (Cambridge, Cambridge University Press, 2021) 225.
Locke, J, *Two Treatises of Government*, P Laslett (ed) (Cambridge, Cambridge University Press, 1988).
—— *An Essay concerning Human Understanding*, (London, Penguin Classics, 1998).
Loh, C, 'Hong Kong: Living on the Fault Line' (11 June 2023) *Pearls and Irritations* (John Menadue Public Policy Journal).
Loughlin, Martin, *Public Law and Political Theory* (Oxford, Oxford University Press, 1992).
—— 'The Concept of the State' in M Sunkin and S Payne (eds), *The Nature of the Crown. A Legal and Political Analysis* (Oxford, Oxford University Press, 1999).
—— *The Idea of Public Law* (Oxford, Oxford University Press, 2003).
—— 'The Functionalist Style in Public Law' (2005) 55 *University of Toronto Law Journal* 361.

—— *Foundations of Public Law* (Oxford, Oxford University Press, 2010).
—— 'The State: *conditio sine qua non*' (2018) 16 *International Journal of Constitutional Law* 1156.
—— 'Dicey and the Making of Common Law Constitutionalism' (2022) 42 *Oxford Journal of Legal Studies* 366.
Low, S, *The Governance of England* (London, T Fisher Unwin, 1904).
Lusztig, M and Knox, C, 'Good Things and Small Packages: Lessons from Canada for the Northern Irish Constitutional Settlement' (1999) 5 *Nations and Nationalism* 543.
McAuslan, P and McEldowney, JF (eds), *Law, Legitimacy and the Constitution. Essays marking the Centenary of Dicey's Law of the Constitution* (London, Sweet and Maxwell, 1985).
McConnell, MW, *The President Who Would Not Be King* (Princeton, Princeton University Press 2020).
MacCormick, N, *HLA Hart*, 2nd edn (Stanford, Stanford University Press, 2008).
MacDonagh, O, 'The Nineteenth-Century Revolution in Government: a Reappraisal' (1958) 1 *Historical Journal* 52.
Macdonald, RA, '… Meech Lake to the Contrary Notwithstanding (Part I)' (1991) 29 *Osgoode Hall Law Journal* 253.
MacFarlane, E, 'The Dilemma of Positive Rights: Access to Health Care and the Canadian Charter of Rights and Freedoms' (2014) 48 *Journal of Canadian Studies* 49.
McLean, I, *What's Wrong with The British Constitution* (Oxford, Oxford University Press, 2010).
McQuillan, L, 'Explainer: Emergencies Act Inquiry – What's Been Said, What Happens Next' (*CBC News*, 23 November 2022).
McWhinney, E, 'The Constitutional Patriation Project, 1980–82' (1984) 32 *American Journal of Comparative Law* 241.
Maciag, D, *Edmund Burke in America: The Contested Career of the Father of Modern Conservatism* (Ithaca, Cornell University Press, 2013).
Maine, HS, *Ancient Law*, 10th edn (Boston, Beacon Press, 1884 [1861]).
—— *Lectures on the Early History of Institutions* (London, John Murray, 1875).
Maitland, FW, *The Constitutional History of England: A Course of Lectures Delivered* (Cambridge, Cambridge University Press, 1908).
Marshall, C, *Political Deference in a Democratic Age. British Politics and the Constitution from the Eighteenth Century to Brexit* (Cham, Palgrave Macmillan, 2021).
Mashaw, J, *Creating the Administrative Constitution: The Lost One Hundred Years of American Administrative Law* (New Haven, Yale University Press, 2012).
Mathen, C, 'The Question Calls for an Answer, and I Propose to Answer it: The Patriation Reference as Constitutional Method' (2011) *The Supreme Court Law Review: Osgoode's Annual Constitutional Cases Conference* 54.
Merrill, T, 'Article III, Agency Adjudication, and the Origins of the Appellate Review Model of Administrative Law' (2011) 111 *Columbia Law Review* 940.
Merrill, TW and Tongue Watts, K, 'Agency Regulations with the Force of Law' (2002) 116 *Harvard Law Review* 467.
Metzger, GE, 'Foreword: 1930s Redux: The Administrative State Under Siege' (2017) 131 *Harvard Law Review* 1.
Mill, J, *Essays on Government, Jurisprudence, Liberty of the Press and Law of Nations* (London, J Innes, 1825).
Mill, JS, *Considerations on Representative Government* (London, Parker, Son & Bourn, 1861).
—— *The Subjection of Women* (London, Longmans, Green, Reader, and Dyer, 1869).
—— *Principles of Political Economy* in *The Collected Works of John Stuart Mill*, vol 3, JM Robson (ed) (Toronto, University of Toronto Press, 1965).
—— *Utilitarianism* in *The Collected Works of John Stuart Mill*, vol 10, JM Robson (ed) (Toronto, University of Toronto Press, 1969).
—— 'Austin on Jurisprudence', *The Collected Works of John Stuart Mill*, vol 21, JM Robson and S Collini (eds) (Toronto, University of Toronto Press, 1984).
—— 'On Liberty' in JS Mill, *On Liberty and Other Essays* (Oxford, Oxford University Press, 2008).

Miners, N and Tuck-Hong Tang, J, *The Government and Politics of Hong Kong*, 5th edn (Oxford, Oxford University Press, 1991).

Moles, RN, *Definition and Rule in Legal Theory. A Reassessment of H.L.A. Hart and the Positivist Tradition* (Oxford, Basil Blackwell, 1987).

Morison, WL, *John Austin* (Stanford, Stanford University Press, 1982).

Morris, J, *Hong Kong: Epilogue to an Empire* (London, Penguin, 1990).

Mulholland, M, 'Revolution and the Rule of Law: Dicey on Irish Home Rule' in A Dickinson, T Endicott, and W Ernst (eds), *Dicey + 100* (Cambridge, Intersentia, 2024).

Munn, C, *Anglo-China: Chinese People and British Rule in Hong Kong, 1841–1880* (Richmond, Curzon Press, 2001).

Nair, C, 'Anti-China Rhetoric is off the Charts: What Explains the Mass Hysteria in the West?' (24 February 2023) *Pearls and Irritations* (John Menadue Public Policy Journal).

Nelson, C, 'The Persistence of General Law' (2006) 106 *Columbia Law Review* 503.

—— 'Adjudication in the Political Branches' (2007) 107 *Columbia Law Review* 559.

Oliver, D, *Common Values and the Public-Private Divide* (Cambridge, Cambridge University Press, 1999).

—— 'Public Law Procedures and Remedies. Do We Need Them?' (2002) *Public Law* 91.

—— 'What, if any, Public-Private Divide Exists in English Law' in M Ruffert (ed), *The Public-Private Divide: Potential for Transformation* (London, BIICL, 2009).

Oliver, PC, *The Constitution of Independence. The Development of Constitutional Theory in Australia, Canada, and New Zealand* (Oxford, Oxford University Press, 2005).

Orth, JV, 'On the Relation between the Rule of Law and Public Opinion' (1982) 80 *Michigan Law Review* 753.

Orwell, G, *The Lion and the Unicorn: Socialism and the English Genius* (London, Secker and Warburg, 1941).

Osman, L, 'Emergencies Act Inquiry Studies Fundamental Rights and Rreedoms at Stake in Protests' (*CBC News*, 28 November 2022).

Padilla, M, *Droit public et doctrine publiciste au Royaume-Uni. Regard critique sur un objet à (re)construire* (PhD thesis, Université de Bordeaux, 2021).

Palgrave, F, *The Rise and Progress of the English Commonwealth* (London, John Murray, 1832).

ParrisPollo, H, 'The Nineteenth-Century Revolution in Government: a Reappraisal Reappraised' (1960) 3 *Historical Journal* 117.

Perelman, C, 'Autorité, idéologie et violence' in *Éthique et droit* (Brussels, Editions de l'Université de Bruxelles, 2012) 399.

Perkin, H, 'Individualism versus Collectivism in Nineteenth-Century Britain: a False Antithesis' (1977) 17 *Journal of British Studies* 105.

Pfander, JE, 'Dicey's Nightmare: An Essay on the Rule of Law' (2019) 107 *California Law Review* 737.

Plaxton, M, 'Police Powers after Dicey' (2012) 38 *Queen's Law Journal* 99.

Plucknett, TFT, '*Bonham's Case* and Judicial Review' (1926) 40 *Harvard Law Review* 30.

Pojanowski, J, 'Neo-Classical Administrative Law' (2020) 133 *Harvard Law Review* 852.

Pollock, F, 'The Science of Case Law', *Essays in Jurisprudence and Ethics* (London, MacMillan, 1882).

—— *The Expansion of the Common Law* (London, Stevens and Sons, 1904).

Poole, T, 'Losing our Religion? Public Law and Brexit' (*UK Constitutional Law Blog*, 2 December 2016).

—— 'The Strange Death of Prerogative in England' (2018) 43 *University of Western Australia Law Review* 42.

Postema, GJ, 'Bentham's Equality-Sensitive Utilitarianism' (1998) 10 *Utilitas* 144.

—— *Legal Philosophy in the Twentieth Century. The Common Law World* (Dordrecht, Springer, 2011).

—— (ed), *Matthew Hale. On the Law of Nature, Reason, & Common Law. Selected Jurisprudential Writings* (Oxford, Oxford University Press, 2017).

—— *Bentham and the Common Law Constitutional Tradition*, 2nd edn (Oxford, Oxford University Press, 2019 [1986]).

Pound, R, 'The Rule of Law and the Modern Welfare State' (1953) 7 *Vanderbilt Law Review* 1.

*Public Law*, *Brexit Special Issue*, November 2017.

Quinn, M, 'A Failure to Reconcile the Irreconcilable? Security, Subsistence and Equality in Bentham's Writings on the Civil Code and on the Poor Law' (2008) 29 *History of Political Thought* 320.

Rajkovic, NM, '"Global Law" and Governmentality: Reconceptualizing the "Rule of Law" as Rule "Through" Law' (2012) 18 *European Journal of International Relations* 29.

Rappaport, MB, 'Replacing Administrative Adjudication with Independent Administrative Courts' (2019) 26 *George Mason Law Review* 811.

Raz, J, *The Authority of Law*, 2nd edn (Oxford, Oxford University Press, 2009).

Reed, R, 'Triremes and Steamships: Scholars, Judges, and the Use of the Past', The Scrymgeour Lecture, University of Dundee, 30 October 2015.

Ritchie, DG, 'On the Conception of Sovereignty' (1891) 1 *Annals of the American Academy of Political and Social Science* 385.

Roberts, D, 'Jeremy Bentham and the Victorian Administrative State' (1958–59) 2 *Victorian Studies* 193.

Robson, R, 'Dicey's Law of the Constitution: A Review' (1939) 38 *Michigan Law Review* 1939.

Robson, WA, *Justice and Administrative Law* (London, Macmillan, 1928).

Rodney, M, 'What Is in Habit?' in M Freeman and P Mindus (eds), *The Legacy of John Austin's Jurisprudence* (Dordrecht, Springer, 2013) 185.

Rosen, F, *Jeremy Bentham and Representative Democracy. A Study of the Constitutional Code* (Oxford, Clarendon, 1983).

—— *Bentham, Byron, and Greece: Constitutionalism, Nationalism, and Early Liberal Political Thought* (Oxford, Clarendon, 1992).

—— *Classical Utilitarianism from Hume to Mill* (London, Routledge, 2003).

Rosenblatt, H, *The Lost History of Liberalism* (Princeton, Princeton University Press, 2018).

Roynier, C, *Le problème de la liberté dans le constitutionnalisme britannique* (Paris, Classiques Garnier, 2019).

Rukavina, S, 'François Legault Says Trudeau's Invoking of Emergencies Act "not necessary" in Quebec' (*CBC News*, 14 February 2022).

Rumble, WE, *The Thought of John Austin* (London, Athlone Press, 1985).

—— *Doing Austin Justice. The Reception of John Austin's Philosophy of Law in Nineteenth Century England* (London, Continuum, 2005).

Russell, B, 'Anti-Suffragist Anxieties' (The People's Suffrage Federation, Queen Anne's Chambers, Broadway, Westminster, London, 1910).

Russell, M, White, H and James, L, *Rebuilding and Renewing the Constitution: Options for Reform* (Report 204, July 2023) https://www.ucl.ac.uk/constitution-unit/publications/reports.

Russell, PH, 'Canadian Constraints on Judicialization from Without' (1994) 15 *International Political Science Review* 165.

Sachs, SE, 'Finding Law' (2019) 107 *California Law Review* 527.

Salmond, JW, *Jurisprudence, or The Theory of the Law* (London, Stevens & Haynes, 1902).

—— *Jurisprudence*, 6th edn (London, Sweet & Maxwell, 1920).

Schneiderman, D, 'A.V. Dicey, Lord Watson, and the Law of the Canadian Constitution in the Late Nineteenth Century' (1998) 16 *Law and History Review* 495.

Schofield, P, *Utility and Democracy: The Political Thought of Jeremy Bentham* (Oxford, Oxford University Press, 2006).

Schwartz, B, *French Administrative Law and the Common-law World* (New York, New York University Press, 1954).

Sedley, S, *Lions Under the Throne: Essays on the History of English Public Law* (Cambridge, Cambridge University Press, 2015).

Shepherd, GB, 'Fierce Compromise: The Administrative Procedure Act Emerges from New Deal Politics' (1996) 90 *Northwestern University Law Review* 1557.

Shinn, RA and Cosgrove, RA (eds), *Constitutional Reflections: The Correspondence of Albert Venn Dicey and Arthur Berriedale Keith* (New York, University Press of America, Inc, 1996).

Sidgwick, H, *The Elements of Politics*, 1st edn (London, MacMillan and Co, 1891).

—— *The Elements of Politics*, 2nd edn (London, MacMillan and Co, 1897).

Sing, M, *Hong Kong's Tortuous Democratization* (Abingdon, Routledge-Curzon, 2004).

Sirota, L, 'Immuring Dicey's Ghost: The Senate Reform Reference and Constitutional Conventions' (2019) 51 *Ottawa Law Review* 313.

Siu-Lai Lau, 'Chinese Familism in an Urban-Industrial Setting: The Case of Hong Kong' (1981) 43 *Journal of Marriage and Family* 997.

—— *Society and Politics in Hong Kong* (Hong Kong, Chinese University Press, 1991).

Smith, DC 'Sir Edward Coke' in RH Helmholz, M Hill (eds), *Great Christian Jurists in English History* (Cambridge, Cambridge University Press, 2017) 93–114.

Smith, H, *The Religions of Man* (San Francisco, Harper & Row, 1964).

Smith, SA de, 'The Prerogative Writs' (1951) 11 *The Cambridge Law Journal* 40.

Smithey, SI, 'Religious Freedom and Equality Concerns under the Canadian Charter of Rights and Freedoms' (2001) 34 *Canadian Journal of Political Science/Revue canadienne de science politique* 85.

Songer, DR, *The Transformation of the Supreme Court of Canada: An Empirical Examination*' (Toronto, Univeristy of Toronto Press, 2008).

Stacey, J and Lazar, NC, 'Emergencies Act Inquiry Final Report is a Reminder that We all have a Role in Upholding the Rule of Law' (*The Conversation*, 21 February 2023).

Stack KM, 'The Constitutional Foundations of Chenery' (2007) 116 *Yale Law Journal* 952.

Stapleton, J, 'Dicey and His Legacy' (1995) 16 *History of Political Thought* 234.

Stephen, L, *The English Utilitarians*, vol 1 (London, Duckworth, 1900).

Stephenson, S, 'Constitutional Reengineering: Dialogue's Migration from Canada to Australia' (2013) 11 *International Journal of Constitutional Law* 870.

Stewart, RB, 'The Reformation of American Administrative Law' (1975) 88 *Harvard Law Review* 1669.

Steyn, Lord, 'Democracy, the Rule of Law and the Role of Judges' (Attlee Foundation Lecture, 11 April 2006).

St-Hilaire, M, Baud, PF and Drouin, ES, 'The Constitution of Canada as Supreme Law: A New Definition' (2019) 28 *Constitutional Forum* 7.

Stubbs, W, *Select Charters and Other Illustrations of English Constitutional History from the Earliest Times to the Reign of Edward I* (Oxford, Clarendon, 1870).

—— *The Constitutional History of England*, vol 1 (Oxford, Clarendon, 1874).

Sunstein, CR and Vermeule, A, 'The New Coke: On the Plural Aims of Administrative Law' (2015) *Supreme Court Review* 41.

—— 'The Morality of Administrative Law' (2018) 131 *Harvard Law Review* 1924.

Suyin, H, *The Crippled Tree: Story of War and Revolution in China* (London, Triad/Panther, 1984).

Taggart M, 'The Peculiarities of the English Law: Resisting the Public/Private Law Distinction' in P Craig and R Rawlings (eds), *Law and Administration in Europe, Essays in Honor of Carol Harlow* (Oxford, Oxford University Press, 2009).

Tarnopolsky, WS, 'The Canadian Bill of Rights and the Supreme Court Decisions in Lavell and Burnshine: A Retreat from Drybones to Dicey' (1975) 7 *Ottawa Law Review* 1.

Tasker, JP, 'Four Highlights from the Emergencies Act Inquiry's Final Report' (*CBC News*, 17 February 2023).

The Common Cause (1909, Online Source).

Thompson, EP, *Whigs and Hunters: The Origins of the Black Act* (London, Penguin, 1977).

Tolley, MC, 'Parliamentary Scrutiny of Rights in the United Kingdom: Assessing the Work of the Joint Committee on Human Rights' (2009) 44 *Australian Journal of Political Science* 41.

Tomkins, A and Scott, P (eds), *Entick v Carrington: 250 Years of the Rule of Law* (Oxford, Hart Publishing, 2015).

Tremblay, LB, 'Two Models of Constitutionalism and The Legitimacy of Law: Dicey or Marshall?' (2006) 6 *Oxford University Commonwealth Law Journal* 77.

Trudeau, PE, 'Convocation Speech at the Opening of the Bora Laskin Law Library' (1991) 41 *The University of Toronto Law Journal* 295.
—— *Trudeau: A Mess that Deserves a Big No: Pierre Elliott Trudeau's Historic Speech at the Eleventh Cité Libre Dinner* (Montréal, Robert Davis, 1992).
Tsang, S, *A Modern History of Hong Kong* (London, IB Tauris, 2007).
Tso, K, 'Fundamental Political and Constitutional Norms: Hong Kong and Macau Compared' (2012) 13 *Australian Journal of Asian Law* 25.
Turégabo Mansilla, I, 'Reconstructing Austin's Intuitions: Positive Morality and Law' in M Freeman and P Mindus (eds) *The Legacy of John Austin's Jurisprudence* (Dordrecht, Springer, 2013) 291.
Tusseau, G, *Les normes d'habilitation* (Paris, Dalloz, 2006).
Tyler, T, *Why People Obey the Law* (New Jersey, Princeton University Press, 2006).
Van Wingerden, SA, *The Women's Suffrage Movement in Britain, 1866–1928* (London, Palgrave Macmillan, 1999).
Verkuil, P, *Valuing Bureaucracy: The Case for Professional Government* (Cambridge, Cambridge University Press, 2017).
Vipond, RC, 'Seeing Canada through the Referendum: Still a House Divided' (1993) 23 *Publius* 39.
Vukovich, DF, *After Autonomy: A Post-Mortem for Hong Kong's First Handover, 1997–2019* (Singapore, Palgrave Macmillan, 2022).
Wade, ECS, 'Introduction' in AV Dicey, *Introduction to the Study of the Law of the Constitution*, 10th edn (London, Macmillan, 1959) xix-cxcviii.
Wade, HWR, 'The Basis of Legal Sovereignty' (1955) 13 *Cambridge Law Journal* 172.
—— 'Law, Opinion and Administration' (1962) 78 *Law Quarterly Review* 189.
—— 'Sovereignty – Revolution or Evolution?' (1996) 112 *Law Quarterly Review* 568.
Wade, HWR and Forsyth, CF, *Administrative Law*, 11th edn (Oxford, Oxford University Press, 2014).
Walker, CJ, 'Constitutional Tensions in Agency Adjudication' (2019) 104 *Iowa Law Review* 2679.
Walker, DM, *The Oxford Companion to Law* (Oxford, Oxford University Press, 1980).
Walker, N, 'Our Constitutional Unsettlement' (2014) *Public Law* 529.
Walters, MD, 'Histories of Colonialism, Legality, and Aboriginality' (2007) 57 *University of Toronto Law Journal* 819.
—— 'Legality as Reason: Dicey, Rand, and the Rule of Law' (2010) 55 *McGill Law Journal* 563.
—— 'Is Public Law Ordinary?' (2012) 75 *Modern Law Review* 899.
—— 'Public Law and Ordinary Legal Method: Revisiting Dicey's Approach to Droit Administratif' (2016) 66 *University of Toronto Law Journal* 53.
—— 'The Judicial Recognition of Indigenous Legal Traditions: *Connolly v. Woolrich* at 150' (2017) 22 *Review of Constitutional Studies* 347.
—— *A.V. Dicey and the Common Law Constitutional Tradition: A Legal Turn of Mind* (Cambridge, Cambridge University Press, 2020).
—— 'Dicey's Legal Constitution' in MD Walters (ed), *A.V. Dicey and the Common Law Constitutional Tradition: A Legal Turn of Mind* (Cambridge, Cambridge University Press, 2020).
Ward, I, *The English Constitution, Myths and Realities* (Oxford, Hart Publishing, 2004).
Weill, R, 'Dicey was not Diceyean' (2003) 62 *Cambridge Law Journal* 474.
Wesley-Smith, P, *Unequal Treaty 1898–1997: China, Great Britain and Hong Kong's New Territories* (Oxford, Oxford University Press, 1983).
—— 'Book Review of Munn's, Christopher, *Anglo-China: Chinese People and British Rule in Hong Kong – 1841–1880*' (2003) *China Perspectives* 74.
Wheare, KC, *Federal Government* (Oxford, Oxford University Press, 1946).
Young, SNM and Cullen, R, *Electing Hong Kong's Chief Executive* (Hong Kong, Hong Kong University Press, 2010).
Zaring, D, 'Personal Liability as Administrative Law' (2009) 66 *Washington & Lee Law Review* 313.
—— 'Towards Separation of Powers Realism' (2020) 37 *Yale Journal of Regulation* 708.
Zhu, H, 'A Chinese Law Wedge into the Hong Kong Common Law System: A Legal Appraisal of the Hong Kong National Security Law' (2023) 21 *Northwestern Journal of Human Rights* 43.

# INDEX

www.ingramcontent.com/pod-product-compliance
Ingram Content Group UK Ltd.
Pitfield, Milton Keynes, MK11 3LW, UK
UKHW020132290926
15471UKWH00003B/436

9 781509 975068